ARIZONA & THE GRAND CANYON

TIM HULL

Contents

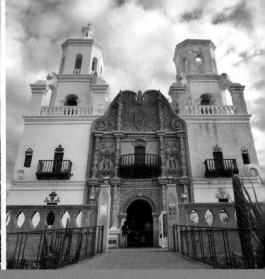

Arizona &
the Grand Canyon

Arizona &
the Grand Canyon

Arizona is authentic. It's too hot to fake it, too rugged to tell tall tales, and too beautiful to commit to the hard sell. All of its institutions, its attractions, and even its mythologies were forged through hard experience, trial, and error.

This is even true of the land, built by the movement and explosion of the earth—canyons ripped open and mountains kicked up over millennia of shaking and oozing. This roiling has provided a wonderland of diversity, building—all at once—hot and verdant desert scrublands, cool evergreen mountain forests, dry sweeping grasslands, and red-rock, river-carved, fairy-tale canyons, all of which merge with a horizon lit most evenings with postcard-ready sunsets. It remains one of the most exotic destinations in North America, with endless variety, iconic scenery, and a dark history of which the world has never tired.

You will be surprised and changed by Arizona. Here you can easily happen upon an old pioneer graveyard, forgotten and ignored, on a strip of undeveloped desert right next to a gathering of just-built dream homes. This may be the perfect image for the dichotomies of this landscape. Everything here is either ancient or five minutes old.

Clockwise from top left: Cactus League baseball; the mission San Xavier del Bac near Tucson; a wind-molded boulder on the Arizona Strip; prickly pear cacti; Hubbell Trading Post in the Navajo Nation; Sedona's historic orchards and famous red rocks.

There's a reason all those road movies feature scenes in the Grand Canyon State. There's no better way to see all the state has to offer than to pile in a car and hit the open road. Less than a day's drive from anywhere, you can discover something unexpected, whether it be the calm and sunny ease of life along the lower Colorado River, where houseboats and water-skiers pass by great monuments to engineering, or a chance meeting with a rare tropical bird hiding out in the riparian mist of a sky island.

In many a traveler's imagination, this place is the home to rattlesnakes, tumbleweeds, and vast tracts of arid wilderness. Luckily, Arizona still has all of these; there are still trackless spaces to explore. But the face Arizona shows to most of the world belies the leaps this once-isolated territory has made. The youngest state in the lower 48 is one of the fastest-growing regions in the nation, and while near-constant growth makes for sometimes rancorous debates about land use and natural resources, it adds to Arizona a dynamism—a flux that perpetuates itself. It is never boring here; it is beautiful and unknowable. There is always something, or someone, being created anew, changing, and blooming.

10 TOP EXPERIENCES

1 **Experience a Wonder of the World:** Hike, bike, raft, or just gaze in awe at the **Grand Canyon** (page 252).

2 **Explore Red Rock Country:** Discover the sculpted red cliffs and buttes around **Sedona** (page 243).

>>>

3 **Take a Hike:** Trails crisscross Arizona, from the **deserts** to the **forests** to the **slickrock canyonlands** (page 21).

<<<

4 **Have a Ball at Spring Training:** Enjoy the Valley of the Sun in March while watching your favorite **Major League Baseball** teams play in intimate, family-friendly ballparks (page 60).

>>>

^^^
^^^

5 **Relax at a Spa Resort:** Treat yourself to the high-style pampering and luxury for which Arizona resorts are known (page 99).

6 **Feast on Mexican Food:** Whether you're craving avocado enchiladas, street-style tacos, or a loaded Sonoran hot dog, Southern Arizona is the place to find it (page 151).

<<<

7 **Take a Scenic Drive through Monument Valley:** Find an otherworldly landscape filled with the eroded sandstone buttes and spires of Navajoland (page 330).

8 Feel the Heat in the Sonoran Desert: Explore this unique and surprising landscape at the **Arizona-Sonora Desert Museum** (page 123) and **Saguaro National Park** (pages 125 and 127).

<<<

9 Journey back in Time on Old Route 66: Drive the remains of the Mother Road to the Colorado River, passing through a time warp along the way (page 392).

>>>

10 Wander around Historic Small Towns: Peruse one-of-a-kind boutiques and art galleries in charming Old West towns like **Bisbee** (page 184) and **Jerome** (page 225).

<<<

Planning Your Trip

Where to Go

Phoenix, Scottsdale, and the Valley of the Sun

Arizona's **largest metro area** has 10 cities linked together to create a sprawling megalopolis of glass high-rises and labyrinthine, stacked freeways spreading out over a hot Sonoran Desert valley. Visitors and residents alike tend to refer to the whole area as the Valley of the Sun, or simply Phoenix, after the valley's largest city. There are pockets of urbanity out in the sprawl, like Scottsdale with its **art galleries,** high-style eateries, resorts, and **golf courses,** and Tempe with its college-town nightlife, shopping, and museums. This area has **some of the state's best resorts and restaurants,** nightlife, museums, and Arizona's largest airport. The rural desert outskirts are home to old mining towns, river canyons, and saguaro forests.

Tucson and Southern Arizona

Tucson, the state's second-largest city and the one with the most character and history, anchors this region of **saguaro forests,** sweeping grasslands, and quirky desert outposts. Towering **sky island** mountain ranges shoot up from the long desert seas, and the nearby Mexican border looms equally large in this region's culture and history. Even better, they say a few of those myths and legends of the **Old West** actually happened here.

Flagstaff, Sedona, and Red Rock Country

Arizona's sap-scented high country begins around mile-high **Prescott** and rises to a great ponderosa pine forest stretching north and east. Even higher is snowy **Flagstaff** and the bald-rock tip of the **San Francisco Peaks,** their slopes variegated by white and yellow aspens among the evergreens. Below the **Mogollon Rim,** the green edge of a great plateau, **Sedona** offers fine dining, self-healing, red-rock buttes, and shady streambeds.

The Grand Canyon and the Arizona Strip

The **Kaibab Plateau** rises in northwestern Arizona; river-cut more than a mile deep into the plateau is **Arizona's signature attraction** and one of the world's most sought-after landscapes—the only canyon on earth deserving of the grand title. Between the canyon's forested rims is the lonely Arizona Strip, empty save for high, barren red cliffs, sagebrush plains, and the water-and-red-rock mazes of **Lake Powell.**

Navajo and Hopi Country

The **high-desert grasslands** in Arizona's northeastern plateau country are dotted with a few old cattle and **railroad towns,** trading posts, and an empty pastel-painted desert strewn with broken swirling-stone trees. The vast Navajo Nation is cut deep with **red-sandstone canyons** in which abandoned cliff-face cities and the tracks of dinosaurs create a timeless atmosphere that can be entrancing. On the edge of **Black Mesa,** the Hopi live on high cold cliffs occupied for more than a thousand years.

The White Mountains and the Gila Valley

Rising in northeastern Arizona near the New Mexico border, the White Mountains region has **small towns,** rental cabins, **trout streams,** cold-water lakes, hiking trails, and wolves. Much of the evergreen, mountainous wilderness is home to the **Western Apache,** and their culture pervades the region, as does that of the Mormon pioneers and cattle ranchers who settled here in the territorial era and never left. Below the highlands, the Gila Valley, where deserts collide and **hot springs** burst from the hot ground, spreads out along the last flowing remains of the once-mighty desert river.

The Lower Colorado River

The Colorado River flows the length of far western Arizona to Mexico, creating a river border through this barren, hot land of **jagged rock mountains** populated by bighorn sheep. The views are long and empty save for the toughest **cacti, scrubs,** and **wildflowers.** The river is a blue-and-green band of rustling, splashing life, and all living things here are drawn to it, whether they be **rare birds** or water-skiers.

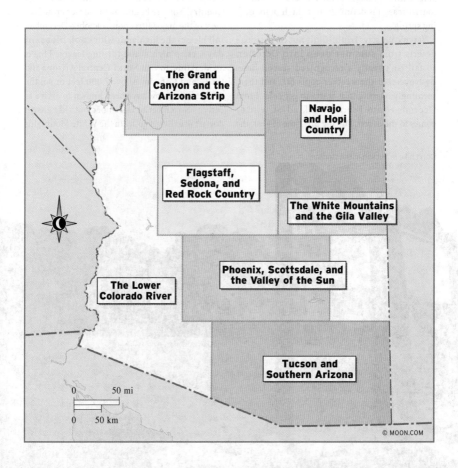

Before You Go

High and Low Seasons

Spring is the best time to be on Arizona's lowland deserts, including Phoenix and Tucson. February-May, the weather is gorgeous, often in the high 70s and 80s. Spring is the desert's bloomtime, when all the dormant **wildflowers** come to life and the spiny cacti burst with vivid color. It's also the season for Major League Baseball in Arizona; fans of the game flock to the Valley of the Sun for **Cactus League spring training** games throughout March. The desert-country tourist season is definitely at its high point during spring.

It typically stays **triple-digit hot** on Arizona's deserts from **summer deep into October,** so fall isn't really a recognized season here. By November the weather cools off; and then, seemingly overnight, it starts to get cold. From December into February a kind of **winter** comes to the desert. During this time of year, the **snowbirds** flock to Arizona from the Midwest, the Northeast, and Canada, crowding the roads, stores, and restaurants of Tucson and the Valley of the Sun.

In **summer,** the high country is warm, tending toward hot during the day, and cool, clear, and star-filled at night. In late summer the rains come, afternoon downpours that clean the air and get the creeks rising. Summer is the **busy tourist season** in this region that includes the Grand Canyon, North-Central Arizona, and Indian Country. You are bound to encounter crowds at most of the major attractions. October-December, **fall** blesses the highlands with **cool, pleasant days,** crisp nights, and turning leaves. This is an ideal time to visit North-Central Arizona and the Grand Canyon. Above 7,000 feet or so, the cold and the snow have been known to arrive as early as November or December, but **ski season** doesn't usually get going in the White Mountains

Don't hike in Tucson in the summer.

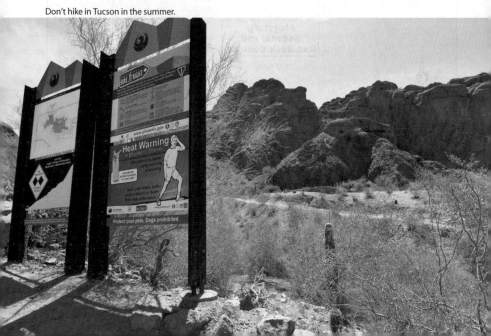

and Flagstaff until January. In winter, especially in a wet year, expect to find the mountain country crowded on the weekends with skiers and snowboarders.

Reservations and Permits

A trip to Arizona requires a certain amount of **advance planning,** especially if you're going to be hiking the **Grand Canyon,** rafting the Colorado's rapids, or renting a houseboat. A permit to spend even one night inside the canyon requires a reservation at least **six months** in advance, more if you want to stay in the canyon's only lodge, **Phantom Ranch.** If you're hoping to float down the Colorado, start planning at least a year in advance. Bring your **passport** along if you're planning to cross the U.S.-Mexico border.

You must have a car, and you'll need to be prepared for a lot of time in it. Towns, sights, and attractions are scattered throughout the state, and most of them are far from the two urban centers of Phoenix and Tucson.

What to Pack

Your luggage should include a few essential items no matter what the season. These include a good pair of **hiking or walking shoes.** Day hikers or at least a pair of tough running shoes or trainers are a necessity. At nearly every national park or national monument, there's some kind of short hike in order to *really* appreciate what you're seeing. A **water bottle** is always nice to have around, and you'll probably want to include a **small pack** for carrying snacks and water on day hikes or sightseeing excursions. **Sunscreen** is a necessity in any season; if you're not in a hot desert, you're in mountain country, where the sun shines hard and dangerous. A **hat** is a must, and one with a brim wide enough to cast a shadow on your neck is recommended. Think about bringing along a pair of **binoculars;** they are always handy when spotting bighorn sheep, petroglyphs, and rare birds.

Even if you're going to be in the desert in the summer, bring along a **light jacket.** In some of the outer and higher regions the nights will be much cooler. In the high country, **layers** will serve you best. It is often warm in the day and cold at night, even in summer.

As for style, think casual and utilitarian. If you're going to be staying or dining at any of the top resorts, a few fancy outfits might be in order. Otherwise, jeans and T-shirts, shorts and tank tops, flip-flops, rock sandals, and general outdoor style are the norm.

The Best of Arizona

The best way to see Arizona is from behind the wheel of your own car. A road trip through the heart of the American Southwest provides a unique opportunity to explore this exotic region from the ground up.

Day 1: Scenic Drive to Cave Creek
70 MILES / 1.5 HOURS

Arrive at **Sky Harbor International Airport** in Phoenix and head to a hotel in central Phoenix, a resort in **Scottsdale**, or **Tempe**. Introduce yourself to the desert by taking a scenic drive along Highway 51 about 35 miles or 45 minutes out to **Cave Creek** and **Carefree**. Have dinner at **El Encanto** in Cave Creek before heading back.

Day 2: Phoenix, Scottsdale, and Prescott
100 MILES / 2 HOURS

Get an early start and spend the morning touring the **Heard Museum**, the **Phoenix Art Museum**, or **Taliesin West.** Leave the city via I-17 to **Prescott.** Stop for a late lunch and a slice of pie midway at the **Rock Springs Café**, north of Phoenix along I-17. Spend the night at one of downtown Prescott's historic hotels or bed-and-breakfasts. Have dinner at **The Raven** and hit up a few **Whiskey Row** watering holes.

Day 3: Prescott and Jerome
35 MILES / 1 HOUR

Get up early and eat breakfast at **The Local.** Walk around downtown Prescott and tour the museums, shops, and galleries. Be sure to visit the **Sharlot Hall Museum.** Head north on scenic Highway 89A to **Jerome.** Stay at the **Jerome Grand Hotel** and have dinner at **The Asylum.**

Day 4: Jerome and Sedona
28 MILES / 40 MINUTES

Have breakfast at **Mile High Grill & Spirits** and take a walk around Jerome. Head down Highway 89A to **Sedona.** Check into your hotel, and

Jerome Grand Hotel

Best Hikes

The wrinkled land of Arizona is a hiker's paradise. The Grand Canyon State's varied landscapes, not to mention the great canyon itself, are crisscrossed with hundreds of well-maintained and well-used trails of various lengths and difficulties. Whether you're looking for an easy walk in the desert or a multiday expedition deep into the canyon's depths, the five hikes listed below are among the best of the best.

- **White House Ruin Trail** (Canyon de Chelly National Monument; 2.5 miles round-trip, 2-3 hours, elevation gain 550 feet, moderate): High sandstone walls tower above as you descend into the Navajo Nation's Canyon de Chelly, where the otherworldly White House Ruin awaits, carved into the cliffs (page 336).

- **Brown Mountain Trail** (Tucson Mountain Park; 4.8 miles round-trip, 2-3 hours, elevation gain 260 feet, moderate): This trail winds through the saguaro forests on Tucson's wild western edge, rising to traverse a ridgeline with spectacular views of the surprisingly verdant Sonoran Desert (page 135).

- **West Fork of Oak Creek Trail** (north of Sedona; 6.5 miles round-trip, 2-3 hours, elevation gain 200 feet, easy): A rare example of a high-desert streamside forest environment, dark green evergreens mingle with red rocks and trickling water here to create an exotic Southwestern Eden (page 248).

- **Humphreys Peak Trail** (Snowbowl Ski Area, Flagstaff; 9 miles round-trip, 5-6 hours, elevation gain 3,833 feet, difficult): This hike isn't easy, but the effort is richly rewarded

Bright Angel Trail

when you're looking out over Arizona from its highest point, more than 12,000 feet above sea level (page 202).

- **Bright Angel Trail to Phantom Ranch** (Grand Canyon Village; 9.6 miles one-way, overnight, elevation gain 4,380 feet, moderate to difficult): Obtain a permit and head down the ancient Bright Angel Trail to the Colorado River and Phantom Ranch, in the mystical depths of the Grand Canyon. It takes a bit of planning, but this is truly the hike of a lifetime (page 292).

then head out to explore the red rocks, galleries, and shops of Sedona. Eat dinner at **Oaxaca Restaurant** in Uptown.

Day 5: Sedona and the Verde Valley
52 MILES / 1.25 HOURS

Spend the day shopping, hiking, sightseeing, and exploring Sedona and the **Verde Valley.** Check

out **Montezuma Castle National Monument,** about 26 miles from town, or hike into red-rock country or take a Jeep tour through the red lands.

Day 6: Oak Creek Canyon and Flagstaff
30 MILES / 1 HOUR

Eat breakfast at the **Coffee Pot Restaurant** in Sedona, then head north on Highway 89A through **Oak Creek Canyon.** Stop for a hike or to splash around in the water at **Slide Rock State Park.** Continue north to **Flagstaff,** about an hour's drive from Sedona. Check into one of the historic hotels downtown. Stroll and shop downtown, then have dinner and beers at **Beaver Street Brewery.**

Day 7: Flagstaff and the High Desert
130 MILES / 3 HOURS

Wake up and head out to visit the **Museum of Northern Arizona** in Flagstaff, about three miles north of downtown on Highway 180, then drive a circuit to take in **Wupatki, Sunset Crater Volcano, and Walnut Canyon National Monuments** via U.S. 89 and the Loop Road. From here drive east for about an hour on I-40 to **Winslow.** Check into **La Posada.** Have dinner in the **Turquoise Room,** and order a box lunch from the restaurant for the next day.

Day 8: The High Desert and Navajo Country
175 MILES / 3.5 HOURS

Spend the morning touring the **Painted Desert** and **Petrified Forest National Park** near

Holbrook, 52 miles or about an hour from Winslow on I-40. Then take I-40 to Highway 191 north to **Chinle** on the Navajo Reservation, a distance of 123 miles, about 2.5 hours. Stay at the **Thunderbird Lodge** near **Canyon de Chelly** or at one of the chains in Chinle.

Day 9: Canyon de Chelly and Monument Valley
150-180 MILES / 3-4 HOURS

Spend the morning hiking into **Canyon de Chelly** to the **White House Ruin** and driving the scenic rim roads, or hire a Navajo guide and go deeper into the canyon. After lunch head north on Highway 191, west on Highway 160, then north on Highway 163 to **Kayenta,** a distance of about 75 miles or about 1.5 hours. Get a hotel room in Kayenta, drive through **Monument Valley** late in the afternoon, and watch the sun set. Monument Valley is 50 miles from Kayenta, a drive that takes about an hour.

Day 10: The Grand Canyon
155 MILES / 3 HOURS

Eat breakfast in Kayenta at the **Blue Coffee Pot Restaurant** and then head west on Highway 160 past Tuba City to U.S. 89 then south to Cameron,

Petrified Forest National Park

about 100 miles or 1.5 hours. Take Highway 64 west 30 miles to **Grand Canyon National Park** and make your way to the east entrance. Check out the **Desert View** sights, then drive on into **Grand Canyon Village** and have lunch at **El Tovar.** Spend the night at El Tovar or the **Bright Angel Lodge.** Get up early and hike down one of the South Rim trails for as far as you feel like going. If you're not a hiker, take a mule ride to the river and back. Spend the remainder of the day looking around the rim and staring into the canyon.

Day 11: Heading to Tucson
340 MILES / 5 HOURS

This day will be spent mostly in the car driving from the high country down to **Tucson** and Southern Arizona. Leave the Grand Canyon early through the South Entrance and take I-40 East to I-17 South. In Phoenix, follow the signs to I-10 South to Tucson. You'll probably arrive in the late afternoon. Check into the **Hotel Congress** or **Hotel McCoy,** or one of the area's bed-and-breakfasts, and then head to **Mi Nidito** for a Mexican-food dinner.

Day 12: Tucson and the Border Region
135 MILES / 2 HOURS

Get up early and spend the morning walking around **Saguaro National Park West** and visiting the nearby **Arizona-Sonora Desert Museum.** Have lunch at the museum's café, or at the **Coyote Pause Café** about five miles

south. Then continue south to see the mission **San Xavier del Bac.** Drive back to your hotel in Tucson, about an hour's drive depending on where you're staying, and relax.

Day 13: Southeastern Arizona
50-150 MILES / 1-3 HOURS

This day is a Southern Arizona grab bag. Drive through the San Pedro Valley or the Mountain Empire. Do some wine-tasting in **Elgin,** shop in **Bisbee,** or drive the dirt roads into the Huachuca Mountains and up to the **Coronado National Memorial.** Visit **Chiricahua National Monument, Cochise Stronghold, Patagonia, Madera Canyon, Kartchner Caverns,** or **Tombstone.** A full, busy day will allow you to make, say, three or four major stops, depending on your personal interests and the amount of time you spend at any one place. You'll likely arrive back at your hotel in Tucson late.

Day 14: Tucson and Back to Phoenix
116-156 MILES / 2-3 HOURS

Wake up early and take a stroll through one of Tucson's downtown neighborhoods or 4th Avenue and the University District. On your way north on I-10 to the airport in Phoenix, a distance of 116 miles, stop off along the way at **Picacho Peak State Park** for a last hike. With more time, you could take a short detour off of I-10 to **Casa Grande Ruins National Monument,** about 20 miles off of I-10, a half-hour drive, for a last look at native Arizona.

The Ruins of Lost Cultures

Arizona and the Southwest are home to many native cultures that are no longer around to tell their stories and legends. Luckily, the ruins of the Hohokam, Ancestral Puebloans, Salado, Sinagua, and others are protected throughout the state by federal law. You could make a whole trip out of visiting these mysterious structures, discovering the lost cultures that once scraped much more than subsistence out of the uncaring land.

THE HOHOKAM AND SALADO

Use Phoenix and the Valley of the Sun as your base as you discover ruins left behind by the Hohokam and Salado tribes.

- **Pueblo Grande Museum and Archaeological Park:** Discover how the Hohokam coaxed an empire out of the Salt River Valley here at the ruin and museum in the middle of the city, near the ruins of the canals the Hohokam built to irrigate the desert (page 45).

- **Tonto National Monument:** Take the backcountry route called the **Apache Trail,** east of the city, and witness a well-preserved cliff dwelling once inhabited by the Salado tribe rising above slopes crowded with saguaros (page 104).

- **Casa Grande Ruins National Monument:** Located between Phoenix and Tucson, this monument is the largest example of Hohokam architecture left, the huge molded-dirt apartment building called Casa Grande (page 105).

THE SINAGUA

Use Sedona or Flagstaff as your base for visiting the awesome ruins of North-Central Arizona's vanished Sinagua.

- **Wupatki National Monument:** Just north of Flagstaff, this monument preserves the ruins of several awesome red-sandstone great houses (page 199).

- **Walnut Canyon National Monument:** East of Flagstaff is a lost world where a long-gone culture once built a busy village on the rim and along the walls of a hidden canyon (page 201).

Casa Grande Ruins National Monument

- **Montezuma Castle National Monument:** This Verde Valley cliff dwelling is one of the best preserved in the Southwest (page 230).

THE ANCESTRAL PUEBLOANS

The abandoned cliff cities of the Ancestral Puebloans are on display in the Navajo Nation.

- **Navajo National Monument:** While visiting Tsegi Canyon, you can spot the ruin called **Betatakin** from the rim, nestled in a rock alcove above a bottomland forest (page 327).

- **Keet Seel:** Sign up for a 17-mile round-trip hike below the rim of Tsegi Canyon to spend the night near the spectacularly preserved ruin hidden deep in the canyon (page 328).

- **Canyon de Chelly National Monument:** Also on Navajoland, don't miss this area where you can hike down a slickrock trail and stand in awe before the **White House Ruin** (page 336).

Grand Canyon Adventure

The Grand Canyon is a backcountry-lover's paradise as well as a fun place to sightsee and contemplate nature. This itinerary includes one night below the rim and so requires you to secure reservations and permits far in advance. The best time to go is spring or October.

Day 1

Take an early-morning flight into Phoenix's **Sky Harbor International Airport,** rent a car, and drive north to **Williams** (170 miles). Park your car and catch the **Grand Canyon Railway** to **Grand Canyon National Park's South Rim.** Check into a cabin at **Bright Angel Lodge,** and then explore and go sightseeing around **Grand Canyon Village,** getting acclimated to the huge gorge in front of you. Eat dinner at **El Tovar.**

Day 2

Tour the South Rim, visiting the **Desert View Watchtower, El Tovar,** and the **Hopi House.**

Have dinner at one of the casual eateries on the South Rim and get a good night's sleep—you'll need it.

If you've got kids ages 4-12, before you start sightseeing, take them to the **South Rim Visitor Center** at Canyon View Information Plaza and get them in the **Junior Rangers** program. The ranger will give them age-appropriate booklets, and throughout the day they'll earn a Junior Ranger badge and patch by fulfilling the fun and educational requirements, which include attending one of the ranger-led programs offered throughout the day.

Day 3

If you are hiking, get a very early start down either the **Bright Angel Trail** or the **South Kaibab Trail.** Don't carry your own bags. Spend a few extra bills to have the mules do it, so you can enjoy the hike and really see the scenery. If you're riding with a mule train to the bottom,

Take your bike to the Grand Canyon's South Rim.

Back to the Old West

The conquistadores, miners, ranchers, outlaws, and mythmakers of the Old West all left an imprint on Arizona, and their descendants do what they can to keep them from fading back into the deserts and the canyons. Listed below are some of the fascinating historical sights you can visit in Arizona.

SOUTHERN ARIZONA

Southern Arizona represents the northern extreme of the Spanish crown's American empire, while southwestern Arizona is full of the legends and kitsch of the Old West. Here you will find the following:

- **Tubac Presidio State Historic Park:** Visit the small park that preserves the memories and artifacts of Spain's American empire (page 172).

- **Coronado National Memorial:** Tour the remote monument in the Huachuca Mountains that marks the trail used by Coronado as he trudged north toward the Seven Cities of Cibola (page 181).

- **Tombstone:** Examine several forensic exhibits on that world-famous seconds-long gunfight that took place in the town's dusty streets (page 182).

- **Bisbee:** Visit an example of an Old West mining town rich with antiques stores and artisan boutiques (page 184).

- **Yuma Territorial Prison State Historic Park:** See what awaited those outlaws and bandits who ran afoul of territorial law (page 410).

NORTH-CENTRAL ARIZONA

- **Riordan Mansion State Historic Park:** Peek into the private lives of two 19th-century Flagstaff lumber barons featured at this state park (page 194).

Allen Street in historic Tombstone

- **Jerome:** Explore the history of the state's mining booms in this preserved mountainside town (page 225).

- **Zane Grey Cabin:** Pay your respects to one of the Old West's greatest mythmakers. Here you can see an exact replica of Grey's hunting cabin (the real one burned down in 1990), complete with period decorations and furniture, and learn all about the prolific author's passion for Arizona's Mogollon Rim region (page 250).

- **Pipe Spring National Monument:** Discover what it was like to live on a lonely fortified ranch in the late 1800s at this Arizona Strip sight (page 305).

South Kaibab Trail

show up at the appointed time and place and saddle up. You'll arrive at **Phantom Ranch** near the **Colorado River** late in the day. (You have to reserve a cabin and meals at the cantina up to a year beforehand. A mule trip will be all-inclusive, but if you're hiking you'll need to make separate reservations.) Take a shower, explore Phantom Ranch, dip your feet in **Bright Angel Creek,** walk to the river, and relax in the inner gorge. Eat a hearty meal at the cantina and attend a ranger-led program before collapsing into bed.

Day 4

Get up early, eat breakfast at the cantina, and spend the day exploring the **inner gorge,** the river, and Phantom Ranch. Ask a ranger for recommendations on the best day hikes and sights in the inner canyon.

Day 5

Wake up early, eat breakfast, and head out, either on a mule or on foot. It'll take you most of the day to get out of the canyon. If you're hiking and you came down the Bright Angel Trail, head up the South Kaibab for a different view. If you came down the South Kaibab, hike out using the Bright Angel so you can see the lush **Indian Garden.** When you make it out of the canyon, treat yourself to a nice dinner and relax and recover for the rest of the day.

Day 6

Spend the morning seeing the canyon for the last time and shopping for souvenirs. Catch the train back to Williams and check into the **Grand Canyon Hotel.** Have dinner at **Rod's Steak House** in Williams, then head back to the hotel to swim or soak in the hot tub.

Day 7

Head south to Phoenix after breakfast at the **Pine Country Restaurant** in Williams. Stop for a late lunch just outside of the city at **Rock Springs Café.** Catch your flight at Sky Harbor, and head home.

Best Scenic Drives

Gas up the car, grab some road food and sodas, make that perfect highway mix for the stereo (pick songs that go well with long, empty views), and hit the road on one of these scenic drives around Arizona.

THE DESERT

Open spaces and strange scenery abound on these routes through the hot, rocky deserts of western Arizona.

- **Historic Route 66:** Drive the remains of the Mother Road on the dry northwestern plains, where you can jump back to a slower time, passing through Kingman, stopping at the **Historic Route 66 Museum,** and spending some time in Seligman, the center of a Route 66 cultural rebirth (page 392).

- **Joshua Tree Forest Parkway:** Take U.S. 60 northwest from Phoenix through Wickenburg and keep going when it turns to Highway 93, known for its stands of Joshua trees (page 401).

THE FOREST

You'll be driving uphill on these scenic drives; watch as the vegetation changes from desert to transitional bushy scrub to highland evergreen forests, all while you sit comfortably behind the wheel.

- **U.S. 60 to the Salt River Canyon:** The forest comes on pretty quickly as you leave the central scrublands around Globe and rise along a twisty highway into the White Mountains. Make sure to stop for a photo op at majestic Salt River Canyon (page 104).

- **Highway 89A from Prescott to Jerome:** Take Highway 89A up over forested **Mingus Mountain,** stopping to enjoy a sweeping view of the Verde River Valley below when you reach the pass at the top of the hill. A little farther on and you're in the old copper mining town of **Jerome,** now home to boutiques and restaurants (page 224).

- **Swift Trail Parkway:** Negotiate a twisting forest road from the desert Gila Valley to the top of **Mount Graham** at over 10,000 feet, the highest of Southern Arizona's sky islands—it's

view of Historic Route 66 and the Cool Springs gas station

the equivalent of driving from Mexico to Canada in about an hour (page 375).

THE PLATEAU

The vast, sparsely populated Colorado Plateau has many lonely, scenic roads. On some of them, the traffic is so thin that you could take a nap on the center stripe.

- **The Vermilion Cliffs Highway:** Perhaps the loneliest of Arizona's lonely routes, this scenic road snakes across the **Arizona Strip** in northwestern Arizona, just below the border with Utah, and passes towering red-rock cliffs and vast bunchgrass plains (page 304).

- **Kayenta to Monument Valley:** The short drive from Kayenta to **Monument Valley Navajo Tribal Park** on the Navajo Reservation is almost as scenic as the famous valley itself, with strangely eroded sandstone monuments rising from the sweeping red-dirt plains (page 330).

Beat the Heat

Most people who don't live in Arizona would say that it's primarily a desert state of cactus, tumbleweeds, and rattlesnakes. Of course, that's only a part of the story. More than one-third of the Grand Canyon State—including the South and North Rims of the Grand Canyon—is covered in evergreen forests. This travel strategy, which starts in Flagstaff, the capital of the state's forested northland, will take you through these forests along cool, secluded, tree-lined highways and to the top of the tallest mountains in the state. The best time to go is in the summer, when the deserts are too hot for comfort.

Day 1

Arrive in **Flagstaff** the night before and stay at one of the historic hotels downtown (the **Weatherford Hotel** or **Hotel Monte Vista**). Wake up early in the morning, have breakfast at the **Morning Glory Café,** and head out to the **San Francisco Peaks.** Hike through the pine-and-aspen forest on the **Humphreys Peak Trail** to the top of Arizona, at 12,600 feet. If you're not into hiking, ride the **Scenic Chairlift** at **Arizona Snowbowl** up to 11,500 feet. After a day in the forest, relax at one of the restaurants or bars in downtown Flagstaff.

Day 2

Get up early and drive to **Williams,** where you'll park your car and hop on the **Grand Canyon Railway.** The historic train will drop you at the forested South Rim of the Grand Canyon, where you can spend the day looking into the canyon, exploring the charming buildings in Grand Canyon Village, and walking along the **Rim Trail** or taking a bike ride to **Hermit's Rest.** Catch the train back to Williams, have dinner at **Rod's Steak House,** and stay the night at **The Lodge on Route 66.**

chairlift at Arizona Snowbowl

Sustainability should have an expansive definition in arid lands. It should include the usual responsible practices—water conservation, recycling, moving toward renewables, and so forth—but also go further to embrace cutting-edge building materials and methods; refurbishing and repurposing old buildings; desert-adapted, native landscaping; and dedication to local farmers, artisans, and traditions. Though there is really no truly green or sustainable hotel in Arizona, these excellent places are moving in the right direction.

- **Bright Angel Lodge,** on the Grand Canyon's South Rim, and most of the other accommodations in Grand Canyon National Park are eco-friendly options thanks to the robust recycling and water-conservation efforts of park concessionaire Xanterra (page 281).

- **Hotel McCoy** makes new use of a forgotten old midcentury motor court in Tucson. The hotel is filled with Tucson-only art; serves only local beer, wine, and coffee; and has been retrofitted with low-flow plumbing fixtures (page 159).

- **Miraval, Life in Balance Resort & Spa,** at the base of Tucson's Santa Catalina Mountains is known the world over as a magical desert paradise dedicated to health and healing. Less known is that the high-end resort operates an on-site water treatment facility, allowing it to reuse nearly 100 percent of the precious resource (page 163).

Bright Angel Lodge

- **Arizona Grand Resort,** located near Phoenix's South Mountain Park, offers sumptuous rooms and inviting pools for relaxing and recovering in the Valley of the Sun. The hotel's parent, Classic Hotels & Resorts, is a member of the 1% for the Planet alliance and strives to use sustainable and recycled materials and organic local foods (page 77).

Day 3

Rise early once again and take Highway 89A through **Oak Creek Canyon** to **Sedona,** stopping along the way to admire the babbling, forested creek. Stay at the **Matterhorn Inn** in Sedona and have dinner at **René at Tlaquepaque.**

Day 4

Have breakfast in Sedona, hit Highway 179 south from Sedona to I-17, and then pick up Highway 260 east to the **Mogollon Rim** region. Drive through the forest along Highway 87, stopping in the small forest communities of **Pine, Strawberry,** and **Payson** to shop, hike, and eat. Check out the **Zane Grey Cabin** in Payson, and consider stopping at the gorgeous **Tonto Natural Bridge State Park.** Stay at the **Majestic Mountain Inn** in Payson and have dinner at **Gerardo's.**

Day 5

Get an early start for a drive across the **Mogollon Rim** to the **White Mountains** region. Drive slowly across the rim along Forest Road 300 for

Grand Canyon Railway

51 miles to the **Mogollon Rim Visitor Center,** where there's a paved trail and some breathtaking views, stopping often to explore and enjoy the forest along the escarpment. Stay the night in Show Low or Pinetop-Lakeside in the White Mountains region.

Day 6

Rise early and lace up your hiking boots for a trek either to the top of **Mount Baldy,** the second-highest peak in the state, or **Escudilla Mountain,** the third-highest peak. Escudilla is the easier hike, and along the way you'll see some of the most beautiful old-growth forests in the state. Have dinner at the **Goob's Pizza** in Springerville and rest up for your last forest drive of the trip.

Day 7

Gas up the car and head south along the **Coronado Trail,** a 120-mile, twisting, forested two-lane from the mountains down to the desert. Stop often to admire the wildflowers growing along the road, and keep a vigilant watch for wildlife. If you feel up to it, there are many hiking trails along the route that lead into the forest.

Phoenix, Scottsdale, and the Valley of the Sun

If you spend enough time in the desert basin known as the Valley of the Sun (often just "the valley"), there will undoubtedly come a time when you will ask yourself, "Why would they build a megalopolis *here*?"

This question will likely come up during the month of July or thereabouts, when it's 110°F in the shade and you're slogging to your car through a heat-storing parking lot somewhere. Don't lose heart, though. There is much in this mostly urbanized valley to do and see, eat and watch, find and buy.

A loose affiliation of cities and suburbs anchored by Phoenix and spreading to the wild northern Sonoran Desert along its edges, the Valley of the Sun is one of the largest metro areas in the nation and

Highlights

Look for ★ to find recommended sights, activities, dining, and lodging.

© MOON.COM

★ **Heard Museum:** This renowned institution is filled with artistic, ceremonial, and daily-life artifacts from both ancient history and modern Native American communities (page 38).

★ **Phoenix Art Museum:** See some of the most spectacular art of the American West—and of the Western world (page 40).

★ **Nightlife in Phoenix:** Like many desert creatures, Phoenicians come out at night. Grab a beer at a laid-back bar, sip cocktails at an ultracool lounge, or dance it up to live music (page 62).

★ **Taliesin West:** Architect Frank Lloyd Wright's desert masterpiece is a rare example of how humans can settle on the wild desert without marring or destroying it in the process (page 89).

★ **Casa Grande Ruins National Monument:** Explore the mysterious remains of a crumbling Hohokam great house (page 105).

Greater Phoenix

SEE "SCOTTSDALE AND VICINITY" MAP

Deadman Wash

Cave Creek

Apache Wash

Lake Bonita

303

N LAKE PLEASANT RD

17

Beardsley Canal

New River

Scatter Wash

Thunderbird Park

101

N 51ST AVE

N 43RD AVE

N 35TH AVE

N 19TH AVE

N 7TH AVE

E UNION HILLS DR

Aqua Fria R.

60

Luke Air Force Base

N 119TH AVE

N 91ST AVE

W UNION HILLS DR

101

Skunk Creek

W BELL RD

W GREENWAY RD

Arizona Canal

W THUNDERBIRD RD

17

Lookout Mountain Preserve

N 32ND ST

N 36TH ST

51

LITCHFIELD RD

N DYSART RD

N EL MIRAGE RD

N 111TH AVE

N 107TH AVE

N 103D AVE

N 99TH AVE

W CACTUS RD

W PEORIA AVE

★ SAHUARO RANCH

W OLIVE AVE

W NORTHERN AVE

Phoenix Mountains Preserve

Luke Air Force Base

Aqua Fria R.

Grand Canal

101

N 91ST AVE

N 83RD AVE

N 75TH AVE

N 67TH AVE

17

CUFF ▼ W GLENDALE AVE

SEE "CENTRAL PHOENIX" MAP

60

W BETHANY HOME RD

N 59TH AVE

N 51ST AVE

N 43RD AVE

N 35TH AVE

W CAMELBACK RD

W INDIAN SCHOOL RD

HEARD MUSEUM ✚

N 82ND ST

N 36TH ST

10

W THOMAS RD

PHOENIX ART MUSEUM ✚

★

CASH NIGHT CLUB AND LOUNGE

W McDOWELL RD

NIGHTLIFE IN PHOENIX

★

PHOENIX-GOODYEAR AIRPORT ✈

W VAN BUREN ST

E MONROE ST

✚

SEE "DOWNTOWN PHOENIX" MAP

N 27TH AVE

E BUCKEYE RD

60

17

60

W LOWER BUCKEYE RD

W BROADWAY RD

Salt River

Western Canal

Gila River

W SOUTHERN AVE

W BASELINE RD

SEE "SOUTH VALLEY" MAP

0   2.5 mi

0   2.5 km

S 75TH AVE

Gila River

W ESTRELLA DR

© MOON.COM

boasts world-class hotels, restaurants, museums, theaters, sports, and shopping.

Phoenix is the logical place to begin an Arizona adventure; it's the transportation, government, and cultural hub of the state. Here you will see the hubris and shortsightedness that have often typified the settling of the urban West. But you will also see novel attempts to live with the desert and its strange beauty, like Frank Lloyd Wright's Taliesin West and the ruins of the ancient canal-building Hohokam civilization.

And if you're here during one of the two or three "springs" that soothe the long summer's violent tendencies, and you're playing golf in December or hiking around the rugged Superstition Mountains in January in shorts, you might end up forgetting that you ever questioned the wisdom of the valley's founders and instead ask yourself, "Why don't I live here?"

PLANNING YOUR TIME

The Valley of the Sun comprises 10 incorporated cities and some 2,000 square miles, but most of the uniform sprawl deserves only pinpointed attention from the visitor. To see the highlights deeply and to taste the desert-city thrills, you'll need a week at least, but a long weekend suffices for a memorable once-over. An extra day could be spent touring the outer desert rings. If you're planning on spending time in other parts of Arizona during your trip, don't spend more than two or three days in Phoenix. It is best used as a transportation hub and jumping-off station—the ideal place to begin but not the main focus of an Arizona journey.

That being said, going deep into the valley's offerings has its rewards. You could spend a week touring the area's museums, especially the Phoenix Art Museum, the Heard Museum, the Arizona Museum of Natural History, the contemporary art museums in Mesa and Scottsdale, and the art and natural

history museums at Arizona State University. You could spend a full day or two checking out the excellent Phoenix Zoo, Phoenix Botanical Garden, Mormon Temple in Mesa, Deer Valley Rock Art Center, and Pueblo Grande archaeological site. A full day could be given over to downtown Scottsdale, shopping and eating, or to downtown Phoenix, looking at the historic buildings, shopping, and lunching. An afternoon spent strolling, shopping, and dining on Tempe's Mill Avenue or in Glendale's historic downtown is never a waste of time. Another full day or more could be spent driving the rugged Apache Trail and exploring the dusty old mining towns on the valley's outer edges.

From May until the end of October, about half of the year, a visit to Phoenix includes the risk of extreme heat. Risk becomes ridiculous folly June-September, when temperatures can and do reach 110°F and higher, and the heat-island effect created by all that concrete and asphalt turns the valley into a monstrous oven that doesn't really cool down even when the moon replaces the angry sun. It is, yes, a dry heat, and it does make a difference—90°F with high humidity feels worse than 110°F with none at all. Still, experiencing Phoenix in the summer is uncomfortable, though these days it's possible to feel the heat only on rare occasions: say, walking from your car through a parking lot and into a store. It is best to avoid daytime outdoor activities during the worst summer, but summer is also a good time to find a deal. If you can take the heat, you'll find prices at the high-class resorts in town drastically reduced, offering a chance for those of us who aren't movie stars and millionaires to experience a little pampering and stylish lounging. The best days to be in the valley are October-November and February-May. These are the "spring" months, when all is right and perfect in the desert. December and January aren't too bad either, though expect

---

Previous: downtown Phoenix; Heard Museum; Casa Grande Ruins National Monument.

to be wearing sweaters and light jackets, especially at night.

ORIENTATION

Phoenix sits at the center of a large basin surrounded by rugged mountain ranges: the McDowell Mountains to the northeast, the White Tank Mountains to the west, the Sierra Estrella to the southwest, the Superstition Mountains to the east, and the South Mountains to the south. In the northeastern portion of the metro area, the Phoenix Mountains provide a convenient landmark in an otherwise rather flat and repetitive urban landscape. The mountains surrounding the Salt River Valley are rocky and dry, topped by cactus and creosote; these are much shorter and hotter than the 9,000-foot and higher sky islands of the southern Sonoran region. The Salt River used to run through the whole basin, but the Roosevelt Dam and other factors long ago dried the river.

Although there are many incorporated towns across the basin, for the purposes of the traveler and tourist, the valley can be conveniently sliced into a few general regions that make the megalopolis easier to digest. These include **Downtown and Central Phoenix,** where you'll find many of the valley's sights and stops, bounded, roughly, by 7th Street on the east and 7th Avenue on the west, and by I-17 on the south and Camelback Road on the north; the **east valley,** which includes

Tempe, Arizona State University, and **Mesa; Scottsdale** and the **north valley,** which includes Scottsdale, just to the northeast of central Phoenix, and the small resort towns of Carefree and Cave Creek; and the **west valley,** which includes Glendale. Even longtime residents rarely distinguish between the towns when they're deciding which restaurant or shopping center to patronize, though it is true that if you live in Tempe or Scottsdale, you're not often found in Glendale. Unless you're paying close attention, you won't notice right away that you've left one city and entered another. The area's many freeways make getting around fairly easy, though you should expect traffic jams everywhere during the rush hours, roughly 6am-10am and 4pm-7pm on weekdays.

I-10 runs east-west through the center of the valley and then turns south along the eastern flank of central Phoenix, skirting Sky Harbor International Airport and heading southeast to Tucson and beyond. I-17 runs east-west from its interchange with I-10 near 7th Street in the east, and then, around 7th Avenue in the west, it moves north through the northwest valley all the way to Flagstaff. The Loop 202 freeway runs mostly east-west through the east valley, continuing east from where the I-10 turns south, and Loop 101 runs north-south and east-west in a loop around the northern, western, and eastern edges of the city.

Sights

DOWNTOWN AND CENTRAL

Downtown Phoenix, the center of the sprawling desert megacity, is roughly bounded by 7th Street on the east, 7th Avenue on the west, Fillmore Street on the north, and Jackson Street on the south. It's the historic heart of the city where you'll find many of the area's best museums, restaurants, theaters, sports arenas, shops, hotels, and parks.

The whole downtown area comes alive 6pm-10pm (or later) every month during the **First Friday Art Walks.** This is the time to see downtown at its most vibrant and creative, as more than 100 galleries and art spaces throw open their doors and put on shows and special performances, and thousands of Phoenicians mingle in the streets of downtown's up-and-coming neighborhoods. Along Roosevelt there's always a block party, with street performers, live bands, and vendors selling all manner of handmade and one-of-a-kind items. The art walk is self-guided and begins at the **Phoenix Art Museum** (1625 N. Central Ave., 602/257-1222), where you can park, pick up a map, talk to a volunteer about what to do, and hop on a free shuttle (or walk or ride a bike). For more information, contact the good folks at **Artlink** (602/256-7539, www.artlinkphoenix.com), who put on this popular event.

Heritage Square

Phoenix was founded by Anglo Americans, most of whom were Victorians through and through, despite their isolation out here in adobeland. With the coming of the railroad in the 1880s, building materials other than mud and rocks became available, and the homes in the valley began to reflect this; suddenly the adobe huts of the early years were replaced by redbrick and lumber homes, some of them big and ornate as anything in the East. The remains of Phoenix's Victorian past can be seen at this downtown collection of museums and restaurants known as **Heritage Square** (115 N. 6th St., 602/262-5071, http://heritagesquarephx.org), especially through a tour of the **Rosson House** (602/262-5029, http://heritagesquarephx.org, 10am-3pm Wed.-Sat., noon-4pm Sun., $9 adults, $4 children under 12), a refurbished Victorian showcase built in 1895 at a cost of about $8,000. The tour takes about 45 minutes and will likely disabuse you of any lingering notions that what passed for the good life in late-19th-century North America didn't find its way out to the frontier.

Arizona Science Center

Kids and adults alike will enjoy the popular, futuristic-looking silver-winged **Arizona Science Center** (602/716-2000, www.azscience.org, 10am-5pm daily, $18 adults, $13 children under 17, planetarium $9 adults, $8 children) in Heritage Square, where you can move a ball with your brain, lie on a bed of nails, and ride a bike across a line rope like a trapeze artist (with a net below, of course). Even teenagers will like this excellent museum, which has a permanent collection of more than 300 hands-on exhibits and a planetarium. There are exhibits on the human body and the brain, solar energy, and the science of flight, plus hands-on displays about gravity and other natural forces.

A few exhibits are somewhat Arizona-specific, but most of the museum is general and geared toward kids. On a weekday during school hours you're liable to run into a rowdy school tour group. There's also an on-site café that's a bit pricey but offers sandwiches and snacks without a lot of grease. Several of the center's more exciting attractions cost extra.

★ Heard Museum

It is possible for the observant visitor to the **Heard Museum** (2301 N. Central Ave.,

Downtown Phoenix

© MOON.COM

Central Phoenix

ZENYARD
GUEST HOUSE ● E MARYLAND AVE
ROKERIJ
N 7TH ST
N 10TH ST
RICHARDSON'S
DICK'S
HIDEAWAY ▼
THE VIG
E BETHANY HOME RD
E MONTEBELLO AVE
N 12TH ST
THE
SWIZZLE
INN
51
E MISSOURI AVE
N 16TH ST
PIESTWA FWY
N 7TH AVE
N 3RD AVE
CENTRAL AVE
POSTINO
CENTRAL
MARICOPA
MANOR
WINDSOR
E COULTER ST
STINKWEEDS
LOLA
TAPAS
BONNS
ROUND
CHERRY BLOSSOM
NOODLE CAFE
E CAMELBACK RD
DUCK AND
DECANTER
CHARLIE'S
LOLA
COFFEE
ROSIE MCCAFFREY'S
IRISH PUB
E HIGHLAND AVE
CHAR'S HAS
THE BLUES
Grand
COUP DES ▼
TARTES
E CAMPBELL AVE
N 3RD AVE
PANE BIANCO/
LUX
Canal
Madison
Park
PHOENIX INDIAN
MEDICAL CENTER
GEORGE & DRAGON
7TH AVENUE
MELROSE DISTRICT
CARL T. HAYDEN VA
MEDICAL CENTER
E INDIAN SCHOOL RD
THE CLARENDON HOTEL/
GALLO BLANCO CAFÉ AND BAR/
CLARENDON ROOFTOOP BAR
THE
RHYTHM ROOM
51
HOLIDAY INN PHOENIX
● DOWNTOWN NORTH
E OSBORN RD
KOBALT ▼
HILTON
SUITES
PHOENIX
Phoenix
Country Club
N 16TH ST
E THOMAS RD
N CENTRAL AVE
WILD
THAIGER
DURANT'S
SWITCH
RESTAURANT
& WINE BAR
BARRIO
CAFE
N 7TH ST
✚ HEARD
MUSEUM
★
✚ PHOENIX
ART MUSEUM
W CULVER ST
E CULVER ST
E MCDOWELL RD
© MOON.COM

Dwight Heard was the onetime publisher of the *Arizona Republican,* now the *Arizona Republic,* the state's largest newspaper both then and now. There was hardly a civic improvement in Phoenix's early 20th-century history that didn't have Dwight's hand in it, including the Roosevelt Dam. It was primarily Maie who developed the museum, however, as Dwight died just before its official opening.

Today the museum has 10 galleries featuring the art, artifacts, and historical narratives of each of the state's tribes. The large display on the Hopi is particularly comprehensive and includes Barry Goldwater's kachina collection. It's not all static history, though. Several galleries feature contemporary art by Native Americans and others. Sculptures dot the grounds while artists demonstrate their methods to onlookers. There are also galleries for kids with hands-on displays about Native American culture, many of them featuring the various ingenious methods native people developed to live well in an arid country. If you're in the market for Native American art (or if you just like looking at it), especially that produced by Hopi and Navajo artists, don't miss the museum's store, which has a good selection of books as well.

The Courtyard Café (602/251-0204, 11am-3pm daily) serves Southwestern-tinged food in the museum's enchanting, shady courtyard, offering appetizing salads, sandwiches, and soups, plus coffee, beer, and wine.

★ Phoenix Art Museum

The state's largest and best art museum and one of the better collections in the Southwest, the **Phoenix Art Museum** (1625 N. Central Ave., 602/257-1222, www.phxart.org, 10am-9pm Wed., 10am-5pm Tues. and Thurs.-Sat., noon-5pm Sun., $18-23 adults, $9-14 children 6-17, prices vary with the number of open galleries) is the high-water mark of the valley's sometimes rather shallow cultural stream. Here you will find exactly what you'd expect

602/252-8848, www.heard.org, 9:30am-5pm Mon.-Sat., 11am-5pm Sun., $18 adults, $7.50 children 6-12) to come away with a rather deep knowledge of the cultures, religions, and histories of the state's indigenous peoples. If you're planning on spending any time in Arizona's other regions, a stop here first will enhance your trip.

This essential Arizona museum was the 1929 brainchild of one of the valley's most influential couples, Dwight and Maie Heard.

1: Heard Museum **2:** St. Mary's Basilica **3:** Rosson House in Heritage Square

from an art museum in the West as well as much that will likely surprise you.

What you'd expect is an excellent collection of Western American art; the museum has that very definitely and is home to the Cowboy Artists of America annual show and sale. There are important and representative works by Eanger Irving Couse—whose arresting *The Captive* should not be missed—Fredric Remington, and other well-known Western artists. One particular highlight is an otherworldly Arizona landscape by the fantasist illustrator Maxfield Parrish, who manages to capture that strange, fantastical vibe the desert sometimes gives off. There's also a worthy collection of Latin American art, featuring paintings by Frida Kahlo, Rufino Tamayo, and others, along with Spanish-era art and religious items. The eclectic modern and contemporary galleries manage to be challenging without becoming ridiculous, and there are interesting displays on fashion and Asian art. The miniatures gallery should not be overlooked, with its little model-room displays on interior design through the ages. Plan on spending several hours or even half a day here.

After you've spent time in the galleries, you can grab a bite or a drink at the museum's restaurant, **Palette** (11am-8pm Wed., 11am-3:30pm Thurs.-Sat., 11am-3:30pm Sunday brunch, $14-18), which serves sandwiches, salads, and desserts made with local, organically grown ingredients as well as a fine selection of Arizona-made beer and wine. The gift shop sells a wide selection of prints, books, and the usual museum store fare. Art lovers would do well to check the museum's website before traveling, as several large special exhibitions are put on every year.

Arizona Capitol Museum and Wesley Bolin Memorial Plaza

A neoclassical copper-domed monument to power on the western edge of downtown, the Arizona Capitol, built in 1901, is no longer the center of day-to-day legislative work here at the bustling state capitol complex. It's now the **Arizona Capitol Museum** (1700 W. Washington St., 602/926-3620, 9am-4pm Mon.-Fri., 10am-2pm Sat. Sept.-May, free), with displays on the state's political history, its flora and fauna, its symbols and industries. Definitely worth seeing are the large paintings with heroic and mythical depictions of Arizona's past, painted by famous local artist Lon Megargee in 1913-1914 to celebrate statehood, and a few exhibits of historic furniture and other items from the territorial days. Just east of the capitol is a large plaza crowded with monuments to various heroes of Arizona and American history, including a large equestrian statue of Padre Kino and a black-wall memorial to the state's Vietnam veterans. This is a good place for a springtime walk, but it isn't worth visiting in the summer unless you have a particular interest in Arizona history. If you do, neither of these sights should be missed.

Wells Fargo Museum

The small **Wells Fargo Museum** (145 W. Adams St., 602/378-1852, www.wellsfargohistory.com, 9am-5pm Mon.-Fri., free) features an intact stagecoach similar to those used by the trailblazing banking and delivery company during the gold rush and subsequent settling of the West. Even if you have no interest in transportation history, you should consider stopping here to see the gallery full of N. C. Wyeth paintings and illustrations. Known for his detailed and iconic illustrations from Robert Louis Stevenson's *Treasure Island* and other classics, N. C. Wyeth was a great interpreter of the Old West in paintings and magazine and book illustrations, and this little museum displays more of his Western-themed work than any other.

Hall of Flame Fire Museum

The **Hall of Flame Fire Museum** (6101 E. Van Buren St., 602/275-3473, www.hallofflame.org, 9am-5pm Mon.-Sat., noon-5pm Sun., $10 adults, $8 children 6-17, $2

1: Arizona Capitol Museum 2: Burton Barr Library

children 3-5) has an engaging collection of relics from the history of firefighting. The almost one-acre museum near Papago Park includes the **National Firefighting Hall of Heroes,** a tribute to firefighters killed in the line of duty, and a display on the history of wildland firefighting, a particularly important occupation in the flame-prone pine forests of Arizona.

Burton Barr Library

Take a quick ride up through the "Crystal Canyon," the five-story glass atrium that divides this star of Phoenix's underrated architecture scene, to the fifth floor's **Great Reading Room** for an expansive view of the Valley of the Sun that nearly beats any vista you'd gain by hiking into the desert mountains. Along the way, make sure to check out the art on the walls—it's an amazing collection, with paintings by some of the Southwest's best artists.

Architect Will Bruder designed Phoenix's main library branch, the **Burton Barr Library** (1221 N. Central Ave., 602/262-4636, www.phxlib.org, 9am-5pm Mon., 1pm-5pm Tues.-Thurs., 9am-9pm Fri.-Sat., free), to suggest one of the great sandstone buttes of Monument Valley on the Navajo Reservation. Step in around noon on June 21, the summer solstice, when round skylights with special lenses project illusory flames; people usually gather to watch the event. The 43,000-square-foot Great Reading Room is one of the nation's largest, and it offers workstations and Wi-Fi. Throughout this beloved local landmark, the sleek, modern, modular furnishings and exposed wires and cables create a futuristic-utilitarian atmosphere that clashes evocatively with those bookshelves full of ancient stories—all of it washed in filtered desert light. A second-floor room holds the library's **Arizona Collection,** a place to get lost in the fascinating history of the Grand Canyon State. The ground floor holds the **Central Gallery,** a space featuring exhibits by mostly local artists, and nearby there's a small store selling used and discarded books at very fair prices.

Civic Space Park

This expanse of greenspace downtown, hovered over by the unique net-sculpture *Her Secret Is Patience,* by artist Janet Echelman, is hopefully an example of the direction urban design in the desert is headed. Opened in 2009, the **Civic Space Park** (424 N. Central Ave., 602/262-4734, 5am-11pm daily), which is right next to the light-rail station on Central Avenue, has solar panels, still-developing shade trees, and pervious concrete that captures rain runoff. The valley's rainstorms are often short and violent, especially during the summer "monsoon" rainy season. With all the paved surfaces that have replaced the thirsty desert floor, not much of the rushing rainwater soaks into the ground. Instead, it runs off quickly into the gutters and is wasted. The pavers and pervious concrete here allow more water to seep in, making the field of cool and inviting green grass seem like a gift for outdoor loungers rather than a waste of precious resources. Solar panels on the roofs of several shade structures provide the electricity for ghostly blue lights that illuminate Echelman's sculpture—which, inspired by the life-giving clouds that so infrequently visit the valley's wide skies, is suspended by cables 38 feet above the ground. A kid-entrancing **Splash Pad** (daily from Memorial Day weekend to Oct. 1) also lights up, though with purplish hues, after the sun goes down, making nighttime ideal for a visit. The historic renovated redbrick **A. E. England Building** within the park has a notable gallery featuring local and national work and hosts the **Fair Trade Café** (602/354-8150, 7am-3pm Mon.-Fri.).

St. Mary's Basilica

St. Mary's Basilica (231 N. 3rd St., 602/354-2100, www.saintmarysbasilica.org, 9am-4pm Mon.-Fri.), the white-stone and red-tile Spanish Revival church downtown, whose tall, cross-topped towers have been points on the valley's skyline for nearly a century, is one of several vital sights in Arizona for the religious soul, though at just under 100 years old, it's also one of the youngest (San Xavier del Bac and Mission Tumacacori in Southern Arizona were founded in the 1600s). The current building, which replaced an older church on the same spot, held its first masses in 1915. The soaring interior, lined and lit by dozens of stained-glass windows (the largest collection in the state, in fact), should be seen by anyone interested in religious architecture. Before visiting Arizona in 1987, Pope John Paul II, who drew thousands of Catholics from the state's rural hinterlands and across the valley to a huge mass at Sun Devil Stadium, made St. Mary's a "minor basilica" (an important church with special ceremonial rights). On the east side of the building the **Via Assisi Gift Shop** (10am-3pm Thurs.-Fri., 10am-6:30pm Sat., 9am-1pm Sun.) sells Catholic gifts.

Children's Museum of Phoenix

Arizona's children's museums have a knack for reusing grand old buildings that have been tossed aside and forgotten by the renewal-mad developers of the urban Southwest. Tucson's small museum for kids took over a stately old Carnegie library, while the larger **Children's Museum of Phoenix** (215 N. 7th St., 602/253-0501, www.childrensmuseumofphoenix.org, 9am-4pm daily, $14.95 adults and children over 1) is housed in the **Historic Monroe School Building,** designed in 1913 by noted California architect Norman Marsh. Half the fun of taking the kids to these hands-on play centers is experiencing the soul of a beautiful old space. Of course, that's not what the kids will say. They'll enjoy scrambling up and all over the 37-foot-high pile of steel, tubes, planks, and passageways called **The Climber,** serving plastic food in the make-believe restaurant, pretending to be a firefighter, doing a shift feeding and changing lifelike dolls in the nursery, or throwing paint in imitation of abstract expressionist master and Monroe Elementary School alumnus Jackson Pollock. Don't expect to make a quick visit. The hands-on, interactive, and deceptively educational activities here will appeal to kids under 10.

Japanese Friendship Garden

A perfect slice of green Japan in the middle of downtown Phoenix, the **Japanese Friendship Garden** (1125 N. 3rd Ave., 602/256-3204, www.japanesefriendshipgarden.org, 10am-4pm Tues.-Sun. Oct.-May, $7 adults, $6 children) celebrates the valley's relationship with Himeji, Japan, Phoenix's sister city, with a sculpted and manicured "strolling garden" with a trickling creek, rushing waterfall, and crowded koi pond. Called *Ro Ho En* in Japanese, the 3.5-acre refuge holds four different vegetation zones (and more than 50 different kinds of plants) that gradually rise into a "mountain zone" above a large pond topped with water lily beds. A creek trickles down from the mountains and spills into the pond over a 12-foot waterfall. It's an enchanting place for a stroll on a warm, breezy fall day in the desert (the garden closes for the torrid summer months). Easy paved paths snake around the deceptively secluded property, past sculpted trees, hanging lanterns, and bamboo fences, and over stone footbridges to the pond, which swarms with large, multicolored koi. The garden also has a traditional Japanese tea garden and an elegant teahouse, where on the second Sunday of every month you can vie for a seat at a traditional **Japanese Tea Ceremony** ($30 pp). It's essential to call ahead for a reservation: The garden hosts just five ceremonies each time, with only eight to nine guests per ceremony.

Pueblo Grande Museum and Archaeological Park

The valley's ubiquitous construction cranes can usually be seen bending and rising at work from the smooth dirt mound tops of the ancient Hohokam ruin at **Pueblo Grande Museum and Archaeological Park** (4619 E. Washington St., 602/495-0900, www.pueblogrande.org, 9:30am-4:45pm Tues.-Sat. May-Sept., 9am-4:45pm Mon.-Sat., 1pm-4:45pm Sun. Oct.-Apr., $6 adults, $3 children under 17), a canal-side city that reached the peak of its power and population just before

The Lost Hohokam Culture

The Sonoran Desert is neither a wasteland of shifting dunes nor a place to make it through at all costs but never to stop and settle. While such may be the popular conception of a desert, first-time visitors to Central and Southern Arizona are often surprised to see so much vegetation, so much diversity, and so much evidence of eons of human habitation.

That's not to say it has always been easy to live here; prior to the damming of the Southwest's rivers, a drought or a flood could wipe out a lifetime's worth of progress, and you never really knew with any confidence if the annual rains would come too heavy, too light, or not at all. There are usually two rainy seasons in the Sonoran Desert: In midsummer the Mexican Monsoon sends moisture north every late afternoon, and in winter the rains come again, hopefully. The twice-a-year rains, though scant compared to nearly every other place (the whole 100,000-square-mile desert gets less than 15 inches per year), allow for myriad dryland-adapted plants and animals to thrive here.

People, too, have thrived here for thousands of years, taking advantage of the once-perennial desert rivers like the Gila, the Salt, the Santa Cruz, and the San Pedro. Because of damming, over-use, and other factors, none of these waterways is much of a river anymore, but each of them long ago provided a healthy, if unpredictable, lifeline for the complex culture of the Hohokam, desert farmers who lived in the Sonoran river valleys from the beginning of the common era (AD 1) to about 1450. They disappeared from the valleys about 100 years before the Spanish arrived, leaving behind great mud ruins and more than 1,000 miles of irrigation canals built with stone and wooden tools.

The Hohokam culture went through several stages before reaching its golden age from around 1150 to 1450, also called the classic period. During this time, the tribe's irrigation farming of the Salt River Valley produced a surplus of maize, beans, squash, and cotton, and the culture grew more complex, the buildings bigger, and the population denser. Ball courts like those found in Mesoamerica were built in Hohokam villages, and pottery became more beautiful and less strictly utilitarian. At the culture's high point, there were as many as 40,000 Hohokam living in the valley, irrigating some 100,000 acres of farmland using canals that were still intact and usable when Anglos arrived in the 19th century. Evidence of this golden age can be seen at ruins like Pueblo Grande in Phoenix and Casa Grande between Phoenix and Tucson.

Then, around 1450, it all fell apart. This is roughly the same time when the Ancestral Puebloan cultures of the Four Corners region were also coming to an abrupt end, and the theories behind both collapses are similar, though by no means universally accepted. The culprits include soil salinization, disease, warfare, flood, drought, climate change, internal unrest, overpopulation, and various combinations thereof. The O'odham cultures, formerly called the Pima and Papago Indians, tell stories about how their ancestors overthrew the Hohokam cities along the Salt River because they had grown arrogant. Many archaeologists believe that the Hohokam were the ancient forebears of today's Sonoran Desert tribes, and oral tradition among the Hopi of north-eastern Arizona links that culture to the Hohokam as well.

it was abandoned around 1450. Here you'll also see the remains of one of the hundreds of canals the Hohokam dug through the valley to harness the Salt River—canals that formed the basis for modern agricultural pursuits as well. A short trail takes you to various points around the main ruin, which looks like a well-worked mound of dirt. Particularly interesting is the collection of Hohokam model homes along the trail, built according to what archaeologists think domestic structures may have looked like in the valley's ancient past. The contrast with today's tract homes and McMansions is striking, to say the least. Though not as large as the spectacular Casa Grande to the east, Pueblo Grande, a rare city-center ruin, is recommended to anyone interested in the Hohokam and to those who want to learn how past cultures have tried to live with the desert rather than against it. A small, informative museum has displays on the Hohokam—who they were, how they developed, and where they went.

Encanto Park

A lush duck-pond park east of the city center, **Encanto Park** (2605 N. 15th Ave., 602/261-8991, 5:30am-11pm daily) was once the place to go on a hot Phoenix afternoon, and it's still a peaceful, green, trickling-water oasis within the heat-island sprawlscape. It borders one of the valley's most tourable residential neighborhoods, the **Encanto-Palmcroft Historic District.** This district, with its winding, manicured streets, each home more elegant and each lawn better landscaped than the next, was Phoenix's first and best garden-style suburb, planned and built in the 1920s by Dwight Heard. It's fun to drive slowly through the neighborhood and see the style and grace that upper-middle-class merchants and city leaders once brought to valley living. The Spanish Colonial Revival and Monterrey Revival homes and the tall palms lining many of the streets—nonnative to Arizona except in a small pocket canyon near Yuma—give the whole neighborhood a dreamy pre-World War II California feel. Over at the park, kids will enjoy the old-school county fair-style rides at **Enchanted Island Amusement Park** (602/254-1200, www.enchantedisland.com, $1.25 for single ride, $21.75 all-day pass for kids under 54 inches tall); check the website for hours, as they change often.

Wrigley Mansion

A mere "winter cottage" to William Wrigley Jr., of the chewing-gum Wrigleys, the shining-white, 16,000-square-foot **Wrigley Mansion** (2501 E. Telawa Trail, 602/955-4079, www.wrigleymansionclub.com), perched on a hill overlooking central Phoenix, is still one of the valley's most beloved reminders of the pre-World War II cityscape. Wrigley, who also owned the Arizona Biltmore Resort just down the hill, built the home in 1931 in a kind of California-Spanish Colonial style with a lot of art deco flourishes. Composer and founder of L.A.'s legendary Village Recording Studio, George "Geordie" Hormel bought the 24-room palace in the 1990s and, after a costly refurbishing, opened a bar and restaurant inside. The place is a "club" that offers memberships for a range of prices, following the letter if not the spirit of the zoning laws. Out-of-town guests can choose a $5 one-month trial membership that allows you to have brunch ($54 pp), lunch ($11-39), or dinner ($18-39) at **Geordie's at Wrigley Mansion** (2501 E. Telawa Trail, 602/955-4079, 11am-3pm and 5pm-9pm Tues.-Sat., 10am-2pm Sun.), a fantastic steak house in the mansion that serves Arizona-bred meat and other locally sourced dishes. It's essential to call ahead for brunch reservations. A lounge and wine bar is also open to members. The most interesting part of a visit to this landmark hilltop, which bicyclists like to climb on weekend mornings, is the one-hour **tour** (10am and 3pm Tues.-Sat., arrive 15 minutes early, reservations required, summer hours may vary, $15), which reveals all the details and flourishes that you couldn't otherwise see. They also offer a lunch-tour package.

Tovrea Castle and Carraro Cactus Garden

Perched on a cactus-covered hilltop just west of the I-10 freeway nearing the east valley and resembling a many-tiered cake made of stone, the Phoenix landmark **Tovrea Castle** (5025 E. Van Buren St., 602/256-3221, www.tovreacastletours.com, tours 7:30am-11am Fri.-Sun., $25) is mostly seen these days from the seat of a car as you fly by at 75 miles per hour. It was built in 1928 by San Francisco businessman Alessio Carraro in a typical fit of passion for the desert but sold soon after to Della Tovrea. The unique home was Tovrea's winter getaway while she lived in Prescott with her second husband, a newspaper publisher, and she used it as her full-time residence after he died until her own death in 1969. The city of Phoenix purchased the large cactus garden, the home, and some adjacent property in the 1990s and has since led a multimillion-dollar

effort to renovate the property. If you want to see the home you must book a tour on the website ($25, 1.5 hours). Tour times vary slightly by season.

Phoenix Zoo

The excellent **Phoenix Zoo** (455 N. Galvin Pkwy., 602/273-1341, www.phoenixzoo.org, 7am-2pm daily June-Aug., 9am-5pm daily Sept.-Nov., 9am-4pm daily Nov. 1-Jan. 14, 9am-5pm daily Jan. 15-May 31, $25 adults, $16.95 children 3-13) in Papago Park was called the "Maytag Zoo" when it first opened in 1962 in honor of its main booster, Robert Maytag, a scion of the appliance family. Today it's the nation's largest privately owned, non-profit zoo, hosting more visitors every year than any other valley attraction. You'll see all the usual suspects here, from the mountain lions and bighorn sheep that stalk Arizona's wildlands to the rare Arabian oryx, which the zoo is credited with saving from near extinction. Along the way, as you walk along three paved trails through the zoo's clean, lush grounds, you'll commune with lions, elephants, camels, giraffes, and too many birds to name. You can catch a ride on a camel, walk through the frenetic Monkey Village, and stare for as long as you want to at the invariably sleepy big cats. A newer exhibit lets you get up close and personal (sort of) with stingrays and even sharks. Don't miss Baboon Kingdom, where you can watch those exceedingly humanlike creatures interact (often hilariously), and be sure to walk the Arizona Trail, where you'll witness what you're missing out there in the desert. Plan on spending at least half of the day here, and happily so.

Desert Botanical Garden

A 50-acre garden in Papago Park, the **Desert Botanical Garden** (1201 N. Galvin Pkwy., 480/941-1225, www.dbg.org, 7am-8pm daily, $25 adults, $13 children 13-18, $8 children under 13) is the very best place to go to learn about the desert's unique flora—other than

1: Phoenix Zoo 2: Desert Botanical Garden

the wild desert itself, of course. Actually, the garden might be even better than the raw desert—you aren't risking your life by coming here in the summer, and there are signs everywhere explaining what each stickery bush and thorn-heavy succulent is called and why. There are several special exhibitions each year, including art installations by visiting artists. You can eat here, at the excellent **Gertrude's** (480/719-8600, www.gertrudesrestaurant.net, 10:30 am-8pm Mon.-Fri., 8am-8pm Sat.-Sun., $18-32), or purchase a strange alien cactus for yourself. If you have any interest in the desert Southwest's unique and always-threatened plantlife, consider spending a few hours strolling the garden's easy pathways. Visiting in the summer can be trying, but it's not completely out of the question, as all that plantlife growing close together gives off a cooling vibe and a shady feeling, even when the sun is beating incessantly.

TEMPE AND THE EAST VALLEY

Tempe, a college town along the banks of the Salt River, is home to Arizona State University, the state's largest university and one of the largest public land-grant schools in the Southwest. The east valley includes Mesa, a seemingly unending band of sprawl east of Tempe that is the third-largest city in Arizona and the part-time home to thousands of snowbirds and RV parks. Mesa was founded in the late 19th century by Mormon pioneers from Utah and has the state's largest Latter-day Saints temple.

Arizona Sealife Aquarium

The colorful, family-oriented **Arizona Sealife Aquarium** (5000 Arizona Mills Cir., Tempe, 480/478-7600, www.visitsealife.com/arizona, 10am-7:30pm Mon.-Sat., 10am-6pm Sun., $24.95 adults, $19.95 children 3-12) at Tempe's Arizona Mills mall is not cheap; indeed, it's a bit pricey for what it is. If you don't have kids with you, it's not worth the price of admission. That being said, kids up to about 12 years old or so will likely enjoy

Tempe

To Double Tree by Hilton Hotel Phoenix Tempe and The Buttes

To Venezio's

W 13TH ST

W 13TH ST

BROADWAY RD

HARDY AVE

ROOSEVELT AVE

HARDY AVE

W HOWE ST

ROOSEVELT AVE

WILSON AVE

Clark Park

Mitchell Park

W UNIVERSITY DR

BECK AVE

W 5TH ST

E 5TH ST

W 1ST ST

Rio Salado Park

202A

TEMPE CENTER FOR THE ARTS

Tempe Beach Park

Moeur Park

MILL AVENUE SHOPPING DISTRICT

CAFFE BOA

HAYDEN FLOUR MILL

TEMPE ST. LUKE'S HOSPITAL

CASEY MOORE'S OYSTER HOUSE

ASU ART MUSEUM

HOUSE OF TRICKS

MISSION PALMS HOTEL

MUNICIPAL BUILDING

★ TEMPE TOWN LAKE

TWIN PALMS

S MILL AVE

ASH AVE

MAPLE AVE

E 5TH ST

E 7TH ST

NELSON FINE ARTS CENTER

GAMMAGE AUDITORIUM

S MYRTLE AVE

E 11TH ST

RIO SALADO PKWY

S RIO SALADO PKWY

Daley Park

S COLLEGE AVE

E 10TH ST

E BROADWAY RD

S MILL AVE

E APACHE BLVD

E ORANGE ST

E PACKARD DR

S MCALLISTER AVE

ARIZONA STATE UNIVERSITY

ASU Karsten Golf Course

Salt River

RED MOUNTAIN FWY

S RURAL RD

S RURAL RD

E VISTA DEL CERRO DR

E SPENCE AVE

E TERRACE RD

E 8TH ST

E UNIVERSITY DR

E DORSEY LN

ALOFT

E BROADMOR DR

S DORSEY LN

DAYS INN

HAJI-BABA'S

S MCCLINTOCK DR

E SPENCE AVE

E ORANGE ST

E GARY DR

FOUR PEAKS BREWPUB

S MCCLINTOCK DR

E HAYDEN LN

E DON CARLOS AVE

E 3RD ST

E RIO SALADO PKWY

E 5TH ST

TEMPE MARKETPLACE

BROADWAY RD

To Arizona Museum of Natural History and Mesa Arizona Temple

E APACHE BLVD

0   400 yds
0   400 m

© MOON.COM

this innovative, educational, and eye-catching attraction. The 26,000-square-foot space features a series of galleries with aquariums in all different shapes and sizes holding more than 5,000 creatures of the sea, including eerie, flat black rays, sharp-toothed sharks, and goofy sea horses. There's a tidal pool display that allows kids to touch a few creatures, and several super-fun observation bubbles get them up close and surrounded on all sides by sealife. At the end of the trail, after you've passed through each gallery and peeked into all 30 tanks, there's a big indoor climbing-and-sliding apparatus that will likely keep you on-site for another hour or so.

Arizona Historical Society Museum at Papago Park

So much of what tourists and historical reenactors find most interesting about Arizona history—cowboys and Indians, placer miners, and improbable gunfights in the streets—happened before the dawning of the 20th century. For many people the state's history stops at the O. K. Corral. But many of the more peculiar events that have occurred in the last state among the lower 48 happened in the 1900s, not the 1800s. The **Arizona Historical Society Museum at Papago Park** (1300 N. College Ave., 480/929-9499, www.arizonahistoricalsociety.org, 10am-5pm Mon.-Thurs., 10am-4pm Fri.-Sat., $12 adults, $8 children 7-17, children 6 and under free, two-for-one admission first Tues. of each month) explains the state's urban, 20th-century history, including how the Valley of the Sun became one of the largest cities in the country and the state's essential role during World War II. Among displays covering the state's singular culture, the one on the memorable local cartoon show hosts Wallace and Ladmo will have longtime Arizonans chuckling with recognition. Don't miss the exhibit on the mass escape of German prisoners of war from the nearby Camp Papago Park. In December 1944, after digging a 176-foot-long tunnel in the hard desert soil, 25 German POWs got away, but the cruel desert expanses proved to be too much for most of them.

Tempe Town Lake

Tempe Town Lake (620 N. Mill Ave., 480/350-8625, www.tempe.gov/lake, free), a large, city-center waterway just off Tempe's main street, represents an ambitious, long-term attempt to bring back a bit of the Salt River, at least for the sake of pedal-boating and waterside jogging, to the valley. It's a pleasant place to stroll, jog, bike, and kayak, or you can even lounge around on the grass at **Tempe Beach Park,** where there's always something going on. You can rent a pedal boat or a kayak, or take an electric-boat cruise on the lake. Kids will love to put on their swimsuits and dash around the cool water features at **Splash Playground** (10am-7pm daily, free), where they'll also learn about water and why it's so important here in the desert. At the western edge of the park, near the inflatable dam that holds the lake together, check out the **Tempe Center for the Arts** (700 W. Rio Salado Pkwy., 480/350-2822, www.tempe. gov), which hosts Broadway-style shows, local theater, music, and dance performances. The Tempe Center for the Arts also has an excellent art gallery, **The Gallery at TCA** (10am-6pm Tues.-Wed., 10am-7:30pm Thurs.-Fri., 11am-7:30pm Sat., free), featuring exhibitions of exciting work by local and regional artists.

Arizona State University (ASU)

A large and innovative public research university, **Arizona State University** (University Dr. and Mill Ave., 480/965-9011, www.asu. edu) has its sprawling, shady main campus in Tempe but belongs to and works on behalf of the entire Valley of the Sun. With more than 40 programs ranked among the top 25 in the United States, a few high-profile sports teams, and, like its rival in Tucson, a role in space exploration, ASU is known around the world. Its focus, though, is primarily local: The university is training a new generation to meet the challenges of climate change, ground zero of which is the great arid Southwest. Students in the first-of-its-kind ASU School of Sustainability work with Phoenix-area

Downtown Mesa

governments, groups, and businesses on sustainability issues and the campus itself is among the most ecofriendly in the country. ASU's main campus is listed as No. 5 on Sierra Magazine's Cool Schools Report and No. 7 on the Sustainable Campus Index.

ASU has about 50,000 students, several times the population of most Arizona towns. The school graduates about 20,000 students every year, and many of Arizona's leaders, lawyers, teachers, artists, and architects were trained here. The main Tempe campus is a pleasant place to stroll and people-watch, and it's worth a visit if only to see Frank Lloyd Wright's **Grady Gammage Auditorium.** But the best reason to stop by is to visit the **ASU Art Museum** (51 E. 10th St., 480/965-2787, www.asuartmuseum.asu.

edu, 11am-5pm Tues.-Wed. and Fri.-Sat., 11am-8pm Thurs., free), a small but memorable museum focused on contemporary art in various media. Housed in an amazing building designed by architect Antoine Predock, who also designed the Arizona Science Center downtown, the museum's permanent collection includes prints by Hogarth, Goya, and Posada and paintings by O'Keeffe, Hopper, Siqueiros, Tamayo, and other notable artists. There's free parking in front of the museum off of Mill Avenue.

Mesa Contemporary Arts Museum

Mesa Contemporary Arts Museum (1 E. Main St., 480/644-6500, www.mesaartscenter. com, 10am-5pm Tues.-Wed., Fri.-Sat.,

10am-8pm Thurs., noon-5pm Sun., free) is highly recommended to anyone who wants to witness the most current moment in painting, sculpture, and other media. Three galleries in this cool, spare space inside the **Mesa Arts Center** show revolving exhibitions featuring primarily artists from the Southwest, California, and Mexico, but not necessarily—in fact, rarely—what most would think of as Southwestern-style art. The shows are typically provocative and singular. This museum, along with a similar contemporary space in nearby Scottsdale, is must-see proof that the valley isn't exactly the cultural graveyard it can sometimes appear to be.

Arizona Museum of Natural History

The valley's only natural history museum, the **Arizona Museum of Natural History** (53 N. MacDonald, 480/644-2230, www. azmnh.org, 10am-5pm Tues.-Fri., 11am-5pm Sat., 1pm-5pm Sun., $12 adults, $7 children 3-12, $8 students over age 13 with ID) has quite a few hulking dinosaur skeletons in its Dinosaur Hall, and its three-story Dinosaur Mountain is definitely something to see, but the most interesting exhibits here are related to the history of the Southwest, including models of a Spanish-era mission and a territorial jail. The exhibition about Arizona in the movies is fascinating, and the exhibit on the Hohokam is one of the best around. This is a great place to stop prior to traveling to other parts of the state, a kind of one-stop lesson on the nature and people of Arizona and the Southwest through the ages—especially recommended to parents who are hoping to sneak a little education into a Southwestern vacation.

Arizona Temple Visitors Center

Non-Mormons can't go inside the beautiful **Arizona Temple** (525 E. Main St., Mesa, 480/964-7164, www.lds.org, 9am-9pm daily, free), on 20 green acres near the original Mesa town site, but those interested in the mysterious and fascinating world of the Latter-day Saints church can stop by and see the outside (which some say resembles the biblical Temple of Herod). Construction on the LDS temple, the first built in Arizona—a state that has welcomed Mormon settlers for generations—began in 1922, and the building was dedicated in 1927. The grounds include a cactus garden and reflecting pools, and the visitors center has some displays and a film about the LDS church.

SOUTH VALLEY
Mystery Castle

From the early 19th century through the mid-20th, American doctors had a simple, if life-altering, prescription for patients suffering from tuberculosis and other chest ailments: seek dry air. As a result, the mountains and deserts of the interior West, especially the arid Southwest, became a popular place for the dying to live out their final days. Phoenix's early boosters did much to attract these "health seekers" to the Valley of the Sun and thus shouldered Arizona and the desertlands early on with a reputation as a wide-open infirmary for the diseased and aged—a reputation the state still can't shake entirely, thanks to its many retirement communities. The American West is littered with the failed and half-realized dream projects of those living in a kind of surrealistic gulf between this and the afterworld, and this 18-room, stacked-stone **Mystery Castle** (800 E. Mineral Rd., 602/268-1581, www.mymysterycastle.com, 11am-3:30pm Thurs.-Sun. Oct.-May, $10 adults, $5 children 5-12, children under 5 free) near South Mountain is one of the more fantastical among them. Something of a masterpiece of folk architecture, the odd, fascinating home was built by the tubercular Boyce Luther Gulley, who came to the valley in 1930 from Seattle, leaving his wife and daughter behind. He spent the remaining years of his life cobbling together the sprawling, fairy-tale house out of stones found around the property and salvaged materials like telephone poles and railroad ties, believing he was constructing a walk-in sandcastle for his daughter. His methods, and the

South Valley

resulting structure, were not that different from the mesa-top stone homes built for centuries by the Hopi of northeastern Arizona, whose methods and aesthetic were copied by Mary Colter, one of the Southwest's finest designers and architects, when she built the famous stone structures that line the South Rim of the Grand Canyon. Gulley's project was unfinished when he died in 1945, but his wife and beloved daughter, Mary Lou Gulley, moved in anyway, and Mary Lou and the home were famously featured in a 1948 article in *Life* magazine.

The home, open for tours October-May, is a truly one-of-a-kind attraction that should be seen by anyone interested in architecture, design, art, or an inspiring and illuminating story of one man's obsession.

Rawhide Western Town at Wild Horse Pass

Pan for gold, ride a mechanical bull, and put the kids on the strong back of a cute burro for a ride around the dusty streets of **Rawhide Western Town** (5700 W. North Loop Rd., Chandler, 480/502-5600, www.rawhide. com, 5pm-10pm Fri., noon-10pm Sat., noon-8pm Sun.), a "replica 1880s" frontier town theme park—though it replicates an average Western movie set more than it does a real Arizona town in the territorial era. But that's certainly not the point here, where you can spend an hour playing in the theme park with the kids and shopping for unique Old West souvenirs and cowboy kitsch and then have a thick steak and some cowboy beans at the steak house. Every night a group of actors has a shoot-out, complete with stunt falls and other high action. It's free to walk around the town, but you have to shell out $5-15 to do anything fun. It costs $4.95 per person to watch the gunfights, which go down nightly at 7pm and 8pm. Rawhide is part of the Wild Horse Pass casino, resort, and golf course complex just off I-10 on the Gila River Indian Community Reservation. You'll find it about 20 miles southeast of downtown on the south side of I-10, Exit 162.

NORTH VALLEY
Musical Instrument Museum

Musicians and music lovers will want to check out the **Musical Instrument Museum** (4725 E. Mayo Blvd., 480/478-6000, www.mim.org, 9am-5pm Mon.-Sat., first Friday of the month open until 9pm, 10am-5pm Sun., $20 adults, $15 children 13-19, $10 children 4-12), a gorgeous museum and concert hall about 20 miles north of downtown via Route 51. This elegant museum showcases musical instruments from around the world and throughout history, offering a free audio tour with admission. A stroll through the museum's galleries reveals the astonishing beauty and variety of musical instruments throughout the world and brings one into close personal contact with the totems of rock and roll. Some of the displays are permanent; others come and go. In recent times the museum has shown a Rickenbacker guitar purchased in 1963 by George Harrison next to the very piano on which John wrote "Imagine." If that's not worthy of a pilgrimage, nothing is. Plan to spend at least two hours here.

WEST VALLEY
Deer Valley Petroglyph Preserve

ASU scholars are researching the forms and meanings of the petroglyphs that cover the Southwest at the **Deer Valley Petroglyph Preserve** (3711 W. Deer Valley Rd., 623/582-8007, http://dvrac.asu.edu, 9am-5pm Tues.-Sat. Oct.-Apr., 8am-2pm Tues.-Sat. May-Sept.,

$9 adults, $5 children 7-12) in the far northwest valley. The more than 1,500 works of rock art on this 46-acre preserve were scraped and scratched by the Hohokam and other tribes that once inhabited the valley, and they are believed to date from about AD 900-1100. A quarter-mile trail around the property has views of some of the state's finest examples of the ancient art form. Consider bringing along binoculars (or you can rent them at the center), as some of the best work is off the trail. The center is about 20 miles northwest of downtown among the volcanic rock piles called the Hedgepeth Hills. The easy trail winds around the black basalt boulders, which seem to have made the perfect canvas for the largely inscrutable but nonetheless fascinating figures and shapes. The steel-and-concrete visitors center, tucked in low among the creosote and cactus, is an attraction itself. It's the work of architect Will Bruder, who also designed the masterful Burton Barr Library downtown.

Historic Sahuaro Ranch

Learn a bit about what it was like to live in Salt River Valley long before the damming of the Colorado River and the invention of air-conditioning on a free tour of **Sahuaro Ranch** (9802 N. 59th Ave., 623/930-4201, glendaleaz.com, weekend tours every half hour, 10am-2pm Fri.-Sat., 1pm-4pm Sun. Sept.-May, 10am-2pm Fri.-Sat. June-July, free). The green and shady 17-acre ranch was active from the 1890s to the 1930s. The main house went up in 1891 and the orchard, palm groves, and rose garden create a lushness that is a world away from the rocky deserts all around. The ranch comprises 13 original buildings and is listed on the National Register of Historic Places. Don't forget to say hello to the peacocks wandering around. The old ranch is also a city park and a great place to walk and have a picnic. Free guided tours take off every half-hour from the main porch. The ranch is closed in August, and it's not a good idea to go during summer in any case.

Sports and Recreation

Phoenicians love to get outdoors—with more than 300 sunny days a year, they really don't have a choice in the matter. They keep their parks and recreation areas immaculate. There are well-trod desert hiking trails a short drive from just about anywhere in town. But Phoenix's official sport is golf, and there are many courses to choose from and play on year-round.

HIKING AND BIKING

The valley's best hiking trails are in a few easily accessible the urban desert preserves, so close to the bustle and yet almost secluded.

Phoenix Mountains

The **Piestewa Peak Summit Trail** (2701 E. Squaw Peak Ln., www.phoenix.gov/parks/trails/location/piestewapeak, 5am-11pm daily), a 1.2-mile one-way hunched-over climb up to what was, prior to the Iraq War, one of the more politically incorrect landmarks in the state—Squaw Peak. The term *squaw* has long had negative connotations for Native Americans, so in 2003 the peak was renamed Piestewa Peak, after Lori Piestewa, a Navajo soldier who was killed in Iraq. You are sure to run into a crowd on the trail on any given day, but if the weather is clear, you can see all of the valley and beyond spread out before you. The Piestewa Peak Summit Trail is an easy, if vertical, hike, and kids won't have a problem with it.

A little bit tougher is the hike up **Camelback Mountain** (www.phoenix.gov/parks/trails/locations/camelback), just a touch higher than its nearby sister at 2,704 feet. Within the **Echo Canyon Recreation Area** (5959 Echo Canyon Dr., 602/256-3220, sunrise to sunset), the mile-long one-way **Summit Trail** is a popular hike, and you may have to wait for a parking spot on weekends. You gain more than 1,000 feet on the way up, so it's not to be taken lightly. There are parts of the trail

that are hewn out of slickrock, with handrails alongside for help. From the top you can see everything, whether you want to or not.

South Mountain Park and Preserve

Forming the valley's southern border, the obviously named South Mountains can't be missed—they are the ones with all the communication towers and antennae shooting up from their peaks like pins in a hard-rock cushion. The 16,000-acre **South Mountain Park and Preserve** (10919 S. Central Ave., www.phoenix.gov/parks, 5am-7pm daily, trails open until 11pm daily) is popular with valley residents as an exercise field; bicyclists in particular enjoy climbing the high, twisting paved road to the lookout peak and then shooting rocketlike back down to the desert floor. One feels a little bad cruising slowly behind them on the curvy drive up to Dobbins Point, the park's highest accessible point at 2,300 feet, which is a favorite pastime of less-active Phoenicians and their visitors. There are several dry, rocky trails through the rugged cactus-and-creosote desert, most of them accessed off the main road up to the top and most of them up-and-down routes that aren't too difficult. Right after the main entrance, there's a trail-map station across from the Civilian Conservation Corps-built rock house, in which you'll find public bathrooms. The trails, nearly 58 miles of them, are open to hikers, mountain bikers, and horses. Mountain bikers will find some fun, moderately tough single-track here. For an easy and representative loop hike or bike ride, try a 3.5-mile round-trip jaunt on the **National Trail** to Hidden Valley. The trail is rough and rocky, and slick from wear in some places, but the views are spectacular and the saguaros

1: Camelback Mountain 2: Hole-in-the-Rock at Papago Park

Papago Park

plentiful. You pick up the trail at the top of the Summit Road at the Buena Vista Lookout. The National Trail crosses the entire park, if you're really feeling ambitious.

Papago Park

A twisting red-rock desert park just east of central Phoenix, **Papago Park** (625 Galvin Pkwy., 602/495-5458, www.phoenix.gov/parks) is a fun place to tear around on a mountain bike for a while or scramble up to **Hole-in-the-Rock,** a big hole in a jutting-rock hill through which the valley opens up beautifully. It's an easy climb up a very short trail, and then you can sit in the little smooth notch—which, the archaeologists will tell you, lines up perfectly with a building at Pueblo Grande a few miles to the southwest—and look out over the land. Facing west, this is a particularly good spot for sunset viewing. Walking

trails crisscross the park, and there are dozens of picnic tables and even a lagoon for fishing.

GOLF

Seen from the air, the Valley of the Sun appears to be stamped illogically with wide swaths of short green grass, all dotted with artificial duck ponds and sandy beach interruptions. The 300-plus days of sunshine enjoyed here allow for year-round golf—the waking dream of your average Rust Belt duffer. As such, an inordinate amount of desert has been rolled over with grass, creating a golfer's paradise and constituting a fairly questionable use of natural resources. The golf lover will likely disagree, however, especially during a bright morning round in November with the raw desert mountains beautifully framing the impossibly green fairways. There are dozens of courses throughout the valley, many of them linked to famous resorts. The valley also has some of the most popular municipal courses in the nation, each of them a bargain compared to the fancier places and competing just fine when it comes to lushness and creative design. Many of the municipal courses host more than 100,000 rounds of golf per year, so it's a good idea to book tee times in advance. You might want to book before traveling—the city's golf course web pages allow for easy online reservations up to eight days in advance.

Perhaps the valley's most environmentally thoughtful course is the municipal **Cave Creek Golf Course** (15202 N. 19th Ave., 602/866-8076, www.phoenix.gov, $12-31 residents, $12-43 nonresidents), a par 72 built on a reclaimed landfill, though you won't notice—it's green, tree-lined, and the valley's most popular public course. One of the oldest courses in the state, built in 1935 near Encanto Park, the city center's lush and attractive oasis, **Encanto Golf Course** (2755 N. 15th Ave., 602/253-3963, www.phoenix.gov, $12-31 residents, $12-43 nonresidents) is a par 70 municipal course lined, like its titular park, with tall shaggy palm trees. At Papago Park in the east valley, the green of the links at **Papago Golf Course** (5595 E. Moreland St., 602/275-8428, www.papagogolfcourse.net, $12-45 residents, $20-44 nonresidents, including cart) contrasts perfectly with redrock hills all around. The par 72 municipal course is very popular and hosts the Phoenix Open qualifying rounds. Just south in Tempe, the **ASU Karsten Golf Course** (1125 E. Rio Salado Pkwy., 480/921-8070, www.asukarsten.com, $19-108) stretches out near the bed of the Salt River, catching the shadow of Sun Devil Stadium—a rolling and twisting course that is particularly difficult.

HORSEBACK RIDING

There's nothing like a slow horseback ride among the saguaro forests to make you feel like a real cowpoke, and there's no better way to meet a real cowboy or cowgirl than to hire one to guide you on a trail ride. The desert preserves around the valley are filled with trails perfect for horseback riding, and there are myriad companies offering one-hour to all-day rides through the unforgettable desert scenery. You can book an early-morning ride to see the desert come alive or a sunset ride to watch it settle down, colorfully as always. There's usually a weight limit of 225-250 pounds, and kids generally need to be eight years old or older. Most of the companies offer full-day rides with lunch or evening rides with dinner around a campfire. It's a good idea to call ahead and make a reservation. Horseback riding in the valley is not recommended during the summer months. Most places are closed for summer anyway.

The best stables, and the ones closest to downtown, are the **Ponderosa Stables** (10215 S. Central Ave., 602/268-1261, www.arizona-horses.com) in South Mountain Park, just before the park's main entrance. They offer trail rides from one to eight hours ($40-150) along the park's many trails, winding among the saguaro, the creosote, and the petroglyphs. They are open year-round, but they suspend rides when the temperatures reach 100 degrees or above, which generally means they are closed during the day for a good part of the summer and open in the early evening for sunset rides. The guides here are friendly and knowledgeable, and if you don't like to hike or tear around on a mountain bike, this is the best way to see South Mountain.

In the western desert, the **White Tanks Riding Stables** (20300 W. Olive Ave., 623/935-7455, http://potagoldadventures.com, one-hour rides 9am, 1:30pm, 3pm, two-hour rides 10:30am Nov.-Apr., $40) offer one- and two-hour rides through the saguaro-dotted **White Tank Regional Park** with guides who are knowledgeable about the desert and its lore.

SALT RIVER TUBING

A leisurely, convivial float down the Salt is a desert-living tradition, especially during the unrelenting shine of summer. **Salt River Tubing and Recreation** (480/984-3305, www.saltrivertubing.com, 9am-6:30pm daily

Cactus League Spring Training

In late February-March, the Valley of the Sun's Cactus League offers baseball fans a unique opportunity to watch their favorite **Major League Baseball** teams, including many recent World Series winners, prepare for the coming season in intimate and family-friendly ballparks scattered around greater Phoenix. Fifteen big-league teams play in the Cactus League:

- **Arizona Diamondbacks** and **Colorado Rockies** play at **Salt River Fields** (7555 N. Pima Rd., Talking Stick Resort, 480/270-5000).

- **Oakland Athletics** are based at **Hohokam Stadium** (1235 Center St., Mesa, 480/644-4451).

- **Chicago Cubs** play at **Sloan Park** (2330 W. Rio Salado Pkwy., Mesa, 480/668-0500).

- **Los Angeles Dodgers** and **Chicago White Sox** share the huge, 13,500-seat **Camelback Ranch Stadium** (10710 W. Camelback Rd., Glendale, 623/302-5000).

- **Cleveland Indians** and the **Cincinnati Reds** share the **Goodyear Ball Park** (1933 S. Ball Park Way, Goodyear, 623/882-3120).

- **Kansas City Royals** and **Texas Rangers** are based at **Surprise Stadium** (15850 N. Bullard Ave., Surprise, 623/222-2222).

- **Milwaukee Brewers** play at **Maryvale Baseball Park** (3600 N. 51st Ave., Phoenix, 623/245-5555).

- **San Diego Padres** and **Seattle Mariners** are based at **Peoria Sports Complex** (16101 N. 83rd Ave., Peoria, 623/773-5700).

- **Los Angeles Angels of Anaheim** are based at **Tempe Diablo Stadium** (2200 W. Alameda Dr., Tempe, 480/350-5205).

- **San Francisco Giants** play at **Scottsdale Stadium** (7408 E. Osborn Rd., Scottsdale, 480/312-2580).

May-Sept., last tube rented at 3pm, $17 pp, per tube, includes shuttle to launch, cash only) rents out tubes all summer, shuttling seekers of cool water to a launch on the Salt River just below Saguaro Lake, east of the city in the Tonto National Forest. You can rent an extra inner tube to hold your ice chest and stock it with cans of beer and soda (no glass allowed) and sandwiches—and make sure to include some water, too. The party can get a bit drunken and adult on some days, especially the weekends. Kids must be at least eight years old and four feet tall to go along. There are some fun rapids and a quick current in places, depending on the water release schedule at the lake, but mostly it's a slow and sunny float along a thin band of shallow, cool, green-blue water, flanked by rock- and saguaro-lined canyon walls and thick riparian greenbelts. There are several beach landings along the way where floaters stop and picnic. Don't expect to be alone, and don't count on quiet or the sounds of nature all the time; a few waterborne revelers along the way will typically blast music, hoot, and yell, depending on how much beer is left. You can choose from two-, three-, and five-hour trips on weekdays, and a six-hour trip is offered on weekends. To get to the rental office, head north for 15 miles from U.S. 60 on the Power Road in Mesa. Always call before going out there, though; the trips are subject to weather and water flow.

Your favorite team's website has all the schedules and links to purchase tickets. Tickets for most of the teams are relatively abundant and affordable, usually starting around $10-15 for lawn or nosebleed seats and going up to $60-70 for great seats. Add $5-10 for parking at the stadium. Many of the ballparks offer package deals that include opportunities to take batting practice and work out with the team.

Depending on the popularity of the team, tickets may sell out quickly, while for others you may be able to get a ticket on the day of. If you're set on seeing a particular match-up, get your tickets as soon as they go on sale. The hottest ticket in town is the Chicago Cubs at Sloan Park, a beautiful, state-of-the-art facility with 15,000 seats, the largest in the Cactus League. There's a waiting list for spring training season tickets to see the Cubs, but it's free to get on it (http://chicago.cubs. mlb.com/chc/sloan-park/spring-training-waiting-list). For individual Cubs games, single tickets go on sale every January. Spring training tickets in general typically go on sale in January, though it could be earlier—as this varies, it's best to check directly with your team's website.

Most of the teams' workouts are open to the public, and if you arrive about 30 minutes before the games, there are usually opportunities to get player autographs. With daytime highs through February and March typically in the mid-70s to low 80s, and the sky always so clear and blue, it's a lot of fun to watch a game, have a beer or two, and kick back on the cool grass next to the couples and families out for a day off.

Before heading to the ballpark, pack your sunglasses and sunscreen—you will need both. Also bring a reusable water bottle. All the ballparks have plenty of water fountains for refills. You will get thirsty out there in the sun, and refillable is the ecofriendly and pocket-friendly way to go.

Many of the ballparks are surrounded by shiny urban entertainment complexes, with all kinds of shopping, hotels, and restaurants close by. As the Cactus League is very popular, plan ahead and book your accommodations early (and expect to pay a high-season rate), just after tickets go on sale.

A great place to start planning your spring training vacation is at www.cactusleague.com, which has all the information and schedules, or you can call individual stadiums for ticket information.

SPECTATOR SPORTS

Everybody in the valley is from somewhere else, or so the conventional wisdom says. The metropolis is indeed a transient city in a transient state; people are always moving in and out, and the new replaces the barely old at a whirlwind clip. This reality is both good and bad for the city's several major league sports clubs. There's always a built-in crowd of local devotees, and casual fans will usually turn out in droves when one of the big Midwestern or Eastern teams is in town. When the Chicago Cubs come to visit every summer, it's sometimes difficult to see the Diamondbacks fans among all those blue shirts. That being said, most of the local teams have been able to

ingratiate themselves with the natives, the longtime residents, and the new arrivals alike simply by doing what a sports team is supposed to do: win.

The Arizona Diamondbacks

One of the more successful of Arizona's teams in recent times has been Major League Baseball's **Arizona Diamondbacks** (602/462-6500, http://arizona.diamondbacks. mlb.com), franchised in 1998 and with a World Series trophy in the clubhouse by 2001. With one of the best scouting programs in the game, lately the D-Backs have skewed younger, introducing future superstars to big-time playoff baseball and beginning a new tradition of smart, fast, and fundamental National League ball that has locals filling the seats at **Chase Field** (401 E. Jefferson St., 602/462-6799 or 800/821-7160, tours offered 9:30am, 11am, and 12:30pm Mon.-Sat. year-round, $7 adults, $5 children under 12) downtown, one of the few ballparks in the world with a retractable roof. The roof is closed during most of the season with the air conditioners blasting—the only way baseball can be played in the desert without killing the athletes. Individual game tickets range in price from $5 for nosebleed seats to $215 for a clubhouse box. A decent seat will cost you $15-40. Though the team is very popular in the valley, most of the time tickets can be purchased the day of the game at the ballpark. If one of the big Midwestern or Eastern teams is in town, like the Chicago Cubs or, during interleague play, the Detroit Tigers, you will need to plan far ahead.

The Phoenix Suns

The quick play of the **Phoenix Suns** (602/379-7900, www.nba.com/suns, $25-55) has made the NBA team a beloved institution in Arizona. The Suns also have a long and storied history, with the likes of Charles Barkley, Dan Majerle (who still has a restaurant in town and now coaches Grand Canyon University's basketball team), Danny Ainge, and Dennis Johnson, and of course Shaquille O'Neal, once wearing the purple and orange. The Suns often battle the L.A. Lakers for supremacy in the Western Conference's Pacific League, and the stands at the huge **Talking Stick Resort Arena** (201 E. Jefferson St.) downtown are always packed with fans.

The Arizona Cardinals

The National Football League's **Arizona Cardinals** (602/379-0102, www.azcardinals.com, $47-148) play in the **University of Phoenix Stadium** (1 Cardinals Dr., Glendale), a flying saucer-shaped building in Glendale, drawing a rabid crowd of football fans from across the state.

ASU Sports

The various teams that play under the name **ASU Sun Devils** (480/965-2381, www.thesundevils.cstv.com, box office open Aug. 16 through school year, 9am-5pm Mon.-Fri., 9am-noon Sat.) are typically pretty good and often especially in baseball and football, very good. The students and the many ASU alumni who stuck around the valley really get into it, and tickets for the bigger games aren't easy to come by. Barry Bonds played his college baseball here, as did many other big leaguers. Jake "The Snake" Plummer, former quarterback for the Arizona Cardinals and then the Denver Broncos, was a college star on the Sun Devil football field.

Entertainment and Events

★ NIGHTLIFE

There are a lot of young people in Phoenix—it's in many ways a very young city. There are also a lot of retirees and even a few people in between. They all manage to come together when the sun goes down. Like so many desert creatures, they love the nightlife. There's upscale and dive-scale, sports bars and ultracool lounges, rock bars, honky-tonks, and hookahs. Hidden somewhere out in that hot sprawl, there's a place that offers what you want. The best way to identify both the new and the classic is with the *Phoenix New Times,* an alternative weekly you'll find free everywhere.

Downtown and Central
BARS AND PUBS

Bookish types just might meet their soul mate at **First Draft Book Bar** (300 W. Camelback Rd., 602/274-0067, www.changinghands.com, 9am-10pm Mon.-Sat., 9am-8pm Sun.), a craft beer and wine bar inside the midtown Phoenix location of the legendary **Changing Hands Bookstore,** which has been one of the brightest literary lights in Arizona for a few generations. The charming bar has a wide selection of craft beer, much of it from Arizona, on draft and in cans and bottles. The menu includes cider, mead, sangria, mimosas, kombucha, coffee drinks, light breakfasts, small plates, sandwiches, and snacks. The bookstore sells new and used books and has an intelligent selection. Happy hour is 3pm-6pm Monday-Friday and 9am-3pm Saturday-Sunday.

Ready-made Irish and English "pubs" have popped up all over the country these days, but central Phoenix's **George & Dragon Pub** (4240 N. Central Ave., 602/241-0018, www. georgeanddragonpub.net, 11am-2am daily) is the real deal, and it has been around forever. A fabulous selection of beers on tap—heavy on the delicious brews of the British Isles—a well-stocked jukebox, billiards, and good eats (the bangers and mash are particularly tasty) make this authentic pub a perfect place to spend an hour or ten. **The Vig Arcadia** (4041 N. 40th St., 602/553-7227, www.thevig.us, 11am-close daily), with its refined interior of redbrick walls, pale wood tables, and chocolate-brown booths, and its cool, shady, and laid-back patio, is one of the best hangouts in the valley. Spend the afternoon or evening drinking on the patio, playing bocce ball, and sampling the wonderful food.

Near downtown's Heritage Square, the British pub atmosphere of **The Rose and Crown** (628 E. Adams St., 602/256-0223, www.theroseandcrownaz.com, 11am-2am Mon.-Sat., 10am-2am Sun.) is all you need most nights. There's a pool table and a dartboard, a convivial atmosphere of fellow beer drinkers downing pints of Guinness, Tetley's, Smithwick's, and the like, The Clash on the stereo and on the wall, and a menu of tasty, rib-sticking pub eats to soak up the booze.

The **Ice House Tavern** (3855 E. Thomas Ave., 602/244-1179, www.icehousetavernphx. com, 1:30pm-2am Mon.-Thurs., 11am-2am Fri.-Sun., sometimes open earlier for college football games) is a casual and fun locals hangout, where you can grab a beer, watch the game, and then stick around and dance to a local garage band. The bar has an ice-hockey theme, and you can watch through a big window as skaters attempt to stay up at the Arcadia Ice Arena.

Head over to the **Valley Bar** (130 N. Central Ave., www.valleybarphx.com, 4pm-2am Mon.-Fri., 6pm-2am Sat.-Sun.) for a large dose of Valley of the Sun culture and history at this fun, inventive, and local-proud bar and dungeon-like live music venue. Just a block from the Adams Street light-rail stop, you can kick back in The Rose Room, a cozy lounge named after Rose Mofford, Arizona's first female governor (who always wore her hair in a fantastic beehive), and sample cocktails named after Arizona politicians past and present. Along with a basement stage for live bands and a game room with pool tables, pinball, and video games, the bar also has food to offer—sandwiches, small plates, and flat bread pizzas—until 1am on weekends and midnight weekdays.

The **Lucky Strike Lanes** (50 W. Jefferson St., Ste 240, 602/732-5490, www. bowlluckystrike.com, 11am-midnight Sun.-Thurs., 11am-2am Fri.-Sat.) in downtown's CityScape development gives new meaning to the usually pejorative term "bowling alley bar." With a posh and civilized interior of low couches and slick surfaces, big screens everywhere, two bars, and DJs spinning the latest, Lucky Strike is a memorable and cool place to hang out. It's a good idea to reserve one of the 12 lanes on the website before you go. If you get sick of bowling, head next door to the **Gypsy Bar** (50 W. Jefferson St., 602/732-5490, www.gypsybarphoenix.com, Fri.-Sat. 11am-2am, Sun. and Thurs. 11am-midnight), a dance place that also has a "game lounge" with all kinds of new and old-school games.

The casual **Bonus Round** (24 W. Camelback Rd., 602/374-6936, bonusround-phx.com, 4pm-midnight Mon.-Thurs., 4pm-2am Fri.-Sat., 4pm-10pm Sun.) pairs craft cocktails with names like the Sarlacc Pit (absinthe, gin, and brown sugar) with 20 classic arcade games, including Ms. Pac Man and Centipede. In other words, there are bound to be a few gamers, Star Wars nuts, and other fun, interesting people hanging out here on any given night. A small menu of pub eats includes flatbread pizzas and veggie sandwiches.

LOUNGES AND WINE BARS

Housed in an old department store downtown that was hailed as a local masterpiece of the International Style when it opened in 1947, the retro-modernist lounge and restaurant **Hanny's** (40 N. 1st St., 602/252-2285, www.hannys.net, 11am-1:30am Mon.-Fri., 5pm-1:30am Sat.-Sun.) is an essential bar-hopping stop for anyone who appreciates urban renewal done the right way. This sophisticated lounge serves food—gourmet pizzas, appetizers, and sandwiches—until 1am and a large menu of creative, expertly mixed (though expensive) cocktails, wine, and beer until 1:30am.

For a top-notch glass of wine, a plate of cheese and olives with bruschetta, and a quiet, laid-back, but elegant atmosphere, head to **Postino** (3939 E. Campbell Ave., 602/852-3939, www.postinowinecafe.com, 11am-11pm Mon.-Thurs., 11am-midnight Fri., 9am-midnight Sat., 11am-10pm Sun.), where they'll squeeze an orange and mix you one of the best mimosas you've ever had. The wine program changes frequently, and they offer a decent selection of beers, most of them in bottles.

Just across Camelback Road from the Biltmore Fashion Park, the upscale **MercBar** (2525 E. Camelback Rd., 602/508-9449, www.mercbar.com, 4pm-2am Mon.-Thurs., 7pm-2am Fri.-Sun.) claims to be "just a bar," but it is far beyond that: It is a civilized and darkly inviting lounge. You might not want to leave once you sit down at a small, round table in a deep leather chair and taste one of the signature concoctions the expert bartenders mix up here. It's pricey, and you should wear your slickest duds, but it is worth it for the atmosphere and the tasty mixes. This is an ideal place to stop for a before- or after-dinner cocktail if you are on a hot date and want to impress.

With its rustic exposed brick and wood floors contrasting against a mid-century-modern-meets-urban-hip decor, the **SideBar** (701 W. McDowell Rd., 602/254-1646, www.sidebarphoenix.com, 4pm-2am Mon.-Thurs., 3pm-2am Fri.-Sun.), at the southwest corner of 7th Avenue and McDowell, has atmosphere to spare. They also take their mixing seriously, with fresh-squeezed juices, perfectly balanced simple syrups, and a range of top-shelf booze both familiar and exotic.

Stop in at **Carly's Bistro** (128 E. Roosevelt St., 602/262-2759, www.carlysbistro.com, 10:30am-1am Mon.-Wed., 10:30am-2am Thurs.-Fri., 10am-2am Sat., 10am-1am Sun.) for a glass of real absinthe, a perfectly made White Russian with soy milk, or a carafe of sangria for the table. This bistro and hangout has a good selection of beers and a warm atmosphere that will keep you sampling from their exciting cocktail menu. Don't forget about **Durant's** (2611 N. Central Ave., 602/264-5967, www.durantsaz.com, 11am-10pm Mon.-Thurs., 11am-11pm Fri., 5pm-11pm Sat., 4:30pm-10pm Sun.), where they have more than excellent steaks and prime rib: They also serve one of the best martinis in town, with an old-school, upscale mood perfect to start a night on the town.

Skydeck/Clarendon Rooftop Bar (401 W. Clarendon Ave., 602/252-7363, http://goclarendon.com, 5am-10pm daily Oct.-early July), on the roof of the Clarendon Hotel, offers amazing views of the valley in an ultra-posh atmosphere, but it's not always easy to get up there. They enforce a strict numbers limit, but it's worth a try for the peace you'll feel looking out over the desert city as the sun dips away, cocktail in hand and coursing through your veins.

GAY AND LESBIAN

The vibe at **Charlie's** (727 W. Camelback Rd., 602/265-0224, www.charliesphoenix.

com, noon-4am Mon.-Thurs. and Sat., 2pm-4am Fri., noon-2am Sun.) is down-home. The home of the Arizona Gay Rodeo Association is all about shuffling your cowboy boots across the floor and getting in on a good line dance, and the DJs often (but not always) spin country hits rather than Lady Gaga. They also have drag shows, proms, and tons of other special events.

In Park Central Mall, **Kobalt** (3110 N. Central Ave., Ste. 125, 602/264-5307, www.kobaltbarphoenix.com, 11am-2am Mon.-Fri., 10am-2am Sat.-Sun.) claims to have the best selection of karaoke music in town. This is a fun, trendy, and popular place; it has a kind of a local watering-hole vibe, hosts all kinds of fun games, offers drink specials, and has a comfortable, open patio.

In 2019, the popular Cash Country Inn changed its tune, moving to a new location and evolving into the **Cash Night Club and Lounge** (1730 E. McDowell Rd., 602/244-9943, www.cashnightclub.com, 9pm-2am Thurs.-Sun.), an urban dance club for the valley's LGBT community, while holding on to the welcoming atmosphere for which it has been known. Now you're more likely to hear hip-hop and Latin music over country-western, and there's a lot of beautiful people and fancy dancing—the whole place has a much more upscale vibe than it did before.

LIVE MUSIC

The **Crescent Ballroom** (308 N. 2nd St., 602/716-2222, www.crescentphx.com, 11am-1am or 2am Mon.-Fri., 5pm-1am or 2am Sat.-Sun.) downtown brings the best artists to the valley, from classic rockers to beloved alternative cult-leaders and contemporary singer-songwriters. It's an intimate little place just a block west of the Van Buren light-rail station. There are no bad seats here; if you're not standing in front of the stage watching spit fly out of the singer's mouth, you're perched middle-center on a small set of bleachers, gulping a martini. The Ballroom's restaurant, **Cocina 10** (11am-midnight Mon.-Fri., 5pm-midnight Sat.-Sun) serves excellent overstuffed burritos with a variety of fillings to choose from. Parking is $5 at a lot next to the Ballroom; bring exact change, or better yet, just take the light-rail.

A hip, wood-and-brick lounge in a converted home, **The Lost Leaf** (914 N. 5th St., 602/258-0014, www.thelostleaf.org, 5pm-2am daily) at 5th Street and Roosevelt offers dozens of beers (many of them Arizona-brewed), meads, ciders, sakes, and wines (also many from Arizona), and hosts the best bands and musicians you've never heard of nearly every night. All the shows are free, and it also costs nothing to look at the astounding, confusing, and haunting art on the walls. **The Blooze Bar** (12014 N. 32nd St., 602/788-4574, www.thebloozebar.com, 9am-2am daily) has rockabilly and alternative rock bands on a regular basis and a young crowd. The **Rhythm Room** (1019 E. Indian School Rd., 602/265-4842, www.rhythmroom.com, 7pm-2am daily) is an excellent venue to catch local and national touring acts playing blues, rock, and country, and on any given night there's likely to be some roots-heavy band tearing up the stage. For blues, jazz, and funk music that you can dance to by some of the tightest groups in the region, check out **Char's House of Blues** (4631 N. 7th Ave., 602/230-0205, www.charshastheblues.com, 8pm-1am Sun.-Thurs., 7:30pm-1am Fri.-Sat.), where you can also watch all the valley's sports teams on big TVs. Music starts nightly at 9pm.

Right next to Stand Up Live in downtown's CityScape development, **Copper Blues** (50 W. Jefferson St., 480/719-5005, www.copperblueslive.com, 11am-10pm Mon.-Tues., 11am-11pm Wed., 11am-midnight Thurs., 11am-2am Friday, 4pm-2am Sat., 4pm-10pm Sun., happy hour 3pm-6pm Mon.-Fri., 4pm-6pm Sat.-Sun.) has more than 60 beers on tap, which you can sample while live local and regional bands rock your socks off. Most of the shows are free, and so are three hours of parking with validation. Copper Blues also serves excellent stone-oven pizzas with all kinds of creative toppings, plus sandwiches, burgers, salads, and much more ($10-20). This fun, laid-back place is located right next to the light-rail stops at Jefferson and 1st Avenue Station and Washington and Central Avenue Station, and it has a comfortable patio for enjoying those perfect Valley of the Sun nights.

COMEDY

Located in the thick of all the downtown action in the bustling CityScape development, **Stand Up Live** (50 W. Jefferson St., 480/719-6100, www.standuplive.com, $10-30) brings A-list comedians to the valley and serves frosty drinks for you to blow out your nose while laughing. Check the club's online calendar for upcoming shows. A ticket to a show comes with a three-hour parking validation, but it's also easy to take the light-rail to either the Jefferson and 1st Avenue Station or the Washington and Central Avenue Station.

Tempe and the East Valley

Head over to **Mill Avenue** in Tempe to party with the ASU crowd; there are several clubs, bars, and restaurants along Mill, and there's bound to be a fashionable, fun, and beautiful crowd anywhere you stop.

BARS AND PUBS

Casey Moore's (850 S. Ash Ave., 480/968-9935, www.caseymoores.com, 11am-2am daily) is a favorite among ASU students, faculty, and still-partying alumni, with a mist-cooled patio, a large selection of beers, and huge plates of oysters. For one of the best handcrafted beers in the valley, try the **Four Peaks Brewing Company** (1340 E. 8th St., 480/303-9967, www.fourpeaks.com, 11am-midnight Mon.-Thurs., 11am-2am Fri., 9am-2am Sat., 9am-midnight Sun.) near campus, but you can also find Four Peaks beers at most of the better bars and restaurants in the valley. At **Dos Gringos South Tempe** (3000 S. Priest, 480/753-4577, 11am-2am daily) you'll think you've died and landed in some beachside town on permanent spring break; a continual college bacchanalian vibe rules here, especially during happy hour and college sports games. The food isn't bad either,

and they serve their hot, filling Mexican grub until 2am.

The Handlebar (6805 Mill Ave., 480/474-4888, www.handlebaraz.com, 11am-2am daily) is a fun, laid-back, bicycle-centric bar along Tempe's bustling main street, Mill Avenue. It has 24 beers on tap, many of them made in Arizona, as well as a huge patio perfect for hanging out on a warm winter day and a kitchen open late that serves brats, sandwiches, burgers, and other delicious food.

LIVE MUSIC

The **Yucca Tap Room** (29 W. Southern, 480/967-4777, http://yuccatap.com, 6am-2am daily) is a legendary ASU-area bar that hosts local and touring rock bands and musicians in a dive-bar setting near campus. A leader in the renowned Tempe music scene of the 1990s, the Yucca Tap Room is still one of the best places in the valley to see live music.

The **Tempe Tavern** (1810 E. Apache Blvd., 480/794-1706, http://tempetavern.com, 10am-2am daily) just south of ASU on Apache Boulevard puts on local and regional bands, from rock to punk to hip-hop, for a mixed crowd. The restaurant here serves pretty good burgers, wings, onion rings, salads, and sandwiches until midnight.

PERFORMING ARTS

The excellent **Phoenix Symphony** (602/495-1999, www.phoenixsymphony.org) puts on dozens of pops and classics concerts throughout the year at downtown's beautiful **Symphony Hall** (75 N. 2nd St.). The hall is also home to the **Arizona Opera Company** (602/266-7464, www.azopera.org), which presents mostly classic, well-known operas with creative set designs and top-notch performers. A few blocks away, the spectacular **Comerica Theatre** (400 W. Washington, 602/379-2800, www.comericatheatre.com) welcomes a constant stream of headlining national acts, including an impressive array of big-name comedians and rock bands. But perhaps the best seat in the valley is at the intimate **Celebrity Theatre** (440 N. 32nd St.,

602/267-1600, www.celebritytheatre.com). The theater's round stage makes every seat in the house a perfect one, and a wide variety of performers appear every year—jazz bands, crooners, rappers, classic rock, and nearly everything else. The acts here aren't usually as big as the ones that play at the Comerica or at the huge outdoor **Ak-Chin Pavilion** (2121 N. 83rd Ave., 602/254-7200, www.cricket-pavilion.com), but you'll want to check the website; if any band or performer you like is playing at Celebrity Theatre, you should definitely think about going.

The valley's premier live theater venue is the **Herberger Theater Center** (222 E. Monroe St., 602/254-7399, www.herbergertheater. org) downtown—you'll know you've found it when you see the fascinating dancing nude sculptures out front. Here you can see original productions by the **Arizona Theatre Company** (502 W. Roosevelt, 602/256-6995, www.aztheatre.org), one of the nation's finest regional theater companies and one that is never daunted by difficult, unique work.

Even if you don't have tickets to see one of the many theater, music, or live performances put on at the classic **Orpheum Theatre** (203 W. Adams St., 602/262-6225, http://orpheum-theater.com), you might want to step into the gorgeous old venue for a look around. The theater, one of the valley's oldest, retains its 1927 glory. If style, beauty, and design are the ultimate criteria, this is probably the best venue in the valley.

CINEMA

For art-house and independent films, Tempe's **Harkins Valley Art** (509 S. Mill Ave., 480/446-7272, www.harkins.com) is the best venue in the valley, showing the films you won't see at the multiplex in a cool, if a bit rickety, old building on Mill Avenue.

COMEDY

Tempe Improv (930 E. University, 480/921-9877, www.tempeimprov.com) welcomes some of the best comedians in the country to its stage, from local talents and touring up-and-comers to *Saturday Night Live* favorites. There's a two-drink minimum, but it's easy to oblige with their long list of cocktails, and the bar-and-grill food is a cut above the usual dinner-theater fare. You must be 21 or older to attend most shows, but some are 18 and over.

CASINOS

For Vegas-style gaming and entertainment in the valley, you can't do much better than

Orpheum Theatre

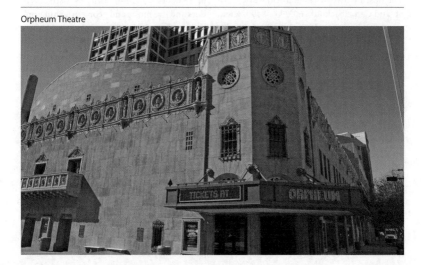

Wild Horse Pass Resort and Casino (5040 W. Wild Horse Pass, 800/946-4452, www.wildhorsepass.com), the biggest American Indian casino in the region. The 100,000-square-foot casino, hotel, and resort on the Gila River Indian Community Reservation, just off I-10 in the southeast valley, has 875 slot machines willing to take your money, plus poker (both live and video) and blackjack tables. Wild Horse Pass also has a buffet for when you need to refuel and live entertainment for when you lose all your money and need a little cheering up.

FESTIVALS AND EVENTS

At the end of December and into the first days of January, the valley celebrates college football with the Fiesta Bowl Parade, Fiesta Bowl Block Party, and, of course, the **Fiesta Bowl** (www.fiestabowl.org) at University of Phoenix Stadium in Glendale. In February the popular **VNSA Book Sale** (602/265-6805, www.vnsabooksale.org) has more than 600,000 used books for sale at the fairgrounds.

In March the **Heard Museum Guild Indian Fair & Market** (602/253-8848, www.heardguild.org) includes more than 600 artists, and spring training and **Cactus League** (www.cactusleague.com) bring MLB teams to the valley for a game every day of the month.

In April **NASCAR Subway Fresh Fit 500** (www.nascar.com) roars into town, bringing the popular sport's top drivers with it.

In October the **Arizona State Fair** and the **Heard Museum Spanish Market** keep locals and visitors busy, and in November the cars return for the **NASCAR Checker Auto Parts 500.** In December, don't miss the popular **Pueblo Grande Museum Indian Market** (602/495-0901, www.pueblogrande.com).

Shopping

DOWNTOWN AND CENTRAL
Shopping Districts

The upscale **Biltmore Fashion Park** (24th St. and Camelback Rd., 602/955-8400, www.shopbiltmore.com) along Camelback Road is the valley's finest shopping mall, with Saks Fifth Avenue, Ralph Lauren, and dozens of other high-end shops. You'll want to spend the whole day here if you're a shopping enthusiast with money to burn, and there are several restaurants to choose from for a memorable lunch or dinner.

On 7th Avenue between Camelback and Indian School Roads, in the **Melrose District,** you'll find retro boutiques, thrift stores, and hip home-decor shops. The increasingly busy and stroll-worthy **Roosevelt Row** (Roosevelt St. between Grand Ave. and 16th St.) has a host of funky locally owned boutiques, cafés, bars, artist studios, and galleries and a pedestrian-friendly vibe that

sets it apart from the valley's strip-mall wastelands. The district hosts the **Second Saturday Sidewalk Sale** (10am-8pm second Sat. of the month), with lots of street vendors and live music and people-watching; and during the popular downtown event known as **First Fridays** (6pm-10pm), this area gets busy and vibrant with revelers, shoppers, and art lovers. The **A.R.T.S. Market** (Roosevelt and 2nd St. and Roosevelt and 5th St.) sets up in the streets on First Fridays as well, featuring crafts, food, vintage items, and fine art.

The Churchill (901 N. 1st St., thechurchillphx.com, 10am-10pm Mon-Thurs., 10am-2am Fri.-Sat.) is a cluster of local shops, restaurants, and bars housed in stylishly refurbished and recycled packing crates that sees itself as a community-driven gathering place; each tenant is required to complete at least four hours a month of community service. The shops face a 9,000-square-foot shaded courtyard, a great place to meet new and old friends. The complex includes several excellent eateries and watering holes, as well as a few artisan and lifestyle shops. Make sure to check out the shop called **State Forty Eight,** which sells Arizona-only clothing and other products.

It's a 30-minute drive to the **Farm at Agritopia** in Gilbert, a former (and, to some extent, current) agriculture community. It's an 11-acre organic farm in a rather Stepford-esque subdivision that looks as if it were built in the Midwest in the early 20th century. A **Farm Store** sells products from the farm, and the eye-catching **Barnone AZ** (3000 E. Ray Rd., Gilbert, 480/988-1238, barnoneaz.com, 7am-9pm Mon.-Wed. and Sun., 7am-11pm Thurs.-Sat.) is an interesting and illuminating spot to visit. A gathering of valley craftspeople in a large Quonset hut, Barnone includes a few innovative farm-to-table eateries and bars, a beauty salon, a gunmaker, a flower shop, a paper shop featuring unique Arizona items, a winemaker, a sign maker, and more.

Farmers Markets

The most popular farmers market in the valley is the **Downtown Phoenix Public Market** (721 N. Central Ave., 602/253-2700, http://phxpublicmarket.com), which gathers hundreds of vendors together downtown to sell locally grown fruits and vegetables, locally prepared foods, arts and crafts, and other items that you can't get anywhere else. There's also usually live music and a lot of interesting people to meet. At the northeast corner of Central and McKinley, the **Open-Air Market** (721 N. Central Ave., 8am-noon Sat. May-Sept., 8am-1pm Sat. Oct.-Apr.) happens all year, even in the summer and the rainy season.

TEMPE AND THE EAST VALLEY

If the clothes at the Biltmore's Saks are too expensive, drive over to Tempe and the **Arizona Mills** (5000 Arizona Mills Cir., 480/491-7300, www.arizonamills.com, 10am-9pm Mon.-Sat., 11am-6pm Sun.), an outlet mall that has a Saks outlet (called Off 5th) and dozens of other outlet shops, including Ann Taylor, Kenneth Cole, and many more. This mall is huge and clean and has a fun gaming center for the kids and several restaurants.

Take a stroll along **Mill Avenue,** where you'll find all kinds of hip shops and boutiques; while Mill used to be quite a bit funkier than it is today, the bigger corporate stores that overtook it about a decade ago still have a lot of good shopping to offer.

WEST VALLEY
Shopping Districts

Historic Downtown Glendale (59th Ave. and Glendale Ave.) and the nearby **Catlin Court Historic District** (bounded by Gardenia Ave., 59th Ave., Palmarie Ave., and 58th Ave.) in the northwest valley offer the valley's quaintest shopping. The streets of downtown Glendale are lined with gas lamps and crowded antiques stores, while Catlin Court is a historic residential neighborhood whose white picket fence-fronted bungalows have been turned into boutiques and restaurants. This area is a must-visit for those who enjoy walking in picturesque small-town settings and finding unique items to take home.

Bookstores

The valley isn't exactly a book-hunter's paradise, but there are a few stores worth checking out. The best bookstore in town is the legendary **Changing Hands Bookstore** (6428 S. McClintock Dr., 480/730-0205, www.changinghands.com, 10am-9pm Mon.-Fri., 9am-9pm Sat., 10am-6pm Sun.) in Tempe, which sells an excellent mixture of new and used books. The statewide chain **Bookmans,** selling all manner of used media, including books, CDs, DVDs, games, and much more, has two well-stocked locations nearby, one in the north valley (8034 N. 19th Ave., 602/433-0255, www.bookmans.com, 9am-10pm daily) and one in Mesa, in the east valley (1056 S. Country Club Dr., 480/835-0505, www.bookmans.com, 9am-10pm daily). All Bookmans locations offer free wireless Internet.

Music

If you prefer browsing in the real world for your CDs and you still enjoy the warm sounds and cover art of vinyl records, there are a few places in the valley that you should not miss. At the Arizona and Nevada chain **Zia Records** (1940 W. Indian School Rd., 602/241-0313, www.zianation.com, 10am-midnight daily) you'll find stacks of new and used CDs in all genres, plus movies, books, and magazines, and a relatively large selection of used vinyl.

Stinkweeds (12 W. Camelback, 602/248-9461, www.stinkweeds.com, 11am-9pm Mon.-Sat., noon-6pm Sun.), at the northwest corner of Central and Camelback, has been a valley favorite since 1987, back when we had little choice other than brick-and-mortar stores to buy our music and the biggest worry of the independent record store was the coming of the superchains. This stubborn little store, which specializes in independent record labels and hard-to-find music, offers hours of browsing potential for new and used CDs and vinyl.

Food

In many ways, Phoenix and the Valley of the Sun began as clean slates, uncluttered by too much history and tradition, available for residents and visitors to scrawl on at will, creating amalgams and collages by cross-pollinating everything they'd seen or heard or tasted before arriving in the desert. The new always finds a foothold here, right up until it is replaced by something else. This is especially true of the area's dining life. But while the details may be changing all the time, the lifestyle remains constant: creative and eclectic, with a particular dedication, like the valley's residents now and throughout history, to fusion.

The daily *Arizona Republic* (www.azcentral.com) keeps an excellent, up-to-the-second guide to the valley's constantly changing dining scene on its website. The alternative weekly *Phoenix New Times* (www.phoenixnewtimes.com) publishes entertaining and knowledgeable reviews and listings on valley eateries.

It's always a good idea to call ahead and attempt to make a reservation, even though for most places you probably won't need one. This is especially smart in the valley, where you may have to drive a ways through busy traffic to get anywhere. Many restaurants here change their hours of operation during the summer, so call ahead if there's any doubt. At most of the area's fancier places, reservations are recommended, if not required. Only the highest-end restaurants are going to have anything approaching a dress code, and that is usually business casual for the most part, but with a jacket. The vast majority of valley hosts and hostesses won't bat an eye at your jeans or even your flip-flops, especially during summer.

DOWNTOWN AND CENTRAL
Mexican

Aunt Chilada's Squaw Peak (7330 N. Dreamy Draw Dr., 602/944-1286, www.auntchiladas.com, 11am-11pm Mon.-Thurs., 11am-2am Fri., 10am-1am Sat., 10am-11pm Sun., $10-15.50) serves delicious Mexican food in a historic building in the shadow of the Phoenix Mountains. **Los Dos Molinos** (1044 E. Camelback Rd., 602/528-3535, www.losdosmolinosphoenix.com, 11am-9pm Tues.-Thurs., 11am-10pm Fri.-Sat., $11-16) near downtown has a fun, cluttered atmosphere and basic northern Mexico favorites.

The **Barrio Café** (2814 N. 16th St., 602/636-0240, www.barriocafe.com, 11am-10pm Tues.-Thurs., 11am-10:30pm Fri., 5pm-10:30pm Sat., 11am-9pm Sun., $10-26) gets quite a bit more creative, serving a rare (for Arizona) modern Mexican cuisine from many different regions. This is not the place for chimichangas and chicken enchiladas. Try the slow-roasted pork, and somebody at the table should order Oaxacan black mole, one of Mexico's famous sauces created by nun-chefs in the 19th century. The bar has over 200 different varieties of tequila.

American and Southwestern

Fez (105 W. Portland St., 602/287-8700, www.fezoncentral.com, 11am-midnight Mon.-Thurs., 11am-1am Fri., 10am-1am Sat., 10am-midnight Sun., $13-15) serves a unique blend of classic American food with the spices and techniques of Morocco and the Mediterranean. A representative example of their approach is the "Tangier Burger": an Angus patty slathered with hummus and herb pesto, held together with ciabatta. The menu has a lot of appealing salads and other burgers, but the most interesting and memorable dishes are the *kisras,* herb-infused flat bread with lamb, chicken, or shrimp and all sorts of enticing spreads and cheeses and vegetables. With its retro-chic lime-green, orange, and brown interiors, large patio, and urban-cool atmosphere, Fez is a fun place for a few drinks and an appetizer even if you're not staying for dinner. The same holds true for the **Tuck Shop** (2245 N. 12th St., 602/354-2980, www.tuckinphx.com, 5pm-10pm Tues.-Sat., $15-30), a serious foodie haven. They bill their inventive, filling, tapas-style dishes as "neighborhood comfort food." The menu is also always changing, and there's an emphasis on fresh, locally sourced ingredients. The restaurant's reformed Desert Modern bungalow is something to see in itself.

★ **Quiessence** (6106 S. 32nd St., 602/276-0601, www.quiessencerestaurant.com, 5pm-close Tues.-Sat., $43-45), an enchanting restaurant in a converted farmhouse, is set among the gardens and organic crops at **The Farm at South Mountain** (near Southern Ave. and 32nd St.), a 10-acre former pecan orchard that features gardens, three restaurants, shops, markets, and events. The restaurant, with its green-grass patio, serves seasonally inspired American cuisine with ingredients from local farms, gardens, ranches, and streams. It also offers unique and delicious cocktails. The menus, changed daily, usually include fish, beef, and vegetable dishes, all made with locally or regionally produced ingredients. This is an ideal place to spend an adventurous, fun, and, yes, educational night with friends, sampling the many foods that are grown, raised, and made in-state, like feta from Snowflake, Arizona.

Another excellent farm-to-table option is **Gertrude's** (1201 Galvin Pkwy., 480/719-8600, www.gertrudesrestaurant.net, 10:30am-8pm Mon.-Fri., 8am-8pm Sat.-Sun., $18-32) at the Desert Botanical Garden. With its wonderful patio and lush, cool garden setting, Gertrude's is a great place for a long valley lunch over a few bottles of wine. It offers a revolving, seasonal menu of American dishes with international flavors, sourced and inspired by Arizona growers.

Windsor (5223 N. Central Ave., 602/279-1111, http://windsoraz.com, 11am-11pm Mon.-Thurs., 11am-2am Fri., 9am-midnight Sat., 9am-10pm Sun., $13-20) serves excellent burgers, sandwiches, and specials, such as a delicious potpie and perfectly prepared fried chicken, all in a stylish central location with a patio and a hip, youngish clientele. Don't miss one of the best decorating flourishes in the valley—a whole wall decorated with old cassette tapes from the 1980s and '90s.

In midtown, try **Switch Restaurant and Wine Bar** (2603 N. Central Ave., 602/264-2295, 11am-10pm Mon.-Thurs., 10am-11pm Sat., 10am-10pm Sun., brunch 10am-3pm Sat.-Sun., $12-26) for lunch, dinner, and brunch on the weekends. This casual-upscale "neighborhood joint" is a place to hang out and eat imaginative takes on classic American food (such as a carved-turkey sandwich with strawberries and provolone, adobo meatloaf, and street corn). You can sample a few inexpensive drinks and small plates during happy hour (4pm-6pm Mon.-Fri.).

An innovative indoor marketplace and food court, ★ **The Churchill** (901 N. 1st St., http://thechurchillphx.com, 10am-10pm

Mon.-Thurs., 10am-2am Fri.-Sat., prices vary by restaurant) is the place to please all the different tastes in your group. Constructed from 19 refurbished shipping containers, this large and exciting gathering place in the Roosevelt Arts District downtown has seven different restaurants and bars gathered around a 9,000-square-foot courtyard with tables. All the eateries are locally owned, and the variety is impressive: pizza, acacia bowls, a Mexican spot serving dishes from Jalisco and Michoacán, a bar with craft cocktails and local beer and wine, and much more.

Breakfast and Lunch

The tasteful diner **Matt's Big Breakfast** (825 N. 1st St., 602/254-1074, www. mattsbigbreakfast.com, 6:30am-2:30pm Tues.-Sun., $6-11) always seems to have a line outside, especially on the weekends. That's because they serve some of the best breakfast food in the valley. The well-prepared, deceptively simple classic breakfasts here will keep you full for most of the day.

Be prepared to wait a bit for a table at tiny **Lo-Lo's Chicken & Waffles** (1220 S. Central Ave., 602/340-1304, www. loloschickenandwaffles.com, 7am-11pm Mon.-Thurs., 7am-11pm Fri.-Sat., 7am-6pm Sun., $5-13), a classic and popular soulfood joint on Central. Lo-Lo's serves crispy Southern-fried chicken and big waffles, macaroni-and-cheese, greens, and many other Southern favorites. But you may find yourself liking the huge "jar of drank" the best: a fruit jar filled with red Kool-Aid, the finest drink on the planet. There's also a Lo-Lo's in Scottsdale (3133 N. Scottsdale Rd., 480/945-1920) that has the same hours.

Head to the **Phoenix Public Market Café** (14 E. Pierce St., 602/253-2700, http:// cafe.phxpublicmarket.com, 7am-9pm Sun.-Thurs., 7am-10pm Fri.-Sat., $8-14) for fresh, local, and thoughtful food at its best. This casual place gets most of its ingredients from

the farmers market nearby and other local sources. It has an inviting, dog-friendly patio and hang-worthy bar serving local beer and wine. For breakfast they have frittatas, quinoa bowls, and steak and eggs, and more; and at lunchtime, it's a vegetarian- and vegan-friendly spot, with beans and rice, roasted vegetable bowls, and more, plus sandwiches, burgers, and unforgettable potpie filled with green chili pork stew.

For an excellent cup of certified fair trade, organic coffee and a bowl of hearty oatmeal—say, after a brisk hike in the desert—head to ★ **Fair Trade Café** (1020 N. 1st Ave., Roosevelt Row, 602/354-8150, www. azfairtrade.com, 6am-10pm daily, $3.50-8.50) downtown. The café has a relaxing patio, local art on the wall, and light, healthy, and delicious breakfast and lunch options. All the baked goods here are made in-house from scratch. Vegetarians and vegans will find much to ponder, including a hummus sandwich and a veggie burrito. The café uses organic, local, and sustainable produce, and all of the cups, napkins, and lids are made with recyclable materials.

Italian and Pizza

Another valley winner of the prestigious James Beard Award, Chris Bianco operates ★ **Pizzeria Bianco** (623 E. Adams St. at Heritage Square, 602/258-8300, www. pizzeriabianco.com, 11am-9pm Mon.-Thurs., 11am-10pm Fri.-Sat., $9-16) out of a historic brick building at downtown's Heritage Square. The pizza is the best in the valley, and, according to many food critics, the best in the nation as well. This is a small, romantic, hip place, and it takes a while to get a table and an equal while to get your pizza. It is all without a doubt worth it. Go here if you love pizza; you'll be sorry to miss it. Next door, **Bar Bianco** (602/528-3699, 11am-9pm Mon.-Thurs., 11am-10pm Fri.-Sat.) has a wide selection of wine and a warm atmosphere, with picnic tables on a grassy, candlelit patio.

1: Barnone AZ, a gathering of craftspeople
2: Pizzeria Bianco

Steaks and Chops

Durant's Fine Foods (2611 N. Central Ave., 602/264-5967, www.durantsaz.com, 11am-10pm Mon.-Thurs., 11am-11pm Fri., 5pm-11pm Sat., 4:30pm-10pm Sun., $19-52) downtown is the archetypal retro-haute steak house and lounge, where you can get a juicy slice of prime rib, a perfectly cooked steak, and an expert martini served by the professional, tuxedoed waitstaff. Durant's has been serving the same food in the same location for more than 50 years and has a loyal following, so you'll probably want to make reservations.

Vegetarian

★ **Loving Hut** (3239 E. Indian School Rd., 602/264-3480, www.lovinghut.us, 11am-2:30pm and 5pm-9pm Tues.-Sat., 4pm-8pm Sun., $6-10) is 100 percent vegan, but you wouldn't know it unless they told you so. The delicious and spicy Asian-style dishes are prepared with all kinds of faux-meat protein that adds depth and zest. Vegetarians and vegans will be in ecstasy here. Loving Hut is closed the last Sunday of every month.

TEMPE AND THE EAST VALLEY

Mexican

The food at **Casa Reynoso** (3138 S. Mill Ave., 480/966-0776, www.casareynoso.com, 11am-8:30pm Tues.-Thurs., 11am-9:30pm Fri.-Sat., 11am-8pm Sun., $8-15) is prepared from old family recipes passed down from an older place in the Central Arizona mining region of Globe-Miami. The Mexican food here is a bit more authentic than your average chimichanga hut, and the hacienda-style building gives the place an Old Mexico aura that makes for a fun night out just slightly north of the border.

American and Southwestern

The New Native American cuisine at **Kai** (5594 West Wild Horse Pass Blvd., reservations accepted noon-5pm Tues.-Sat. at 602/385-5726, outside these times 602/225-0100, www.wildhorsepassresort.com, 5:30pm-9pm Tues.-Thurs., 5:30pm-9:30pm Fri.-Sat. early Sept.-late July, $46-56), one of the most unusual five-star restaurants in the West, seems at first completely foreign, but you soon realize that most of the ingredients are actually as native as can be. Indeed, the chefs at Kai, which means "seed" in the local O'odham language, are so dedicated to the local-food revolution that they serve baby lettuce handpicked by children from the Gila River Indian Reservation. The menu is fascinating, and the decor is proof that Native American motifs can be made new and surprising again. Business casual dress: no T-shirts, shorts, hats, or open-toed sandals for gentlemen, and denim is not preferred.

The enchanting atmosphere at the **House of Tricks** (114 E. 7th St., 480/968-1114, www.houseoftricks.com, 11am-10pm Mon.-Sat., $26-33), housed in a 1920s-era cottage and adjacent 1903 adobe house just off Mill Avenue, with a patio shaded by old trees and a warm, homey vibe, is nearly as attractive as the New American cuisine cooked up in its kitchen. The seasonally inspired menus, which change often, feature the freshest meats, fish, and produce all mixed up into eclectic and creative dishes you won't find anywhere else.

Burgers and Steaks

Rustler's Rooste (8383 S. 48th St., 602/431-6474, www.rustlersrooste.com, 5pm-10pm daily, $15-30) is a cowboy-style steak house that seeks to recreate a rough-hewn ranch mess hall near South Mountain. Here you'll get pots of cowboy beans and steaming ears of corn, thick steaks, an always-celebratory atmosphere, and expansive views of the desert and city. This place is great for families and has a relatively inexpensive kids' menu offering small steaks and ribs. If you're just visiting Arizona, this may be your one chance to try fried rattlesnake.

You won't find many handcrafted microbrews better than the varieties served at **Four Peaks Brewing Company** (1340 E. 8th St., 480/303-9967, www.fourpeaks.com,

11am-2am Mon.-Sat, 10am-2am Sun., $10-15), near campus in Tempe, and the pub eats and entrées—burgers, sandwiches, pizzas, and some really excellent starters—are equally good. Happy hour is 2pm-6pm daily.

The **Pedal Haus Brewery** (730 S. Mill Ave., 480/314-2337, http://pedalhausbrewery.com, 11am-11pm Mon.-Thurs., 11am-1am Fri.-Sat., 11am-10pm Sun., $12-24) is a cavernous brewery and restaurant off Mill Avenue with a huge, stylish patio and front-row booths for watching the lonely brewmaster work his trade. Like all working breweries, this one has that wet-hops smell, but it's soon replaced by the beefy deliciousness of the burgers and sandwiches. The decor is about bikes and beer, two things that Tempe residents enjoy and celebrate. The brewery offers about a dozen handmade beers, delicious and inventive in their variety.

Indian

Perhaps the best Indian food in the state is served out of the **Delhi Palace** (933 E. University Dr., #103, 480/921-2200, www.delhipalacetempe.us, 11am-2:30pm, 5pm-10pm Mon.-Fri., 11am-3pm, 5pm-10pm Sat.-Sun., $9-15) near ASU, offering well-prepared standards. The service can be patchy, but you will never leave unsatisfied, especially after partaking in the lunch buffet (11am-2:30pm Mon.-Fri., 11am-3pm Sat.-Sun.).

The foods and flavors of Punjab are served at **The Dhaba** (1874 E. Apache Blvd., 480/557-8800, www.the-dhaba.com, 11am-2:30pm, 5pm-10pm Mon.-Fri., noon-10pm Sat.-Sun., $8-20), a spectacular Indian restaurant named for the casual, road-food joints that line the highways of India and Pakistan. Enjoy meats cooked in the restaurant's authentic tandoors (clay ovens) as well as many appetizing rice dishes and vegetarian options.

Italian

Caffe Boa (398 S. Mill Ave., 480/968-9112, www.cafeboa.com, 11am-10pm Sun.-Wed., 11am-11pm Thurs.-Sat., 10am-3pm Sun.,

$15-30) serves the east valley's best Italian and Mediterranean food in an intimate setting in the busy Mill Avenue District. The panini here are particularly good for lunch, and there's a new dinner menu every month, always featuring delectable and creative pasta dishes grounded in tradition.

Middle Eastern

★ **Haji-Baba Middle Eastern Food** (1513 E. Apache Blvd., 480/894-1905, 10am-8pm Mon.-Sat., noon-4:30pm Sun., $10-15), a storefront in a strip mall just south of the ASU campus in Tempe, serves without a doubt the best Middle Eastern food in Arizona. The baba ghanoush is amazing, as are the hummus, gyros, kabobs, and falafel. The place is laid-back and casual, with a busy grocery store operating behind a thin partition; it's often packed, and the service can be a bit lackadaisical, but the food is perfect and cheap.

Vegetarian

The folks at **Green** (2240 N. Scottsdale Rd., 480/941-9003, www.greenvegetarian.com, 11am-9pm Mon.-Sat., $9-10), a "New American Vegetarian" restaurant, use mock meats and fresh vegetables and sauces to create 100 percent vegan meals. This is a place that even avid meat eaters will enjoy. They've got the best vegan chili fries and vegan chicken wings in town, and the "no harm chicken parm sandwich" is so tasty that it's difficult to believe *no* harm was done in its creation.

The **Udupi Café** (1636 N. Scottsdale Rd., 480/994-8787, www.udupiaz.com, 11am-3pm and 5pm-9:30pm Sun.-Thurs., 11am-3pm and 5pm-10pm Fri.-Sat., $9-16) is a fantastic option for vegetarians and vegans who like Indian food. The casual restaurant concentrates on dishes from different regions of the subcontinent, offering delicious vegetarian vindaloos, curries, and the like. Udupi will typically make a dish vegan for you if it isn't already on offer as such. It also has an excellent lunch buffet daily ($10 pp).

WEST VALLEY

While strolling and shopping in downtown Glendale, stop by **Cuff** (5819 W. Glendale, 623/847-8890, www.cuffglendale.com, 11am-9pm Mon.-Thurs., 11am-10pm Fri.-Sat., $8-15), a casual but sophisticated bistro and bar with an eclectic menu of burgers, sandwiches, salads, tacos, brisket, shrimp and grits, and more. Vegetarians and vegans will like this spot (offerings include green chili jackfruit tacos and black bean burgers), and several dishes can be made vegan and gluten free.

Try the relaxing and well-stocked bar during happy hour (3pm-6pm Mon.-Fri.). There's also an event space here that regularly hosts comedy and bands (http://offthecuffdowntown.com).

If you're in the northwest valley around breakfast time, don't miss **Kiss the Cook Restaurant** (4915 W. Glendale Ave., 623/939-4663, 6am-2:30pm Mon.-Fri., 7am-3pm Sat., 7am-1pm Sun., $5-9), which serves the old American favorites in an antique-shop interior.

Accommodations

The accommodations scene in the valley is ruled by the big chains and resorts. If you're hoping to find something a bit more distinctive and independent, expect to pay for it accordingly. The best time to find bargains is in summer, when nearly every big hotel and resort slashes its prices to attract business to the infernal desert.

Downtown Phoenix is a great place to stay for most visitors. It's centrally located and home to the best accommodations, restaurants, and nightlight in the valley. It's also relatively pedestrian friendly and convenient to Tempe's main street, Mill Avenue, by light-rail. Scottsdale's downtown and Old Town neighborhoods are also good options, with fun places to stay and some areas that are pedestrian friendly—but never really cheap. If you're visiting Arizona State University or one of its students, you can stay in the lively areas of Tempe around the university campus and Mill Avenue.

If you're staying at one of the resorts on the edges of the city, expect to do a lot of driving to get to most of the sights around the valley.

DOWNTOWN AND CENTRAL
$50-100
The best deal in town is the **Hosteling International Phoenix** (1026 N. 9th St.,

602/254-9803, www.phxhostel.org, $30-85), but you really have to be a hostel kind of person to enjoy it. You can stay in a dorm room or pay extra for a private room, but you share the bathrooms and kitchen area. There's a shady courtyard, coin-operated laundry, and a common area with a piano; the staff is friendly and laid-back, and the house is located downtown in the Roosevelt Row arts district.

$100-250
The most distinctive accommodation in the valley is the historic ★ **Hotel San Carlos** (202 N. Central Ave., 602/253-4121, www.hotelsancarlos.com, $189-300), located right downtown with a facade that brings back the golden age of big-city hotels. The San Carlos, opened in 1928, was a favorite stop of Hollywood stars during the first half of the 20th century, and it was one of the first high-rise hotels in the Southwest with full air-conditioning and electric elevators. The hotel now celebrates its glory days with themed rooms and memorabilia. Rooms are comfortable and chic, and the whole place has a kind of overstuffed, retro-cool ambience that you'll get nowhere else. Despite being charmingly old-school, Hotel San Carlos has an ecofriendly soul: it's a member of the Arizona Green Chamber of Commerce, which works to promote sustainable economic

development, and certified "Green Platinum" by the national Green Business Bureau. The certification is the result of the hotel's efforts to make sustainability an integral part of daily operations.

The charming Mission-style **Maricopa Manor** (15 W. Pasadena Ave., 602/264-9200, www.maricopamanor.com, $189-239) offers the best in B&B-style accommodations in the valley. Located in North-Central Phoenix just minutes from everything, this historic hideaway has lush, grassy grounds and a beautifully tiled pool area with a waterfall, spa, and several shady ramadas for lounging. The inn offers six rooms, each with a private bath and free Wi-Fi, and many of them open onto the pool area and patio. In the morning, don't worry about getting dressed to face the other guests around a communal table; here breakfast is delivered to your doorstep in a basket. If you want to stay here, you need to book long in advance.

Over $250

The **Foundre Phoenix** (1100 N. Central Ave., 602/875-8000, http://foundrehotels.com, $189-349) rises at the corner of Central and Portland downtown, and even if you can't afford to stay here (it's cheaper in the summer, pretty expensive in the high season), you should take a look inside, especially if you're an art lover. This place takes its walls so seriously that it has a curator on staff. You will find work by major Arizona artists throughout this strange and wonderful place. The loft-style rooms are individually decorated with a kind of industrial craftsman style. This is probably the hippest, coolest hotel in Phoenix. Check it out if only to see the huge and cheeky painting of the great Burt Reynolds. The hotel has won best of Phoenix awards from several local and national magazines. Parking is $25 per night.

The ★ **Arizona Biltmore** (2400 E. Missouri Ave., 602/955-6600, www.arizonabiltmore.com, $400-450), covering 39 acres at the base of the Phoenix Mountains, is the valley's most famous, and still in most

ways its best, resort. Other places may come and go, but this Frank Lloyd Wright-inspired (and, many contend, designed—Wright received a consulting fee on the project) "Jewel of the Desert" just keeps getting better with age. There are 738 guest rooms, including one- and two-bedroom villas, eight swimming pools, seven tennis courts, two 18-hole golf courses at the country club next door, a spa, an enormous outdoor chess set, and four restaurants.

The **Renaissance Phoenix Downtown** (50 E. Adams St., 602/333-0000, www.mariott.com, $299) is downtown's biggest and nicest high-rise, right in the middle of everything and offering spacious, tasteful rooms—style, elegance, and haute comfort galore. The **Ritz-Carlton** (2401 E. Camelback Rd., 602/468-0700, www.ritzcarlton.com, $349-429), along the Camelback Corridor, is a gorgeous hotel with large, comfortable rooms and great views of the mountains and valley. It has all the amenities one would expect for the price, including a truly spectacular pool area.

The **Clarendon Hotel** (401 W. Clarendon Ave., 602/252-7363, www.theclarendon.net, $600) is a popular hangout owing to its amazing rooftop deck that overlooks the city and the desert. It also has gorgeous, spacious rooms with cool and comfortable beds and a pool area to beat any in the valley. This is one of the hippest places you can stay in the valley, and it's a favorite of visiting pop stars and other luminaries.

Located near South Mountain Park, the ★ **Arizona Grand Resort** (8000 S. Arizona Grand Pkwy., 602/438-9000, www.arizonagrandresort.com, $229-300) has well-appointed, comfortable rooms, a golf course for the adults, a water park for the kids, a health club, a spa, six pools, and seven restaurants. It's a great place to take the family for an unforgettable getaway. The resort is "Certified Green" by the Arizona Hotel & Lodging Association under the Green Lodging Program. Also, the hotel's parent company, Classic Hotels & Resorts, is a

member of the 1% for the Planet alliance. A vigorous recycling program, electric vehicle charging stations, low-flow shower heads, and many other water- and energy-saving strategies are a regular part of the hotel's operation.

The **Royal Palms** (5200 E. Camelback Rd., 602/840-3610, www.royalpalmshotel. com, $450-600), right by the Phoenician at the base of Camelback Mountain, is a lush hideout with all the amenities and then some. The rooms are all decorated with antiques and other stylish touches; the grounds resemble some king's well-kept gardens, with Camelback Mountain shining in the background. This wonderful resort offers comfortable rooms, private casitas, and sprawling villas, plus the usual pool, spa, fitness center, and excellent gourmet dining. The Royal Palms is Certified Green by the Arizona Hotel & Lodging Association under its Green Lodging Program.

The kids will love the **Pointe Hilton at Squaw Peak** (7677 N. 16th St., 602/997-2626, www.pointehilton.com, $250-300) for its **Hole-in-the-Wall River Ranch,** a four-acre watery playground of linked pools, waterslides, spas, cabanas, and all sorts of other watery fun. This is a very nice place that is also relatively affordable, especially during summer, when they offer cut-rate deals that no family in need of a vacation should pass up. Also a great place for families is the **Pointe Hilton Tapatio Cliffs Resort** (11111 N. 7th St., 602/866-7500, www.pointehilton. com, $250-300), which has a gorgeous series of pools and cabanas called the **Falls Water Village,** with several waterfalls, whirlpools, a waterslide, and hidden, romantic spots to soak up the sun. There's also a golf course, a spa, and several restaurants. The Tapatio Cliffs is Certified Green by the Arizona Hotel & Lodging Association under its Green Lodging Program.

1: Hotel San Carlos **2:** Foundre Phoenix **3:** Arizona Biltmore

TEMPE AND THE EAST VALLEY
$150-250

Formerly known as the Fiesta Inn, the remodeled **DoubleTree by Hilton Hotel Phoenix Tempe** (2100 S. Priest Dr., Tempe, 480/967-1441, http://doubletree3.hilton.com, $169-200) remains a favorite among visiting ASU parents. It isn't the only valley hotel to call itself Frank Lloyd Wright-inspired, but it is certainly the most affordable. This high-end but not-too-pricey resort has tasteful Old Southwest-style rooms and common areas, acres of saltillo tile, and sharp, rustic-looking decor all around. It has a big, glistening blue pool (heated in winter), a great restaurant and lounge with complimentary finger foods at happy hour, and service that rivals much pricier places.

★ **Graduate Tempe** (225 E. Apache Blvd., 480/967-9431, www.graduatehotels. com, $180-200) is right across from the ASU campus and close to all the action in Tempe. It's a stylish, art-filled place with distinctive, comfortable, and memorable rooms. The hotel also has two restaurants, a large pool, and free bikes for exploring the campus. Plus, this is a very pet-friendly hotel—dogs stay free and are welcomed in style. This a great place to stay if you're visiting ASU or shopping and partying on Mill Avenue.

Near Tempe Town Lake, **Aloft** (951 E. Playa Del Norte Dr., 480/621-3300, www. alofttempe.com, $140-180) is a contemporary, chic destination with complimentary spa products in your room and a plug-and-play station to charge your gadgets. The hotel offers free wireless, superbly comfortable beds, a hip bar, oversize showerheads in sleek walk-in showers, and so much style that you'll want to take photos of your room and the lobby.

As its name suggests, **The Buttes** (2000 Westcourt Way, 602/225-9900, www.marriott. com/phxtm, $200-250) overlooks the east valley from atop a 25-acre promontory in Tempe. This gorgeous resort offers free Wi-Fi, sumptuously comfortable rooms, two large swimming pools with a waterslide, a full-service spa, and all manner of other fun and relaxing amenities.

Over $250

The **Tempe Mission Palms** (60 E. 5th St., Tempe, 480/894-1400, www.missionpalms.com, $250-300) in downtown Tempe is a beautiful property, with a huge pool and tennis courts on the roof overlooking the entire valley. It has its own cozy bar and restaurant and is within walking distance to the shops and restaurants on Mill Avenue. The rooms have a Southwest style, and the courtyards are lush and watered. This is one of the most luxurious places to stay in Tempe and a bit less pricey than similarly appointed places in Phoenix and Scottsdale. The Mission Palms is Certified Green by the Arizona Hotel & Lodging Association under its Green Lodging Program.

WEST VALLEY

The historic ★ **Wigwam Hotel** (300 E. Wigwam Blvd., Litchfield Park, 623/935-3811, http://wigwamarizona.com, $220-350), which opened in 1929 and still has some of its original adobe casitas, offers a bit of classic Arizona in the west valley. The citrus trees that used to crowd the valley before the population boom still live on at this retro resort, and the whole place smells like oranges and lemons. It's far from the action but worth the drive for the classic touches and historic feel. The resort has the Red Door Spa, a golf course, and all the other amenities you'd expect from a legendary desert hideaway.

At Glendale's **Westgate** complex, just a few miles west of historic downtown on Glendale Avenue, you'll find several big chain hotels right next to the stadiums—homes of the NFL's Arizona Cardinals and the NHL's Phoenix Coyotes. The Westgate center also has a host of midrange and upscale shopping and eating options, all conveniently located right next to the stadiums.

Information and Services

TOURIST INFORMATION

The Downtown Phoenix Visitor Center (125 2nd St., 877/225-5749, www.visitphoenix.com, 8am-5pm Mon.-Fri.) has stacks of information and literature, and the helpful staff will answer all your questions.

MEDIA

The two best newspapers in the valley, and in the state for that matter, are the daily *Arizona Republic* (www.azcentral.com), the largest newspaper in Arizona, and the weekly *Phoenix New Times* (www.phoenixnewtimes.com), which is the best source for investigative reporting, off-center opinions, and cultural coverage.

HOSPITALS AND EMERGENCY SERVICES

If you get hurt in the valley or have any kind of emergency medical situation, the simplest thing to do is call 911. There are several top-notch hospitals around the valley, and many of them have satellite centers in every major subregion around the basin. **St. Joseph's Hospital and Medical Center** (350 W. Thomas Rd., 602/406-3000) is a Catholic hospital started by the Sisters of Mercy in the late 19th century and is consistently ranked one of the top hospitals in Arizona. It operates a Level 1 trauma center, one of just a few in Arizona.

St. Luke's Medical Center (1800 E. Van Buren, 602/251-8100, www.stlukesmedcenter.com) is located near downtown Phoenix and has an updated and state-of-the-art emergency room that includes an innovative Chest Pain Emergency Center dedicated to preventing heart attacks. **Maricopa Medical Center** (2601 E. Roosevelt St., 602/344-5011, www.mihs.org) is one the nation's top hospitals, offering a full range of services including a Level 1 trauma center and an infant ICU.

Transportation

All the information in this section applies to the entire Valley of the Sun, not just Phoenix proper. If you spend time in the sprawling valley, you'll soon realize that it is easier to view it as one big city rather than many midsize cities. Though each of the cities around the valley has something unique to offer, in terms of transportation, the differences are negligible. If you're going to be in the valley more than a day, you are going to need a car. The bus system is reliable and comfortable, but it is not realistic to employ it for sightseeing tours. The light-rail system moves past most of the downtown and central sights, restaurants, and accommodations.

AIR

Phoenix Sky Harbor International Airport

Phoenix Sky Harbor International Airport (PHX, 3400 E. Sky Harbor Blvd., 602/273-3300, www.skyharbor.com) is one of the Southwest's largest, with three terminals served by 17 domestic and international airlines offering flights to about 80 domestic and 22 international destinations, most of them in Mexico and Canada. If you're traveling to Arizona by air, you will likely land at Sky Harbor.

AIRPORT TRANSPORTATION

Sky Harbor is just five miles or so east of downtown Phoenix. If you're leaving the airport in a rental car, head east on Sky Harbor Boulevard to Route 143 South. Go south on Route 143 and after about two miles take Exit 1B and get on I-10 going west. It should take about 10 minutes, or up to 20 in traffic, to get downtown from the airport. If you're headed to Tempe and Arizona State University, take Sky Harbor Boulevard east to North Priest Drive. Turn right onto North Priest and then turn left on West University Drive. The airport is about five miles from

campus, which could take up to 15 minutes in traffic.

The **Metro Light Rail** goes to the airport ($2 per ride)—take the light-rail to the 44th Street and Washington Valley Metro Station to get to terminals 2-4. From the Metro station, you can catch the free **Sky Train** to get to the terminals and the economy parking lots. The Sky Train runs all day and night, and there's never a wait of more than five minutes or so. There's also a **free shuttle** that travels from the economy parking lots to the terminals.

SuperShuttle (602/244-9000, www. supershuttle.com) offers rides to the airport from destinations all over the valley. Sky Harbor contracts with the shuttle giant to provide the service, and the ride is typically reliable and not unpleasant. You have to make a reservation. Shuttles run every 15 minutes 9am-9pm daily. Expect to pay $12-38 for the first person in your party, depending on how far you are from the airport, and $7 for each additional passenger regardless of where you are. Catch the shuttle from terminal 2 on the north curb; from terminal 3, wait at the north or south curbs; and from terminal 4, head down to the first floor and wait at the north or south curb.

Three **taxicab** companies contract with Sky Harbor to provide transportation at a set rate ($5 first mile, $2.30 each additional mile, $23 per hour traffic delay, $15 minimum fare, $1 per trip surcharge): **Apache Taxi** (480/557-7000), **AAA/Yellow Cab** (480/888-8888), and **Mayflower Cab** (602/955-1355).

You can meet a taxi on the north curb outside terminal 2's door 8, on the north curb of terminal 3, outside door 8, or on the first floor of terminal 4 on the north curb, outside door 7.

You can get a taxi to take you anywhere in the valley; however, considering the long distances involved, they can get expensive pretty quickly. On the weekends you'll find taxis waiting outside of popular drinking and partying areas like downtown Phoenix, Scottsdale, and Tempe, but most of the time you're going to have to call a company and arrange for a pickup. Ultimately, taxis are not really an efficient way of getting around the valley.

Uber, Lyft, and other ride-share companies serve Sky Harbor as well. Each terminal has a specified pickup location.

CAR

The easiest way to get to, from, and around Phoenix and Arizona is by car. Phoenix's charms are a mere preamble to the wonderland that is Arizona, and the best way to see that wonderland is in your own car, preferably with your road-trip mix on the stereo.

I-10 passes through the valley's heart and lungs on its way to and from the California coast. Phoenix is 372 miles east of Los Angeles, a straight five-hour shot on I-10. Continue east on I-10 another 100 miles or so and you're in Tucson, Arizona's second city. The valley is connected to the I-40 east-west corridor by I-17, which runs north 150 miles from central Phoenix to Flagstaff, an I-40 town and one of the gateways to the Grand Canyon. The trip north from the desert of Phoenix to the cool pines of Flagstaff takes just over two hours.

Car Rental

It is easy to rent a car at the airport, but the exorbitant airport taxes and fees make doing so a bad idea; you'll get price shock that will ruin your trip in advance. That said, Sky Harbor provides a free **Rental Car Shuttle** from the baggage claim at each terminal to the **Rental Car Center** (1805 E. Sky Harbor Circle South, 602/683-3741), just west of the airport. All the major rental companies are represented at the center, including **Hertz** (602/267-8822 or 800/654-3131, www.hertz.com) and **Budget** (800/527-7000, www.budget.com).

It's better to head outside the airport to rent a car. Try the locally owned **Phoenix Car Rental** (2934 E. McDowell Rd., 602/269-9310 and 3625 W. Indian School Rd., 602/269-9310, www.rentacarphoenix.com). The McDowell Road site is about seven miles from the airport. Take Sky Harbor Boulevard east to Priest, then get on the 202 Loop to exit 1C or 32nd Street, then turn left on McDowell. You can also arrange for them to pick you up.

Metro Light Rail

LONG-DISTANCE BUS

Phoenix's **Greyhound bus station** (2115 E. Buckeye Rd., 602/389-4200) is located near Sky Harbor International Airport. **Arizona Shuttle** (800/888-2749, www.arizonashuttle. com, $48 pp, one-way) offers several daily trips between Flagstaff's Amtrak station and Sky Harbor International Airport.

TRAIN

The **Amtrak** *Sunset Limited* (800/872-7245, www.amtrak.com), which runs along the southern route and dry desert Southwest three times a week from New Orleans, stops in Maricopa, Arizona, about 30 miles east of Phoenix. However, as of this writing, transportation options from Maricopa to Phoenix are tough to come by and expensive.

PUBLIC TRANSPORTATION

Bus

Valley Metro (602/253-5000, www.valley metro.org), the valley's public transportation authority, runs bus service ($2 per ride) everywhere, including Glendale, Scottsdale, Tempe, and Mesa.

Metro Light Rail

The best thing to happen to the valley since affordable air-conditioning, the sleek **Metro Light Rail** (602/253-5000, www. valleymetro.org) is transforming the city's one-person, one-car culture into something more sustainable. The current system is nearly 30 miles long, beginning in the northwest at Montebello and 19th Avenue, where there's a large parking lot, and traversing the valley all the way to Mesa in the east. Along the way the futuristic people mover stops at or near most of the valley's top sights, including downtown's Heard and Phoenix Museums and Tempe's Mill Avenue and Town Lake. It's a great way to get around and to see the sights without having to get in and out of a car every 20 minutes, let alone find parking (though this strategy is recommended only in spring and winter). Fares start at $2 per ride, $4 for an all-day pass, and the last trip begins at 11pm Sunday-Thursday and 2am Saturday and Sunday. See the website for a complete map and fare schedule.

Scottsdale

Scottsdale suffers somewhat from its reputation as being high-toned, high-dollar, and maybe even a little pretentious. This isn't the case, however, in most corners of the city, which has won numerous national awards for being generally livable, clean, and attractive. It's true that you see more Beemers and Jags within Scottsdale's city limits than in other parts of the valley (save Paradise Valley, a mostly residential community that is one of the richest in the nation), but a day's visit here will likely reveal that there is much more to Scottsdale than beautiful rich people and their high-walled resorts.

SIGHTS

Downtown

Visitors to Scottsdale, a citrus-growing suburb turned international resort destination and art center, primarily come to stroll, shop, and eat in the city's bustling downtown area (www.downtownscottsdale.com), which includes Old Town, Fifth Avenue, and the Arts District, among others. There are dozens of Native American and Western art galleries and trading posts, boutiques selling Southwestern-style items both authentic and touristy, contemporary art galleries with a flair for the most current styles, restaurants

Scottsdale and Vicinity

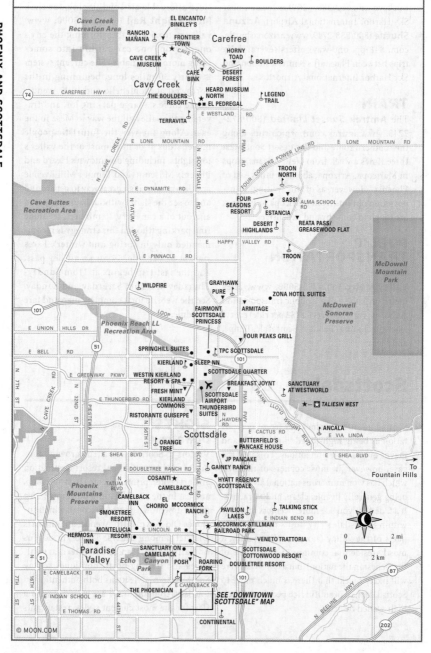

Cave Creek Recreation Area

RANCHO MAÑANA

EL ENCANTO/BINKLEY'S

FRONTIER TOWN

Carefree

CAVE CREEK MUSEUM

HORNY TOAD

BOULDERS

CAVE CREEK RD

CAFE BINK

DESERT FOREST

E CAREFREE HWY

Cave Creek

THE BOULDERS RESORT

HEARD MUSEUM NORTH

LEGEND TRAIL

EL PEDREGAL

74

E WESTLAND RD

TERRAVITA

E LONE MOUNTAIN RD

E LONE MOUNTAIN RD

N SCOTTSDALE RD

N CAVE CREEK RD

N PIMA RD

FOUR CORNERS POWER LINE RD

TROON NORTH

Cave Buttes Recreation Area

E DYNAMITE RD

N TATUM BLVD

FOUR SEASONS RESORT

SASSI

ALMA SCHOOL RD

ESTANCIA

DESERT HIGHLANDS

REATA PASS/ GREASEWOOD FLAT

E HAPPY VALLEY RD

E PINNACLE RD

TROON

McDowell Mountain Park

WILDFIRE

GRAYHAWK

PURE

ZONA HOTEL SUITES

101

FAIRMONT SCOTTSDALE PRINCESS

ARMITAGE

McDowell Sonoran Preserve

LOOP 101

Phoenix Reach LL Recreation Area

E UNION HILLS DR

51

FOUR PEAKS GRILL

E BELL RD

SPRINGHILL SUITES

TPC SCOTTSDALE

101

N 7TH ST

N CAVE CREEK RD

E GREENWAY PKWY

KIERLAND

SLEEP NN

SCOTTSDALE QUARTER

WESTIN KIERLAND RESORT & SPA

N 32ND ST

PIESTEWA PKWY

E THUNDERBIRD RD

FRESH MINT

BREAKFAST JOYNT

SANCTUARY AT WESTWORLD

KIERLAND COMMONS

SCOTTSDALE AIRPORT

TALIESIN WEST

N FRANK LLOYD WRIGHT BLVD

RISTORANTE GUISEPPE

THUNDERBIRD SUITES

N HAYDEN RD

N 16TH ST

ORANGE TREE

ANCALA

E VIA LINDA

Scottsdale

BUTTERFIELD'S PANCAKE HOUSE

E CACTUS RD

E SHEA BLVD

E SHEA BLVD

N SCOTTSDALE RD

N PIMA RD

To Fountain Hills

E DOUBLETREE RANCH RD

JP PANCAKE

COSANTI

GAINEY RANCH

N TATUM BLVD

CAMELBACK

HYATT REGENCY SCOTTSDALE

Phoenix Mountains Preserve

CAMELBACK INN

EL CHORRO

MCCORMICK RANCH

PAVILION LAKES

TALKING STICK

E INDIAN BEND RD

SMOKETREE RESORT

E LINCOLN DR

MCCORMICK-STILLMAN RAILROAD PARK

0   2 mi

MONTELUCIA RESORT

0   2 km

HERMOSA INN

VENETO TRATTORIA

51

Paradise Valley

SANCTUARY ON CAMELBACK

SCOTTSDALE COTTONWOOD RESORT

87

N 7TH ST

N 16TH ST

Echo Canyon Park

POSH

ROARING FORK

DOUBLETREE RESORT

E CAMELBACK RD

THE PHOENICIAN

E CAMELBACK RD

101

SEE "DOWNTOWN SCOTTSDALE" MAP

E INDIAN SCHOOL RD

N 44TH ST

E THOMAS RD

CONTINENTAL

202

N BEELINE HWY

© MOON.COM

from hamburger huts to highbrow gourmet destinations, and lots of coffeehouses and cool watering holes.

Downtown Scottsdale is roughly defined by Chaparral Road on the north, Osborn Road on the south, Miller Road on the east, and 68th Street on the west. Within these general boundaries there are several distinct districts, though they do meld into one another. The attractions here are art-searching, shopping and window-peering, eating and drinking, and general strolling and people-watching. In the Arts District, between Goldwater Boulevard and Scottsdale Road, you'll find a collection of art galleries to rival any other artsy block in the Southwest; the neighborhood is home to a popular Art Walk every Thursday night. On Fifth Avenue you'll find more than 80 boutiques and shops selling mostly Southwestern and Native American items. Here you'll also find **Bob Parks's Horse Fountain,** a collection of wild, galloping stone horses jumping out of a large fountain. There are several kiosks scattered around downtown that are stuffed with pamphlets, free magazines, and handouts about visiting Scottsdale.

HISTORIC OLD TOWN SCOTTSDALE

The stretch of downtown where Scottsdale's founder, Eastern banker Albert G. Utley, first staked out a town site (roughly bounded by Scottsdale Rd., Brown Ave., Indian School, and 2nd St.) has a collection of shops and eateries, some of them with Old West-style facades and hitching posts out front. The main shopping, sauntering, and people-watching area is along Main Street just before Brown Avenue. In the old days Main Street here was lined with homes, but in the 1940s Scottsdale began selling itself as "The West's Most Western Town," and the homes were turned into businesses with faux frontier-era facades. Main Street ends at the 21-acre **Scottsdale Civic Center Mall,** prime strolling grounds with lots of grass, shade-giving trees, and public art both silly and thought provoking. Just as you reach the mall off Main Street, look for the **Little Red Schoolhouse,** also known as

the **Scottsdale Historical Museum** (7333 E. Scottsdale Mall, 480/945-4499, www. scottsdalemuseum.org, 10am-2pm Wed.-Sun., Sept.-June, 10am-5pm Wed.-Sun., Oct.-May). Inside this charming brick structure, built in 1909 and used as the town's school, city hall, courthouse, and library at various times over the years, there are several exhibits on Scottsdale's history. Every Tuesday at 10am January-March, a docent leads a one-hour **Downtown Historic Walking Tour** that begins at the schoolhouse. All around Old Town and in the other touristy districts of downtown, you'll see quite a few horses doing draught duty in front of some restored carriage or wagon, loaded down with couples and kids.

SCOTTSDALE MUSEUM OF CONTEMPORARY ART

It's fitting that the only art museum in Arizona dedicated strictly to the new and the now is in Scottsdale, one of the magnetic centers of art in the Southwest. You won't find any howling coyotes or Kokopelli here; the works are edgy, sometimes confusingly avant-garde, and always interesting. **SMoCA** (7374 E. 2nd St., 480/874-4666, www.smoca.org, noon-5pm Tues.-Wed. and Fri.-Sun., noon-9pm Thurs., $10 adults, $7 students, children under 15 free, free admission Thurs.) is located just across the street from the Center for the Arts and has five galleries in a spare, modern space that used to be a movie theater. Special shows and exhibitions rotate often, and there's always at least one gallery showing work from the museum's permanent collection.

WESTERN SPIRIT: SCOTTSDALE'S MUSEUM OF THE WEST

Located in downtown Scottsdale's arts district, **Western Spirit: Scottsdale's Museum of the West** (3830 N. Marshall Way, 480/686-9539, 9:30am-5pm Tues.-Sat., 9:30am-9pm Thurs., 11am-5pm Sun., adults $13, children 6-17, $8) should be visited by anyone interested in the art, culture, and history of the Old West. Focused on the art and

Downtown Scottsdale

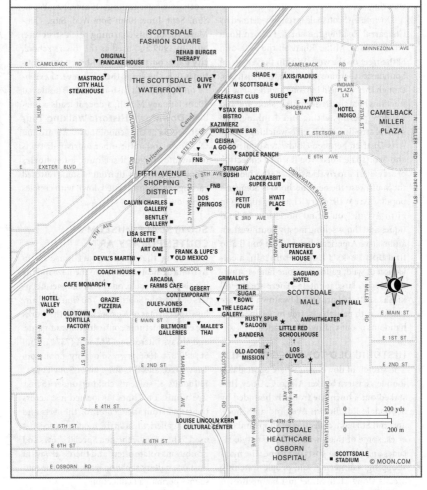

images of the Western frontier, it offers several unique exhibitions each year on subjects such as the Cowboy Artists of America, the Grand Canyon in painting, Native American pottery, Western films, and much more.

OLD ADOBE MISSION

The **Old Adobe Mission** (7655 E. Main St., 480/947-4331, www.olphaz.com, 10am-4pm daily Nov.-Apr., free), a small chapel in the heart of the Old Town district, was built in 1933 by a group of Mexican and Yaqui Indian families. If it looks a bit like a miniature San Xavier del Bac, that's because it's supposed to: They say architect Robert Evans had Tucson's famous "White Dove of the Desert" in mind when he designed this little Mission-style gem. It was built by volunteers with some 14,000 adobe bricks made from a mixture of dirt, straw, and horse manure. Local tinsmith Barnebe Herrera made—and signed—the church's stained-glass windows. There's often a volunteer on-site to talk about the building, its history, and the important effort to save it.

Central Scottsdale and Paradise Valley
COSANTI

Known for his visionary, utopian architecture, the late Paolo Soleri, founder of the living architecture research facility in Central Arizona called Arcosanti, was a powerful figure in the valley, if only because he represented what could be when it comes to humans living in resource-sparse environments. His round, organic, fairy-world structures, which seem to have been waiting there in the desert for some mad genius to tell them to rise up, are part Frank Lloyd Wright (who brought Soleri to the valley to study at Taliesin West), part Native American, and part artistic fantasy. His Paradise Valley desert complex, established in 1956, has a gallery, studio, living spaces, and a foundry, where students make the famous **Soleri Windbells,** which are sold throughout the world to fund the ongoing urban design experiments at Arcosanti. You can watch the bells being made most weekday mornings. An ideal way to visit **Cosanti** (6433 E. Doubletree Ranch Rd., 480/948-6145, www.cosanti.com, 9am-5pm Mon.-Sat., 11am-5pm Sun., free) is to combine it with a tour of Taliesin West, which is located only about eight miles to the northeast.

MCCORMICK-STILLMAN RAILROAD PARK

Kids and train enthusiasts will love **McCormick-Stillman Railroad Park** (7301 E. Indian Bend Rd., 480/312-2312, www.therailroadpark.com, generally 10am-6pm daily, free), dedicated to the old iron horse. Rides on the train and carousel cost $1-2 each. A replica of a Colorado narrow-gauge railroad called **The Paradise and Pacific Railroad** makes you feel like a giant as it moves around a one-mile track running through the green park. There are also several old trains in the park that are worth a look as well as a museum featuring exhibits on the history of the railroad and how it changed the valley—housed in a 1914 Santa Fe Railroad baggage car. Another highlight is a presidential Pullman car used by Eisenhower and FDR. Don't skip a ride on the restored old carousel—pure joy. The park's hours vary slightly by season, so call ahead or visit the website to verify before heading over.

North Scottsdale
ODYSEA IN THE DESERT

A family entertainment complex, **OdySea in the Desert** (9500 E. Via De Ventura off the 101 Freeway, 480/291-8000, http://odyseainthedesert.com) has a pleasant courtyard with a soaring metal structure, a fountain, and several restaurants, bars, and shops to hang out in and peruse before or after you check out the sea creatures at the huge **OdySea Aquarium** (480/291-8000, www.odyseaaquarium.com, 9am-7pm Mon.-Wed., 9am-8pm Thurs.-Sat., 9am-6pm Sun., adults $22, kids 3-12 $15) or the butterflies and reptiles at **Butterfly Wonderland** (www.butterflywonderland.com, 480/800-3000, 9am-5pm daily, adults $22, children 3-12 $15). Kids will love the **Laser and Mirror Maze** (480/270-6200, www.odyseamirrormaze.com, 10am-7pm Sun.-Fri., 10am-8pm Sat., $4-13), a fun playland with challenging games that have you scooting around to avoid green lasers—like some kind of secret agent or cat burglar. The complex also has super-fun **bumper boats** (10am-6pm daily, 1 ride $4).

HUHUGAM KI MUSEUM

In an adobe building on the **Salt River Pima-Maricopa Indian Community,** two of the state's river-bred tribes preserve their history and cultural customs. "Huhugam Ki" means "House of the Ancestors," and the ancestors they are talking about are the mysterious Hohokam, who irrigated and grew crops in the Salt River Valley hundreds of years ago. The **Huhugam Ki Museum** (10005 E. Osborn Rd., 480/362-7400, www.srpmic-nsn.gov/history_culture/museum.asp, 9:30am-4:30pm Mon.-Fri., free) tells the stories and

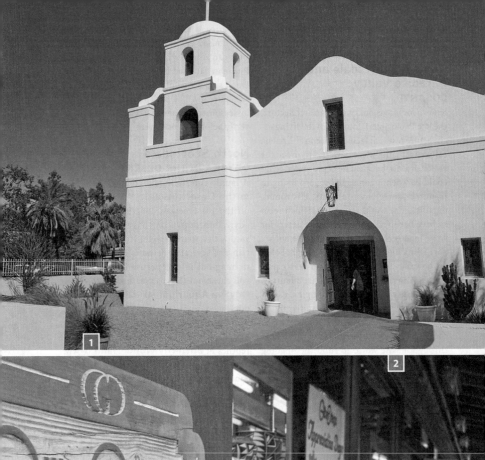

Frank Lloyd Wright in the Valley of the Sun

In 1940 Frank Lloyd Wright published an essay in *Arizona Highways* in which he eloquently pleaded for a different kind of architecture for the desert, one not based on previous models but on the unique colors and contours of the desert itself: "The ever advancing human threat to the integral beauty of Arizona might be avoided if the architect would only go to school in the desert," he wrote, "and humbly learn harmonious contrasts or sympathetic treatments that would, thus, quietly, belong."

Certainly the best of the very few real-world examples of what Wright had in mind is his own **Taliesin West,** Wright's most famous desertland building. He designed a few other distinctive structures in the valley, and some of them are accessible to fans of the nation's greatest architect. In addition to a church and an auditorium, Wright built nine private homes in the valley, eight of which still exist. One of the finest of his private homes is a small bungalow Wright designed for his friend Raymond Carlson, once the editor of *Arizona Highways.*

Many critics and scholars include the 1928 **Arizona Biltmore** (2400 E. Missouri Ave., Phoenix), then as now the state's most stylish resort, on the short list of public structures Wright designed in the valley. Though the architect of record is his former apprentice, Albert Chase McArthur, Wright was paid a consulting fee on the project and left his mark on the design, as anyone with even a passing knowledge of Wright's quirks and obsessions will see during a stroll around the magnificent "Jewel of the Desert."

Wright created the design for the north valley's **First Christian Church** (6750 N. 7th Ave., 602/246-9206, www.fccphx.com) in 1950 as part of the Classical University commission that never got off the ground. In 1972, church leaders obtained the unused plans and started construction on the sanctuary, considered by many the best example of Wright's church architecture. You can stop in for a look around, or attend one of the services held Sundays at 9am and 10:30am.

Wright originally designed Arizona State University's **Grady Gammage Memorial Auditorium** (1200 S. Forest Ave., Tempe, 480/965-5062) as an opera house for Baghdad, Iraq. In 1957, when Wright was 90 years old, the king of Iraq commissioned him to design several public buildings in Baghdad. Unfortunately, the king was killed the next year, so the project fell apart. Later, the design for the Baghdad opera house was changed a bit to become Gammage Auditorium. It is not one of the critics' favorites—a bit puffy and sappy for some tastes—but the acoustics, as in all of Wright's performance spaces, are absolutely perfect.

Journalist Lawrence Cheek wrote a slim but comprehensive book about Wright's desert work, *Frank Lloyd Wright in Arizona* (Rio Nuevo, 2006), which should be read by anybody interested in Wright's Western masterpieces.

---

histories of the Pima Indians, now commonly referred to in their own language as the Akimel O'odham (River People)—cousins to Southern Arizona's Tohono O'odham (Desert People)—and the Maricopa, or Xalychidom Piipaash, a tribe that migrated to the valley from the banks of the Gila and Colorado Rivers, through exhibits, old photographs, pottery, and other artifacts. The Akimel O'odham are known for their basket making,

and a highlight of a visit to this small museum is the live demonstrations of the intricate art by tribal members.

★ TALIESIN WEST

Architect Frank Lloyd Wright spent the money he made from his masterpiece Fallingwater on a large swath of desert northeast of Scottsdale, and from about 1937 onward he spent a portion of each year living in the desert with his apprentices and building what would become **Taliesin West** (12621 Frank Lloyd Wright Blvd., 480/860-2700, recorded tour info 480/860-8810, www.franklloydwright.

1: Old Adobe Mission 2: Gilbert Ortega Gallery & Museum, a gallery and shop featuring Native American arts org, 9am-4pm daily). If every house built in the desert used the natural landscape in the same way as this wondrous complex does, the valley would be a very different, better place today. Familiar Wright motifs, like his ubiquitous compression-and-release entranceways, Oriental touches, and native-rock-and-mortar aesthetic, are on display at this truly unique and important attraction.

You can see Taliesin only by tour, and the guides are knowledgeable and enthusiastic about Wright's work and legacy. Since the complex is still used and lived in today by fellows of Taliesin Associated Architects, a group carrying on the spirit of Wright's work, some buildings may be off-limits during a given tour. You have several tours to choose from, including an in-depth, three-hour, behind-the-scenes look around ($75). The most popular is the 90-minute **Insights Tour** (8:45am-4pm daily, every half hour Nov.-Apr., every hour May-Oct., $35 adults, $19 children 12 and under), which includes a look at the beautiful Garden Room and the living quarters as well as all of the sights included in the one-hour **Panorama Tour** (10:15am and 2:15pm daily, $24 adults, $12 children under 12). The tour schedules changes sometimes, so it's a good idea to call before you go. Arrive a little early so you can check out the excellent bookstore and gift shop, which sells Frank Lloyd Wright-inspired knickknacks and just about every book ever published by or on the master.

CAREFREE AND CAVE CREEK

Drive north on Scottsdale Road (about 15 miles from Phoenix) through a beautiful, if disappearing, stretch of desert to these tiny resort-style towns full of galleries, antiques stores, restaurants, and artisan shops—a perfect daylong escapade to the valley's northeastern outer reaches. Along the way, watch for the large signs on the side of the road pointing out various representative Sonoran Desert flora. In January and March, the **Carefree Fine Art & Wine Festival** attracts artists, artisans, and wine lovers from across

the nation. This drive is very popular with motorcycle groups, and on any given weekend (though not so much in the summer) the area is likely to be somewhat crowded.

SPORTS AND RECREATION

Scottsdale is a bit greener than many desert cities, and there are quite a few parks and open spaces within the relatively small area of the town. One of the best of these is the long multiuse trail that winds through the center of the mostly residential neighborhoods along Hayden Road from Indian Bend Road south to Tempe—about 13 miles of greenspace for bikers, joggers, walkers, and skaters called the **Indian Bend Wash Greenbelt** (Scottsdale Parks and Recreation, 7340 Scottsdale Mall, 480/312-7957, www.scottsdaleaz.gov). Along this unique flood-control system, which channels intermittent desertland floods—mostly in the late-summer monsoon season—into Indian Bend Wash while at the same time creating a fine exercise and recreation belt through the length of the town, you'll see a steady stream of bikers, in-line skaters, and joggers, especially in the mornings. The path passes through several city parks and golf courses as it makes its way south all the way to Tempe Town Lake. There's not really a set-aside, signed starting block for the greenbelt, but a good place to pick it up is at **Chaparral Park** (5401 N. Hayden Rd., 480/312-2353).

Hiking and Biking
MCDOWELL MOUNTAIN REGIONAL PARK

If you'd like to get out of the city a bit and into the desert, head out to **McDowell Mountain Regional Park** (16300 McDowell Mountain Park Dr., 480/471-0173, www.maricopa.gov/parks/mcdowell), a 21,000-acre desert preserve northeast of Scottsdale proper with miles of desert hiking, biking, and equestrian trails. This is an excellent setting for getting to know the Sonoran Desert. To get to the park from Scottsdale, take Shea Boulevard east to Fountain Hills Boulevard, which heads north and turns into McDowell Mountain Road leading into the park. If you've got some extra time, think about stopping in the retirement haven of Fountain Hills and seeing the world's biggest fountain; continue on Shea past Fountain Hills Boulevard, and then turn north on Saguaro Boulevard, which will take you right past **Fountain Park** and **The Fountain** and then meets with Fountain Hills Boulevard, which leads to the preserve.

Inside the park, there are various trails for hiking, biking, and horseback riding; one of the more popular short hikes is the 3-mile North Trail. The 15-mile Pemberton Trail is the toughest and longest hike in the park.

MCDOWELL SONORAN PRESERVE
McDowell Sonoran Preserve (various trailheads around Scottsdale, 480/312-7013, www.scottsdaleaz.gov/preserve, sunrise-sunset daily, free) in Scottsdale holds back the sprawling cityscape from some 27,000 acres of beautiful desert around the McDowell Mountains. The area is northeast of the city center and has dozens of varied trails for hiking, all of them fairly near each other. The largest and most developed trailhead is the **Gateway Access Area** (18333 N. Thompson Peak Pkwy.), about 15 miles north of downtown Scottsdale via the Route 101 Loop. Other access areas with trails include **Lost Dog Wash** (12601 N. 124th St.), 14 miles north of downtown via the 101 Loop; **Quartz** (10215 E. McDowell Mt. Ranch Rd.), also 14 miles north on the 101; **Ringtail** (12300 block of N. 128th St.), 14.5 miles north on the 101; **Sunrise** (12101 N. 145th Way), 16 miles north of downtown via the 101, and **WestWorld** (15939 N. 98th St.), 13 miles from downtown on the 101.

The **Gateway Loop Trail** (Gateway Access Area) is a relatively easy 4.5-mile loop through a beautiful Sonoran Desert setting—and an excellent primer on desert hiking. More difficult is the **Tom Thumb Trail** (23015 N. 128th St.), a 4.5-mile climb to a promontory that provides spectacular views of the desert and the city. The **Brown's Ranch Trail** (30301 N.

Alma School Pkwy.) is an easy three-mile hike through an old ranch property.

Golf

There are about 200 golf courses in the Valley of the Sun, and about 50 of them are in Scottsdale, a town as famous for its golf as for its galleries and resorts. You'll likely find the golf courses in Scottsdale to be a bit more challenging and considerably more beautiful and dramatic than those in surrounding communities, but they are also considerably more expensive. For a true golf lover, though, this is where you'll want to splurge.

Kierland Golf Club (15636 N. Clubgate Dr., 480/922-9283, www.kierlandgolf.com) is a gorgeous 27-hole, par 36 desert course along Scottsdale Road just south of Frank Lloyd Wright Boulevard. It's part of the Weston Kierland Resort and Spa but is open to the public. The greens are shocking against the hard desert scenery, which has been left to itself along the edges of the greenery, making for a uniquely Arizona golfing experience. It's not cheap: It'll cost you about $170-190 in the high season, and about $44-74 during the hottest days of the summer. The course offers some twilight hour prices that are significantly cheaper, however. You can book a tee time online, and it's recommended that you do so before traveling if you want to play any of Scottsdale's courses.

The fabulous **Troon North Golf Club** (10320 E. Dynamite Blvd., 480/585-5300, www.troonnorthgolf.com) in the far northeast valley is a much-sought-after golfing experience for duffers the world over. It's probably the most beautiful public course in the valley, though one could say that about many fairways here. There are two courses at the club, both lined with desert boulders and saguaro; the Monument Course, the better of the two, is so named because of the 14-foot boulder rising off the fairway. Expect to pay $50-80 in summer and around $200 in the high season.

Starfire at Scottsdale Country Club (11500 N. Hayden Rd., 480/948-6000, www.

starfiregolfclub.com) is a more centrally located course—head north on Hayden Road and you'll find it—and more reasonably priced than some of the fancier desert courses north of the city. The 27-hole course, lined with eucalyptus and palm trees, was designed by Arnold Palmer and is moderately challenging. Expect to pay about $20 for a round in summer, and about $40-50 during the high season.

TPC of Scottsdale (17020 N. Hayden Rd., 480/585-4334, http://tpc.com/scottsdale) is where the PGA pros play one of the most popular tournaments of the year in late January; the **Waste Management Open** (www.phoenixopen.com), formerly the Phoenix Open, is one of the oldest tournaments on the pro tour and draws some of the biggest crowds of any tournament. In the off-season you're likely to see one of the local PGA tour members practicing on the two exquisite courses. The Scottsdale Princess Resort is linked with the club. To stay and play here is to engage in the height of luxury and enjoy challenging golf, but it's going to cost you. Greens fees will run you more than $200 in the high season and about $80 in the deep summer, with discounts for evening play.

Spas

Scottsdale is known far and wide as a place to pamper your body and soul. There are dozens of spas in this upscale desert burg, and many of them are associated with the city's many world-famous resorts. A half day or a full day at one of these spas may be just what you need to get your life back on track or to celebrate how on-track your life already is. Regardless, it's going to cost you. Check the individual websites for current pricing, but don't expect to do anything, or have anything done to you, for much under $100, and that's just to get started. During the summer months, however, most of the spas, like their parent resorts, cut prices somewhat to attract business to the hot valley. It's a good idea to call ahead for a reservation in any season.

The Phoenician Spa (6000 E. Camelback Rd., 480/843-2392, www.thephoenician.com, 7am-7pm daily) takes your health and comfort very seriously. They offer 75 different treatments at this 22,000-square-foot spa that will put you through a vigorous workout, give you a facial, massage, and a makeover, and then send you on your way after you've stopped at the "waters bar" and found your center in the meditation room.

The Spa at Camelback Inn (5402 E. Lincoln Dr., 800/922-2635, www.camelbackspa.com, 6:15am-7:30pm daily, appointment required) has a gorgeous spa, with plunge pools, Turkish baths and saunas, and a beautiful pool area where you can rent a spa cabana for a day of relaxation. They offer all manner of body wraps and facial treatments, massages, and other bodywork in a truly stunning setting. They also have exercise classes, personal training and consultations, and a spa restaurant serving healthy and wholesome foods.

At **The Sanctuary Spa at Sanctuary Resort** (5700 E. McDonald Dr., Paradise Valley, 480/607-2326, www.sanctuaryoncamelback.com, 6am-8:30pm daily) you can get a variety of Asian treatments, such as the medicinal herb massage called "luk pra kope," as well as acupuncture, Reiki, shiatsu, and Thai reflexology. This refined, tranquil space on the grounds of the Sanctuary Resort also offers a host of other treatments, including Swedish massage, facials, makeovers, and personal training.

If you're in downtown Scottsdale and find yourself in need of a massage, facial, and sauna, stop into **The Lamar Everyday Spa** (5115 N. Scottsdale Rd., 480/945-7066, www.thelamar.com, 10am-7pm Sun.-Thurs., 9am-7pm Fri.-Sat.), which offers massages, facials, pools and saunas, and all the other soothing treatments in a friendly, coed atmosphere that was voted one of the valley's best places for a romantic date. The prices here are generally a bit lower than those of the resort spas.

ENTERTAINMENT AND EVENTS

Nightlife

Scottsdale is known as a playground for the beautiful and the rich, and some quarters of town focus on dancing to repetitive beats and peeking into VIP rooms to espy some minor celebrity. But there are a lot of down-to-earth watering holes and scenes here, too. Last call is usually 2am, per the state legislature, but many bars and clubs stay open for hours afterward, offering late-night menus and after-hours fun. Dress is generally casual, unless you're going to the highest of the high-end places. Most of the restaurants listed under the Food section double as nightspots as well.

Downtown's **Entertainment District** (roughly bounded by Camelback Rd., Scottsdale Rd., Miller Rd., and 6th Ave.) is as good a place as any to start your night on the town in Scottsdale, and you'll likely find enough clubs, bars, and lounges to keep you busy for quite a while.

BARS AND PUBS

The **Living Room at the W Scottsdale** (7277 E. Camelback Rd., 480/970-2100, 4pm-midnight Sun.-Thurs., 4pm-2am Fri.-Sat.) provides a perfect introduction to the high-end Scottsdale nightlife scene, with its moneyed and tanned patrons, high-priced, handcrafted cocktails, and swanky Modernist-fusion interiors. You might even see a few celebrities staying at the hotel.

If you're looking for something a bit more rowdy, try the cowboy-dive **Rusty Spur Saloon** (7245 E. Main St., 480/425-7787, www.rustyspursaloon.com, 10am-1am Mon.-Thurs., 10am-2am Fri.-Sat.), a historic Scottsdale saloon housed in a building that opened first in 1921 as a bank. The vault is still here, but they keep booze in it now, and there's all kinds of cool old Western memorabilia on the walls and a relaxed, neighborhood-joint atmosphere here. They serve heaping plates of rib-sticking bar food and offer live bands as well.

Vines & Hops (4216 N. Brown Ave., 480/748-4460, http://vinesandhopsbar.com, 3pm-10pm Mon.-Tues., noon-11pm Wed.-Thurs., noon-midnight Fri.-Sat., noon-10pm Sun.) specializes in beers made in Arizona, with 19 of them on tap. The slick, stylish interior and fun games (darts, cards, and board games) make this a great place to hang out in central Scottsdale, and one that's hard to leave once you get comfortable. Along with the AZ-centric beer list, the bar offers a long and varied wine list, along with creative small plates and sandwiches. Bring your dog along; they are most welcome here.

Rockbar (4245 N. Craftsman Circle, 480/331-9190, www.rockbarscottsdale.com, 3pm-2am daily) in Old Town Scottsdale is a fun place to see local and touring rock bands, kick back a cocktail or two, and chomp up some excellent pizza. Check the bar's website for a schedule of bands coming up.

CASINOS

The **Salt River Pima-Maricopa Indian Community** operates two casinos in Scottsdale, though both require a bit of a drive from downtown. **Casino Arizona at Salt River** (524 N. 92nd St., 480/850-7777, www.casinoarizona.com), east of the Loop 101 at McKellips, has 900 slots, 34 gaming tables, keno, and a showroom that hosts touring acts and a review featuring look-and-sound-alikes of the superstars of American music. At the **Casino Arizona at Talking Stick** (9700 E. Indian Bend Rd., 480/850-7777, www.talkingstickresort.com), about a mile east of the Loop 101 on Indian Bend Road, there are 700 slots and 50 gaming tables. This is a good option if you're in town for spring training; the casino is right next to the spring home of the Arizona Diamondbacks.

Performing Arts

The **Scottsdale Center for the Performing Arts** (7380 E. 2nd St., 480/499-8587, www.scottsdaleperformingarts.org) is a huge complex of theaters, classrooms, and grassy knolls right downtown. Inside, the **Virginia G. Piper Theater** and a few smaller spaces nearby host a wide range of theater, dance, comedy, and music—mostly classical and jazz. Acts like Laurie Anderson and Arlo Guthrie have performed here, as have jazz legend Dave Brubeck and many others.

Festivals and Events

More than 100 artists, many of them internationally known in art circles, participate in the popular **Arizona Fine Art Expo** (Scottsdale Rd. and Jomax Rd., www.arizonafineartexpo.com) from January through March, during which you can stroll in and out of galleries and cabanas set up streetside and watch the artists at work. Also in January, the famous **Barrett-Jackson Antique Auto Auction** (7400 E. Monte Cristo Ave., 480/421-6694, www.barrett-jackson.com) gets underway, selling auction-style the most expensive and spectacular automobiles in existence. Hundreds of white tents go up at Scottsdale Road and the Loop 101 from January through March for the **Celebration of Fine Art** (www.celebrateart.com), while inside, juried artists create their works before your eyes and sell them directly.

The **Scottsdale Arabian Horse Show** (Westworld, 16601 N. Pima Rd., www.scottsdaleshow.com) brings equestrian enthusiasts from all over the world to town in February, and in March the **Scottsdale Arts Festival** (75th St. and Main St., www.scottsdaleperformingarts.org) attracts about 10,000 visitors to the Scottsdale Center for the Performing Arts for three days of art sales, demonstrations, and performances. In April, just before it starts to get hot, the shining stars of the eating scene gather for the **Scottsdale Culinary Festival** (www.scottsdaleculinaryfestival.org).

SHOPPING
Shopping Centers and Districts

If you're a serious shopper with serious money, don't miss the upscale centers for which this part of the valley is famous. Even if you don't have sacks of money, it's fun to walk around these always well-landscaped and fashionable shopping centers, bustling with beautiful people and stocked with luxury items from all over the globe, to get an idea of how the other 1 percent lives. Scottsdale's busy downtown areas provide the best shopping in town, and nearby **Scottsdale Fashion Square** (7014 E. Camelback Rd., 480/945-5495, www.fashionsquare.com, 10am-9pm Mon.-Sat., 11am-6pm Sun.) is the largest enclosed mall in the Southwest, featuring high-end department stores, boutiques, and restaurants.

Kierland Commons (6166 N. Scottsdale Rd. and Greenway Pkwy., 480/348-1577, www.kierlandcommons.com, 10am-5pm Mon.-Sat., noon-6pm Sun.) has about 70 upmarket shops and eateries, including Anthropologie and Crate & Barrel.

The Shops at Gainey Village (Scottsdale Rd. and Doubletree Ranch Rd., www.theshopsgaineyvillage.com, 10am-6pm Mon.-Sat., noon-6pm Sun.) is perhaps the most stylish of them all, featuring unique boutiques, interior design shops, and furniture stores with custom-made items you won't find anywhere else.

Close to downtown, check out **Scottsdale Quarter** (15059 N. Scottsdale Rd., 480/270-8123, http://scottsdalequarter.com, 10am-9pm daily), a civilized and therapeutic wonderland of high-end retail and restaurants. Along the Arizona Canal, the **Scottsdale Waterfront** (7135 E. Camelback Rd., 480/247-8071, http://scottsdalewaterfrontshopping.com, hours vary) has midrange stores, shops, restaurants, and a pleasant atmosphere for strolling and people-watching.

Downtown
CLOTHING

It might be hard to swallow Scottsdale's claim as "The West's Most Western Town" when you are, say, sipping a cocktail in some urban-chic lounge. But when you visit **Saba's Western Wear** (3965 N. Brown Ave., 480/947-7664, www.sabas.com, 10am-7pm Tues.-Fri., 10am-6pm Sat., 11am-5pm Sun.), a fixture in Old Town since back when it was merely "town," you might start to sympathize a bit. Members of the Saba family, longtime valley merchants with nine stores (including one just across the street), still sell the finest, most authentic working-cowpoke Western wear you can find—plus an unparalleled selection for the equally authentic urban cowboy and cowgirl.

NATIVE AMERICAN ARTS

Scottsdale has long been known as one of the three or four top places in the Southwest to see and buy Native American arts. There are several galleries and shops along Main Street downtown, and the **Gilbert Ortega Gallery & Museum** (3925 N. Scottsdale Rd., 480/990-1808, 10am-6pm Sun.-Tues., 10am-9pm Wed.-Sat.) is worth a perusal.

For Hopi kachina dolls, Hopi and Zuni pottery, and Zuni fetishes, don't miss the **River Trading Post & Traditional Pueblo Arts** (7033 E. Main St., Ste. 102, 480/444-0001, www.rivertradingpost.com, 11am-5pm Tues.-Sat., noon-4pm Sun.). This museum-like shop has a superior collection of Navajo rugs, sculptures, and frontier-era furniture. The **Old Territorial Indian Arts** (7100 E. Main St., #3, 480/945-5432, www.oldterritorialshop.com, 10am-4pm Mon.-Sat.) is a classic gallery that has been selling and showing wonderful antique Navajo rugs, Hopi pottery and kachina dolls, and Native American jewelry, folk art, and baskets, for more than 40 years.

FARMERS MARKET

Every Saturday the **Old Town Farmers Market** (7am-11am Sat. late Oct.-late May), in the city parking facility at the corner of Brown Avenue and 1st Street, features local farmers and artists, food artisans, and food lovers selling and promoting their unique wares.

GALLERIES

Scottsdale is second only to Santa Fe as a center for the Southwestern art scene. The **Scottsdale Arts District** (west of Scottsdale Rd. to 70th St., north along Marshall Way to 5th Ave.) has more than 100 galleries, many of them featuring the work of classic Southwestern artists and contemporary

masters. But it's not all about regional expectations; be prepared to see a lot that defies preconceived notions about what Southwestern art is and should be. It's not all about Southwestern art, either. There are several galleries that have little to do with it at all, displaying instead a general contemporary style that is always intriguing. One of the best ways to see all that the downtown Scottsdale art scene has to offer is to embark on the famed Thursday night **Scottsdale Artwalk** (480/377-9366, 6:30pm-9:30pm Thurs.). Every Thursday for three hours (and sometimes longer), the galleries along Main Street, Marshall Way, Stetson, and 6th Avenue throw open their doors to hundreds of art lovers, and you can walk along the lit-up streets, stop in for a drink at one of the area's many watering holes, and dip in and out of dozens of galleries. The weekly event has been going on since 1976 and is one of the nation's oldest art walk events. For more information, and for a complete list of galleries, check out the **Scottsdale Gallery Association** website (www.scottsdalegalleries.com).

The **Wilde Meyer Gallery** (4142 N. Marshall Way, 480/945-2323, www.wildemeyer.com, 10am-5:30pm Mon.-Fri., 10am-6pm Sat.) shows an eclectic mix of paintings by mostly contemporary artists, many of whom have infused the Southwestern landscape with a surreal sensibility. The work here is some of the most exciting and baffling in the Arts District. At the **Trailside Galleries** (7330 Scottsdale Mall, 480/945-7751, www.trailsidegalleries.com, 10am-5:30pm Mon.-Sat.) on Scottsdale Mall, which has been around since 1963, you'll find mostly realistic Western art in the form of bucking-bronc bronzes, noble Indian chiefs, and tired old cowboys lounging on their saddles. They also have a fine collection of landscape paintings. At **Bonner David Galleries** (7040 E. Main St., 480/941-8500, www.bonnerdavid.com, 10am-5:30pm Mon.-Sat., open until 9pm Thurs.) you'll find a thrilling mix of abstracts, landscapes, and realistic sculpture.

If you're a film fan, and especially if you love old movies, don't miss the **Femmes Fatales & Fantasies Art Museum & Gallery** (7013 E. Main St., 480/429-6800, www.fffmovieposters.com, www.sherrygoldbergart.com, 10am-6pm, Tues., Wed., Fri., Sat., 1pm-9pm Thurs.), where they have a spectacular collection of framed, original movie posters from *The Big Sleep* to *Back to the Future* and pretty much everything in between.

FOOD

Scottsdale has many of the valley's poshest restaurants, and the scene is always changing and evolving. You'll find enough variety here to make your head and your palate spin. It's not all high-toned and intimidating, though; most of the best restaurants here are serious about food, design, and service, but they don't take themselves too seriously. Many of Scottsdale's restaurants serve late-night menus and have busy bars as well as packed dining rooms. Reservations are always a good idea.

Mexican

Don't leave Cave Creek without stopping for lunch or dinner at **El Encanto** (6248 E. Cave Creek Rd., 480/488-1752, www.elencantorestaurant.com, 11am-10pm daily, $7-17), serving what is perhaps the valley's best Mexican food from comfortable booths that look out on an enclosed Spanish-style courtyard with a pond, atop which elegant swans float lazily. Try the prickly pear margarita—sweet and delicious with a perfect kick.

Downtown's **Old Town Tortilla Factory** (6910 E. Main St., 480/945-4567, www.oldtowntortillafactory.com, 5pm-9pm Sun.-Thurs., 5pm-10pm Fri.-Sat., $14-29) has an enchanting patio and serves gourmet Southwestern-style creations with pork, fish, chicken, shrimp, and beef. The tortillas are made on-site, come in several different flavors, and are served hot and fresh. The margarita menu is excellent, offering mango, raspberry, blue agave, and other creative takes, along with the classic original.

The Tex-Mex food at **Old Town Gringos** (4209 N. Craftsman Ct., 480/423-3800, www.oldtowngringos.com, 11am-2am daily, $10-15) downtown is delicious and filling, but it's the patio-party atmosphere that draws daytime drinkers here. The sunny rooftop patio, the chips and salsa and burritos, the buckets of Corona on the tables—how can you resist?

American and Southwestern

Chef Charleen Badman of **FnB** (7125 E. 5th Ave. Ste. 31, 480/284-477, www.fnbrestaurant.com, 5pm-10pm Mon.-Sat., 5pm-9pm Sun., June-Aug. only open Wed.-Sat., $12-36, credit cards only) won a 2019 James Beard Award for Best Chef Southwest, a category for which she's been in the running four years in a row. FnB has also been lauded by national magazines and newspapers as a leader in Arizona's culinary scene. The menu changes often but always features wonderful and strange dishes with ingredients sourced from local farms and food artisans. Reservations are a must.

★ **Arcadia Farms Café** (7014 E. 1st Ave., 480/941-5665, www.arcadiafarmscafe.com, 7am-3pm daily, $10-20) is a casual farm-to-table spot with tasty American food with a regional twist. Menu offerings include warm chopped vegetable salad; chicken and vegetable quesadilla; and chicken, wild mushroom, and leek crepes. Arcadia Farms gets a large portion of its ingredients from local and organic farms and food purveyors. The café's on-site market sells a variety of local foods.

Rehab Burger Therapy (7210 E. 2nd St., 480/621-5358, http://rehabburgertherapy.com, 11am-9pm Sun.-Tues., 11am-10pm Wed.-Thurs., 11am-11pm Fri.-Sat., $7.50-18) serves a wide selection of creative craft-burgers in a casual atmosphere. The burgers go very well with a big basket of sweet potato fries. They also serve salads, wings, and sandwiches that will not disappoint. Rehab has locations in Phoenix and Tempe as well.

AZ 88 (7353 Scottsdale Mall, 480/994-5576, www.az88.com, 11:30am-12:30am daily,

$11-19) is an ultracool lounge and restaurant with delicious, simple dishes like hamburgers and chicken sandwiches, DJs spinning many nights, and consistently interesting art on the walls, changed out regularly.

★ **Rancho Pinot** (6300 N. Scottsdale Rd., #101, 480/367-8030, www.ranchopinot.com, 5:30pm-9pm Tues.-Sat., $13-35) is a leading light of the locavore movement in the valley, serving a seasonally based, always-fresh menu of truly feel-good food. This is Arizona-bred eating at its best. Chef Chrysta Robertson started the Phoenix chapter of Slow Food and has been a pioneer in sustainable, local cuisine for 25 years. The menu changes often but generally features small plates like grilled quail with polenta and stuffed squash blossoms, and large plates like spinach fettucine and grilled lamb chops with mint pesto.

★ **Lon's at the Hermosa** (5532 N. Palo Cristi Rd., 602/955-7878, www.lons.com, 7am-10am, 11:30am-2pm, and 5:30pm-10pm Mon.-Fri., 7am-2pm and 5:30pm-10pm Sat.-Sun., $29-52) offers "comfort cuisine" carefully prepared with regional flair and ingredients, including many grown in the organic gardens on the grounds of this boutique resort, which was built out of the original desert studio of renowned valley artist Lon Megargee. The desert hideaway atmosphere enhances the spectacular New American cuisine. The tortilla soup is a classic, and you really must try the "truffle-scented" macaroni-and-cheese.

The **Sugar Bowl** (4005 N. Scottsdale Rd., 480/946-0051, www.sugarbowlscottsdale. com, 11am-10pm Sun.-Thurs., 11am-midnight Fri.-Sat., $6-12) has been a Scottsdale institution since it opened in 1958, serving delicious and filling sandwiches, soups, chili, burgers, and dogs, as well as decadent ice cream treats, in a family atmosphere. Bill Keane, who lived in nearby Paradise Valley, featured the Sugar Bowl several times in his famous "Family Circus" cartoon.

ACCOMMODATIONS

In Scottsdale, world-class accommodations and pampering are available to a great degree, but only to those who have the resources to buy them; those who don't, however, can still find a middle ground here, and there are even a few places for the budget-minded traveler. If you don't mind braving the heat, summer prices at the top resorts and getaways dip down into the real world.

$100-250

The **3 Palms** (7707 E. McDowell Rd., 800/450-6071, www.scottsdale-resort-hotels. com, $115-275) is a middle-brow resort-style accommodation in Scottsdale, offering most of the comforts and style of the more expensive places with just a slightly less ritzy sheen. This boutique hotel has cool, contemporary interior design in all the rooms and a large pool area perfect for lounging in the hot sun while sipping drinks. The **Aloft Scottsdale** (4415 N. Civic Center Plaza, 480/941-9400, www.scottsdalehiphotel.com, $199-215) is an upscale boutique hotel with tasteful rooms featuring big, comfortable beds and retro-chic couches. The pool area and the outdoor lounge are perfect places to gather for drinks around a fire.

The **Magnuson Hotel Papago Inn** (7017 E. McDowell Rd., 480/947-7335, www. papagoinnscottsdale.com, $108-120) is a centrally located boutique hotel with lush grounds, a big blue pool, and a throwback style with a lot of mid-century desert-style touches. It's a comfortable and affordable place to stay in the middle of all the action in Scottsdale and the valley. A room comes with free wireless Internet, a fridge, and a free breakfast buffet.

Located in Old Town within easy walking distance of the best Scottsdale has to offer, stylish, upscale **Saguaro** (4000 N. Drinkwater Blvd., 480/308-1100, http:// thesaguaro.com, $194-230) has a spa and gym, a gorgeous pool, a fantastic restaurant, and enough elegance and luxury to stick in your memory long after you've returned home.

Over $250

Built up over many decades from the Paradise

Valley studio of famed valley artist Alonzo "Lon" Megargee, the **Hermosa Inn** (5532 N. Palo Cristi, 602/955-8614, www.hermosainn. com, $400) is one of the most enchanting places to stay in Arizona. With its 34 detailed, high-rustic hacienda-style rooms, its gorgeous pool and myriad hidden outdoor spaces, and the surrounding desert scenery, it's truly a desert original. The 1930s-era Arizona details, reflecting Megargee's time, add to the pervading romance and enchantment here.

The Scott Resort & Spa (4925 N. Scottsdale Rd., 480/945-7666, www. thescottresort.com, $275-330) is a sumptuous, gardenlike place downtown with all kinds of secluded and secret spots—lagoons, hot tubs, and cozy cabanas—leather chairs and flat-screen TVs in the rooms, and a full-service spa. The Scott is Certified Green by the Arizona Hotel & Lodging Association under its Green Lodging Program. Also, the resort's parent company is a member of the 1% for the Planet alliance.

The **Fairmont Scottsdale Princess** (7575 E. Princess Dr., 480/585-4848, www.fairmont. com/scottsdale, $500-700) is a five-diamond resort in downtown Scottsdale with unbelievably comfortable and richly decorated rooms, suites, and casitas as well as golf courses, three restaurants, and one of the top spas in the nation. The Fairmont is Certified Green by the Arizona Hotel & Lodging Association under its Green Lodging Program.

The Boulders Resort and Golden Door Spa (34631 N. Tom Darlington Dr., Carefree, 480/488-9009, www.theboulders.com, $550-700), out in the wild desert of Carefree, has been named America's top spa more than a dozen times. This unique desert property offers gorgeous suites, casitas, villas, and haciendas in a secluded setting outside of the city. It goes far beyond the norm in comfort, style, and recreation.

The spectacular ★ **Sanctuary Camelback Mountain Resort and Spa** (5700 E. McDonald Dr., Paradise Valley, 480/607-2326, www.sanctuaryoncamelback. com $550-700) is on 53 acres of preserved and manicured desert in Paradise Valley, with elegant, private casitas tucked among the rocks, all watched over by the jagged dry mountain and with the valley spread out below. Inside the casitas, with their wood and limestone interiors, you'll find huge beds and deep tubs, and the spa and exercise regime will have you rejuvenated in no time, if lounging by the pool in your own private cabana doesn't do the trick. Voted by *Condé Nast* readers as the best resort in the nation, the Sanctuary is a prime and triumphant example of all a desert resort can be.

The ★ **Hotel Valley Ho** (6850 E. Main St., 480/248-2000, www.hotelvalleyho.com, $350-525) recalls the days of mid-20th-century high-end hipster style. It's a beautiful structure right in the middle of downtown Scottsdale, within easy walking distance of all the restaurants and bars and galleries. The upscale atmosphere here is infectious, and after a few hours you begin to feel like you deserve it all. The hotel has a wonderful pool made for lounging, with cabanas and daybeds, and a relaxing spa made for pampering. Hotel Valley Ho is Certified Green by the Arizona Hotel & Lodging Association under its Green Lodging Program.

The Phoenician (6000 E. Camelback Rd., 480/941-8200, www.thephoenician.com, $365-775), along the Camelback Corridor, has an excellent golf course, high-end style, and the Center for Well-Being spa. The Phoenician is Certified Green by the Arizona Hotel & Lodging Association under its Green Lodging Program.

The Camelback Inn (5402 E. Lincoln Dr., 480/596-7040, $415-525) has well-appointed guestrooms with French doors that open onto a private patio. The long pool, with luxurious lounging areas, looks out over unspoiled desert scenery, and the spa offers relaxation and balance in a secluded, peaceful setting.

The **Four Seasons Resort Scottsdale at Troon North** (10600 E. Crescent Moon Dr., 480/515-5700, www.fourseasons.com/ scottsdale, $600-800), just below jagged Pinnacle Peak, is a stunning resort that takes

Luxurious Retreats

Arizona is known around the world for the high-luxury resort accommodations offered in Scottsdale, Phoenix, Tucson, Sedona, and elsewhere. The best of these spa resorts appear to require their own zip code and guidebook, and those who frequent them can spend weeks in Arizona without venturing beyond the gates. Here are some of the best of the bunch:

- **Wigwam Hotel:** Southwestern elegance at its best is on display at this historic resort west of Phoenix, where you can experience all of today's luxuries while immersed in stylish reminders of yesterday (page 80).

- **Sanctuary Camelback Mountain Resort and Spa:** On 53 acres around Camelback Mountain in Paradise Valley, this aptly named sanctuary has amazing views of the desert, upscale lodgings, and opportunities for renewal (page 98).

- **Canyon Ranch:** Nestled in the desert foothills of the Santa Catalina Mountains above Tucson, this famed resort offers nothing less than a life-transforming experience (page 163).

- **Miraval, Life in Balance Resort & Spa:** This ultraexclusive desert hideaway at the base of Tucson's Santa Catalina Mountains has lots of green and shady spots for yoga and meditation, and it also has a big green heart. Among many other sustainable practices, Miraval operates its own treatment facility and reuses 99 percent of its water (page 163).

- **Amara Creekside Resort:** Set among the red rocks of Sedona, this oasis-like hideaway is the perfect place to relax the body and renew the spirit (page 242).

---

full advantage of its desert setting, with casitas set among the creosote and saguaros. The whole place has a whitewashed hacienda look, with exposed vigas, ironwork touches, and fireplaces. Many of the rooms have balconies that look out over the desert, and the pool area is spectacular and watched over by the landmark peak.

The Westin Kierland Resort & Spa (902 E. Greenway Pkwy., 480/624-1000, www.kierlandresort.com, $500-700) makes a great choice for families looking for different resort experiences: golf, spa treatments, and a super-fun waterslide, the holy trinity of modern family happiness. The Westin Kierland is Certified Green by the Arizona Hotel & Lodging Association under its Green Lodging Program.

Cave Creek

Not surprisingly, this mid- to high-end burg has not a few bed-and-breakfasts. The **Spur Cross Bed & Breakfast** (38555 N. School House Rd., Cave Creek, 480/473-1038, www.

spurcrossbnb.com, $250) rents four nice rooms with outside entrances and has a hot tub and wireless Internet.

INFORMATION

The **Scottsdale Convention & Visitors Bureau** (www.experiencescottsdale.com) operates a **tourist center** at **Scottsdale Fashion Square** (7014 E. Camelback Rd., 480/421-1004, 800/782-1117, 9am-6pm Mon.-Sat., 10am-5pm Sun).

TRANSPORTATION

The best way to get from Phoenix to Scottsdale is to take one of the surface streets east from downtown; that way you'll get to see more of the ground-level city instead of breezing past everything on the freeways. If you take Camelback Road east from downtown Phoenix, you'll run right into downtown Scottsdale. If you're heading from Scottsdale to Tempe, take Scottsdale Road south, and you'll run right into the college town.

Valley Metro (602/253-5000, www.

valleymetro.org), the valley's public transportation authority, provides bus service ($2 per ride) throughout the area, including to Glendale, Scottsdale, Tempe, and Mesa.

Each downtown district in Scottsdale runs

into the next and is easy to walk to, and there's a **free trolley** (11am-6pm daily, Thurs. evenings until 9pm, runs every 15 minutes) that will take you all around the downtown area if you prefer.

Around the Valley of the Sun

On the far eastern edge of the spreading cityscape, the desert holds a strong line in the Tonto National Forest. In this cactus, creosote, and mesquite wilderness, dashed with fallen slabs and boulders covered in faded-green dry lichen, you will experience the real Central Arizona outback, a rugged and storied stretch of the upper Sonoran Desert. If you have an SUV or a similarly high-clearance vehicle (or even, most of the time, a regular car), don't hesitate to drive the Apache Trail (State Rte. 88), a mostly dirt route that takes you deep into the desert, past several artificial lakes to one of the state's huge reclamation-era dams. You can then loop around to U.S. 60, where you'll cruise through several old mining towns and past the jagged Pinal Mountains before heading back into the city. Or detour north for about 40 miles on U.S. 60 from Globe to get a jaw-dropping look at Salt River Canyon. All along the way there are pull-offs and stops, trailheads, and historic markers. You can tour these eastern and northeastern reaches of the valley in one long day, unless you want to hike; then you'll need to mount a separate expedition.

If you're headed to Southern Arizona from the valley along I-10, veer off the main route for a few hours and visit the mysterious Casa Grande, the largest remaining Hohokam ruin. Or stop at Picacho Peak State Park just off the interstate to hike along a ragged rock spine towering over the desert.

About 60 miles northwest of the city on U.S. 60 you'll find the old mining town of Wickenburg, which still has a bit of Old West charm. Continue north on U.S. 89 for a twisting and scenic, mostly two-lane drive through

the chaparral and scrub midlands, through a lush ranching region, and on up to the pine forests of Prescott. And if you're taking the quick route to the northland along I-17, consider stopping at Arcosanti, an ongoing experiment in architecture and living.

THE SUPERSTITION MOUNTAINS

These rugged desert mountains rise to about 5,000 feet off the desert floor and are the main component of the 160,000-acre **Superstition Wilderness Area** in the Tonto National Forest. The Superstitions pale in comparison to other Arizona mountains both in elevation and diversity, but they are an ideal place to get an introduction to the Sonoran Desert and spend some time in a wilderness close to the city. The trails are rocky, and some are quite worn in places; the landscape is rough, gray-green desert, crowded with mobs of saguaro reaching into the always clear blue and huge sky, and carpeted with creosote, brittlebush, prickly pear, and all the other desert familiars. In February and March, especially after a winter of plentiful rainfall, and from April through June, large patches of the desert pop open with purple, red, yellow, and blue—everything that was waiting dormant explodes into bloom. This is the best time to be in the Superstitions. Don't go in the deep summer.

It is possible to get very far away from the city and everything else by going far into the wilderness area. Most, however, stick to the well-trodden but still impressive sights along the popular **Peralta Trail,** a moderately difficult, approximately 6-mile round-trip hike that leads to a saddle with a fine view of

The Valley of the Sun

Weavers Needle, a fantastically eroded butte. From Phoenix take U.S. 60 east through Gold Canyon, then turn east on Peralta Road and drive about 8 miles to the trailhead for the Peralta and the **Dutchman's Trail,** on which you can take an 18-mile journey through the wilderness area. Expect to pay a user fee ($6 per vehicle) in the Tonto. For more on hiking in the Superstitions, check out the Tonto National Forest's online **trail guide** (www. fs.fed.us/r3/tonto).

Lost Dutchman State Park

A stop at small **Lost Dutchman State Park** (6109 N. Apache Trail, 480/982-4485, http:// azstateparks.com, sunrise-10pm daily, $7 per vehicle) at the base of the Superstitions is a good way for families and day hikers to see the range and to spend some time walking around the desert on relatively easy trails. The park has 70 campsites ($15-20 no hookups, $25-35 with electric) with showers, as well as tables and grills perfect for picnics. The **Treasure Loop Trail** is an easy way to see the park and get an idea of what the desert is like at about 2,000 feet. It's 2.4 miles round-trip, moderate, and well marked, starting and beginning at either picnic area. Using the **Siphon Draw Trail,** you can climb up to about 5,000 feet, first to a high overlook spot called the Flatiron and then on to the top of Superstition Peak, a hard 5-mile round-trip hike that rewards the tough with some striking desert views.

Superstition Mountain Museum

The small **Superstition Mountain Museum** (4087 N. Apache Trail, 480/983-4888, www.superstitionmountainmuseum.org, 9am-4pm daily, $5), at the beginning of the Apache Trail just outside of Apache Junction, makes for an interesting stop if you have an extra half hour to an hour. The displays on local mining legends, especially the infamous whopper about the **Lost Dutchman Mine** (which people still hunt for today, believing that 1890s prospector and "Dutchman" Jacob Waltz died before

revealing the route to the world's richest gold mine somewhere deep in the Superstitions), and other Old West history lessons will enhance and contextualize the backcountry drive you're about to take.

Goldfield

Heading out of Apache Junction, the Apache Trail passes the Old West-show tourist trap **Goldfield** (4650 N. Mammoth Mine Rd., 480/983-0333, www.goldfieldghosttown.com, 10am-5pm daily, $4-10), a rebuilt 1890s town on the site of what used to be a mining camp with about 5,000 people, settled after gold was discovered in the Superstitions and depopulated soon after the mining stopped. It's a kind of mining-camp theme park now, with a working narrow-gauge railroad, theme shops along a boardwalk main street, a couple of cowboy-style restaurants, a saloon, a mine tour, gold panning, staged gunfights, and Jeep tours into the Superstitions. Kids will likely enjoy this attraction; everybody else should move on down the trail.

THE APACHE TRAIL AND VICINITY

A tour of the Apache Trail (Rte. 88) and the Old West Highway (U.S. 60), a 120-mile round-trip loop along the wild edges of the sprawl-choked valley, begins just outside Apache Junction and eventually winds around the Superstition Mountains to Roosevelt Dam and then on through the Pinal Mountains and a few old mining towns.

The route follows in places the course of the Salt River, the damming of which first made all that sprawl possible but also created several desert lakes, each improbably beautiful and surrounded by an arid army of saguaros peering down from jagged-rock cliffs into the miragelike waters, wondering what all the fuss is about. The Apache Trail itself came about as a result of the dam, built as it was to cart materials and workers to and from the great construction site, though the route had been regularly traversed by native inhabitants long before the reclamation project began.

The best place to eat and get gas is at Globe, at the trail's end. However, if you find yourself in a bind, there's a good, fun restaurant at Tortilla Flat, plus restaurants and gas at each of the marinas along the route. Make sure you bring water with you, and check your tires and fluids before you go.

Apache Junction, a sprawling suburb east of Phoenix at the base of the Superstition Mountains, marks the beginning of the Apache Trail from the west, and it ends at Tonto National Monument, 49 miles from Apache Junction and just outside of Globe. To reach Apache Junction from downtown Phoenix, go 40 miles east on U.S. 60, a drive of about an hour. The Apache Trail, which is well marked, is Route 88, which is right off of U.S. 60.

At the time of writing, portions of the Apache Trail were closed from the 2019 Woodbury Fire and subsequent flooding; keep potential road closures in mind as you approach Tortilla Flat, Apache Lake, and Roosevelt Dam and Lake. Consult the **Arizona Department of Transportation** website (https://azdot.gov; search for Apache Trail or Route 88) for the latest updates. To reach destinations on the Apache Trail from Tortilla Flat to Tonto National Monument, you might have to drive the loop counterclockwise from U.S. 60 near Globe, rather than clockwise from Apache Junction.

Needle Vista to Tortilla Flat

The wild portion of the Apache Trail really gets started about 8 miles outside of Apache Junction at **Needle Vista,** which provides a sweeping view of the rough country and a good look at Weavers Needle, a distinctive rock formation. There are bathrooms here. Continuing east on the paved road, you next come to **Canyon Lake,** about 12 miles from Apache Junction. The smallest of the Salt River Project lakes, and the first you come to along the trail from Phoenix, Canyon Lake has 950 surface acres and 28 miles of shoreline. The headquarters here is the

Canyon Lake Marina and Campground (16802 NE Hwy. 88, 480/288-9233, www. canyonlakemarina.com), which has a restaurant and campground with sites for tents and RVs with hookups, tables, grills, fire rings, and showers ($35 for waterfront campsite, two tents per site, six people, one vehicle; $60 for pull-through RV site with hookups; $20 each for additional vehicles). You're allowed to ride personal watercraft and water-ski on Canyon Lake, and there's even an excursion steamboat and dinner cruise.

About five more miles east and you're at the old **Superstition Restaurant and Saloon** (20909 E. Apache Trail, 480/984-1776, 11am-9pm Mon.-Fri., 9am-5pm Sat.-Sun. June-Sept., 9am-6pm daily Oct.-May, $8-20) at **Tortilla Flat** (http://tortillafl ataz.com), which was once a stage stop and is now a . . . well, a stage stop—only now its burgers, homemade chili, Mexican food, beers, and saddle-topped bar stools are popular with Harley riders, who haunt the trail in large numbers on the weekends. This strange, charming little place, restored from the original but still romantically rustic, is named after a butte nearby that looks a bit like stacked tortillas.

Apache Lake

Continuing on the trail another five miles east, a saguaro and scrub forest spreads out on either side, boulders strewn about and rising from the earth, the Superstitions looming like the petrified rock remains of giant jagged teeth; then the route descends precipitously just before it turns to dirt and washboards near spectacular Fish Creek Canyon, where you'll probably want to stop and take a few photos. Then it's on to the next of the desert lakes, Apache Lake, where the **Apache Lake Marina and Resort** (Rte. 88, 928/467-2511, www.apachelake.com) rents clean and basic lakeside rooms at the **Apache Lake Motel** ($90-105), including suites with kitchenettes. The 17-mile-long lake is popular with Phoenicians who enjoy waterskiing, riding personal watercraft, and fishing for small- and largemouth bass.

Roosevelt Dam and Roosevelt Lake

After Apache Lake, the dirt trail follows a narrow band of river below the dam. Then it climbs up a bit, and that sheer rock wall holding back the river comes into sight, about five miles from the last lake. You can stop here, read some plaques about the dam, and look at it from a promontory. Then the road passes the large **Roosevelt Dam Bridge** and the highway heading north to Payson and the Rim Country. The largest of the Salt River Lakes with a peak fill of 22,000 surface acres, Roosevelt Lake can be accessed through the **Roosevelt Lake Marina** (28085 N. Hwy. 188, 602/977-7170, www.rlmaz.com, $6 day use, $4 boat fee, campsites $10/night first-come, first-served). There are four motels near the lake and an RV park. You can rent a boat here, skid around on personal watercraft, or explore hidden coves and fishing spots.

Tonto National Monument

Pass Roosevelt Lake and turn at the sign to get to **Tonto National Monument** (8am-5pm daily, 928/467-2241, www.nps.gov, $5), a picturesque cliffside ruin once inhabited by the Salado people from about 1150 to 1450. It's so well preserved it appears—from far away, at least—as if people could still live here in the cool shade of a natural rock alcove high above the saguaro and cholla. The paved **Lower Ruin** trail is about a mile round-trip, most of it straight up, and open to the public. The visitors center below the ruin has some interesting artifacts of the Salado and a good bit of information on this often-overlooked tribe. Tonto is about 49 miles from Apache Junction and marks the end of the Apache Trail from the west and its beginning from the east.

Globe and Superior

Follow Route 88 through several old Central Arizona mining towns and then head back west on a scenic stretch of U.S. 60 called the Old West Highway. Both Globe and Superior, in the shadow of the rocky Pinal Mountains, have quaint old downtowns that have yet to

be discovered by hippies, artists, shop owners, and shoppers—sort of like Bisbee before the craft boom. They are mostly boarded up now but seem ripe for discovery, especially Superior, which has a few really cool but disused buildings (long ago fancy hotels and shops) that could be expensively hipped up for the ever-growing retro-loving crowd.

In Globe, the kids will have fun climbing around the largely rebuilt Hohokam and Salado ruins at **Besh-Ba-Gowah Archaeological Park** (1324 Jess Hayes Rd., 928/425-0320, www.globeaz.com, 9am-4:30pm daily, $5 adults, children under 12 free). Unlike most ruins in Arizona, these modest reconstructed pit houses and courtyards are open for scrambling and exploring, and there's a small but interesting museum with exhibits on the lifestyles of those long-lost tribes.

If you're feeling hungry, try **Guayo's on the Trail** (14249 S. Hwy. 188, Globe, 928/425-9969, www.guayosrestaurants.com, 10:30am-9pm Mon. and Wed.-Sat., 10:30am-8:30pm Sun., $6.50-15), which serves up outstanding traditional Mexican food based on old family recipes. This casual place has been around since 1938, and it's very popular with Apache Trail travelers, especially the motorcycle crowd.

Salt River Canyon

Take a detour north on Route 77 (which doubles as U.S. 60 for this stretch) from Globe along the edge of the Apache Mountains for about 40 miles to spectacular **Salt River Canyon,** one of the more impressive roadside natural wonders in a state chock-full of them. Once used as a hideout by the Apache during the Indian wars, this 2,000-foot-deep jagged desert gorge is where the Salt River runs free and wild. There's a parking area before the bridge where you can learn about the canyon and take pictures, and easy paved trails lead down to the flowing river. If you've got a four-wheel-drive vehicle, you can head off on a riverside Jeep trail and explore the canyon in more depth. The traffic along Route 77 near the canyon bridge can get heavy and frustrating, especially on the weekends.

Boyce Thompson Arboretum State Park

A stroll around the unique **Boyce Thompson Arboretum** (37615 U.S. Hwy. 60, 520/689-2811, http://ag.arizona.edu/bta, 6am-3pm daily May-Sept., 8am-5pm daily Oct.-Apr., $15 adults, $5 kids 5-12) is the perfect capstone to an Apache Trail tour. Just three miles west of Superior along U.S. 60, the arboretum was developed in the early 20th century by wealthy do-gooder and mining magnate Colonel William Boyce Thompson. He built his own dreamland here, a kind of desert-country Hearst Castle, and endeavored to grow several different ecosystems on his property. Here you can walk on well-trodden and easy paths leading through otherworldly cactus gardens, across a cottonwood-covered stream, along the shores of a desert lake, and even through an Australian eucalyptus forest, all surrounded by the huge, telltale boulder-mountains of the Central Arizona outback. This is not recommended in summer.

West to Phoenix

Phoenix sits about 60 miles west of the arboretum via U.S. 60, a scenic stretch that skirts the edge of the Superstition Mountains and passes through Florence Junction and Gold Canyon. There's not much to look at along the route back to Phoenix save for awesome desert scenery. U.S. 60 becomes the Superstition Freeway once you're back in the city.

FROM PHOENIX TO TUCSON

The small towns southeast of the metro area are a snapshot of rural America in a state of flux, adapting to the city's spread and trying to hold on to some kind of identity as commuters move in and take over. The southeast, known to most Arizonans as the area you have to drive through to get from Phoenix to Tucson, was once dedicated to agriculture, though these days many of those fields are

covered not with cotton but with stuccoed homes and RV parks. The area is prone to blowing dust storms, especially during the summer rainy season.

★ Casa Grande Ruins National Monument

An ancient and fragile molded-mud apartment building just outside of the old farming town of Coolidge, **Casa Grande Ruins National Monument** (1100 W. Ruins Dr., 520/723-3172, www.nps.gov/cagr, 9am-5pm daily, $5 adults, children under 15 free) is all that remains of one of the largest prehistoric structures ever built in North America. It's an easy 10- to 15-minute detour off I-10 (Exit 211 halfway between Phoenix and Tucson—watch for signs).

There are still a lot of unanswered questions about how and why Casa Grande grew to dominate the Salt River Valley and beyond at its peak in about 1350, and even more questions about what caused its catastrophic decline around 1450. It's an amazing sight nonetheless—almost like a huge, human-sized sandcastle covered by a towering metal roof to keep out the elements. The monument's excellent museum interprets and explains what we do know about the Hohokam, those ancient arid-land agriculturists who inspired the valley's modern-day settlers to attempt to turn the desert into an Eden.

Picacho Peak State Park

Small **Picacho Peak State Park** (just off I-10, Exit 219, 520/466-3183, http://azstateparks.com, 5am-10pm daily, $7 per car, camping $25-30, trails close at sunset), about 40 miles north of Tucson and 60 miles south of Phoenix, sits in the shadow of a dramatic 1,500-foot rock upcropping in the middle of an otherwise mostly flat desert plain. **Picacho Peak** has always been a natural landmark in this part of the state, and nearby, in 1862, soldiers fought Arizona's only Civil War battle, an event reenacted at the park every year. There are several good trails that lead up and along the rough spine of the peak; the area

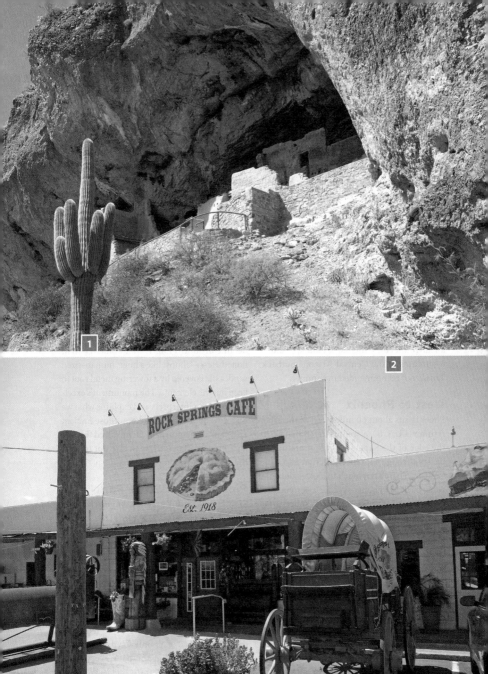

is particularly popular in spring, when the *bajada* stretching out from the cliffsides is often carpeted with multicolored wildflowers. Try the four-mile round-trip **Hunter Trail,** a rather difficult and steep route to the top that begins on the north side and requires negotiation of steel cables anchored into the rock in some places. The three-mile round-trip **Sunset Vista Trail** is a bit easier but longer, starting on the south side and heading to the top. Either way, the views from the top are amazing and well worth the climb.

WICKENBURG

This old mining town northwest of the valley on U.S. 60 still has a bit of Old West charm and makes for a fun day trip from Phoenix or a couple of hours' detour during a drive north. If you're headed to Prescott from Phoenix, consider taking the back way along U.S. 60 through Wickenburg, then on to Route 89 north, cruising along a twisting rural two-lane through a sleepy but scenic mining and ranching region that most visitors miss.

Sights

Fans of Western art will want to spend an hour or so at the **Desert Caballeros Western Museum** (1 N. Frontier St., 928/684-2272, www.westernmuseum.org. 10am-5pm Mon.-Sat., noon-4pm Sun., closed Mon. June-Aug., $12), a very decent regional art museum that has some unique exhibits on life in the Old West.

Hikers and birders shouldn't miss the beautiful riparian area at the 770-acre **Hassayampa River Preserve** (49614 U.S. 60, www.nature.org, 7am-11am Fri.-Sun. in summer, 8am-5pm Wed.-Sun. in winter, $5) just outside of Wickenburg. The preserve is run by the Nature Conservancy, and you can walk along a creek beneath cottonwoods and willows and watch for all manner of water-loving birds darting among the bushes.

1: Tonto National Monument 2: historic Rock Springs Café

Food

A good place to stop for lunch in Wickenburg is **Anita's Cocina** (57 N. Valentine Dr., 928/684-5777, http://anitascocina.com, 8am-9pm Mon.-Fri., 7am-9pm Sat.-Sun., $8-16), a popular place with locals where they serve delicious and inexpensive Mexican favorites in a casual atmosphere.

NORTH ON I-17

If you've got a little time to spare during a drive north to Prescott, Sedona, or Flagstaff along I-17, stop by ★ **Rock Springs Café** (35769 S. Old Black Canyon Hwy., I-17 Exit 242, 623/374-5794, www.rockspringscafe. com, 7am-9pm Sun.-Thurs., 7am-10pm Fri.-Sat., $10-21), an old cowboy-style saloon, historic general store, soda fountain, and café that serves locally famous hamburgers, steaks, barbecue, and homemade pies that you'll want to send home in a refrigerated crate. The whole place has a kind of dark, wood-and-stone air of historic authenticity, and it's been the site of one dusty travelers' wayside or another since the late 19th century. Once a month from October to June, Rock Springs Café puts on a **Hogs 'n' Heat Barbecue,** featuring delicious barbecue ($12 all you can eat), live country music, and plenty of draft beer. Check the website for exact dates.

A bit farther north on I-17, the **Agua Fria National Monument** (623/580-5500, www. blm.gov, free) offers a relatively easy hike through a lush riparian area, which includes access to a petroglyph site. The trailhead is about 40 miles north of downtown Phoenix via I-17. Get off the interstate at Exit 256, Badger Springs, and follow the dirt road for about a mile east to the parking area at the trailhead. The trail runs through Badger Springs Wash, which you may find to be filled with a bit of water outside of deep summer and follows the wash for about two miles one-way.

As the ever-reaching imprint of the valley's insatiable growth begins to disappear and the midland desert scrublands open up wide, veer off at the Cordes Junction exit (Exit

262) and follow the signs to take a tour of the fascinating "urban laboratory" being built by the followers of the late artist Paolo Soleri at **Arcosanti** (928/632-7135, www.arcosanti.org, 9am-5pm daily, tours $15-30). The sweeping high desert locale adds to its evocative otherworldliness. The one-hour and two-hour tours take you through the settlement, as a guide explains the history and philosophy of the project. There's a small café and a gift shop where you can buy one of the world-famous handmade bells that support this ongoing experiment in "arcology"—an architectural theory that seeks to lessen our imprint on the earth by bringing together architecture and ecology.

Tucson and Southern Arizona

The Sonoran Desert's soft greens and yellows
can appear monotonous. But look closely and you'll find staggering
variety. So it is with the culture in Tucson and Southern Arizona.

If there's a melting pot in the United States, it bubbles here. While
traveling the region, it's difficult to escape constant reminders that
not too long ago this land was considered not the southern end of the
United States but rather the northern end of Mexico. The Anglo and
Hispanic settlers have since come to terms with each other, for the most
part, and their mixing has created a unique culture that can only be
described as Southwestern. While this true Southwestern experience
can be explored in a few other places, nowhere is it more authentic and
dynamic than in Southern Arizona. Proof of this in the region's food,

Highlights

Look for ★ to find recommended sights, activities, dining, and lodging.

★ **Arizona-Sonora Desert Museum:** See the region's animals—mountain lions, wolves, bighorn sheep, and other rare Sonoran natives—up close (page 123).

★ **Saguaro National Park East:** Drive, walk, or ride a bike through the Sonoran Desert's unique saguaro forests (page 127).

★ **Santa Catalina Mountains:** Drive to the top of a sky island peak and cool off in the high green forests (page 130).

★ **San Xavier del Bac:** See Arizona's answer to the Sistine Chapel, a white jewel of a mission on the desert (page 133).

★ **Kartchner Caverns:** Enter an otherworldly cave still being formed by slowly dripping water (page 182).

★ **Bisbee:** Explore an old mining boomtown, now an enclave for artists and antiques shops (page 184).

★ **Chiricahua National Monument:** Marvel at the "Land of Standing Up Rocks," a forest of hoodoos high in the evergreen mountains (page 188).

art, music, and writing, all of which thrive on the arid climate and cultural complexity.

The landscape is dominated by desert, stretching out like a vast forgotten sea. It rains here only rarely, yet in spring the land bursts with otherwise dormant wildflowers, like a one-night-only command performance, and during the summer monsoon season this so-called arid region is positively lush. Increase your elevation into one of the region's sky islands, and you will be hunting for tropical birds in a misty creekbed, or, if you go high enough, clamping on a pair of skis. Take a short drive south and you'll experience the dynamic border region with all its bustling and color. Go east and you'll find the remains of the Old West at its most iconic. Look a little closer and you'll find the new as well, in the artists and artisans who find Southern Arizona's quaint towns like Tubac and Bisbee so inviting. This is a fascinating, exotic region, and one in which you might find yourself happily lost.

PLANNING YOUR TIME

You can do Tucson and Southern Arizona in one busy week; to sample some of the sky island trails and hideaways, take two weeks. The best times to visit are March-May and September-November. The weather is very hot in the desert in summer but perfect in the mountains, and in July and August count on near-daily late-afternoon thunderstorms. Though hot and humid during the day, the months of the monsoon are a wonderful time to be alive in the Sonoran Desert. It's best to use Tucson as a base and explore the outlying areas by car unless you have more than a week or two to explore. All of the major sights in this region are within a few hours of the city.

Tucson's charms deserve at least three days of concentration. Spend a full day visiting the West Side's Saguaro National Park, Tucson Mountain Park, the Arizona-Sonora Desert Museum, and San Xavier del Bac, and

another day hanging around downtown and 4th Avenue, sampling the desert's urban side. Then head up the Sky Island Highway to Mount Lemmon to see a completely different view of Southern Arizona from the forested mountain heights. You can visit the Santa Cruz Valley and the Border Region, and even take a stroll into Mexico at Nogales, in a long day trip from Tucson. You can also drop by Bisbee, Tombstone, the Amerind Foundation, and even Chiricahua National Monument in a long, rather exhausting day. However, these and the other fascinating sites along the Cochise Trail, especially the wondrous Kartchner Caverns, are best explored slowly and carefully, and Bisbee, which is relatively close to all the sites, is a romantic and memorable place to spend a night or two.

ORIENTATION

The Tucson metropolitan area encompasses several small towns as well as the city of Tucson. In this section of the guide, sights, accommodations, and restaurants are listed according to their proximity to downtown.

Tucsonans have tried to hold on to a semblance of the small, funky city character that once dominated the Old Pueblo, and there are still no real freeways in the city as a result. I-10 provides the only quick thruway, and I-19 is the primary route south to the Santa Cruz Valley. Most of the time, plan to slog along busy surface streets. Traffic is moved along with some speed, however, thanks to the left arrow lights at most major intersections.

The main commercial corridors run west to east—22nd Street, Broadway Boulevard, Speedway Boulevard, and Grant Road. Dozens of hotels, motels, and restaurants can be found along any of these main roads in the city's midtown section, bordered roughly on the east by Wilmot Road and on the west by I-10. South Tucson is a separate incorporated city, a mile square, south of downtown Tucson.

Previous: Saguaro National Park; San Xavier del Bac; Santa Catalina Mountains.

Tucson and Southern Arizona

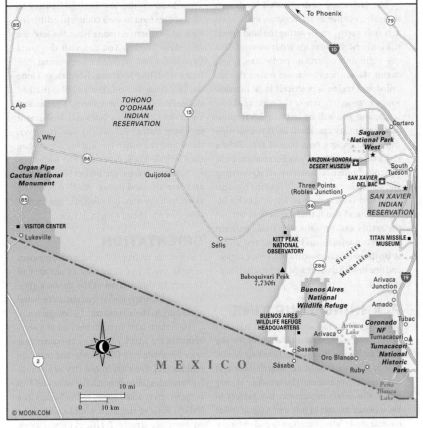

North of the city, on Oracle Road/Route 77, the small towns of Oro Valley, Catalina, and Oracle nestle in the back foothills of the Santa Catalina Mountains. To the southeast is the old mining and ranching district of Vail and the Rincon Valley, now peppered with suburban housing developments, and beyond that the communities along the Cochise Trail. South on I-19 are the big open-pit copper mines, the bedroom community of Sahuarita, the retirement haven of Green Valley, the artist colony and shops of Tubac, and then on to the U.S.-Mexico border.

Tucson itself is surrounded by mountains, with the mighty Santa Catalinas to the north, the Rincon Mountains to the east, and the Tucson Mountains to the west. Far south in the Santa Cruz Valley along I-19 are the Santa Rita Mountains. If you remember that the Santa Catalinas, the most imposing range around the valley, are generally to the north, Tucson isn't too difficult to navigate.

Sights

DOWNTOWN AND CENTRAL

Downtown Tucson is where the city first rose from the desert. The general area can be expanded to include 4th Avenue and the historic neighborhoods of El Presidio, Armory Park, and Barrio Historico, as well as those around the University of Arizona. The Sun Link Streetcar serves all of these areas, and most of them are pedestrian friendly—something rare in a Southwestern cityscape. The streetcar also goes to the westside Mercado San Agustin and MSA Annex, which are both part of the greater downtown area.

Tucson Museum of Art and Historic Block

The permanent collection at the **Tucson Museum of Art** (140 N. Main Ave., 520/624-2333, www.tucsonmuseumofart. org, 10am-5pm Tues.-Sat., noon-5pm Sun., $12 adults, $10 seniors, $7 students) features

Tucson

© MOON.COM

TOHONO O'ODHAM INDIAN RESERVATION
SAN XAVIER DISTRICT

El Presidio Historic District

El Presidio Historic District is where Tucson began as a place of human habitation, a mixture of adobe row houses and Victorian mansions that is several chapters in the city's history writ in architecture. The district is bounded roughly by Granada on the west, 6th Street on the north, Church Street on the east, and Alameda Street on the south.

Though turned back to desert now, the royal Presidio de San Agustín del Tucson once stood here, the farthest north the Spanish crown dared to go. The presidio, or fort, had 12-foot-high adobe walls and covered 11 acres, housing a small contingent of soldiers and their families, a population that spent a good deal of its time fearing and fighting Apaches. Much later, archaeologists discovered that the fort had been built close to a Hohokam site that flourished from about AD 700-900, proving humans had made their lives on the banks of the Santa Cruz River for as long as nearly anywhere else in the country. A self-guided tour pamphlet of this district and other downtown-area historic sites is available at the Tucson Visitor Center at 811 N. Euclid Ave., near the University of Arizona's Main Gate.

When the Americans took over in 1856, the fort was dismantled and its walls used to build homes and businesses for new arrivals. As more Anglos settled in, the district became a mixture of adobe row houses and eastern-style mansions for early-20th-century Tucson's rich and powerful. Many of these old mansions and adobes have been restored and now serve as offices and private residences.

TUCSON
SIGHTS

the mysterious artifacts of the Americas prior to Columbus's arrival, the art of the American West, and contemporary art, often with a Latin and Southwestern flavor. This is a good place to introduce yourself to that tricultural mixing that makes Southern Arizona unique. The museum puts on several special exhibitions every year; recent years have seen a Warhol retrospective and the largest showing of the Arizona paintings of Maynard Dixon anywhere. Five historic homes built in the last half of the 19th century survive next to the museum. Just beyond the museum's wide Main Avenue entrance is the oldest of the Historic Block's buildings (and probably the oldest building in Tucson), La Casa Cordova, its two west rooms built several years before the Gadsden Purchase made Tucson part of the United States in 1854. The home is a perfect example of the style of Mexican townhouse that once lined the city's core, with its central courtyard and entrance right on the street. A shady courtyard behind the museum's main building, The Plaza of Pioneers, has a wall honoring Tucson pioneers from the Spanish, Mexican, and Anglo periods.

Arizona Historical Society Museum Downtown

Until shopping malls began to proliferate in midtown starting in the 1960s, downtown Tucson was the commercial and social heart of the city, a fact that the **Arizona Historical Society Downtown History Museum** (Wells Fargo Building, 140 N. Stone Ave., 520/770-1473, www.arizonahistoricalsociety. org, 11am-3pm Wed.-Fri., free or donation) celebrates. These days Tucson's downtown has returned to something like it was—a bustling, mixed-use area with locally owned boutiques, hotels, restaurants, and theaters lining the narrow streets, the sidewalks crowded with people working, shopping, living, and playing all within the same few blocks.

This small museum, tucked away in the Wells Fargo building on Stone Avenue, shows artifacts from the early days of downtown through to its desertion, with large, rare photographs and ephemera from different eras of the city's history. An especially interesting installation tells the history of the Dillinger gang's capture in Tucson in the 1930s. You'll find free validated parking in the Wells Fargo garage on Alameda Street.

El Presidio Park and Pima County Courthouse

The sea-green tiled dome of the **Pima County Courthouse** (115 N. Church St., 8:30am-noon and 1pm-5pm Mon.-Fri.), built in the late 1920s, is a landmark of the Old Pueblo's modest skyline, and it's worth a walk around the grounds of the city's government bee-hive to take in the Spanish Colonial Revival touches and, on weekdays, to see downtown at its most industrious. Walk across the front courtyard through a few arches and you'll be in **El Presidio Park,** with its foun-tains, conquistador statue, and memorial to the Mormon Battalion, which occupied the presidio briefly in late 1846. There are also memorials and statues in this large urban gov-ernment center park honoring WWII veter-ans, John F. Kennedy, and various pioneers of the Old West. There's usually a hot-dog cart on the plaza, and the area offers plenty of op-portunities for people-watching and shade.

Presidio San Agustín del Tucson

Experts on the history, lifeways, and architec-ture of the early Spanish settlers have recreated a portion of the old **Presidio San Agustín del Tucson** (at the downtown corner of Washington and Church Sts., 520/884-4214, www.tucsonpresidio.com, 10am-3pm Thurs.-Sun. May-Sept., 10am-4pm Wed.-Sun. Oct.-Apr., $5, children 6-14 $1). Within the adobe walls there's a large mural depicting daily life in and around the fort. There are a few dark, cool adobe rooms set up in period style to show visitors what life was like on the far, lonely northern edge of the Spanish Empire in 1775, when an Irishman working for the Spanish rode north from Tubac to establish the fort. During the week parking is available in a nearby parking garage on Alameda Street; metered parking is available on nearby streets.

Barrio Historico

The photogenic Sonoran-style row houses in the **Barrio Historico** (bordered by Stone Ave., I-10, Cushing St., and 18th St.) on the southwest edge of downtown are well adapted to the desert environment. Their front en-trances hug the property line (unlike their Anglo counterparts, with large front and back yards) to make space for central court-yards hidden from the street, which provide a shaded outdoor living space within the home. Many of the adobes here have been lovingly and colorfully restored and now serve as of-fices, working galleries, and private resi-dences. Sometimes called Barrio Viejo (the Old Neighborhood), the barrio has been on the National Register of Historic Places since the 1970s. It dates from the mid-1850s and, as its dominant architecture suggests, has tradi-tionally been a Mexican enclave. Once, several neighborhoods sprawled out here to create a large quarter referred to as Barrio Libre (Free Neighborhood), due either to the anything-goes atmosphere in some corners or because the Mexican population was mostly left alone to follow its own rules and culture. Much of the quarter was razed in the late 1960s to make way for the "urban renewal" program that built the Tucson Convention Center. The best examples of the adobe row houses can be found along Myer, Main, and Cushing. Along Myer look for the old Teatro Carmen, a Spanish-language theater that opened in 1915. The adobe building, which over the years served as a movie house, a boxing arena, and an Elks Lodge, still retains the charm and his-toric interest that once pervaded this district.

El Tiradito Shrine

Roadside shrines are common in Southern Arizona even in the most out-of-the-way places, but only one is dedicated to a folk saint who was, by the church's standards, an unre-deemed sinner. **El Tiradito** (The Castaway, 221 S. Main Ave.) dates to the 1870s, when Juan Oliveras, a young shepherd, fell in love with his mother-in-law, and the two gave in to an illicit passion. They were discovered by her ax-wielding husband, who killed Oliveras and tossed his dead body away on the land that now holds the shrine (such is the tradi-tion, anyway). The church wouldn't allow the doomed lover to be buried on consecrated land, so the people of the barrio interred him where he was "cast away" and erected a shrine. Some say that if you make a wish at the shrine by night, leave a lit candle, and find it still burning in the morning, your wish will come true—this is why El Tiradito is sometimes called the "Wishing Shrine."

St. Augustine Cathedral

Facing Stone Avenue on the eastern edge of the Barrio Historico, **St. Augustine Cathedral** (192 S. Stone Ave., 520/623-6351, http://cathedral-staugustine.org, mass at 7am and noon Mon.-Fri., church open all day Sat.-Sun.), dedicated to Tucson's patron saint, was built in 1896 and remodeled several times over the years. The facade has stone-carved yucca, saguaro, and horned toad flourishes, and there are statues of the Virgin Mary and the titular saint near the big, heavy-wood entrance. Catholics or anyone interested in regional variations on the mass should attend the lively mariachi mass, held at 8am every Sunday. Inside, one of the bells formerly used in the original Spanish-era cathedral is preserved in the vestibule.

Tucson Children's Museum

Housed downtown in Tucson's original Carnegie Library, the **Tucson Children's Museum** (200 S. 6th Ave., 520/792-9985, www.childrensmuseumtucson.org, 9am-5pm Tues.-Fri., 10am-5pm Sat.-Sun., $9 adults and children, free for infants under 1), a nonprofit, interactive learning center, is a local family favorite. Parents will appreciate the creativity and attention to detail. There are 12 permanent exhibits here, all of them hands-on and featuring some kid-mesmerizing subjects like dinosaurs, electricity, ocean life, and trains. There's also a beautiful garden that was planted by Tucson's most famous chef, Janos Wilder. It's not always easy to find parking because the museum has no lot of its own; there are metered spaces around the museum, and $1 will get you an hour.

Southern Arizona Transportation Museum

When the railroad reached the isolated town of Tucson in the 1880s, it transformed the city and the region. The small **Southern Arizona Transportation Museum** (414 N. Tooele Ave., 520/623-2223, www.tucsonhistoricdepot.org, 11am-3pm Tues.-Thurs. and Sun., 10am-4pm Fri.-Sat., free) at the refurbished 1940s rail depot downtown explains all the myriad ways the railroad, and later the car and the interstate system, changed Tucson and the Southwest, opening it up to visitors and settlers and linking it more with the United States than with Mexico, as it had been before the train's arrival. There's a lifelike statue of Wyatt Earp and Doc Holliday nearby and a plaque that tells the story of a bit of revenge and/or murder that went down right here back in the old violent days of the territory.

The Diamondback Bridge

Artist Simon Donovan designed this work of public art (spanning Broadway near Euclid) in 2002 to be a kind of memorable entrance to a downtown that has been undergoing a slow revitalization for at least the past 20 years. **The Diamondback Bridge,** spanning Broadway Boulevard just as the busy street dips into the central city, has since become a popular local landmark. In 2003 it won the prestigious American Public Works Project of the Year award. The bridge, which looks like a monster-size rattlesnake taking it easy, albeit with its jaw perpetually stretched open, is 300 feet long and cost about $2.7 million to build. There's a small, pleasant park on either end of the snake. The easiest way to see it is to pull over at Euclid and Broadway, park, and walk across. Just after the snake bridge, as you enter downtown, you'll see huge black-and-white photographs on both sides of the underpass. These are photographs from the 1940s and 1950s of Tucsonans walking, shopping, and generally bustling about downtown.

Sunshine Mile

Pass under the Diamondback Bridge heading east and you're at the start of the **Sunshine Mile** along Broadway Boulevard between Euclid and Country Club (https:// sunshinemile.com). Starting with a soaring 1964 Googie diner, now an excellent farm-to-table restaurant, the Sunshine Mile features a host of well-preserved **Mid-Century Modernist architecture.** Built up during the post-war boom years along the city's main east-west corridor, this stretch of modernist style is for anyone interested in 20th century car-culture and the clean lines and optimistic, space-age details of classic American architecture. Most of the eye-catching storefronts still host locally owned business. Particularly interesting examples include the Kelly Building at 2343 E. Broadway, Chase Bank at 3033 E. Broadway, and Broadway Village, a charming shopping plaza just opposite the bank. A delightful example of the regional amalgam called Sonoran Modern, Broadway Village was designed by Tucson's favorite architect, Josias Joesler.

4th Avenue District

Lined with chic thrift stores, exotic clothing boutiques, smoke shops, restaurants, and cocktail lounges, **4th Avenue** is an ideal place to people-watch, and there are some really good places to eat and treasures to be found in the quirky shops. Twice a year, in fall and spring, the area closes to vehicle traffic for a street fair featuring artisan booths, concerts, and greasy food galore. Located between downtown and the University District, 4th Avenue is just a short walk from campus, and on Friday and Saturday nights expect hordes of college kids out looking for inebriation. It's best to avoid driving in this area on weekend nights altogether.

Tours

Tucson Bike Tours (215 N. Hoff Ave., 520/488-4446, http://tucsonbiketours.com, 9am, noon, 3pm, 6pm, $50 for 2.5 hours) offers invigorating and informative bike tours around Tucson's historic neighborhoods, including downtown, Barrio Viejo, and 4th Avenue. Your guide leads you on an easy 9- to 11-mile ride over flat and well-paved streets, pointing out interesting and historical details along the way. You'll ride a comfortable Civia neighborhood cruiser with a single gear and hand brakes. It's easy, safe, and a lot of fun. Tours start October 1 and close down in early May.

UNIVERSITY OF ARIZONA (UA)

Since it rose from the desert in 1885 as the first institution of higher learning in the Arizona Territory, the fate of the University of Arizona and that of its host pueblo have been linked. It's difficult to imagine what Tucson would be without the shady central campus. A land-grant school that has educated countless Arizona leaders and citizens, UA has nearly 37,000 students (more populous than most Arizona towns) and is active in the U.S. space program, specifically in Mars exploration. The school is world renowned for its arid-land research, and it has a center for integrative medicine founded by best-selling healer-doctor Andrew Weil. It's also the place where anthropology, archaeology, and many other disciplines were revolutionized through the discovery of tree-ring dating.

The university is becoming known for its contributions to the ongoing exploration of outer space. Check out the displays on the HiRISE Mars Camera, the Phoenix Mars Lander, and Cassini mission to Saturn at the **Sonett Visitor Center** (northwest corner of University Blvd. and Cherry St., 520/626-7432, 9am-5pm Mon.-Fri., free).

On campus you'll find a number of museums and galleries, and the entire campus itself is an arboretum. Indeed, the green central campus claims to be the "oldest continually maintained green space in Arizona." Flora

---

1: Sonoran Desert **2:** giant tiki head on Tucson's 4th Avenue **3:** Old Main, the original building on the University of Arizona campus

enthusiasts can stroll around the campus and take in a cactus garden, a collection of rare tropical trees, and various arid-land species that have been brought to UA from all over the world. If you want to learn more about the campus's natural wonders, go by the **Campus Arboretum** at Herring Hall (520/621-7074, http://arboretum.arizona.edu, 9am-5pm Mon.-Fri., free). Don't miss the **Joseph Wood Krutch Cactus Garden** in the center of the campus's long, grassy mall.

Kids will enjoy the hands-on exhibits, laser shows, and sky-watching at **Flandrau: The UA Science Center** (1601 E. University Blvd., 520/621-4516, www.flandrau.org, 9am-5pm Mon.-Thurs., 9am-10pm Fri., 10am-10pm Sat., noon-5pm Sun., $16 adults, $12 children 4-17); admission includes entry to the science center, mineral museum, and one planetarium show. Downstairs at Flandrau, you'll find the **UA Mineral Museum** (520/621-4516, www.uamineralmuseum.org, 9am-5pm Mon.-Thurs., 9am-10pm Fri., 10am-10pm Sat., noon-5pm Sun., free), which has on display a wondrous collection of rocks from Arizona and beyond.

There are also numerous public art installations on campus. One that should not be missed is the hulking commentary *Border Dynamics,* created by artists Alberto Morackis and Guadalupe Serrano. It's not always easy to find parking on campus, and it's impossible during sporting events. Visitors can pay to park at the Park Avenue Garage at the corner of Park and Helen Street and at the Main Gate Parking Garage at Euclid Avenue and East 2nd Street.

Arizona Historical Society Museum

Just south of the main gate wall along North Campus Drive is the **Arizona Historical Society Museum** (949 E. 2nd St., 520/628-5774, www.arizonahistoricalsociety.org, 9am-4pm Mon.-Thurs., 9am-8pm Fri., 11am-4pm Sat., $10 adults, $5 students 7-13), the largest of the Arizona Historical Society's three Tucson museums. Exhibits include a full-scale reproduction of the cramped canvas-tent home early miners lived in and a walk through a dark underground mine. There's also an old Studebaker on display; this make of car was once so popular with Arizona's sheriffs that the car company sent an author to the young state to write a public relations pamphlet including exciting stories of frontier law enforcement. This is an interesting stop for Arizona history buffs, and there are several hands-on exhibits for the kids.

Arizona State Museum

Established in 1893, the **Arizona State Museum** (1013 E. University Blvd., 520/621-6302, www.statemuseum.arizona.edu, 10am-5pm Mon.-Sat., $5) is the oldest anthropology museum in the Southwest. Here you'll find several rooms of fascinating displays on the state's various Native American tribes and the world's largest collection of Southwest Indian pottery, including many contemporary pieces that prove pottery making is certainly not a lost art. Every year in February the museum's grassy grounds play host to the Southwest Indian Art Fair, one of the more important and well attended of such events in the Southwest. A permanent exhibition inside the stately old building explains the origins and histories of 10 of Arizona's Native American groups, including the Hohokam, the O'odham, and the Apache, each of whom once thrived in Southern Arizona. Park in the garage at either Euclid Avenue and Second Street or North Tyndall Avenue and Fourth Street; both are free on weekends.

University of Arizona Museum of Art

The permanent collection of the **University of Arizona Museum of Art** (UA campus near Park Ave. and Speedway Blvd., 520/621-7567, http://artmuseum.arizona.edu, 9am-5pm Tues.-Fri., noon-4pm Sat.-Sun., $8) houses works by Tintoretto, Piazzetta, Goya, Brueghel, Rodin, Picasso, Hopper, Pollock, Rothko, O'Keeffe, and many more. Asian and Latin American traditions are also well

Howard Hughes in Tucson

Many have heard about those weird few years that Howard Hughes spent hiding out on the top floor of a Las Vegas hotel, going mad.

Well, there are hints that the Old Pueblo could have been the site of Hughes's infamous hideout instead of Vegas. Bob Maheu, Hughes's right-hand man and official public face during the Vegas years, told Geoff Schumacher, author of the 2008 book *Howard Hughes: Power, Paranoia, and Palace Intrigue,* that in the mid-1960s before moving to Vegas Hughes first considered moving to Tucson, where he'd already set up a manufacturing plant in 1951.

Hughes loved the desert, considering it free of the germs that stalked him. There's a great scene in *The Aviator* in which the young Hughes, played by Leonardo DiCaprio, sees a stand of saguaros in a film he's watching and whispers something like, "so clean." Ultimately, though, Hughes soured on the desert around Las Vegas due to his inability to stop nuclear testing at the Nevada Test Site, fallout from which he obsessively feared.

Though he never moved to Tucson, Hughes did have a presence here. Hughes Aircraft built the Falcon, the world's first air-to-air guided missile, and many other missiles and weapons here, employing thousands of workers. Hughes Missile Systems was eventually bought by Raytheon, which is today Southern Arizona's largest private employer.

represented. Special shows often feature the work of well-known local, national, and Mexican artists. The museum has an impressive collection of Spanish medieval art, the signature piece of which is the 26-panel *Retablo of Ciudad Rodrigo,* an altarpiece depicting the sweep of biblical events from Genesis through the life of Jesus Christ to the Last Judgment.

Center for Creative Photography

UA's **Center for Creative Photography** (1030 N. Olive Rd., 520/621-7968, www.creativephotography.org, 9am-4pm Tues.-Fri., 1pm-4pm Sat., free) has one of the largest photography collections in the world; it holds the archives of Ansel Adams, Edward Weston, and other major artists. The center mounts a few exhibitions a year, so it's a good idea to check the website before traveling to see what's on display. You can even make an appointment by phone to personally view a few of the 80,000 prints accessible to the public.

MIDTOWN

Reid Park Zoo

Take Broadway Boulevard east to Randolph Way at Reid Park to Tucson's small but prestigious **Reid Park Zoo** (1100 S. Randolph Way, 520/791-4022, www.tucsonzoo.org, 9am-4pm daily winter, 8am-3pm daily summer, $10.50 adults, $8.50 seniors, $6.50 children 2-14). The zoo specializes in giant anteater breeding and preservation, and there are several of these strange beasts to look at here. The zoo also features elephants, bears, various big cats, and much more.

Make sure to take the kids to the **Giraffe Encounter** (10am-10:45am Mon.-Fri. in winter, 9:30am-10:15am Mon.-Fri. in summer, $3 pp), where you can feed the long-necked residents, who stick out their long, purple tongues, dripping with saliva, to capture the morsel. If you get to the zoo early enough, you might catch a glimpse of the elegant black jaguar lounging in the cool of the morning.

A gift shop sells all kinds of zoo-related stuffed animals, shirts, and books, and a fast-food-style eatery serves hamburgers, corn dogs, and the like. The zoo is small enough that little kids aren't likely to get too tired out. Plan about three hours, less if you don't have kids. Check out the cameras on the zoo's website to get a preview of the some of the animals.

Tucson Botanical Gardens

Gardeners and anybody who appreciates beauty should stop at the **Tucson Botanical Gardens** (2150 N. Alvernon Way, 520/326-9686, www.tucsonbotanical.org, 8:30am-4:30pm daily winter, 7:30am-4:30pm daily summer, $15 adults, $8 children 4-17), a mid-town oasis, for a few hours. Easy walking trails wind around the nearly six-acre property, which feels secluded and hidden away even though it's right in the path of busy midtown. There are benches throughout on which to sit and contemplate the various gardens, each showcasing a different gardening tradition. A cactus and succulent garden has examples of cacti not just from the nearby deserts but also from around the world, and the xeriscape garden demonstrates how you can grow desert-adapted plants without using a lot of water.

If you go between October and March, you'll get to see **Butterfly Magic,** a live tropical butterfly exhibit. Call ahead for times and availability. For the price of admission you can take advantage of one of several tours of the gardens. Different tours are offered throughout the month, and not every tour is offered every day, so it's best to call ahead or check the website. The **Garden Gallery** has rotating art shows that can be viewed 8:30am-4:30pm daily.

Mini Time Machine Museum of Miniatures

Built by passionate collectors, the charming **Mini Time Machine Museum of Miniatures** (4455 E. Camp Lowell Dr., 520/881-0606, www.theminitimemachine.org, 9am-4pm Tues.-Sat., noon-4pm Sun., $10.50 adults, $7 children 4-17) in midtown is a great place to take kids, who generally find all the tiny objects and detailed dioramas endlessly fascinating. They'll also like the Enchanted Tree, with its big face and fairy-tale trunk life. The museum has a permanent collection of nearly 300 miniatures, both contemporary and antique, and presents special exhibits from time to time that explore a particular theme or style in depth and, of course, in miniature.

WEST OF DOWNTOWN

Take Speedway Boulevard west under I-10. The road becomes Gates Pass Road and then runs into Kinney Road. Follow the signs to each of the following sights, some of Tucson's most representative attractions. You can do it in one long day, though the Desert Museum and Saguaro National Park stand up to a full day each. To get to the Desert Museum, take Speedway Boulevard west for about 12 miles through the desert and then turn right onto Kinney Road. The International Wildlife Museum is along the way, and Old Tucson is nearby as well.

Sentinel Peak and Tumamoc Hill

Also called "A" Mountain for the large white letter "A" repainted on its face every year by University of Arizona students (a tradition that began in 1915), **Sentinel Peak** (1000 S. Sentinel Peak Rd., 8am-8pm Mon.-Sat., 8am-6pm Sun.) served the early populations of the Tucson Valley with spring water and black basalt. When Father Kino first rode into the valley in the 1690s, he found the native population living in the small peak's shadow, and it was surely an important landmark in the basin for eons before that. During the presidio days it earned its name as a promontory from which soldiers would scan the desert for Apaches. Now there's a park on the peak, reached by a paved, winding road to the top. Take Congress Street west under I-10 and follow the signs. There are a few short trails around the park, a little rock shelter to sit under, charcoal barbecues, and some great views of the valley. The hill just to the north of Sentinel Peak, called **Tumamoc Hill** (Tumamoc Hill Rd.), is the home to a desert laboratory founded in 1903. For thousands of years indigenous residents of the Tucson Valley farmed on and around Tumamoc Hill, as evidenced by numerous archaeological sites found there. Among the legends of the Tohono

O'odham is the story of a giant horned lizard that threatened to devour the tribe had not the god I'itoi, in response to prayers, turned the great reptile into a hill, hence the name Tumamoc (horned lizard) Hill.

International Wildlife Museum

As you drive west toward Gates Pass and the Tucson Mountains, off on the north side of the road, partly obscured by the thick desert, a large, castlesque building holds the impressive taxidermy collection of the **International Wildlife Museum** (4800 W. Gates Pass Rd., 520/629-0100, www.thewildlifemuseum.org, 9am-5pm Mon.-Fri., 9am-6pm Sat.-Sun., $10 adults, $5 children 4-12), a private, nonprofit natural history museum. There are more than 400 stuffed and preserved mammals, birds, insects, and spiders here, including "Big Terror," a stuffed tiger who still looks a bit hungry. The mighty beast was killed in 1969 in India, after he'd reportedly devoured between 8 and 12 people. This is a fun and educational place to bring kids, but if you have limited time, skip it in favor of the Arizona-Sonora Desert Museum a few miles up the road, where the mountain lions, rattlesnakes, beavers, and scorpions are all indigenous, and alive.

Tucson Mountain Park and Gates Pass Scenic Overlook

Robert Gates was a typical Southwestern frontier entrepreneur: He did a little mining, a little ranching, a bit of saloon keeping, and some homesteading. In 1883, in order to connect his Avra Valley mine with his other interests in Tucson, he set about building a precipitous route over the Tucson Mountains, and in the process set the stage for local officials, about 50 years later, to establish one of the largest public parks of its kind in the nation. Thus we have the 37-square-mile Sonoran Desert preserve called **Tucson Mountain Park** (Speedway west from downtown over Gates Pass to Kinney Rd., 7am-10pm daily, free). The 20,000 acres of wild desert features one of the largest saguaro

forests in the world and has something like 62 miles of trails for hiking and mountain biking. The park has a rifle and pistol range, three large picnic areas with grills, ramadas, and picnic tables, and within its boundaries is the world-renowned Arizona-Sonora Desert Museum. If all these activities seem a bit sweaty and active for your taste, at least make it to the top of the road named for the man who conquered the comparatively short Tucson Mountains at **Gates Pass.** You can drive to the pass and park at a large lot, which offers bathrooms, a ramada, and two little stacked-rock huts decorated inside with eons of graffiti. There are short trails out to a promontory from which you can see the whole sweeping expanse of the desert below. It's one of the best views in Arizona—a state that has no shortage of sweeping views. If you want to stay the night at the park, the **Gilbert Ray Campground** (8451 W. McCain Loop, off Kinney Rd., 520/883-4200, $10-20) has sites with RV hookups, picnic tables, restrooms, and a dumping station.

TOP EXPERIENCE

★ Arizona-Sonora Desert Museum

A big part of the fun of a visit to the **Arizona-Sonora Desert Museum** (2021 N. Kinney Rd., 520/883-2702, www.desertmuseum.org, 7:30am-5pm daily Mar.-Sept., until 10pm Sat. June-Aug., 8:30am-5pm daily Oct.-Feb., $21.95 adults, $8.95 children 3-12) is getting there. Driving west out of Tucson over dramatic Gates Pass, you'll see thousands of saguaros standing tall on the hot, rocky ground below, surrounded by pipe-cleaner-like ocotillo and fuzzy cholla, creosote, and prickly pear.

But the saguaro forests of Tucson Mountain Park and Saguaro National Park West, both of which surround the Desert Museum, are only one of several distinctive desert life zones you'll see and learn about at this world-famous museum and zoo, where native mammals, birds, reptiles, amphibians,

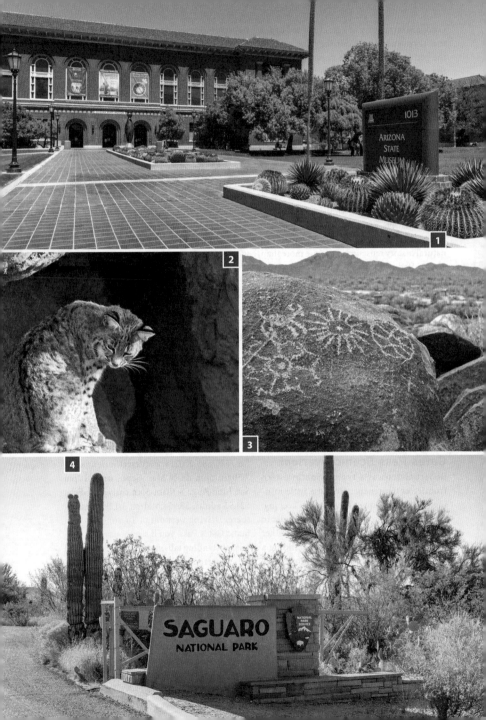

fish, and arthropods live in displays mimicking their open-desert habitats.

This is the best place to learn about both the general structure and the minute details of the surrounding desert, and it is probably your only realistic chance to see all of the unique creatures that call it home.

Easy trails wind through the beautiful 21-acre preserve, passing exhibits of semidesert grasslands and mountain woodlands similar to those surrounding and growing on the Sonoran Desert's high mountain ranges. The Desert Loop Trail leads through a lowland scrub and cacti landscape with javelina and coyote. In Cat Canyon, a bespeckled ocelot sleeps in the shade, and a bobcat lounges on the rocks. A mountain lion can be seen close up through a viewing window, and a black bear strolls along an artificial stream and sleeps on a rock promontory. There are also rare Mexican wolves, white-tailed deer, bighorn sheep, and adorable prairie dogs in their commune.

A riparian habitat has beavers and otters, water lovers that were once abundant in the Southwest. There's a desert garden exhibit, a cactus and succulent garden, and a butterfly and wildflower display. There are also displays on desert fish and dunes, and a walk-in aviary that holds dozens of native birds. Docents are scattered throughout the complex to help with questions and give presentations on special topics. All this, plus a restaurant, snack bars, and a gift shop that sells excellent Pueblo Indian crafts, make the Desert Museum Tucson's very best attraction. If you're planning on doing any exploring in the desert, do so after a trip to the Desert Museum, where you'll get a comprehensive minicourse in desert ecology.

Old Tucson Studios

Since 1939 **Old Tucson** (201 S. Kinney Rd., 520/883-0100, www.oldtucson.com,

1: Arizona State Museum 2: a bobcat at the Arizona-Sonora Desert Museum 3: ancient petroglyphs in Saguaro National Park West 4: Saguaro National Park East entrance

10am-5pm daily Oct.-May, $19.95 adults, $10.95 children 4-11, extras cost more) has been the setting for more than 400 film productions, the majority of them Westerns. It was originally constructed to make the film *Arizona*, starring Jean Arthur and William Holden, which tells the story of Tucson's territorial days.

In the 1950s, impresario Bob Shelton bought the disused property and rebuilt its circa-1860s town, again drawing productions west from Hollywood, several starring Shelton's friend John Wayne. It remained popular as a movie set as long as Westerns were popular at the box office and so went through boom-and-bust periods along with the genre. Shelton added gunfight shows and other family-oriented tourist attractions to ride out the lean times. Today a rebuilt Old Tucson (the town burned to the ground in the 1990s) is again used by filmmakers, and various rides, games, and performances recreate a movie-house version of the Old West for tourists.

Make sure to check out the collection of vintage posters from the films produced at the studio. Tours talk about the history of the studio and the stars who walked its dusty streets, and musical acts and vaudeville-style revues go on all day. There are several restaurants onsite, including **Big Jake's,** which serves up good barbecue and beans. If you're a Western-film buff, you'll find the film-related aspects worth a look. Kids will enjoy the rides and the gunfights, but the entry price is rather expensive for what you get.

TOP EXPERIENCE

Saguaro National Park West

This is where the icon of arid America holds court. The split **Saguaro National Park** (www.nps.gov/sagu, 7am-sunset daily, visitors center 9am-5pm daily, $20 per car, receipt valid for seven days, good at both sections) has a western section at the base of the Tucson Mountains and a larger eastern section at the base of the Rincon Mountains. Both are worth visiting, but if you have time only for one, go to the eastern section, which is older and larger. (Then again, there are a few other sights around the western portion, while the eastern is a bit on its own, save for nearby Colossal Cave.) Together they protect about 91,300 acres of magnificent Sonoran Desert landscape, including large and crowded saguaro forests surrounded by a thick underbrush of ocotillo, prickly pear, cholla, mesquite, and paloverde. If you want to see an accessible and wondrous example of the Sonoran Desert at its best, there are few better places to go.

The saguaro (pronounced sa-WAH-ro) is much more than a strange-looking plant to the native inhabitants of the Sonoran Desert, be they cactus wrens, coyotes, screech owls, or Tohono O'odham people. It is so supremely adapted to the arid environment, in which the rains come but twice a year, that it anchors an entire busy community of living things, providing food and shelter to all sorts of desert creatures.

The great cactus-tree grows slowly, and only during the summer rainy season. After living, shaded and protected by a mesquite tree, for 15 years, a saguaro is still only about a foot tall. But then again, these green, ribbed giants can live to be 150 years old or more, so there's really no hurry. Not until it reaches 75 years old does a saguaro even begin to sprout its identifying arms, so when you see a tall and fat one with many arms—and there are many in both sections of the park—know that it is a venerable old plant.

The place to start your tour of the western park is the **Red Hills Visitor Center** (2700 N. Kinney Rd., 520/733-5158), where you can learn about the ancient symbiotic friendship between the Tohono O'odham and the saguaro. Here you'll find a guide to the park's 40 miles of trails, and you can also book a tour with a naturalist and peruse the bookstore stocked with titles on local history and nature.

A good way to see the park, especially in the heat of summer, is to drive the six-mile **Bajada Loop** through a thick saguaro forest.

The route is graded dirt and can get dusty, but you can also walk or bike the loop. Or you can drive the loop and stop at the **Valley View Overlook Trail,** an easy one-mile round-trip trail off the loop road that rises to an expansive view of the Avra Valley, the saguaro-lined desert, and the skulking rock mountains. A half-mile round-trip walk to the **Signal Hill Picnic Area** offers a look at ancient petroglyphs. Both trails can be accessed off the Bajada Loop drive and are well marked. There are also a few very short, paved walks around the visitors center featuring interpretive signs about the saguaro and other desert fauna.

Ironwood Forest National Monument

A 129,000-acre wild Sonoran Desert preserve about an hour's drive northwest of Tucson, **Ironwood Forest National Monument** (520/258-7200, www.blm.gov, free) is a great place to encounter the desert up close. Its namesake tree will likely appear a bit underwhelming to the uninitiated. The gray-green monotony of the surface-level desert blurs the vision, and one bushy little tree tends to look a lot like another. As it usually is, however, the truth is in the details. The ironwood, which can live as long as 800 years, anchors a deceptively busy desert ecosystem, providing shade and succor for a whole host of flora and fauna unique to the region. Like most of Arizona's BLM-monitored national monuments, Ironwood Forest is a vast and empty place, inviting to hikers, hunters, campers, and other outdoor types. There's no visitors center, campgrounds, or rangers. It is a perfect place for a long daytime drive through the desert on its dirt roads, which are mostly smooth and accepting of regular cars, although coming in an SUV is best. More so than even Saguaro National Park, Ironwood is a place where the wild desert is there for you to discover—unvarnished, uncultivated, and unforgiving. It's not a good idea to venture out here in the summer. If you want to head out to this wilderness, the easiest way to see it is to drive slowly along the dirt roads that traverse part of the monument, stopping here and there to look into the details. The best way to do this is to take I-10 north to Avra Valley Road and then follow the road until it turns to dirt around the waste-pile remainders of the Silverbell Mine. Just follow the road through the monument, passing the mine, the Silverbell Mountains, Ragged Top Mountain, and Wolcott Peak. Take Silverbell Road out of the monument and back to the interstate. The whole trip could take all day if you stop enough to look around. Archaeologists say that people have been living out here for about 5,000 years, though these days there are usually only campers and hunters hanging around this glorious desert outback.

EAST AND NORTH OF DOWNTOWN

The north end of Tucson, on the *bajada* and the foothills of the Santa Catalinas, is known for its Mission Revival and Spanish Colonial homes, many of them designed by famed architect Josias Joesler, and its high-end accommodations. The mighty mountains, reaching nearly 10,000 feet and an entirely different world from the desert below, rise northeast of downtown and are easily reached by taking Grant east from midtown to Tanque Verde (Catalina Highway) and then the Mount Lemmon Highway north into the range. To the east you'll find caves, mountains, and saguaros as far as the eye can see.

TOP EXPERIENCE

★ Saguaro National Park East

The eastern portion of **Saguaro National Park** (3693 S. Old Spanish Trail, 520/733-5153, 7am-sunset daily, visitors center 9am-5pm daily, $20 per car, receipt valid for seven days, good at both sections) is backed by the 8,600-foot Rincon Mountains. The visitors center has a bookstore and exhibits about the desert. The easiest way to see this section is to stroll, bike, or drive very slowly along the paved Cactus Forest Drive, an eight-mile one-way that begins at the visitors center and

winds up and across the *bajada*. The desert here is gorgeous, especially after a rainstorm or early in the morning during the bloom months. There are more than 100 miles of trails here, including one that goes to Rincon Peak above 8,000 feet. The park's newspaper guide has a full description of the major trails.

Vista del Rio Cultural Resource Park

Before the Spanish arrived in Southern Arizona and even before the Tohono O'odham and the Apache ruled this desert, it was home to the Hohokam people, arid-land farmers who lived in the Sonoran Desert's river valleys, building a highly complex culture that survived for centuries. Though the Tucson Valley doesn't have any spectacular Hohokam ruins on the order of Casa Grande just off I-10 halfway between Tucson and Phoenix, **Vista del Rio Cultural Resource Park** (7575 E. Desert Arbor St., dawn-dusk daily, free), a four-acre archaeological park on the east side, preserves the humbler ruins of a village occupied by the Hohokam from about AD 1000 to 1150. Even if you're less than fascinated by the dirt-mound ruins, this is a quiet and peaceful park with walking paths and sitting areas, perfect for relaxation and contemplation among the ghosts of a long-lost nation.

Colossal Cave Mountain Park

Sure it's a "dead cave," and certainly it has become in recent years a poor cousin to the living underground wonderland that is Kartchner Caverns State Park just a few dozen miles to the southeast; but **Colossal Cave Mountain Park** (16721 E. Old Spanish Trail, 520/647-7275, www.colossalcave.com, 8am-5pm daily, park entry $5 per car with up to five people, cave tours $18 adults, $9 children 5-12) near Vail, about a half-hour drive through the desert east of Tucson, has many charms nonetheless. The cave has been used as a shelter, an altar, a hideout, and a tourist attraction by various bands of natives and colonists for the last 1,000 years—this according to prehistoric artifacts and historic local newspaper accounts. In the 1930s the Civilian Conservation Corps (CCC) built a few structures near the cave's entrance in that inimitable native-stone style and installed lights and railings through a half mile of the sprawling grotto. The typical tour follows this route, while the guide narrates a general natural history of the cave with a bit of human history (including a tale of outlaws) peppered in. It's all very interesting and really fun, especially with kids.

After the cave tour, there's a gift shop, a café, and long views of the desert. A few miles down the road but still within the park, the mid-1870s **La Posta Quemada Ranch** offers more activities, particularly for children. In addition to pony rides ($5), a petting zoo ($5), trail rides ($38-87) and a gift shop, the ranch features a large sundial, displays on the cave and the CCC's work in the park, and a habitat for desert tortoises Shelly and Cienega. It's unlikely you'll see either tortoise unless you arrive in the morning, especially during the hotter months. There are plenty of shady and peaceful places to picnic here, and you can even camp ($7.50 per night) if you make a reservation.

Trail Dust Town

The best way to visit **Trail Dust Town** (6541 E. Tanque Verde Rd., 520/296-5442, www. traildusttown.com, 5:30pm-9pm daily, $2.50-6 for each attraction), an Old West-themed family attraction on the east side, is to wrap it up with a cowboy steak-and-beans dinner at Pinnacle Peak Steak House. If you don't have kids, rethink the entire venture. I'm not saying that there's nothing for the adult at Trail Dust Town; anyone interested in big-screen notions of Old West culture might get a kick or two here—there's some movie-set-style buildings, a miniature train that circles the property, a few on-cue gunfights in the dusty streets, and various shops and displays featuring touristy gifts and frontier artifacts. There's also a gold-panning game, a shoot-out gallery, and a lot of other commotion. If you have young or even youngish children,

though, you and the spouse can sit in the saloon and wait for your table while the kids explore the attractions.

St. Philips Church in the Foothills

St. Philips Church in the Foothills (4440 N. Campbell Ave., 520/299-6421, www. stphilipstucson.org) was originally designed in 1936 by Josias Joesler, a Swiss-born architect who designed many other foothills structures and who is responsible for the amalgam of native and revival architecture sometimes known as the Tucson Style. Joesler's structures usually mimic Mexican, Spanish, and Moorish styles with upscale flourishes, many of them stylish desertland haciendas on the *bajada* of the Catalinas, an area long reserved for the region's wealthy. A longtime Tucson architect said that Tucson, at least when it came to architecture, divorced itself from Mexico (and thereby Spain and its Moorish traditions) too quickly; these styles, with their courtyards, native materials, and passive solar heating, are ideal for living in the hot, dry Sonoran Desert, certainly much better than the cheaply built tract homes that proliferate in the valley these days. Very few Tucsonans build homes in the Joesler style anymore (to do so, or to live in one that's already built, is out of the financial question for most of us), and that's too bad. St. Philip's is along the busy River Road corridor and yet retains a peaceful atmosphere, with gardens and fountains behind thick, silent walls. The building and grounds have been added to and changed over the years, but always with respect paid to the original vision. Church officials welcome visits from students of architecture and anybody else who wants to look around. It's best not to go on a Sunday if you're just looking, and arrive before 4pm on weekdays if you want to talk to someone about the church and its history.

Tohono Chul Park

Tohono Chul Park (7366 N. Paseo del Norte, 520/742-6455, www.tohonochulpark.

org, 8am-5pm daily, $15 adults, $13 seniors, $6 children 5-12), a 49-acre desert preserve, is worth the short drive north on Oracle Road, into Tucson's sprawl. Turn left on Ina Road, then right on Paseo del Norte, and you'll find native-plant gardens with easy trails punctuated by interpretive signs. The **Ethnobotanical Garden**, with rows of maize and other crops once planted by the O'odham and the Spanish settlers, demonstrates the different methods used by each group to coax subsistence out of the dry ground.

If you stay quiet and sit by one of the many fountains or other water features on the grounds, you might get a glimpse of the many bobcats or javelina that call the preserve home. One night a year, in June or July, the garden's **night-blooming cereus** comes to life, an event so rare and spectacular that there's a hotline (520/575-8468) for visitors to keep up to date on the expected bloom timing.

There are gift shops and galleries on the property, and exhibits generally feature Native American and Hispanic folk and fine arts. **The Garden Bistro** (520/797-1222, 8am-4:30pm daily brunch, $15-20) has an excellent, Southwestern-inspired brunch menu; it's the perfect place to lounge before or after exploring the grounds, sipping a mimosa or a prickly pear margarita.

Roy P. Drachman Agua Caliente Regional Park

Approaching the shock of wet greenery among the otherwise gray green of the foothills, it's easy to see why this spring-fed oasis has been a popular spot for humans for the last 5,000 years or more. Now **Roy P. Drachman Agua Caliente Regional Park** (12325 E. Roger Rd., 520/749-3718, 7am-sunset daily; visitors center and art gallery 1pm-4pm Wed.-Fri., 8am-4pm Sat.-Sun. Nov.-Apr.), a 100-acre public park with a visitors center, gallery, nature shop, and wildlife-attracting spring water ponds, the site has over the millennia been a stopover for hunter-gatherers and the farming Hohokam culture as well as a ranch and

a resort built to exploit the supposedly curative powers of the springs. Much of the vegetation here, as along with the fish and the log-lounging turtles you'll see everywhere, is decidedly nonnative. The shaggy palms encircling the ponds like some spice-road camp were planted long ago, but the 200-year-old mesquite tree next to the former ranch house, a tree that hosts a whole ecosystem of its own, is native to the area and one of the oldest mesquites in the valley. This is a contemplative, peaceful spot, a good place for a walk, a picnic, or a long talk by the 87-degree ponds, with lazy turtles listening in.

DeGrazia Gallery in the Sun

A lot of art lovers turn up their noses at Ettore "Ted" DeGrazia. His little sad-eyed native children are ubiquitous here, on mugs and Christmas ornaments and whatever else. All the work can look the same and seems to offer little in the way of depth. A visit to the **DeGrazia Gallery in the Sun** (6300 N. Swan Rd., 520/299-9191, http://degrazia.org, 10am-4pm daily, $8 adults, $5 children 12-18), the amazing foothills home and gallery that he largely built himself, changes many opinions of the artist. When you see the home he built and get a close up look at the more serious paintings that hang throughout the gallery—epic cycles about the Mexican Revolution, the "founding" of the Southwest by Cabeza de Vaca and his doomed companions, and the lives and traditions of the Tohono O'odham, to name just a few—you may conclude that DeGrazia actually created some of the most enduring impressionistic visions in the Southwest. A native of Southern Arizona, DeGrazia attended UA and published his first work in *Arizona Highways* magazine. He went on to study in Mexico with muralists Diego Rivera and Jose Clemente Orozco. He died in 1982 at the age of 73, but the DeGrazia Foundation carries on his memory at the Gallery in the Sun, DeGrazia's first studio and gallery in Tucson, built in honor of Padre Kino and dedicated to Our Lady of Guadalupe. A mission on the grounds features DeGrazia murals, with a roof open to the sky. The gallery has a gift shop stocked with DeGrazia reproductions for sale. Even if you can't muster an appreciation of this admittedly overexposed artist's work, go for the native architecture and design to be found at his Gallery in the Sun, which may, after all, be DeGrazia's greatest work of art.

★ Santa Catalina Mountains

Drive about 40 miles (about 1 hour) up a twisty, paved two-lane from the desert floor northeast of midtown, and you're at nearly 10,000 feet—the trip, it is often said, is like traveling from Mexico to Canada in one short, scenic drive. It wasn't until the 1930s that Tucsonans could reach the cool heights in great numbers, when former U.S. postmaster general Frank Hitchcock called in some federal favors and secured money and convict labor to begin building a road into the mountains. The indomitable Civilian Conservation Corps eventually finished the job, and in the 1940s real estate agents began selling lots in what is now **Summerhaven,** a little cabin village at 7,840 feet with a few gift shops and cafés. Just up a bit from the village are the 22 runs of **Ski Valley** (10300 Ski Run Rd., 520/576-1321, snow report 520/576-1400, www.skithelemmon.com, 10am-4:30pm Mon. and Thurs.-Fri., 9am-5pm Sat.-Sun., $27-47), the nation's southernmost ski hill. The season runs, roughly, mid-December-early April in a good year. The chairlift ($12 adults, $9 youths) operates year-round, and it's fun to ride it to the green and cool mountaintop in the summer while the rest of the world sweats below.

Dozens of trails are on the range, along with several public bathrooms, campgrounds, and lookout points. The trails in the Santa Catalina Mountains move through dense pine and aspen forests, along high ridges overlooking the hazy valley and the city spread out below, and through mazes of boulders and along trickling creeks. It's very different up here in the forest from the desert valley below, and it snows here in the winter, limiting access by car for brief periods throughout the season.

It's a good idea to stop at the **Palisade Visitor Center** (520/749-8700, 8:30am-4:40pm daily) at 7,200 feet, which has trail maps, a bookstore, and displays about the mountain's ecology.

Don't expect to be alone when you're exploring the Catalinas; this is an extremely popular area among locals for picnicking and hiking, especially in the spring and summer. That being said, while the weekends are sometimes bumper to bumper, on weekdays, even in the summer, it's possible to avoid large crowds.

Sabino Canyon

Sabino Creek starts as springs high up in the mountains, gathering snowmelt and runoff as it descends into the foothills. There it rushes through Sabino Canyon with sometimes deadly vigor, creating a riparian oasis of cottonwoods, willow, walnut, sycamore, and ash; saguaro, barrel cactus, prickly pear, and cholla dominate the rocky canyon slopes away from the creek's influence. It is a truly spectacular place that should not be missed.

Sabino Canyon Recreation Area (8:30am-4:30pm daily, $5 per car), about 13 miles northeast of downtown Tucson, is easily accessible, user friendly in the extreme, and much used—best estimates say 1.25 million people visit every year. Many locals use the canyon's trail system for daily exercise, and hikers, picnickers, and sightseers usually pack the canyon on any given day in any given season.

A paved road rises nearly four miles up into the canyon, crossing the nearly always running creek in several places. During Southern Arizona's summer and winter rainy seasons, it is nearly impossible to cross the small bridges without getting your feet wet. The Forest Service closed the road to cars in 1978. It's a relatively easy walk along the road to the top of the canyon, which offers access to trails that go far into the Santa Catalinas. If you

1: Sabino Creek in Sabino Canyon **2:** Tohono Chul Park **3:** Biosphere 2 **4:** San Xavier del Bac

don't feel like walking, the **Sabino Canyon Shuttle** (https://rpcshuttle.org, $10 adults, $5 children 3-12, children under 2 free), an ecofriendly electric tram, runs 45-minute, narrated trips into the canyon all day, pausing at nine stops along the way to take on or let off hikers at various trailheads. From July through mid-December the shuttle runs 9am-4pm weekdays and 9am-4:30pm on weekends and holidays. From mid-December to June it runs 9am-4:30pm daily.

From the last tram stop 3.8 miles up in the canyon, hikers can get off and take an easy stroll down the road, crossing the creek at nearly every turn, or try the **Phoneline Trail** winding along the canyon slopes and overlooking the riparian beauty below. Perhaps the most popular trail in the entire Tucson Valley is the hike through nearby **Bear Canyon** to **Seven Falls,** a wonderful series of waterfalls and collecting pools. You can access the **Bear Canyon Trail** from just outside the visitors center, or take the shuttle to a trailhead 1.5 miles on. To the falls it's a total of 3.8 miles one-way and worth every step, though it is moderately difficult, rocky, and rather steep. The Bear Canyon shuttle leaves the visitors center every hour on the hour, 9am-4pm daily ($4 for adults, $2 children 3-12).

The **Sabino Canyon Visitors Center and Bookstore** (520/749-8700, www.fs.fed.us/r3/coronado, 8am-4:30pm daily) has trail guides and sells gifts and books. There are bathrooms, drinking fountains, and dozens of tucked-away picnic areas throughout the canyon, and many of the trails link up with one another, so it is easy to cobble together a loop hike that will take you through all of the various life zones. The canyon is open from sunup to sundown every day, and bikes are allowed in the canyon only before 9am and after 5pm, never on Wednesday or Saturday, and never on trails that lead into the **Pusch Ridge Wilderness Area.**

To get to the canyon from midtown, take Speedway Boulevard east until it turns into Tanque Verde Road and then turn north on Sabino Canyon Road to the recreation area, just north of Sunrise Road. There's a $5-per-car fee for one day, or $10 for a week. An annual pass can be had for $20.

Catalina State Park

Catalina State Park (State Hwy. 77, mile marker 81, 520/628-5798, http://azstateparks.com, 5am-10pm daily, $7 per car), a popular desert reserve just north of Tucson in the saguaro-dotted foothills of the Santa Catalinas, is heavily used, especially on weekends. Hikers shouldn't be surprised to pass large families carrying coolers and bags of chips up the trail.

The 5,500-acre park has eight trails—most of them easy to moderate—picnic areas, charcoal grills, and a small gift shop. It's an easily accessible place to see the desert, lush here thanks to the runoff and snowmelt that barrel down from the mountains through boulder-strewn washes. In the early spring and late summer there are many natural pools that fill up with runoff, some of them deep enough to be called swimming holes.

The seven-mile **Romero Canyon Trail** will take you to an array of natural pools—and you don't have to hike the whole trail to get there. If you want to get off the beaten track a little, veer right about a mile into the trail near a bench, pick your way down into the wash, and then follow a footpath up the wash that leads to some out-of-the-way, less-used pools. For an easy walk, take the half-mile round-trip **Romero Ruin Interpretive Trail** to an ancient Hohokam site. The ranger station/gift shop has a guide to all the park's trails, some of which link up to other trails all the way up into the mountains.

Biosphere 2

In the early 1990s eight scientists took up residence in **Biosphere 2** (32540 S. Biosphere Rd., 520/838-6200, www.b2science.org, 9am-4pm daily, $21 adults, $14 children 5-12), a 3.14-acre simulation of the earth (which would, of course, be Biosphere 1), in hopes of lasting two years and gaining important knowledge about how humans will survive in the future. They weren't able to remain self-contained, owing to problems with the food supply, but two members of the team did fall in love. The unique laboratory may yet save the world, however, as the UA is now running experiments under the dome and researching ways to combat climate change.

While the science is fascinating—there are actually small savannas, rainforests, deserts, and even an ocean under the glass—many who take the tour seem more fascinated by the doomed experiments in togetherness. Indeed, the tour takes you into the "Biospherians'" apartments, kitchen, and garden, and guides field more questions on this part of the tour than all the others. The tour lasts about 45 minutes and is not wheelchair accessible. The Biosphere is in a beautiful 35-acre desert setting about 30 minutes north of Tucson near the small town of Oracle.

Oracle

This small, historic town about 30 miles north of Tucson on the northeastern slopes of the Santa Catalina range has a few historic buildings and a proliferation of high-desert-dwelling artists. The **Acadia Ranch Museum** (825 Mount Lemmon Rd., 4pm-6pm Thurs., 1pm-4pm Sat., free) tells the colorful history of the ranch—once a sheep ranch and later a sanatorium for sufferers of TB and other ailments—and of the town, which today has about 3,500 people, many of them artists and other desert runaways. The **Oracle Union Church** (695 E. American Ave.) is on the National Register of Historic Places and worth a look, as is a nearby state park. There are several restaurants, including a historic steak house, and even a few little B&Bs, if you'd rather stay out here in the relative cool of 4,000 feet.

SOUTH OF DOWNTOWN

Head south from downtown and you reach South Tucson, a largely Latino community incorporated as a separate city. The airport is farther south, and to the southeast is the Pima Air and Space Museum, on the southwest

edge of Davis Monthan Air Force Base. To the southwest, reached via I-19, is San Xavier del Bac.

Pima Air and Space Museum

One of the largest museums of its kind in the West, the **Pima Air and Space Museum** (6000 E. Valencia Rd., 520/574-0462, www.pimaair.org, 9am-5pm daily, $16.50 adults, $13.75 seniors/military, $10 children 5-12) has interesting exhibits and an impressive number of decommissioned aircraft that tell the story of our fascination with defying gravity. Nearly 300 rare airplanes, many of them military, rest on the grounds and in six different hangars.

The Air and Space Museum is operated by the same group that operates the Titan Missile Museum near Green Valley, and for one price you can see both attractions. Warplane enthusiasts will want to take the hour-long bus tour to the **Aerospace Maintenance and Regeneration Center (AMARC)** to see the hundreds of dust-gathering planes ending their days in this "boneyard."

★ San Xavier del Bac

Founded in 1692 by Father Eusebio Francisco Kino and then built slowly over decades by other priests, missionaries, and natives, the mission **San Xavier del Bac** (1950 W. San Xavier Rd., 520/294-2624, www.sanxaviermission.org, 7am-5pm daily, free, donations encouraged) sits pure white against the perpetually blue sky about nine miles south of Tucson on the Tohono O'odham's San Xavier Indian Reservation. It is considered by many to be the foremost example of Mission architecture remaining in the United States, blending elements of Moorish, Byzantine, and late Mexican Renaissance architecture.

Few Arizona landmarks have received as much worldwide attention as the "White Dove of the Desert," which has been called America's answer to the Sistine Chapel. Mass is still celebrated daily in the church (check website for times), but non-Catholic visitors are encouraged and welcomed.

Most days there are tables and booths set

up in the mission's plaza selling burritos, fry bread, and other delicious eats, and across from the mission to the south is a small shopping area called **San Xavier Plaza,** with a snack bar and several shops selling Native American crafts.

Statues and paintings of St. Francis Xavier and the Virgin of Guadalupe decorate the cool, dark interior of the domed church. A continuous videotape about the mission runs throughout the day as a self-guided tour, and there's a gift shop on site that sells religious items and books about the history of the mission and the region. A small museum presents the history of the area's native inhabitants and the construction and ongoing rehabilitation of the mission. The mission is continually being worked on, but the seemingly ever-present scaffolding doesn't detract too much from its grandeur.

Sports and Recreation

It's certainly true that Tucson is an active, outdoorsy, sunburned kind of place. On any given weekday, let alone during the crowded, busy weekends, you'll see Tucsonans decked out in colorful, skintight Lycra outfits, pedaling with all their might up and down the steep mountain roads and along the bike routes through the city; you'll also see them hiking on desert trails among the saguaro forests and exploring the sky island mountain ranges that encircle the valley. If you're coming to Tucson to find some similar action, you won't have to look far.

PARKS

Some might say that there is neither river nor park at **Santa Cruz River Park** (south from Grant Rd. to 29th St.), but still it's as good a vantage as any other from which to view what remains. The Santa Cruz, like most Southwestern desert rivers, was never a deep, swollen river, but it at least had a perennial flow. It sustained a few different indigenous communities for eons and was the green and cool home of beaver, otter, native fish species, and all manner of wild riparian life. Now look at it. It's not *all* our fault; the region is prone to long droughts, and most desert rivers have wildly fluctuating, even intermittent, flows. But it was largely the pumping of groundwater throughout the region that sent the river underground for good a few generations ago. Every now and then, if the late-summer monsoon comes on blessedly strong, the water rises and flows past this pleasant, artificial green space just west of downtown, where you can ride your bike, take an early-morning jog, or just gaze at the dry, rocky bed.

A 131-acre greenscape on the southern end of midtown, **Gene C. Reid Park** (900 S. Randolph Way, 520/791-4873, www.tucsonaz. gov/parksandrec, 6am-10:30pm daily) is probably the city's favorite nondesert playground, with plenty of shade from imported trees and cool Bermuda grass for lounging and forgetting. The park has, among dozens of other attractions, two small duck-topped lakes (no swimming), a band shell and amphitheater for concerts under the stars, and an off-leash dog park. The playground equipment involves cool submarine-style passageways, twisting slides, fire poles, and sky-reaching swing sets, and several layers of soft woodchips and some bouncy outdoor foam flooring provide for soft landings. Hi Corbett Stadium is located on the park's grounds, as are the Reid Park Zoo, a large, modern recreation and aquatics center, a tennis facility, and a golf course. Kids love the "splash pad" at **Brandi Fenton Park** (3482 E. River Rd., http://brandifentonmemorialpark. org), between River Road and the Rillito, and it's a worry-free good time for parents as well. Just push the button, and for 15 minutes at a time cool water sprays out of fountains, falls from buckets, and bubbles and sprays up out of the ground, allowing water-resistant tykes to get the hang of a wet face before tackling the pool. The splash pad is open from mid-April until October 31, and it's free.

GOLF

It's not easy to justify the existence of golf courses in the arid Southwest from a perspective that recognizes the region's rather obvious resource deficiencies. It is, however, somewhat easier from the average golfer's point of view. For golfers, what most see as the region's primary deficiency—its aridity—is instead its greatest attribute, allowing them to play 36 holes on Thanksgiving morning with their envy-rotten visitors from Chicago. And so the courses proliferate. The city of Tucson operates five public courses in town, all of them excellent, though older and less dramatic than most of the resort and private courses invading the desert. The city's somewhat humbler courses come with the added benefit of being ecologically defensible: They are all irrigated with reclaimed water. The city maintains a helpful website (www.tucsoncitygolf.com) where you can see maps of all the courses, get rates (they are generally quite low, varying from $25 to $75 for 18 holes depending on premiums, season, time of day, and residency), and book tee times. All of the city courses have clubhouses, lighted driving ranges, carts, pros, and pro shops. The two most popular courses in Tucson's municipal system are **Randolph Golf Course** and **Dell Urich Golf Course** (600 S. Alvernon Way, 520/791-4161, www.tucsoncitygolf.com, 5am-7pm daily, $23-72 for 18 holes, price depends on season and residency), side-by-side courses at midtown's Reid Park. Randolph, the city's flagship course and the longest at 6,500 yards from the regular tees, has been the site of numerous PGA and LPGA tournaments and is green, spacious, and tree lined. Dell Urich, a par-70 course a bit to the south of Randolph, opened in 1996 and is probably the most popular in town. Both make for easy-access, in-town, and relatively inexpensive play year-round.

HIKING

Tucson and its surrounding sky island ranges have hiking trails for all experience levels. Desert trails tend to be rather flat and rocky, while the mountain trails are steep and usually offer some spectacular views.

The **Arizona Trail** (various trailheads around Southern Arizona, www.aztrail.org) is a nearly 1,000-mile network of mostly existing trails that one could follow on foot, horse, or mountain bike (if you want to carry your bike through the Grand Canyon and other federal wilderness areas along the way), from the border with Mexico to the border with Utah. There are 43 "passages" that make up the trail, each between 11 and 35 miles; more than a dozen of these are in Southern Arizona, within easy reach of Tucson. The trail through Southern Arizona traverses all of the region's biomes, from the scrubby desert to the dry grasslands to the cool, green mountains—it's a great way to get to know all of the natural wonders around Tucson. The nonprofit **Arizona Trail Association** (www.aztrail.org) is responsible for upkeep and trail building, and their website has a complete map and detailed descriptions of the trail.

Some of the best desert hiking in the region can be found at **Tucson Mountain Park** (www.pima.gov), a sprawling, saguaro-crowded park west of the city. Here the trails are rocky and sandy, moderately flat, and thickly lined with desert vegetation. The nearly five-mile round-trip **Brown Mountain Trail** leads through a cactus forest along the sandy bottomlands between the mountains, then rises gradually to a ridgeline that looks out on the hard country all around. Keep an eye out for lazy desert tortoises, who are known to sun themselves on the trail early in the morning. You can access the trailhead at the Brown Mountain Picnic Area or the Juan Santa Cruz Picnic Area, both just southeast of the Arizona-Sonora Desert Museum off Kinney Road. Just before you reach the valley after the steep descent from Gates Pass, there's a parking lot and trailhead where you can pick up the 5.5-mile

The Lemmon Rock Lookout

Arizona still has 72 active or semiactive fire lookouts, meaning they are staffed at least intermittently, especially during fire season or times of high risk and emergency. Only Oregon, with 106, and Florida, with 130, have more, according to the Forest Fire Lookout Association, a group that advocates for the preservation of lookouts and their traditions. What's more, Arizona has a higher ratio of active to standing lookouts than most states—72 active or semiactive out of 83 still standing. Contrast that with California, where 198 lookouts still stand but just 50 of those are active.

Only a small handful of lookouts classified as active are still staffed full-time for the entire fire season, roughly April 1 to September 1, and one of these rare huts happens to be lashed to a rock overhang in the Santa Catalinas above Tucson, overlooking the Wilderness of Rocks and, beyond that, the unfurled basin and range territory as far as the urban haze will allow. The Lemmon Rock Lookout, at 8,820 feet, has been occupied for about five months a year since 1928. On the face of the 14-by-14-foot lookout shack, the side that stares down on the vast pine and boulder land below, someone stenciled long ago the words "No Diving," as if aware of the risks of so much war with oneself.

Fire lookouts like Lemmon Rock have been around, in one form or another, for a very long time, but they really started to proliferate in the 1930s with the advent of the Civilian Conservation Corps and the U.S. Forest Service's all-or-nothing suppression policy. Responding to several huge, unprecedented backcountry forest fires that plagued the nation during the first third of the 20th century, government foresters enacted the 10am policy, decreeing that every fire on public lands must be quelled by 10am the morning after its initial spark. The fire lookout was an integral component of that policy. There is still some debate about the scientific efficacy of suppression, and we are, in many ways, paying for it now with overgrown, drought-ridden forests just waiting for a slash of dry lightning or a tossed cigarette to molt and be reborn, in the process ripping through the million-dollar homes we build in the forest hoping old Smokey the Bear will keep us safe from nature's cycles. Around the same time, the stock market crashed and so too the job market, hence the birth of the New Deal and the CCC, which put thousands of out-of-work Americans in the national forests building trails, firebreaks, and, in some of the remotest areas in the country, fire lookouts. Lemmon Rock was built by a CCC crew in the early 1930s, replacing a more primitive lookout on Mount Lemmon that had stood since 1913.

You can take a look at the Lemmon Rock Lookout for yourself and, during the summer months, sit down and have a high-altitude chat with the friendly current occupant of the little hut. To get there, drive up the Sky Island Highway to Ski Valley and park at the trailhead parking lot at the top of Mount Lemmon (keep going past the ski slopes and take the dirt road after the pavement ends). Once you park, pick up the short Lemmon Rock Trail.

David Yetman Trail, named for the host of the PBS show *The Desert Speaks*. There's another trailhead at Camino de Oeste—and if you leave a car at both ends you won't have to do a more-than-10-mile there-and-back trudge. Pima County's Natural Resources Department keeps a map of the trails around Tucson Mountain Park on their website.

The dozens of trails around and on 9,157-foot Mount Lemmon and the Santa Catalina Mountains (Coronado National Forest, 520/670-4522, www.fs.usda.gov/coronado, $5 per car), about an hour's drive up the winding Sky Island Highway from central Tucson and into another world entirely, are beloved among all those Tucsonans sweating away in the hot valley down there, dreaming of a weekend day spent scrambling around the evergreen forests and cool streams up on the mountain. Since there are so many trails to choose from (many of them lead into and branch off one another), consider the following eight-mile loop composed of portions of several trails, which is designed to take you through some of the best areas the mountain has to offer: At Summerhaven, turn onto the Sabino Canyon Parkway and follow it down to Marshall Gulch; leave your car at the small streamside parking lot. Start on Trail #3 (Marshall Gulch Trail) behind the bathrooms and follow it up through the shady forest for 1.2 miles to Marshall Saddle, at 7,920 feet. At Marshall Saddle branch off on Trail #44, which will take you down about 700 feet into the beautiful **Wilderness of Rocks** for 1.7 miles. At the junction take Trail #12 (the Lemmon Rock Lookout Trail) as it rises and rises for about two miles to near the very peak of Mount Lemmon at 9,157 feet, where you'll be among metal towers essential to life down below. Along the way you can stop off and look at the Mount Lemmon Lookout, which offers one the best views in the region. You'll see the ski lift near the top, but don't get on. Instead, hike along **Radio Ridge** using the Mount Lemmon Trail (Trail #5) for a mile or so to its junction with Trail #93 (the Aspen Trail). Follow that downhill for 1.3 miles, and you'll find yourself back at Marshall Saddle, where it's 1.2 miles back to the car. The climbs on this loop can be a bit brutal, but you're definitely rewarded for the effort. For information on other trails and more suggestions on which ones to try, stop by the Palisades Visitor Center on your way up the hill. There you can talk to rangers and pick up a map of the trail system.

Both sections of **Saguaro National Park** (Red Hills Visitor Center, 520/733-5153, www.nps.gov/sagu) offer superior desert hiking. In the **Tucson Mountains** district west of town, a strenuous but beautiful hike up to 4,687-foot **Wasson Peak,** the highest in the Tucson Mountains, is a great way to spend a Sonoran Desert morning. You can get there by picking up the **King Canyon Trail** just across Kinney Road near the Arizona-Sonora Desert Museum. It's about 3.5 miles to the top of the peak, hiking on switchbacks through typical *bajada* desert; then you can make it a loop by heading down the **Hugh Norris Trail** to its junction with the **Sendero Esperanza Trail** and taking the **Gold Mine Trail** back to the car. The whole adventure is about 7.5 miles total. There are certainly easier and less steep trails around the park as well. An easy

one to take with kids is the half-mile **Signal Hill Petroglyphs Trail,** a modest climb to a collection of boulders with several petroglyphs on display. If you continue on from here on the flat, easy trail, you'll go through some wonderful desert with a good chance to see wildlife. In the park's eastern section, at the base of the **Rincon Mountains,** there are several three- to five-mile loop hikes that will take you through all of the best parts of the sprawling cactus forests; for a two-mile round-trip walk, the **Cactus Forest Trail** is an easy, mostly flat trail among the green-armed giants. The visitors centers at both the western and eastern sections have complete trail guides and rangers on duty who can help you decide the best routes, and the park's website has detailed maps and trail guides as well.

BIKING

The **3rd Street Bike Route** is an easy, flat way to get from midtown to downtown on a bike—it goes from Wilmot on the eastern edge of midtown all the way through the University of Arizona to downtown. The **Rillito River Park Bike Route** is a flat and easy 11-mile route following the sandy-bottomed Rillito River, a great route for exercise and commuting across the north end of Tucson. Sure, the river is dry on top, but it's still a relatively green and shady path. The path runs from near I-10 all the way to Craycroft Road, and along the way it passes several parks, always hugging the parched riverbed, colored here and there with seeping lushness. The Rillito Park Bike Route is one of the more popular sections of an ambitious project called **The Loop** (www.pima.gov/TheLoop), which, when complete, will comprise some 130 miles of connected paths for bikers and walkers. At the time of writing, about 120 miles of The Loop were complete, connecting the Rillito River Park with Santa Cruz River Park downtown, and with other parks on the east and south sides. Pima County has a map of the entire Loop on its website, and hard-copy maps are available at most of the library branches and at the visitors center downtown.

Serious road cyclists proliferate in Tucson, and a few teams even do their winter training here. One of their favorite rides on a warm weekend morning is the **Dan Yersavich Memorial Bikeway** along Old Spanish Trail from Broadway all the way to Saguaro National Park East. Another favorite route is the long, hard climb up the Catalina Highway, also called the **Brad P. Gorman Memorial Bikeway,** and into the cool heights of the mountains. The ride up and over Gates Pass and into the Tucson Mountains region west of downtown is another favorite.

Local mountain bikers love **Fantasy Island** (south end of Harrison where it intersects with Irvington), a system of trails on a swath of scrubby state trust land southeast of midtown. While none of the trails and loops is very long, they are all fun and relatively easy—a great place for beginners and novices to ride. There's a detailed trail map set up at the entrance. You need to purchase a permit to recreate on state trust land in Arizona, and you should always have it with you while you're riding, just in case. To purchase one ($15 for a year) go to www.land.state.az.us.

Tucson's downtown and central neighborhoods can be easily explored by bike. For rentals, check out the **Tugo Bike Share** (http://tugobikeshare.com), a program sponsored by local business Tucson Electric Power. There are 36 stations in more than 13 neighborhoods throughout Tucson—about 330 bikes! A 30-minute station-to-station trip costs $4, or you can take an unlimited number of 3-hour trips over 24 hours for $15. For locations check out the website.

HORSEBACK RIDING

The horse has been an integral part of daily life in Tucson and Southern Arizona since the Spanish introduced it to the Southwest back in the 1500s. The useful animal transformed the lives and cultures of the native peoples here virtually overnight, and still

today there is a distinct subculture of "horse people" in the Old Pueblo whose lives are dedicated to the care and enjoyment of the equestrian kind. There are quite a few such people who will rent you a usually friendly, docile horse and guide you and your new friend deep into the desert on trails once traversed by conquistadores, ranchers, and Indians. Most places require that kids be at least six years old to ride, and most have a 230-pound maximum weight limit, but call ahead to make sure. Spring rides are the best, especially when the desert's in bloom. Summer is different—go early in the morning, or book one of the fun evening or nighttime rides many places offer. Always wear long pants and closed-toe shoes, and always bring a hat, though it doesn't necessarily have to be the cowboy type.

About 13 miles southeast of town, out in the shaggy cactus-and-scrub desert not far from Saguaro National Park East, the friendly folks at **All Around Trail Horses** (various areas near Saguaro National Park East, 520/298-8980, http://fareharbor.com/horsingaroundarizona, 8am-5pm daily winter, 8am-noon, 4pm-6:30pm daily summer, $43 one hour, $138 three hours, $75 1.5-hour sunset ride) will take you out and make you feel like a real cowhand. The desert out this way is beautiful and thick, and if you go when the cacti are blooming, you are in for a spectacular show. It's a good idea to call ahead for a reservation.

SPECTATOR SPORTS

The biggest sports draws in the region are the teams of the **University of Arizona.** With perennial powerhouses in basketball, volleyball, and baseball, and a Pac-10 football team that holds its own in a tough division, there's always something to cheer for on campus. For ticket information call the UA's **McKale Center** (520/621-2287, www.arizonaathletics.com). Don't expect it to be easy.

FC Tucson (Kino Sports Complex, 2801 N. Ajo Way, 520/600-3095, www.fctucson.com) is the Old Pueblo's scrappy USL League 1 soccer

1: golfing in Gene C. Reid Park **2:** The Loop, a popular bike route around the city team. They are a lot of fun to watch, and most of the seats are just $10. The team plays from late April to early October, and the action on the field is usually quite exciting as promising young talents compete furiously for a future in the beautiful game.

Entertainment and Events

NIGHTLIFE

Tucson's most vibrant nightlife takes place on three blocks within easy walking, or stumbling, distance of each other: Congress Street downtown, 4th Avenue, and Main Gate Square near the UA. There are always plenty of cabs waiting around outside the bars in these neighborhoods, especially on the weekends. When school's in session these areas are typically packed with students. But Tucson's nightlife and entertainment scene is fairly casual and mixed, drawing college kids, postcollege slackers and go-getters, thirtysomething urban workers, hip parents who still haunt the alt-rock shows, and professors and professionals of indeterminate age. There's really something for everybody out there.

Second Saturdays

Once a month on **Second Saturdays** (www.2ndsaturdaysdowntown.com, 5pm-10:30pm), the streets of downtown Tucson come alive as thousands of Old Pueblo residents head to the city's traditional heart to meet and mingle. The event, which, as its name suggests, goes down on the second Saturday of every month, features street vendors, performers, food, bands, art shows and more, and all the downtown stores, bars, clubs, and restaurants along Congress Street are usually hopping with activity. This is the best time to see downtown Tucson at its most active and interesting.

Bars, Pubs, and Lounges
DOWNTOWN AND
UNIVERSITY DISTRICT

The **Tap Room** (311 E. Congress St., 520/622-8848, www.hotelcongress.com, 11am-2am daily) has been around since 1919 and still packs them in, especially when there's a band playing at Club Congress, to which the Tap Room serves as a kind of hideout from the crush and noise. But if you belly up here of an afternoon, or on a slow midweek night, you'll notice the details: the retro booths and stools; the scratchy juke in the corner; and especially the cowboy-life art of Pete Martinez, one of several lauded Western artists who once called Tucson home. Martinez, who lived in Tucson from 1935 until his death in 1971, was neighbor to the painter and illustrator Maynard Dixon and friend to Ted DeGrazia, and he reportedly spent a good deal of his time drinking at the Tap Room. People always used to say that he would from time to time trade his work for his drinks, and that's how they got on the bar's walls. But the management says that's just a rumor, and that the artist gifted the paintings to his favorite bar.

The **Playground Bar & Lounge** (278 E. Congress St., 520/396-3691, http://playgroundtucson.com, 4pm-2am Mon.-Fri., noon-2am Sat.-Sun.) is a hip, fun place to hang out, drink and eat, listen to DJs, and meet locals and students downtown. Located at Congress Street and 5th Avenue, this sleek space with old chain-and-wood swings decorating the ceiling has an urban vibe combined with the historic warmth of a tastefully refurbished old building. The wonderful rooftop patio should not be missed, nor the long views of the Old Pueblo. For sports fans, there's often a soccer game on the big TVs.

Scott & Co. (49 N. Scott Ave., 520/624-4747, www.47scott.com, 4pm-11pm Tues.-Thurs., 4pm-midnight Fri.-Sat., 4pm-8pm Sun.) is the bar at on downtown's popular bistro. The emphasis here is on the drink in your hand. The expert bartenders at Scott &

Co. take their jobs very seriously. The menu of unique and creative drinks, many of them updated twists on classic cocktails, changes often, but the ingredients are always top shelf and house made.

★ **Borderlands Brewing Co.** (119 E. Toole Ave., 520/261-8773, http://borderlandsbrewing.com, noon-9pm Wed.-Thurs., noon-10pm Sat., noon-5pm Sun.) is the place to sample some of the best microbrews the Old Pueblo has to offer. The brewers here use local ingredients and follow in the footsteps of beer-loving Germans who settled in the Southwest in the 1800s. They serve several different beers in a beautifully refurbished old redbrick warehouse near the train tracks, including a superior IPA, a prickly pear wheat beer, and a rich "noche dulce" porter. A food truck is usually parked outside while a local band rocks the house inside. Check out the jaguar mural by artist Kati Astraeir across the street.

Pueblo Vida Brewing Company (115 E. Broadway Blvd., 520/623-7168, http://pueblovidabrewing.com, 4pm-10pm Mon.-Thurs., 1pm-10pm Fri., noon-11pm Sat., noon-8pm Sun.) serves amazing craft beers, brewed on-site, in a fun and convivial tap room with lots of windows and sunlight. This is very much a representative downtown Tucson hangout: it is particularly dog friendly, allowing well-behaved pups to join the party, and caters to the bike crowd, letting you park your ride inside. Bring your own food or have some delivered from one of the nearby restaurants. They also sell many of their craft brews in four-pack cans to go.

Ermanos Craft Beer and Wine Bar (220 N. Fourth Ave., 520/445-6625, http://ermanosbrew.com, 11am-midnight Mon.-Thurs., 11am-1am Fri.-Sat., 11am-10pm Sun.) is a laid-back and comfortable beer-and-wine bar in a refurbished historic space on 4th Ave. They offer about 25 different wines, 34 draft beers, and a wide assortment of bottles and cans, a list so varied that you are pretty much guaranteed to discover something new and quite possibly life-altering. The scratch food

here is several steps above the usual pub fare (panko crusted avocado fries, five-cheese grilled cheese sandwich, etc., $15-25), including jackfruit asada and other excellent vegetarian options.

Bar Toma at **El Charro** (311 N. Court Ave., 520/622-1922, www.elcharrocafe.com, noon-9pm Sun.-Thurs., noon-10pm Fri.-Sat.), one of the Old Pueblo's oldest and best-loved restaurants, has patio seating and a small but stylish bar that is a laid-back and civilized place to drink a margarita or five.

Sneak into Herbert Alley behind The Rialto Theatre to find **R Bar** (350 E. Congress No. 110, 520/305-3599, http://rbartucson.com, 7pm-2am daily), an intimate and stylish lounge serving craft beer, wine, and some very creative cocktails (the "Wes Anderson Fans Are Insufferable": bourbon, cappelletti, cinnamon syrup, and IPA). Done up all in deep red and cushions, the walls graced with Tucson-themed murals, this is a convenient and memorable spot to have a few drinks before or after a show at the Rialto.

Mr. Head's Art Gallery and Bar (513 N. 4th Ave., 520/792-2710, noon-2am daily) draws a mixed 4th Avenue-style crowd of college kids and frolicking urbanites with live bands; curious, glorious, and strange artwork; and a large selection of Arizona microbrews. The patio here is particularly nice.

Not exactly a hangout for revolutionaries in the Che Guevara mode, **Che's Lounge** (350 N. 4th Ave., 520/623-2088, www.cheslounge.com, noon-2am daily) is instead a small, inviting hangout for a vast array of 4th Avenue denizens, from college kids to fortysomethings. Local and touring bands regularly play on the lounge's patio.

Next to Brooklyn Pizza on 4th Avenue, **Skybar** (536 N. 4th Ave., 520/622-4300, www.skybartucson.com, 9am-2am daily) is a "solar powered café by day" and an "astronomy bar by night." The open, airy bar, with a patio from which you can watch all the people sauntering along 4th Avenue, is ideal for kicking back with a drink and a slice of New York-style pizza from next door (which they'll bring to you). The "astronomy bar" title comes from the telescopes they set up come nightfall, allowing patrons to peer into the nearly-always-clear skies above Tucson. They also show deep-space images on a big screen. From 5pm to 8pm daily the happy hour prices kick in, and throughout the week they offer theme nights as well as live music, DJs, open mic nights, and dance parties.

MIDTOWN
The Tucson Valley played a major role in the Cold War: For years ICBMs ringed the city, locked and loaded beneath the desert and aimed directly at various targets in the USSR. While there's a museum south of town where you can learn all about the Old Pueblo's atomic age bona fides, **The Shelter** (4155 E. Grant Rd., 520/326-1345, 3pm-2am daily) is the best place to celebrate, so to speak, the era and its two coolest cold warriors. It's dark and cool like a shelter should be, with plenty of good booze and always a campy cult film playing out silently on a TV in the corner. The walls are covered with Jack and Bobby, and the pinball machines ding and flap.

The **Casa Film Bar** (2905 E. Speedway Blvd., 520/326-6314, www.casafilmbar.com, 10am-1am daily) is a fun bar inside Tucson's last and favorite video store, which is still going strong thanks to the city's significant population of microbrew-loving film nerds. It's a great place to hang out, knock back a few local and regional beers, order in pizza from a nearby restaurant, watch a foreign film on the TV screens, and meet like-minded locals.

Tucson Hop Shop (3230 N. Dodge Blvd., 520/908-7765, www.tucsonhopshop. com, 2pm-9pm Mon.-Thurs., noon-11pm Fri.-Sat., noon-8pm Sun.) is a laid-back and stylishly utilitarian beer and wine bar in the Metal Arts Village, a small collection of artists' studios and shops near the Rillito River bike path, The Loop. This "bicycle friendly business" encourages patrons to ride, and to bring the kids along too. The outdoor beer garden is a great place to kick back after a long ride. The metal building is cool and comfortable inside, with plenty of seating, records on the turntable, and beer-loving bartenders. About 20 beers are typically on tap, from around the world, including a few from Arizona.

FOOTHILLS
The **Cascade Lounge at Loews Ventana Canyon Resort** (7000 N. Resort Dr., 520/299-2020, www.loewshotels.com, 3pm-10pm

Mr. Head's Art Gallery and Bar

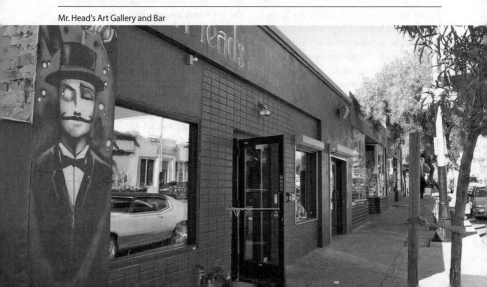

Mon.-Thurs., 3pm-midnight Fri.-Sat., 11am-10pm Sun.) is an eminently tasteful and upscale place to drink, with warm and earthy colors, thick and comfortable furniture, low, flattering lighting, and 30-foot windows offering commanding views from Ventana Canyon's high perch in the Catalina Foothills. One of Tucson's most romantic night spots, Cascade offers a nightly happy hour (5:30pm-7pm) with affordable drinks and small plates, and music Wednesday-Saturday.

Sipping a martini among stylish and stimulating surroundings while watching the desert city fade to black from high above the valley is just as much of a typical Tucson experience as scrambling up some rocky trail shadowed by saguaros. One of the best places to do the former is the **Azul Lounge** (3800 E. Sunrise Dr., 520/742-6000, www.westinlapalomaresort. com, 2pm-midnight daily), a rather upscale but not forbidding lounge at the **Westin La Paloma Resort** in the Catalina Foothills. The lounge, decorated all in blue and washed by music that registers but doesn't get in the way, offers top-notch cocktails and delicious small plates, all complemented with a view that can't be beat. The least expensive time to go is during happy hour, weekdays from 5pm to 7pm.

Live Music

Most of the bars, pubs and lounges in downtown and along 4th Avenue host local bands and performers throughout the week.

Club Congress (311 E. Congress St., 520/622-8848, www.hotelcongress.com, 9pm-1am Sun.-Mon., 10pm-1am Tues.-Sat., cover varies), inside the historic Hotel Congress, is the city's premier spot for touring alternative rock and alt-country bands. Most nights if there's not a band playing, there's a DJ and dancing. Music geeks and college-town rock and rollers frequent the shows here, and it's a kind of headquarters for the thriving downtown music scene—the stage new local bands aspire to get to. If you're not in the mood for sweaty crowds, guitars, or breakbeats, there's a somewhat quieter lounge in the lobby, but

the music is the club's reason for being, and thank the gods for that.

The nicest Quonset hut you've ever danced in, **The Hut** (305 N. 4th Ave., 520/623-3200, www.huttucson.com, 4pm-2am Mon.-Fri., noon-2am Sat.-Sun., cover varies) books in the weird and the rocking in equal measure, with roots, rock, blues, reggae, and even spoken-word performance art filling the faux-tropical bar most nights. It has a kind of slum-tiki vibe, laid back and beach bound with a lot of frozen drinks on the menu. Don't miss taking a picture of the three-story cement tiki head out front.

Head up to the foothills to see a tight jazz band at the **Terraza Garden Patio and Lounge** on the enchanting grounds of the historic **Hacienda del Sol Guest Ranch Resort** (5501 N. Hacienda del Sol Rd., 7am-10:30pm daily). The large and usually bustling patio hosts jazz trios and quartets, singers, and pianists every night of the week. During the popular happy hour (3pm-6pm daily), when the expensive drinks ($15 for a craft cocktail, try the "Day Spa," one of the bar's signature drinks) and tapas are slightly less expensive, you're likely to meet some locals, some tourists, and maybe even a few European travelers. On a cool evening sit out on the couches by the fire and look at the dark and looming Santa Catalina Mountains. Then you'll know what Tucson is all about.

THEATERS AND VENUES

A furbished theater from the 1920s, the **Rialto** (318 E. Congress St., 520/740-1000, www.rialtotheatre.com, box office open noon-6pm Mon.-Fri.) books an eclectic list of acts, everything from Steve Earl to 2 Chainz. It's a great place to catch your favorite alt-rock and alt-country bands on tour. Across Congress Street from the Hotel Congress downtown, the historic building has over the years been a vaudeville house, a Spanish-language cinema, and for five years in the 1970s, a porn theater.

191 Toole (191 E. Toole, 520/445-6425, http://191toole.com, times and prices vary by show) hosts hard-working touring bands

The Day of the Dead

In the Arizona borderlands these days it's difficult to find a boutique, gift shop, or gallery that doesn't sell *calavera* (skeletons doing human things) statues, paintings, T-shirts, and all manner of other consumer goods featuring the Day of the Dead aesthetic. Generally these art objects recreate the work, or at least the spirit of the work, of Posada, a late-19th-century and early-20th-century Mexican printmaker and illustrator whose broadsides and newspaper illustrations employed the *calavera* and Day of the Dead traditions in social commentary. While Posada's work had the immediacy of journalism, it has outlasted its original intent and is more popular today than ever before. His style and overt political commentary influenced Diego Rivera and other Mexican muralists of the first half of the 20th century.

The Day of the Dead, El Día de los Muertos, falls on November 2, but the celebrations begin on November 1 or even before that. It is roughly meant to coincide with the traditional Catholic holidays of All Saints Day and All Souls Day, but the tradition is far older than the Spanish conquest of Mexico. It is like most Latin American rites a deep-time amalgam of pre-Columbian and Spanish traditions whose origins reach far back into the mist.

The Day of the Dead reminds us that death and the dead have a profound influence on the living. The details of the celebrations vary from region to region, from town to town and from the big city to the rural areas. Generally they include feasts in graveyards with a dead relative's favorite dishes prepared and set aside. There are also parades and marches, candles and altars, sugar skulls, and sweet breads shaped like skulls and skeletons.

For many years the Day of the Dead has been marching north, so much so that it now rivals

and other performers in a cavernous old space downtown. You can buy tickets to specific shows at the door one hour before show time, or at the Rialto Theater box office.

From the 1930s to the 1970s, the **Fox Theatre** (17 W. Congress St., 520/624-1515, www. foxtucsontheatre.org, box office open 11am-6pm Mon.-Fri., 11am-2pm Sat.) was the place to go in Tucson to see Hollywood's latest offering, and the theater's art deco style nearly matched the glamour on the screen. Along with many other once-famous and much-used buildings downtown, the Fox fell into disrepair until the late 1990s, when a group raised money to refurbish the old movie house. Now the theater, beautifully restored to its original grandeur, shows classic films several times a month and hosts concerts and events.

The **Temple of Music and Art** (330 S. Scott Ave., 520/884-4875) is a beautiful old theater and playhouse built in 1927 downtown. It is the main stage for the **Arizona Theatre Company** (www.arizonatheatre. org) and hosts concerts and shows throughout the year.

PERFORMING ARTS

The **Arizona Theatre Company** (330 S. Scott Ave., 520/622-2823, www. arizonatheatre.org) puts on an excellent season of plays September-May at the Temple of Music and Art, and the **Arizona Opera** (520/293-4336, www.azopera.org) presents some of the best regional opera in the country October-April at the **TCC Music Hall** (260 S. Church Ave.). The **Tucson Symphony** (520/882-8585, www.tucsonsymphony.org) holds concerts September-May also at the TCC Music Hall.

CINEMA

The best theater in town is **The Loft Cinema** (3233 E. Speedway Blvd., 520/795-0844, www. loftcinema.com), showing art-house, classic, cult, and foreign films, and offering free showings of classic films on Sunday afternoons and Monday nights. There's always something worth seeing at this remodeled old theater, and you can buy a beer and a slice of pizza to go with all the soul searching on the big screen.

Cinco de Mayo as the Southwestern Anglo's favorite Mexican import. But the spectacles surrounding the holiday have long been a subject of fascination for tourists, especially those from the United States. As far back as the 1970s, Mexican observers were complaining that in places like Mixquic and Patzcuaro, towns famous for their Day of the Dead celebrations, "cameras had come to outnumber candles in the cemeteries."

Throughout November there's usually a traditional Day of the Dead altar at **Tolteca Tlacuilo** (186 N. Meyer, 520/623-5787, 10am-4pm Mon.-Sat., 11am-4pm Sun. June-mid-Sept., 9:30am-5:30pm Mon.-Sat., 11am-5pm Sun. mid-Sept.-May) in Tucson's Old Town Artisans complex, and the **Tucson Museum of Art** (140 N. Main Ave., 520/624-2333, www.tucsonmuseumofart.org, 10am-5pm Tues.-Sat., noon-5pm Sun.) typically celebrates the ancient rite with a family event on November 2, with the usual music, food, arts and crafts, an altar, a parade, and big-headed puppets.

skeleton statue

Roadhouse Cinema (4811 E. Grant Rd., 520/468-7980, http://roadhousecinemas.com) in midtown shows all the big movies and serves great food, microbrews, and cocktails while you watch. Perhaps the best thing about Roadhouse is the comfortable chairs that lean back and cradle you to sleep if you're not attentive. The food here is pretty good—finger foods and burgers and fries, quesadillas and jalapeño popcorn—and the servers go out of their way to stay out of the way while the movie is on. You have to reserve seats, and they are often sold out, so plan ahead. There's also a Roadhouse in Scottsdale.

COMEDY

Touring stand-up comedians from around the country stop at **Laffs Comedy Club** (2900 E. Broadway, Ste. 154, 520/323-8669, www.laffscomedyclub.com, $12.50-17.50). Thursday night is open mic, and comedians hit the stage 8pm and 10:30pm Friday and Saturday. The club also serves food and drinks.

CASINOS

Take I-19 south to Pima Mine Road for the fun **Desert Diamond Casino & Hotel** on Tucson's south side (7350 S. Nogales Hwy., 520/294-7777 or 866/332-9467, www.desertdiamondcasino.com), operated by the Tohono O'odham tribe. It has slot machines, blackjack, poker, keno, and bingo, several restaurants, and a hotel. **The Agave Restaurant** here serves wonderful, eclectic lunches and dinners 11am-9pm daily. There's also a constant stream of talent moving through Desert Diamond's intimate concert venues, often hosting top-name acts like Willie Nelson and Bob Dylan.

West of I-19 on Valencia Road, the Pascua Yaqui tribe operates **Casino Del Sol** (800/344-9435, www.casinodelsol.com), a Mediterranean-influenced fun land with poker, slots, bingo, blackjack, and keno. The complex has several places to eat and drink, including an excellent upscale steak house. Stick around after the gaming for a concert in the casino's amphitheater, which regularly hosts major touring acts.

THE ARTS

The creative class is well represented in Tucson. There are probably more artists and artisans living in or near the Old Pueblo than in any other Arizona locale save the Navajo and Hopi Reservations. Some top galleries in Tucson also have sister galleries in Santa Fe, New Mexico, or Sedona in Northern Arizona. You don't have to appreciate the sometimes overly romantic depictions of the famed Old West to enjoy looking at art in Tucson. There are all kinds of galleries, especially those in the downtown area, that show art from a more experimental, contemporary Southwest, and there are few cowboys left these days. But if you do love Western and Southwestern art, from the conservative to the experimental, there are few better places to be. Head to the foothills around Campbell and Skyline for galleries showing the best of the genre. Check with the **Tucson-Pima Arts Council** (www.tucsonpimaartscouncil.org) for a complete calendar of all the arts-related stuff going on in town at any given moment.

Galleries

For anyone enraptured by the classic art of the Southwest—from the photographs of Edward Curtis to the modernist paintings of Maynard Dixon; from the ceremonial kachinas of the Hopi people to the elegant yellow-brown pottery of Nampeyo—**Mark Sublette's Medicine Man Gallery** (6872 E. Sunrise, 520/722-7798, www.medicinemangallery.com, 10am-5pm Tues.-Sat. May-Sept., 10am-5pm Mon.-Sat. Oct.-late Nov., 10am-5pm Mon.-Sat., 1pm-4pm Sun. late Nov.-Apr.) is an absolute must-visit. The huge gallery also features the **Maynard Dixon Museum,** with a wide selection of often obscure paintings, illustrations, and ephemera from throughout the great artist's career. There's also a contemporary art gallery here featuring the best in new Western art by the likes of the fabulous Navajo artist Shonto Begay.

True to a long tradition of repurposing old buildings in downtown Tucson, **MOCA Tucson** (265 S. Church Ave., 520/624-5019, www.moca-tucson.org, noon-5pm Wed.-Sun. $8 winter, $5 summer) used to be a fire station. MOCA puts on several exhibits each year, mixing paintings, photography, and installations. When they say contemporary here, they really mean it: You will see art done this afternoon by working, struggling, and inspired artists confronting aesthetic and social themes in all kinds of interesting and confusing ways. It's a small museum but worth the time.

More than 70 local artists display and sell their work at the **Southern Arizona Arts Guild (SAAG) Gallery of Gifts** (2905 E. Skyline Dr., 520/437-7820, http://southernarizonaartsguild.com, 10am-7pm Mon.-Wed., 10am-8pm Thurs.-Sat., 11am-6pm Sun.) at La Encantada shopping center. The large gallery has paintings and photography by Sonoran Desert artists, and also ceramics, jewelry, handbags, and textiles created by members of Tucson's notable arts community. With an emphasis on decorative and Southwestern-themed pieces, this is a great spot to look for a unique souvenir or gift.

FESTIVALS AND EVENTS

In January the multicultural **Family Arts Festival** (Tucson-Pima Arts Council, 520/624-0595, www.familyartsfestival.org) features exhibits, concerts, and performances. February is dominated by the biggest local event of them all, **Tucson Gem & Mineral Show** (520/322-5773, www.tgms.org), which brings thousands of visitors to the Old Pueblo. The busy month also welcomes **La Fiesta de Los Vaqueros** (800/964-5662, www.tucsonrodeo.com), Tucson's famed rodeo and parade—the longest nonmechanized parade in the world. The **Southwest Indian Art Fair and Market** (520/621-6302, www.statemuseum.arizona.edu) in February brings the region's top jewelers, potters, weavers, and carvers from the Navajo, Hopi, Zuni, and other tribes.

In March Civil War enthusiasts recreate the Battle of Picacho Pass during the **Civil War in the Southwest** (http://azstateparks.com). Also in March, the Tohono O'odham hold their annual gathering at Mission San Xavier del Bac during the **Wa:k Powwow** (520/294-5727, www.powwows.com). Cinephiles file into town in April to catch the **Arizona International Film Festival** (520/628-1737, www.azmac.org).

The Tucson Kitchen Musicians put on their signature event, the always fun (and free) **Tucson Folk Festival** (www.tkma.org), in May. With the heat of June come prayers and dances for rain on **Día de San Juan,** a series of festivals and rituals celebrating John the Baptist and the saint's historical relationship with the desert's summer rainy season.

Ski Valley on Mount Lemmon celebrates **Oktoberfest on Mount Lemmon** (520/885-1181) a month early, in September. In early October, the Tucson Historic Preservation Foundation sponsors **Tucson**

Modernism Week with events that celebrate the Old Pueblo's mid-century style (http://preservetucson.org). Another October event is the **Tucson Culinary Festival** (www.tucsonculinaryfestival.com), which features top local and national chefs and lots of good food. Also during the Halloween month, Old Tucson Studios hosts its popular annual horror show called **Nightfall** (520/883-0100, www.nightfallaz.com).

The **All Souls Procession** (www.allsoulsprocession.org), held the first weekend in November, has brought the artful traditions of the Day of the Dead to downtown Tucson since 1990. The celebration, organized by the nonprofit arts group Many Mouths One Stomach, culminates in a colorful and rather spooky nighttime parade through the downtown streets, featuring ghouls, ghosts, skeletons, big-headed puppets and myriad other walking works of art. Throughout the weekend, art shows and other events take place at venues around the city—all celebrating the impermanence of life and the glory of human-made art.

Shopping

In the Old Pueblo you just might find that authentic artifact that has long eluded you. Here you'll find merchants with Mexican imports, folk arts, Western Americana, and Indian jewelry; boutiques with clothes you'll find nowhere else; and galleries featuring the work of artists from Tucson and the rest of the world.

SHOPPING CENTERS AND DISTRICTS

Main Gate Square (University Blvd., 520/622-8613, www.maingatesquare.com) is right next to the University of Arizona and so is frequented by students. There are 52 stores and restaurants on this block, the likes of Urban Outfitters and American Apparel mixed in with local shops and bars, all of them skewing young for the university crowd. This

is a good place to walk around and have lunch, and there's always something new opening or moving in. Be careful about parking; instead of braving the back-in-only metered parking, go to the **Main Gate Parking Garage** (815 E. 2nd St.) and leave your car in shade and safety.

The **Lost Barrio** (Park Ave. south of Broadway Blvd., www.thelostbarrio.com, 10am-6pm Mon.-Sat., noon-4pm Sun.) is a series of rustic old warehouses tucked away on Park Avenue just before you enter downtown from Broadway. Here you'll find six shops selling unique items such as handcrafted and imported furniture, folk arts, antiques, and locally sourced home decor. The oldest and best of the stores here is **Rustica,** which has gorgeous Mexican and Peruvian furniture and Talavera pottery.

Even if you don't have any room in your budget for pottery, Mexican folk arts, and turquoise jewelry, you should still find time to visit shady, historic **Old Town Artisans** (201 N. Court Ave., 520/623-6024, www. oldtownartisans.com, 9:30am-5:30pm Mon.-Sat., 11am-5pm Sun. Sept.-May, 10am-4pm Mon.-Sat., 11am-4pm Sun. June-Aug.) downtown across from the Tucson Art Museum. Six shops and galleries are gathered in the 150-year-old adobe structure, each one opening onto the verdant Mexican-style courtyard with a fountain and tables. There's a good restaurant here as well, and there are often festivals and live music going on in the courtyard, which is a fine place to sit and rest with a beer. The import shop **Tolteca Tlacuilo** (www.toltecatlacuilo.com) here sells some of the best Día de los Muertos items in town. There are nearly 20 shops and restaurants at **Plaza Palomino** (southeast corner of Swan and Fort Lowell Rds., 520/320-6344, www. plazapalomino.com, 10am-6pm Mon.-Sat.), an upscale midtown shopping center, including purveyors of Native American arts and crafts, Southwestern-style items and home decor, furniture, jewelry, fine art, and high-style women's clothing.

West of downtown, the **Mercado San Agustín** (100 S. Avenida del Convento, 520/461-1107, http://mercadosanagustin. com, daily, hours vary by shop) is a stylish open-air market and shopping center in the burgeoning westside Mercado District, featuring a Mexican-style bakery that sells knee-buckling donuts, and a Sonoran snow-cone spot. With several boutiques, a great restaurant, and a bright and sunny coffee spot, the Mercado is popular with locals. On a Saturday or Sunday morning there are bound to be a host of resting bikers and active families having fun in the shade. Just a few steps outside the Mercado is the **MSA Annex** (267 S. Avenida del Convento, 520/461-1107, http://mercadodistrict.com), home to 13 locally owned businesses, all of them housed in stylishly rusted, recycled shipping containers. With added floors and windows and

doors, of course, the surprisingly elegant and eye-pleasing boutiques and restaurants face shaded open spaces with tables and chairs. Don't miss the tiny bike shop and the charming store that sells Tucson-specific items.

The ideal upscale shopping experience can be found in the foothills at Skyline Drive and Campbell Avenue. **La Encantada** (2905 E. Skyline Dr., 520/299-3556, 10am-7pm Mon.-Wed., 10am-8pm Thurs.-Sat., 11am-6pm Sun.) has posh shops like Tiffany & Co., Louis Vuitton, Crate & Barrel, and dozens more in a lush, two-level outdoor setting.

Drive west from downtown over dramatic Gate's Pass and through the saguaro forests to **Cat Mountain Station** (2740 S. Kinney Rd., 520/578-4272, www.catmountainstation.com, 8am-8pm daily), an oasis of taste and style that's close to the Tucson Desert Museum and Saguaro National Park. The enchanting station with gorgeous desert landscaping and a shady courtyard hosts a Buffalo Exchange boutique offering fashionable second-hand clothing, along with a store selling hand-made jewelry and local art, a Southwestern art gallery, and a shop featuring handmade, Tucson-only gifts and souvenirs. There's also a restaurant and bed-and-breakfast, and a small observatory for guided tours of the inky-black desert sky.

ANTIQUES

The **Grant Road Antique District** (Grant Rd. between Campbell Ave. and Craycroft Rd.) has more than half a dozen antiques and resale shops on both sides of Grant Road between Campbell and Craycroft, the best of which is the **American Antique Mall** (3130 E. Grant Rd., 520/326-3070, www. americanantiquemall.com, 10am-5pm Tues.-Sat.). A visit here will give you a good idea of the kinds of antiques, collectibles, and generally interesting junk available at most of the Old Pueblo's resale places—a crowded mix of cowboy-life and Southwestern collectibles and kitsch; Native American jewelry and artifacts (not all of them authentic); furniture from the common to the rare, the handmade and colonial, the retro and modern; old but not necessarily collectible books (*a lot* of Westerns); and all the varied possessions and ephemera left behind by several generations of snowbirds and retirees who spent their final days warm and content in the desert. Though it is not really recognized locally as such, there is a kind of **Speedway Antiques District** along both sides of busy Speedway Boulevard, roughly between Country Club and Wilmont, where you'll find half a dozen or more shops, both small and large, selling used furniture, antiques, and other used and historic treasures.

CLOTHES

"Vintage clothing for New Bohemians" is how the founder of **The Buffalo Exchange** (2001 E. Speedway, 520/795-0508, www. buffaloexchange.com 10am-8pm Mon.-Fri., 10am-7pm Sat., 11am-6pm Sun.) describes her first store in Tucson. Now the chain has spread throughout the country to college towns and bohemian enclaves from Tempe to Brooklyn, but it all started in midtown Tucson in the early 1970s. This boutique, which has a few Tucson locations, offers some of the most unique used clothes you'll ever find.

NATIVE AMERICAN ARTS

First opened in 1952 by Tom Bahti, father of current owner Mark Bahti, **Bahti Indian Arts** (4330 N. Campbell Ave., Ste. 72, 520/577-0290, www.bahti.com, 9:30am-6pm Mon.-Sat., 9am-4pm Sun.), though no longer in its original location, is now the oldest shop of its kind in the Old Pueblo. The small shop at St. Philip's Plaza, at River and Campbell, sells some of the finest examples of Navajo, Hopi, and Pueblo textiles, kachinas, jewelry, basketry, pottery, paintings, sculptures, and fetishes in the state, as well as an assortment of art and artifacts from tribes outside the Southwest. Mark himself is a noted expert on Native American arts, as his father was before him. He sells many useful books and guides at his store, including

his own *Silver + Stone: Profiles of American Indian Jewelers.* **Morning Star Traders** (2020 E. Speedway Blvd., 520/881-2112, www. morningstartraders.com, 10am-6pm Mon.-Sat.) has a fabulous collection of the high-end Indian arts—kachinas, Navajo textiles, pots and baskets, carvings, and historical artifacts—from the Southwestern traditions and others as well. The friendly, knowledgeable folks at **Mac's Indian Jewelry** (2400 E. Grant Rd., 520/327-3306, www. macsindianjewelry.com, 9am-5pm Mon.-Fri., 10am-5pm Sat.), longtime purveyors of Indian art and crafts in Tucson, will help you find that playful kachina doll, that delicately wrought basket, or that substantial silver-and-turquoise heirloom you've always wanted.

FOLK ARTS

The Old Pueblo has its fair share of resident artists, and, contrary to popular belief, not all of them are struggling to find the most evocative pose for a sunset-lit cowboy atop his horse. **Native Seed Search** (3061 N. Campbell Ave., 520/622-5561, www.nativeseeds.org, 10am-5pm daily) has uniquely Southwestern items, from heirloom seeds for nearly lost regional crops to one-of-a-kind gifts and videos and handmade crafts and soaps (yucca root soap, for example)—all with a link to the region and its past. A perfect gift to take back home is one of the gift baskets sold here, with all kinds of locally and regionally produced foods, soaps, and balms. This store also has an excellent selection of books about Tucson and the Southwest.

The concept of "upcycling" is a relatively new one, but it makes a lot of sense in our cluttered world. The artists selling their wares at the charming 4th Avenue boutique **Popcycle** (422 N. 4th Ave., 520/622-3297, www.popcycleshop.com, 11am-6pm Mon.-Thurs., 11am-7pm Fri.-Sat., 11am-5pm Sun.) take old pop-culture artifacts—old record albums, found art, advertising, etc.—and create new and exciting items out of the detritus of the culture. You won't believe what a creative mind can come up with, given just a bit of time spent in the attic or thrift store.

BOOKS, MAPS, AND OUTDOOR SUPPLIES

Book lovers can't miss **Bookmans** (6230 E. Speedway Rd., 520/748-9555, www.bookmans.com, 9am-10pm daily), a Southern Arizona original, which now has clones throughout the state. There are three Bookmans stores in Tucson, all of them featuring thousands of used books, CDs, videos, DVDs, and video games, but the relatively new Speedway location has become the firm's flagship store. Prices are cheap compared to smaller, boutique-style used bookstores, and the selection is absolutely without compare. This is one of the West's best used bookstores. **The Book Stop** (214 N. 4th Ave., 520/326-6661, www.bookstoptucson.com, 10am-7pm Mon.-Thurs., 10am-10pm Fri.-Sat., noon-5pm Sun.) is one of the last independent bookstores in Tucson. Open since the late 1960s, it's been on 4th Avenue since 2007. They have a decent selection of used and out-of-print books, including a substantial section on the Southwest. The books are a bit pricey in comparison to the bigger Bookmans, but when you're inside this classic store and nestled deep in the heady world of dusty old books, you feel a million miles away from the present.

You'll find topographical maps and hiking guides, bedrolls, backpacks, outdoor clothing, and everything else you might need for a desert adventure, at the locally owned **Summit Hut** (5251 E. Speedway Blvd., 520/325-1554, www.summithut.com, 9am-8pm Mon.-Fri., 9am-6:30pm Sat., 10am-6:30pm Sun.).

Food

The Old Pueblo's culinary scene is famously dominated by the ranchland comfort food available at the dozens of Mexican eateries in town, most of them serving classic variations of a cuisine formed in Mexico's arid northern states and on the hot, dry coastlines of the nearby Sea of Cortez. While such home-style Mexican food represents one of the most popular cuisines in the United States, in Tucson it has a kind of authenticity and diversity of taste that's available nowhere else—except perhaps just across the border, about an hour's drive from the city. UNESCO apparently agrees with this assessment: In 2015 the group named Tucson a "City of Gastronomy."

While you could spend a lifetime here eating carne asada, chiles rellenos, and enchiladas exclusively, you'd not only gain more weight than you'd like to but also miss out on sampling the work of some of the most creative, adventurous chefs and restaurateurs in the Southwest. The amorphous hodgepodge that is Southwestern-inspired American cuisine thrives in Tucson through an impressive array of mid- to high-end, locally owned restaurants throughout the city. If none of the spots below sends you craving, check out the list of locally owned eateries at "Tucson Originals" (http://tucsonoriginals.com).

To be totally honest, though, when you've got year-round outdoor patio dining—with gentle heaters when it's chilly, and cold-water-spitting "misters" when it's hot—and the sky above that patio is ever blue and clear, and the views from that patio are of looming high mountains and sweeping desert valleys, the quality of the food in front of you often becomes a secondary issue. Whenever you can, barring something unlikely like rain or cold, ask to sit on the patio or in the Spanish-style courtyard—scores of restaurants here have them, and alfresco dining in, say, February is one of the great joys of desert living.

Fast Food

A homegrown enterprise, **Eegee's** (21 locations throughout Tucson, www.eegees.com) has been a favorite among Tucsonans

From *Machacas* to *Menudos*: Mexican Cuisine in Arizona

Because so many Arizona residents are from somewhere else, you'll find all the world cuisines well represented in even the most seemingly out-of-the-way places. However, one style reigns supreme: Mexican food. The cuisine of Mexico is very popular throughout the United States these days, and travelers to Arizona and the border region are likely to have at least a passing knowledge of the favorites. But Tucson and Nogales (especially if you cross "the line" and try one of the restaurants in the tourist section of Nogales, Sonora, Mexico) are the best places in the state to eat Mexican food. In Tucson you'll find dozens of restaurants featuring a variety of regional Mexican foods, but the most prevalent is the style of northern Mexico, "El Norte"—after all, it wasn't that long ago that this region was not the extreme south of the United States but rather the extreme north of Mexico.

Mexican cuisine

A ranching frontier, northern Mexico (specifically the states of Sonora and Chihuahua) has a cuisine based on beef, beans, cheese, and chilies—the comfort foods of Mexico. You are more likely to find flour tortillas in northern Mexico than in the central and southern regions, as the desert and semidesert land is harder on corn than on wheat. A popular ranchland delicacy is *machaca,* also called *carne seca*—dried, shredded beef that is available at nearly every restaurant as a filling for burritos and tacos or on its own. Many Tucson restaurants are famous for their **carne asada,** or grilled meat—thin strips of beef spiced and grilled and then stuffed in tacos or burritos or served on their own with rice and beans. Another popular northern dish is **menudo,** available at many taco stands and restaurants around Tucson as well as Phoenix. It's a kind of soup made with tripe, hominy, and cow's foot that's said to cure hangovers—it is often offered only on the weekends.

Originating in Hermosillo, the capital of the Mexican border state of Sonora, the so-called **Sonoran hot dog** is a decadent variation of the great American street food. You can find them all over Tucson and Phoenix at restaurants and from vendors on street corners, and you really must try one if you like hot dogs. The classic version is a grilled hot dog wrapped in bacon and then couched in a fluffy Mexican-style bun (*bolillo*), and topped with beans, salsa, tomatoes, onions, creamy mayonnaise, and mustard.

Throughout the southern portion of the state it's also easy to find excellent **Mexican seafood.** Tucson is only four or five hours from the Sea of Cortez, and many locals have vacation homes along the desert coast. Places serving fish tacos, shrimp cocktail, and other seafood delights abound. There are also a few restaurants in the state that serve a more complex, gourmet version of Mexican cuisine. At these places, you'll be able to sample the intricate moles and chicken and pork dishes of central and southern Mexico.

since 1971. The most popular items on the menu are the frozen drinks—multiflavored shaved ice in a Styrofoam cup goes down very easy on a hot summer day in the desert. My favorite is still the one they started with: lemon. They serve excellent deli-style sandwiches—many of them hot—french fries, and similar fare. The ranch fries, a heap of sliced and deep-fried potatoes smothered in ranch dressing and topped with bacon bits, are a delight if you can risk the coronary. There's one of these Tucson-only joints on a corner near you wherever you are in the Old Pueblo.

DOWNTOWN AND UNIVERSITY DISTRICT
Mexican and Latin American

Featured far and wide in gourmet and lifestyle magazines, **Cafe Poca Cosa** (110 E. Pennington St., 520/622-6400, www.cafepocacosatucson.com, 11pm-9pm Tues.-Sat., $15-30) is one of the Old Pueblo's top eateries. Reservations are basically required, and the menu changes twice daily. The food is usually an adventurous, learned, and creative hybrid—a kind of gourmet Mexican food created by Chef Suzana Davila, a native of Guaymas on the Sea of Cortez. Eat here if you want something on the far creative edge of Mexican cuisine. The interior is done up in a smooth, cool style with contemporary art—including a painting by the great Daniel Martin Diaz—peppered throughout.

El Charro Café (311 N. Court Ave., 520/622-1922, www.elcharrocafe.com, 11am-9pm Sun.-Thurs., 11am-10pm Fri.-Sat., $6-18) makes the city's most beloved Mexican food in a building once lived in by Julias Finn, a French stonemason who came to Tucson to work on the cathedral. The restaurant has a bar, ¡Toma!, with half-price drinks and appetizers (delicious Mexican favorites like cheese crisps and quesadillas) 3pm-6pm daily.

Do you like loud music while you eat, waitresses who kiss and hug their customers, and a bit of attitude with your chiles rellenos? The food is so spectacular at ★ **The Little One** (151 N. Stone Ave. at Alameda St., no phone, 8am-2pm Mon.-Fri., $7.50-10) you might be willing to put up with just about anything to get the simple Mexican and Latin American fare at this beloved lunch spot. The hugs and even the cheek kisses from the waitresses are all right with a belly full of goodness. Make sure to tip big; a large percentage of everything goes to various good causes. They take only cash, no exceptions.

The carne asada and the Mexican (also called Sonoran) hot dogs are the specialties

of the house at ★ **El Guero Canelo** (5201 S. 12th Ave., 520/295-9005, www.elguerocanelo.com, 10am-11pm Sun.-Thurs., 10am-midnight Fri.-Sat., $4-7), which replicates better than any other Old Pueblo Mexican restaurant the tastes and atmosphere of casual eating south of the border. If you're a fan of hot dogs, you really have to try the Sonoran variation—a skinny, grilled dog hidden in a thick, rich, soft white bun, lathered with beans, mayo, salsa, and whatever else you want to add. It's amazing, but it rarely sparks ambivalence—people seem to either love it or hate it. The restaurant has **two additional locations** (North Midtown: 2480 N. Oracle Rd., 520/882-8977; Eastside: 5802 E. 22nd St., 520/790-6000).

American and Southwestern

A restaurant and bar in the refurbished old Southern Pacific train depot downtown, **Maynards Market & Kitchen** (400 N. Toole Ave., 520/545-0577, http://maynardstucson.com, 11am-10pm Sun.-Wed., 11am-midnight Thurs.-Sat., market 7am-8pm Mon.-Sat., 9am-8pm Sun., $15-30) is cool and stylish and looks out on the railroad tracks and the graffiti-covered trains rolling by. Globally inspired cuisine, with a slight emphasis on Southwestern traditions (best side: pima corn grits), have made Maynard's one the bright lights of Tucson's foodie scene. Here you'll also find one of the best happy hours (4pm-6pm Tues.-Sat.) in the city features small plates of poutine, shrimp cocktail, burgers, and more, while the bartender makes an amazing martini featuring olives hand stuffed with blue cheese, bacon, and jalapeños. The market here has really good sandwiches.

The ★ **Cup Café** (311 E. Congress St., 520/798-1618, 7am-10pm Sun.-Thurs., 7am-11pm Fri.-Sat., $7.50-24) serves an eclectic blend of American food with a dash of several ethnic traditions. Inside the Hotel Congress downtown, the Cup is a popular weekend breakfast destination but also a perfect choice for lunch and dinner anytime. The menu features dishes such as dates stuffed with chorizo and wrapped in bacon, fish tacos, burgers with

Arizona-raised beef (also a wonderful veggie burger), and Thai Fisherman's Stew. Not only does the restaurant have a range of unique and memorable creations, many of them are gluten-free and vegan, making it an ideal place for foodies and vegetarians to share a meal.

Chef Janos Wilder was among the first local chefs to focus on reforming and repurposing regional ingredients and styles in the 1980s. He's credited with reimagining Southwestern cuisine, infusing it with French mechanisms and a New American ethos. His influence can be seen in restaurants all over the Old Pueblo. These days, Janos, who is something of a local celebrity, serves a creative, seasonal menu heavy with local and regional ingredients and strong links to the various flavors of Mexico, Italy, and Asia at **Janos Downtown Kitchen and Cocktails** (135 S. 6th Ave., 520/623-7700, http://downtownkitchen.com, 11am-2pm and 5pm-10pm Mon.-Fri., 5pm-10pm Sat.-Sun., $10-26). The stylish streetside patio and open, modernist interior make this restaurant and bar one of downtown's best places to kick back, sample unique dishes, and toss back a few expertly made cocktails.

Hidden away behind a nondescript storefront on downtown's Scott Avenue, **47 Scott** (47 N. Scott Ave., 520/624-4747, www.47scott.com, 4pm-close Mon.-Fri., 10am-10pm Sat., 10am-9pm Sun., $15-30) has a romantic, brick-walled patio that's lit subtly after dark. The menu is seasonally adjusted, but they generally serve a familiar but no less appetizing take on New American comfort food. To know what's going on here you need only order the phyllo-wrapped chicken—a juicy breast cased in toasted phyllo dough, stuffed with goat cheese and spinach, drizzled with a rich and hearty chicken jus, flanked by smashed potato cakes and sage carrots. It's a wonderful kind of deconstructed chicken potpie.

The **Hub Restaurant and Ice Creamery** (266 E. Congress Street, 520/207-8201, http://hubdowntown.com, 11am-midnight daily, $11-25) has a hipster style and the soul of a great American diner. The food is certainly a few cuts above the usual countertop fare:

fries smothered in prime rib and cheese sauce, shrimp and grits, chicken potpie, lobster mac-and-cheese. . . . So is the decor: white faux-leather booths, thick ropes like vines on the redbrick walls, and upside-down house lamps hanging from the exposed rafters.

In a glorious and lovingly refurbished 1964 Googie on the eastern edge of downtown, the ★ **Welcome Diner** (902 E. Broadway Blvd., 520/622-5100, welcomediner.net, 8am-9pm Sun.-Thurs., 8am-10pm Fri.-Sat., $7.50-16) puts on a feast of style, flavor and goodness not to be missed. Its mid-century style stands out even along Tucson's Sunshine Mile, a stretch of classic mid-century architecture along Broadway Boulevard that the Welcome either begins or ends, depending on which way you're going. And that's just the outside. Inside, the chicken and biscuits, fried green tomato sandwiches, burritos with native tepary beans, full bar and friendly people will keep you around. The folks at Welcome Diner make their delicious and creative dishes with organic and local produce, chicken, bread, coffee, tortillas, and more. About the farthest from Arizona they go is to nearby California, where they buy their beef from a small ranch with sustainable and humane practices.

Italian and Pizza

There's nothing better than a greasy slice (from $3) of authentic New York-style pizza after a night of hitting the bars, and **Brooklyn Pizza** (534 N. 4th Ave., 520/622-6868, www.brooklynpizzacompany.com, 11am-11pm Mon.-Sat., noon-10pm Sun.; slices served 11pm-2:30am Fri.-Sat., $7-22) serves them late into the night (or rather, morning) on the weekends. The pizza here almost rivals anything you can find back East, and the meatball subs, calzones, and gelato are the best in town. What's more, this little pizza place is completely solar powered.

Caruso's (434 N. 4th Ave., 520/624-5765, www.carusositalian.com, 11:30am-11pm Tues.-Sun., $7-12) has been serving delicious Italian favorites on 4th Avenue since 1938. Sit on the shaded patio next to a trickling fountain and enjoy the pasta dishes and pizzas created here. It's nothing fancy—just well-prepared Italian favorites in a laid-back atmosphere with, of course, checkered tablecloths and fat bottles of chianti.

Some of the most toothsome pizza in town is served by **Reilly Craft Pizza and Drink** (101 E. Pennington St., 520/882-5550, www.reillypizza.com, 11am-11pm daily, $10-18) out of a tastefully refurbished circa-1908 building that once housed a funeral home downtown. The restaurant kept the funeral home's name and sign but little else. With an urban-cool interior and sophisticated menu, Reilly is a standout in the ever-expanding downtown culinary scene. The "craft pizzas" have a thick-but-light toasted crust and come with a variety of toppings far removed from the usual slice-on-the-corner variety (fennel pollen, truffle cheese, eggplant, fontina, etc.). Reilly also serves pasta dishes and extraordinary salads. Try the one with watermelon and goat cheese; it's truly something special.

Vegetarian

Café Desta (758 S. Stone Ave., 520/370-7000, http://cafedesta.com, 11am-9pm daily, $10-45), a bright café on the southern edge of downtown, serves exceptional Ethiopian cuisine, much of it vegan, and has a full coffee bar. Bring your own bottle of wine and a few friends and try the "vegan signature plate" ($30, serves up to three people), a sampling of several spicy and exotic vegan dishes featuring mushrooms, lentils, cabbage, onions, collard greens, spinach, and more, served with rice and the spongy Ethiopian flatbread *injera* (which is also vegan). If you have carnivores in tow, Desta also has flavorful dishes with beef, lamb, and fish.

Small and always busy, **Tumerico** (402 E. 4th St., 520/270-2055, and 2526 E. 6th St., 520/240-6947, www.tumerico.com, 9am-8pm Thurs.-Sat., 9am-3pm Sun., $13-18) has two locations offering unique and inspiring plant-based Mexican food in a casual, counter-service setting. The chef, who started out selling her creations from a cooler at local events, makes plant-based dishes a world away from the usual cheese-and-sauce-smothered hot plate. The small, regularly changing menu often includes classic dishes with a vegetarian twist, such as jackfruit tacos, green enchiladas, and vegan tamales, all made with local ingredients. Try the Tumerico lemonade; it's amazing. You can take a free yoga class at the 4th Street location (corner of Fourth Ave. and 4th St.) at 9am on Sat. and Sun.

★ **Beaut Burger** (267 S. Avenida del Covento, 520/344-5907, www.beautburger.com, 11:30am-8:30pm daily, $6-9) serves an array of fantastically tasteful scratch-made veggie burgers—made from grains, beans, vegetables, walnuts, and spices—from a re-purposed shipping crate. Head over to the westside MSA Annex near the Mercado San Juan, which is a bustling complex of wasteful shipping crates made over into stores and eateries. Consider trying the tasty burger named "B10" with tomatillo salsa, chiltepin, and cheddar cheese. At $9 it's the most expensive item on the menu, but all the proceeds are donated to the Center for Biological Diversity, a Tucson-based environmental group that has for decades worked around the world on behalf of endangered species and their (our) habitats. Eating this veggie burger, or at least buying it, is one of the greener things you can do in Tucson.

MIDTOWN
Mexican

A recognized leader among the Old Pueblo's many purveyors of the Sonoran hot dog, **BK Carne Asada & Hot Dogs** (2680 N. 1st Ave., 520/207-2245, www.bktacos.com, 9am-11pm Sun.-Thurs., 9am-midnight Fri.-Sat.), with a cozy midtown location, is the perfect place to have, say, 30 of the bacon-wrapped, bean-heaped dogs, and maybe a few dozen carne asada tacos, and an indeterminate number of cold beers. BK also serves awesome "caramelos." Apparently a local creation, they're a

1: Beaut Burger 2: Maynards Market & Kitchen
3: The Parish 4: The American Eat Co.

sort of grilled tortilla sandwich, usually over-stuffed with meat, cheese, chilies, and other staples. They also have a **Southside location** (5118 S. 12th Ave., 520/295-0105, 9am-midnight Sun.-Thurs., 9am-2:30am Fri.-Sat.).

The Arizona home of the Sonoran hot dog is ★ **El Guero Canelo** (2480 N. Oracle Rd., 520/882-8977, www.elguerocanelo.com, 10am-11pm Sun.-Thurs., 10am-midnight Fri.-Sat., $4-7), which has been serving authentic and fast Mexican "street" food in the Old Pueblo for two decades. The restaurant serves what many believe to be the city's best Sonoran dogs—a grilled beef hot dog wrapped in bacon, nestled deep in a thick, rich bun, and smothered in beans, onions, mustard, mayo, and salsa. It's a decadent meal, especially because it's nearly impossible to have just one. Another must-try here would be the carne asada tacos, and don't forget to wash it all down with a bottle of Mexican soda. They also have **two other locations** (Southside: 5201 S. 12th Ave., 520/295-9005; Eastside: 5802 E. 22nd St., 520/790-6000).

American and Southwestern

The genius baker behind ★ **Barrio Bread** (18 S. Eastbourne Ave., 520/327-1292, http://barriobread.com, 9am-5pm Tues.-Fri., 9am-2pm Sat.), Don Guerra, was a semifinalist for the 2019 James Beard Award. Yeah, he's that good. He's also fascinated with local and heritage grains and uses them to make some of the best bread in Arizona. Located in Broadway Village along Broadway Boulevard's Sunshine Mile, Barrio Bread features a dizzying selection of fresh loaves that generally don't last long, including the signature Heritage loaf made with a blend of Southwestern heritage flours and embossed with a charming saguaro. Guerra also bakes a loaf called the pan de Kino using white Sonora wheat. Padre Kino first brought this kind of wheat to Southern Arizona in the late 1600s, and it's still grown and milled locally for Barrio Bread at a small farm in nearby Marana. You'll know you've found it when you see the line out the door. Try either of the two midtown locations

of **Prep & Pastry** (2660 N. Campbell Ave., 520-326-7737 and 6450 E. Grant Rd., Unit 160, 520/838-0809, www.prepandpastry.com, 7am-3pm Mon.-Fri., 7am-3pm Sat.-Sun. brunch, $7-13.50) for a breakfast any day and brunch on the weekends. The chefs here use local and seasonal ingredients to create inspired and unique breakfast dishes like herb-cheddar biscuits smothered in duck fat gravy, spicy tri-tip, scrambled egg and arugula on a croissant, asparagus toast, and of course plain old pancakes—it's a bright and busy spot for foodies and their hungry friends. Prep & Pastry is also a great place for lunch. Brunch here is fantastic and popular. Get your name on the waiting list early by going to the website.

Cielos at Lodge on the Desert (306 N. Alvernon Way, 520/320-2000, www.lodgeonthedesert.com, 7am-10:30am, 11am-2pm, and 5pm-10pm daily, $12-36) has become one of the city's most esteemed eateries. The midtown restaurant and bar, deep within the confines of the boutique hotel's property, exudes a kind of Old West high-walled coziness that pairs perfectly with a regional take on New American cuisine. It has a daily happy hour (3pm-7pm).

High-piled gourmet burgers in a casual setting—it's a rather simple concept that seems like a stroke of genius when you're trying to bite into your towering, inventive **Monkey Burger** (5350 E. Broadway Blvd., 520/514-9797, www.monkeyburgerrestaurant.com, 11am-9pm Mon.-Sat., noon-7pm Sun., $10-11). They offer a dozen or so signature burgers and a few not-so-usual sides (fried pickles, sweet potato fries, roasted corn on the cob), plus draft beer and thick shakes.

The best greasy spoon in Tucson, and perhaps the greasiest, is ★ **Frank's/Francisco's** (3843 E. Pima St., 520/881-2710, 6am-2pm, 5pm-10pm Mon.-Thurs., 6am-2pm, 5pm-midnight Fri., 7am-2pm, 5pm-midnight Sat., 8am-2pm, 5pm-10pm Sun., $5-10), whose motto is "Elegant Dining Elsewhere." You can sit at a rickety table or belly up to the bar and watch your hash browns cook on the grill. The breakfast menu has all you'd expect, with the addition of Mexican favorites that come highly recommended. There's nothing like getting all spiced up early in the morning. At night Frank's becomes Francisco's, serves Michoacán-style Mexican food, and gives away free slow-cooked pinto beans to go.

Huge and delicious omelets can be had at the **Blue Willow** (2616 N. Campbell Ave., 520/327-7577, www.bluewillowtucson.com, 7am-9pm Mon.-Fri., 8am-9pm Sat.-Sun., $11-20), serving out of a cute old house with a large covered patio in Campbell Avenue's busy commercial district. The emphasis here is on the fresh, homemade, and all-natural. A gift shop sells funny stickers, buttons, and knick-knacks about politics and gender issues.

Vegetarian

Govinda's Natural Food Buffet (711 E. Blacklidge Dr., 520/792-0630, www.govindasoftucson.com, 5pm-9pm Tues., 11:30am-2:30pm, 5pm-9pm Wed.-Sat., 11am-2:30pm Sun., $2-10) puts out a tasty, expertly prepared, and inexpensive all-you-can-eat vegetarian and vegan buffet. On Thursday nights everything is vegan, and on Tuesdays authentic Indian food is served. Sundays they offer brunch from 11am to 2:30pm featuring pancakes, home fries, and scrambled tofu. The restaurant is located at the Chaitanya Cultural Center, its name referring to one of Krishna's many incarnations; you will be among Tucson's Hare Krishna community here, in a peaceful and always friendly atmosphere that may spark a meditative mood—post-buffet, of course.

FOOTHILLS
American and Southwestern

An admirable restaurant in an incomparable setting, the **Flying V Bar and Grill** (7000 N. Resort Dr., 520/299-2020, www.loewshotels.com, 5:30pm-9pm Mon.-Thurs., 5pm-10pm Fri.-Sat., 5pm-9pm Sun., $18-45) at Loews Ventana Canyon, a gorgeous Catalina Foothills destination resort, combines all the best elements of Tucson's dining scene in one place: awesome views, a romantic terrace,

guacamole made to order tableside by a "guacamoliere," and inspired comfort food with a dollop of Southwestern flavor.

An upscale pub on the edge of the foothills, **Union Public House** (4340 N. Campbell Ave., 520/329-8575, www.uniontucson.com, 11am-2am Mon.-Sat., 10am-2am Sun., $11-33) has outstanding food and one of the best patios in town, looking out on St. Philip's Plaza, with its shady trees and trickling fountain. The menu features creative variations on comfort classics—potpie, chicken and waffles, fish-and-chips, burgers, and flatbread pizzas.

For those who could exist on beef alone, and who believe that beef is best served ground, in patty form, and between two warm buns, there is **Zinburger** (1865 E. River Rd., 520/299-7799, www.foxrestaurantconcepts.com, 11am-10pm Sun.-Thurs., 11am-11pm Fri.-Sat., $8-16), a gourmet homage to the good old burger joint. Not surprisingly, the Kobe burger (with cheddar cheese and wild mushrooms) is quite popular, as is the Samburger, with maple bacon, American cheese, and Thousand Island dressing—a kind of dressed-up Big Mac. The sides alone are worth a visit: sweet potato chips, zucchini fries, double truffle fries. Thick shakes, crème brûlée, and bananas Foster are among the perfectly paired desserts offered in this sleek and bright burger house.

A unique pairing of South-by-Southwest food styles, **The Parish** (6453 N. Oracle Rd., 520/797-1233, www.theparishtucson.com, 11am-midnight Sun.-Thurs., 11am-2am Fri.-Sat., $14-29) calls itself a "Southern fusion gastropub." That generally means New Orleans meets Tucson, and it's a meeting that anybody who loves food will want to be present for. Try the crawfish hush puppies; you may end up eating a dozen. Or sample the house-made pork rinds, or the bacon popcorn . . . and that's just the appetizers. The entrées include various steaks, fish, and burgers, all prepared with Southern methods and just a dash of Southwestern spice. The Parish also has a creative cocktail menu and a wide selection of beers on tap.

Steaks and Chops

★ **El Corral Restaurant** (2201 E. River Rd., 520/299-6092, www.elcorraltucson.com, 5pm-10pm Mon.-Thurs., 4:30pm-10pm Fri.-Sun., $15-30) is a charming, historic choice for prime rib, a thick steak, and big bowl of cowboy beans. In a low-ceilinged, stone-and-wooden-beam territorial ranch house with flagstone floors along River Road, this restaurant's been a Tucson institution since 1926. The setting is almost as inviting as the sizzling beef and barbecue ribs, with Technicolor portraits of movie-house cowboys on the walls and several rooms that offer romantic, fireside dining.

SOUTH OF DOWNTOWN

If you only have the time or inclination to eat at one of Tucson's famous Sonoran-style Mexican restaurants, consider ★ **Mi Nidito** (1813 S. 4th Ave., 520/622-5081, www.minidito.net, 11am-10:30pm Wed.-Thurs. and Sun., 11am-2am Fri.-Sat., $10-18); Bill Clinton did. While on a short stopover in Tucson during his presidency, Clinton, known for his love of food (especially the comfort variety), stopped at Mi Nidito (My Little Nest), sampling pretty much one of everything. His order is preserved as a special on the menu still. It's difficult to say what it is about this bright South 4th Avenue restaurant, with its tropical decor and friendly, albeit always harried, staff, that sets it apart from the dozens of other similar eateries in the Old Pueblo. It is the best; that's all there is to it. *Tucson Weekly* readers invariably name it the top (or at least among the top) Sonoran joints in town in that publication's annual Best of Tucson poll, and you shouldn't be surprised to see a line of people waiting to be seated at 10:45am on a Wednesday. On a weekend night, figure on at least a half hour on the porch, waiting anxiously for your name to ring out.

Head south on 6th Ave. out of downtown to South Tucson (about 2 miles from Congress St.) and ★ **The American Eat Co.** (1439 S. 4th Ave., 520/867-8700, http://americaneatco.com, 11am-9pm Mon.-Thurs., 11-10pm Fri.-Sat., prices vary by restaurant), a food court featuring 10 different local businesses, including a coffee house, a beer-and-wine bar, and a butcher shop. The counter-service restaurants here offer an eclectic selection of foods—burgers, ribs, pizza, poke bowls, etc. There's also a spot serving "Chicano comfort food" from South Tucson. You can take your food to go or sit down with the locals at the large family-style tables.

WEST OF DOWNTOWN
American and Southwestern

The ideal place to refuel after exploring the desert in and around Tucson Mountain Park, Saguaro National Park, and the Arizona-Sonora Desert Museum, **Coyote Pause Café** (2740 S. Kinney Rd., 520/883-7297, www.coyotepausecafe.com, 7:30am-2:30pm daily, $6-12) is a casual diner-style eatery serving classic American rib-stickers with a few nods to the territory. It's in a refurbished 1950s-era desert outpost called Cat Mountain Station and an easy drive from all of the main west-side attractions. The "Coyote Burger," with house-made prickly pear barbecue sauce (you might want to take home several dozen bottles) and thick, crunchy onion rings, will restore any energy that you left out on the saguaro-lined trails nearby. They serve a number of vegetarian, vegan, and gluten-free dishes, including a spicy, locally inspired "Sonoran Veggie Burger."

Accommodations

There aren't a lot of inexpensive accommodations in Tucson worth taking a chance on. There is one hostel, in a clean and friendly house near downtown. It's the best choice for budget travelers. On the I-10 frontage road just west of downtown there is a long row of chain hotels, some of them inexpensive. This isn't the Old Pueblo's most charming district, however. Throughout midtown and on to the east side there are dozens of big chain hotels to choose from, and of course there are many more around the south side near the airport.

For most tourists and casual visitors, downtown and the University District is the best place to stay. This is the best area for walking, sightseeing, eating, and drinking, and it's close to I-10 and the road out to Saguaro National Park and the Arizona-Sonora Desert Museum. Midtown has the largest selection of accommodations, most of them chains of varied quality and price. For a truly memorable Tucson experience, consider staying in one of the small (though often relatively pricey) B&Bs and inns in one of the city's many historic neighborhoods, such as the El Presidio and Sam Hughes neighborhoods; the latter is a residential neighborhood on the eastern edge of the University of Arizona campus popular with students and professors. The northwest side and foothills have most of the high-end resorts, most of which are at least a half-hour drive from the city center.

During the summer months, roughly late May-late September, nearly all of the hotels, resorts, and inns in Tucson slash their prices—some by as much as 50 percent, but most by around 20 percent. If you're planning on coming to town during those torpid, quiet months, you might just be able to afford to live like a robber baron for a few days. Also, it pays to explore the websites of the larger chains listed below; most of them offer all kinds of different packages, one of which will likely save you some money. If you're coming

to town in February or March, book early and plan to pay a bit more; those two perfect-weather months feature several very popular festivals, events, and conventions in the Old Pueblo, and most places are booked solid.

DOWNTOWN AND UNIVERSITY DISTRICT
$100-250

Built in 1919 and extensively remodeled since then, ★ **Hotel Congress** (311 E. Congress St., 520/622-8848 or 800/722-8848, www.hotelcongress.com, $89-149) is a historic downtown hotel that offers charm and atmosphere; it's listed on the National Register of Historic Places and is right in the center of downtown's bar and music scene. Though the rooms are a bit creaky, the beds are comfortable, and the historic atmosphere more than makes up for the lack of sumptuous amenities (plus, it's the best value in town if you value personality in your sleeping quarters). There is noise some nights coming from the Club Congress downstairs (it's not too bad, but a slight thumping comes through the walls). The club is a venue for alternative bands and alt-country bands from across the nation, and the Tap Room bar will make you feel like a ranch hand on his day off. The Cup Café off the beautiful old lobby has an eclectic mix of gourmet and Southwestern-style food for breakfast, lunch, and dinner. Rates are about $10 less in summer, beginning at the end of May. Congress has been a leader in sustainability for many years. The hotel is Certified Green under the Arizona Hotel & Lodging Association's Green Lodging Program and has been retrofitted with water-saving technology. Congress is also a member of One-Less Straw, a nonprofit that helps keep plastic straws out of landfills and the oceans.

About a mile south of downtown and with easy access to I-10, the ★ **Hotel McCoy** (720 W. Silverlake Rd., 844/782-9622, https://

hotelmccoy.com, $89-120) offers clean, comfortable rooms, some with kitchenettes, in a resurrected mid-century motor court made into a traveler's haven with creative zest, retro style, and a local vibe and value that's hard to resist. Tucson-made art fills the rooms and the lobby, which has an all-local beer-and-wine bar and, in the morning, a nutritious, filling, free and delicious oatmeal bar. Not a very scenic location but it's close to everything and the staff here is working hard to make the hotel sustainable and affordable. Not only have they made fine use of an old building, they installed low-flow water fixtures, drip irrigation, drought-tolerant landscaping, and LED lighting. If you stay for three or more nights, you can choose to skip housekeeping in exchange for $10 gift certificate. Hopefully this place represents the future of midpriced, locally flavored, and ecofriendly independent accommodations.

Downtown Clifton Hotel (485 S. Stone Ave., 520/623-3163, https:// downtowntucsonhotel.com, $99) is a perfectly located small independent motel in a lovingly restored 1947 motor lodge on Stone Avenue., near the intersection known as five points. It's close to all of downtown's historic and walkable neighborhoods, and has clean and comfortable rooms with free Wi-Fi, minifridges, microwaves, and smart TVs. The rooms are spacious, old but remodeled with polished concrete floors and brick walls. Guests receive a free meal at the nearby 5 Points Café and Market.

The Catalina Park Inn (309 E. 1st St., 520/792-4541 or 800/792-4885, www. catalinaparkinn.com, $125-195 late Sept.- late May) in the West University Historic District was built in 1927 and has beautiful mixed gardens with many native plants in a private, peaceful walled courtyard. There are six rooms, two of which are detached from the main house and open onto the lush courtyard. This inn is close to the UA campus, downtown, and midtown. Breakfast here is always

an elegant, gourmet affair, and there's Wi-Fi throughout the property. Each individually decorated room has a private bath, cable television, big thick bathrobes, and more. The inn is popular with parents visiting their kids at the nearby University of Arizona; as such, in mid-May during graduation and in early October for Parents Day, they require a three-night minimum stay and raise the rates on their rooms by about $20-30 per night. This is true during Gem Show (first two weeks in Feb.) as well. The inn is closed June 15-September 25.

The enchanting **El Presidio Inn Bed & Breakfast** (297 N. Main Ave., 520/623-6151, www.elpresidiobbinn.com, $142-179), in the Julius Kruttschnitt House, built in 1886 and remodeled over the years in various architectural styles, is one of the city's best small inns. It's located in "Snob Hollow" in the historic El Presidio neighborhood, the same block on which Tucson's wealthy pioneers used to live in their mansions. The inn has a wonderful garden courtyard that is cool, lush, and peaceful, with a babbling fountain, cobblestone walkways, and shade-casting trees. The inn has four rooms, two of which—the Carriage House and the Gate House—open onto the courtyard and have kitchenettes. **The Royal Elizabeth Bed and Breakfast Inn** (204 S. Scott Ave., 877/670-9022, www. royalelizabeth.com, $169-325) is also in a historic home, this one known as the Blenman House, built in 1878 in Tucson's El Presidio district. There are six large rooms to choose from, all elegantly decorated in an old-world style, with big, sweeping beds and footed stand-alone bathtubs. There's also a pool, hot tub, and gorgeous gardens. They only allow kids over 13 years old, and they don't allow pets or smoking. There is a two-night minimum stay October-May.

MIDTOWN
$100-250

A charming Spanish Revival B&B in midtown's quiet, tree-lined Sam Hughes neighborhood, the **Sam Hughes Inn Bed and**

1: Hotel Congress 2: Hotel McCoy

Breakfast (2020 E. 7th St., 520/861-2191, www.samhughesinn.com, $90-145) is within walking distance to the University of Arizona and close to downtown and midtown. The inn has four distinctively decorated rooms with free wireless Internet and private bathrooms. The enclosed courtyard out back is something to see: green, cool, and perfect for relaxing and watching the sun dip away.

Originally built in 1931, **The Lodge on the Desert** (306 N. Alvernon Way, 520/325-3366, www.lodgeonthedesert.com, $179-199) has a beautiful and stylish lobby and restaurant on top of its great hacienda-style rooms offering free wireless Internet, comfortable beds, and big, cushy bathrobes. The grounds are green and private, and the patio lounge is one of the best in the city.

Over $250

The historic ★ **Arizona Inn** (2200 E. Elm St., 520/325-1541, www.arizonainn.com, $329-359), a boutique hotel in central midtown founded in the 1930s by Arizona's first-ever congresswoman and still owned and operated by the same family, is the best place to stay in Tucson—as long as you have fairly deep pockets. It offers several different kinds of rooms, all of them decorated in the inimitable 1930s Southwestern style. The grounds and lobby have a lot of charm—there's a 60-foot pool, old-school tennis courts, and all kinds of little quiet corners in the verdant, retreatlike setting behind high pink walls.

WEST OF DOWNTOWN

If you want to stay out in the desert west of downtown Tucson, near Saguaro National Park and The Sonoran Desert Museum, try ★ **Cat Mountain Lodge and Roadside Inn** (2727 S. Kinney Rd., 520/578-6085, http://catmountainlodge, $218-298), an enchanting desert oasis with both lodge and roadside motel rooms (including rooms named after and inspired by icons Frida Kahlo and Diego Rivera). The tasteful and regionally decorated rooms include free Wi-Fi and minifridges, and come with free breakfast or lunch at the nearby Coyote Pause Café. Many rooms open onto a shady and peaceful courtyard, and an on-site observatory offers star tours for an extra fee. Striving to be sustainable and eco-friendly, the owners built the lodge using the latest green materials and repurposed an old, neglected structure to build the roadside inn. They have also installed tanks on the property for rainwater harvesting, use their gray water for landscaping, purchase recycled products, and the lodge is Certified Green under the Arizona Hotel & Lodging Association's Green Lodging Program. Don't forget to introduce yourself to the resident desert tortoise, Juan Wayne.

FOOTHILLS
Resorts

Visitors and émigrés have sought healing in Southern Arizona since at least the early 19th century. Any tubercular patient lucky enough to flee the crowded, disease-ridden tenements of the Northeast or the malarial bottomlands of the South was invariably advised to seek the high and dry air of the Southwest. Nineteenth-century medicine being what it was, physicians had little else but this general, somewhat specious advice to offer the scores of Americans who suffered from TB, fevers, dysentery, and other ailments of the chest and the blood.

Scholar Billy Jones, in his book *Health-Seekers in the Southwest 1817-1900*, estimates that some 20-25 percent of those who moved to the Southwest during the great migrations of the 19th and 20th centuries did so hoping to cure some ailment, creating a "Health Frontier" that, in Tucson, resulted in the haphazard construction of vast tent cities on the outskirts of town populated by consumptives and often destitute folk not long for the world.

Medical science has since cured most of the diseases that once brought sickly travelers to the desert, but that hasn't stopped today's visitors from seeking health of a different breed. Tucson has long rivaled its ritzy northern neighbors Scottsdale and Sedona as a place where the afflicted, both physically and psychically, can find solace—usually very expensive solace. The high season at most resorts in Tucson lasts from around late September-to late May or early June. During the hot summer months many resorts drop their prices precipitously. However, in this season you may find the service standards somewhat lowered, the staff slightly lackadaisical, and even some amenities and features shut down. And you will not want to do much outdoors after about 10am.

★ **Miraval, Life in Balance Resort & Spa** (5000 E. Via Estancia Miraval, Catalina, 520/825-4000 or 800/232-3969, www.miravalresorts.com, $579-1,300) is a secret and magical desert hideaway, a place where everybody loves and wants to help you get fit, well, happy, and tuned in. The Catalinas tower over 400 acres of bushy desert and elegant, sustainable buildings with rooms and suites featuring beehive fireplaces and private patios. There are myriad quiet spaces made by nature for meditation, yoga, and spiritual contemplation, and you'll eat nothing but gourmet food made with organic ingredients grown on the property. During the last 15 years this once-in-a-lifetime retreat has drastically reduced its impact on the desert by using sustainable materials both new and ancient, including rammed earth and adobe walls. The water heaters are solar, and an on-site treatment facility allows Miraval to reuse about 99 percent of its water. To further conserve water, guests get a reusable water bottle to refill at fountains around the resort.

Perhaps Tucson's most famous resort, **Canyon Ranch** (8600 E. Rockcliff Rd., 520/749-9000 or 800/742-9000, www.canyonranch.com, $1,100 and up pp per night) is not mere resort. It's more of a life-affirming pleasure dome out of which you're meant to emerge changed for the better. Here you can not only pamper yourself silly with spa treatments (an activity sure to lead to optimum, albeit temporary, good health) but also schedule appointments with a staff nutritionist, spiritual guide, acupuncturist, and physician. A personal trainer will work with you on keeping in shape in the long term, while a meditation class will help you get in tune with your spirituality. After one of your three gourmet (but healthy) meals a day, you can attend lectures and classes and retreats on various topics in healthful living. For an experience so potentially meaningful, it's not surprising that you're going to have to spend accordingly.

Founded in 1929 and displaying the elegant Spanish Colonial architecture of a more civilized age, ★ **Hacienda del Sol Guest Ranch Resort** (5601 N. Hacienda del Sol Rd., 520/299-1501 or 800/728-6514, www.haciendadelsol.com, $200-416) reflects more than any other local accommodations (save perhaps the Arizona Inn) the beauty and rustic chic of the high-style Southwest of yesteryear. Each distinctive room comes with custom-made furniture and a story all its own. There's even a "Tracy-Hepburn Casita," with two bedrooms, two bathrooms, and a kitchen, where Spencer Tracy and Katharine Hepburn used to stay. The small, comparatively inexpensive Historic Rooms look out on the enchanting and lush courtyard, and there are two inviting outdoor pools and hot tubs that look out over the bushy desert toward the looming Santa Catalina Mountains. Like its younger foothills neighbors, this resort has a full-service spa, riding stables, and an excellent restaurant and patio bar.

One of the best things about **Loews Ventana Canyon Resort** (7000 N. Resort Dr., 520/299-2020 or 800/234-5117, www.loewshotels.com, $136-429) is its view—anywhere you stand on the grounds you get a long, clear look beyond the sweeping golf course off to the valley below. With a fabulous restaurant, a top-notch spa, tennis courts, hiking trails, and one of the most scenic golf courses in the Southwest, it's no wonder this world-renowned hotel and spa was rated number 31 of the top 100 golf resorts in the nation by *Condé Nast* magazine. The resort also has a popular stargazing program and a desert setting you won't soon forget. Ventana Canyon is Certified Green under the Arizona Hotel & Lodging Association's Green Lodging Program.

Guests of **The Westin La Paloma Resort & Spa** (800 E. Sunrise Dr., 800/937-8461, www.westinlapalomaresort.com, $195-279) are allowed to use the facilities of the nearby country club, which has a 27-hole Jack Nicklaus-designed golf course. The rooms here are spacious and have private patios looking out over the desert, huge sink-in beds, and some have fireplaces and sunken spa tubs. The resort's **Elizabeth Arden Red Door Spa** will pamper you after a few sets on one of 10 championship tennis courts. There are also indoor racquetball courts, a huge pool area, Pilates and yoga studios, and an exercise room. La Paloma is Certified Green under the

Arizona Hotel & Lodging Association's Green Lodging Program.

First built as a private home in 1912, the hacienda-style **Westward Look Resort** (245 E. Ina Rd., 520/297-1151 or 800/722-2500, www.westwardlook.com, $329-344) has Southwestern charm to spare. Though it has been built up and remodeled over time, the older, adobe portions still have the exposed vigas made from wood brought down from Mount Lemmon. The 241 guest rooms and suites have all the usual high-end luxuries, and the resort offers horseback riding, tennis, spa treatments, and 80 acres of desert foothills grounds with nature trails, stargazing programs, and exhibits about the desert's natural history and native peoples. Westward Look is Certified Green under the Arizona Hotel & Lodging Association's Green Lodging Program.

Loews Ventana Canyon Resort

Information and Services

VISITORS CENTER
Near the University of Arizona's Main Gate area, the **Tucson Visitor Center** (811 N. Euclid and University Blvd., 800/638-8350, www.visittucson.org, 8am-5pm Mon.-Fri., 9am-4pm Sat.-Sun.) has advice, maps, brochures, and other resources for tourists and travelers.

FOREST CONTACTS
Most of the public lands around Tucson and Southern Arizona are administered by the **Coronado National Forest.** The main office in Tucson (300 W. Congress St., 520/388-8300, www.fs.usda.gov/coronado, 8am-4:30pm Mon.-Fri.) can direct you to a specific field office.

The **Bureau of Land Management** (12661 E. Broadway, 520/258-7200, www.az.blm.gov, 8am-4pm Mon.-Fri.) controls much of the public land that is not within the national forest.

If you have any trouble with wild animals or need to report a poaching incident, call the **Arizona Game and Fish Department** (555 N. Greasewood Rd., 520/628-5376, www.azgfd.gov, 8am-5pm Mon.-Fri.).

HOSPITALS
Dial 911 for emergencies anywhere in Southern Arizona. **University Medical Center** (1501 N. Campbell Ave., 520/694-0111) has the region's only Level 1 trauma center, so if you are seriously hurt anywhere in Southern Arizona, you are likely to be treated by the capable staff there.

MEDIA
The morning daily newspaper *The Arizona Daily Star* (www.azstarnet.com) has a local focus but isn't provincial by any means. The weekly alternative tabloid *Tucson Weekly* (www.tucsonweekly.com) is the place to go for news on arts, entertainment, politics, and local news. You'll find it free throughout the city.

Transportation

AIR
Tucson International Airport (TUS, 7250 S. Tucson Blvd., 520/573-8100, www.flytucson.com) hosts six airlines (including American, Delta, Southwest, and Alaska Airlines) flying to 18 destinations. It's a small but efficient airport, with free wireless Internet and daily nonstop flights to Atlanta, Chicago, Minneapolis, Houston, Albuquerque, Denver, Salt Lake, Vegas, Seattle, San Francisco, L.A., and San Diego. If you're coming in from or headed to a city not on this list, it's likely you'll stop first at the state's major airport, **Sky Harbor International Airport,** in Phoenix, and then desert-hop, as it were, for about 45 minutes south (probably after waiting more than an hour or so at the terminal). If you find yourself at Sky Harbor and don't feel like boarding an absurdly short flight, you can rent a car there and make the easy 1.5-hour drive down I-10 across the desert—though the scenery along the I-10 is certainly not representative of what you're in for when you get to Tucson. Or, you can call **Arizona Shuttle Service** (520/795-6771 or 520/795-6775, www.arizonashuttle.com, $43 one-way), which offers many daily trips between Phoenix and Tucson.

CAR
A car is necessary to truly visit Tucson the way it deserves to be visited. To get out into the

desert you need your own vehicle, though it need not be a four-wheel drive.

The main national route to and from Tucson is I-10, which acts as a kind of in-town freeway as well. Tucson is rather isolated from the east-west route to the north, I-40. It's a four-hour, 263-mile drive from Tucson to Flagstaff, which is along I-40 and one of the best gateway cities for a visit to the Grand Canyon. Phoenix is just 100 miles or so up I-10, a drive of about two hours. The Old Pueblo is connected to its former owner, Mexico, via I-17, a straight one-hour shot (70 miles) south through the beautiful Santa Cruz Valley.

Car Rental

If you're flying into Tucson and don't have friends or relatives to chauffeur you around the typically sprawling Southwestern city, you'll need to rent a car. The airport has several counters from which to choose. For a local option, try **A.P.S. Auto Rental** (3747 E. Speedway Blvd., 520/750-9776, www.tucsonautorental.com, 9am-5pm Mon.-Sat.), which rents used but well-maintained compacts, sedans, SUVs, and passenger vans. The lot is about 10 miles, or 20 minutes, from the airport.

LONG-DISTANCE BUS

For bus service from Tucson to all points on the map, there's the **Greyhound Bus Station** (801 E. 12th St. near Broadway and Euclid, 520/792-3475, www.greyhound.com).

TRAIN

The **Amtrak Station** (400 N. Toole Ave., 520/623-4442, www.amtrak.com) downtown is served by the *Sunset Limited* and *Texas Eagle* lines.

PUBLIC TRANSPORTATION

Bus

The city of Tucson operates the **Sun Tran** (4220 S. Park Ave., 520/623-4301, www.suntran.com) bus line. It has stops all over the

Old Pueblo and operates 6am-7pm weekdays and 8am-5pm weekends. Full fare is $1.25, with children under five riding free.

Modern Streetcar

The **Sun Link Modern Streetcar** (www.sunlinkstreetcar.com, 7am-10pm Mon.-Wed., 7am-2am Thurs.-Fri., 8am-2am Sat., 8am-8pm Sun., $1.50 one-way, 24-hour pass $4) is a sleek light-rail system that traverses several city-center neighborhoods. It has transformed the Old Pueblo's downtown and entertainment districts since it opened in summer 2014.

The railcars shoot through the streets of downtown, 4th Avenue, Main Gate Square near the University of Arizona, and all the way to the Mercado District west of I-10— connecting all of the neighborhoods to each other. The seven streetcars, each with a 180-passenger capacity, run the route every 10-15 minutes in daytime and every 20 minutes in evening, making 17 stops along the way.

Cab and Shuttle

Cab rides can get expensive in Tucson because everything is so spread out. Expect to spend about $20 for a ride from midtown to restaurants and bars downtown or on 4th Avenue. **Uber** and **Lyft** also operate in Tucson and may be cheaper.

Cool Cabs (520/308-1536, www.thecoolcab.com) operates locally and provides rides to and from the airport for a fair price. You can reserve a ride on its website or call them. Also try **Yellow Cabs** (520/300-0000, www.yellowcabaz.com), which also accepts reservations or calls. Expect to pay about $30-40 depending on where you're headed in town. Unless you're staying near the airport, the ride will be at least 10-15 miles and take 20-30 minutes.

Arizona Shuttle Service/Groom Transportation (520/795-6771 or 520/795-6775, www.arizonashuttle.com, $43) offers 18 daily trips between Tucson International Airport and Phoenix's Sky Harbor International Airport.

Santa Cruz Valley

Heading south out of Tucson on I-19 you enter the Santa Cruz Valley, a storied landscape through which the Spanish took some of their first steps into the vast north.

This is the land of the trailblazing Father Eusebio Kino, who in the later 1600s traveled through Pimeria Alta, the "land of the upper Pima," as the Spanish called this region, referring to one of the many native populations that called the valley home for eons before Europeans arrived. The Tohono O'odham, formerly called the Papago, live here; their San Xavier Indian Reservation stretches out west of the interstate. Kino, a Jesuit with a penchant for roughing it, founded several missions in Pimeria Alta, two of which, on the Arizona side of the border, still stand and still hold masses. One of the oldest continually inhabited villages in North America can be found at Tubac, now an artist colony and tourist stop where they celebrate the legacy of the Basque adventurer Juan Bautista de Anza the younger, who attempted to tame the valley and its hostile Apaches and eventually led the expedition west that established San Francisco, California.

The valley has always been a ranching area, even during Kino's time, and after the Gadsden Purchase several Anglo ranches were established and thrived for generations. Much of the former ranchland has been sold to establish conservation areas and wildlife refuges in this rare ecosystem. During the Cold War, intercontinental ballistic missiles (ICBMs) were cocked and ready in underground missile silos throughout the valley, an era celebrated with a museum. The area has also long been home to large open-pit copper mines, and the towering tailings piles rise like ziggurats to the west of the retirement community of Green Valley. And in Ambos Nogales—the name meaning, roughly, "both Nogaleses"—you'll witness the teeming U.S.-Mexico border region in all its fascinating chaos.

The Santa Rita Mountains to the east attract subtropical birds on the move from Mexico and points farther south to their sky island heights, a fact that in turn attracts birding enthusiasts from around the world. You can hike to the top of 9,453-foot Mount Wrightson and see the whole world on a clear day, or stay in one of Madera Canyon's small lodges and take a tour of an observatory where scientists are trying to discover the beginnings of the universe.

GREEN VALLEY AND SAHUARITA

Sahuarita is a bedroom community about 15 miles south of Tucson, the site of the largest pecan-growing operation in the world. Green Valley is one of Arizona's best retirement communities, home to about 25,000 year-round residents and many more part-time snowbirds from the frozen north. Together the two towns make up a relatively large population center between the dry Santa Cruz River to the east and the copper mines to the west.

Asarco Mineral Discovery Center

Take Exit 80 off I-19 and drive west of the casino to reach the **Asarco Mineral Discovery Center** (1421 W. Pima Mine Rd., Sahuarita, 520/625-8233, www.mineraldiscovery.com, 9am-3pm Tues.-Sat., exhibitions free, mine tour $9 adults, $6 children 5-12). This illuminating sight, using exhibits, old mining equipment, and films, explains how all the huge piles of dirt flanking the valley's west side got there.

The copper in the Santa Cruz Valley takes a lot of earth-moving to get at; a one-hour bus tour will take you up into the hills to the sprawling Mission Mine to show you how it's done. From the bus you'll see the vast pit and the postapocalyptic landscape created by large-scale copper mining, and you'll drive

Santa Cruz Valley

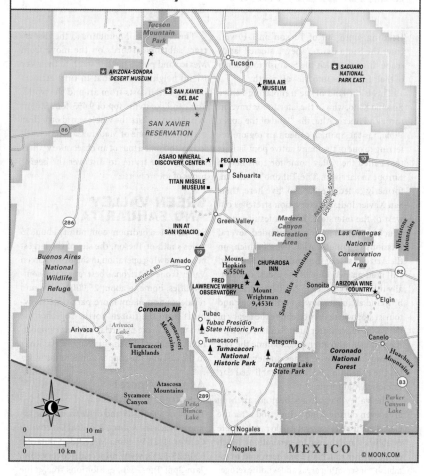

© MOON.COM

through a working mill. Back at the Discovery Center, a gift shop sells souvenirs. Call ahead to make sure the tour is being offered; it runs Saturdays only in summer.

Titan Missile Museum

This deactivated missile site, one of several missile facilities staffed with underground-dwelling cold warriors in what was once referred to as the Titan Valley, had its Titan II aimed squarely at the USSR from 1963 to 1982. The site was decommissioned in 1986 and became a National Historic Landmark in 1994.

The one-hour tour of the **Titan Missile Museum** (1580 W. Duval Mine Rd., Sahuarita, 520/625-7736, www.titanmissilemuseum.org, 8:45am-5pm daily, $10.50 adults, $7 children 5-12) takes you deep underground, and volunteer guides, some of them former crew members, explain what daily life was like for workers at the silo. The highlight of the tour for many is seeing an actual Titan II still waiting there in the launch duct. Guides also simulate the launch sequence that crew members hoped they would never have to complete. The visitors center provides context with a Cold War timeline and artifacts from the era, and a gift shop sells souvenirs and books.

Shopping

Drive east on Sahuarita Road past the pecan groves—roll down your windows and feel how much cooler the trees make the air—and you'll come to the **Pecan Store** (1625 E. Sahuarita Rd., Sahuarita, 520/791-2062 or 800/327-3226, www.pecanstore.com, 9am-5pm Mon.-Sat.), an outlet of Farmers Investment Corp., which operates one of the largest pecan-growing and packaging operations in the world (some 400,000 trees on 5,000 acres) and sells, of course, pecans and pecan accessories.

SANTA RITA MOUNTAINS

Black bears, mountain lions, ring-tailed cats, deer, and too many birds to count call this sky island range home, where mining and logging once were legitimate pursuits but now outdoor recreation rules. The range's highest peak is 9,453-foot Mount Wrightson. Most visitors to the Santa Ritas head to Madera Canyon and its trails to the peak's summit.

Madera Canyon

Madera Canyon is the part-time home to many subtropical bird species that stop off on their migrations north to mate along a cool mountain creek in conditions not dissimilar from more tropical climes to the south. Consequently, the canyon is a kind of mecca for serious birders fulfilling their life lists. It is one of a very few places in North America one can see the fat green-and-red elegant trogon, a relative of the quetzal and the source of much thrill and consternation for birders visiting from points far away. The great variety of hummingbird species flitting about the canyon also draws visitors from far and wide.

A paved two-lane road leads from the desert floor up to about 6,000 feet, where well-used and relatively steep trails climb the slopes of **Mount Wrightson** all the way to its bare and rocky 9,453-foot peak. The most popular trail to the top is the 10.8-mile round-trip **Old Baldy Trail,** which is fairly steep but much shorter than the more gradual, 16-mile round-trip **Super Trail.** Both trails are well marked, heavily used, and start near the Mount Wrightson Picnic Area at the top of the canyon. Both trails also take you over **Josephine Saddle,** at about 7,000 feet, and **Baldy Saddle,** not far below the peak at more than 8,000 feet, which make good places to stop and rest. At Josephine Saddle make sure to look at the makeshift memorial to a group of Boy Scouts who got caught in a snowstorm on the mountain in the 1950s and never returned. If you're coming up the Super Trail, stop and rest at Sprung Spring just before you reach the saddle, which has delicious mountain water trickling from a spigot.

To see the lushness that a little trickling water can inspire, hit the 5.8-mile **Bog Spring-Kent Spring Loop,** which leads over some old mining roads in the lower reaches of the canyon onto some fairly steep and skinny trails along a windswept ridge, providing some pretty spectacular views of the valley below. The trail eventually leads deep into the forest, where sycamores thrive on the edges of green and spongy clearings. Also try the 4.4-mile one-way **Nature Trail,** a fairly steep but relatively easy way to see the entire canyon, from the desert grasslands at its entrance at the **Proctor Parking Area,** where you can pick up the trail, all the way up to the woodlands at the top. Small signs along the way point out notable flora and fauna, and the highest point on the trail, high above the canyon floor, offers a unique perspective.

The average summertime temperature in the canyon is about 85°F, 15-20°F cooler on any given summer day than it is down in the valley. It gets cold in the high country October-April, and it regularly snows up there in deep winter. Madera Canyon is an extremely popular day-use area and hiking destination for Tucson and Santa Cruz Valley residents, so expect to see quite a few people on the trails and using the three developed picnic areas, all of which have tables, bathrooms, and charcoal grills. You can pick up a trail map at any of the lodges in the canyon, or you can get one at the welcome station at the canyon's entrance, but it is staffed irregularly. There's a $5 per car user fee, or you can purchase a $20 annual pass.

Mount Hopkins Fred Lawrence Whipple Observatory

The Smithsonian Institution operates the **Fred Lawrence Whipple Observatory** atop 8,550-foot Mount Hopkins, where astronomers take advantage of the dark Southern Arizona sky to scan space for very faint objects. The **MMT**, the largest single-mirror telescope in North America, is one of four you can see up close during a six-hour tour of the facility (Mon., Wed., and Fri. mid-Mar.-Nov., $10 adults, $5 children 6-12, no children under 6). It's a good idea to make reservations far in advance. The **visitors center** (520/670-5707, www.cfa.harvard.edu, 8:30am-4:30pm Mon.-Fri.) near Amado has displays about the work being done on the mountain and the history of the telescope.

Accommodations and Camping

Madera Canyon used to be dotted with summer homes and getaway cabins, but beginning in the 1970s the U.S. Forest Service tore them down and converted the treasured ecosystem into a federal recreation area. Now only a scattered few homes remain on historic mining claims. Three of the lasting structures are lodges that welcome visitors year-round. As you're driving up the canyon's only road, first you come upon the **Santa Rita Lodge** (520/625-8746, www. santaritalodge.com, $125-205), offering several casitas and freestanding cabins with private decks. The lodge, the oldest in the canyon, has beautiful grounds along Madera Creek, where feeders attract birds and there are benches for viewing. There's also a gift shop, but no food, so bring your own or plan to eat in Green Valley about 12 miles away. March through May the lodge can fix you up with an experienced birding guide by appointment. Tours start early and last about four hours ($20 pp).

Next you'll see the A-frame **Madera Kubo** (520/625-2908, www.maderakubo. com, $145-160), which has four cozy cabins and a gift shop but no food. Near the top of the canyon is the ★ **Chuparosa Inn** (520/393-7370, www.chuparosainn.com, $200-275, two night minimum), with four beautiful rooms, a great bird-watching area, a barbecue, and friendly hosts. The Chuparosa serves a hearty continental breakfast, but you're on your own for lunch and dinner. If you prefer to rough it, the **Bog Springs Campground** (turn left off Madera Canyon Rd. at sign, 520/281-2296, www.fs.usda.gov/coronado, $10) has campsites year-round on a first-come, first-served basis.

Information

The area is managed by the **Coronado National Forest Nogales Ranger District** (303 Old Tucson Rd., Nogales, 520/281-2296, 8am-4:30pm Mon.-Fri.). The forest's main office in Tucson has information on this area as well. From I-19, exit at Ruby Road, then turn east.

BUENOS AIRES WILDLIFE REFUGE

This remote 118,000-acre refuge preserves large swaths of endangered semidesert grassland, home to the pronghorn. The refuge's flagship program was once the reintroduction of the rare masked bobwhite quail to the grasslands, but the program was transferred to a private organization in 2007. Its proximity to the U.S.-Mexico border has caused some

---

1: standing at the peak of Mount Wrightson
2: Tumacacori National Historic Park

trouble on the refuge, and portions are indefinitely closed to the public because of smuggling activity.

One the most accessible portions of the refuge is the **Arivaca Cienega,** a swamplike desert wetland just outside the tiny village of **Arivaca.** The easy two-mile loop trail includes boardwalks over the wetter portions, and birds, frogs, and snakes abound. Take Arivaca Road about 20 miles from Exit 48 off I-19 until you see the sign for the Cienega, just east of Arivaca. At the western end of town, turn at the Y and drive 2.5 miles to Arivaca Creek, also managed by the refuge, where there's easy creekside hiking among cottonwood and mesquite. Far off to the northwest in the Baboquivari Mountains is Brown Canyon, a riparian area accessible only with a guide and by appointment.

To get to **refuge headquarters** (520/823-4251, www.fws.gov, 7:30am-4pm Mon.-Fri. June-mid-Aug., 7:30am-4pm daily mid-Aug.-May), go through Arivaca to Highway 286, head south four miles, and then turn left at milepost 7.5. There's also a satellite office that's open intermittently in downtown Arivaca next to the mercantile.

TUBAC AND TUMACACORI

These two villages along the Santa Cruz River are steeped in the history of the Spanish expeditions in Pimeria Alta. Padre Kino established the mission at Tumacacori in 1691, and Tubac, a Piman village, became a mission farm and ranch. By the 1730s Spanish colonists had arrived from the south to farm and ranch the fertile river valley. In 1751 the violent Piman revolt convinced the Spanish crown to establish the Presidio San Ignacio de Tubac, which was founded the next year. The famous Basque Juan Bautista de Anza II was the second commander of the presidio, and in 1776 he led the first of two overland journeys to establish a fort at San Francisco, California, taking along about 60 colonists from Tubac. In 1860 silver strikes nearby briefly made Tubac the largest town

in the Arizona Territory. It eventually fell into obscurity but was discovered again as an artist colony during the second half of the 20th century, and today its many galleries and shops are a draw for tourists and locals alike.

Crowds flock to Tubac during the week-long **Tubac Festival of the Arts** in February, during which artisans and artists from around the country set up booths. Music and the smell of greasy, delicious food fill the village.

Tubac Presidio State Historic Park

Arizona's first state park, founded in 1959, **Tubac Presidio State Historic Park** (520/398-2252, http://azstateparks.com, 9am-5pm daily, $5 adults, $2 children 7-13) preserves the history and foundations of the Presidio San Ignacio de Tubac. You can see the fort's original foundation and peruse a museum that explains what life was like for the natives, settlers, and soldiers. Guided tours and hands-on interpretation programs are available on request. The park's annual **Anza Days** celebration around the third week of October honors the fort's most famous commander with historical recreations, music, and food. The Tubaquenos, a historical reenactment society, put on living history demonstrations at the park 1pm-4pm Sunday, October-March.

Tumacacori National Historic Park

Padre Kino founded **Mission San Jose de Tumacacori** in 1691, and much of it still stands today on 310-acre **Tumacacori National Historic Park** (three miles south of Tubac on the eastside Frontage Rd., 520/398-2341, www.nps.gov/tuma, 9am-5pm daily, $5 adults over 16). You can explore the mission and its grounds, which include an old graveyard, an orchard, and a recreated Piman shelter. A museum tells the history of the mission and Pimeria Alta, and most days you can buy tortillas and refried beans made right before your eyes in the traditional fashion. A gift shop sells a wide assortment of books on local history.

The mission at Tumacacori still holds masses on holidays, but the two other missions protected by the park are mostly in ruins. The ruins of mission **San Cayetano de Calabazas,** normally closed to the public, can be visited on monthly guided tours for $10 per person. Reservations are required (520/398-2341).

Juan Bautista de Anza National Historic Trail

There's a 4.5-mile portion of the **Juan Bautista de Anza National Historic Trail,** the route used to take colonists and their stock animals from northern Mexico to Northern California in 1775-1776 between the presidio and the mission, that makes for an easy and shady riverside hike, though there's often a lot of trash along the route as a result of illegal migration and seasonal flooding of the northward-flowing Santa Cruz River. The route crosses private ranchland, and you're bound to see cattle. It leads from just outside the state park to just outside the national park, or vice versa, and is a route historically used to travel between the two landmarks.

Shopping

Tubac has more than 100 shops and galleries, many of them selling Mexican and South American imports. Pick up an illustrated map of the shopping district at any of the shops or at the visitors center.

Food

Open since 1944 and still run by the same family, **Wisdom's Café** (1931 E. Frontage Rd., Tumacacori, 520/398-2397, www.wisdomscafe.com, noon-3pm and 5pm-8pm Mon.-Sat., $6-17) may be the best restaurant in the Santa Cruz Valley, serving Mexican food from handed-down family recipes. Don't miss the famous fruit burrito for dessert. Head south on Frontage Road toward the mission and look for the big chicken statue out front.

Accommodations

Tubac Golf Resort and Spa (1 Ave. de Otero, Tubac, 520/398-2211, www.tubacgolfresort.com, $259-329) is a historic, upscale resort and golf course with casitas and rooms of various sizes and styles, two restaurants, a pool, a hot tub, and spa treatments. Once part of the sprawling Otero cattle ranch, the hotel and golf course opened on 500 lush acres along the Santa Cruz River in 1959. Bing Crosby was one of the original owners. New owners completed a $40 million restoration of the historic gem in 2007. Check the website for great package deals; prices drop considerably in summer. The **Tubac Country Inn** (12 Burruel St., Tubac, 520/398-3178, www.tubaccountryinn.com, $120-190) is situated right in the heart of the village and offers suites with kitchenettes, TVs, and Wi-Fi.

Tumacacori Highlands

This huge wilderness of semidesert grasslands, rugged mountains, and riparian canyons west of the valley can best be accessed using Ruby Road (I-19 Exit 12) just north of Nogales. West about 11 miles is **Peña Blanca Lake,** where bass and catfish can be lured in but not eaten because of high mercury content. There's a boat ramp and trail around the lake. Branch off on Forest Road 39 for the **White Rock Campground,** which has sites year-round, but no water ($5). Continue another five miles along Forest Road 39 to the trailhead for the **Atascosa Lookout Trail.** The popular, steep trail to the 6,255-foot peak, a six-mile round-trip, takes you to a decommissioned fire lookout which, for a few months in 1968, was manned by writer **Edward Abbey.**

There's a sign pointing to the trailhead for the **Sycamore Canyon Trail** on Forest Road 39 about 10 miles in from Peña Blanca Lake. This trail leads deep into a watered canyon, with steep walls dotted with saguaro, white sycamore trees shading the creekbed, and jagged rocks jutting out from above. It's a five-mile one-way hike to the U.S.-Mexico border, marked by a barbed-wire fence. The trail isn't always well marked, as the creek often overtakes it, and you will certainly have to wade in parts. During the rainy season some sections may be impassable. The canyon is a major corridor for drug smuggling, and you are likely to see a lot of trash and other evidence of the trade.

The Border Region

Anywhere you are in Cochise or Santa Cruz Counties, you're never more than a few miles from Mexico. Small towns like Bisbee and Douglas each have a Mexican twin right across the line, and traffic between the two generally flows pretty easily (though they are fraternal twins; the Mexican-side counterparts are larger and more populous). The easiest way to visit our neighbors to the south for the day is to walk across the border at the Mariposa Port of Entry in Nogales, Arizona, about an hour south on I-19 from Tucson. The Arizona side of what locals call Ambos Nogales (both Nogaleses) is a somewhat sleepy government center and produce-warehousing town with about 20,000 souls, while the sprawling industrial city just across the border has about 300,000 residents. Most visitors stick to the tourist-friendly blocks just beyond the port of entry. A good portion of the nation's produce passes through the port of entry in Nogales, Arizona, as does a large quantity of illegal drugs.

Further west you'll find the desert homeland of the Tohono O'odham, and to the east the grasslands and cottonwood forests of the Mountain Empire.

NOGALES
Nogales, Mexico, Tourist District

Nogales, Sonora, Mexico, is a modern shipping center for factory and produce, but it's also a very popular tourist destination. It's easy to get there: Just walk across the international border in downtown Nogales, Arizona, after parking at one of the many pay lots (about $4 per day) near the port of entry. There's a tourist area of about a square mile just south of the border, with restaurants, curio shops, and, if you want, drugstores. You can drive into Mexico, but the lines of cars driving north into the United States are long and slow. If you need to ride, there are cabs everywhere, and the drivers speak English; they, like everyone else who deals with tourists, accept U.S. dollars.

In recent years more and more merchants in Nogales's tourist district are competing for fewer and fewer tourist dollars, making a slow, fun stroll along the narrow streets and souvenir-crowded shops an impossibility. Everybody puts on the hard sell these days; be prepared to be accosted at every step and begged repeatedly to have a look at this or that shop, all of which contain similar if not identical items. There's lots of leather and silver, Mexican handicrafts, Day of the Dead items, ceramics, Mexican vanilla, and cheap booze, but is it worth putting up with the incessant barking of the increasingly desperate hawkers? Not really. But if you've never been to Mexico before, this is an easy and generally safe way to do so. There are *farmacias,* dentists, and doctor offices on every block, and their services are offered for a fraction of the price of their U.S. counterparts. Most of them have barkers standing outside, calling you to come in and spend your dollars.

Nogales, Arizona

This small town named, like its cross-border sister, for the walnut trees that once thrived in the area, has long been Santa Cruz County's seat. The beautiful old neoclassical, shiny-domed **Santa Cruz County Courthouse** (2150 N. Congress Dr.), built in 1904 out of stone quarried locally, lends it a historic feel that belies the constant comings and goings of a border town. The **Old City Hall** building, built in 1914, now houses the **Pimeria Alta Historical Society** (Grand Ave. and Crawford St., 520/287-4621, 10am-4pm Wed.-Sun., free), with several interesting exhibits and artifacts on the history of the region. The town's historic downtown along **Morley Avenue** has a few stores that were established in the early 1900s and are still being run by descendants of pioneer merchants.

Food

With dozens of authentic Mexican restaurants within an easy walk across the border, don't spend too much time eating on the Arizona side. If you insist, try the steaks and Sonoran-style food at **Las Vigas Steak Ranch** (180 W. Loma St. at Fiesta Market off Arroyo Blvd., 520/287-6641, 10:30am-8:30pm Tues.-Thurs., 10:30am-9:30pm Fri., 9am-9:30pm Sat., 8am-8pm Sun., $19-25) or the excellent Mexican seafood at **Cocina La Ley** (226 W. 3rd St., 520/287-4555, http://cocinalaley.com, 8am-4pm daily, $5-15).

Across the border, the main north-south street is Obregon, two blocks west of the border-crossing station. Popular restaurants include **La Roca** (84010 Plutarco Elias Calles, 520/313-6316, www.larocarestaurant.com; 11am-6pm Mon.-Tues., 11am-midnight Wed., 8am-midnight Thurs.-Sat., and 8am-6pm Sun. June-Oct.; Mon.-Wed. 11am-midnight, Thurs.-Sat. 8am-midnight, and 8am-6pm Sun. Nov.-May; $16-22) east of the railroad tracks in downtown; **El Toro,** a steak house, about two miles south of the border on Lopez Mateos; and **La Palapa,** a no-frills seafood place 1.5 miles south on Lopez Mateos. **The Oasis** has an outdoor balcony overlooking where two main thoroughfares, Lopez Mateos and Obregon, merge; it is reminiscent of Times Square, but much smaller. Sit there, enjoy shrimp in a warm cheese sauce, and watch the traffic. And yes, you can drink the water, but most restaurants will put a bottle of it on your table.

Accommodations

There are several chain hotels in Nogales, Arizona, along Mariposa Road and along Grand Avenue, both major thoroughfares. If you're looking for something special, there's the historic **Hacienda Corona de Guevavi** (348 S. River Rd., 520/287-6503, www.haciendacorona.com, $199-239), a historic inn along the Santa Cruz River that once hosted John Wayne and other stars. The inn features murals by Salvador Corona, a famous artist and bullfighter, and offers B&B-style rooms and stand-alone casitas. It has a swimming pool and offers horseback riding, stargazing, and many other activities.

Information

For visitor information go to the **Nogales-Santa Cruz Chamber of Commerce** (23 W. Kino Park Pl., 520/287-3685, www.nogaleschamber.com, 9am-5pm Mon.-Fri.).

There's a **U.S. Consulate** (Calle San José s/n, Fraccionamiento Los Alamos, Nogales, Sonora, Mex. tel. 631/980-0522, U.S. tel. 844/528-6611, 8am-3pm Mon.-Fri.; after-hours emergencies: Mex. tel. 555/080-2000, U.S. tel. 301/985-8843) in Nogales, Sonora, on Calle San José, about five miles south of the border. If you get in trouble on the weekend, there's a consulate officer who checks the Nogales, Mexico, jail daily—Monday through Friday.

You must have a valid passport or passport card to cross into and out of Mexico.

THE WESTERN DESERT
Tohono O'odham Nation

Southwest of Tucson, the vast desert homeland of the Tohono O'odham stretches out, a hot wasteland where few dare to venture. You can head out to this 4,400-square-mile borderland reservation via Highway 286 west of Tucson, but there isn't much out here except gorgeous, mostly untouched desert. Straddling the border, the reservation is a popular, albeit deadly, corridor for illegal migrants heading north, and dozens die crossing the area every year. Only the O'odham know how to live out here.

KITT PEAK NATIONAL OBSERVATORY

About 90 minutes west of Tucson along Highways 86 and 386 (follow the signs) you'll find another of Southern Arizona's famous observatories. **Kitt Peak National Observatory** (Hwy. 386, 520/318-8726, www.noao.edu, 9am-3:45pm daily, donation) operates 23 telescopes—the world's largest collection—atop the 6,875-foot peak in the reservation's Quinlan Mountains. Docent-led tours are available at 10am, 11:30am, and 1:30pm and last about an hour ($2 adults, $1 children over 6), or you can pick up a pamphlet and take a self-guided tour. The visitors center has exhibits on astronomy and a gift shop selling star- and planet-related items and O'odham baskets. Far off to the south, look for 7,700-foot Baboquivari Peak, the home of I'itoi, the tribe's sacred "elder brother" god.

EVENTS

During the first weekend in February, O'odham cowboys join in the **All Indian Rodeo and Fair,** during which locals set up food booths, play music, march in a parade, dance, and show off and sell their crafts.

FOOD

The reservation capital, Sells, is a small outpost about 58 miles southwest of Tucson on Highway 86. There's a supermarket, a few businesses, offices, and a school. Try the chimichangas and other Mexican, American, and Native American fare at the **Papago Café** (Hwy. 86, 520/383-3510, 8am-9pm Mon.-Fri., $5-10, cash only) along Highway 86.

Continue through the thick desert west on Highway 86 and then north on Highway 85 and you'll hit Ajo, a copper mining community with a few restaurants that's a good place to see the scars strip mining leaves open on the land.

Organ Pipe Cactus National Monument

South of Ajo on Highway 85, past the tiny town of Why, you'll find Organ Pipe Cactus National Monument. This rugged, beautiful monument along the border protects what amounts to pretty much all of the organ pipe cacti in North America, along with many other species of cactus, and is a popular area for seeing spring wildflowers in bloom. The **Kris Eggle Visitor Center** (520/387-6849) is open 8am-5pm daily. There's a **campground** ($12 per night) with 208 sites that offers drinking water but no hookups or facilities. The 21-mile Ajo Mountain Drive, on a twisty dirt road that's usually passable, will take you into the monument's center, where you can see the many-armed cacti up close.

THE MOUNTAIN EMPIRE: PATAGONIA, SONOITA, AND ELGIN

With an average elevation between 4,000 and 5,000 feet and average annual rainfall around 20 inches, the grasslands and creek beds of the "Mountain Empire" on the eastern side of the Santa Rita range are much cooler than Tucson, and the landscape is unlike any other in Arizona. The towns here are tiny, but they serve an increasingly popular tourist spot, so little out-of-the-way inns are plentiful. In Patagonia, the largest town in the area with only about 800 people, there's a yellow train depot in the center of town, built in 1900, and a nearby butterfly garden. A few shops sell unique locally made items and other treasures.

Transportation

There are two ways to get to the grassland seas and cottonwood forests of the Mountain Empire, a historic ranching and mining district between the Santa Rita, Patagonia, Mustang, and Huachuca Mountains. If you're coming from the Santa Cruz Valley, take Highway 82 from Nogales 19 miles northeast to Patagonia and then on to Sonoita, where

Highway 83 branches off north to I-10. If you're coming from Tucson, take I-10 east to Highway 83.

Telles Grotto Shrine

Just southwest of Patagonia along Highway 82, near milepost 15.9, there's shrine built into the rock face of the mountain. It's worth taking a few minutes to climb the steps and take a peek inside, where there will likely be candles burning and messages written to the dead. The shrine was built in the 1940s by the Telles family, whose matriarch vowed she would construct and keep up the shrine if her five boys returned safely from World War II. They did, and the shrine is still in use today.

Patagonia Lake State Park

About seven miles south of Patagonia on Highway 82 is Southern Arizona's largest lake, 2.5-mile-long **Patagonia Lake** (400 Patagonia Lake Rd., 520/287-6965, http:// azstateparks.com, 4am-10pm daily, $15-20 per car), where you can fish for bass, bluegill, and catfish; camp; rent a boat; swim; lie around Boulder Beach; water-ski (though not on weekends); and hike around the 5,000-acre Sonoita Creek State Natural Area. The campground has 72 campsites and 34 hookups ($27 with water and electric, $17-20 boat site), and there are boat launches, restrooms, showers, a dump station, and a camp supply store. In March, crowds head to the park to see the annual Mariachi Festival. From Nogales head 12 miles northeast on Highway 82; then turn left at the sign and drive 4 miles to park entrance.

Patagonia-Sonoita Creek Preserve

The Nature Conservancy protects a Fremont cottonwood-Gooding willow riparian forest—one of the best and last remaining examples of this lush landscape in Arizona—on about 750 acres along perennial Sonoita Creek. A small green paradise, the **Patagonia-Sonoita Creek Preserve** (150 Blue Heaven Rd., Patagonia, 520/394-2400, www.nature.org, 7:30am-4pm Wed.-Sun. Oct.-Mar., 6:30am-4pm Wed.-Sun. Apr.-Sept., $6 pp) has six miles of easy trails leading through the forest, with its 100-foot tall, 130-year-old cottonwoods—the biggest and oldest in the country—and along the creek. The birding here is excellent, and it's not uncommon to see deer, bobcats, toads, and frogs in this verdant preserve. Friendly Conservancy volunteers lead nature walks every Saturday morning at 9am. This is an extremely rare ecosystem, one that was once abundant in Southern Arizona but now has all but disappeared.

Wine Country

With soil and growing conditions often likened to those in Burgundy, France, the Sonoita-Elgin grasslands have become a well-known winemaking region. It's fun to drive through the open landscape sampling wines, but consider taking along a designated driver.

In Sonoita just east of the crossroads on the east side of Highway 82, the **Dos Cabezas Wineworks** (3248 Hwy. 82, 520/841-1193, www.doscabezas.com) is open for tasting 10:30am-4:30pm Thursday-Sunday. The tasting room and gift shop at **Sonoita Vineyards** (290 Elgin-Canelo Rd., 520/455-5893, www.sonoitavineyards.com, 10am-4pm daily) is located three miles south of Elgin. Also along the Elgin Road is **Callaghan Vineyards** (336 Elgin Rd., 520/455-5322, www.callaghanvineyards.com, tasting room 11am-4pm Thurs.-Sun.). The **Village of Elgin Winery** (471 Elgin Rd., 520/455-9309, www.elginwines.com) has tastings 9am-8pm Thursday-Saturday. In April locals turn out in Elgin for the annual **Blessing of the Vine Festival.**

Food and Accommodations

The Velvet Elvis Pizza Co. (292 Naugle Ave., Patagonia, 520/394-2102, 4pm-8:30pm Wed., 11:30am-8pm Thurs.-Sat., 11:30am-8:30pm Sun., $5-25) serves fabulous pizza among interesting pictures of the King and the Virgin. The **Steak Out Restaurant**

& Saloon (junction of Rte. 82 and Rte. 83, Sonoita, 520/455-5205, www.azsteakout. com, 5pm-9pm Mon.-Thurs., 5pm-10pm Fri., 11am-10pm Sat.-Sun., $10-25) has pretty good steaks, ribs, and other hearty favorites.

The Sonoita Inn (3243 Hwy. 82, Sonoita, 520/455-5935, www.sonoitainn.com, $109-149) at the crossroads of Highways 82 and 83 has 18 rooms with Western ambience, all with great views of the grasslands and mountains.

Southeastern Arizona

The small towns in southeastern Arizona offer many sights and attractions, mostly of the Old West variety, and are good bases for exploring the spectacular natural areas around them, mostly of the riparian and mountainous variety.

THE COCHISE TRAIL

Named after the indomitable Apache chief Cochise, who waged war against the United States in the 1860s and 1870s, the region was also home to probably the most famous Apache of them all, the warrior and medicine man Geronimo, who was the last of his kind to surrender to the reservation. Miners, ranchers, outlaws, and even a few gunfighters lived here, too, and their brief reign is still celebrated in touristy Tombstone. But many people come for the vistas, the birds, and the trails that can be found in the accessible Huachuca and Chiricahua mountain ranges.

Transportation

The Cochise Trail and its environs are best traveled by car. If you want to avoid the interstate, a good road trip can be made by heading east out of Tucson on I-10 and then going south on Highway 83, which will take you through the grasslands of the Mountain Empire to the heights of the Coronado National Memorial (on some dirt roads), into the Huachuca Mountains, and then on to the San Pedro River Valley. Exit at Highway 90, Highway 80, or Highway 191 to make loop drives to all the best sights in the area.

Sierra Vista and Fort Huachuca

Much of the war against the Apaches was fought from Fort Huachuca, founded in 1877 in a canyon that had historically served as an escape route for the West's final holdout tribe. Currently the fort is a major center for military intelligence training. Both stories are told at two museums here. The Fort Huachuca Museum (Building 41401, 520/533-5736, 9am-4pm Tues.-Sat., $5 suggested donation) has exhibits about army life on the Southwestern frontier, the famous battles with the Chiricahua Apaches, and the Buffalo Soldiers—African American cavalry whose story is one of the most fascinating of the West. The U.S. Army Intelligence Museum (9am-4pm Tues.-Sat., $5 suggested donation) tells the 200-year story of the army's underrated intelligence corps. The museum is located two doors down from the Fort Huachuca Museum. Check the museum's website or call before visiting to learn about procedures for accessing the base where the museums are located.

The military town of Sierra Vista, though the largest town in the valley, the fort's host, and sitting at the base of the Huachuca Mountains, has little charm in and of itself. There are a lot of well-known U.S. chain hotels and restaurants, and it's close to the southern end of the San Pedro River. It makes a good base if you're planning on spending some quality time in the mountains, but otherwise it's just a drive-through.

1: Kitt Peak National Observatory **2:** Allen Street in Tombstone

The Cochise Trail

© MOON.COM

FOOD AND ACCOMMODATIONS

There is no shortage of chain hotels and restaurants in Sierra Vista, especially along Fry Boulevard, the town's main drag. But if you want to stay in the mountains—and who wouldn't?—there are several bed-and-breakfasts nestled in the range's canyons. The riverside **Casa de San Pedro** (8933 S. Yellow Ln., Hereford, 520/366-1300 or 888/257-2050, www.bedandbirds.com, $175-295) is a territorial-style home with a central courtyard, a pool, a hot tub, and all kinds of activities geared toward birders and nature lovers. **Ramsey Canyon Inn** (29 Ramsey Canyon Rd., Hereford, 520/378-3010, www.

ramseycanyoninn, $135-175) just outside the Ramsey Canyon Preserve, has six rooms named for hummingbird species, delicious breakfasts, and a setting that can't be beat.

INFORMATION

Check out the **Sierra Vista Convention and Visitors Bureau** (1011 N. Coronado Dr., 520/417-6960 or 800/288-3861, http://visit.sierravistaaz.gov, 9am-5pm daily) for information about this area.

Huachuca Mountains

Ranging in elevation from 3,934 feet at the base to 9,455 feet at the top of Miller Peak, the

Huachucas are another of Southern Arizona's signature sky island ranges. You'll see the common transition from semidesert grasslands at the base, up into arid scrub, on to mixed oak forests, and all the way up to cool ponderosa pine forests in the higher reaches. There are dozens of trails in the range, plus rough roads that lead deep into the outback. If you're looking to put together a backpacking or camping adventure, talk to the staff at the **Coronado National Forest Sierra Vista Ranger District** (4070 S. Avenida Saracino, Hereford, 520/378-0311, 8am-4:30pm Mon.-Fri.).

Ramsey Canyon

You'll pass the ranger station as you head up to the 300-acre **Ramsey Canyon Preserve** (27 Ramsey Canyon Rd., 520/378-2785, www.nature.org, 8am-5pm daily Mar.-Oct., 9am-4pm daily Nov.-Feb., $6), an easily accessible, stream-influenced canyon protected by the Nature Conservancy. This is a very popular with area with birders, who come to see the more than 14 species of hummingbird and other avian species that stop over in the cool riparian canyon, fed by babbling Ramsey Creek, protected by high canyon walls, and crowded with sycamores, maples, and columbines.

The upper part of the canyon is within the **Miller Peak Wilderness Area.** Make sure you stop at the Nature Conservancy's visitors center, which has maps, trail guides, books, T-shirts, and helpful, friendly volunteers. It's a good idea to get there early; this area is very popular, and the parking lot only has 23 first-come, first-served spaces. To reach the preserve, take Ramsey Canyon Road west from Highway 92 south of Sierra Vista (six miles south of Fry Blvd.); the preserve is at the end of the road, four miles west of the highway.

Also along Ramsey Canyon Road, before you reach the preserve, you'll find the **Arizona Folklore Preserve** (520/378-6165, www.arizonafolklore.com), a quaint little theater along the creek where Arizona State Balladeer and nationally known folkie Dolan Ellis and others put on acoustic folk concerts at 2pm on Saturdays and Sundays. The shows are popular, so call ahead for a reservation.

Coronado National Memorial

Named in honor of the Spanish conquistador Francisco Vasquez de Coronado, who trudged north in 1540 searching for the Seven Cities of Cibola—which turned out to be nothing more than a few hardscrabble pueblos—this beautiful landscape along the U.S.-Mexico border, on the southern end of the Huachuca Mountains, has a **visitors center** (Coronado Memorial Rd., 5 miles from Hwy. 92, 520/366-5515, www.nps.gov/coro, 9am-5pm daily) with exhibits about its namesake, local history, and natural history. Three miles west of the visitors center there's a scenic overlook at Montezuma Pass, with expansive, windswept views of the San Pedro and San Rafael Valleys and Mexico. You can have a picnic here or hike around on a number of trails leading to and from the lookout, but there's no camping allowed. To get there, go south on Highway 92 about 20 miles to S. Coronado Memorial Drive; then it's 5 miles to the visitors center. (At the visitors center, you can purchase a trail map of the Huachucas for $5.)

San Pedro Riparian National Conservation Area

This 58,000-acre preserve protects some 40 miles of the upper San Pedro River between St. David and the border. There are about 400 species of birds here, 82 mammal species, and 45 reptile and amphibian species, some of which you're likely to see if you stay vigilant and quiet while exploring. Beavers, once plentiful in the now nearly extinct riparian habitats of Southern Arizona, have been reintroduced here. The **Friends of the San Pedro River** have converted a 1930s-era ranch house—in the shade of a beautiful 120-year-old Fremont cottonwood tree—into the **San Pedro House** gift shop and bookstore (9800 Hwy. 90, 520/508-4445, 9:30am-4:30pm daily), where you can pick up information and pamphlets for a self-guided river walk and other trails as well as get advice from the volunteers here. You'll also find the **Murray Springs Clovis Site and Trail,** a kind of stone-age butcher shop frequented by Clovis people 8,000-11,000 years ago. Scientists have dug up the fossils of several huge extinct mammals here, some of which are currently housed at the Museum of Natural History in New York.

★ Kartchner Caverns

Kartchner Caverns (2980 AZ-90, Benson, 520/586-2283 for reservations, 520/586-4100 for information, http://azstateparks. com, 8am-6pm daily, free with tour reservation, $7 per vehicle up to four people, $2 each additional person) were discovered in the early 1970s by two cave-loving University of Arizona students. Gary Tenen and Randy Tufts knew right away that they had shimmied down a sinkhole in the Whetstone Mountains into caving immortality, because the small, wet cave—meaning that it is still forming drip by drip, in a very real sense "alive"—is one of the most spectacular water-on-rock formations of its kind. And yet the explorers managed to keep their find a secret for several years in an effort to protect it from cavers less responsible than themselves. They called it Xanadu, after the great English poet Samuel Taylor Coleridge's famous unfinished poem "Kubla Khan," a name given to the Throne Room's 58-foot main column, which is formed not so much by drips as by torrents of water flowing into the cave over millennia, producing the largest cave column in Arizona.

Eventually Tenen and Tufts told the property owners what they'd found, and the Kartchner family quickly joined those who wanted to see the cave preserved. A pre-tour film in the park's **Discovery Center** tells the whole story and explains what makes this cave unique. There's also an interesting museum and a gift shop; just outside the Discovery Center, a native-plant butterfly garden is worth a stroll.

There are two different tours you can take through the caverns. The **Big Room Tour**

(1.5 hours, $23 adults, $13 children 7-13, no children under 7) is offered only October 15-April 15. During the summer months a large colony of bats returns to the big room, as they have likely done for eons, to give birth to and rear their single pups. The **Rotunda/Throne Room Tour** (1.5 hours, $23 adults, $13 children 7-13) is offered year-round and is more than enough to satisfy even the most discerning spelunker.

Because the cave is still "alive," much is made of its conservation. Visitors are warned repeatedly not to touch any of the formations, and guides are not shy about telling kids to stand back and keep their hands to themselves. The tour information is repetitive if you've just watched the pre-tour movie.

If a tour of the cave isn't enough, the park offers campsites with electric hookups, water, a dump station, and restrooms with showers ($15-50), as well as camping cabins ($35-75).

Benson

The **Horseshoe Café** (154 E. 4th St., Benson, 520/586-3303, 6am-8pm Mon.-Sat., 6am-2pm Sun., $5-15) serves pretty good steaks, burgers, and Mexican favorites—including big, sloppy, and tasty burritos. It's been around since 1938 and is right on Benson's main drag; it's decorated with all kinds of portraits of horses and a few antiques. Author Neil Miller, in his recent history of the nearby caverns, reports that every time Gary Tenen and Randy Tufts would visit their secret cave during the many years they kept the discovery a secret, they'd invariably stop at the Horseshoe for a bite to eat before returning to Tucson. For some reason, nobody in the restaurant seemed to think it was strange that the two spelunkers always came in covered in mud.

TOMBSTONE

Just outside the green and lush Mormon village of St. David, Highway 80 rises onto the dry, scrubby plane where Ed Schieffelin struck silver in 1879, defying the soldiers who'd predicted he'd find only his own tombstone out there.

The town of the same name became one of the largest, rowdiest, and most deceptively sophisticated locales in the Southwest for a time, a place where legends were created daily by overheated journalists and where a 30-second gunfight of dubious legality became a defining frontier myth. These days about 1,600 residents call Tombstone home, many of them retirees or working in some capacity for the town's tourism industry, which attracts visitors, many of them from Europe, year-round.

Boothill Graveyard

Reportedly, many of Tombstone's gunfighters, along with their victims, lie alongside prostitutes, settlers, and obscure passers-through in the hilltop **Boothill Graveyard** (7:30am-6pm daily, donations welcome). You can walk among the more than 300 uniformly bland and refurbished graves and read short messages on some of them that illuminate what death was like on the frontier. It doesn't feel authentic in the least, despite claims to the contrary, but it is free. Boothill is just off Highway 80 at the north end of town.

Allen Street and National Historic District

Closed to cars and lined with wood-plank sidewalks, Western kitsch shops, and even a few genuine historical attractions, Allen Street *is* Tombstone to most. There are several saloons and restaurants here, and faux-gunfighters and saloon girls (some of them with somewhat anachronistic tattoos) mill about next to the working stagecoach replicas of **Old Tombstone Historical Tours** (520/457-3018, http://oldtombstonetours.net, 9am-5pm daily, $10 adults, $5 children). The National Historic District includes several streets off of Allen, including Toughnut, Fremont, and 6th Streets.

Within this historic district you'll find the **Tombstone Epitaph Museum** (5th St., 520/457-2211, 9:30am-5pm daily, free), where you can see the original press used to print the perfectly named *Epitaph,* first published in 1880 and still going, and other printing-related exhibits. The **O.K. Corral and Historama** (Allen St., 520/457-3456, www.ok-corral.com, 9am-5pm daily, $10 with gunfight, $6 without) has all the information you'll need on the famous, albeit short, gunfight between the Earps and Clantons. You can see a historical reenactment of the fight and watch a show on the major events in Tombstone history.

Among the saloons in the district, the **Crystal Palace Saloon** and **Big Nose Kate's Saloon** are worth a look, with Kate's being a fine place to knock back a few and look at all the pictures on the walls if you have the time. Both are on Allen Street. One of the best sights on Allen is the **Bird Cage Theatre** (Allen and 6th Sts., 520/457-3421, 8am-6pm daily, $6 adults, $5 children 8-18), an 1881 dance hall, brothel, saloon, theater, and casino that has been spectacularly preserved. A self-guided tour takes you through the building, which looks much as it did when it closed in 1889. On Fremont and 6th Streets the **Tombstone Western Heritage Museum** (520/457-3800, 9am-5pm Mon.-Sat., 12:30pm-5pm Sun., $5 adults, $3 children 8-18) has many relics of Tombstone's past, including a few personal items once owned by the Earps.

Tombstone Courthouse State Historic Park

A more sober treatment of Tombstone's history is presented inside the preserved 1882 **Tombstone Courthouse** (3rd and Toughnut Sts., 520/457-3311, http://azstateparks.com, 9am-5pm daily, $7 adults, $2 children 7-13). The museum features artifacts, pictures, and ephemera from the territorial days, and there's a rebuilt gallows in the building's courtyard. Particularly interesting are the two nearly forensic accounts of the gunfight, with slightly differing details.

Rose Tree Museum

Planted way back in 1885, this Lady Banks' rose, sent all the way from Scotland to Tombstone as a gift, is believed to be the world's largest rose tree at 8,700 square feet and is listed in the *Guinness Book of Records*. The white blossoms are usually at their best in early April. The small **Rose Tree Museum** (4th and Toughnut Sts., http://tombstonerosetree.com, 11am-5pm Sun.-Fri., 10am-5:30pm Sat., $5) exhibits photos and furniture owned by the tree's planter, who moved to the territory in 1880. There's also an excellent bookstore here with a lot of books about the history of the region.

Festivals and Events

In March, Tombstone celebrates its founder during **Ed Schieffelin Territorial Days.** In April the **Tombstone Rose Tree Festival** shines the light on the record-making rose tree, and in May Tombstone's most famous citizen gets his own party during **Wyatt Earp Days.** The anniversary of that infamous gunfight warrants a celebration every year in October. Contact the **Tombstone Chamber of Commerce** (109 S. 4th St., 520/457-9317, www.tombstonechamber.com, 8am-4:45pm Mon.-Fri.) for more information.

Food

Nellie Cashman Restaurant (5th and Toughnut Sts., 520/457-2212, 7:30am-9pm daily, $3-9), the oldest restaurant in Tombstone, is named for the so-called "angel of the camp" Nellie Cashman, known throughout the mining camps of the American West for her work aiding sick and distressed miners. She opened a hotel and restaurant in Tombstone in 1882. Today the spot serves delicious and filling home-style breakfasts and burgers, sandwiches, and salads for lunch and dinner.

Accommodations

There are a few easy-to-locate chain hotels in Tombstone and a variety of bed-and-breakfasts. The **Tombstone Boarding House B&B** (108 N. 4th St., 520/457-3716 or 877/225-1319, $59-89) offers comfortable rooms in two adobe houses that date to the 1880s.

One of the nicer options in this small town is the **Tombstone Grand Hotel** (580 W. Randolph Way, 855/904-7263, http://tombstonegrand.com, $98-150), which offers clean and comfortable rooms with refrigerators as well as free breakfast and a pool.

Information

Make sure to stop by the **Visitor Information Center** (4th and Allen Sts., 520/457-3929, 10am-4pm daily), where you'll find a nearly overwhelming amount of information about the town and its sights.

TOP EXPERIENCE

★ BISBEE

The most charming town in Cochise County began life in the 1880s as a copper mining camp. Eventually several billion pounds of the useful ore would be taken out of the ground here, and by 1910 Bisbee was said to be the biggest city between the Midwest and West Coast.

Flooding in the 1,000-foot-deep tunnels and the boom-and-bust nature of the mining economy closed the mines by the 1970s, and the town, with its labyrinthine staircases and cozy little bungalows built precariously on the slopes of the Mule Mountains, was nearly moribund when it was discovered by hippies, artists, and artisans, a group that funkified the town into what it is today. Retired miners, retirees from elsewhere, county government workers, and sons and daughters of the pioneers also call Bisbee home. **Old Town Bisbee,** centered around Main Street and Brewery Gulch, is stuffed full of shops, galleries, restaurants, historic landmarks, and some of the best old hotels in the West. Perhaps the most fun to be had in Bisbee comes from just walking around, climbing the scores of off-kilter steps, and exploring its back alleys and narrow streets.

Mining History Sights

Driving in on Highway 80, just after the intersection with Highway 92, you can stop at a turnout along the side of the road and witness the **Lavender Pit Mine** and the huge tailings surrounding the largest open-pit mine in the state, now closed.

Bisbee is still proud of its history as the queen of all mining towns, and you can learn all about it at the **Bisbee Mining and Historical Museum** (Copper Queen Plaza, junction of Main St. and Brewery Gulch, 520/432-7071, www.bisbeemuseum. org, 10am-4pm daily, $8 adults, $3 children 4-16), housed in the building formerly occupied by the headquarters of the Copper Queen Consolidated Mining Company. Now an affiliate of the Smithsonian Institution, the museum has exhibits on local history and culture during territorial days, with an emphasis on the history and science of copper mining.

You can see for yourself what it was like descending into the earth every day to coax the ore out of the mountain on the 75-minute **Queen Mine Tour** (478 N. Dart Rd., 520/432-2071 or 866/432-2071, www. queenminetour.com, 9am, 10:30am, noon, 2pm, and 3:30pm daily, $13 adults, $5.50 children 6-12). Retired miners lead these tours and will regale you with stories of what it was really like underground as you ride deep beneath the earth on an old mine car, wearing a yellow slicker, a hard hat, and a headlamp. It's about 47 degrees in the shaft, so think about taking something warm to wear.

Events

Like most of the old mining towns in Arizona and northern Mexico, much of Old Town Bisbee is perched rather precariously on the sides of a mountain, and the early residents installed steps all over town so folks could reach their homes. These days the steps are more atmospheric than useful; they contribute much to Bisbee's quaint character. Every October strange characters from all over the world gather in Old Town to run up and down these stairs during the **Bisbee 1,000 Stair Climb** (www.bisbee1000.org, $55-100).

You too can join in, but the event fills up fast, so register early.

Shopping

Old Town Bisbee has dozens of unique shops, and there always seem to be new ones opening. There are jewelry stores, shops selling local and Mexican folk art, a bookstore with both new and used books, including a large selection by local authors, and several multilevel antiques and junk shops that you can get lost in for hours.

Food

The best breakfast in town can be found at the **Bisbee Breakfast Club** (75A Erie St., 520/432-5885, www.bisbeebreakfastclub. com, 7am-3pm daily, $10-14), serving huge American-style breakfasts, along with a bit of Mexican spice, of course, in a refurbished old building on the largely abandoned historic block next to the huge pit. You might have to wait to get a table, but the food is worth it.

Santiagos (5 Howell Ave., 520/432-1910, www.santiagosmexican.com, 11am-9pm daily, $10-26), a small, often busy Mexican restaurant in Old Town Bisbee, serves impeccable dishes in a new traditionalist style. Everything here is familiar (ceviche, chiles rellenos, enchiladas, etc.), but it's so well made—the ingredients fresh and local, the sauces soothing and surprising all at once— that you'll swear you never had its like before. They also make a huge, mean margarita.

Be warned: When you visit the **Old Bisbee Brewing Co.** (200 Review Alley, 520/432-2739, www.oldbisbeebrewingcompany.com, noon-10:30pm Mon.-Thurs., noon-11:30pm Fri.-Sat.), which is well situated in Bisbee's old "Brewery Gulch," if it is pleasant out (which it so often is) as you imbibe one or more of the delicious beers brewed on-site, and if you are sitting in the sun on the patio looking out over the quaint old town, you probably aren't going anywhere for a while. The brewery also serves bratwurst and vegetarian chili.

Accommodations

There are all manner of accommodations in Bisbee, and bed-and-breakfasts proliferate along the narrow, twisty roads of Old Town.

The **Bisbee Grand Hotel** (61 Main St., 520/432-5900 or 800/421-1909, www.bisbeegrandhotel.com, $94-175) is in a Victorian building in Old Town. It offers small, well-decorated, themed rooms with private baths, and a full breakfast is served on the veranda. It has wireless Internet and a saloon frequented by tourists and locals. **The Copper Queen Hotel** (11 Howell Ave., 520/432-2216, www.copperqueen.com, $140-200) is an institution in Bisbee, built in 1902 and still in beautiful shape but almost certainly haunted, as anyone in Bisbee will tell you. It has a solar-heated pool, a saloon, and a restaurant.

For a truly unique experience, rent one of the 1950s vintage trailers at **Shady Dell RV Park** (1 Old Douglas Rd. 520/432-3567, www.theshadydell.com, $95-115), each beautifully refurbished and decorated. Many have interiors of polished chrome and wood and include black-and-white TVs and phonographs complete with 45 singles from the era.

The oldest brick building in Bisbee now houses the elegant, friendly, and truly memorable **Letson Loft Hotel** (26 Main St., 520/432-3210, www.letsonlofthotel.com, $125-150). This small boutique hotel in the heart of Old Town offers romantic, high-end, but affordable accommodations in a gorgeously remodeled and tastefully decorated space. All of the rooms have modern amenities and are quiet and cozy, despite being located right in the thick of the action along Bisbee's narrow, shop-lined main drag, onto which some of the rooms look down from on high, giving the dweller a bit of a sense of what the old town was once like in its busy urban heyday.

Information

At the **Bisbee Chamber of Commerce & Visitor Center** (1 Main St., Copper Queen Plaza, 520/432-5421 or 866/224-7233, www.bisbeearizona.com, 9am-5pm Mon.-Fri., 10am-4pm Sat.-Sun.) you'll find brochures on self-guided walking tours and loads of information on what to do and see.

Parking isn't easy, especially on weekends, so it's a good idea to find a space, stick with it, and explore the town on foot.

WILLCOX AND VICINITY

Though the former railroad and ranching town has seen better days, the canyons, mountains, and grasslands around Willcox are worth the 80-mile drive east on I-10 from Tucson. Willcox today has a few boarded-up buildings and abandoned motels along its main thoroughfare, but its historic downtown holds some interest and is worth a mosey. The famous singing cowboy Rex Allen grew up in the area; a museum and an annual festival honor that fact. Willcox is also known as the place where Wyatt's brother, Warren Earp, met with a bullet in 1900, later to be buried in the Historic Willcox Cemetery.

Historic Downtown and Railroad Avenue

This area used to be where life in Willcox happened, and even today it's the most interesting part of town. There's a shady, grassy park with a big bronze statue of native son Rex Allen, and across the street on Railroad Avenue the singing cowboy's life and career are celebrated at the **Rex Allen Arizona Cowboy Museum** (150 N. Railroad Ave., 520/384-4583 or 877/234-4111, www.rexallenmuseum.org, 10am-1pm Mon., 11am-3pm Tues.-Sat., $2), which also displays a **Cowboy Hall of Fame** honoring area ranchers and cowboys. Every Monday the museum features free concerts by local musicians. Just down the sidewalk a bit is the **Willcox Commercial Store,** which claims to be the oldest continually operating store in the state. The **Willcox Rex Allen Theater**

1: Bisbee Grand Hotel **2:** Chiricahua National Monument

(134 N. Railroad Ave., 520/384-4244), a 1935 art deco movie house, still runs new movies daily, and at the end of Railroad Avenue is the **Southern Pacific Depot,** built way back in 1880 and now used by the city of Willcox. The depot's lobby has exhibits on the history of the area and the railroad, and Rex Allen narrates a video played on a loop (8:30am-4:30pm Mon.-Fri.). The small town honors its most famous native with **Rex Allen Days** the first week in October every year.

Just around the corner from Railroad Avenue, the **Chiricahua Regional Museum** (127 E. Maley St., 520/384-3971, 10am-5pm Mon.-Sat., $2 pp, $3 per couple, $5 per family) exhibits mining artifacts, weapons used by Native Americans and the cavalry, and rocks and minerals found in the region. There's also an excellent display on the history of the Chiricahua Apaches.

Apple Annie's Orchard

The Sulphur Springs Valley outside of Willcox has the perfect growing conditions for the apple, peach, pear, and Asian pear orchards at **Apple Annie's Orchard** (2081 N. Hardy Rd., Willcox, 520/384-2084, www.appleannies.com, 8am-5pm daily July 3-Oct.). From July to late October every year people flock to the "U-Pick" farm to pick and purchase fruit by the bucketful. The farm also serves delicious hamburgers and cowboy beans for lunch, and you can buy all kinds of homemade preserves, sauces, condiments, and pies in the farm store. Take I-10 to Exit 340, turn west on Ft. Grant Road, and travel 5.5 miles to the Apple Annie's sign.

Amerind Museum

On your way east on I-10, get off at the Dragoon Exit (318) to visit the **Amerind Museum** (2100 N. Amerind Rd., Dragoon, 520/586-3666, www.amerind.org, 10am-4pm Tues.-Sun., $10 adults, $8 children 10-17), an excellent little museum in beautiful Texas Canyon. Established in 1937, the Amerind Foundation (a contraction of "American" and "Indian") preserves and

studies Native American cultures from prehistory all the way to the Chiricahua Apache and beyond. It is commonly thought to hold one of the best private ethnological collections in the nation. The museum is fascinating, and the location, among the imposing boulders of Texas Canyon, makes it well worth the stop.

Cochise Stronghold

A bit farther east on I-10, Exit 331 takes you to the **Cochise Stronghold,** the former hideout of Cochise and his band in the strange Dragoon Mountains. The great Apache chief is said to be buried somewhere out here, but nobody knows precisely where. As you look around, it seems an ideal place to hide, with plenty of bluffs from which to watch the plains for the oncoming army. There are a few easy trails at the Stronghold, including a short nature trail and a paved history trail with information about the Chiricahua Apache. A few campsites ($10) are sheltered by the same high boulders that once kept the Chiricahua hidden. If you want to hike deeper into the canyon, try the six-mile round-trip Cochise Stronghold Trail that veers off the nature trail. To get there, head southeast on Highway 191 and then west nine miles on Ironwood Road. The last four miles are on a dirt road.

★ Chiricahua National Monument

This place simply has to be seen to believed. Precarious rock spires jut into the sky in this strange, wonderful landscape, called the "Land of Standing Up Rocks" by the Apache. About 38 miles southeast of Willcox (120 miles from Tucson) on Highway 186, the **Chiricahua National Monument** (520/824-3560, www.nps.gov, 8am-4:30pm daily, free) protects one of the most unusual areas in Arizona. There's a visitors center two miles from the monument entrance on Bonita Canyon Road, a paved two-lane road. Drive six gorgeous miles up to **Massai Point** and one of the most spectacular overlooks this side of the Grand Canyon. The visitors center has an excellent free guide with information on all the trails within the monument, and there's a free hikers' shuttle available. You can camp at the Bonita Campground a half mile from the visitors center for $12 per night (no hookups). Bring your own food and water to this special place because none is available for miles in any direction. For information and advice on getting out into the less accessible regions of the Chiricahua range, contact the **Douglas Ranger District** (1192 W. Saddleview Rd., 520/364-3468, 8am-4:30pm Mon.-Fri.), 2.2 miles north of Highway 80 on Highway 191 in Douglas.

Flagstaff, Sedona, and Red Rock Country

Famed Red Rock Country, one of the world's

most celebrated landscapes, is in between Flagstaff, the hub of the northland, and the quaint town of Prescott, with posh Sedona at the center.

The landscape is a red, pink, and green-dotted geologic canvas, with the green bursts of Oak Creek Canyon and the often ignored but gorgeous Verde Valley right nearby. Just to the north is the Mogollon Rim, a 200-mile-long cliff that marks the southern border of the vast plateau. The Rim, as it's called locally, drops 2,000 feet in some places and provides some inspiring views. Those same views inspired the likes of the writer Zane Grey, who called the region home on occasion.

Exploring this region, you'll find a different Arizona, one that most

Highlights

Look for ★ to find recommended sights, activities, dining, and lodging.

★ **Museum of Northern Arizona:** Learn about the plants, animals, geology, and people that make the northlands such a fascinating landscape (page 198).

★ **Sunset Crater Volcano and Wupatki National Monuments:** Explore the foothills of a silent black-rock crater and the 800-year-old red-rock apartment buildings rising from the dry scrublands (page 199).

★ **Walnut Canyon National Monument:** In this enchanting, lush canyon the Sinagua people built limestone-and-clay apartments into the cliffsides (page 201).

★ **Jerome:** This haunted mining town is now a funky mountain getaway, with bed-and-breakfasts, hotels, eclectic restaurants, and one-of-a-kind boutiques (page 225).

★ **Montezuma Castle National Monument:** See the mysterious ruins of the Southern Sinagua culture's high point—a cliff-wall castle molded out of limestone (page 230).

★ **Oak Creek Canyon:** Drive along a shady creekside with red-and-white-rock walls towering on each side, where birds, butterflies, and people flock to the babbling water sliding over pink slickrock (page 245).

★ **Hiking in Red Rock Country:** Find otherworldly scenery and maybe even some inner peace on the high-desert trails around Sedona (page 247).

★ **The Mogollon Rim:** Sit on the very edge of the Colorado Plateau overlooking a deep-green sea of pine treetops, with all of lowland Arizona spread out before you (page 249).

Flagstaff, Sedona, and Red Rock Country

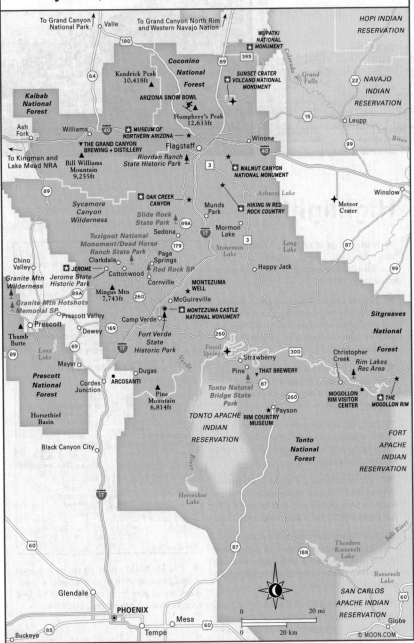

HOPI INDIAN
RESERVATION

To Grand Canyon
National Park   Valle

To Grand Canyon North Rim
and Western Navajo Nation

WUPATKI
NATIONAL
MONUMENT

180

Coconino
National
Forest

64

395

89

SUNSET CRATER
VOLCANO NATIONAL
MONUMENT

Colorado

Grand
Falls

NAVAJO
INDIAN
RESERVATION

22

Kendrick Peak
10,418ft

ARIZONA SNOW BOWL

Kaibab
National
Forest

Ash
Fork

Williams   40

Humphrey's Peak
12,633ft

15

Leupp

MUSEUM OF
NORTHERN ARIZONA

Winona

River

99

THE GRAND CANYON
BREWING + DISTILLERY

Flagstaff

40

To Kingman and
Lake Mead NRA

Bill Williams
Mountain
9,255ft

Riordan Ranch
State Historic Park

3

WALNUT CANYON
NATIONAL MONUMENT

89

Sycamore
Canyon
Wilderness

OAK CREEK
CANYON

Munds
Park

Ashurst Lake

HIKING IN RED
ROCK COUNTRY

Meteor
Crater

Winslow

Slide Rock
State Park

89A

Sedona

Mormon
Lake

3

Chino
Valley

Tuzigoot National
Monument/Dead Horse
Ranch State Park

Clarkdale

Page
Springs

179

Stoneman
Lake

Long
Lake

Happy Jack

87

99

JEROME

Granite Mtn
Wilderness

Jerome State
Historic Park

89A

Cottonwood

Red Rock SP

Cornville

MONTEZUMA
WELL

Granite Mtn Hotshots
Memorial SP

Mingus Mtn
7,743ft

260

McGuireville

Prescott   Camp Verde

MONTEZUMA CASTLE
NATIONAL MONUMENT

Sitgreaves

National

Thumb
Butte

89

Lynx
Lake

Dewey

169

Fort Verde
State
Historic Park

Verde

260

Fossil
Springs

300

Forest

Christopher
Creek

Rim Lakes
Rec Area

Mayer

69

17

Strawberry

Pine

THAT BREWERY

MOGOLLON
RIM VISITOR
CENTER

THE
MOGOLLON RIM

Cordes
Junction

Dugas

ARCOSANTI

Pine
Mountain
6,814ft

Tonto Natural
Bridge State
Park

87

RIM COUNTRY
MUSEUM

Payson

River

TONTO APACHE
INDIAN
RESERVATION

Tonto
National
Forest

FORT
APACHE
INDIAN
RESERVATION

Black Canyon City

Horseshoe
Lake

17

188

Theodore
Roosevelt
Lake

Roosevelt
Lake

60

Glendale

SAN CARLOS
APACHE INDIAN
RESERVATION

PHOENIX

87

Salt River

60

Globe

Buckeye   85

Mesa   60

Tempe

0   20 mi

0   20 km

© MOON.COM

of the clichéd ideas about the state don't account for. Don't miss contemplating the ruins of the Sinagua culture scattered all over this land. And bring your hiking boots, mountain bikes, skis, canoes, kayaks, and tents; this is outdoor country at its best. But there are also cleaner and more comfortable things to do: Sedona, Flagstaff, Prescott, Jerome, and other towns in the region offer unique accommodations and dining as well as a variety of shops and boutiques selling arts and crafts, antiques, and souvenirs of the arid West's high country, once the province of miners and lumberjacks, ranchers and shepherds.

PLANNING YOUR TIME

This region attracts visitors regardless of the season, mostly because, unlike lowland Arizona, it actually has a few seasons. In the summer, the pine forests of the transition zone offer cool respite from the desert: Prescott, the Verde Valley, and Rim Country on average are about 10-20°F cooler than the lower Sonoran region of the state. Flagstaff and, to the east, the White Mountains can seem like another country altogether; in these high places, winter snowfall makes skiing and snow play a popular attraction. In the fall, the turning leaves throughout the region are glorious; the orange and yellow of the scattered deciduous trees look like fire flares among the dominant stands of ponderosa pine.

A comprehensive trip to the region, one touching on all its charms and sights and including backcountry hikes and off-the-track exploring, would take about two weeks. A week would suffice to see everything, indulge your sensual whims, and explore the pinelands, red rocks, and mountaintops a bit.

Flagstaff makes an ideal base for a visit to this region, as it is within a two-hour drive (often less) of all the sights to see and adventures to be had in North-Central Arizona. The quaint town of Prescott is good for a day trip from Flagstaff or Phoenix (it's about two hours each way from both), or a weekend if you're going to explore the pine forests that surround it. Sedona, a popular day trip from Phoenix (two hours each way), is only about an hour's scenic drive from Flagstaff and can be easily done in a long day from either. However, consider staying overnight or over a weekend in Sedona so you can explore the red rocks and riparian canyons. A visit to Payson and Rim Country is best done in a weekend or as a day trip from Phoenix or Flagstaff.

Flagstaff and Vicinity

The San Francisco Peaks, Arizona's tallest mountains and the Olympus of the Hopi kachina, watch over this highland hub, the long-ago waterless home of the Sinagua and the Colorado Plateau's Arizona capital. Cinder rocks from centuries of volcanic activity crunch beneath your feet here. The town's scent is a potpourri of pine sap, wet leaves, and wood smoke mixing with incense, patchouli oil, train smoke, and beer. The redbrick, railroad-era downtown sits at around 7,000 feet, and the whole area from mountains to meadows is covered under about 100 inches of snow every year. In the summer temperatures are mild, in the 70s and 80s mostly, but it gets cold pretty fast from September to December, when, in wet years, the first snow falls. In the deep winter and on into early April, daytime temperatures are cold, and nighttime lows dip well below freezing.

Always a crossroads, Flagstaff is especially so these days, thriving as a tourism gateway to the Grand Canyon, Indian Country, and the Colorado Plateau. It is also a college town attracting students from all over the world and a major pull-off along I-40. Despite all that, it has managed to retain a good bit of its small mountain-town charm and Old West-through-Route 66 character. Its picturesque qualities, combined with its myriad opportunities for outdoor adventuring, make Flagstaff a major northland tourist draw in its own right.

Flagstaff was founded on July 4, 1876, but didn't really get going until the Santa Fe Railroad arrived in the 1880s, establishing the present-day downtown area and allowing for the ranching and lumber industries to exploit the surrounding forests and grasslands. Today Flagstaff is home to about 65,000 residents, and it's surrounded by nearly 2 million acres of the Coconino National Forest. Though tourism and the service industry are the town's major lifelines these days, the railroad is still very much a part of Flagstaff. As many as 80 trains a day chug through the heart of town, dividing it in two and often stopping traffic. The wail of train horns is so ubiquitous that many residents don't even notice it anymore. There's something romantic and evocative about being in a warm bed on a cool, star-bright forest night and hearing the plaintive whine of a westbound train.

SIGHTS
Historic Downtown District

Flagstaff has managed to hold on to many of its historic downtown redbrick buildings and quaint storefronts that served the needs of the railway and its passengers, housed and kept Route 66's argonauts, and marked the social and commercial heart of the town for generations. Its many restaurants, shops, and bars make it an ideal spot for tourists. On the National Register of Historic Places since the 1980s, many of the buildings in the downtown area date from the late 19th and early 20th centuries, including the Babbitt Brothers Building, which was constructed in 1888, and the Coconino County Courthouse, built in 1894. Just across Route 66 from the downtown area is the old Santa Fe Depot, built in the Tudor Revival style in 1926.

Downtown is a pleasant place to be any time of year, and the traveler will find myriad places to eat, drink, and hunt for all manner of artistic and handmade treasures. Take a half a day or so and walk along Humphreys Street, Beaver Street, Leroux Street, San Francisco Street, and Route 66 (also called Santa Fe) across from the train depot, ducking in and out of shops, galleries, watering holes, and eateries. **Heritage Square** (Aspen Ave. between Leroux and San Francisco Sts., 928/853-4292, www.heritagesquaretrust.org) hosts live music, outdoor movies, and arts and crafts fairs on weekends during the warmer months.

Southside Historic District

After exploring downtown, walk south of the tracks, where there are more shops, restaurants, and bars in the Southside Historic District, which is a bit shaggier than downtown and offers a look at Flagstaff's left-of-center scene. It's just south of downtown and bordered by Route 66 and the Santa Fe Railroad, the Rio de Flag, and Northern Arizona University (NAU). The neighborhood was added to the National Register of Historic Places in 2010. Check out the ruins of the **Historic Basque Handball Court** (east side of San Francisco St.) built in 1926 by tourist-home owner Jesus Garcia, who migrated to Flagstaff from Spain in 1912. The building has been wonderfully restored and is now an excellent restaurant and bakery. The ruins of the 40-foot-high sandstone court remain. It's said to be the last such court standing in Arizona and one of only a few in the nation. Route 66 enthusiasts will want to seek out the imaginative mural on a wall along West Phoenix Avenue. The nearby Flagstaff Visitor Center offers a free walking guide to other historic Route 66 sites around downtown and the Southside.

Riordan Mansion State Historic Park

Riordan Mansion State Historic Park (off Milton Rd. at 409 W. Riordan Rd., 928/779-4395, http://azstateparks.com, 9:30am-5pm

Flagstaff

MUSEUM OF NORTHERN ARIZONA

To Arizona Snowbowl, San Francisco Peaks, and Grand Canyon

ARIZONA HISTORICAL SOCIETY'S PIONEER MUSEUM

FORT VALLEY RD

Buffalo Park

McPherson Park

GEMINI DR

CEDAR AVE

FOREST AVE

0   0.5 mi
0   0.5 km

Thorpe Park

FLAGSTAFF MEDICAL CENTER

TURQUOISE DR

ELDEN TRAILS BED & BREAKFAST

LOWELL OBSERVATORY

MARS HILL RD

THORPE

SANTA FE AVE

CHERRY AVE

ELM AVE

HUMPHREYS

SEE DETAIL

SWITZER CANYON DR

To WALNUT CANYON NATIONAL MONUMENT

COTTAGE AVE

E ROUTE 66

BUS 40

BUTLER   AVE

ENTERPRISE RD

I-40 EXIT 198

W ROUTE 66

BUS 40

RIORDAN RD

RIORDAN MANSION STATE HISTORIC PARK

BUSTER'S

NORTHERN ARIZONA UNIVERSITY

WOODLANDS VILLAGE

MILTON RD

KNOLES DR

FOREST MEADOWS ST

McCONNELL CIR

San Francisco ST

McCONNELL DR

To Arboretum at Flagstaff

BEULAH BLVD

I-40 EXIT 195, I-17 EXIT 340

I-40 EXIT 339

LAKE MARY RD

To Sedona   To Phoenix   To Payson

Detail

0   0.1 mi
0   0.1 km

PARK   ST

KENDRICK ST

DATE   ST

ELM   AVE

THE INN AT 410 B&B

ASPEN   AVE

SITGREAVES ST

BIRCH   AVE

Wheeler Park

HUMPHREYS   ST

CHERRY AVE

BEAVER   ST

LEROUX   ST

Heritage Square

HOTEL MONTE VISTA

E RTE 66

WEATHERFORD HOTEL

FLAGSTAFF VISITOR CENTER

CHARLY'S PUB AND GRILL

FLAGSTAFF BREWING COMPANY

AGASSIZ ST

MOTHER ROAD BREWING CO

THE STATE BAR

PHOENIX

BEAVER STREET BREWERY

SAN FRANCISCO ST

MIKES PIKE

MACY'S EUROPEAN COFFEE HOUSE

GRAND CANYON INTERNATIONAL HOSTEL

COTTAGE

TOURIST HOME CAFE

BENTON

© MOON.COM

FLAGSTAFF AND SEDONA
FLAGSTAFF AND VICINITY

daily, $10 adults, $5 children 7-13) is a rock-and-log mansion sprawled amid a stand of pines in the middle of Flagstaff's commercial section and abutting the NAU campus. Its origin is a great American success story that would have been perfectly depicted in Technicolor. Two brothers, Michael and Timothy Riordan, make it big on the Western frontier, denuding the Arizona northland of its harvestable lumber. The boys are rich, powerful, and run in Flagstaff's founding circles, helping to build a lasting American community out of a rough, arid wilderness. The close brothers marry close sisters, Caroline and Elizabeth Metz, and the two fledgling families get on so well that they decide to build a 40-room, 13,000-square-foot Arts and Crafts-style masterpiece and live in it together. They hire El Tovar designer Charles Whittlesey to design two mansions in one, each shooting off in separate directions and linked by a pool hall and communal space. They decorate their majestic home with Stickley furniture, stained glass, and enough elegant details to draw crowds of visitors for the next 100 years. And everybody lives happily ever after.

The park offers **tours** (on the hour 10am-4pm, reservations recommended) of the Arts and Crafts treasure, one of the best examples of the distinctive architecture that left a stylish stamp on the Southwest in the late 19th and early 20th centuries. Only a small portion of the structure is included in the tour, but it's full of original furniture and displays about the family and life in Flagstaff's formative years.

Lowell Observatory

The hilltop campus of **Lowell Observatory** (1400 W. Mars Hill Rd., 928/774-3358, www.lowell.edu, 10am-10pm Mon.-Sat., 10am-5pm Sun., $17 adults over 17, $12 on Sundays, $10 children 5-17, $6 on Sundays) just west of downtown, occupied by tall straight pines and a few small white-domed structures with round concrete bases, has had a good deal

of influence over the science of astronomy since its founders began searching the clear rural skies over Flagstaff in 1894. The historic viewpoint has had something to do with contemporary ideas about the beginnings of the universe as well.

It was here between 1912 and 1914 that Vesto Slipher discovered that the universe's galaxies are moving away from earth, a phenomenon measured by changes in the light spectrum called redshifts. This in turn helped Edwin Hubble and others confirm that the universe is expanding, thus providing the first observable evidence for the Big Bang. Another historic distinction came a few years later in 1930, when 24-year-old Clyde Tombaugh looked out from atop Mars Hill and discovered Pluto.

Today the campus welcomes the public with 45-minute tours offered on the hour, 10am-4pm in summer and 1pm-4pm in winter. The tours include a look through a solar telescope to view spots and flares on the sun, a duck into the Pluto Telescope building, and a look at some of fascinating historical documents and artifacts. The **Steele Visitor Center** shows a movie about the observatory and has interesting exhibits on astronomy. If you visit at night, you can take part in galactic viewing sessions with staff astronomers.

Though smaller and less sleek and impressive than the more state-of-the-art telescopes in Southern Arizona, Lowell is worth the trip for its historical import (it's one of the oldest observatories in the nation, deemed a National Historic Landmark in 1965) and its picturesque location in the shadowy pines at the border of Flagstaff's Thorpe Park. Don't miss checking out **Percival Lowell's tomb,** a neoclassical, observatory-shaped mausoleum that honors the observatory's founder, whose popular writings led many Americans to suspect that there was a series of canals, and by implication life, on Mars.

1: Historic Basque Handball Court in the Southside Historic District 2: the telescope at Lowell Observatory 3: Sunset Crater Volcano National Monument 4: Wupatki National Monument

★ Museum of Northern Arizona

A couple of well-educated and adventurous easterners, Mary and Harold Colton, an artist and a zoologist, respectively, who first came to Northern Arizona on their honeymoon, founded the **Museum of Northern Arizona** (3101 N. Fort Valley Rd., U.S. 180 three miles north of downtown, 928/774-5213, www.musnaz.org, 10am-5pm Mon.-Sat., noon-5pm Sun., $12 adults, $8 children 10-17) in 1928 to preserve and encourage the indigenous arts and crafts of the Colorado Plateau. Since then this essential museum has become the cultural and scientific center of the Four Corners region, collecting, interpreting, and displaying the natural history, art, and artifacts of timeless landscapes and human cultures.

The museum's main building is itself a dark-wood and river-rock work of art, set among the pines along the shallow Rio de Flag, with Arts and Crafts-era touches such as the handmade tile borders by Hopi potter Sadie Adams around the main entrance. Inside there are comprehensive exhibits on the Four Corners region's ancient and current biomes and its buried and blowing strata, plus one of the better introductions to Ancestral Puebloan and Puebloan cultures you'll find, with displays from the Basket Makers up to the Hopi and Navajo of today. Volunteer docents stroll about eager to discuss and supplement any of the exhibits. The collection of Pueblo Indian pottery, jewelry, kachina, and basketry is the museum's high point; but the galleries showing contemporary Hopi and Pueblo art, including oil paintings, watercolors, and sculpture, tend to open one's eyes to the vibrancy of the region's current cultural moment. Those who appreciate design should stroll into the lounge to see the Arts and Crafts flourishes in this cozy living-room setting. There's also a beautiful and relatively easy **nature trail** on the museum's forested grounds. Maps to the half-mile trail are available at the front desk.

Arizona Historical Society-Pioneer Museum

Stop at the **Arizona Historical Society-Pioneer Museum** (2340 N. Fort Valley Rd., 928/774-6772, www.arizonahistoricalsociety.org, 10am-5pm Mon.-Sat., 10am-4pm Sun., $6 adults, $3 ages 7-17) near the Museum of Northern Arizona to see how the early Anglo settlers lived in Flagstaff and Northern Arizona. It's rather fascinating, after just learning about the ancient plateau lifeways of the Hopi and other tribes, to see how a completely different culture adapted to the same relatively harsh conditions. The building is something to see in itself: It's the old Coconino County Hospital for the Indigent, built in 1908. The museum has several displays on, among other things, frontier farming, education, transportation, and medicine, including a bedroom kept exactly as a hardworking nurse would have left it a century ago. There's also a retired steam train and various old farming implements parked on the beautiful forested grounds, where the museum puts on a host of events throughout the spring and summer.

Coconino Center for the Arts

Not a few artists and artisans lurk among the tall pines in Flagstaff, and many more sit atop the Hopi Mesas nearby, carving kachinas out of cottonwood root, while others walk the wide, empty roads of Navajoland and then recreate the landscape. Throughout the year the local arts group Flagstaff Cultural Partners gathers them together for a series of art exhibitions and concerts at the **Coconino Center for the Arts** (2300 N. Fort Valley Rd., 928/779-2300, http://flagartscouncil.org, 11am-5pm Tues.-Sat.), a sleek, modern gallery that looks somewhat futuristic among the trees and contrasted with the historical architecture of the nearby Museum of Northern Arizona and the Pioneer Museum. Check the website for an up-to-date calendar of events at this, the "cultural hub of Flagstaff."

The Arboretum at Flagstaff

A 200-acre botanical garden and research station spotlighting the flora (and, if you're lucky, the fauna) typical of the Colorado Plateau, **The Arboretum at Flagstaff** (4001 S. Woody Mountain Rd., 928/774-1442, www.thearb.org, 9am-4pm Wed.-Mon. Apr. 15-Oct. 31, $10 adults, $5 children 3-17) offers 50-minute guided walking tours daily at 11am and 1pm and shows off birds of prey at noon and 2pm (Sat.-Thurs.). The forested property on the volcanic lands southwest of downtown Flagstaff has easy, winding trails, tall, shaggy trees, a pond, a tree-ring maze, and much more. A few hours here and you'll be able to recognize and appreciate the unique plants and animals that flourish in this high and dry plateau country. The arboretum is about four miles south of Route 66 on Woody Mountain Road, only the first mile of which is paved. The rest is OK for all vehicles.

Elden Pueblo Heritage Site

The **Elden Pueblo Heritage Site** (Townsend-Winona Rd. off Hwy. 89, 928/527-3452, free), a Sinagua ruin in the shadow of 9,280-foot Elden Mountain, on Flagstaff's eastern edge, was once a bustling trading center related to the more dramatic Wupatki and Walnut Canyon settlements to the north and east. These easily accessible volcanic-rock ruins were first studied in 1926 by the great Southwestern archaeologist and ethnologist Jesse Walter Fewkes, who also supervised digs at Casa Grande in Southern Arizona and Mesa Verde in southern Colorado. The settlement in its heyday, from about AD 1100 to 1275, had 60-70 rooms and hosted a fairly well-connected population: Archaeologists have found macaw skeletons and other evidence of trade with the far south. The site is still being studied and excavated today, often with the help of students and volunteers. Tall ponderosa pines guard the ruin along the 250-yard dirt path (ADA accessible) that circles the site. This is a perfect first stop on a daylong tour of the Sinagua ruins around Flagstaff. There's a sign for the parking lot on Townsend-Winona

Road, one mile north of the Flagstaff Mall on the west side of Highway 89.

★ Sunset Crater Volcano and Wupatki National Monuments

Sunset Crater Volcano isn't really a volcano at all anymore but a nearly perfectly conical pile of cinder and ash that built up around the former volcano's main vent. Sunset Crater erupted, probably several different times, between 1049 and 1100. The eruptions transformed this particularly arid portion of the not exactly lush Colorado Plateau, and now huge cinder barrens, as surprising as an alien world the first time you see them, stretch out along the loop road leading through these popular national monuments. You can't climb the crater cone anymore—years of scarring by the crowds saw to that—but you can walk across the main lava field at the crater's base, a cinder field with scattered dwarfed, crooked pines and bursts of rough-rock-adapted flowers and shrubs, all the while craning up at the 1,000-foot-high, 2,550-foot-wide cone.

Along with turning its immediate environs into a scorched but beautiful wasteland, the volcano's eruptions may have inadvertently helped the Sinagua culture thrive for a brief time in this formidable environment, the subject and object of Sunset Crater's sister monument, Wupatki. The series of eruptions spewed about a ton of ashfall over 88 square miles, and closer to the source the ash created a kind of rich mulch that, combined with a few years of above-average rainfall, may have stimulated a spike in population growth and cultural influence. Archaeological findings in the area suggest that the five pueblos in the shadow of the crater, especially the large Wupatki, were at the center of a trading crossroads and the most important population center for 50 miles or more, with about 2,000 people living within a day's walk from the sprawling red-rock apartment building by 1190. Times seem to have been good for about 150 years here, and then, owing to a variety of factors, everybody left. The Hopi

Who Were the Sinagua... and Where Did They Go?

The Sinagua left their architecture and masonry all over North-Central Arizona, from the red-rock apartment buildings rising from the cinder plains below the San Francisco Peaks, the sandstone cliff hideouts of Walnut Canyon, the limestone castles in the lush, easy-living Verde Valley, and the brick-stone rooms leaning against Sedona's red walls.

We don't really know what they called themselves, but we call them, according to tradition more than anything else, the Sinagua, Spanish for "without water"—which alludes to the name used by early Spanish explorers for this region of pine-covered highlands still stuck somehow in aridity: *Sierra Sin Agua* (mountains without water).

Their cultural development followed a pattern similar to that of the Ancestral Puebloans in the Four Corners region. They first lived in pit houses bolstered by wooden beams and made a living from small-scale dryland farming, hunting, and gathering piñon nuts and other land-given seasonal delicacies. They made strong and stylish baskets and pottery (though they didn't decorate theirs in the manner of the Ancestral Puebloans and others); they were weavers, craftspeople, and traders.

Around AD 700 a branch of the Sinagua migrated below the Mogollon Rim to the Verde Valley and began living the good life next to fish-filled rivers and streams that flowed all year around; these migrants are now called the Southern Sinagua, and the ones who stayed behind are called the Northern Sinagua. When, around AD 1064, the volcano that is now Sunset Crater, northeast of Flagstaff, erupted, there were Sinagua villages well within reach of its spewing ash and lava, though archaeologists have found evidence that nearby pit houses had been disassembled and moved just before the eruption, leading to the assumption that they probably knew the big one was coming.

and other Pueblo people consider Wupatki a sacred place, one more in a series of former homes their ancestors kept during their long migrations to Black Mesa. Today you can walk among the red and pink ruins, standing on jutting patios, looking out over the dry land, wondering what that waterless life was like, and marveling at the adaptive, architectural, and artistic genius of those who came before.

VISITING THE MONUMENTS

The monuments sit side by side on an arid sweep covered with clump grass, humps of volcanic remains, pine stands, and, if you're lucky, blankets of yellow wildflowers, about 12 miles north of Flagstaff along Highway 89. Turn onto the Sunset Crater-Wupatki Loop Road, which will lead you across the cinder barrens, through the forest, out onto the red-dirt plains and the ruins, and then back to Highway 89. One ticket is good for both monuments.

Heading north from Flagstaff, you'll get

to the **Sunset Crater Volcano National Monument Visitor Center** (6082 Sunset Crater Rd., 928/526-0502, www.nps.gov/sucr, 9am-5pm daily Nov.-June., 8am-5pm daily June-Oct., $25 per vehicle for 7-day pass to both monuments) first, about two miles from the junction. Take a few minutes to look over the small museum and gift shop; there are several displays about volcanoes and the history of the region. Pick up the guidebook ($1, or free if you recycle it) to the one-mile loop **Lava Flow Trail** out onto the **Bonito Lava Flow** and head up the road a bit to the trailhead. This is an easy walk among the cinder barrens, a strange landscape with a kind of ruined beauty about it—only squat pines will grow, but there are surprising flushes of life throughout, small niches in which color can find a foothold. The trail skirts the base of the great crater cone and takes about an hour or so.

Another 16 miles on the loop road and you're at the **Wupatki National Monument**

The eruption would not be the end of the Sinagua—quite the contrary. Though the reasons are debated—it could have been that crops grew to surplus because a posteruption cinder mulch made the land more fertile, or it could be that the years following the big blow were wetter than normal, or it could be a bit of both—after the eruption Sinagua culture began to become more complex, and soon it would go through a boom time. From roughly 1130 to 1400 or so, Sinagua culture flourished as the Sinagua lands became an important stop in a trade network that included Mexico to the south, the Four Corners to the north, and beyond. At pueblo-style ruins dating from this era, archaeologists have found shells, copper bells, and macaw bones, all from Mexico. Sinagua architecture became more Puebloan, and villages often had Mexican-style ball courts and kivas similar to those of the Ancestral Puebloans. It is from this era that the famous ruins protected throughout this region date.

Then it all ended. Owing to drought, disease, war, civil strife, a combination of these, or some other strange tragedy we may never learn about, by the early 1400s the Sinagua culture was on the run. By 1425, even the seemingly lucky farmers of the Verde Valley had abandoned their castles. The survivors and stragglers mixed with other tribes, their kind never to be seen again. Lucky for us they were such good builders.

To learn more about the Sinagua, check out the easy-to-read booklet *Sinagua*, written by Rose Houk, part of the Western National Park Association's series Prehistoric Cultures of the Southwest. This and many other booklets in the series are available at Wupatki and other Sinagua sights near Flagstaff and in the Verde Valley. There are also displays on the Northern and Southern Sinagua at all of the ruins near Flagstaff and in the Verde Valley. The information above comes from various museum displays and Houk's excellent booklet.

FLAGSTAFF AND SEDONA
FLAGSTAFF AND VICINITY

Visitor Center (25137 N. Wupatki Loop Rd., 928/679-2365, www.nps.gov/wupa, 9am-5pm daily, $20 for both monuments), a total of 21 miles from the junction, near the last of the five pueblos, the titular Wupatki. The other pueblos before Wupatki are reached by two separate short trails, each with its own parking lot along the loop road. At Wupatki, you can purchase a guidebook ($1, or free if you recycle it) to the half-mile **Wupatki Pueblo Trail,** which leads around the village complex and back to the visitors center. If you don't have time to see all five pueblos, head straight to Wupatki, the biggest and best of them all.

★ Walnut Canyon National Monument

Not far from Wupatki, another group of Sinagua people farmed the forested rim and built stacked limestone-and-clay apartments into the cliffsides of Walnut Canyon, a 20-mile-long, 400-foot-deep gathering of nearly every North American life zone in one relatively small wonderland. Near the rim, a huge island of rock juts out of the canyon innards, around which residents constructed their cells, most of them facing south and east to gather warmth. Depending on how much sunlight any one side of the island received, the Sinagua could count on several seasons of food gathering, from cactus fruit to piñon nuts and wild grapes. A creek snakes through the canyon's green bottomlands, encouraging cottonwoods and willows. The Sinagua lived in this high, dry Eden for about 125 years, leaving finally for good around 1250. This is an enchanting, mysterious place that should not be missed.

VISITING THE MONUMENT

Take I-40 east from Flagstaff for 7.5 miles to Exit 204. Then it's three miles south to the canyon rim and the **Walnut Canyon Visitor Center** (928/526-3367, www.nps.gov/waca, 9am-5pm daily Nov.-June, 8am-5pm daily June-Oct., $15 for 7-day pass), where there are a few displays, a small gift shop, and a spectacular window-view of the canyon. An hour or more on the Island Trail, a one-mile loop past 25 cliff dwellings (close enough to examine in detail) and into several different biomes high above the riparian bottomlands, is essential to a visit here, but it's not entirely easy; you must climb down (and back up) 240 rock-hewn steps to get to the island, descending 185 feet. Once you're on the island, though, it's an easy, mostly flat walk, and one that you won't soon forget. There's also a short trail up on the rim with some great views.

SPORTS AND RECREATION
Hiking

Head north on Highway 180 eight miles to the San Francisco Peaks for the best hikes in the area. There are dozens of lesser hikes around the peaks, but the most memorable, essential hike in these sylvan, volcanic lands is the Humphreys Peak Trail (Snow Bowl Rd./ Forest Road 516, 10 miles round-trip, strenuous). The tough hike leads to the highest reaches of Humphreys Peak at 12,633 feet—the very top of Arizona and near to the sacred realms wherein the Hopi kachina dwell and watch. The 10-mile round-trip is very strenuous but beautiful and thrilling. The trail moves through a shady aspen forest and up above the tree line to a windy and rocky alpine stretch. Be careful of altitude sickness if you're a habituated lowlander. The trailhead is signed along Snow Bowl Road (Forest Road 516). The Kachina Trail (Snow Bowl Rd./ Forest Road 516, 10 miles round-trip, moderate), which begins at the dead end of Snow Bowl Road, is a less vertical walk and popular with locals. It's a 10-mile round-trip stroll along mostly flat land—you're at 9,500 feet anyway, so why go up any more?—through thick stands of conifers and aspens with sweeping views at every corner. This is a particularly beautiful route in the fall, with fiery yellows and reds everywhere.

Contact the Coconino National Forest (1824 S. Thompson St., 928/527-3600, www.

fs.usda.gov/coconino, 8am-4pm Mon.-Fri.) for information on hiking in the San Francisco Peaks, and see the national forest's website for other hikes in the volcanic highlands and more detailed trail descriptions.

Mountain Biking

Mountain biking is very popular in Flagstaff, and many of its trails are up-and-down exciting and technical to the point of mental and physical exhaustion. Enthusiasts will want to head straightaway to the series of moderate-to-difficult interconnected trails of the Mount Elden Trail System northeast of town along Highway 89. There are enough loops and mountainside single-tracks in this area to keep you busy for a while.

The Flagstaff Biking Organization (http://flagstaffbiking.org) offers information on northland biking events and issues. The experts at Absolute Bikes (202 E. Route 66, 928/779-5969, www.absolutebikes.net, 9am-7pm Mon.-Fri., 9am-6pm Sat., 10am-4pm Sun. Apr.-Dec., 10am-6pm Mon.-Sat., 10am-4pm Sun. Jan.-Mar.) have info on some of the best local trails on their website. They also have a store in the nearby slickrock paradise of Sedona, and they rent out mountain bikes in both areas.

Arizona Snowbowl

On the slopes of the San Francisco Peaks, the Arizona Snowbowl (Snow Bowl Rd. off Hwy. 180, 928/779-1951, www.arizonasnowbowl. com, all-day lift tickets $75) offers skiers and snowboarders over 2,300 feet of vertical drop and 32 scenic trails that cover 777 acres. In wet years the first snow usually falls in December, but in recent, drought-ridden years the snow has stayed away until late in the season. The resort recently prevailed in a dispute with Native Americans over artificial snow and has commenced building a system to make powder from reclaimed water when Mother Nature won't play along. The Hopi and other regional tribes consider the mountains sacred.

In the summer, the ski lift becomes the

Scenic Chairlift (10am-4pm Fri.-Mon., $19 adults and children over 12, $15 children 6-12), lifting passengers slowly up to 11,500 feet, where you need a jacket in July and the hazy flatland stretches out for eternity.

DISC GOLF

The Snowbowl also has a challenging high-mountain disc golf course (9am-5pm daily summer, disc rental $3-8) that opens during the summer months. It takes 3-5 hours to complete the 18 holes. The course has some steep climbs and, of course, gorgeous scenery. Come up here to hike around a bit and enjoy the views.

Flagstaff Nordic Center

A complex of trails and sledding hills, the Flagstaff Nordic Center (Hwy. 180, mile marker 232, 928/220-0550, www.flagstaffnordiccenter.com) is a popular place for cross-country skiing, sledding, snowshoeing, and all manner of snow play as long as there's snow on the Coconino National Forest at the base of the peaks. Equipment rental, lessons, and races are available.

There's even more to do here in the summer. The high-meadow trails here offer excellent hiking and biking during the cool mountain days, and if you just can't stand to leave, camp in a yurt or rustic cabin ($50-60) for an unforgettable night in the starlit forest, with the majestic San Francisco Peaks watching over your slumber.

ENTERTAINMENT AND EVENTS

Nightlife

BARS, BREWPUBS, AND LOUNGES

Most of Flagstaff's favorite nightspots can be found in and around the historic downtown, the Southside Historic District, and on the edges of the Northern Arizona University campus. The nightlife here is naturally full of college students, but you'll find plenty of older locals and tourists in the mix.

The Monte Vista Cocktail Lounge (100 N. San Francisco St., 928/779-6971, www. hotelmontevista.com, 1pm-2am daily) is a genial and historic place to sip cocktails or cry into your beer, with live music on the weekends, DJs, and pool. It's in what feels like the low-ceilinged basement of the Monte Vista Hotel, built way back in 1928. On entering this little old-school joint down the steps from the hotel lobby, you can smell fourscore years of spilled beer and general revelry imprinted deeply into the walls and floor. They say there are even a few ghosts still hanging around, unwilling to go home. Also off the Monte Vista's lobby is the more modern-minded Rendezvous Coffee House and Martini Bar (100 N. San Francisco St., 928/779-6971, www.hotelmontevista.com, 6:30am-2am daily), a coffeehouse-cum-cocktail lounge with an impressive selection of spirits and creative cocktail creations. The coffee here is superior, but don't be surprised if you start drinking early after looking at all of those bottles as you sip your brew. The sleek, elegant interior and big windows that look out on bustling downtown Flagstaff encourage lounging and a "let's have another" attitude.

The State Bar (10 E. Route 66, 928/266-1282, 3pm-midnight Sun.-Thurs., noon-2am Fri.-Sat., noon-midnight Sun.) proves that the locavore movement is alive and well in Arizona, serving a surprisingly wide selection of beer and wine made right here in the Grand Canyon State.

Charley's Pub (23 N. Leroux St., 928/779-1919, www.weatherfordhotel.com, 8am-10pm daily) and The Gopher Hole Pub (5pm-close daily), both in the historic Weatherford Hotel downtown, are historic and fun places to have a beer or cocktail, hang out for happy hour, and watch live rock and blues bands.

Flagstaff Brewing Company (16 E. Route 66, 928/773-1442, www.flagbrew.com, 11am-2am daily), along Route 66 in downtown, offers expertly crafted microbrews in a pub-style setting where locals and tourists meet and mix. Try the dark-as-midnight Sasquatch Stout and sit on the patio, letting the strong beer and high-country air adjust your outlook on the laid-back mountain town.

Mother Road Brewing (7 S. Mikes Pike, 928/774-9139, www.motherroadbeer.com, 2pm-9pm Mon.-Thurs., noon-10pm Fri.-Sat., noon-9pm Sun.), just across the train tracks in the Southside, has a casual tasting room, a patio with a fire pit, and a rotating menu of creative small-batch beers. Order a pizza from Pizzicletta next door or bring your own food if you prefer. Mother Road also has a tap room at its 20-barrel brewhouse at 1300 Butler Avenue.

Beaver Street Brewery (11 S. Beaver St., 928/779-0079, www.beaverstreetbrewery.com, 11am-11pm Sun.-Thurs., 11am-midnight Fri.-Sat.), on the historic Southside, serves award-winning microbrews and fantastically delicious pizzas in a bar-and-grill setting. IPA lovers should not miss the HopShot IPA served here. Connected on the inside and owned by Beaver Street Brewery, a fun atmosphere prevails at Brews & Cues (11am-1am Sun.-Wed., 11am-2am Thurs.-Sat.), where a few games of eight ball provide the perfect complement to the tasty ales.

The Green Room (15 N. Agassiz St., 928/226-8669, http://flagstaffgreenroom.com, 5pm-2am Mon.-Thurs., 3pm-2am Fri.-Sun.) has a super-fun happy hour, a big dance floor, and a party vibe nearly every night. On the weekends this dance club and live music venue brings in local and touring bands and has karaoke.

Flagstaff is a ski town, and the Southside's Altitudes Bar & Grill (2 S. Beaver St., 928/214-8218, www.altitudesbarandgrill.com, 11am-10pm daily) celebrates that fact with its snow-sports decor and "Skishots," a convivial way to get hammered quickly. A friendly bartender, perhaps with a full cold-weather beard and a wool cap, serves three or four shots of your favorite spirit affixed to an old ski. You and your drinking buddies must cooperate to sink them, a task that becomes increasingly tricky as the night progresses. Altitudes also offers a good selection of local beers and live music and serves a sufficiently tasty American grill-style menu until 10pm.

Collins Irish Pub & Grill (2 N. Leroux St., 928/214-7363, www.collinsirishpub.com, 11am-2am daily) downtown is a decent place to watch the game and sock back a few pints of Guinness. The emphasis here is on sports, and the menu of pub food is a strange amalgam (Irish nachos?). But if you forget that it's supposed to be an Irish pub, it turns instantly into a regular old American joint with a friendly crowd and all sorts of fun distractions.

Vino Loco (22 E. Birch Ave., 928/226-1764, www.vinolocoflag.com, noon-close daily) is a charming little bar and shop downtown that features wines made by Arizona's many small vineyards, including those in the Verde Valley just an hour or so south of Flagstaff. There's live music here Thursdays and Fridays.

LIVE MUSIC

Flagstaff's a pretty laid-back town, and it has its share of mountain men, bohemians, and creative types. Northern Arizona University's more than 20,000 students, many from abroad, help give the old frontier town a dash of do-it-yourself cosmopolitanism. It's not surprising, then, that the area attracts headlining acts and smaller indie favorites to its bars and theaters at a steady clip. If you're a fan of alternative pop, alt-country, classic country, bluegrass, classic rock, and just plain rock and roll, it's a good idea to check the websites of the following venues before making your travel plans. Odds are some funky act you love or have barely heard of will be playing during your visit.

The Orpheum (15 W. Aspen St., 928/556-1580, www.orpheumpresents.com), a retro-cool theater and bar that was Flagstaff's first movie house, hosts practitioners of modern music from Ozomatli to Modest Mouse and shows classic, neoclassic, and first-run movies on special nights each month. True to Flagstaff's crunchy reputation, the venue hosts a party every year on Jerry Garcia's birthday. The Pepsi Amphitheater (2446 Fort Tuthill Loop, 928/774-0899, www.pinemountainamphitheater.com) out in the pines at Fort Tuthill Park is the region's best

1: Brews & Cues 2: The Orpheum

outdoor venue and attracts great bands from all over, many of the bluegrass and country persuasion. **Prochnow Auditorium** (Knoles Dr., North Campus, Northern Arizona University, 928/523-5638 or 888/520-7214) at NAU books national and international acts into an intimate setting.

Festivals and Events

Flagstaff hosts a variety of cultural events, mostly during its cool springs and warm summers.

During Flagstaff's year-round **First Friday Artwalk** (6pm-9pm) downtown comes alive with local art, crafts, music, and food. Students and townies mix it up and celebrate the vibrancy of the northland's culture at this fun monthly street festival. A walking guide to participating galleries is available on the **Flagstaff Art Council's website** (http://flagartscouncil.org). In the summer, it joins forces with **Downtown Friday Nights/First Friday,** a monthly street festival on the first Friday of every month May-October with live bands, artwalks, food, and crowds of northlanders seeking fun and diversions. The party is centered at Heritage Square.

In May, world-renowned authors come to town for lectures, signings, readings, and panel discussions at the **Northern Arizona Book Festival** (928/380-8682, www. nazbookfest.org).

The **Museum of Northern Arizona Heritage Program** (928/774-5213, www. musnaz.org) puts on several important and well-attended cultural festivals each year, featuring native arts and crafts markets, food, history displays, and entertainment: the **Hopi Festival of Arts and Culture** in early July; the **Navajo Festival of Arts and Culture** in early August; and, in late October, **Celebración de la Gente,** marking Día de los Muertos (Day of the Dead). In late May, the museum puts on the **Zuni Festival of Arts and Culture.** The second week in September, just before it starts to get cold in the north country, Flagstaff ushers in **Route 66 Days** (www.flagstaffroute66days.com), celebrated with a parade, a classic car show, and all manner of special activities along the downtown portion of the Mother Road. In October the **Flagstaff Mountain Film Festival** (www. flagstaffmountainfilms.org) screens the year's best independent films with an environmental, outdoor-adventure, and social-justice bent at The Orpheum.

If you find yourself in the northland on New Year's Eve, head over to the historic downtown **Weatherford Hotel** (23 N. Leroux) for the popular local party known as the **Pine Cone Drop.** Among rocking bands and general revelry, the hotel lowers a six-foot-tall, lit-up pinecone from its roof, as if this little railroad town in Arizona were Times Square. Thousands attend to meet the new year with cheer and watch the fireworks that attend the pinecone's fall. They do it twice: once at 10pm to coincide with the party on the East Coast and again at midnight.

SHOPPING

The best place to shop for distinctive gifts, souvenirs, decorations, clothes, and outdoor gear is Flagstaff's historic downtown. You'll find Native American arts and crafts, Western wear, New Age items, art galleries specializing in handmade objects, antiques stores, and more.

Outfitters

Babbitt's (12 E. Aspen Ave., 928/774-4775, www.babbittsbackcountry.com, 9am-8pm Mon.-Sat., 10am-6pm Sun.) sells top-notch outdoor gear from a famous old building with a famous old northland name. The store's 1880s-era, local sandstone building once housed the state's largest general store, built by a pioneer family of traders. The knowledgeable staff here can help you plan a northland backcountry adventure and will recommend the best gear for the conditions; they also have an excellent map and book section. Another locally owned outfitter downtown, **Aspen Sports** (15 N. San Francisco St., 928/779-1935, http://aspensportsflagstaff.com, 9am-7pm Mon.-Fri., 8am-7pm Sat., 10am-5pm

Sun.), sells the best in outdoor, hiking, skiing, snowboarding, and trekking gear and has an experienced staff of experts, all of whom would likely rather be skiing the peaks or hurling themselves into a canyon somewhere nearby. In this wilderness those are the folks you want on your side.

Books
Bookmans (1520 S. Riordan Ranch Rd., 928/774-0005, www.bookmans.com, 9am-10pm daily), Arizona's original used-media supercenter, is the best bookstore in Northern Arizona bar none, with a huge selection of used books, CDs, vinyl records, DVDs, and musical instruments.

Galleries
Stop by the **West of the Moon Gallery** (14 N. San Francisco, 928/774-0465, www.westofthemoongallery.com, 10am-5pm daily) in Flagstaff's downtown to see the best work of contemporary painters, artists, and artisans from around the region, including both classic and experimental work from Navajo artists. This is one of several places in Arizona to see and purchase the luminous, swirling, mysterious paintings of Shonto Begay, one of the best Native American artists working today.

FOOD
Mexican and Latin American
★ **Criollo Latin Kitchen** (16 N. San Francisco St., 928/774-0541, http://criollolatinkitchen.com, 11am-10pm Mon.-Fri., 9am-10pm Sat.-Sun., $10-30), in Flagstaff's historic downtown, creates an eclectic, ever-changing menu of gourmet, Latin-inspired dishes for brunch, lunch, and dinner from sustainable ingredients grown regionally on small farms and ranches. The sleek and refined interior, with eye-catching paintings and small tables that look out on downtown through a glass front, creates an urbane atmosphere that complements the creative food and somewhat belies the rural mountain setting.

American and Southwestern
The **Tourist Home Café** (52 S. San Francisco, www.touristhomecafe.com, 928/779-2811, 6am-8pm daily, $8-14) is a bright and airy counter-service eatery on the Southside serving scratch baked goods, breakfast burritos, fish tacos, and a variety of sandwiches and other fare. With tables inside and outside this wonderfully refurbished 1926 boarding house for Basque shepherds, it's not a place to just take-and-go. The bakery here entices to an almost criminal degree, and the "breakfast bar" with twisted mimosas and Bloody Marys may convince you not to rush off.

For the very best burgers in the northland, head to **Diablo Burger** (20 N. Leroux St., #112, 928/774-3274, www.diabloburger.com, 11am-9pm Sun.-Wed., 11am-10pm Thurs.-Sat., $10-13), which serves a small but stellar menu of beef raised locally on the plains around Flagstaff. All the finely crafted creations, such as the "Cheech" (guacamole, jalapeños, and spicy cheese), or the "Vitamin B" (bleu cheese with bacon and a beet), come on Diablo's branded English muffin-style buns alongside a mess of Belgian fries. They also have a terrific veggie burger.

Brandy's Restaurant and Bakery (1500 E. Cedar Ave., #40, 928/779-2187, www.brandysrestaurant.com, 6:30am-3pm daily, $6-10) often wins the Best Breakfast honors from readers of the local newspaper, and those readers know what they're talking about. The homemade breads and bagels make everything else taste better. Try the Eggs Brandy, two poached eggs on a homemade bagel smothered in hollandaise sauce. For lunch there are crave-worthy sandwiches (Brandy's Reubens are some of the best in the business), burgers, and salads. They also serve beer, wine, and mimosas.

Josephine's Modern American Bistro (503 N. Humphreys St., 928/779-3400, www.josephinesrestaurant.com, 11:30am-2pm and 5pm-9pm Mon.-Fri., 10am-2pm and 5pm-9pm Sat., 9am-2pm Sun., $10-30) offers a creative fusion of tastes for lunch and dinner, such as the roasted pepper and hummus grilled-cheese sandwich and the chile relleno with sun-dried cranberry guacamole, from a cozy historic home near downtown. This is one of the best places in town for brunch.

Charly's Pub and Grill (23 N. Leroux St., 928/779-1919, www.weatherfordhotel. com, 8am-10pm daily, $11-26), inside the Weatherford Hotel, serves Navajo tacos, enchiladas, burritos, and a host of other regional favorites for breakfast, lunch, and dinner. Their Navajo taco, a regional delicacy featuring fry bread smothered in chili and beans, might be the best off the reservation. Try it for breakfast topped with a couple of fried eggs. Charly's also has more conventional but appetizing bar-and-grill food such as hot, high-piled sandwiches, juicy burgers, steaks, and prime rib.

★ **Brix Restaurant & Wine Bar** (413 N. San Francisco St., 928/213-1021, http://brixflagstaff.com, 5pm-close Tues.-Sun., $18-36) operates out of a historic building a few blocks north of downtown and serves creative and memorable food using local and sustainable ingredients. The menu here changes often based on what's new at Arizona's small farms, ranches, and dairies. The New American cuisine that results is typically spectacular. They also have fine selections of wine, a slew of creative cocktails, and desserts that should not be missed.

The **Tinderbox Kitchen** (34 S. San Francisco St., 928/226-8400, www. tinderboxkitchen.com, 5pm-10pm daily, $18-26) in the Southside District serves a revolving menu of gourmet takes on familiar American favorites and has an elegant lounge (4pm-close daily) where you can wait for your table with a martini. The chef uses seasonal ingredients, and there's always something new and exciting here—like venison served with blue cheese grits, bacon creamed corn, or jalapeño mac-and-cheese. It's one of those places where the chef is limited only by ingredients and imagination, and the chef here is lacking in neither.

Asian

Consistent with its role as a port of call for canyon-country visitors from all over the world, Flagstaff has two excellent Thai restaurants, both stars of this atypical small town's varied and cosmopolitan food scene. **Swaddee Thai** (115 E. Aspen Ave., 928/773-1122, 11am-3pm and 5pm-9pm Tues.-Thurs., 11am-3pm and 5pm-9:30pm Fri.-Sat., $8-16), in Flagstaff's historic downtown right across from the Weatherford Hotel, serves fresh and authentic Thai dishes in an elegant setting. It's a clone of a restaurant that opened in the Phoenix area in 2007 and has quickly become one of the state's most acclaimed Thai eateries. The food here is unassailable: flavorful, consistent, and filling without being heavy. They also deliver.

Just a short stroll south sits **Dara Thai** (145 San Francisco St., 928/774-0047, www. darathaiflagstaff.com, 11am-10pm Mon.-Sat., $10-17), in the Southside neighborhood. Part of a small regional chain with sister restaurants in Williams, Anthem, Santa Fe, and Taos, Dara Thai has been a beloved local institution since 1992. Close to campus, it's popular with students and locals for its rich, tasty, and perfectly spiced dishes. Both Dara Thai and Swaddee Thai offer a relatively wide range of vegetarian options.

Italian

Named Flagstaff's favorite pizza since 2002, **Fratelli Pizza** (119 W. Phoenix Ave., 928/774-9200, www.fratellipizza.net, 10:30am-9pm daily, $10-20) swears by its "stone deck oven" and eschews the "conveyer belt" mentality of the chains. The results are sublime. Try the popular Flagstaff, with basil pesto, sun-dried tomatoes, and artichoke hearts. You can also build your own pie from among dozens of fresh toppings or stop in for a huge slice ($3). They also serve salads, antipasti, and calzones and offer a decent selection of beer and wine. They also have a location on **4th Street** (2120 N. 4th St., 928/714-9700, 10:30am-9pm daily).

The wonderful **Pizzicletta** (203 W. Phoenix Ave., 928/774-3242, www.pizzicletta. com, 5pm-close Tues.-Sun., $11-15) in the Southside neighborhood offers soppressata rather than pepperoni and prosciutto di Parma rather than ham. Among the carefully chosen, rather spare list of toppings are almonds and charred kale. But it's the dough that makes the pizza here so good. They also serve fantastic bread, beer, wine, and housemade gelato.

Diners

For a big breakfast of eggs, bacon, and potatoes, or an omelet stuffed with cheese, a hot cup of coffee, and friendly service, head over to the **Downtown Diner** (7 E. Aspen Ave., 928/774-3492, 6am-6pm daily, $5-15) right across from Heritage Square. This clean little greasy spoon also has good burgers, shakes, and hot dogs. There's similar fare at local favorite **Miz Zip's Route 66 Diner** (2924 E. Route 66, 928/526-0104, 6am-9:30pm Mon.-Sat., 7am-2pm Sun., $5-15) on Flagstaff's eastside. Open since the 1950s, they are still serving the same diner classics of the golden age, such as hot open-faced sandwiches smothered in rich gravy, juicy burgers, and filling breakfasts. They only take cash.

The **Crown Railroad Café** (3300 E. Route 66, 928/522-9237, http://thecrownrailroadcafes.com, 6am-9pm daily, $8-12) celebrates the golden era of the railroad. Sit among model trains, iron road memorabilia, and Navajo blankets while enjoying the huge, three-egg "Route 66 omelet," expertly prepared huevos rancheros, and a fresh homemade biscuit. They also have a location on **Woodlands Village Boulevard** (2700 S. Woodlands Village Blvd., Ste. 600, 928/774-6775).

Vegetarian

The **Morning Glory Café** (115 S. San Francisco St., 928/774-3705, http://morningglorycafeflagstaff.com, 10am-2:30pm Tues.-Fri., 9am-2:30pm Sat.-Sun., $8-11) serves natural, tasty vegetarian eats from a cozy little spot on San Francisco Street. Try the hemp burger for lunch, and don't miss the blue corn pancakes for breakfast. With local art on the walls, free wireless Internet, and friendly service, this is an ideal place to get to know the laid-back Flagstaff vibe. There are a lot of vegan and gluten-free options here. They don't take credit cards, so bring some cash.

Macy's European Coffee House (14 S. Beaver St., 928/774-2243, www.macyscoffee.net, 6am-8pm daily, $5-10) south of the tracks is the best place to get coffee and a quick vegetarian bite to eat, or just hang out and watch the locals file in and out.

ACCOMMODATIONS

Being an interstate town close to several world-renowned sights, Flagstaff has all the chain hotels. A good value and a unique experience can be had at one of the historic downtown hotels. Along Route 66 as you enter town from the east, there are a large number of chain and locally owned small hotels and motels, including several old-school motor inns, and a few places that are likely inexpensive for a reason. East Flagstaff, while it lacks the charm of the downtown area, is an acceptable place to stay if you're just passing through. If you're a budget traveler and don't mind students, hippies, and folks from other lands, try the hostels in Flagstaff's Southside Historic District.

Under $50

The **Grand Canyon International Hostel** (19 S. San Francisco St., 888/442-2696, www.grandcanyonhostel.com, $26-78) is a clean and friendly place to stay on the cheap, located in an old 1930s building in the Southside neighborhood, in which you're likely to meet some lasting friends, many of them foreign tourists tramping around the Colorado Plateau. The hostel offers bunk-style sleeping arrangements and private rooms, mostly shared bathrooms, a self-serve kitchen, Wi-Fi, free breakfast, and a chance to join in on tours of the region. It's a rustic but cozy and welcoming hippie-home-style place to stay. The same folks operate the **Motel DuBeau** (19 W. Phoenix St., 800/398-7112, www.modubeau.com, $26-75), a clean and charming hostel-inn with a small dorm and eight

private rooms. They offer a free breakfast, Wi-Fi, and a friendly atmosphere in an old motor hotel built in 1929. Make sure to spend some time at the on-site **Nomad's Global Lounge** (4:30pm-10pm Mon.-Thurs., 4pm-11pm Fri.-Sat., 4pm-9pm Sun.), kicking back a few cold ones with your new friends.

$100-250

The **Weatherford Hotel** (23 N. Leroux St., 928/779-1919, www.weatherfordhotel. com, $80-190) is one of two historic hotels downtown. It's basic but romantic, like stepping back in time when you head off to bed. There are no TVs or phones in most of the rooms, the cheapest of which share a bathroom. While the whole place is a little creaky, the location and the history make this a fun place to rest. With live music at the hotel's two pubs and the odd wedding or private party in the historic ballroom, the Weatherford can sometimes get a bit noisy. It's not for those looking for the tranquility of the surrounding pine forest.

The ★ **Hotel Monte Vista** (100 N. San Francisco St., 928/779-6971 or 800/545-3068, www.hotelmontevista.com, $85-125 Apr. 15-Nov. 5, $50-175 Nov. 6-Apr. 14), the other historic downtown hotel, is a retro-swanky, redbrick high-rise, built in 1927, which once served high-class and famous travelers heading west on the Santa Fe Railroad. These days it offers comfortable and convenient rooms with historic charm, cable TV and private bathrooms. There are also hostel-style rooms with a shared bathroom. There's a cocktail lounge and sleek coffee bar off the lobby. As with many of the grand old railroad hotels, there are lots of tales to be heard about the Hollywood greats who stayed here and the restless ghosts who stayed behind. Parking is not easy downtown, so if you have a big rig consider staying somewhere else.

The Inn at 410 Bed and Breakfast (410 N. Leroux St., 928/774-0088 or 800/774-2008,

www.inn410.com, $195-325) has eight artfully decorated rooms in a classic old home on a quiet, tree-lined street just off downtown. This is a wonderful little place, with so much detail and stylishness. Breakfasts are interesting and filling, often with a Southwestern tinge, and tea is served every afternoon. You certainly can't go wrong here. Booking far in advance, especially for a weekend stay, is a must.

The stately **England House Bed and Breakfast** (614 W. Santa Fe Ave., 928/214-7350 or 877/214-7350, www. englandhousebandb.com, $149-219) is located in a quiet residential neighborhood near downtown at the base of Mars Hill, where sits the famous Lowell Observatory. This beautiful old Victorian has been sumptuously restored, and its rooms are booked most weekends. If you're just passing through, the innkeepers are happy to show you around, after which you will probably make a reservation for some far future date. They pay as much attention to their breakfasts here as they do to details of the decor. This is one of the best little inns in the region.

The hosts at ★ **Elden Trails Bed & Breakfast** (6073 Snowflake Dr., 928/266-0203, www.eldentrailsbedandbreakfast.com, $149-169 d, $40 per night each additional adult) are committed to living a sustainable-as-possible lifestyle, including growing a lot of their own food in a large garden and greenhouse full of native plants and organic crops. Both ecotourists and foodies will feel at home in this comfortable and inspiring B&B at the base of Mount Elden, about five miles east of downtown Flagstaff. It's a small place, just one detached studio suite that sleeps four adults. A healthy, organic, and if you prefer vegan breakfast is served in the studio's sunny nook, and your new home-away-from-home sits amid tall pines and hiking trails. Make reservations far in advance.

Forest Inns

The **Ski Lift Lodge** (6355 N. Hwy. 180, 928/774-0729 or 800/472-3599, www.

1: England House Bed and Breakfast 2: Diablo Burger

arizonasnowbowl.com, $109-179) has simple, rustic cabins and rooms with cozy fireplaces and a good restaurant. Best of all, it's in the forest beneath the San Francisco Peaks, about seven miles northwest of downtown, right near the road up the peaks to the Snowbowl. It's dark out there, and you can see all the stars in the galaxy on many nights. This lodge is a good bet if you're skiing or engaging in other snow-related activities. Make reservations in advance for ski season, as there are few other places to stay in the immediate area. The drive from Flagstaff proper is about 10-20 minutes, longer in inclement weather. Prices are considerably lower on weekdays.

The **Starlight Pines Bed and Breakfast** (3380 E. Lockett Rd., 928/527-1912 or 800/752-1912, www.starlightpinesbb.com, $169-179) is located about three miles northeast of town in the forest at the foot of Mount Elden, offering four rooms stuffed with antiques and style in a Victorian-era home. There's a porch swing, deep tubs perfect for bubble baths, and fresh-cut flowers in every room but no TVs. They'll even bring your breakfast to your room for you. This is a perfect place for couples looking for a romantic mountain getaway.

For a touch of wilderness adventure with all the comforts, try the **Arizona Mountain Inn** (4200 Lake Mary Rd., 928/774-8959, www.arizonamountaininn.com, $137-247), offering 17 rustic but comfortable family-perfect cabins ($135-600) in the pines not far from town as well as four B&B-style rooms ($120-160). Dogs are welcome in most rooms and cabins.

INFORMATION

The **Flagstaff Visitor Center** (1 E. Route 66, 928/774-9541 or 800/379-0065, www. flagstaffarizona.org, 8am-5pm Mon.-Sat., 9am-4pm Sun.), located in the old train depot in the center of town, has all kinds of information on Flagstaff and the surrounding area.

TRANSPORTATION

Air

Flagstaff's small **Pulliam Airport** (FLG,

928/556-1234, www.flagstaff.az.gov), located about five miles south of downtown, offers five flights daily to and from Sky Harbor in Phoenix through **American Airlines** (800/443-7300, www.aa.com). It's a roughly 50-minute flight, as opposed to a 2.5-hour drive from Phoenix, and generally costs about $400. This is not your best option, as you must rent a car to explore the northland properly. If you are coming from Phoenix, it's best to rent a car there and make the scenic drive north.

Car

The best and, really, the only easy way to properly see Flagstaff and the surrounding country is by car. From Phoenix, take I-17 north for about 2.5 hours (142 miles), and you're in another world. The scenic route to Flagstaff from I-17 starts at Highway 260 in the Verde Valley, about 100 miles (1.5 hours) north of Phoenix near Cottonwood. Get off the interstate at Exit 287, heading west toward Cottonwood. About 12 miles on, take State Highway 89A north through Sedona and Oak Creek Canyon and all the way to the mountains and the pines. It's only about 50 miles from Cottonwood to Flagstaff, but it takes at least an hour and probably more to drive the scenic route through the verdant riverside valley and past the otherworldly red rocks of Sedona. You can also pick up Highway 89A at the Village of Oak Creek, which is 39 miles from Flagstaff, and take it straight north through Sedona and Oak Creek Canyon. This route is spectacular, as it includes about eight miles of travel on Highway 179 past some of the Sedona area's most famous eroded-rock attractions. Get off the interstate at Exit 298 (Hwy. 179) and pick up Highway 89A about eight miles north at Sedona. From there, Sedona and Flagstaff are separated by about 30 slow miles of winding two-lane road with amazing views.

Once in "Flag," as the locals sometimes call this mountain town, you're ideally situated to visit a long list of unique attractions. Chief among these is Grand Canyon National Park's South Rim, a mere 81 scenic miles away. Take Highway 180 north from downtown, driving through the pine forest in the shadow of the towering San Francisco Peaks. Pick up Highway 64 east at the tiny, windswept roadside stop known as Valle, about 50 miles from Flagstaff. From there it's a straight shot across a barren plain to the South Rim gate. The whole trip takes about 1.5 hours, making Flagstaff a logical place to base your Grand Canyon visit if you don't want to stay in the park. A trip to the North Rim from Flagstaff takes quite a bit longer. Take Highway 89 north across the volcanic cinderlands, through the western edge of the vast Navajo Reservation, and into the lonely landscape near the Utah border known as the Arizona Strip. After about two hours (123 miles), pick up U.S. 89A going west at Bitter Springs. Cross the Colorado River at Marble Canyon and skirt the edge of Vermilion Cliffs National Monument toward the Kaibab Plateau, climbing to the forested highlands and Jacob Lake, the center of plateau life. The 50-mile drive from Bitter Springs to Jacob Lake usually takes an hour or more. When you pass the hotel and restaurant at Jacob Lake, you have another 45 miles to go on State Highway 67, a drive that takes an hour or more through a mountain forest of evergreens and aspen, with patches blackened by fire. The whole gorgeous, unforgettable, 208-mile drive will take you at least four hours and probably longer. It's not a great idea for a day trip from Flagstaff unless you want to spend all day in the car. It's a better idea to take two days and stay overnight in the park or at Jacob Lake.

The sights closest to town are Meteor Crater, 45 miles east on I-40; Sunset Crater and Wupatki, 14 and 39 miles north on Highway 89, respectively; and Walnut Canyon, a quick, seven-mile drive east on I-40. These places attract visitors from around the world and are easy to find. You can't miss them if you follow the signs along the highway and the interstate. The Navajo Nation's reservation begins about 50 miles north of Flagstaff on Highway 89, and Lake Powell spreads across the hard land 136 miles to the north on the same route.

The Petrified Forest and Painted Desert are about 115 miles east on I-40.

The 467-mile drive from Los Angeles to Flagstaff typically takes about seven hours, most of it along I-40. If you're starting from Las Vegas, take Highway 93 past Hoover Dam and over the Colorado River to I-40. The 252-mile drive takes about four hours.

CAR RENTAL

Most of the major car-rental companies have a presence at Flagstaff's small **Pulliam Airport** (928/556-1234, www.flagstaff. az.gov), about five miles south of downtown. **Avis Downtown Flagstaff Car Rental** (175 W. Aspen Ave., 928/714-0713, www.avis.com, 7am-6pm Mon.-Fri., 8am-4pm Sat., 9am-1pm Sun.) is located right in the middle of all the action at the corner of Aspen Avenue and Humphreys Street. **Budget** (800/527-7000, www.budget.com) operates out of the same facility with the same hours and phone number. **Enterprise Rent-A-Car** (213 E. Route 66, 928/526-1377, www.enterprise.com, 8am-6pm Mon.-Fri., 9am-noon Sat.) is located on the eastern edges of town along I-40.

If you're looking for a mythic Southwestern experience, stop by **EagleRider Flagstaff** (800 W. Route 66, 928/637-6575, www. route66rider.com, 8am-6pm daily, $109-145 per day) and rent a Harley-Davidson.

Long-Distance Bus

Flagstaff's **Greyhound Bus Lines** (800 E. Butler Ave., 928/774-4573, www.greyhound. com) station is located along the industrial wasteland that is East Butler Avenue. The company offers bus service to Flagstaff from most points on the map. **Groome Transportation-Arizona Shuttle** (928/350-8466, https://groometransportation.com/ arizona, $48 pp one-way) offers several daily trips between Flagstaff's Amtrak station and Sky Harbor International Airport.

Train

The **Amtrak *Southwest Chief* route** (800/872-7245, www.amtrak.com), which mirrors the old Santa Fe Railway's *Super Chief* route of the grand Fred Harvey days, stops twice daily (one eastbound, one westbound) at Flagstaff's classic **downtown depot** (1 E. Route 66), the former Santa Fe headquarters and also the town's visitors center. The route crosses the country from Chicago to L.A., dipping into the Southwest through northern New Mexico and Northern Arizona.

Public Transportation

Flagstaff's city bus, the **Mountain Line** (928/779-6624, www.mountainline.az.gov, $1.25 per ride or $2.50 for a day pass), runs 6am-10pm weekdays and 7am-8pm weekends to stops all over town.

Bike

Flagstaff is a relatively bicycle-friendly city, with a well-established and active bike culture. You'll likely see a lot of people riding mountain bikes around town, even in the winter. It's pretty easy to get around most of the town on a bike following a network of trails of multiuse paths laid out in the **Flagstaff Urban Trails and Bikeways Map,** available for free at the **Flagstaff Visitor Center** downtown. You can pedal from downtown to the east side of town while avoiding the always busy traffic along Route 66 using the popular **Route 66 Trail.** The 4.4-mile paved trail runs along the south side of Route 66 east from downtown and is popular with bike commuters. The ambitious 42-mile **Flagstaff Loop Trail** is about half finished. The trail will someday circle the town and feed smaller, spoke-like paths to various points in town.

Prescott

With more than 700 buildings on the National Register of Historic Places and a rough Old West history full of political chicanery and violence, Prescott has much to recommend it to tourists, especially those fascinated by the 19th-century Anglo West and Victorian architecture. Prescott has become "Everybody's Hometown," a slogan printed on signs and flags throughout the picturesque downtown. The town has a sizable population of well-off retirees and a hard-to-miss group of young back-to-nature bohemian residents, many of them students at Prescott College, a private liberal arts school.

Prescott's lasting draw for those living in the lowlands is its four-season climate—hot in summer, perfect in spring, cool in fall, and cold, sometimes even snowy, in winter. The Prescott National Forest hugs the outskirts of town in a sappy embrace, traversed by hundreds of trails and ideal for all manner of outdoor retreats and recreation.

SIGHTS
Downtown and the Courthouse Plaza

Most of Prescott's charm is centered on a few blocks in the **downtown area** (Gurley, Montezuma, Cortez, and Goodwin Sts.), among dozens of shops, boutiques, antiques stores, and art galleries (many of them with an Old West theme, and most in the middle to high end of the price range) and the town's best restaurants and bars, most of them frequented by visitors and locals alike. The whole scene surrounds the big, tall-pillared stone **Yavapai County Courthouse,** built in 1916 out of locally quarried stone, and its grassy grounds lined by imported trees; there's always something going on—square dancing, craft shows, live theater, a few families or couples lounging on the grass with a picnic, kids playing with Frisbees and Hacky Sacks, and exercisers doing laps on the cobblestone walkways, led quickly by their dogs.

Large **bronze statues** grace three sides

Prescott

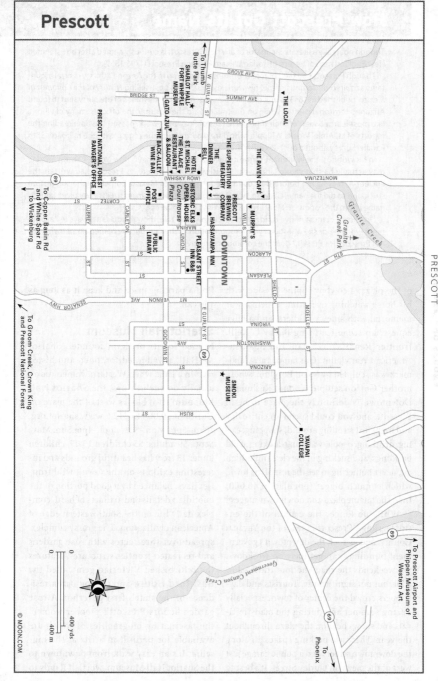

To Thumb
Butte Park

GROVE AVE

SUMMIT AVE

THE LOCAL

BRIDGE ST

SHARLOT HALL
FORT WHIPPLE
MUSEUM

EL GATO AZUL

W GURLEY ST

McCORMICK ST

THE SUPERSTITION
THE MEADERY

THE RAVEN CAFÉ

MONTEZUMA

THE
DINNER
BELL

PRESCOTT NATIONAL FOREST
RANGER'S OFFICE

THE
BACK ALLEY
WINE BAR

ST

ST

CORTEZ

AUBREY

CARLETON

ST

ST

ST

POST
OFFICE

PUBLIC
LIBRARY

MARINA

UNION

ST

ST

ST

MT VERNON AVE

E GURLEY ST

GOODWIN ST

AVE

WASHINGTON

ARIZONA

RUSH

ST

ST

ST

ST

ST

ST

89

To Copper Basin Rd
and White Spar Rd
to Wickenburg

SENATOR HWY

To Groom Creek, Crown King
and Prescott National Forest

ST MICHAEL
THE PALACE
RESTAURANT
& SALOON

HOTEL

(WHISKY ROW)

HISTORIC ELKS
OPERA HOUSE

Courthouse
Plaza

PRESCOTT
BREWING
COMPANY

HASSAYAMPA INN

PLEASANT STREET
INN B&B

PLEASANT STREET

DOWNTOWN

MURPHY'S

WILLS ST

ALARCON

SHELDON

VIRGINIA

MOELLER

ST

6TH ST

US 89

Granite
Creek
Park

Granite Creek

Government Canyon Creek

SMOKI
MUSEUM

YAVAPAI
COLLEGE

89

89

69

To Phoenix

To Prescott Airport and
Phippen Museum of
Western Art

0   400 yds

0   400 m

© MOON.COM

How Prescott Got Its Name

Though not really a literary incubator of any note, Prescott is curiously named after an esteemed New England man of letters, historian William Hickling Prescott (1796-1859).

Though Prescott had died before the remote little camp in the Arizona's thirsty central mountains acquired his famous name, his work, especially his best-selling *History of the Conquest of Mexico,* published in 1843 to universal acclaim, was much on the minds of the party sent to found Arizona's territorial capital. While on the trail toward the territory, the officials, many of whom, like most learned men of their time, were fans of Prescott's work, passed the time reading the reports of Lt. Amiel Weeks Whipple, who'd trekked through the region with the railroad's 35th Parallel Survey about a decade earlier.

In his writings, the lieutenant suggests several times that what is now North-Central Arizona may actually be that vague land to the "northwest" from where, as Prescott had written, the ancient Aztecs hailed before they conquered the Valley of Mexico. Somehow the suggestion stuck, and so did the name. Likewise, two of downtown Prescott's main streets were given famous names from the conquest: Montezuma Street and Cortez Street.

Don't expect most native residents to know this little tale, though you can always tell a long-timer when he or she questions your pronunciation of their cryptically named hometown. "It's not Prescott, it's Preskit," goes the common corrective.

of the plaza: a cowboy supine fireside with his horse watching over him, a lifelike war memorial with sinewy soldiers, and a huge equestrian scene featuring Bucky O'Neill, frontier Renaissance man and Spanish-American War victim. This famous area landmark was sculpted by Solon Borglum, whose brother Gutzon sculpted Mount Rushmore. Downtown is definitely the place to be in Prescott, and you could spend an entire day and night just strolling around, shopping, eating, drinking, people-watching, looking at old buildings, and sucking in the clean mile-high air, never bothering to see the rest of the town, which is much bigger (population 40,000) than the quaint plaza and downtown suggest.

While no longer the capital of the entire territory, Prescott is seat of the Yavapai County, and as such the downtown's government buildings can get busy on weekdays. On weekends the road and foot traffic slow a bit, but not significantly. Tourists and day-trippers crowd the center of town, especially during summer and during the many festivals and shows held on the plaza throughout the year. There are parking spaces all along the downtown streets and a public garage just west of the plaza on Gurley Street. It's best to find a parking space and keep it as long as you can.

Sharlot Hall Museum

Named for its brilliant founder, Sharlot M. Hall, a writer, editor, poet, and historian in a time when Western women didn't usually do such things, the **Sharlot Hall Museum** (two blocks west of the plaza on Gurley St., 928/445-3122, www.sharlot.org, 10am-5pm Mon.-Sat., noon-4pm Sun. May-Sept., $9 adults, $5 children 13-17, children under 13 free) has beautiful grounds and interesting exhibits on the town's wild frontier days, balanced by a good portion of the quotidian details and artifacts of hard, complex daily life on the Southwestern edge of American civilization. The grassy complex, spread over three acres with rose gardens and recreated frontier structures, features the refurbished Victorian gem called the **Bashford House** and the log-cabin residence of the state's first governor. A rose garden honors Prescott's pioneer women, the fascinating biographies of which are available for perusal in a file at the museum. It's an easy walk from downtown to the Sharlot Hall Museum, worth it if only to see the pretty green grounds and the mansions of another age.

Fort Whipple Museum

The Sharlot Hall Museum also operates the small **Fort Whipple Museum** (500 N. Hwy. 89, Bldg. 11, Veterans Administration campus, 928/445-3122, 10am-4pm Thurs.-Sat., free, donations encouraged) about four miles north of downtown on the tree-lined campus of the VA Hospital, formerly home to Fort Whipple, a major base for General Crook's war against the Apache. The museum, housed in an old Victorian home once used as officers' quarters, displays the memorabilia and daily items of frontier military life and puts on historical reenactments on the third Saturday of February, May, August, and November.

Smoki Museum

For 70 years, from 1920 to 1990, the builders of this little puebloesque building a few miles east of downtown off Gurley Street—a group of Prescott businesspeople who called themselves the Smoki People—covered their half-naked bodies in a shade of brownish-red and sold tickets to an annual fairground performance of dances and ceremonies based on Hopi religion, including even the famous Snake Dance with its live props. The group's museum preserved and displayed some excellent examples of Pueblo, Navajo, and Yavapai arts, crafts, and artifacts, along with items from tribes throughout the West. Not exactly a politically correct organization, the Smoki People were protested out of existence in 1990 by the Hopi, who were fed up with having their sacred culture co-opted and, as they saw it, mocked by Anglos. The whole story is told through a fascinating and frank exhibit in the **Smoki Museum** (147 N. Arizona St., 928/445-1230, www.smokimuseum.org, 10am-4pm Mon.-Sat., 1pm-4pm Sun., $7 adults, children under 12 free), now dedicated to interpreting the Smoki phenomenon—extremely popular among locals here for many years—and preserving some of the wonderful treasures collected over the years. This

is a quirky and illuminating attraction, and the building itself should be seen by lovers of unique structures. The museum is part of the Prescott Armory Historic District, which includes nearby Ken Lindley Field, the old Prescott National Guard Armory, and the Citizens' Cemetery, each of which will be of at least passing interest to history buffs and enthusiasts of quirky architecture.

The Phippen Museum of Western Art

Prescott's only art museum, **The Phippen Museum of Western Art** (4701 Hwy. 89 N., 928/778-1385, www.phippenartmuseum. org, 10am-4pm Tues.-Sat., 1pm-4pm Sun., $7 adults, children under 12 free) is an essential stop for those who appreciate the Cowboy Artists of America school of painting and bronze sculpture. The museum's namesake, the artist George Phippen, was that famous group's cofounder and first president, and the collection features many of the luminaries of the movement as well as Native American arts and crafts and about four special Western-related exhibits every year. The drive out to the hilltop museum is as stimulating as all the oil paintings of cattle drives and bronze bucking broncos inside put together. The building overlooks a little dry-grass valley just past the strangely piled giant boulders of Granite Dells and the reedy confines of Watson Lake nearby, a scenic seven miles north from downtown.

RECREATION
Prescott National Forest

The **Prescott National Forest** (www. fs.usda.gov/prescott), more than a million acres of desert scrub, chaparral, piñon, juniper, and pine-carpeted rolling hills, dry-grass flatlands, and rocky mountains, is the western edge of the largest ponderosa pine forest in the world, the beginning of the great Arizona Pine Belt that stretches across and below the Mogollon Rim all the way to New Mexico.

Just a few miles from downtown, the forest around Prescott is a perfect place for a high-altitude hike over pine needle-strewn

trails, an afternoon picnic, a cool-breeze glide across a tucked-away forest lake, or an overnight camping trip beneath the tall, sap-scented woods. The forest has long been used for small-scale mining, ranching, and outdoor recreation, and in some places it shows its wear and tear. There are more homes on this forest than one usually sees on federal land, mostly owing to the fact that owners of mining claims are allowed to build on public lands, and there are a lot of still-active mining claims in those mineraled mountains. Old mining and logging roads are now used by mountain bikers and hikers, and, in some areas, off-road vehicle enthusiasts.

The forest's **headquarters** (344 S. Cortez St., 928/443-8000, 8am-4:30pm Mon.-Fri.) just outside downtown has a kiosk with free single-sheet descriptions and maps of every trail on the forest. It's really a good idea to stop here if you're going to be doing anything in the forest—there's simply too much information to pass up. Staff rangers at the office can help you with any questions.

Lynx Lake Recreation Area (day use 6am-8pm Apr.-Sept., 7am-6pm Oct.-Mar., $5 parking), just north of town off Highway 69, is a 55-acre lake surrounded by ponderosa pines and stocked with trout. You can float your own boat out on the lake and fish or rent a craft and gear at the **Lynx Lake Store and Marina** (928/778-0720). The surrounding forest has several hiking and biking trails. The 4.3-mile hike to **Salida Gulch** will get you to the **Gold Pan Day Use Area,** where you can engage in the occupation that put the forest around Prescott on the map. The area has two basic campgrounds ($18 per night, no reservations).

In the forest just outside town along Senator Highway is **Goldwater Lake,** a popular place for picnicking, kayaking, and canoeing. Out along Highway 89, about five miles north of downtown, **Watson Lake** is surrounded by giant, otherworldly boulder

piles, an area called **Granite Dells.** The five-mile **Peavine Trail,** an old railroad right-of-way that takes you through the heart of the amazing rock piles, is a highlight of this area and can be hiked or biked with ease. If you didn't bring your mountain bike, you can rent one from **Ironclad Bicycles** (710 White Spar Rd., 928/776-1755, www.ironcladbicycles.com, 10am-5:30pm Mon.-Sat., 10am-2pm Sun., $12-16 per hour). If you forgot your canoe or kayak, or if you want to try either of these activities for the first time, call **Prescott Outdoors** (928/925-1410, www.prescottoutdoors.com, 8am-3pm Wed.-Sun. at Watson Lake and 9am-4pm Sat.-Sun. at Goldwater Lake, closed in winter).

Granite Basin Recreation Area ($5 parking fee) is a boulder-and-pine wilderness west of town off Iron Springs Road, the home of 7,600-foot-high Granite Mountain, the stained sheer rock face of which is a preferred residence of peregrine falcons. The area has a small lake with fishing and a popular, basic campground ($18, no hookups or reservations) as well as miles of hiking and biking trails.

Hiking and Mountain Biking

You could spend years hiking and biking the Prescott National Forest and still not get to every trail and hidden, trickling-water canyon. If you've got years to spare, go down to the forest headquarters, pick up all of the handy free maps, and get hiking. If you have only a few days, however, try one of the popular and beautiful hikes described below. Most forest trails that aren't in a wilderness area are open to hikers, bikers, and horseback riders; all trails are closed to motorized vehicles unless expressly set aside for off-road recreation.

The steep but relatively easy two-mile round-trip hike up to a saddle at the base of **Thumb Butte,** Prescott's favorite natural monument, provides awesome views of the town all nestled among the pines. Several trails around the popular **Thumb Butte Picnic Area** (three miles west of downtown on Gurley St., which becomes Thumb Butte

1: Yavapai County Courthouse 2: Granite Dells in the Prescott National Forest

Rd., $3 or America The Beautiful card) lead into the forest, along creeksides, and off to highlands from which you can see the San Francisco Peaks way up north.

The four-mile one-way hike up to the big boulders waiting atop **Granite Mountain** (three miles west of downtown off Iron Springs Rd., $2 parking fee) is highly recommended for those who don't mind a steep trudge. It's one of the most popular trails in the Prescott area, and for good reason. Peregrine falcons nest on the mountain's rock face, so bring binoculars. The trail winds up the mountain from a manzanita and piñon forest up through to the pine and on to the rocky peak at 7,600 feet. It gets pretty cold in the early spring, fall, and winter, and there's likely to be snowpack in the higher regions in the winter. This is a wilderness area, so no mountain bikes are allowed, and some of the areas around the cliff face are closed in spring and winter so the falcons can go about their nesting in peace.

The **Groom Creek Loop Trail** extends through the forest and up more than 1,000 feet to the top of Spruce Mountain, where there's a fire lookout and a few promontories from which you can just about see the top of every tree in the land. The winding single-track heading downhill makes this a wild ride on a mountain bike, nearly worth the difficult climb up. Head out Senator Highway via Mount Vernon Avenue, lined with intricate old Victorian homes, for about six miles until you see the sign for Groom Creek Horse Camp. The trailhead parking lot is on the east side of the road.

ENTERTAINMENT AND EVENTS

Nightlife

Although these days there are more galleries and boutiques than saloons, gambling halls, and brothels along the short stretch of Montezuma Street known since territorial days as **Whiskey Row** (www.prescott. com/whiskey-row), downtown is still the best place to party in Prescott. To get a sense of what it was like on this infamously raucous street back in the old days, step into the **The Palace Restaurant and Saloon** (120 S. Montezuma St., 928/541-1996, www. historicpalace.com, 11am-9:30pm Mon.-Thurs., 11am-10:30pm Fri.-Sat., $12-36). It was known throughout the region as a rowdy and even dangerous place to be on any given night. Though the old heavy-wood bar remains, and it can still get a little hectic with drunk tourists and locals mixing together, the Palace is today mostly a good restaurant. But back in the heyday of the drunken territory, everybody drank at the Palace—from the Earp brothers on up to Steve McQueen, who made a movie in Prescott. His time spent in the town is celebrated with several pictures on the wall. A big part of the fun of a stop here is looking at all the artifacts and memorabilia of days past.

The **Superstition Meadery** (120 W. Gurley St., 928/458-4256, www. superstitionmeadery.com, 11am-9pm Mon.-Thurs., 11am-10pm Fri.-Sat., 11am-6pm Sun.) serves a wide variety of complex and delicious mead and hard cider made with the help of local bees. This might be the most interesting bar in the northland. Head down the stairs from a gift shop in a historic building downtown into the dark and romantic underground space and sample a flight of the ancient "honey-wine." They also offer good tapas, including charcuterie, bruschetta, hummus, cheese plates, and the like.

The **Back-Alley Wine Bar** (156 S. Montezuma, in the alley behind Whiskey Row, 480/570-5131, https://backalleywinebar. business.site, 2pm-9pm Mon.-Thurs., 2pm-10pm Fri.-Sat., noon-6pm Sun.) serves a selection of wine, beer, and hard cider in a casual atmosphere and with an emphasis on those made in Arizona. You can bring your own food, and there's live music and karaoke on the weekends.

Performing Arts

The **Historic Elks Opera House** (928/777-1370, www.prescottelkstheater.com) is on

Gurley Street downtown, on Elks Hill right across from the Hassayampa Inn. The stylish old opera house, which still has a good bit of its grandeur, books acts throughout the year.

Festivals and Events

The Courthouse Plaza hosts several large shows and festivals every year, including the **Mountain Artist Guild Summer Arts and Crafts Festival** (http://prescottartfestivals. com, Aug.) in early August and the **Phippen Museum Western Art Show & Sale** (www. phippenartmuseum.org, May) over Memorial Day weekend, both big events in the regional Western art world. Also in early August, literary cowpunchers get together and put on readings and performances at the **Arizona Cowboy Poets Gathering** (Yavapai College, http://azcowboypoets.org, Aug.).

In late June, major touring acts show up in town for the **Prescott Bluegrass Festival** (www.prescottbluegrassfestival.com, June).

Prescott is famous, and used to be a bit infamous, for the wild public revelry of the Fourth of July weekend, when **Prescott Frontier Days and the World's Oldest Rodeo** (www.worldsoldestrodeo.com, July) puts the populace and the many visitors in the mood to party.

SHOPPING

Prescott is a great place to find antiques, art, and that unique, indescribable item you always knew you needed but never could find. Downtown is the best place to search for such treasures. The streets flanking the Courthouse Plaza (Gurley, Montezuma, Cortez, and Goodwin Streets) and continuing on for several blocks in every direction are crowded with shops, boutiques, and galleries selling cowboy-style Western art, Mexican folk arts, handmade jewelry and crafts, gifts, Western clothing, and even contemporary furniture and home decorations. **Cortez Street** especially is a kind of antiques row, with several big stores stacked with the fascinating leftovers of past generations, the members of which usually constructed their

daily-life items to last—and to look beautiful and stylish while doing so.

FOOD
American

Near the small campus of Prescott College, which is renowned for its emphasis on environmental and social justice, **The Local** (520 W. Sheldon St., 928/237-4724, 7am-2:30pm daily, $11-16) offers a full vegan menu and gets many of its ingredients from Prescott-area farms and ranches. Open for breakfast and lunch, The Local serves familiar but Southwest-inspired dishes and one of the best veggie-burgers in the known universe.

The long and fascinating menu of small plates at tiny **El Gato Azul** (316 W. Goodwin St., 928/445-1070, www.elgatoazulprescott. com, 11am-close Mon.-Fri., noon-close Sat.-Sun., $7-22) might cause you a little stress when it's time to order, but push through it and choose more than one. The dozens of creative and mouthwatering tapas here, including many seafood and vegetarian selections, rarely disappoint. Better yet, weekdays from 4pm to 6pm most plates are $2 off. They also serve delicious margaritas and sangria. Make a reservation and ask to sit on the patio as the micro dining room is a bit cramped.

Park Plaza Liquor & Deli (402 W. Goodwin St., 928/541-9894, http:// parkplazaliquor.com, 10:30am-9pm Sun.-Wed., 10:30am-10pm Thurs.-Sat., $9-19) is a casual place inside a liquor store on the edge of downtown. The locally owned restaurant and bar, a favorite with locals, represents the laid-back, beer-loving, outdoorsy vibe that pervades Prescott. Sit out on the patio and enjoy the cool northland evenings and sample the excellent sandwiches, fantastic pizzas, mac-and-cheese, and burgers, as well as, of course, the long list of craft brews.

The ★ **Raven Café** (142 N. Cortez St., 928/717-0009, www.ravencafe.com, 7:30am-11pm Mon.-Thurs., 7:30am-midnight Fri.-Sat., 8am-3pm Sun., $9-15), with its dark-wood interior, decorative-tin ceiling, and fantastical local art on the walls, is a true Prescott

Granite Mountain Hotshots Memorial State Park

It happened in Yarnell, a village scattered among the boulders and scrub about 35 miles down Highway 89 from Prescott. Before the interstate you had to pass through this old mining area on the slow drive from Phoenix to the northland, keeping a few gas stations and cafés in business. But those days were long gone in the summer of 2013, when Yarnell became synonymous with the deadliest wildland fire in Arizona's history.

Sparked by lightning on June 28, 2013, the Yarnell Hill Fire took the lives of 19 elite firefighters with the Granite Mountain Hotshots, a group based in Prescott and named after the boulder mountain rising from the flatlands north of town. By the time the blaze was contained on July 10, it had burned more than 8,400 acres and changed Yarnell and Prescott forever.

Though it's not easy to visit, the **Granite Mountain Hotshots Memorial State Park** (Hwy. 89, 4 miles south of Yarnell, 877/697-2757, http://azstateparks.com, always open, free) tells the story of the fire and the lives it took in a powerful way, requiring of visitors a small amount of the drive and stamina needed to fight such wild and remote blazes.

The 2.85-mile one-way **Hotshots Trail** climbs and winds through brush and boulders to an observation deck above the spot where the 19 firefighters died. Along the way, plaques attached to rocks tell the story of each hotshot. From the deck you can pick up the 0.75-mile one-way **Journey Trail** down to the "fatality site," which is circled by large rock walls.

Round-trip the hike is about 7 miles, and there are a few steep areas. There are no bathrooms along the trail, and no shade or water. May through September it's very hot in this area, so prepare yourself for a hard hike of four hours or more. Take water, and make sure you have your dog leashed. There are bathrooms at the trailhead along with a bronze statue of a hotshot in full gear, but no visitors center.

original and the center of café culture in this small, historic burg. All the food is fresh, and many of the ingredients are local or regional. The breakfasts here are amazing, including thick cuts of bacon, local eggs, and flavorful potatoes. They have an excellent beer selection, top-notch coffee, free Wi-Fi, and a patio for lounging around on a beautiful mile-high day. The Raven has earned a 3-star certification from the Green Restaurant Association based on the café's use of recycled materials, energy efficient equipment, and plant-based foods.

If you love beer, don't miss the **Prescott Brewing Company** (130 W. Gurley St., 928/771-2795, www.prescottbrewingcompany.com, 11am-10pm daily, $8-15), right across Gurley from the Courthouse Plaza. While serving rib-sticking pub fare like bangers and mash and shepherd's pie, along with a wide assortment of lighter dishes, the brewpub offers up some of the best beers in the territory.

The Peacock Room (122 E. Gurley St., 928/778-9434, http://hassayampainn.com, 7am-9pm Sun.-Thurs., 7am-9:30pm Fri.-Sat., $10-32) inside the Hassayampa Inn is a great place for a long, lazy lunch or a romantic candlelit dinner. Puffy booths line the walls, art deco lines define the interior, and the chef serves up good steak, lamb, and fish dishes, along with Southwestern-tinged specials.

ACCOMMODATIONS

A tourist haven, Prescott has many chain hotels (one or two of them nearly upscale), not a few smaller independents, and a growing number of bed-and-breakfast establishments. Most of the accommodations can be found along Gurley Street from one end of town to the other. The **Tourist Information Center** (800/266-7534, www.prescott.org) downtown has reams of pamphlets and brochures on various area accommodations. It's best to make reservations before arriving, especially in the summer.

The historic **Hotel St. Michael** (205 W. Gurley St., 928/776-1999, www.stmichael hotel.com, $109-139) is right downtown on the corner of Whiskey Row and Gurley Street, a redbrick reminder of another era. Built in 1901 with gargoyles staring down from its facade, the hotel has an excellent bistro and individually decorated rooms, cable TV, free Wi-Fi, and air-conditioning. The comfortable old building still operates an elevator installed in 1925. A room comes with breakfast in the bistro.

The **Hotel Vendome** (230 S. Cortez St., 928/776-0900 or 888/468-3583, www. vendomehotel.com, $109-149) is a delightful, historic, and finely detailed place to stay in one of Prescott's central, tree-lined neighborhoods, with beautiful relics of the Victorian heyday on every lot. Within easy walking distance to downtown, the Vendome, a Registered Historic Landmark built in 1917, offers 20 rooms with big bathtubs and all the comforts you could ever want and still feel good about yourself. There's also an elegant and cozy bar on-site serving Arizona beers and wines.

As historic Prescott hotels go, however, the ★ **Hassayampa Inn** (122 E. Gurley St., 928/778-9434, www.hassayampainn.

com, $89-139) is the star. Built in 1927 atop Elks Hill, a high-class gateway to downtown, the landmark hotel has a kind of redbrick, modified Spanish Colonial Revival style, with a bell tower and a covered passageway from the street to the lobby doors. Off the lobby there's a great restaurant, the Peacock Room, and a cozy dark-wood lounge where a jazz band often plays. The rooms are old, but classic, comfortable and stylish. All the rooms have free Wi-Fi, TVs and air-conditioning, which the likes of D. H. Lawrence and Greta Garbo lacked when they stayed here.

A few blocks up Montezuma from downtown and Whiskey Row, **The Motor Lodge** (503 S. Montezuma St., 928/717-0157, http:// themotorlodge.com, $129-189) is a wonderfully refurbished homage to midcentury road culture. A lot of little touches make it a fun and retro-reality experience—like the classic cars sitting out front, the old neon, and the period furniture and knickknacks—and yet its comforts are all up-to-date and stylish, with 12 motor-court-style rooms each with their own eclectic decor, free Wi-Fi, cable TV, and private porches.

The Grand Highland Hotel (154 S. Montezuma, 928/776-9963, http://

Hotel St. Michael

grandhighlandhotel.com, $99-189), right downtown on Whiskey Row, is a charming boutique hotel that brings back a little of what it must have felt like to a be frontier dandy in town for a spree. Sumptuous, historic and ideally located, this is a memorable place to stay in the heart of Prescott, a few steps from bars, restaurants, and shops, and perfectly located for evening strolls around the shady courthouse square just across the street.

INFORMATION AND SERVICES

The **Prescott Chamber of Commerce** (117 W. Goodwin St., 928/445-2000 or 800/266-7534, www.prescott.org, 9am-5pm Mon.-Fri., 11am-2pm Sat.-Sun.) has friendly volunteers and tons of free information on the area. A volunteer offers free guided historical tours of the downtown at 10am Friday-Sunday out of the chamber building.

The Verde Valley

In the Verde Valley—an ancient oasis fed and greened by water falling headlong off the Mogollon Rim—you can't walk a mile without seeing some fallen ruin or artifact left behind by the conquistadores, miners, agriculturists, and speculators who've been drawn to this fertile valley and its surrounding mountains over the centuries. Most people came here after rumors of ore; others grew crops and orchards and raised livestock. The area continues to grow at a steady pace, as more and more refugees from the Phoenix sprawl hunt out the remaining rural enclaves. It's still rather quiet here, though that is likely to change in the next decade or so. The area has long been known for one ruin in particular, the spectacular, if misnamed, Montezuma Castle. This must be seen. There's a good bit of outdoor fun to be had in the valley, including tubing and boating down wild stretches of the Verde River and hiking into beautiful Sycamore Canyon. But even before you reach the valley, you'll get a chance to shop, eat, and stay in some memorable stores, restaurants, and hotels in Jerome, a former copper boomtown that is too cool to pass up. The Verde Valley is one of several regions in Arizona that produces wine. There are at least seven vineyards along the Verde River and Oak Creek. You can sample and tour local vineyards on the **Verde Valley Wine Trail** (www. verdevalleywines.org), but if you just want to drink the wine you'll find tasting rooms in Jerome, Old Town Cottonwood, and Sedona.

MINGUS MOUNTAIN

The best way to start a tour of the Verde Valley is to drive up and over the mountain that watches over it from the west, 7,743-foot **Mingus Mountain**, part of the Black Hills range and Prescott National Forest. Take **Highway 89A** from the mountain's base—either from the Verde Valley on the east side or Prescott Valley on the west—and slowly negotiate the switchbacks along the two-lane road, towered over by cliffs and overlooking deep, pine-swept draws. It's a **scenic drive**, one of the region's most stunning, usually taking about an hour to go the 30 miles or so over the mountain, through the old mining metropolis of Jerome and down the other side. The drive is understandably popular with motorcycle enthusiasts and sports car pilots, so you might have to pull over and let some of them pass.

Near the top of the mountain, you'll find **Mingus Mountain Recreation Area** (www. fs.usda.gov), where there are a few high forest campgrounds (basic spots, $10, no reservations) and the eight-mile round-trip hike along the **Woodchute Trail** into the Woodchute Wilderness and up around to the north side of Woodchute Mountain, from which the boomtown Jerome got the wood to build itself. It's a pretty easy hike through an open pine and juniper forest that allows for some spectacular views. If you don't feel like hiking but still want to see the valley from way up high, head about three miles on the dirt road to the recreation area, where there's a promontory from which you can see mile after hazy mile spreading out in various shades of green and brown, as you sit high above on a granite outcropping.

★ JEROME

More than 1,000 years ago the Sinagua took minerals out of the cliffs that Jerome would one day cling to, engaging in prehistoric small-scale mining for precious stones and paints. This established the primary use of Cleopatra Hill, where Spanish conquistadores, too, would dig for what was precious to their culture—gold and silver. But it wasn't until copper became one of the most useful metals of the modern age that the "Million Dollar Copper Camp" really got going. At its zenith in the 1920s, Jerome had about 15,000 residents.

Throughout the late 19th and early 20th centuries, Jerome was known for its moral subjectivity; prostitution and other common territorial sins were tolerated, albeit regulated, well into the 1940s. Mining, no matter what mineral you're after, is always going to be a boom-and-bust enterprise, and by the 1950s the bust had descended. Phelps Dodge left, never to return. The town turned ghostly around 1953, when it had fewer than 50 full-time residents and a lot of abandoned and crumbling homes, hotels, and shops.

By the 1970s, however, hippies, artists, dropouts, and crafters had found the picturesque old town and begun its resurgence as a colorful hilltop village of creative people, the kind of funky tourist haven and hideaway one finds all over the old mining frontier. Today dozens of shops, many of them carrying one-of-a-kind creations made by Jerome's bevy of resident artists and artisans, line the narrow, twisting streets through town, and saloonesque bars, historic boutique hotels,

and New American eateries occupy the old buildings that once served as saloons, hardware stores, hospitals, and hotels during the town's busy mining years, when the pits were worked around the clock. A couple of hours walking Jerome's streets, shopping for gifts and souvenirs, and eating at one of its excellent restaurants make for a fine way to spend an Arizona day.

Jerome Historical Mine Society Museum

The small **Jerome Historical Mine Society Museum** (200 Main St., 928/634-5477, www. jeromehistoricalsociety.com, 9am-6pm daily, $2 adults, children free) has exhibits on Jerome's exciting and sometimes violent history. It has ephemera and artifacts from the town's various eras, from its boom days through the big bust in the 1950s and beyond. There's a hefty touch of the lurid here, with a lot about violence, illicit sex, and the social consequences of each—the most fascinating displays in the building, naturally. There's also a small gift shop that sells books on the history of Jerome and souvenirs of the region.

Jerome State Historic Park

The Douglas family ruled mining in Jerome for decades, and in 1916 patriarch James "Rawhide Jimmy" Douglas built this palatial adobe house above his Little Daisy Mine, the better to welcome mine investors and company officials to town with the kind of style and comfort not always expected in western wildlands. The mansion is now **Jerome State Historic Park** (Douglas Rd. off Hwy. 89A, 928/634-5381, http://azstateparks.com, 8:30am-4:45pm Thurs.-Mon., $7 adults, $4 children 7-13, children under 7 free), dedicated to Jerome's history, and it's worth a visit just to see the building; the library has been beautifully restored and evokes what it was like to live comfortably and richly in an otherwise rough mining town. There are also several interesting displays on Jerome's history and a lot of rusty old mining equipment sitting around the grounds. A short

A Northland Road Trip

This is ideal road-trip country, its scenic treasures nearly always represented not only deep in the wilderness but right there on the roadside, too.

Starting from Phoenix, the most scenic road trip, and one on which you'll hit all the wonders and sights, goes first to Prescott, where you'll pick up State Highway 89A, twisting up and over Mingus Mountain through Jerome and then coming down the other side to the Verde Valley.

After seeing the ruins and lush riverine spectacle of Verde country, continue on Highway 89A to Sedona, through Oak Creek Canyon, and up to Flagstaff, where it becomes U.S. 89 and leads to Wupatki and Sunset Crater. Then head south to I-40 and east a little way to Walnut Canyon. Continue on the interstate to Winslow, where you'll pick up State Highway 87 south through the pines to Payson and Tonto Natural Bridge, just below the Mogollon Rim.

After exploring below the rim, take Forest Road 300 (a dirt road but easily traversed) across the rim to State Highway 260 (if you want to skip the dirt-road backcountry, pick up Highway 260 in Payson), which becomes the White Mountain Scenic Highway and leads through the high forest and meadow country to U.S. 191, the Coronado Trail. Slowly twist and turn down the forest-lined, two-lane road, through the tiny mountain towns, down to the desert grasslands of southeastern Arizona. Then take I-10 west through Tucson and back to Phoenix.

If you don't stop too long at any one place, such a drive-through, best-of-the-region's scenery road trip makes for a memorable and busy long weekend.

video, narrated by a friendly ghost, tells the story of Jerome, and a cool 3-D model of the town shows what the tunnels looked like under it.

Nightlife

Though these days Jerome is no longer known as one of the "wickedest" places in the territory and illegal narcotics aren't regularly ingested from the town's bar tops as in the 1970s and 1980s, Jerome's nightlife can still get a little rowdy—and therefore fun. The **Spirit Room Bar** (166 Main St., 928/634-8809, www.spiritroom.com, 11am-1am daily) offers deep cocktails and live music Saturday and Sunday afternoons and into the night.

Shopping

There are dozens of shops, boutiques, galleries, and antiques stores in Jerome, and there are always new ones opening up as the tourist traffic through town increases. Along with all the usual shops with gifts and crafts and a Southwestern flare, you'll find contemporary fine art, handmade wines, fudge, pottery, copper and turquoise jewelry, and all sorts of other treasures in Jerome, where shopping is

really the primary activity. Make sure to check out the amazing collection of kaleidoscopes at **Nelly Bly** (136 Main St., 928/634-0255, www.nelliebdyscopes.com, 9:30am-5:30pm Sun.-Thurs., 9:30-6pm Fri.-Sat.). Stick to Main Street to find most of the shops, although others can be found on Clark Street, Hill Street, and Jerome Avenue.

Food

Mile High Grill & Spirits (309 Main St., 928/634-5094, www.milehighgrillandinn. com, 8am-4pm Tues.-Thurs., 8am-9pm Fri.-Sat., $10-15) serves great breakfasts until noon and offers steaks, prime rib, sandwiches, and salads for lunch and dinner. The bar has a great beer selection and makes some unique, locally inspired specialty drinks. The walls are decorated with the work of local artists. Sit at one of the window tables and watch people walk by while you kick back a few cold ones. Or you could sit at one of the candlelit tables overlooking the Verde Valley at ★ **The Asylum** (200 Hill St., 928/639-3197, www.theasylum.biz, 11am-3:30pm and 5pm-9pm daily, $13-32) up on a hill inside the Jerome Grand Hotel.

The restaurant bills itself as "a restaurant on the fringe," meaning that they are cooking on the cutting edge of New American cuisine. The menu has an interesting mix of the familiar and the exotic fused together to create some delicious meals, and the wine selection is as impressive as the elegant, view-centered interior.

Accommodations

Jerome has several boutique hotels and bed-and-breakfast inns, most of them in refurbished historic buildings with at least one or two ghosts in residence.

★ **Jerome Grand Hotel** (200 Hill St., 928/634-8200, www.jeromegrandhotel.net, $185-295) used to be a hospital, and from the outside it has the character of an old sanatorium, perched on a hill and heavy with secrets. Inside, the rooms are tastefully decorated and comfortable, with nice showers and tubs, TVs, and some with views of the valley below.

The **Connor Hotel of Jerome** (164 Main St., 928/634-5006, www.connorhotel.com, $125-185), a high-class establishment for boomtown visitors, has been around in one form or another in the same location since 1898. Today it's a charming, comfortable place to stay in downtown Jerome, with 12 rooms, each with TV, minifridge, private bath, and Wi-Fi. The rooms above the Spirit Room Bar are sometimes noisy, especially on the weekends.

The **Mile High Inn** (309 Main St., 928/634-5094, www.milehighgrillandinn.com, $85-130), a comfy, historic, and friendly place occupying a redbrick storefront on Main Street, has five rooms individually decorated with a Southwestern Victorian style, not all with private baths. All of the rooms have air-conditioning and free Wi-Fi but not TVs.

Information and Services

Check out the **Jerome Chamber of Commerce** (310 Hull Ave., 928/634-2900, www.jeromechamber.com, 9am-5pm Mon.-Fri.) for up-to-date information about all the goings-on in Jerome and environs.

CLARKDALE AND THE VERDE CANYON RAILROAD

Founded in 1912 by the United Verde Copper Company for workers at a nearby smelter, Clarkdale remains largely unreconstructed today, though the smelter and the company shut down long ago. It's said that the quiet town was the first master-planned community in Arizona, a state that would one day suffer from a surfeit of that breed. There's not much here save **The Verde Canyon Railroad** (300 N. Broadway, 800/582-7245, www.verdecanyonrr.com, $65-90), an excursion train that runs on tracks formerly used to bring ore from Jerome to the smelter in Clarkdale. The four-hour round-trip ride takes its passengers from Clarkdale to Perkinsville Ranch and back, snaking through Verde Canyon, an inaccessible, bald eagle-populated notch with ochre cliffs towering on one side and the green river meandering on the other. It's a slow but unforgettable route, at one point disappearing into a dark, 680-foot tunnel. There's a small café and a gift shop at the Clarkdale depot.

The least expensive fare is an adult coach ticket at $65, which is a basic and comfortable ride through the spectacular canyon. A first-class ticket starts at $90 and includes open-air viewing cars, a complimentary glass of champagne, supremely comfortable seats, and a full bar. For $129 you can book passage for special events, including wine-tasting and sunset trips.

TUZIGOOT NATIONAL MONUMENT

Just outside of Clarkdale, **Tuzigoot National Monument** (100 Main St., off Broadway between Clarkdale and Old Town Cottonwood, 928/634-5564, www.nps.gov/tuzi, 8am-6pm daily summer, 8am-5pm daily winter, $10 adults, children under 16 free, entrance fee also good at Montezuma Castle), a 120-room, stacked-stone pueblo ruin on top of a hill overlooking the lush river valley, is the first of three federally protected sites in the Verde Valley that preserve what remains of the disappeared Sinagua culture. A museum has some good exhibits on Sinagua culture and the natural history of the area. You can walk up to the roof of the building and see the green valley with Sinagua eyes. The site is not as dramatic as Montezuma Castle or Well, but it is a fascinating and important place nonetheless.

SYCAMORE CANYON WILDERNESS AREA

Hikers should make it a point not to leave the valley before taking a jaunt into the **Sycamore Canyon Wilderness Area,** one of Arizona's most beloved and beautiful natural treasures, often called, as are other lesser canyons in the state, "the other Grand Canyon." It is the state's second-largest canyon and one of the first to enjoy federal wilderness protection.

You can reach the southern rim of the canyon by taking the road to Tuzigoot, then turning left after the bridge on Sycamore Canyon Road, and then heading about 10 miles to the rim.

The best day trip into the canyon from this end starts at the **Parsons Trailhead** on the rim. You descend about 500 feet into the bottomlands, where you'll walk along the creek, with cottonwood and willow and other water-loving flora all around. Deep, still pools catch falling leaves in the fall, and the riverside shade is life saving in the summer. Dark, high walls tower over you, closing in ever tighter. You can backpack through the entire 11-mile canyon bottom, but the day-use portion of the Parsons Trail ends about four miles in at a deep pool—the spring that feeds the creek. From there, return the way you came, climbing back up to the rim. Expect to get your feet wet crossing the creek in a few places and expect to not want to leave the canyon bottom and return to dry reality.

OLD TOWN COTTONWOOD

This pleasant and short stretch of State Highway 89A (Main Street) through downtown Cottonwood, just a few miles east of the road to Tuzigoot, was once the commercial and social heart of the valley. Some of the old buildings remain; others have been rebuilt and replaced several times over the generations. Along the clean, refurbished sidewalks are a few shops, antiques stores, cafés, and galleries and a couple of really good restaurants. The Old Town area is on the National Register of Historic Places and worth a stroll and a stop for lunch or dinner. Along the Old Town's quaint row you'll also find several comfortable and stylish **Verde Valley Wine Trail** (http://vvwinetrail.com) tasting rooms.

Food and Accommodations

Jerome and Sedona offer proximity to more abundant dining and sleeping options, but you'll find a few charming hotels and some excellent restaurants in Cottonwood's historic Old Town.

The 1950s-style **Bing's Burger Station** (794 N. Main St., 928/649-1718, www. bingsburgers.com, 10am-8pm Mon.-Thurs., 10am-9pm Fri.-Sat., 10am-8pm Sun., $4.50-10.25) is housed in a retro gas station in Old Town and serves some of the best burgers in the region. Fans of the old-school roadhouse diner should see this place, with its road-culture antiques and simple, filling, well-prepared comfort food. The **Tavern Grille** (914 N. Main St., 928/634-6669, http://thetaverngrille.com, 11am-9pm daily, $12-24) serves an eclectic selection of burgers, sandwiches, steaks, pasta, and salads, and offers cocktails, craft beers, and wines from Arizona and elsewhere.

The **Iron Horse Inn** (1034 N. Main St., 928/634-9455, http://ironhorseoldtown.com, $119) has been a motor court-style hotel along

1: Jerome State Historic Park **2:** Tuzigoot National Monument **3:** Montezuma Castle National Monument **4:** rock carvings at the V-Bar-V Ranch Petroglyph Site

Cottonwood's Main Street since the 1930s. It still has a good bit of retro charm, but also offers all the modern amenities and comforts. Rooms come with wireless Internet, TVs, and refrigerators. The Iron Horse is in a great location, within walking distance to the river and Old Town's tasting rooms. As is the **Tavern Hotel** (914 N. Main St., 928/634-6669, http://thetavernhotel.com, $169), a boutique hotel for the wine trail crowd, with upscale touches and a stylish atmosphere.

DEAD HORSE RANCH STATE PARK

The near-jungle of **Dead Horse Ranch State Park** (675 Dead Horse Ranch Rd., Cottonwood, 928/634-5283, http://azstateparks.com, 8am-5pm daily, $7 per car up to four people), just a few blocks from Old Town Cottonwood, provides easy access to the riparian wonders of the Verde River. Here you can walk streamside for miles, below weeping cottonwoods and hanging willows, and through all kinds of vines and branches teeming out of proportion. You'll completely forget that you are in the arid West here. If you want to camp and fish one of the artificial lagoons, there are dozens of spots with hookups, bathrooms, and showers ($15-55 per night). But the park is best used for a riverside day trip to spend a few hours exploring the source of all life in the valley, maybe with a picnic and some bird-watching. The best hike is the 1.5-mile loop along the **Verde River Greenway**, a six-mile stretch of lush life along the Verde between the Tuzigoot and Bridgeport bridges meant to preserve the riparian ecosystem, one of only a few remaining in the state. Unlike the park's creepy name, the Verde River Greenway's name is descriptive to perfection—that's exactly what it is, a greenway, and it is all the more beautiful for being so rare and threatened.

FORT VERDE STATE HISTORIC PARK

One of several outposts in the central highlands from which General Crook battled the Apache and others, **Fort Verde State Historic Park** (125 E. Hollamon St., Camp Verde, 928/567-3275, http://azstateparks. com, 9am-5pm daily, $7 adults, $4 children 7-13, children under 7 free) will be of interest to history lovers and those wondering what a poor soldier's life was like serving on what must have felt like the very edge of the world. You can stroll the grounds and look into a few old buildings set up with original fort artifacts, furniture, and daily-life items that give one a feeling for late-19th-century Anglo-West life and a connection to the officers, surgeons, and soldiers who must have wondered every day how they got all the way out here.

VERDE RIVER SCENIC AREA

The **Verde River Scenic Area** is a wild stretch of the river that is popular with canoers, kayakers, and other boating types. The beautiful, sometimes rough and rapid stretch from **Beasly Flat to Childs** offers a true river adventure. The best way to prepare for a trip is to get ahold of the **Boater's Guide to the Verde River,** which you can download for free at www.fs.usda.gov. Or contact the **Verde Ranger District** (300 E. Hwy. 260, Camp Verde, 928/567-4121, 8am-4:30 Mon.-Fri.).

★ MONTEZUMA CASTLE NATIONAL MONUMENT

If you have time to make only one stop in the Verde Valley, make it the **Montezuma Castle National Monument** (I-17 Exit 289, 928/567-3322, www.nps.gov/moca, 8am-5pm daily winter, 8am-6pm daily summer, $10 for 7-day pass, children under 16 free, entrance fee also good at Tuzigoot National Monument). The five-story, 20-room limestone castle, built about AD 1200, looks down on Beaver Creek and the former farmlands of its builders from an improbable niche in the cliffside. It seems like it *was* a castle of some kind, the home of a ruler or a god, but it was

The Verde Backcountry

Forest Road 708, also known as **Fossil Creek Road,** is a 26-mile dusty washboard of a road below the Mogollon Rim, deep in the river valley outback between Camp Verde and Strawberry. Take this out-of-the-way route to find deep collecting pools for swimming, warm smooth rocks for sunbathing, and a tough but beautiful semidesert hike. Or detour off down to the banks of the Verde and take a short walk along the river past a decommissioned power plant to the ruins of an old resort, its hot springs still spilling and steaming out of the ground. You may find parts of this backroad route closed from time to time. Check the **Coconino National Forest website** (www.fs.usda.gov/coconino) before heading out. Note that the Forest Service recommends a high-clearance or four-wheel-drive vehicle.

Verde Hot Springs

Verde Hot Springs: Take Forest Road 502 off of Forest Road 708 (signed from the west but not the east), about 12 miles from Strawberry. Drive about 6.5 miles south to the Verde, where the old power plant molders, and take a short hike against the river flow along the road beyond the ruined plant. After about a mile you'll see the ruined baths of the old Verde Hot Springs Resort across the green river, now a hidden public art gallery decorated with generations of graffiti and wall paintings. It's not likely that the baths are cleaned too often, and you might, on any given day, run into a few naked or nearly naked refugees from the world, drinking beer and enjoying the solitude of one of the stranger of the famous Verde Valley ruins.

Waterfall Trail: The most popular hike in the wild and beautiful area known as Fossil Creek would have to be this two-mile in-and-out trail. Access is 14 miles down Forest Road 708, and the creekside trail ends at an enchanting waterfall and swimming hole, a lush and cool area that's the very definition of an oasis. If it's a nice, warm day, and it usually is, you will not be alone. It is difficult to get a parking permit during the April 1-October 1 high season, so reserve a **permit** (www.recreation.gov) one month before your trip.

Fossil Springs Trail No. 18: At the end of Forest Road 708 you'll find a parking lot for this moderate-strenuous trail, also in the Fossil Creek area, fed by Fossil Springs. It's an eight-mile round-trip hike down an old wagon road to the creek (dropping about 1,500 feet), with its deep pools of inviting water and ceaseless flow rushing over rocks past the lush and shady banks. Going back up is not easy, especially if it's hot. There are signs all up and down the trail warning people to be prepared, and still several rescues are required every season. It's a wonderful place to go, and one of the last places to see a wild and unaltered high-desert riparian area in all its special glory. A parking permit is also required here April 1-October 1, and again is not easy to come by; reserve a **permit** (www.recreation.gov) one month before your trip. This is also a nice hike in the winter, when the parking lot is nearly empty and the riverside trees naked.

more likely the apartment-style shelter for a group of Sinagua who found the creek and the sheltered cliffs to their liking. There's not much to do here other than walk along the short trail and look up at the ruin, but it is something that really should be seen. Imagine being the first explorer to come upon the abandoned castle. When you walk out of the small visitors center and behold the cliff-side for the first time, it's a breath-catching moment.

Montezuma Well

The **Montezuma Well** (I-17 Exit 293,

928/567-4521, 8am-6pm daily June-Aug., 8am-5pm daily Sept.-May, free), a sister monument just up the interstate from the castle, is often overlooked, but it's a fascinating, quiet stop that will leave you in a bit of awe at nature's strangeness. The "well" is actually a sinkhole into which 1.5 million gallons of 74°F springwater has flowed daily for untold stretches of flowing time, ringed by rough cliffs into which the Sinagua built apartments. You can walk a short, twisting path down to the water's edge and explore the rock-wall rooms.

BEAVER CREEK RECREATION AREA

If you find the streamside red rocks of Sedona and Oak Creek too busy, try **Beaver Creek Recreation Area** (I-17 Exit 298), a rather out-of-the-way oasis at the dirt-road southern end of Forest Road 618, about two miles from the interstate. Here red-rock banks and tree shade await, lining Wet Beaver Creek. The warm red-rock slabs make perfect jumping boards into the pools along the creek, great for splashing around and soaking your feet. There's a **campground** (928/203-2900, $16 per night) with nice creekside spots if you can't bear to leave this beautiful spot.

V-Bar-V Ranch Petroglyph Site

Most of the hundreds of rock-carved symbols, animals, and mysterious beings at the **V-Bar-V Ranch Petroglyph Site** (I-17 Exit 298, www. redrockcountry.org/heritage, 9:30am-3:30pm Fri.-Mon.) were created between AD 900 and AD 1300 by the Sinagua, the same people who built Montezuma Castle and other ancient sites around the Verde Valley. Here you can walk along an easy, level creekside trail, shaded by cottonwoods and willows, and get up close to the strange rock carvings. There is usually a knowledgeable docent around to explain things; otherwise, there are several information panels scattered around the site. Plan on spending an hour or more here, and make sure to bring your own water. You need a Red Rock Pass to visit, which you can buy here for $5. To reach the site, which was the V-Bar-V Ranch until it was purchased by the Forest Service in the 1990s to preserve the astonishing petroglyphs, drive two miles south on Forest Road 618 from I-17 Exit 298 and cross over Wet Beaver Creek.

Sedona

Second only to the Grand Canyon as a favorite Arizona destination, Sedona and its red rocks resemble the great canyon in several ways. Like the canyon, Sedona's rare beauty is the result of geologic circumstance—the slow work of wind, rain, trickling water, and the predictable restless rocking of the Colorado Plateau. The little resort town sits at the base of the plateau, and its red-rock monuments sit dramatically alone, rising into the light-blue sky.

Also like the canyon, this landscape seems so otherworldly that it's a struggle not to go a little beyond yourself here. For most, all other explanations fail, which can explain why the spiritual instincts come alive for many who visit, and why there are hordes of spiritual entrepreneurs ready to exploit those instincts. Here you can stay in extreme comfort, bordering on the decadent, or rough it to a certain degree. You can purchase a world-class work of art and jostle through the backcountry in a pink Jeep. There will be crowds—some four million tourists come to the red rocks every year, searching for one thing or another. It's easy to forget that, despite its international reputation as a life-list destination, Sedona is really just a small, somewhat rural town with only about 10,000 year-round residents. It just happens to be stuck in a geologic wonderland.

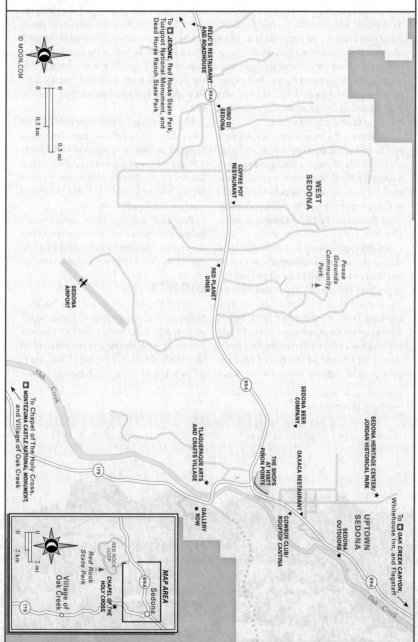

Sedona

© MOON.COM

0   0.5 km
0   0.5 mi

To **JEROME**, Red Rocks State Park,
Tuzigoot National Monument, and
Dead Horse Ranch State Park

RELIC'S RESTAURANT
AND ROADHOUSE

VINO DI
SEDONA

COFFEE POT
RESTAURANT

WEST
SEDONA

SEDONA
AIRPORT

Posse
Grounds
Community
Park

RED PLANET
DINER

SEDONA BEER
COMPANY

OAXACA RESTAURANT

SEDONA HERITAGE CENTER/
JORDAN HISTORICAL PARK

THE SHOPS
AT HYATT
PINON POINTE

COWBOY CLUB/
ROOFTOP CANTINA

SEDONA
OUTDOORS

UPTOWN
SEDONA

To **OAK CREEK CANYON**/
Whitehouse Inn, and Flagstaff

TLAQUEPAQUE ARTS
AND CRAFTS VILLAGE

GALLERY
ROW

Oak Creek

To Chapel of The Holy Cross,
MONTEZUMA CASTLE NATIONAL MONUMENT,
and Village of Oak Creek

0   2 km
0   2 mi

RED ROCK
LOOP

Red Rock
State Park

CHAPEL
OF THE
HOLY CROSS

MAP
AREA

Sedona

Village of
Oak Creek

PLANNING TIPS

Sedona is a popular destination for day trips as its highlights can be seen in a few hours, and most people who visit this spectacular landscape spend only a brief time within it. Those who spend the most time here are hiking or mountain biking enthusiasts, spiritual seekers, or guests at high-end resorts. In the summer, the cool waters of Oak Creek and Wet Beaver Creek call to desert dwellers, who then throng to their sandy red banks.

Uptown is the busiest and most touristy section of Sedona, making parking challenging (especially during the spring and summer weekends). **West Sedona** is more of a "real town," spread out along Highway 89 in a series of shopping centers, strip malls, and stand-alone businesses. Red Rock Country is accessible from both.

Sedona can be easily and somewhat thoroughly enjoyed in an unhurried day trip; it's less than an hour from Flagstaff and just two hours from the Grand Canyon and Phoenix. The best way to do it is to arrive by, say, mid-morning. Drive along the **Red Rock Scenic Byway** on your way into town from I-17, take a stroll on one of the trails around **Bell Rock,** stop at the **Chapel of the Holy Cross** and poke around Uptown before having lunch

there or in West Sedona. After lunch, take the **Red Rock Loop Road** down to **Red Rock Crossing** to see the creek and the warm red rocks. Lastly, on your way back to Highway 179 and the interstate, drive up to **Airport Mesa** for one last look at the region. If you're visiting from Flagstaff, you may want to skip the Red Rock Loop Road and instead drive through Oak Creek Canyon on State Highway 89A.

It's easy to fit a visit to **Montezuma Castle** into a day trip to Sedona from Phoenix or Flagstaff. It's just 26 miles away via Highway 179 and I-17 and doesn't take long to see. Ideally, you would visit it before you arrive in Sedona; that way you are less likely to be tired and blow it off on the way home.

For those with more time and interest, a Sedona dream vacation would last from three days to one week, with plenty of time for hiking, biking, and exploring the backcountry.

SIGHTS

Nature is the main attraction here, but all of Sedona and its environs qualify as a "sight," so to speak. Still, you'll want to make sure you get a look at the famous **Chapel of the Holy Cross** (780 Chapel Rd., three miles south of the Y at Chapel Rd., www.

view from Uptown Sedona

chapeloftheholycross.com, 9am-5pm Mon.-Sat., 10am-5pm Sun., free), part of the Roman Catholic Diocese of Phoenix. The towering, cross-faced chapel appears to be emerging full born from a red-rock cradle southwest of town (and supposedly near a vortex). In keeping with the self-conscious spiritual vibe in Sedona, many visitors come here to quietly commune with the view, encouraging the emotion all that stained sandstone naturally inspires.

To learn a little local history, at least from the Anglo point of view, check out the **Sedona Heritage Museum** (735 Jordan Rd., 928/282-7038, www.sedonamuseum.org, 11am-3pm daily, $7 adults, $10 with audio tour, $3 children under 13) in Uptown's **Jordan Historical Park,** where there's an old fruit orchard and a few disused artifacts from the agricultural past. The museum features a historic cabin, built in the 1930s by fruit growers and now restored with some original furnishings, wherein is told the story of early Sedona from the 1880s on. The best exhibit is the **Movie Room,** all about the many films that have been made amid the red rocks (Zane Grey's *Call of the Canyon, Johnny Guitar,* etc.).

To see the whole strange landscape laid out before you in miniature, make the short drive up **Airport Mesa** (the end of Airport Rd.). On the side of the road leading to this small rural airport and lodge, some 500 feet above the town, there's a lookout spot that is simply breathtaking and a logical place to take a few pictures. You can park for free at a nearby lot.

ENTERTAINMENT AND EVENTS
Nightlife

If you're looking to be around people, have a few drinks, and enjoy some conversation, try the rooftop cantina at **Oaxaca Restaurant** (321 N. Hwy. 89A, 928/282-4179, www.oaxacarestaurant.com, 11am-9pm daily) in Uptown. The shaded patio bar, which looks down on Sedona's main tourist strip, provides long, romantic views of the red rocks that seem to get more beautiful with every round

of margaritas. The crowd here is the typical northland mix of hometown locals, tourists from all over creation, canyon-and-river rats, and spaced-out vortex hunters. It's likely to be crowded, noisy, and fun on a weekend night in season.

The ★ **Sedona Beer Company** (465 Jordon Rd., 928/862-4148, www.sedonabeerco.com, noon-9pm Thurs.-Mon.) brews a fantastic line of craft beers using local ingredients, including barley grown on a family farm in nearby Camp Verde with support from the nonprofit Sinagua Malt (http://sinaguamalt.com). To combat the Verde River's declining flow, Sinagua Malt helps local farmers move away from summer crops that need a lot of water and replace them with comparable late-winter and spring crops that don't. Such as malt barley, a key ingredient in beer—leading to a powerful partnership between Arizona's family farmers and craft brewers. Sedona Beer Company has a tap-room vibe, great beers, and delicious, well-prepared pub-style food.

The **Oak Creek Brewery** (2050 Yavapai Dr., 928/204-1300, www.oakcreekbrew.com, noon-close daily) attracts a lot of locals and is an enjoyable place to hang out. The brewery offers some of the best microbrews in the state in a laid-back, tasting-room atmosphere, with jam sessions, drum circles, dance parties, and live music throughout the week. It is a place to let loose, listen to live local music, and chow down on some fantastic tamales, quesadillas, and other Southwestern bar food. This casual place, which is in West Sedona away from the more touristy sections of the town, should not be confused with **Oak Creek Brewery and Grill** (336 Hwy. 179, 928/282-3300, www.oakcreekpub.com, 11:30am-8:30pm daily) at upscale Tlaquepaque Village, which is also a fun place to kick back a few of the Oak Creek-brand microbrews.

Vino Di Sedona (2575 W. 89A, 928/554-4682, www.vinodisedona.com, 8pm-10pm Mon., 11am-11pm Tues.-Thurs., 11am-midnight Fri.-Sat., 11am-10pm Sun.) only works with Arizona's family-owned, small batch wineries and breweries. This fun and

What's a Vortex... and Why Should You Care?

Hanging around the Sedona Visitor Center in the summer, one hears more than once the suggestions of local volunteers trying to get out-of-towners, especially first-time visitors, interested in the little town's story beyond the famous vortexes. "But we came out here from Boston, and we want to see the vortexes."

Well, you can't really see them. A vortex, they say, is a place with a special energy, a space in a landscape that gathers energy from all around it, concentrating, perhaps to be manipulated by someone in touch with the earth's languages. The red rocks around Sedona are said to be rotten with them, and a hike or drive to a vortex site has become the most popular New Age activity here in recent years. Don't worry; you can still get your tarot cards read, have your aura photographed, your past lives remembered, and your crystals recharged at storefronts all over town.

The vortex movement, according to Dwight Garner of the *New York Times,* began in 1987, "the year of the Harmonic Convergence when believers flocked to mystical places across the planet, hoping for a global awakening of harmony and love." Reportedly some 5,000 true believers descended on Sedona, understood as one of those "mystical places," probably owing more to its unique scenery than anything else, and many of them never left. These days there's no shortage of guides who will take you out into the red rocks and introduce you to the vortexes and, perhaps, your spiritual self.

Suzanne McMillan and her staff at **Sedona Vortex Tours** (150 Hwy. 79, Stes. 2-3, 928/282-2733 or 800/943-3266, www.sedonavortextours.com, $159-239 pp for 3-5 hours) promise to "teach you how to feel the vortex energy." McMillan has been leading tours since 1988, taking seekers out in vans or on hikes to vortexes and on Medicine Wheel Tours. Linda Summers of **Sedona Spirit Journeys** (928/282-8966, www.sedonaspiritjourneys.com, $188 pp for 2 hours) has a degree in Native American studies and guides a "Sedona Vortex Healing Journey," during which she shares the history of the vortex sites and offers "guided meditation, drumming, and a special crystal and Reiki healing energy in the beauty of nature." Cynthia Tierra of **Healing from the Heart** (928/821-0989, www.healingone.net, $100 per hour) has 25 years of experience as a holistic health practitioner and Reiki master. She will guide you to both well-known and "secret" vortexes, and she gives psychic readings as well. **Sedona Spirit Yoga & Hiking** (928/282-9900 or 888/282-9901, www.yogalife.net, $89-225 pp for 3-4 hours), run by Johanna (Maheshvari) Mosca, who calls herself "Madame Vortex," offers guided vortex hikes that include yoga sessions on the red-rock buttes.

For more on this scene, check out the **Sedona Metaphysical Spiritual Association** (928/300-7796, www.sedonaspiritual.com).

---

casual place offers live music every night, and great tapas, pizza, sandwiches, and sliders. Vino Di Sedona is also an excellent, well-stocked wine store.

Festivals and Events

Cinephiles will enjoy drinking wine with indie film stars during the **Sedona International Film Festival** (928/282-1177, www.sedonafilmfestival.org, Feb.-Mar.), five days in late February and early March filled with cutting-edge and independent films, discussions, and workshops.

The arts take over in October, with the renowned **Sedona Arts Festival** (Sedona Red Rock High School, 995 Upper Red Rock Loop Rd., 928/204-9456, www.sedonaartsfestival. org, Oct., $12) and the **Sedona Plein Air Festival** (Sedona Arts Center, 15 Art Barn Rd., 928/282-3809 or 888/954-4442, www. sedonapleinairfestival.com, Oct.). Both festivals feature local and national artists interpreting the painting-worthy landscapes of Sedona and the greater Southwest.

1: Chapel of the Holy Cross 2: orchard in Jordan Historical Park

SHOPPING AND GALLERIES

Contemporary eclectic, mid- to high-end arts and crafts with a fetish for the Southwestern legendary, Native American jewelry and spiritual objects, Mexican colors and religious items, or a heavy-framed painting of a cowboy sleeping next to a campfire, his worn old hat pulled down a bit over his eyes. . . . This is pretty much what you'll find in Sedona's many shopping districts, though there are notable exceptions. After a while, one boutique, gallery, and fancy "trading post" tends to meld into the next. Shopping here is great fun and probably the second-most-popular activity around, just below staring dumbfounded at the rocks. It's doubtless even more fun if you have the wallet to afford the best pieces, which, sadly, always cost the most, and sometimes even more than that.

Start at the **Uptown Shops** (N. Hwy. 89A), the original Sedona shopping district. Both sides of Highway 89 have several levels of little touristy shops, souvenir stands, boutiques, and jewelry stores. If you feel like going hiking and didn't plan for it, look for **Sedona Outdoors** (267 N. Hwy. 89A, Ste. 5, 928/282-0296, 9am-8pm daily), where you can get pretty much any gear you need.

The high-end **Shops at Hyatt Piñon Pointe** (intersection of Hwy. 89A and Hwy. 179, 928/204-8828, http://hyattpinonpointe. hyatt.com) are worth a stroll. Make sure to stop at **Visions Fine Art Gallery** (101 N. Hwy. 89A, Ste. E24, 928/203-0022, www. visionsfineart.com, 11am-5pm daily), one of Sedona's best galleries.

Sedona's true shopping treasure, **Tlaquepaque Arts & Crafts Village** (336 Hwy. 179, 928/282-4838, www.tlaq.com) is an enchanting collection of Mexican-style courtyards with all kinds of unique shops and the best restaurant in town, René at Tlaquepaque. There's even a little white stucco chapel in the "village," as if you're in an upscale version of Old Mexico, with beautiful stained glass and a mural above the altar. There are more than 40 shops and galleries among the courtyards

and shade trees, including **Feliz Navidad** (928/282-2752, www.feliznavidadsedona.com, 10am-5:30pm Sun.-Tues., 10am-7pm Wed.-Sat.), dedicated to Christmas ornaments with a Mexican aesthetic.

Across the street from Tlaquepaque is **Gallery Row** (Hwy. 179 and Schnebly Hill Rd.), where you'll find Sedona's best Native American art. **Kopavi** (411 Hwy. 179, Garland Building upstairs, 928/282-4774, www. kopaviinternational.com, 10:30am-5pm Mon.-Sat., noon-5pm Sun.) has the best items made by Hopi artists. It is a good idea to call first to make sure they are open. Also check out the **Lanning Gallery** (Hozho Center, 431 Hwy. 179, 928/282-6865, www.lanninggallery. com, 10am-6pm Mon.-Sat., 11am-5pm Sun.) for tasteful Southwestern styles.

The **Hillside Sedona** (671 Hwy. 179, 928/282-4500, www.hillsidesedona.net) complex is also in this area and deserves a look, especially the **Gallery of Modern Masters** (888/282-3313, www.galleryofmodernmasters. com, 10am-5pm daily), which has some spectacular pieces by some of the all-time greats.

FOOD

A favorite with the locals, the ★ **Coffee Pot Restaurant** (2050 W. Hwy. 89A, 928/282-6626, www.coffeepotsedona.com, 6am-2pm daily, $8-11) is great for breakfast and lunch, with filling home-style American and Mexican food in big portions. It serves breakfast all day, especially from a signature list of "101 Omelettes." It may be that a few of them were desperation choices: The final entry on the list comes with peanut butter, jelly, and banana. Nonetheless, there are at least 70 others worth trying. Located in West Sedona along Highway 89A, not far from Coffee Pot Rock, this popular restaurant also has a shaded patio and an eclectic gift shop. Expect a crowd and a bit of a wait on weekend mornings.

The **Cowboy Club** (241 N. Hwy. 89A, 928/282-4200, http://cowboyclub.com,

---

1: Tlaquepaque Arts & Crafts Village 2: Cowboy Club in Uptown Sedona

11am-9pm daily, $14-37) in Uptown Sedona is a perennial favorite, a Western-style place with buffalo meat and rattlesnake on the menu along with great burgers and steaks. Founding members of the Cowboy Artists of America used to hang out here long ago when it was called the Oak Creek Tavern, and their memory is kept alive in the many paintings on display throughout the restaurant.

One of the better Mexican restaurants in the northland is ★ **Oaxaca Restaurant** (321 N. Hwy. 89A, 928/282-4179, www. oaxacarestaurant.com, 11am-9pm Mon.-Fri., 8am-9pm Sat.-Sun., $13-24). This popular restaurant in Uptown Sedona has a spectacular patio and excellent food that's both pleasingly familiar and a bit off kilter.

★ **René at Tlaquepaque** (336 Hwy. 179, 928/282-9225, www.rene-sedona.com, 11:30am-2:30pm and 5:30pm-8:30pm daily, $11-16 lunch, $28-45 dinner), with its Mexican courtyard ambience and outrageously tasty food, has long been one of Sedona's top spots to dine. Try the baked French onion soup and the sweet potato ravioli, or the venison, or the . . . just try the whole menu and go back again and again if you can.

If you're headed up to Airport Mesa to view all of Sedona spread out before you, and you should be, stop by the **Mesa Grill** (1185 Airport Rd., 928/282-2400, www. mesagrillsedona.com, 7am-9pm daily, $16-26) for a bite to eat or a drink (happy hour 3pm-6pm daily). The small, sleek restaurant and bar looks out on the airport's runway through large, view-framing windows. The eclectic menus feature pasta dishes, hamburgers, and seafood.

As the name says, **Nick's Westside** (2920 Hwy. 89A, 928/204-2088, www.nickswestside. com, 7am-9pm Mon.-Sat., 8am-2pm Sun., $7-23) is in West Sedona, along Highway 89A. It's popular with locals for breakfast, lunch, and dinner. This place serves exceedingly satisfying home-style food: ribs, brisket, burgers, sandwiches, burritos, tacos, and enchiladas. Nick's tends to be busy for breakfast on weekend mornings.

The **Oak Creek Brewery and Grill** (336 Hwy. 179 at Tlaquepaque Village, 928/282-3300, www.oakcreekpub.com, 11:30am-8:30pm daily, $12-24) serves excellent bar-and-grill-style fare, including fantastic barbecue ribs, fish-and-chips, and a large selection of pizzas. Then there's the enchanting setting within the charming confines of Tlaquepaque Village. Sit on the patio if weather permits, and it usually will. The locally brewed beer on tap here is some of best in the state.

ACCOMMODATIONS

There are dozens of hotels and resorts in Sedona, some of them like little towns themselves. Many of the resorts are outlandishly well-appointed, with golf courses and all kinds of spa treatments, workshops, and spiritual rituals.

Some of the most romantic and secluded spots are about 2-4 miles north of Uptown Sedona on State Highway 89A, in Oak Creek Canyon along the shady banks of Oak Creek.

$50-100

The clean and inexpensive **Sedona Village Lodge** (105 Bellrock Plaza, 800/890-0521, www.sedonavillagelodge.com, $69-119) is a good choice for hikers and those who are more interested in red rocks than gift shops. It's across from Bell Rock, a name given to an eroded mound of rock that looks vaguely like a bell, about six miles south of downtown along Highway 179—close enough but also a bit far away, which is the ideal place to be. The rooms are comfortable, the hosts are friendly, and the Wi-Fi is free. It's a good idea to reserve a room far in advance.

Another great value is the **Sugar Loaf Lodge** (1870 W. Hwy. 89A, 928/282-8451 or 877/282-0632, www.sedonasugarloaf.com, $75-95), a little 15-room motel just a mile or so west of the junction of Highways 89A and 179. It's close to everything and offers a clean, comfortable room with a refrigerator and television. With its pool, hot tub, and budget-friendly price, Sugar Loaf is one of the best deals in a town where bargains are often hard to find.

$100-250

The **Whitehouse Inn** (2986 W. Hwy. 89A, 928/282-6680, www.sedonawhitehouseinn. com, $115-130) is an affordable and basic place to stay, offering a clean and central base for a visit without the huge price tag, mud baths, or chakra healing.

The **Arroyo Pinion Hotel** (3119 W. Hwy. 89A, 928/204-1146 or 800/789-7393, www. ascendcollection.com, $166-196) is an excellent choice for hikers and mountain bikers. It's located in West Sedona, a bit away from the tourist bustle of Uptown and Tlaquepaque. The location provides easy access to backcountry roads that lead to the trails around Chimney Rock and Sugarloaf. There's a free continental breakfast, and the rooms are well appointed with flat-screen TVs, free Wi-Fi, refrigerators, and big, comfortable beds perfect for resting your bones after a day in the wilderness.

Located right in the middle of all the action in Uptown Sedona, the ★ **Matterhorn Inn** (230 Apple Ave., 800/372-8207, www. matterhorninn.com, $185-199) is one of the best places to stay if you're hoping to experience all that Sedona has to offer. The small hotel sits among dozens of shops and restaurants and yet still manages to provide amazing views of the beautiful, exotic Sedona landscape. The Southwestern-style rooms offer comfort, free Wi-Fi, and private balconies from which to stare at the red rocks. Don't miss the solar-heated pool and hot tub next to a romantic outdoor sitting area with a fireplace. The Matterhorn is also one of Sedona's greener hotels. It has undergone extensive renovations with a focus on conservation, including installing low flow toilets, water efficient faucets and showerheads, timers on outdoor lighting, dry landscaping, and on-demand hot water heaters.

The **Oak Creek Terrace Resort** (4548 N. Hwy. 89A, 928/282-3562 or 800/224-2229, www.oakcreekterrace.com, $120-289) is tucked into the greenery along Highway 89A just south of Slide Rock State Park in Oak Creek Canyon. Arizonans love Oak Creek Canyon because it is one of the last easily accessible riparian areas left in the state, and its green and shady nature is shocking for its rarity. It seems impossible that one could improve on the natural splendor of this place, but the folks at Oak Creek Terrace have made an honest and successful go of it. The little bungalows and cabins on this beautiful property have fireplaces, in-room hot tubs, outdoor barbecues, and kitchenettes. This is a perfect place for families looking to get out of the city and back to nature without giving up any of the comforts of home.

The **Sky Ranch Lodge** (1105 Airport Rd., 928/282-6400 or 888/708-6400, http:// skyranchlodge.com, $124-157) offers something a little different: It's located on top of Airport Mesa, 500 feet above the red land, set next to the small Sedona Airport. Its best feature is its location high above the rest of Sedona, and the views, especially at sunrise and sunset, are spectacular and right outside your door. They offer a variety of rooms, including large ones with kitchens for families and cozy, romantic hideaways with fireplaces. Don't worry about noise from planes. It's an airport, yes, but a very small one that serves mostly private planes, corporate jets, and airtour companies. The Sky Ranch Lodge also has a decent restaurant and bar, so it's conceivable that you could stay up here and never go down again.

The **Wildflower Inn** (6086 Hwy. 179, 928/284-3937 or 888/494-5335, www. sedonawildflowerinn.com, $89-199) in the Village of Oak Creek looks out at Bell Rock and offers rooms with fireplaces and in-room whirlpool tubs—a little bit of decadence at a relatively affordable price.

The **Orchards Inn** (254 N. Hwy. 89A, 928/282-2405 or 800/341-5931, www. orchardsinn.com, $249 and up) has a pool and whirlpool tub, plus wonderful rooms, many with fireplaces and patios with views of the red rocks. The central location in Uptown is hard to beat. Stay here and you can walk to all the shops and restaurants on the main tourist strip of 89A and leave your car parked.

The **El Portal Sedona** (95 Portal Ln., 800/313-0017, www.elportalsedona.com, $199 and up) is an amazing 12-room hacienda in the rustic-elegant style, with deep comfort, great food, and furniture you'll want to pack up and take home. Most of the rooms have private patios and fireplaces, and all of them have televisions and free wireless Internet. This fabulous little inn is next to the Los Abrigados Resort and Tlaquepaque Village, and if you stay at El Portal, you are allowed to use the resort's pool and spa.

Over $250

The enchanting **Orchard Canyon on Oak Creek Lodge** (8067 Hwy. 89A, 928/282-3343, www.garlandslodge.com, $285-385) has 16 charming and comfortable cabins of various sizes set on 10 acres along Oak Creek, on the edge of the Red Rock Secret Mountain Wilderness. The lodge has a renowned restaurant, and the price of a room includes breakfast, dinner, and tea. This wonderful place is surrounded by orchards and a lush, green lawn on which they serve cocktails every evening. The lodge is open April 1 through November 15 and has a two-night minimum. Some people love this place so much that they make a habit of returning year after year, so you must call far, far ahead of time to book a spot, and you might end up on a waiting list. Something to consider: There are no televisions or telephones in the rooms.

★ **Amara Creekside Resort** (310 N. Hwy. 89, 928/282-4828, www.amararesort. com, $326-432) is one of those Sedona places you've heard about: Lovely beyond reason and intimidatingly tasteful, this retreat on the banks of Oak Creek has a full-service spa and all the other amenities you'd expect from a five-diamond hideaway.

INFORMATION

The **Sedona Chamber of Commerce** has a very energetic and organized tourism bureau

that operates a well-stocked and well-staffed visitor center. The **Visitor Information Center** (331 Forest Rd., 928/282-7722 or 800/288-7336, www.visitsedona.com, 8:30am-5pm Mon.-Sat., 9am-3pm Sun.) in the Uptown shopping area is easy to spot.

TRANSPORTATION

Since it's a small town with a huge population of visitors, driving and parking in Sedona can be an adventure; nonetheless, it's easy to find your way around. The first thing you have to know is that there are four distinct zones in and around Sedona, all of them accessible using just two connecting roads. State Highway 89A runs right through the heart of town, north to Oak Creek Canyon, and eventually to Flagstaff. The portion of this road north of its junction with State Highway 179, the town's main intersection, called the "Y" among locals, is called Uptown. The stretch of Highway 89A west of the Y is called West Sedona. Highway 179 heads southwest from the Y and continues through the red rocks, eventually intersecting with I-17. The stretch of Highway 179 between Schnebly Hill Road and Canyon Drive is called Gallery Row. The Village of Oak Creek is about five miles southwest of Sedona along Route 179.

Car

You really must have a car to see Sedona and Red Rock Country right, and it would be ideal to have an SUV or a four-wheel-drive vehicle. A regular sedan will work just fine, though, and if you still want to explore the inaccessible backcountry, you can book a Jeep tour.

The best and quickest way to get to Sedona from Phoenix is to take I-17 north to State Highway 179, which will take you past some amazing scenery and right into the small town's heart. The 116-mile drive from Phoenix to Sedona, about 90 percent of it on the interstate, usually takes about two hours.

Coming from Flagstaff to the north, take State Highway 89A through Oak Creek Canyon, one of the most scenic routes in the state. Much of the road is slow and twisty, so expect the 44-mile drive to take at least an hour. You can also take I-17 south from Flagstaff to Highway 179, about 90 miles or 1.5 hours. This route, though longer, is probably the safest way to go during inclement weather.

A lot of travelers combine a visit to Sedona with stops at Montezuma Castle, the quaint old mining town of Jerome, and Prescott. The Sinagua ruins are about 30 miles south of Sedona. Take Highway 179 out of Sedona to I-17, and look for the Montezuma Castle sign at Camp Verde, right near the casino. If you want to stay off the interstate and take a look around the Verde Valley on your way to Montezuma Castle, take Highway 89A southwest to Cottonwood, about 19 miles, then take State Highway 260 to Camp Verde, a distance of about 12 miles. You can reach Prescott from Sedona, a distance of about 67 miles, by taking Highway 179 to I-17. The interstate moves through and then climbs out of the river valley for about 20 miles. As you reach the top of the hill, look for Highway 169 on the west side of the freeway. This road, also called the "Cherry Cut-Off," leads to Highway 69, which goes to Prescott, about 40 miles from the intersection of I-17 and Highway 169. The whole trip takes about an hour and a half. A much more scenic route to Prescott from Sedona takes you up over Mingus Mountain and through the bustling old "ghost town" of Jerome. Take Highway 89A west out of Sedona and follow it up to the top of the mountain, about 27 miles away. Follow the road out of Jerome as it twists and turns through the forest down to plains below and then into Prescott, which is 36 miles from Jerome. The whole drive from Sedona is likely to take two hours or more despite its relatively short distance.

Public Transportation

Once you've made it to town, if you don't feel like driving around, hop on the **Sedona Trolley** (928/282-5400, www.sedonatrolley.com, $17 adults, $12 children under 12) for two different 55-minute "best-of" tours offered between 10am and 4pm daily.

Red Rock Country

TOP EXPERIENCE

Red Rock Country's towering natural monuments were once a part of the Colorado Plateau, the connection eaten away by erosion, that ingenious sculptor that makes all of Arizona its medium over millions of years. High concentrations of iron oxide, or rust, in the sediment layers stain the rock statues many shades of red as a finishing flourish. The result is one of the most beautiful and sought-after landscapes on earth.

Many of the red-rock buttes, spires, and monuments around Sedona have been given names over the years. Some of the more famous rocks can be seen from the road at designated pull-offs, and most of them have relatively easy trails around them if you want to get closer. On State Highway 89A heading into Sedona from the west, look for **Chimney Rock** off to the north, roughly around Andante Drive. A little farther east and far off to the north around Soldiers Pass Road, keep an eye out for **Coffee Pot Rock.** Many people recognize in a rock monument near Schnebly Hill Road and Highway 179 the shape of Snoopy relaxing with Woodstock on his nose, and thus call it **Snoopy Rock.**

Red Rock Pass

Before you do anything in Red Rock Country, stop by the ranger station or the Sedona visitors center and purchase a **Red Rock Pass** ($5 per day, $15 per week, or $20 per year), which you're required to have even if you're only going to be motoring around the rocks and stopping every now and again. The fees go to the upkeep of this heavily used national forest. An America the Beautiful Interagency

Pass, the $80 federal pass to all parks, works here as well.

For all the information on driving, hiking, and biking in Red Rock Country, stop by the **Red Rock Ranger District visitors center** (8375 Hwy. 179, mile marker 304.7, six miles north of I-17 junction, 928/282-4119 or 928/203-2903, www.fs.usda.gov/coconino, 8am-5pm daily).

RED ROCK SCENIC BYWAY

The best way to enter Sedona is from the south, from I-17 to State Highway 179. Along this route, roughly between Wet Beaver Creek and Oak Creek, about 10 miles or so, you'll see some otherworldly scenery along both sides of the road. This short stretch, if driven slowly with stops in between for photographs and strolls, could take a few hours, or it could be passed by at a brisk pace, mouth gaping open. Either way, it is along this paved, busy road that Sedona's red rocks reveal their strange splendor; if you're only passing through, do it along this stretch of Highway 179. The always busy route has a series of roundabouts as it moves through the Village of Oak Creek that must be navigated with great care. Also, make sure to keep extra distance between you and the car ahead; people tend to stop abruptly here.

There are two developed pullouts along the road. The first, if you are moving from the south, is the **Bell Rock Pathway and Vista Southern Trailhead,** on the east side of the road. Pull over here for views and photographs of **Bell Rock** and **Courthouse Butte** to the east. To the southwest sit **Cathedral Rock** and **The Three Nuns.**

Just beyond the parking lot, there are popular and easy hiking and mountain biking trails that lead into the high-desert red lands and up close to the rocks. There's a trail map and bathrooms at the turnout. Just 2.6 miles up the road, again on the east side of the road, you'll see the **Little Horse Trail and Bell Rock Pathway Northern Trailhead,** the second pullout along the route. This stop

provides a different vantage point from which to view the rocks, and there's parking for and access to hiking trails. There is a trail map and a bathroom near the parking lot.

RED ROCK LOOP ROAD

This short loop drive is an easy way to see the red rocks, and it also provides access to beautiful Red Rock Crossing and Red Rock State Park. Most regular passenger cars can make it with no problems; the route is paved except for one short stretch.

Head west on State Highway 89A for about seven miles from Uptown and turn south on Upper Red Rock Loop Road, also called Forest Road 216. Now, open your eyes. There's red and green everywhere, various in shade and mood. There are a few undeveloped scenic pullouts, and not a few homes, along this road. About 1.5 miles in you'll see signs for the **Crescent Moon Recreation Area** and **Red Rock Crossing** ($10 per car), reached by turning left on Chavez Ranch Road. This is a very popular creekside oasis where people go to splash around in Oak Creek and soak up the warm mercy of the red rocks. Get there early, especially on the weekend in the summer, if you want a picnic table. The area has bathrooms and drinking fountains, but you should bring your own water. Also bring your camera: Red Rock Crossing provides some spectacular views of **Cathedral Rock,** not to mention dark green water lapping against red rock. The road continues and becomes Lower Red Rock Loop Road, which provides access to Red Rock State Park. It then leads back around to Highway 89A.

Red Rock State Park

The 286-acre **Red Rock State Park** (Lower Red Rock Loop Rd., 928/282-6907, http://azstateparks.com, 8am-5pm daily, visitors center 9am-5pm daily, $7 per vehicle) is a pleasant place to see Oak Creek, which runs through the park and provides water for huge cottonwoods and willows under which you can lounge and walk. There are about five miles of short streamside hiking trails, situated into loops with truly inspiring scenery.

Every day at 10am a ranger leads an hour-long **nature walk** through the riparian ecosystem. The main thrust here is environmental education, and this is the best place to really get to know the ecology of the area. This is also a really good choice for families with young kids. The trails are easy and provide a kind of introductory hiking experience.

PALATKI HERITAGE SITE

Palatki Heritage Site (928/282-3854, www.fs.usda.gov/coconino, 9:30am-3pm daily), a small Sinagua cliff dwelling in the Sedona backcountry, isn't as dramatic as Montezuma Castle or the Northern Sinagua dwellings near Flagstaff, but it's still very much worth visiting for the beauty of the area and the amazing petroglyphs and pictographs left behind on the soft sandstone walls. The site was occupied by a small group of Sinagua, who hunted, farmed, and built strange stone cities throughout the Verde Valley, from about AD 1100 to 1300.

A great pioneer of Southwestern archaeology, Jesse Walter Fewkes, visited Palatki, which means "Red House" in the Hopi language, as part of an archaeological expedition to Arizona in the 1890s. He described the cliff dwelling as showing a "degree of architectural skill, which, while not peculiar to the cliff dwellings of the Red-rocks, is rarely found in southern cliff houses." Not much is left, but by hiking the short but relatively steep step-trail to the dwelling you can still get an idea of how the Sinagua lived and the skill with which they built. Most visitors will find the walk of moderate difficulty; make sure you have some good walking shoes and bring along water. The view from the high dwelling of the Sedona landscape, all rust-red and pine-green, is something to remember—and photograph. Another moderately steep trail leads to the petroglyphs and pictographs, which are an essential part of a visit here.

You must purchase a Red Rock Pass ($5) to visit Palatki, and you have to call ahead to reserve a spot, as parking is limited to 20 cars. The drive to the ruin is over dirt roads, though most regular sedans can make it without problems. Take State Highway 89A west from Sedona and go five miles past the last traffic light. Turn right on Forest Road 525. It's 10 miles from the turnoff to the ruin, with signs along the way to guide you. Once there, you'll find knowledgeable docents and a small visitors center with bathrooms and bookshop. No pets are allowed. You don't need a reservation to visit the smaller **Honanki** ruin about five miles from Palatki. Meaning "Bear House" in Hopi, Honanki is not as well-preserved as Palatki and is recommended only to those with an extremely deep interest in the Sinagua.

★ OAK CREEK CANYON

Arguably the most beautiful drive in the state is the twisty, streamside drive north on State Highway 89A through Oak Creek Canyon and back up to the plateau. Head north out of Sedona, over the large bridge hovering high over Oak Creek, and just drive and look, slowly, taking great pains not to veer into oncoming traffic as you're craning to see the towering red rocks, topped with white caps, greenery peppered throughout. The creek is so inviting that you may want to stop along the side of the road and put your feet in. It's illegal to park along most stretches of the road, but there are a few pull-offs and several lodges and stores along the way where you can stop. The best and easiest place to get in the creek is at **Slide Rock State Park** (6871 N. Hwy. 89A, 928/282-3034, http://azstateparks.com, 9am-6pm daily winter, 8am-6pm daily summer, $10 per vehicle, $20 summer) where you can try out the 80-foot natural red-rock slide, walk around the short nature trails, picnic, or just soak in the creek and lie around on the warm rocks. There will likely be crowds in the summer, including many, many families with children.

★ HIKING

Red Rock Country is high country, high desert populated by evergreen junipers and piñon pines, always dusted with a bit of red sand. The landscape holds famous rusty buttes, red slickrock, mystical slot canyons, and lush and shady creeksides. It's a unique place, and one that rewards the traveler who trades the scenic highway for rocky trails with a deeper understanding and appreciation of the natural wonders here.

There are several areas around Red Rock Country where you can access various trailheads in one place, and get a taste of the area's most beautiful and memorable spots. Many of the trails around Sedona are open to hikers, equestrians, and mountain bikers. Trailheads often have a large map for reference, but you can also pick up a fairly comprehensive guide to the region's trails at the **Red Rock Ranger District Visitor Center** (8375 Hwy. 179, 928/203-2900, www.fs.usda.gov, 9am-4:30pm daily). Always take water and a hat with you.

Just south of the intersection of Highways 179 and 89A (known as the Y) south of Uptown, take the traffic-circle exit for Schnebly Hill Road. About a mile in, you'll find the parking lot for **Huckaby & Margs Draw Trails,** which gives access to hikes that wind around the highlands above Uptown. A good option here is **Margs Draw Trail No. 163,** an easy 2-mile one-way hike with great views of Snoopy Rock, Camel Head, and Steamboat Rock. Allow about two hours for the hike. The **Huckaby Trail** is a fantastic 2.8-mile one-way hike down to Oak Creek and back up to higher land after passing beneath the dramatic Midgely Bridge. You have to cross the creek, hopping over boulders, and the trail is steep in a few places. This route provides great views of Uptown Sedona, Oak Creek, and, of course, the red-rock buttes. Plan on about 2.5-3 hours for the hike.

From Uptown Sedona, take Highway 179 south for about eight miles and you'll

1: Pink Jeep Tours 2: Courthouse Butte along the Red Rock Scenic Byway 3: Oak Creek Canyon 4: Tonto Natural Bridge State Park

find the **Bell Rock Area Trails,** a series of mostly easy, flat trails that lead around Bell Rock and Courthouse Butte, two of the most famous rocks in town. The **Bell Rock Pathway and Vista** is an easy 3.6-mile out-and-back trail that gets you up close to both Bell Rock and Courthouse Butte. Most of the trail is fairly flat and wide, and mountain bikers often speed by. If you want to get better-than-average photographs of these famous eroded rocks, you'll need to hike in a bit. About 0.5 mile into the trail you'll see an offshoot for the **Courthouse Butte Loop,** a 3.6-mile loop around the hulking red rocks, moderately strenuous and a bit steep in a few places. This is a great introduction to Red Rock Country. Both trails take about 2.5 hours total to hike.

Off the north side of Highway 89A, the **Soldier Pass Trails** can be accessed by turning right on Soldier Pass Road heading west from Uptown Sedona. A good option here is the **Soldier Pass Trail No. 66,** a 4.5-mile loop that passes through the Red Rock Secret Mountain Wilderness and near a natural arch. You'll gain some great views of Red Rock Country from the high vistas on this hike, but you have to walk up some fairly steep and rocky trails to enjoy them. It's a moderate hike and takes about 2.5 hours.

For sweeping, in-town views, take an easy hike on the 3.3-mile round-trip **Sugarloaf/ Coffee Pot Trail,** a walk that's perfect for families. The trail winds through red lands and residential neighborhoods to the top of **Sugarloaf Rock,** where you can get some excellent pictures of Coffee Pot Rock and Thunder Mountain. From the Y intersection of Highway 89A and Highway 179, go west on 89A for about two miles to Coffee Pot Drive and turn right. Take a left on Sanborn after about 0.5 mile; then turn right on Little Elf, which ends at Buena Vista, where you'll see parking for the trailhead.

A bit farther west on Highway 89A from Uptown Sedona, turn right onto Dry Creek Road and continue on it as it becomes Boynton Pass Road, turning right at the juncture for the

Dry Creek Trails parking lot. The most popular trail in this area is the **Boyton Canyon Trail,** an easy five-mile round-trip to a vortex through the Red Mountain Secret Wilderness, where you'll see canyon walls more than 1,000 feet high and maybe even waterfalls if it's a wet time of year. The trailhead is just outside Enchantment Resort. Allow about two hours for this hike.

For some streamside hiking, try the **West Fork of Oak Creek Trail,** 6.5 miles round-trip, which takes you through a riparian wonderland mixed with red rocks and deep-green pools. It's a popular trail, so expect crowds. The trailhead is at milepost 385 along Highway 89A in Oak Creek Canyon, north of Uptown Sedona. It's an easy, mostly flat hike that takes about 2-3 hours, but you'll probably get your feet wet crossing the creek a few times. It costs $10 to park at the trailhead, and the parking lot and trail closes when full, which is usually early during the high season—the parking lot opens at 9am and fills up by 9:30am.

MOUNTAIN BIKING

One of the best biking areas is the **Bell Rock Loops,** a series of red-dirt single-tracks among the petrified sand dunes out in the rocks near the Village of Oak Creek. The northland biking authorities at **Absolute Bikes** (6101 Hwy. 179, 928/284-1242 or 877/284-1242, www.absolutebikes.net, 8am-6pm Mon.-Fri., 8am-5pm Sat., 8am-4pm Sun.), right near the Bell Rock Loops trailhead, can give you some pointers and ideas about where to go.

JEEP TOURS

One of the most famous tour companies in the Southwest, **Pink Jeep Tours** (204 N. Hwy. 89A, Uptown Sedona, 800/873-3662, www.pinkjeep.com, 7am-6pm daily, $95) operates under a special permit with the Forest Service to take their gaudy open-air four-wheel-drive Jeeps, filled with eager and excited tourists, out into the red lands. Founded in 1960, it's pretty much an institution, and the guides are usually friendly, entertaining, and knowledgeable. Unless you have your own four-wheeler, this is the best way to see the less accessible portions of the backcountry in a vehicle. There are a lot of Jeep tour companies to choose from in Sedona, but Pink Jeeps is one of the oldest and certainly the most conspicuous.

Payson and Rim Country

Just a short, scenic 1.5-hour drive north of Phoenix on State Highway 87, also known as the Beeline Highway, and you're in a different world. Payson, a small town of about 15,000 people, sits about 5,000 feet above sea level and is surrounded by the Tonto National Forest and the Sierra Ancha and Mazatzal Mountains. The town is tucked below the 7,000-foot-high Mogollon Rim. Visitors to this region can access the heights of the Rim via a historic dirt road about 30 miles north of the small forest town. The road parallels the Rim for about 50 miles and ends in the White Mountains region, within the vast Apache-Sitgreaves National Forests. Along the two-lane highway between the Rim and Payson, you'll pass through a few tiny, quaint forest settlements, but this area is mostly about the pine-and-aspen forest, the long, sweeping views above the treetops, and the cool, clean high-country air.

Founded in 1882 by miners and ranchers, Payson, which stretches out along Highway 87 about 90 miles north of Phoenix, used to be called Green Valley, and it's easy to see why. The little town is popular with Phoenicians escaping the summer heat, and as such it has several chain hotels and restaurants, all of which you can find on the main drag along the highway. This is an inviting region if you're interested in Old West history and forest sports such as hiking, mountain biking, camping, and fishing. Otherwise, its scenic value and cool breezes, even in the summer, are enough to recommend it for a day trip from Phoenix.

SIGHTS
★ The Mogollon Rim

The 7,000-foot-high southwestern edge of the Colorado Plateau, the Mogollon Rim (pronounced "Mug-ee-yun") is a dramatic rock escarpment that runs west-to-east across Arizona's high country for some 200 miles. Also called the Tonto Rim and featured in Westerns by Zane Grey and Louis L'Amour, the escarpment's topside is covered with pine-and-aspen forests and small lakes. The easiest way to see it, and to view a sea of pine trees spread out below its heights, is to take a several-hour drive along the General Crook Trail, an ancient route across the rim that's also known as the Rim Road.

Made from a trail that was once used by General George Crook to run supplies from Fort Verde, near Prescott, to Fort Apache in the White Mountains during the Apache wars of the 1870s, the Rim Road (Forest Road 300) is not paved, but neither is it too rough; most sedans will make it just fine. In places the road parallels the Rim exactly, and you can stop, walk right up to the edge, and feel the pine-scented wind on your face. The 51-mile one-way drive across the Rim from Highway 87 to the **Mogollon Rim Visitor Center** (Hwy. 260, about 32 miles east of Payson and 27 miles west of Heber/Overgaard, 9am-3pm Thurs.-Sun. May 19-Labor Day) takes several hours. Expect the drive to take at least two hours one-way, but it could take twice that depending on how many times you want to stop and explore the forest. Make sure to gas up, check your tires and fluids in Payson before you head out, and pack food and water with you; there's little but beautiful views along the way.

Drive north out of Payson on State Highway 87 (also designated as State Highway 260 westbound) for 29 miles until you see the sign for Forest Road 300 on the right side of the road, not far after Highway 260 separates and continues west. Turn east on Forest Road 300 and drive all the way across the Rim to the visitors center, where there's a paved trail and some breathtaking views right at the edge of the White Mountains region, near an eastern portion of Highway 260. You can make a loop back to Payson by taking Highway 260 from the Mogollon Rim Visitor Center southwest 34 miles back to town. You could also start the trip from Payson going northeast on Highway 260 eastbound and then drive west on Forest Road 300 across the rim to Highway 87.

Along the Rim Road you'll see the effects of the huge wildfires that have threatened this region repeatedly over the last few decades. Blackened stands of deadwood and new green growth are everywhere along the escarpment. The whole region is generally bone dry and drought-ridden, and it is usually subject to campfire restrictions in the summer.

Rim Lakes

In the forest just north of the Rim along Forest Road 300, there are several small, pine-encircled artificial lakes that are stocked with trout and bass and offer camping spots and plenty of easy trails to the Rim's edge.

The best of these is **Woods Canyon Lake,** a gorgeous little 55-acre lake not far from the Rim Visitor Center. There are four **campgrounds** (Apache-Sitgreaves National Forests, Black Mesa Ranger District, Overgaard, 928/535-7300, www.fs.usda.gov/asnf, 877/444-6777, $22 per night) near the lake, offering a total of about 150 sites, some of which can take trailers up to 32 feet long. There's also a country store that sells all kinds of supplies, a dump station, picnic tables, and bathrooms, and there's a company that rents boats. The lake is open April 1-October 15 and quite popular. The easiest way to reach Woods Canyon Lake and the other nearby Rim lakes is to take Highway 260 northeast from Payson 30 miles to Forest Road 300, which is paved on this stretch. Then drive about four miles west and turn right on Forest Road 105. The lake is a mile farther on.

INFORMATION

For more information on the Rim and its lakes and trails, try the **Apache-Sitgreaves National Forests, Black Mesa Ranger District** (Overgaard, 928/535-7300, www. fs.usda.gov/asnf). Another good source for information about hiking, biking, and camping in this region is the local website www. rimcountry.com.

Zane Grey Cabin

Even if you've never read any of Zane Grey's more than 130 books, a look at the **Zane Grey Cabin** (700 Green Valley Pkwy., 928/474-3483, 10am-4pm Wed.-Mon., $5) is a must when you're in the small town of Payson. The famous, beloved writer of Westerns loved this area, which he called the Tonto Rim, and came here to write and hunt often between 1918 and 1929. The original cabin burned down in the 1990 Dude Fire, but a local group rebuilt it exactly and furnished it according to surviving pictures. There's also a small **Rim Country Museum** next door with exhibits on Grey and what life was like for the Anglo pioneers who settled this piney area below the great rim.

Tonto Natural Bridge State Park

The **Tonto Natural Bridge State Park** (11 miles north of Payson on Hwy. 87, 928/476-4202, http://azstateparks.com, 8am-5pm daily, last entry at 5pm, $7 adults, $4 children 7-13) is the major stop in Rim Country other than the Rim itself. The world's largest natural travertine bridge, the strange and wondrous sight can be hiked to or over on short trails. Though the trail going to the dripping, moss-covered inner bridge is steep going back up, it's short and should really be taken to get the full experience. Hike down and sit on the wet rocks, watching water drip off the bridge's arch high above. A visit here typically takes about an hour but could go much longer.

Pine and Strawberry

Tucked just below the Rim north on Highway 87 about 20 miles from Payson, the tiny towns of **Pine** and **Strawberry** have a few antiques stores, small inns and restaurants, and a historic, rural atmosphere.

Pine comes first as you drive north from Payson on Highway 87. The **Pine-Strawberry Museum** (15 miles north of Payson on Hwy. 87, 928/476-3547, www. pinestrawhs.org, 10am-2pm Wed.-Sat., $1, children under 11 free) located here is worth a short stop. Housed in a former Mormon chapel that dates from 1917, the museum has an interesting collection of information and artifacts on the area's prehistoric cultures and its later settling by several tough Mormon families in the 1880s.

Strawberry is located just three miles north of Pine along Highway 87. About a mile into town is the **Fossil Creek Road,** which leads to the Verde Valley from the Rim Country. About two miles to the west on Fossil Creek Road from Highway 87, you'll find Arizona's "Oldest Standing Schoolhouse," a pine-log cabin called the **Strawberry Schoolhouse** (10am-4pm Sat., noon-4pm Sun. mid-May-mid-June and early Aug.-mid-Oct., 10am-4pm Mon.-Sat., noon-4pm Sun. mid-June-early Aug., free). Built in 1882 to serve a few pioneer families in the area, the small pine-plank, one-room schoolhouse has been preserved and restored by locals and now presents a 19th-century frontier school room as it would have looked to the kids filing in from the forest trails so long ago.

FOOD

There are a lot of chain restaurants and hotels around Payson, Pine, and Strawberry to serve Phoenicians escaping the heat, as it's a mere 1.5-hour drive from Phoenix. Most of the services are along the main route through town.

The chili and burgers at **Macky's Grill** (201 W. Main St., 928/474-7411, 10am-8pm Sun.-Wed., 10am-9pm Thurs.-Sat., http:// mackysgrill.com, $10-20) are excellent, and the menu is stocked with all kinds of other dishes, including a vegetarian burger and other nonmeat options. This place is popular with locals and has a fun, kitschy cowboy decor. The patio here is the place to eat on a cool high-country afternoon.

★ **That Brewery** (3270 AZ Hwy. 87, Pine, 928/476-3349, www.thatbrewery.com, 11am-8pm Mon.-Sat., 11am-7pm Sun., $10-20), along winding Highway 87 through the dusty pine forest, deserves a stop around lunch or dinner time for some delicious pub-style food, including vegetarian and gluten-free options, as well as superior craft beers. This out-of-way gem sits among the tall, cool pines and has a volleyball court and a shady patio. The restaurant is serious about sustainability, with a vigorous recycling ethic that includes building and decorating a second Cottonwood location with repurposed materials and found items. They also use only grass-fed, Arizona-raised beef, and donate 5 percent of all sales from their AZ Trail Ale brand to the nonprofit Arizona Trails Association. And, like other craft brewers in the northland, That Brewery buys its grain from a small farm in Camp Verde, helping local farmers to grow a lucrative crop while using less water.

ACCOMMODATIONS

Payson and the Rim work best as a drive-through or a day trip, but if you want to stay longer, there are several chain hotels along Highway 87, the main drag through town. You can't go wrong staying at the small **Majestic Mountain Inn** (602 E. Hwy. 260, 800/408-2442, www.majesticmountaininn.com, $119-189), which has clean, comfortable rooms, free wireless Internet, in-room refrigerators, and a heated pool. A few of the rooms have hot tubs next to the bed.

The Tonto Apache Tribe operates the **Mazatzal Hotel and Casino** (Hwy. 87 Mile Marker 251, 800/777-7529, www.

mazatzalcasino.com, $150 and up), which has very nice all-suite rooms, clean with comfortable beds, refrigerator, and microwave. Mazatzal has the somewhat desperate and depressing atmosphere unique to gambling halls, smoky and cheap. It's a fine place to stay nonetheless, and in a great location for anything you want to do in rim country. Eat elsewhere; the food here is overpriced.

TRANSPORTATION
Car

Payson and the Mogollon Rim are easy to visit by car from Phoenix. It's only 90 miles from Phoenix to the pine forests below the Rim. The best route is State Highway 87, also called the Beeline Highway. It usually takes about 1.5 hours to make the trip, but traffic can be slow on weekends in the summer, when everybody gets the same idea to head to the mountains out of the heat. Fill up before you leave Phoenix, as gas is likely to be more expensive along the road.

To reach this region from the Verde Valley and Sedona, take State Highway 260, east from Camp Verde 36 miles to Strawberry; then it's 30 miles south on the dual-designated Highway 260/Highway 87 to Payson, or only a few yards to Forest Road 300, which leads across the Rim to the White Mountains.

From Flagstaff, head south to the Verde Valley on State Highway 89A, through Sedona, and then take Highway 206 to Payson from Camp Verde. Another scenic route is to take Forest Road 209, also known as Lake Mary Road, out of Flagstaff, through the forest, past Happy Jack and Clints Well to Highway 87 near the Rim Road. The incredibly beautiful forest drive is about 100 miles long and takes more than two hours. The road sometimes closes in winter.

To reach the White Mountains region from Payson, simply take Highway 260 east for 90 miles to Show Low.

The Grand Canyon and the Arizona Strip

There's a reason why Arizona's official nickname is "The Grand Canyon State." Any state with one of the true wonders of the world would be keen to advertise its good luck.

The canyon must simply be seen to be believed. If you stand for the first time on one of the South Rim's easily accessible lookouts and don't have to catch your breath, you might need to check your pulse. Staring into the canyon brings up all kinds of existential questions; its brash vastness can't be taken in without conjuring some big ideas and questions about life and humanity. Take your time here—you'll need it.

The more adventurous can make reservations, obtain a permit, and enter the desert depths of the canyon, taking a hike, or even a mule ride, to the Colorado River or spending a weekend trekking rim to

Highlights

Look for ★ to find recommended sights, activities, dining, and lodging.

★ **Hermit Road:** Make your way west along the forested rim to the enchanting stone cottage called Hermit's Rest, stopping to see the setting sun turn the canyon walls into fleeting works of art (page 267).

★ **Desert View Watchtower:** See one of architect Mary Colter's finest accomplishments—a rock tower standing tall on the edge of the canyon (page 274).

★ **Rim Trail:** Walk along the rim on this easy, accessible trail, past historical buildings, famous lodges—and the most breathtaking views in the world (page 275).

★ **Bright Angel Trail:** Hike down the most popular trail on the South Rim, its construction based on old Native American routes (page 276).

★ **Grand Canyon Lodge:** This rustic old lodge balances on the edge of the gorge, where

you can sink into a chair and gaze out at the multicolored canyon (page 286).

★ **Pipe Spring National Monument:** At this wisely preserved ranch and homestead, guides will show you what life was like on the lonely 19th-century frontier (page 305).

★ **Cliff Dwellers and House Rock Valley:** Stop along the highway and walk among these strange, thrilling little structures built of red rock (page 309).

★ **Lee's Ferry:** This is one of the few places in the canyonlands where you can dip your toes in the mighty Colorado River without first hiking deep into the Grand Canyon (page 309).

★ **Glen Canyon National Recreation Area:** Rent a houseboat or fish the waters of Lake Powell, an artificial lake formed by the Glen Canyon Dam (page 314).

The Grand Canyon and the Arizona Strip

Beaver Dam Mountains

Santa Clara
St. George
Washington

UTAH

59

Cottonwood
Point
Wilderness

Hildale

Beaver Dam
Mountains
Wilderness

VIRGIN RIVER
CANYON
RECREATION AREA

Colorado City

Cane Beds

Kaibab

Vermilion

Littlefield

Paiute
Wilderness

389

PIPE SPRING
NATIONAL
MONUMENT

Mesquite

Virgin River

15

▲ Mt Bangs
8,012ft

ARIZONA

Hurricane Cliffs

Virgin Mountains

Grand Canyon-
Parashant National
Monument

Hidden Canyon

Shivwits Plateau

Kanab

Grand Wash
Cliffs
Wilderness

Poverty
Mountain
6,791ft

Mount
Trumbull

Mt
Trumbull
8,028ft
▲

NEVADA

Mt Trumbull
Wilderness

Grand Canyon
National Park

Mt Logan
Wilderness

Parashant Canyon

Lake Mead
National
Recreation
Area

Supai

★ TOROWEAP

HUALAPAI
HILLTOP

Lake
Mead

Mt Dellenbaugh
7,072ft
▲

Colorado River

Lake Mead
National
Recreation Area

GRAND
CANYON WEST ★

Sanup Plateau

Coconino

White Hills

Grand Canyon

North Rim

Aubrey Cliffs

18

★ DIAMOND CREEK

Dolan
Springs

Red
Lake

Mt Tipton
Wilderness

Grand Wash Cliffs

Music Mountains

HUALAPAI INDIAN
RESERVATION

Peach Springs Canyon

▲ Mt Tipton
7,148ft

Peach
Springs

Chloride

Cerbat Mountains

Truxton

GRAND
CANYON
CAVERNS

66

93

Valentine

Hackberry

Cottonwood Mountains

Peacock Mountains

Seligman

Golden
Valley

Kingman

40

66

40

0   10 mi

0   10 km

© MOON.COM

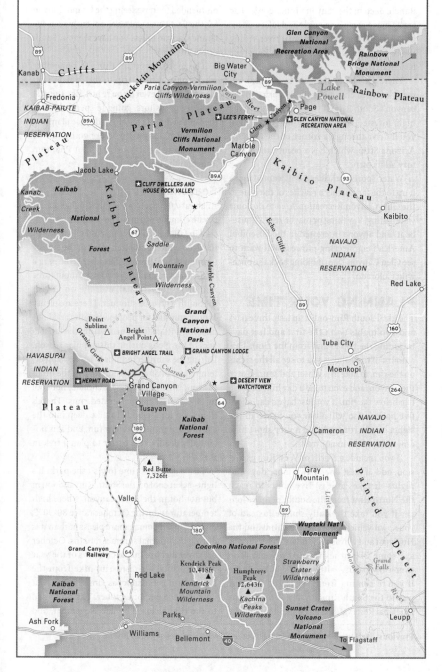

rim with an overnight at the famous Phantom Ranch, deep in the canyon's inner gorge. The really brave can hire a guide and take a once-in-a-lifetime trip down the great river, riding the roiling rapids and camping on its serene beaches.

There are plenty of places to stay and eat, many of them charming and historic, on the canyon's South Rim. If you decide to go to the high, forested, and often snowy North Rim, you'll drive through a corner of the desolate Arizona Strip, which has a beauty and a history all its own.

Water-sports enthusiasts will want to make it up to the far northern reaches of the state to the Glen Canyon Recreation Area to do some waterskiing, kayaking or maybe rent a houseboat, and anyone interested in the far end of America's engineering prowess will want to see Glen Canyon Dam, holding back the once-wild Colorado.

PLANNING YOUR TIME

The ideal South Rim-only trip lasts three days and two nights (with the first and last days including the trip to and from the rim). This amount of time allows you to see all the sights on the rim, to take in a sunset and sunrise over the canyon, and even to do a day hike or mule trip below the rim. If you just have a day, about five hours or so will allow you to see all the sights on the rim and take a very short hike down one of the major trails.

If you include a North or West Rim excursion, add at least one or two more days and nights. It takes at least five hours to reach the North Rim from the South, perhaps longer if you take the daily shuttle instead of your own vehicle, and the West Rim and the Hualapai and Havasupai Indian Reservations are some 250 miles from the South Rim over slow roads—although it makes sense if you're coming from Vegas and on your way to the South Rim anyway. A visit to the Hualapai Reservation's Skywalk should not be

substituted for the South Rim (and isn't recommended to those seeing the Grand Canyon for the first time; you have not truly seen the Grand Canyon unless you have seen the South or North Rim).

The most important thing to remember when considering a trip to the canyon is to plan far ahead, even if you're just, like the vast majority of visitors, going to spend time on the South Rim. Six months' advance planning is the norm, longer if you are going to ride a mule down or stay overnight at Phantom Ranch in the inner canyon.

Seasons

At about 7,000 feet, the South Rim has a temperate climate: warm in the summer months, cool in fall, and cold in the winter. It snows in the deep winter and often rains in the late afternoon in late summer. Summer is the park's busiest season, and it is *very* busy. About three million visitors from all over the world visit the South Rim each summer. There are plenty of opportunities for people-watching and hobnobbing with fellow tourists from the far corners of the globe during this popular season. During the summer months (May-September) temperatures often exceed 110°F in the inner canyon, which has a desert climate, but cool by 20-30°F up on the forested rims. There's no reason for anybody to hike deep into the canyon in summer. It's not fun, and it is potentially deadly. It is better to plan a trek in the fall.

Fall is a perfect time to visit the park: It's light-jacket cool on the South Rim and warm but not hot in the inner canyon, where high temperatures during October range 80-90°F, making hiking much more pleasant than it is during the infernal summer months. October or November are the last months of the year during which a rim-to-rim hike from the North Rim is possible, as rim services shut down by the end of October. The only road to the rim is closed by late November, and

---

Previous: the North Rim; Bright Angel Trail; Desert View Watchtower on the South Rim.

often before that, due to winter snowstorms. It's quite cold on the North Rim during October, but on the South Rim it's usually clear, cool, and pleasant during the day and snuggle-up chilly at night. A winter visit to the South Rim has its own charms. There is usually snow on the rim January-March, contrasting beautifully with the red, pink, and dusty green canyon colors. The crowds are thin and more laid-back than in the busy summer months. It is, however, quite cold, even during the day, and you may not want to stand and stare too long at the windy, bone-chilling viewpoints.

What to Take

Take along an easy-to-carry receptacle to re-fill at the water fountains situated throughout the park. A water bottle, CamelBak, or canteen is simply required gear for a visit; you are going to get thirsty in the high, dry air along the rim. You might even bring along a cooler with cold water and other drinks, which you can leave in your car and revisit as the need arises. Consider taking a hat, binoculars, and a camera along with your water bottle. The canyon's vastness can only be considered for so long before you start to notice the details hidden in plain sight; binoculars and cameras come in handy in such circumstances.

Even in summer, bring along a light jacket, for the nights at 7,000 feet can turn somewhat chilly. In the winter, when it is 70-something in Phoenix, the South Rim is cold and often snowy. Several layers of cold-weather clothing will serve you well October-May.

Gateways to the Canyon

Grand Canyon National Park, especially its South Rim, has some of the most interesting accommodations in the entire national park system, but it's not always possible to get reservations. The park's lodging rates are audited annually and generally compare favorably to those offered outside the park, but you can sometimes find excellent deals at one of several gateway towns around canyon country. Using one of these places as a base for a visit to the canyon makes sense if you're planning on touring the whole of the canyonlands and not just the park. Besides offering affordable and even a few luxurious places to stay and eat, these gateways are often interesting in their own right and deserving of some attention from the traveler, especially those interested in the history of this hard and spacious land.

Flagstaff, 79 miles southeast of the park's main South Rim entrance, was the park's first gateway town, and it's still in many ways the best. The home of Northern Arizona University is a fun, laid-back college town with a railroad and Route 66 history. In the old days, Eastern tourists detrained at Flagstaff and then faced an all-day stagecoach trip across the forest and the plains, just for a glimpse at the canyon and a few nights in a white canvas tent. These days you just hop in your rental car or your family road-trip wagon, take U.S. 180 northwest to Route 64, and about 1.5 hours later, there you are. The route is absolutely (with apologies to desert rats who prefer the eastern Desert View approach) the most scenic of all the approaches to the canyon, passing through Coconino National Forest and beneath the San Francisco Peaks, the state's ruling mountain range.

CAMERON

About 50 miles north of Flagstaff along Highway 89, near the junction with Route 64 (the route to the park's east gate), sits the more than 100-year-old ★ **Historic Cameron Trading Post and Lodge** (800/338-7385, www.camerontradingpost. com, $79-199). It's only about a 30-minute drive from the Desert View area of the park and is a good place to start your tour. Starting from the East Entrance, you'll see the canyon gradually becoming grand. Before you reach the park, the Little Colorado drops some 2,000 feet through the arid, scrubby land, cutting through gray rock on the way to its marriage with the big river and creating the **Little Colorado Gorge.** Stop here and get a barrier-free glimpse at this lesser chasm to prime yourself for what is to come. There are usually a few booths set up selling Navajo arts and crafts and a lot of touristy souvenirs at two developed pull-offs along the road.

The Cameron Lodge is a charming and affordable place to stay and makes a perfect base for a visit to the Grand Canyon, Indian Country, Lake Powell, and the Arizona Strip. It has a good restaurant (6am-9:30pm daily summer, 7am-9pm daily winter, $7-16) serving American and Navajo food, including excellent beef stew, heaping Navajo tacos, chili, and burgers. There's also an art gallery, a visitors center, a huge trading post/gift shop, and an RV park ($35 full hookup, no bathroom or showers). A small grocery store has packaged sandwiches, chips, and sodas. The rooms are decorated with a southwestern Native American style and are very clean and comfortable, some with views of the Little Colorado River and the old 1911 suspension bridge that spans the stream just outside the lodge. There are single-bed rooms, rooms with two beds, and a few suites that are perfect for families. The stone-and-wood buildings and the garden patio, laid out with stacked sandstone bricks with picnic tables and redstone walkways below the open-corridor rooms, create a cozy, history-soaked setting and make the lodge a memorable place to stay. The vast, empty red plains of the Navajo Reservation spread out all around and create a lonely, isolated atmosphere, especially at night; but the rooms have cable TV and free wireless Internet, so you can be connected and entertained even way out here.

If you're visiting in the winter, the lodge drops its prices significantly during this less crowded touring season. In January and February, you can get one of the single-bed rooms for about $79.

WILLIAMS

This small, historic town along I-40 (what used to be Route 66), surrounded by the Kaibab National Forest, is the closest interstate town to Route 64 and thus has branded itself "The Gateway to the Grand Canyon." It has been around since 1874 and was the last Route 66 town to be bypassed by the interstate (not until 1984). As a result, and because of a resurgence over the last few decades owing to the rebirth of the Grand Canyon Railway, Williams, with about 3,000 full-time residents, has a good bit of small-town charm—the entire downtown area is on the National Register of Historic Places. It's worth a stop and an hour or two of strolling about, and there are a few good restaurants. It's only about an hour's drive to the South Rim from Williams, so many consider it a convenient base for exploring the region. The drive is not as scenic as either Route 64 from Cameron or U.S. 180 from Flagstaff. This is the place to stay if you plan to take the **Grand Canyon Railway** to the rim, which is a highly recommended way of reaching the South Rim. It's fun, it cuts down on traffic and emissions within the park, and you'll get exercise walking along the rim or renting a bike and cruising the park with the wind in your face.

Williams Historic District

On a walk through the **Williams Historic Business District** you'll see how a typical pioneer Southwestern mountain town might have looked from territorial days until the railroad died and interstate came. Williams wasn't bypassed by I-40 until the 1980s, so many of its old buildings still stand and have been put to use as cafés, boutiques, B&Bs, and gift shops. Walk around and look at the old buildings; shop for Native American and Old West knickknacks, pioneer-era memorabilia, and Route 66 souvenirs you don't need; and maybe stop for a beer, cocktail, or a cup of coffee at an old-school, small-town saloon or a

1: winter at the Grand Canyon **2:** Rod's Steak House in Williams **3:** downtown Williams

dressed-up café. The district is bounded on the north by Railroad Avenue, on the south by Grant Avenue, and on the east and west by 1st and 4th Streets, respectively. About 250 acres, the district has 44 buildings dating from 1875-1949 and an array of Route 66-era business signs and midcentury commercial architecture worth a few snapshots. Old Route 66 is variously termed Bill Williams Avenue, Grand Canyon Avenue, and Railroad Avenue, and it splits into parallel one-way streets through the historic downtown before meeting up to the west and east.

Bearizona Wildlife Park

Don't be surprised if a big brown bear, gone lazy from living the easy life in beautiful pine-covered **Bearizona Wildlife Park** (1500 E. Route 66, I-40 Exit 165, 928/635-2289, www.bearizona.com, 8am-5pm daily, $25 adults, $23 seniors, $15 children 4-12), decides to lounge on his back in front of your car; it's best to drive around the old beast, one of the many rescued animals that call this family-friendly drive-through wildlife park home. Along the three-mile drive through the forested park, which the park insists be done with windows up, you'll see many brown and black bears wrestling and lounging in the meadows, as well as wolves, bison, bighorn sheep, and other classic Western animals. A walk-through section at the end of the drive called **Fort Bearizona** features adorable baby animals frolicking with innocence and wonder, along with a few regal birds of prey that would probably like to eat all those fuzzy little morsels.

Kids absolutely love this place, and it makes for an easy side trip on the way to the Grand Canyon: It's located just outside of Williams near the junction of I-40 and Route 64, right on the route to the South Rim. Allow about two hours to visit this fun park; many of the animals here have a bit of personality, and you might get hooked if you stay *too* long. Bearizona is busiest in the summer, but the park is open year-round. The hours may vary according to season and weather, so call before driving out there just to make sure. As always, bring your own water no matter the season.

Recreation

The alpine ski runs at the Arizona Snowbowl in the San Francisco Peaks are only a quick hour's drive from downtown Williams.

Events

In June, classic car enthusiasts gather in Williams for the **Historic Route 66 Car Show,** which includes a retro evening of cruising a two-mile loop around town showing off refurbished masterpieces.

Northland kids wait all year for the Grand Canyon Railway's celebration of author Chris Van Allsburg's classic holiday story *The Polar Express.* The always sold-out **Polar Express and Mountain Village Holiday** (800/848-3511, www.thetrain.com, 5:30pm and 7:30pm daily mid-Nov.-early Jan., $45-58 adults, $33-45 children 2-15) features a one-hour nighttime pajama-party train ride, complete with cookies and hot cocoa, to a lit-up Christmastown that kids ooh and ahh at from their train seats. Riders dressed up like characters in the book read the story as kids follow along in their own copies. Then Santa boards the train and gives each kid some individual attention and a free jingle bell like the one in the famous book. On the return trip, everybody sings Christmas carols, while the younger tykes generally fall asleep. This annual event is *very* popular with kids and their families from all over Northern Arizona, and tickets generally sell out early (even as early as August).

Shopping

There's a gathering of boutiques and gift shops in Williams's quaint, historic downtown area, between Railroad, Grant, 1st, and 4th Streets.

Don't miss **Native America** (117 E. Route 66, 928/635-4600, 8am-9pm summer, 8am-6pm winter), a Native American-owned shop with Hopi and Navajo arts and crafts and some fun and interesting Old West kitsch sculptures holding up the front porch.

Food

A northland institution with some of the best steaks in the region, ★ **Rod's Steak House** (301 E. Route 66, 928/635-2671, www.rodssteakhouse.com, 11am-9:30pm Mon.-Sat., $12-25) has been operating at the same site since 1946. The food is excellent, the staff is friendly and professional, and the menus are shaped like steers.

The **Pine Country Restaurant** (107 N. Grand Canyon Blvd., 928/635-9718, http://pinecountryrestaurant.com, 6:30am-9:30pm daily, $8-19) is a family-style place that serves good diner-style food and homemade pies. Check out the beautiful paintings of the Grand Canyon on the walls.

Cruiser's Route 66 Bar & Grill (233 W. Route 66, 928/635-2445, www.cruisers66.com, 11am-9pm daily, $7-18) offers a diverse menu, with superior barbecue ribs, burgers, fajitas, pulled-pork sandwiches, and homemade chili. They have a full bar and offer live music most nights. During the summer evenings the patio is lively and fun.

For something a bit more upscale and romantic, try the **Red Raven Restaurant** (135 W. Route 66, 928/635-4980, www.redravenrestaurant.com, 11:30am-2pm and 5pm-close daily, $11-25), a charming little place along Route 66 with big windows looking out on the bustling sidewalk and the tourists strolling by. It serves delicious and inventive dishes: steak wraps, Guinness stew, tasty lamb, sweet potato fries, and Southwest egg rolls, to name just a few. The restaurant also has a deep beer list with selections mainly from Arizona and Colorado, and a good wine selection heavy on Italy and California. Make a reservation for dinner.

The vegetarian's best bet this side of downtown Flagstaff is the **Dara Thai Café** (145 W. Route 66, 928/635-2201, 11am-2pm and 5pm-9pm Mon.-Sat., $7-15), an agreeable little spot in the Grand Canyon Hotel. They serve a variety of fresh and flavorful Thai favorites and offer quite a few meat-free dishes.

Brewing and serving craft beers in a cavernous building near the railroad tracks, **The Grand Canyon Brewing + Distillery** (301 N. 7th St., 800/513-2072, www.grandcanyonbrewery.com, 2pm-close daily, $9-22) is a favorite with locals and tourists alike. It gets pretty busy here at times, especially around quitting time. Along with several excellent craft beers, they serve pub-style food and pizzas that do not disappoint.

Accommodations

Williams has some of the most affordable independent accommodations in the Grand Canyon region as well as several chain hotels.

It's difficult to find a better deal than the clean and basic **El Rancho Motel** (617 E. Route 66, 928/635-2552 or 800/228-2370, www.elranchomotelwilliams.us, $80-125), an independently owned, retro motel on Route 66 with few frills save comfort, friendliness, and a heated pool open in season.

The **Canyon Country Inn** (442 W. Route 66, 928/635-2349, www.thecanyoncountryinn.com, $89-115) is an enchanting little place right in the heart of Williams's charming historic district. Its country-Victorian decor is not for everyone, but it's a comfortable and friendly place to stay while exploring the canyon country.

The **Grand Canyon Railway Hotel** (235 N. Grand Canyon Blvd., 928/635-4010, www.thetrain.com, $169-189) stands now where Williams's old Harvey House once stood. It has a heated indoor pool, two restaurants, a lounge, a hot tub, a workout room, and a huge gift shop. The hotel serves riders on the Grand Canyon Railway and offers the highest-end accommodations in Williams.

The original **Grand Canyon Hotel** (145 W. Route 66, 928/635-1419, www.thegrandcanyonhotel.com, $79-195) opened in 1891, even before the railroad arrived and made Grand Canyon tourism something not just the rich could do. New owners refurbished and reopened the charming old redbrick hotel in Williams's historic downtown in 2005, and now it's an affordable, friendly place to stay with a lot of character and a bit of an international flavor. Spartan single-bed rooms go for $79 a night with a shared bathroom, and individually named and eclectically decorated double rooms with private baths are $93-105 a night—some of the most distinctive and affordable accommodations in the region. There are no televisions in the rooms. Several larger rooms with private baths and other amenities go for $150-195. There are also hostel rooms for $33-38.

The **Red Garter Bed & Bakery** (137 W. Railroad Ave., 928/635-1484, www.redgarter. com, $175-199) makes much of its original and longtime use as a brothel (which, like many similar places throughout Arizona's rural regions, didn't finally close until the 1940s), where the town's lonely, uncouth miners, lumberjacks, railway workers, and cowboys met with unlucky women, ever euphemized as "soiled doves," in rooms called "cribs." The 1897 frontier-Victorian stone building, with its wide, arching entranceway, has been beautifully restored with a lot of authentic charm, without skimping on the comforts—like big brass beds for the nighttime and delightful, homemade baked goods, juice, and coffee in the morning. Famously, this place is haunted by some poor unquiet, regretful soul, so you might want to bring your night-light along.

★ **The Lodge on Route 66** (200 E. Route 66, 877/563-4366, http://thelodgeonroute66. com, $99-189) has stylish rooms with sleep-inducing pillow-top mattresses; it has a few civilized two-room suites with kitchenettes, dining areas, and fireplaces—perfect for a family that's not necessarily on a budget. The motor court-style grounds, right along the Mother Road of course, feature a romantic cabana with comfortable seats and an outdoor fireplace. No pets.

Information and Services

Stop at the **Williams-Kaibab National Forest Visitor Center** (200 W. Railway Ave., 928/635-1418 or 800/863-0546, 8am-6:30pm daily spring-summer, 8am-5pm daily fall-winter) for information about Williams, the Grand Canyon, and camping and hiking in the Kaibab National Forest.

TUSAYAN

About a mile outside Grand Canyon National Park's south gate, along Route 64/U.S. 180, Tusayan is a collection of hotels, restaurants, and gift shops that has grown alongside the park for nearly a century. The village makes a decent, nearby base for a visit to the park, especially if you can't get reservations at any of the in-park lodges. Although there are a few inexpensive chain hotels here, a stay in Tusayan isn't on the whole cheaper than lodging in the park. There are however many more places to eat in Tusayan than there are inside the park.

Sights

Tusayan is perhaps best known as the home of the **Grand Canyon Visitors Center** (Rte. 64, 928/638-2468, www.explorethecanyon. com, 8am-10pm daily Mar.-Oct., 10am-8pm daily Nov.-Feb., IMAX tickets $13 over age 10, $10 children 6-10, children under 6 free), which has been a popular first stop for park visitors since the 1980s. You can purchase a park pass here, book tours, and check out some displays about the canyon, but the center wouldn't be worth the stop if not for its **IMAX Theater.** The colossal screen shows the 35-minute movie *Grand Canyon—The Hidden Secrets* every hour at half past. The most popular IMAX film ever (some 40 million people have reportedly seen it), the movie is quite thrilling, affording glimpses of the canyon's remoter corners that feel like real time, if not reality. If you can afford the admission price, this is a fun way to learn about what you're about to see in the park. It's also a convenient place to book tours—everything from Jeep rides to helicopter tours to river rafting adventures. If you're going budget, skip it and drive a few miles up the road, where you're likely to forget about both movies and money while staring dumbfounded into that gorge.

Food

Nobody would go to Tusayan specifically to eat, but it makes for a decent stop if you're hungry. A lot of tour buses stop here, so you might find yourself crowded into waiting for a table at some places, especially during the summer high season. Better to eat in the park or in Flagstaff or Williams, both of which have many charming and delicious local restaurants worth seeking out. It's only about an hour's drive to either place, so you might be better off having a snack and skipping Tusayan altogether.

Sophie's Mexican Kitchen (110 Hwy. 64, Grand Canyon Village Shops, 928/638-4654, 10am-9pm daily, $10-15) is a great option for vegetarians, including vegans—and anyone who likes Mexican food. You'll find a fun, festive atmosphere here. It's a popular place with delicious margaritas and good fajitas, chimichangas, and the like.

If you're craving pizza after a long day exploring the canyon, try **We Cook Pizza & Pasta** (125 E. Rte. 64, 928/638-2278, www.wecookpizzaandpasta.com, 11am-10pm daily Mar.-Oct., 11am-8pm daily Nov.-Feb., $10-30) for an excellent, high-piled pizza pie. It calls to you just as you enter Tusayan coming from the park. The pizza, served in slices or whole pies, is pretty good considering the locale, and they have a big salad bar with all the fixings, plus beer and wine. It's a very casual place, with picnic tables and an often harried staff. It gets really busy in here during the high summer season.

The Coronado Room (74 Rte. 64, 928/638-2681, 5pm-10pm daily, $15-25) inside the Grand Canyon Squire Inn serves tasty steaks, seafood, pasta, and Southwestern-inspired dishes.

Accommodations

Most of Tusayan's accommodations are of the chain variety. Though they are generally clean and comfortable, few of them have any character to speak of, and most are rather overpriced for what you get. Staying in either Flagstaff or Williams is a better choice if you're looking for an independent hotel or motel with some local color, and you can definitely find better deals in those gateways.

Before you reach Tusayan you'll pass through Valle, a tiny spot not far off Route 64, where you'll find one of the better deals in the whole canyon region. The **Red Lake Campground and Hostel** (8850 N. Rte. 64, 928/635-4753, $20 pp/night), where you can rent a bed in a shared room, is a very basic but reasonably comfortable place sitting lonely on the grasslands next to a gas station; it has shared bathrooms with showers, free Wi-Fi, a common room with a kitchen and a TV, and an RV park ($25) with hookups. If you're going super-budget, you can't beat this place, and it's only about 45 minutes from the park's south gate.

The **Red Feather Lodge** (300 Rte. 64, 928/638-2414, www.redfeatherlodge.com, $220-240), though more basic than some of the other places in Tusayan, is a comfortable, affordable place to stay with a pool, hot tub, and clean rooms in separate hotel and motel complexes.

The **Grand Hotel** (149 Rte. 64, 928/638-3333, www.grandcanyongrandhotel.com, $200-400), resembling a kind of Western-themed ski lodge, has very clean and comfortable rooms, a pool, hot tub, fitness center, and beautiful lobby. One of the more luxurious places to stay in the region, with prices to match, the hotel also has a large saloon and steak house.

The **Best Western Grand Canyon Squire Inn** (74 Rte. 64, 928/638-2681, www.grandcanyonsquire.com, $197-239) has a fitness center, pool and spa, salon, game room, bowling alley, and myriad other amenities—so many that it may be difficult to get out of the hotel to enjoy the natural sights.

The South Rim

The reality of the Grand Canyon is often suspect even to those standing on its rim. "For a time it is too much like a scale model or an optical illusion," wrote Joseph Wood Krutch, a great observer and writer of the Southwest. The canyon appears at first, Krutch added, "a man-made diorama trying to fool the eye." It is *too big* to be immediately comprehended, especially to those visitors used to the gaudy, lesser wonders of the human-made world.

Once you accept its size and understand that a river full of dry rocks and sand carved this mile-deep, multicolored canyon into the Colorado Plateau, the awesome power and wonder of it all is bound to leave you breathless and wondering what you've been doing with your life. If there are any sacred places in the natural world, this is surely one. The canyon is a water-wrought cathedral, and no matter what beliefs or preconceptions you approach the rim with, they are likely to be challenged, molded, cut away, and revealed—like the layers of primordial earth that compose this deep rock labyrinth and tell the history of the planet, a geology textbook for new gods. And it is a story in which humans appear only briefly, if at all.

Visitors without a spiritual connection to nature have always been challenged by the Grand Canyon's size. It takes mythology, magical thinking, and storytelling to see it for what it really is. The first Europeans to see the canyon, a detachment of Spanish conquistadores sent by Coronado in 1540 after hearing rumors of the great gorge from the Hopi people, at first thought the spires and buttes rising from the bottom were about the size of a man; they were shocked, upon gaining a different perspective below the rim, to learn that they were as high or higher than the greatest structures of Seville. Human comparisons do not work here. Preparation is not possible.

Never hospitable, the canyon has nonetheless had a history of human occupation for around 5,000 years, though the settlements have been small and usually seasonal. It was one of the last regions of North America to be explored and mapped. The first expedition through, led by the one-armed genius John Wesley Powell, was completed at the comparatively late date of 1869. John Hance, the first Anglo to reside at the canyon, explored its depths in the 1880s and built trails based on ancient Native American routes. A few other tough loners tried to develop mining operations here but soon found out that guiding avant-garde canyon tourists was the only sure financial bet in the canyonlands. It took another 20 years or so and the coming of the railroad before it became possible for the average American visitor to see the Grand Canyon.

Though impressive, the black-and-white statistics—repeated throughout the park on displays and interpretive signs along the rim and at the various visitors centers—do little to conjure an image that would do the canyon justice. It is some 277 river miles long, beginning just below Lee's Ferry on the north and ending somewhere around the Grand Wash Cliffs in northwestern Arizona. It is 18 miles across at its widest point and an average of 10 miles across from the South to the North Rim. It is a mile deep on average; the highest point on the rim, the north's Point Imperial, rises nearly 9,000 feet above the river. Its towers, buttes, and mesas, formed by the falling away of layers undercut by the river's incessant carving, are red and pink, dull brown, and green-tipped, though these basic hues are altered and enhanced by the setting and rising of the sun, changed by changes in the light, becoming throwaway works of art that astound and then disappear.

It is folly, though, to try too hard to describe and boost the Grand Canyon. The consensus, from the first person to see it to

The Canyon and the Railroad

Musing on the Grand Canyon in 1902, John Muir lamented that, thanks to the railroad, "children and tender, pulpy people as well as storm-seasoned travelers" could now see the wonders of the West, including the Grand Canyon, with relative ease. It has always been easy for storm-seasoned travelers to begrudge us tender, pulpy types a good view—as if all the people who visit the canyon every year couldn't fit in its deep mazes and be fairly out of sight. Muir came to a similar conclusion after actually seeing the railway approach the chasm: "I was glad to discover that in the presence of such stupendous scenery they are nothing," he wrote. "The locomotives and trains are mere beetles and caterpillars, and the noise they make is as little disturbing as the hooting of an owl in the lonely woods."

It wasn't until the Santa Fe Railroad reached the South Rim of the Grand Canyon in 1901 that the great chasm's now-famous tourist trade really got going. Prior to that, travelers faced an all-day stagecoach ride from Flagstaff at a cost of $20, a high price to pay for sore bones and cramped quarters.

For half a century or more the Santa Fe line from Williams took millions of tourists to the edge of the canyon. The railroad's main concessionaire, the Fred Harvey Company, enlisted the considerable talents of Arts and Crafts designer and architect Mary Colter to build lodges, lookouts, galleries, and stores on the South Rim that still stand today, now considered to be some of the finest architectural accomplishments in the entire national parks system. Harvey's dedication to simple elegance and Colter's interest in and understanding of Pueblo Indian architecture and lifeways created an artful human stamp on the rim that nearly lives up to the breathtaking canyon it serves.

The American love affair with the automobile, the rising mythology of the go-west road trip, and finally the interstate highway killed train travel to Grand Canyon National Park by the late 1960s. In the 1990s, however, entrepreneurs revived the railroad as an excursion and tourist line. Today, the Grand Canyon Railway carries more than 250,000 passengers to the South Rim every year, which has significantly reduced polluting automobile traffic in the cramped park.

yesterday's gazer, has amounted to "You just have to see it for yourself." Perhaps the most poetic words ever spoken about the Grand Canyon, profound for their obvious simplicity, came from Teddy Roosevelt, speaking on the South Rim in 1903. "Leave it as it is," he said. "You cannot improve on it; not a bit."

EXPLORING THE SOUTH RIM

The South Rim is by far the most developed portion of **Grand Canyon National Park** (928/638-7888, www.nps.gov/grca, 24 hours daily, $30 per car for seven-day pass, $25 motorcycles, $15 walk-ins and bikes, rates subject to change annually) and should be seen by every American, as Teddy Roosevelt once recommended. Here you'll stand side by side with people from all over the globe, each one breathless on their initial stare into the canyon and more often than not hit suddenly

with an altered perception of time and human history. Don't let the rustic look of the buildings fool you into thinking you're roughing it. The food here is above average for a national park. The restaurant at El Tovar offers some of the finest, most romantic dining in the state, and all with one of the great wonders of the world just 25 feet away.

Before you drive into the South Rim section, remember that parking is not easy to find during the high season, and that driving around the park can be slow, a bit dangerous, and frustrating. Consider parking outside the park in Tusayan and taking the free shuttles into and around the park. Or you can ride your bicycle from a parking lot in Tusayan into the park, and then use the paved trails to get around. If you do take your car into the park, you can still use the free shuttles to get around; it's much easier and will allow you to see more of the park.

Visitors Centers

Canyon View Information Plaza (9am-5pm daily) near Mather Point, the first overlook you pass on entering the park's main South Entrance, is the perfect place to begin your visit to the park. You get there by walking the short path from the Mather Point parking lot or by hopping off the free shuttle, for which the plaza serves as a kind of central hub. Throughout the plaza there are displays on the natural and human history of the canyon and suggestions on what to do, and inside the **South Rim Visitor Center,** the park's main welcome and information center, there are displays on canyon history and science. Rangers are always on duty to answer questions, give advice, and help you plan your visit. Head to the visitors center's 200-seat theater and watch the thrilling *Grand Canyon: A Journey of Wonder,* a 20-minute orientation film that takes you on a daylong journey through the canyon and around the park and explains the basics of the canyon's natural and human histories. The movie is free and starts on the hour and half hour.

Another information center, **Verkamp's Visitor Center** (8am-5pm daily), sits near El Tovar and the Hopi House in Grand Canyon Village. Verkamp's was a souvenir shop, the park's first, from 1906 to 2008.

The farthest-flung of all the park's South Rim information centers, **Desert View Visitor Center and Bookstore** (9am-5pm daily), sits on Desert View Point about 25 miles east of Grand Canyon Village. It is staffed by helpful rangers and has information and displays on visiting the canyon; this is the natural place to stop for those entering the park from the quieter East Entrance.

As you enter the park you'll receive the *Grand Canyon Pocket Map & South Rim Services Guide,* including a free map and information about the South Rim and the canyon. It also has a shuttle schedule and map with shuttle stops. Make sure you read through it; it's fairly comprehensive and will likely answer most of your questions.

Entrance Stations

Unless you choose to ride the chugging train from Williams, there are only two ways, by road, in and out of the park's South Rim section. The vast majority of visitors to Grand Canyon National Park enter through the **South Entrance Station** along Route 64 from Williams. U.S. 180 from Flagstaff meets up with Route 64 at Valle, about 30 miles south of the South Entrance; it's about 55 miles along scenic Highway 180 from Flagstaff to Valle. Route 64 from Williams to the South Entrance is 60 miles of flat, dry grass and windswept plain, dotted with a few isolated trailers and manufactured homes and gaudy for-sale signs offering cheap "ranchland." Entering through the busy South Entrance will assure that your first look of Grand Canyon is from **Mather Point,** which is as a result one of the most iconic views.

A lesser-used but certainly no less worthy park entrance is the **East Entrance Station,** in the park's **Desert View** section. About 25 miles east of Grand Canyon Village and all the action, this route is a good choice for those who want a more leisurely and comprehensive look at the rim, as there are quite a few stops along the way to the village that you might not otherwise get to if you enter through the South Entrance. To reach the East Entrance Station take U.S. 89 for 46 miles north of Flagstaff, across a wide big-sky landscape covered in volcanic rock, pine forests, and yellow wildflowers, to Cameron, on the red-dirt Navajo Reservation. Then head west on Route 64 for about 30 miles to the entrance station.

Tours
MOTORCOACH TOURS

Xanterra, the park's main concessionaire, offers in-park **Motorcoach Tours** (888/297-2757, www.grandcanyonlodges.com, $28-80 pp). Options include Sunrise and Sunset tours, and longer drives to the eastern Desert View area and the western reaches of the park at Hermit's Rest. This is a comfortable, educational, and entertaining way to see the park, and odds are you will come away with a few new friends—possibly even a new email pal from abroad. Only pay for a tour if you like being around a lot of other people and listening to mildly entertaining banter from the tour guides for hours at a time. It's easy to see and learn about everything the park has to offer without spending extra money on a tour; as in most of the national parks, the highly informed and friendly rangers hanging around the South Rim's sites offer the same information that you'll get on an expensive tour, but for free. Also, if you like being on your own and getting out away from the crowds, a tour is not for you.

AIRPLANE AND HELICOPTER TOURS

Three companies offer helicopter tours of the canyon of varying lengths. One of the better operators is **Maverick Helicopters** (888/261-4414, www.maverickhelicopter.com, $300 for 45-minute fly-over, $469 for 4-hour tour from Las Vegas). Though not ideal from the back-to-nature point of view, a helicopter flight over the canyon is an exciting, rare experience and can be well worth the rather expensive price—a chance to take some unique photos from a condor's perspective.

Maverick and five other plane and helicopter tour companies operate out of **Grand Canyon Airport** (www.grandcanyonairport. org) along Route 64 in Tusayan. They all prefer reservations.

Driving Tours
★ **HERMIT ROAD**

March-November the park's free shuttle goes all the way to architect and Southwestern-design queen Mary Colter's **Hermit's Rest,** about seven miles from the village along the park's western scenic drive called the Hermit Road. It takes approximately two hours to complete the loop, stopping at eight viewpoints along the way. On the return route buses stop only at Mohave and Hopi Points. The Hermit Road viewpoints are some of the best in the park for viewing the sunsets. To make it in time for these dramatic solar performances, catch the bus at least an hour before sunset. There is often a long wait at the **Hermit's Rest Transfer Stop** just west of the Bright Angel Lodge. The bus drivers generally know the times of sunrise and sunset. The route is open to cars beginning in December, when you can drive to most of the viewpoints and stare at your leisure.

Each of the Hermit Road lookouts provides a slightly different perspective on the canyon, whether it be a strange unnoticed outcropping or a brief view of the white-tipped river rapids far, far below. The first stop along the route is the **Trailview Overlook,** from which you can see the Bright Angel Trail twisting down into the canyon and across the plateau to overlook the Colorado River. The next major stop along the route is **Maricopa Point,** which provides a vast, mostly unobstructed view of the canyon all the way to the river. The point is on a promontory that juts out into the canyon over 100 feet. To the west you can see the rusted remains of the Orphan Mine, first opened in 1893 as a source of copper and silver—and, for a few busy years during the height of the Cold War, uranium. Consider taking the 10- to 15-minute hike along the Rim Trail west past the fenced-off Orphan Mine and through the piney rim world to the next viewing area, **Powell Point.** Here stands a memorial to the one-armed explorer and writer John Wesley Powell, who led the first and second river expeditions through the canyon in 1869 and 1871. The memorial is a flat-topped pyramid, which you can ascend and stand tall over the canyon. You can't see the river from here, but the views of the western reaches of the gorge are pretty good, and this is a strong candidate for a sunset-viewing vantage point. About a quarter of a mile along the Rim Trail from Powell Point is **Hopi Point,** which offers sweeping, open views of the western canyon. As a result, it is the most popular west-end point for viewing the sun dropping red and orange in the west. North from here, across the canyon, look for the famous mesas named after Egyptian gods—Isis Temple, off to the northeast, and the Temple of Osiris to the northwest. The next viewpoint heading west is **Mohave Point,** from which you can see the Colorado River and a few white-tipped rapids. Also visible from here are the 3,000-foot red-and-green cliffs that surround the deep side canyon, appropriately named **The Abyss.** Right below the viewpoint you can see the red-rock mesa called the Alligator. The last viewpoint before Hermit's Rest is **Pima Point,** a wide-open view to the west and the east, from which you can see the winding Colorado River and the Hermit Trail twisting down into the depths of the canyon.

DESERT VIEW DRIVE

One more Mary Colter construction—arguably her greatest—and a Puebloan ruin are located along Desert View Drive, the 25-mile eastern scenic drive from the village. The viewpoints along this drive, which one ranger called the "quiet side of the South Rim," gradually become more desertlike and are typically less crowded. The free shuttle goes only as far as **Yaki Point,** a great place to watch the sunrise and near the popular South Kaibab Trailhead. Yaki Point is at the end of a 1-mile side road northeast of Route 64. The area is closed to private vehicles. Along Desert View Drive, make sure not to miss the essential **Grandview Point,** where the original canyon lodge once stood long ago. From here the rough Grandview Trail leads below the rim. The viewpoint sits at 7,400 feet, about 12 miles east of the village and then a mile on a side road. It's considered one of the grandest views of them all, hence the name; the canyon spreads out willingly from here, and the sunrise in the east hits it all strong and happy. To the east, look for the 7,844-foot monument called the Sinking Ship, and to the north below look for Horseshoe Mesa. This is a heavily wooded area, so for the best view hike a bit down the Grandview Trail. The steep and narrow trail is tough, but if you're prepared to hike, you can descend three miles to Horseshoe Mesa.

Moran Point, east of Grandview, is just eight miles south of Cape Royal (as the condor flies) on the North Rim and offers some impressive views of the canyon and the river. The point is named for the great painter of the canyon, Thomas Moran, whose brave attempts to capture the gorge on canvas helped create the buzz that led to the canyon's federal protection. Directly below the left side of the point you'll see Hance Rapid, one of the largest on the Colorado. It's three miles away, but if you're quiet you might be able to hear the rushing and roaring. Farther on the Desert View Drive you'll come to **Lipan Point,** with its wide-open vistas and the best view of the river from the South Rim. At Desert View, from the top of the watchtower, you'll be able to catch a faraway glimpse of sacred Navajo Mountain near the Utah-Arizona border, the most distant point visible from within the park.

SIGHTS

Though you wouldn't want to make a habit of it, you could spend a few happy hours at **Grand Canyon Village Historical District** with your back to the canyon. Then again, this small assemblage of hotels, restaurants, gift shops, and lookouts offers some of the best viewpoints from which to gaze comfortably at all that multicolored splendor. Here is a perfect vantage from which to spot the strip of greenery just below the rim called **Indian Garden,** and follow with your eyes—or even your feet—the famous **Bright Angel Trail** as it twists improbably down the rim's rock face. You can also see some of the most interesting and evocative buildings in the state, all of them registered National Historic Landmarks.

The Bright Angel Lodge

The village's central hub of activity, rustic **Bright Angel Lodge** was designed in 1935 by Mary Colter to replace the old Bright Angel Hotel, which was built by John Hance in the 1890s, and the Bright Angel Camp tent-city near the trail of the same name. Originally meant to attract more middle-class tourists to the park, the lodge is still a romantic and comfortable place to stay, resembling a rough-hewn hunting lodge constructed of materials found nearby.

In a room off the lobby there's a small museum with fascinating exhibits about Fred Harvey, Colter, and the early years of Southwestern tourism. You'll see Colter's "geologic fireplace," a 10-foot-high re-creation of the canyon's varied strata. The stones were collected from the inner canyon by a geologist and then loaded on the backs of mules for the journey out. The fireplace's strata appear exactly like those stacked throughout the canyon walls, equaling a couple of billion years of earth-building from bottom to rim. The lodge includes a collection of small cabins just to the west of the main building. The cabin closest to the rim was once the home of **Bucky O'Neill,** an early canyon resident and prospector who died while fighting with Teddy Roosevelt's Rough Riders in Cuba.

El Tovar

Just east of the lodge is **El Tovar,** the South Rim's first great hotel and the picture of haute-wilderness style. Designed in 1905 by Charles Whittlesey for the Santa Fe Railroad, El Tovar has the look of a Swiss chalet and a log-house interior, watched over by the wall-hung heads of elk and buffalo; it is at once rustic, cozy, and elegant. This Harvey Company jewel has hosted dozens of rich and famous canyon visitors over the years, including George Bernard Shaw and presidents Teddy Roosevelt and William Howard Taft. On the rim side, a gazebo stands near the edge. While it is a wonderfully romantic building up close, El Tovar looks even more picturesque from a few of the viewpoints along the Hermit Road, and you can really get a good idea of just how close the lodge is to the rim by seeing it from far away. Inside you'll find two gift shops and a cozy lounge where you can have a drink or two while looking at the canyon. El Tovar's restaurant is the best in the park, and it's quite pleasant to sink into one of the arts-and-crafts leather chairs in the rustic, dark-wood lobby.

Hopi House

A few steps from the front porch of El Tovar is Colter's **Hopi House,** designed and built in 1905 as if it sat not at the edge of the Grand Canyon but on the edge of Hopi's Third Mesa. Hopi workers used local materials to build this unique gift shop and Native American arts museum. The Fred Harvey Company even hired the famous Hopi-Tewa potter Nampeyo to live here with her family while demonstrating her artistic talents and Hopi lifeways to tourists. This is one of the best places in the region for viewing and buying Hopi, Navajo, and Pueblo art (though most of the art is quite expensive), and there are even items made by Nampeyo's descendants on view and for sale here.

Lookout Studio

Mary Colter also designed the **Lookout Studio** west of the Bright Angel Lodge, a little stacked-stone watch house that seems to be a mysterious extension of the rim itself. The stone patio juts out over the canyon and is a popular place for picture taking. The Lookout was built in 1914 exactly for that purpose—to provide a comfortable but "indigenous" building and deck from which visitors could gaze at and photograph the canyon. It was fitted with high-powered telescopes and soon became one of the most popular snapshot scenes on the rim. It still is today, and on many days you'll be standing elbow to elbow with camera-carrying tourists clicking away. As she did with her other buildings on the rim, Colter designed the Lookout to be a kind of amalgam of Native American ruins and backcountry pioneer utilitarianism. Her formula of using found and indigenous materials, stacked haphazardly, works wonderfully. When it was first built, the little stone hovel was so "authentic" that it even had weeds growing out of the roof. Inside, where you'll find books and canyon souvenirs, the studio looks much as it did when it first opened. The jutting stone patio is still one of the best places from which to view the canyon.

Grand Canyon Village

Mohave Point ★

Hopi Point ★

To Hermits
Rest (8 miles) →

POWELL
MEMORIAL ★

⭐ RIM TRAIL

Maricopa
Point ★

⭐ BRIGHT ANGEL TRAIL

DELI IN
THE PIINES ▾

G r a n d

→ To Phantom Ranch

Bright Angel Trail

★ TRAILVIEW
OVERLOOK

⭐ HERMIT ROAD

HERMIT RD

SEE DETAIL

HARVEY HOUSE
CAFE   ARIZONA STEAKHOUSE

GATE ↓

VILLAGE LOOP

GATE

🅿

POWELL WELL RD

TONTO

NAVAJO

APACHE ST

MASWIK LODGE
AND CAFETERIA ●

🅿

BOULDER ST

MASWIK TRANSPORTATION
CENTER AND
BACKCOUNTRY OFFICE

CENTER RD

■ KENNELS

🅿

ALBRIGHT AVE

BRIGHT ANGEL
TRAILHEAD/
KOLB STUDIO ★

LOOKOUT STUDIO ★

EL TOVAR HOTEL
AND RESTAURANT ●

HOPI HOUSE (NATIVE
AMERICAN ART) ★

The Rim
Trail

BRIGHT ANGEL LODGE
& RESTAURANTS ●

THUNDERBIRD
LODGE ●

KACHINA
LODGE ●

VERKAMP'S
VISITOR CENTER ■

GATE ↓

🅿

RIM

HISTORIC
RAILROAD ★
STATION

DR

VILLAGE LOOP

PUBLIC
LIBRARY ■

PUBLIC
GARAGE ■

© MOON.COM

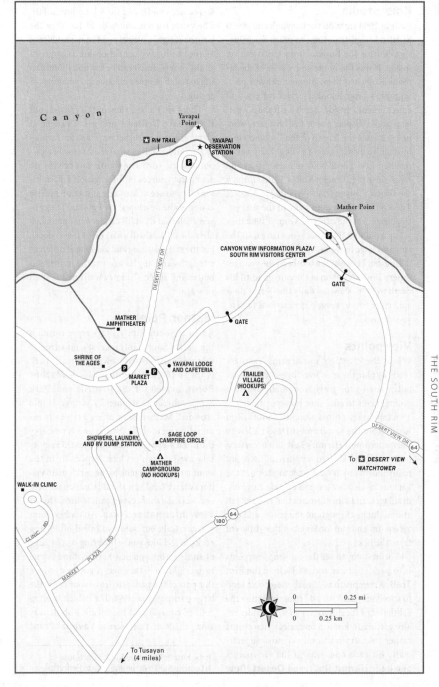

Canyon

Yavapai Point ★

★ RIM TRAIL

★ YAVAPAI
OBSERVATION
STATION

P

Mather Point ★

DESERT VIEW DR

P

CANYON VIEW INFORMATION PLAZA/
SOUTH RIM VISITORS CENTER

GATE

MATHER
AMPHITHEATER

GATE

SHRINE OF
THE AGES

P

MARKET
PLAZA

P

YAVAPAI LODGE
AND CAFETERIA

TRAILER
VILLAGE
(HOOKUPS)

DESERT VIEW DR

64

To ✦ DESERT VIEW
WATCHTOWER

SHOWERS, LAUNDRY,
AND RV DUMP STATION

SAGE LOOP
CAMPFIRE CIRCLE

MATHER
CAMPGROUND
(NO HOOKUPS)

WALK-IN CLINIC

CLINIC RD.

180   64

MARKET PLAZA RD.

0   0.25 mi
0   0.25 km

To Tusayan
(4 miles)

Kolb Studio

Built in 1904 right on the canyon's rim, **Kolb Studio** is significant not so much for its design but for the human story that went on inside. It was the home and studio of the famous Kolb Brothers, pioneer canyon photographers, moviemakers, river rafters, and entrepreneurs. Inside there's a gift shop, a gallery, and a display about the brothers, who, in 1912, rode the length of the Colorado in a boat with a movie camera rolling. The journey resulted in a classic book of exploration and river-running, Emery Kolb's 1914 *Through the Grand Canyon from Wyoming to Mexico.* The Kolb Brothers were some of the first entrepreneurs at the canyon. Around 1902 they set up a photography studio in a cave near the rim and later moved it to this house. After a falling-out between the brothers, the younger Emery Kolb stayed on at the canyon until his death in 1976, showing daily the film of their epic river trip to several generations of canyon visitors.

Viewpoints

While the canyon's unrelenting vastness tends to blur the eyes into forgetting the details, viewing the gorge from many different points seems to cure this; however, there are 19 named viewpoints along the South Rim Road, from the easternmost Desert View to the westernmost Hermit's Rest. Is it necessary, or even a good idea, to see them all? No, not really. For many it's difficult to pick out the various named buttes, mesas, side canyons, drainages, and other features that rise and fall and undulate throughout the gorge, and one viewpoint ends up looking not that different from the next.

The best way to see the canyon viewpoints is to park your car and walk along the **Rim Trail.** Attempts to visit each viewpoint tend to speed up your visit and make you miss the subtleties of the different views. Consider really getting to know a few select viewpoints rather than trying to quickly and superficially hit each one. Any of the viewpoints along the **Hermit Road** and **Desert View**

Drive are candidates for a long love affair. The views from just outside **El Tovar** or the **Bright Angel Lodge,** right in the middle of all the bustling village action, are as gorgeous as any others, and it can be fun and illuminating to watch people's reactions to what they're seeing.

There isn't a bad view of the canyon, but if you have limited time, ask a ranger at Canyon View Information Plaza or Yavapai Observation Station what their favorite viewpoint is and why. The shuttle bus drivers are also great sources of information and opinions. Try to see at least one sunset or sunrise at one of the developed viewpoints. The canyon's colors and details can seem monotonous after the initial thrill wears off (if it ever does), but the sun splashing and dancing at different strengths and angles against the multihued buttes and sheer, shadowy walls makes it all new again.

Mather Point

As most South Rim visitors enter through the park's South Entrance, it's no surprise that the most visited viewpoint in the park is the first one along that route—**Mather Point,** named for the first National Park Service director, Stephen T. Mather. While crowded, Mather Point offers a typically astounding view of the canyon and is probably the mind's-eye view that most casual visitors take away. It can get busy, especially in the summer. If you're going to the park's main visitors center (and you should), park near here and walk the short paved path to the **Canyon View Information Plaza.** At Mather Point you can walk out onto two railed-off jutting rocks to feel like you're hovering on the edge of an abyss, but you may have to stand in line to get right up to the edge. A good way to see this part of the park is to leave your car at the large parking area at Mather (which is often full, of course) and then walk a short way along the Rim Trail west to **Yavapai Point**

1: the historic El Tovar lodge **2:** Hopi House **3:** Lookout Studio **4:** the entrance to Hermit's Rest

and the **Yavapai Observation Station,** the best place to learn about the canyon's geology and get more than a passing understanding of what you're gazing at. It's a good idea to check out the informative displays on canyon geology here before you hit any of the other viewpoints (unless you are coming in from the East Entrance).

Yavapai Observation Station

First opened in 1928, **Yavapai Observation Station** and **Geology Museum** (8am-6pm daily winter, 8am-8pm daily summer, free) is the best place in the park to learn about the canyon's geology. This limestone-and-pine museum and bookstore is a must-visit for visitors interested in learning about what they're seeing. The building itself is of interest. Designed by architect Herbert Maier, the stacked-stone structure, like Colter's buildings, merges with the rim itself to appear a foregone and inevitable part of the landscape. The site for the station, which was originally called the Yavapai Trailside Museum, was handpicked by canyon geologists as the best for viewing the various strata and receiving a rimside lesson on the region's geologic history and present. Inside the building you'll find displays about canyon geology. Particularly helpful is the huge topographic relief map of the canyon—a giant's-eye view that really helps you discern what you're seeing once you turn into an ant outside on rim.

Hermit's Rest

The final stop on the Hermit Road is the enchanting gift shop and rest house called **Hermit's Rest.** As you walk up a path through a stacked-boulder entranceway, from which hangs an old mission bell, the little stone cabin comes into view. It looks as if some lonely hermit stacked rock upon rock until something haphazard but cozy rose from the rim—a structure from the realm of fairy tales. Inside, the huge, yawning fireplace, tall and deep enough to be a room itself, dominates the warm, rustic front room, where there are a few chairs chopped out of stumps, a

Navajo blanket or two splashing color against the gray stone, and elegant lantern-lamps hanging from the stones. Outside, the views of the canyon and down the Hermit Trail are spectacular; but something about that little rock shelter makes it hard to leave.

Tusayan Museum and Ruin

The **Tusayan Museum** (daily 9am-5pm, free) has a small but interesting exhibit on the canyon's early human settlers. The museum is located near an 800-year-old Ancestral Puebloan ruin with a self-guided trail and regularly scheduled ranger walks. Since the free shuttle doesn't extend this far east, you have to drive to the museum and ruin; it's about 3 miles west of Desert View and 22 miles east of the village. It's worth the drive, though, especially if you're going to be heading to the Desert View section anyway (which you should). There are several interesting displays on the history of human life in the region. While the canyonlands haven't been exactly hospitable to humans over the eons, the oldest artifacts found in the Grand Canyon date back about 12,000 years. They include little stick-built animal fetishes and other mysterious hints at what life was once like on the rim and inside the canyon. Imagine living along the rim, walking every day to the great gorge, tossing an offering of cornmeal into the abyss, and wondering what your hidden canyon gods were going to provide you with next.

★ Desert View Watchtower

What is perhaps the most mysterious and thrilling of Colter's canyon creations, the **Desert View Watchtower** is an artful homage to smaller Ancestral Puebloan-built towers found at Hovenweep National Monument and elsewhere in the Four Corners region, the exact purpose of which is still unknown.

You reach the tower's high, windy deck by climbing the twisting, steep steps winding around the open middle, past walls painted with visions of Hopi lore and religion by Hopi artist Fred Kabotie. Pick up *The Watchtower Guide* free in the gift shop on the bottom floor

Hiking the Grand Canyon... the Easy Way

One of the first things you notice while journeying through the inner canyon is the advanced age of many of your fellow hikers. It is not uncommon to see men and women in their 70s and 80s hiking along at a good clip, packs on their backs and big smiles on their faces.

At the same time, all over the South Rim you'll see warning signs about overexertion, each featuring a buff young man in incredible shape suffering from heatstroke or exhaustion, with the warning that most of the people who die in the canyon—and people die every year—are people like him. You need not be a wilderness expert or marathon runner to enjoy even a long, 27-mile, rim-to-rim hike through the inner canyon. Don't let your fears hold you back from what is often a life-changing trip.

There are several strategies that can make a canyon hike much easier than a forced march with a 30-pound pack of gear on your back. First of all, don't go in the summer; wait until September or October, when it's cooler, though still quite warm, in the inner canyon. Second, try your best to book a cabin or a dorm room at Phantom Ranch rather than camping. That way, you'll need less equipment, you'll have all or most of your food taken care of, and there will be a shower and a beer waiting for you upon your arrival. Also, for $70 each way, you can hire a mule to carry up to 30 pounds of gear for you, so all you have to bring is a day pack, with water and snacks. This way, instead of suffering while you descend and ascend the trail, you'll be able to better enjoy the magnificence of this wonder of the world.

for interpretations of the figures and symbols. From the top of the watchtower, the South Rim's highest viewpoint, the whole arid expanse opens up, and you feel something like a lucky survivor at the very edge of existence, even among the crowds. Such is the evocative power, the rough-edged romanticism, of Colter's vision.

RECREATION
Hiking

Something about a well-built trail twisting deep into an unknown territory can spur even the most habitually sedentary canyon visitor to begin an epic trudge. This phenomenon is responsible for both the best and worst of the South Rim's busy recreation life. It is not uncommon to see hikers a mile or more below the rim picking along in high heels and sauntering blithely in flip-flops, not a drop of water between them. It's best to go to the canyon prepared to hike, with proper footwear and plenty of water and snacks. You'll probably want to hike a little, and since there's no such thing as an easy hike into the Grand Canyon, going in prepared, even if it's just for a few miles, will make your hike a pleasure rather

than chore. Also, remember that there aren't any loop hikes here: If you hike in a mile—and that can happen surprisingly quickly—you also must hike out (up) a mile, at an oxygen-depleted altitude of 6,000 to 7,000 feet.

★ RIM TRAIL

Distance: 12.8 miles
Duration: all day
Elevation gain: about 200 feet
Effort: easy
Trailhead: Grand Canyon Village east to South Kaibab Trailhead or west to Hermit's Rest

If you can manage a 13-mile, relatively easy walk at an altitude of around 7,000 feet, the **Rim Trail** provides the single best way to see all of the South Rim. The trail, paved for most of its length, runs from the South Kaibab Trailhead area on the east, through the village, and all the way to Hermit's Rest, hitting every major point of interest and beauty along the way. The path gets a little tough as it rises a bit past the Bright Angel Trailhead just west of the village. The trail becomes a thin dirt single-track between Powell Point and Monument Creek Vista, but it never gets too difficult. It would be considered an easy, scenic walk by just about anybody, kids included. But perhaps the best thing about the Rim Trail is that you don't have to hike the whole 13 miles—far from it. There are at least 16 shuttle stops along way, and you can hop on and off the trail at your pleasure. Dogs are allowed on Rim Trail with a leash, but you can't take them on the shuttle buses.

Few will want to hike the entire 13 miles, of course. Such an epic walk would in fact require twice the miles, as the trail is not a loop but a ribbon stretched out flat along the rim from west to east. It's better to pick out a relatively short stretch to walk, starting from the village and ending back there after turning around. Toward the west, try walking the roughly 2.2-mile stretch from the village to Hopi Point. This would be an ideal hike toward the end of the day, as Hopi Point is a famed spot for viewing the sunset. You could then hike back by flashlight or take the free shuttle bus. Eastward, hike the Rim Trail from the village to Yavapai Point, a distance of about two miles one-way. This route will take you past stunning views of the canyon to the Yavapai Observation Station.

★ BRIGHT ANGEL TRAIL

Distance: 1.5-9.6 miles
Duration: a few hours to overnight
Elevation gain: 4,380 feet
Effort: moderate to difficult
Trailhead: Grand Canyon Village, just west of Bright Angel Lodge

Hiking down the **Bright Angel Trail,** you quickly leave behind the piney rim and enter a sharp and arid landscape, twisting down and around switchbacks on a path that is sometimes all rock underfoot. Step aside for the many mule trains that use this route, and watch for the droppings, which are everywhere. Because this trail is so steep, it doesn't take long for the rim to look very far away, and you soon feel like you are deep within a chasm and those rim-top people are mere ants scurrying about.

The Bright Angel Trail is the most popular trail in the canyon owing in part to its starting just to the west of the Bright Angel Lodge in the village center. It's considered by park staff to be the "safest" trail because it has two rest houses with water. The Bright Angel was once the only easily accessible corridor trail from the South Rim.

Many South Rim visitors choose to walk down Bright Angel a bit just to get a feeling of what it's like to be below the rim. If you want to do something a little more structured, the three-mile round-trip hike to the **Mile-and-a-Half Resthouse** is a good introduction to the steep, twisting trail. A little farther on is **Three-Mile Resthouse,** a six-mile round-trip hike. Both rest houses have water seasonally. One of the best day hikes from the South Rim is the nine mile round-trip to beautiful **Indian Garden,** a cool and green oasis in the arid inner canyon. This is a rather punishing day hike, not recommended in the summer. The same goes for the 12-mile round-trip trudge down to **Plateau Point,** from which you can see the Colorado River winding through the inner gorge.

SOUTH KAIBAB TRAIL

Distance: 1.5-7 miles
Duration: several hours to all day
Elevation gain: 4,780 feet
Effort: moderate to difficult
Trailhead: near Yaki Point

Steep but relatively short, the seven-mile **South Kaibab Trail** provides the quickest, most direct South Rim route to and from the river. It's popular with day hikers and those looking for the quickest way into the gorge, and many consider it superior to the often-crowded Bright Angel Trail. The trailhead is located a few miles east of the village near Yaki Point; take the shuttle bus on the Kaibab Trail Route. The 1.8-mile round-trip hike to **Ooh Aah Point** has great views of the canyon from steep switchbacks. **Cedar Ridge** is a three-mile round-trip hike down the trail, well worth it for the views of O'Neill Butte and Vishnu Temple. There's no water

---

1: Desert View Watchtower **2:** Bright Angel Trail

anywhere along the trail, and there's no shade to speak of. Bighorn sheep have been known to haunt this trail, and you might feel akin to those dexterous beasts while hiking the rocky ridgeline, which seems unbearably steep in a few places, especially on the way back up. If you are interested in a longer haul, the six-mile round-trip hike to **Skeleton Point,** from which you can see the Colorado River, is probably as far along this trail as you'll want to go in one day, though in summer you might want to reconsider descending so far. Deer and California condors are also regularly seen along the South Kaibab Trail.

HERMIT TRAIL TO DRIPPING SPRINGS

Distance: 6.2 miles
Duration: 5-6 hours
Elevation gain: 1,400 feet
Effort: moderate
Trailhead: just west of Hermit's Rest

Built by the Santa Fe Railroad as a challenge to the fee-charging keeper of the Bright Angel Trail, the **Hermit Trail** just past Hermit's Rest leads to some less visited areas of the canyon. This trail isn't maintained with the same energy as the well-traveled corridor trails, and it has no potable water. You could take the Hermit Trail 10 miles deep into the canyon to the river, where Fred Harvey built the first below-rim camp for tourists, complete with a tramway from the rim, the ruins of which are still visible. But such a trudge should be left only to fully geared experts. Not so the 6.2-mile round-trip hike to the secluded and green **Dripping Springs,** which is one of the best day hikes in the canyon for midlevel to expert hikers. Start out on the Hermit Trail's steep, rocky, almost stair-like switchbacks, and then look for the **Dripping Springs Trailhead** after about 1.5 miles, once you reach a more level section dominated by piñon pine and juniper. Veer left on the trail, which begins to rise a bit and leads along a ridgeline across Hermit Basin; the views are so awe-inspiring and so unobstructed that it's difficult to keep your eyes on the skinny trail.

Continue west once you come to the junction with the Boucher Trail, after about one mile; then it's about 0.5 mile up a side canyon to the cool and shady rock overhang known as Dripping Springs. And it really does drip: a shock of fernlike greenery creeps off the rock overhang, trickling cold, clean spring water at a steady pace into a small collecting pool. Get your head wet, have a picnic, and kick back in this out-of-way, hard-won oasis. But don't stay too long. The hike up is nothing to take lightly: The switchbacks are punishing, and the end, as it always does when one is hiking up a trail in the Grand Canyon, seems to get farther away as your legs begin to gain fatigue-weight. There's no water on the trail, so make sure to bring enough along and conserve it.

GRANDVIEW TRAIL

Distance: 8.4 miles to the river
Duration: a few hours to overnight
Elevation gain: 4,792 feet
Effort: difficult
Trailhead: Grandview Point, 12 miles east of Grand Canyon Village

A steep, rocky, and largely unmaintained route built first to serve a copper mine at Horseshoe Mesa and then to entice tourists below the forested rim, the **Grandview Trail** should be left to midlevel hikers and above. Though you can take the trail all the way to the river and Hance Rapid, more than eight miles in, for day hikers the 6.4-mile round-trip trek to Horseshoe Mesa and the mine's ruins is probably as far as you'll want to go. This trail is definitely not safe for winter hiking. Hiking back up, you won't soon forget the steep slab-rock and cobblestone switchbacks, and hiking down will likely take longer than planned as the steepest parts of the route are quite technical and require heads-up attention. Park staff are not exactly quick to recommend this route to casual hikers. Don't be surprised if you meet a ranger hanging out along the trail about 1.5 miles in, who may tell you to turn around if they don't think you have the proper gear or enough water to continue on.

Biking

Riding bikes in the national parks seems to get easier and more popular every year, and the Grand Canyon is no exception to the trend. It's now possible to ride from outside the park near Tusayan to the visitors center, and then on across the park to Hermit's Rest, on either paved trails or roads closed to cars. This long round-trip ride, starting and ending about 6.5 miles outside the park at the **Tusayan Greenway** trailhead, is about 32 miles. It's probably not for everyone, but it's also not that difficult. The easy paved trails undulate across the park, so you're never too far away from a gentle downhill.

Bikes are not allowed on the Rim Trail except for a 2.8-mile section called the **Hermit Road Greenway Trail.** The paved trail begins at Monument Creek Vista along the Hermit Road and ends close to Hermit's Rest. This is about as close as you can get to the rim on a bike, and it's a fun and beautiful stretch of trail highly recommended to bicyclists. To get to the very edge of the rim, you have to park your bike and walk a bit, but never very far, and there are bike racks at each developed viewpoint.

While the main park roads are open to bikes, they don't have wide shoulders or bike lanes, so it's best to stick to the Greenway Trail. The exception is **Hermit Road,** which is closed to cars during peak season. Seven miles one-way between the village and the western end of the park at Hermit's Rest, the Hermit Road is the best and most popular bikeway on the South Rim. The only traffic you'll have to deal with on this rolling ride of tough ups and fun downs is the occasional shuttle bus. Just pull over and let them pass.

The free *Pocket Map* includes a map of bike routes around the park.

Bright Angel Bicycles and Café (928/814-8704, www.bikegrandcanyon.com, 6am-8pm daily Apr.-Nov., 7am-7pm daily Dec.-Mar., adult rental $12.50 for 1 hour, $31.50 for 5 hours, $40 for full day, child rental $9.50 for 1 hour, $20 for 5 hours, $31.50 for full day) rents comfortable, easy-to-ride bikes as well as safety equipment and trailers for the tots. They also offer guided bike tours of the South Rim, including a 5.5-mile, three-hour ride along Hermit Road ($47-65) and a 6-mile, 3.5-hour ride along the rim to Yaki Point ($42-55). Both rides are relatively easy, though the Hermit Road tour has more ups and downs. Also remember that you are at 7,000 feet. The friendly staff members are quick to offer suggestions about the best places to ride. The little café serves excellent coffee and sells premade sandwiches and other snacks. Bright Angel Bicycles is located right next to the **Grand Canyon Visitors Center** near the South Entrance and Mather Point.

MOUNTAIN BIKING ON THE RIM

The **Tusayan Bike Trails** are a series of single-track trails and old mining and logging roads organized into several easy to moderate loop trails for mountain bikers near the park's South Entrance. The trails wind through a forest of pine, juniper, and piñon. The longest loop is just over 11 miles, and the shortest is just under 4 miles. There's a map at the beginning of the trails that shows the various loops. Pick up the trails on the west side of AZ 64 north of Tusayan, about one mile south of the park entrance.

LECTURES AND PROGRAMS

Every day the park offers numerous ranger-guided hikes and nature walks, as well as lectures and discussions on the animals, human history, and geology of the canyon, at various spots around the park; check at the visitors center or on the park's website for specific programs.

Most nights during the summer, there's a typically fascinating Evening Ranger Program at the **Mckee Amphitheater.** This varied program of lectures and night walks, on subjects ranging from astronomy to the Colorado River to "Surviving the Apocalypse at the Grand Canyon," is usually very popular, so it's best to plan ahead. You must get a ticket to secure a spot, starting at 7:30pm at the Shrine of the Ages venue near the park headquarters for an 8:30pm program. The amphitheater is just east of the Shrine of the Ages and the across the road from Canyon Village Market Plaza, 1.4 miles east of the village. Other times of the year ranger programs are held daily and nightly at Shrine of the Ages and elsewhere around the park, and they are always free.

SHOPPING

There are more than 16 places to buy gifts, books, souvenirs, supplies, and Native American arts and crafts at the South Rim. Nearly every lodge has a substantial gift shop in its lobby, as do Hermit's Rest, Kolb Studio, Lookout Studio, and the Desert View Watchtower.

For books, the best place to go is **Books & More** at the Canyon View Information Plaza, operated by the nonprofit Grand Canyon Association (GCA). You'll find books about canyon science and history for both adults and children. All of the gift shops have a small book section, most of them selling the same selection of popular canyon-related titles published by the GCA. If you're in need of camping and hiking supplies to buy or rent—including top-of-the-line footwear, clothes, and backpacks—try the general store at the **Canyon Village Market Plaza.** Here you'll also find groceries, toiletries, produce, alcoholic beverages, and "I hiked the Grand Canyon" T-shirts.

Whether you're a semiserious collector or a first-time dabbler, the best place on the South Rim to find high-quality Native American arts and crafts is Mary Colter's **Hopi House.** Shop here for baskets, overlay jewelry, sand paintings, kachina dolls, and other regional treasures. Don't expect to find too many great deals—most of the best pieces are priced accordingly.

FOOD

Xanterra Parks and Resorts runs most of the hotels and eateries at Grand Canyon National Park. The company has a relatively strong sustainability program that includes creating a "single stream" trash and recycling program at the park to reduce use of local landfills, as well as efforts to save water and energy, reduce pollution in the park, and design and retrofit buildings to make them greener.

★ **El Tovar Dining Room** (928/638-2631, ext. 6432, www.grandcanyonlodges.com, 6:30am-11am, 11:30am-2pm, and 5pm-10pm daily, $10-40, reservations highly recommended) truly carries on the Fred Harvey Company traditions on which it was founded more than 100 years ago. A serious, competent staff serves fresh, creative, locally inspired and sourced dishes in a cozy, mural-lined dining room that has not been significantly altered from the way it looked back when Teddy Roosevelt and Zane Grey ate here. The wine, entrées, and desserts are all top-notch and would be appreciated anywhere in the world—but they always seem to be that much tastier with the sun going down over the canyon. Pay attention to the specials, which usually feature some in-season local edible; they are always the best thing to eat within several hundred miles in any direction. If you only have one nice dinner planned for your trip, choose El Tovar over The Arizona Room. El Tovar has greater historical and aesthetic interest and is not that much more expensive than The Arizona Room.

The Arizona Steakhouse (928/638-2631, www.grandcanyonlodges.com, 11:30am-3pm and 4:30pm-10pm daily Mar.-Dec., $14-36), next to the Bright Angel Lodge, serves locally sourced, Southwestern-inspired steak, prime rib, fish, and chicken dishes in a stylish but still casual atmosphere. There's a full bar, and the steaks are excellent—hand-cut and cooked just right with unexpected sauces and marinades. The Arizona Room is closed for dinner in January and February and closes to the lunch crowd November-February.

★ **Harvey House Cafe** (928/638-2631, www.grandcanyonlodges.com, 6:30am-10pm daily, $9-22), just off the Bright Angel Lodge's lobby, is a perfect place for a big, hearty breakfast before a day hike below the rim. It serves all the standard, rib-sticking dishes amid decorations and ephemera recalling the Fred Harvey heyday. At lunch there's stew, chili, salads, sandwiches, and burgers, and for dinner there's steak, pasta, and fish dishes called "Bright Angel Traditions," along with a few offerings from The Arizona Room's menu. Nearby is the **Bright Angel Fountain** (11am-5pm daily in season), which serves hot dogs, ice cream, and other quick treats.

Maswik Food Court (928/638-2631, www. grandcanyonlodges.com, 6am-10pm daily, $5-15) is an ideal place for a quick, filling, and delicious meal. You can find just about everything—burgers, salads, country-style mashed potatoes, french fries, sandwiches, prime rib, chili, and soft-serve ice cream, to name just a few of the dozens of offerings. Just grab a tray and pick your favorite dish, and you'll be eating in a matter of a few minutes.

Yavapai Lodge Restaurant (www. visitgrandcanyon.com, 6am-10pm daily, $10-20) has decent food in a cafeteria setting where you order from a computer. Sandwiches, both hot and cold, dominate the limited menu.

ACCOMMODATIONS

The park's lodging rates are audited annually and compare favorably to those offered outside the park, but you can sometimes find excellent deals at one of several gateway towns around canyon country. Using one of these places as a base for a visit to the canyon makes sense if you're planning on touring the whole of the canyonlands and not just the park. There are six lodges within Grand Canyon National Park at the South Rim, most of them operated by Xanterra (www. grandcanyonlodges.com). The hotels within the park are a relatively green and sustainable choice; Xanterra has a fairly robust sustainability program aimed at conserving water and energy, reducing pollution, and increasing recycling while decreasing use of landfills.

A stay at ★ **El Tovar** (303/297-2757, www. grandcanyonlodges.com, $217-263 standard room, $442-538 suite), more than 100 years old and one of the most distinctive and memorable hotels in the state, would be the secondary highlight—after the gorge itself—of any trip to the South Rim. The log-and-stone National Historic Landmark, standing about 20 feet from the rim, has 78 rooms and suites. The hotel's restaurant serves some of the best food in Arizona for breakfast, lunch, and dinner, and there's a comfortable cocktail lounge off the lobby with a window on the canyon. A mezzanine sitting area overlooks the log-cabin lobby, and a gift shop sells Native American art and crafts as well as canyon souvenirs. If you're looking to splurge on something truly exceptional, there's a honeymoon suite overlooking the canyon.

When first built in the 1930s, the ★ **Bright Angel Lodge** (303/297-2757, www.grandcanyonlodges.com, $95-210) was meant to serve the middle-class travelers then being lured by the Santa Fe Railroad, and it's still affordable and comfortable while retaining a rustic character that fits perfectly with the wild canyon just outside. Lodge rooms don't have TVs, and most have only one bed. The utilitarian "hikers" rooms have refrigerators and share several private showers, which have lockable doors and just enough room to dress. Bright Angel is the place to sleep before hiking into the canyon; you just roll out of bed onto the Bright Angel Trail. The lodge's cabins just west of the main building have private baths, TVs, and sitting rooms. Drinking and dining options include a small bar and coffeehouse, a Harvey House diner, and a restaurant with big windows framing the canyon.

Standing along the rim between El Tovar and Bright Angel, the **Kachina Lodge** (303/297-2757, www.grandcanyonlodges. com, $225-243), offers basic, comfortable rooms with TVs, safes, private baths, and refrigerators. There's not a lot of character, but its location and modern comforts make the Kachina an ideal place for families to stay. The **Thunderbird Lodge** (303/297-2757, www.grandcanyonlodges.com, $225-243) is in the same area and has similar offerings. Both properties have some rooms facing the canyon.

Maswick Lodge (303/297-2757, www.

grandcanyonlodges.com, $215) is located on the west side of the village about 0.25 mile from the rim. The hotel has a cafeteria-style restaurant that serves just about everything you'd want and a sports bar with a large-screen TV. The rooms are motel-style basic but clean and comfortable, with TVs, private baths, and refrigerators, but there's no elevator. In spring 2018, the lodge's two-story south section was torn down to make way for a new building. The project is expected to take two years, so you may want to think twice before booking here, as there's likely to be construction noise and parking hassles.

About five miles from the park entrance on the road to Canyon Village Market Plaza, **Yavapai Lodge** (11 Yavapai Lodge Rd., 928/638-4001 or 877/404-4611, www.visitgrandcanyon.com, $150-200) is basic but clean and comfortable. The East Section has clean and comfortable rooms with air-conditioning, refrigerators, and TVs, and the King Family Room is a great option for families with a king bed and twin bunk beds. The West Section, a retro motel-style structure, lacks air-conditioning but has pet rooms for an extra $25.

Camping
★ **Mather Campground** (877/444-6777, www.recreation.gov, $18 Mar.-Nov., $15 Dec.-Feb.) takes reservations up to six months ahead for the March-November 20 peak season and thereafter operates on a first-come, first-served basis. Located near the village and offering more than 300 basic campsites with grills and fire pits, the campground typically fills up by about noon during the summer busy season. It has restrooms with showers, and coin-operated laundry machines. The campground is open to tents and trailers but has no hookups and is closed to RVs longer than 30 feet. Even if you aren't an experienced camper, a stay at Mather is a fun and inexpensive alternative to sleeping indoors. Despite its large size and crowds, the campground gets pretty quiet at night. Even in summer, the night takes on a bit of chill,

making a campfire not exactly necessary but not out of the question. Bring your own wood or buy it at the store nearby. A large, clean restroom and shower facility is within walking distance from most sites, and they even have blow-dryers. Everything is coin operated, and there's an office on-site that gives change. Consider bringing bikes along, especially for the kids. The village is about a 15-minute walk from the campground on forested, paved trails, or you can take the free tram from a stop nearby. Pets are allowed but must be kept on a leash, and they're not allowed on shuttle buses.

About 25 miles east of the village, near the park's East Entrance, is **Desert View Campground** (first-come, first-served, May-mid-Oct. depending on weather, $12), with 50 sites for tents and small trailers only, with no hookups. There's a restroom with no showers and only two faucets with running water. Each site has a grill but little else. Pets are allowed but must be kept on a leash.

If you're in a rolling mansion, try **Trailer Village** (888/297-2757, www.xanterra.com, $45) next to Mather Campground, near the village, where you'll find hookups for trailers up to 50 feet long.

GETTING THERE
Car
The majority of Grand Canyon visitors drive here, reaching the South Rim from either **Flagstaff** or **Williams** and entering the park through the south or east gates. The South Entrance is usually the busiest, and during the summer traffic is likely to be backed up somewhat. The quickest way to get to the south gate by car is to take Route 64 from Williams. It's about a 60-mile drive across a barren plain; there are a few kitschy places to stop along the way, including Bedrock City, a rather dilapidated model of the Flintstones' hometown with an RV park and a gift shop.

From Flagstaff take U.S. 180 through the forest past the San Francisco Peaks. The road merges with Route 64 at Valle, for a total distance of about 80 miles from Flagstaff to the park gate. Or, to reach the East Entrance, take U.S. 89 north from Flagstaff to Cameron, then take Route 64 west to the entrance. This longer route is recommended if you want to see portions of Navajo Country on your way to the canyon, and entering through the East Entrance will put you right at Desert View, the Desert View Watchtower, and Tusayan Museum and Ruin—sights that otherwise you'll have to travel 25 or so miles east from Grand Canyon Village to see.

The Grand Canyon's South Rim is 224 miles from **Phoenix,** which has in Sky Harbor International Airport the closest major airport to the park. The best way to reach the canyon from out of state is to fly into Phoenix, rent a car, and drive north on I-17. Once you reach the northland, you can either take the route through Williams along Route 64 or the Flagstaff route along U.S. 89 and Route 64. Both will lead you to the canyon's edge within about an hour from their respective towns, though the latter is more scenic. Expect the drive from Phoenix to take about 3.5 hours, barring heavy traffic on the interstate.

The roughly five-hour drive from **Las Vegas** to the South Rim—a very popular trip—is relatively short one by Southwestern standards. Even if you get a late-morning start and make a few stops along the way, you're still likely to arrive at the park by dinnertime. If you feel like stopping overnight—and perhaps it is better to see the great canyon with fresh morning eyes—do so in Williams. It's just an hour or so from the park's South Entrance, has a bit of Route 66 charm, and offers several distinctive and memorable hotels and restaurants, all of which you'll miss if you breeze through town in a hurry. Stick to I-40 after leaving Kingman. The speed limit on most sections of I-40 in Arizona is 75 mph, so all that highland forest scenery flashes by unless you stop a few times to take it in. Most summer weekends you'll find the route crowded but manageable. At all times of the year you'll be surrounded by 18-wheelers barreling across the land.

If you are inclined to visit the **Hualapai Reservation's Skywalk,** remember that it's only 125 miles from Las Vegas (about a 2.5-hour drive), so it makes sense to include this remote side trip if you're headed to the South Rim from Vegas anyway. To reach Grand Canyon West from Las Vegas, take U.S. 93 out of the city, heading south for about 65 miles to mile marker 42, where you'll see the Dolan Springs/Meadview City/Pearce Ferry exit. Turn north onto Pearce Ferry Road. About 30 miles in, turn east on Diamond Bar Road. Then it's about 20 miles, 7 or so miles of it unpaved, to Grand Canyon West.

To continue on to the South Rim, head to Peach Springs along Old Route 66. You can stop here for the night, at the **Hualapai Lodge,** or continue on for about an hour east on Route 66 to **Seligman,** which has several small hotels and a few good restaurants. Then head east on Route 66 to Ash Fork, where you can pick up I-40 east to Williams, the gateway to the South Rim.

Grand Canyon National Park's South Rim is 494 miles from Los Angeles, the capital of the American West. Most of the seven- or eight-hour drive is along I-40. It's an approximately two-hour drive north on I-15 from L.A. to Barstow, where I-40 begins (or ends, if you're coming from the east), but it's sure to take considerably longer on the weekends and during the morning and evening rush hours, which in Southern California tend to be interminable. Expect snarls and delays around Barstow as well.

PARKING

If you're just visiting for the day, you can drive into the village and park your car in the **El Tovar** parking lot. More often than not, especially in the summer, the lot at El Tovar will be full. You can also park at the large lot at **Canyon Village Market Plaza** and then take the shuttle bus around the park. The **Backcountry Information Center** (928/638-7875) also has a large parking lot, the southern portion of which can accommodate RVs and trailers.

Air

Grand Canyon Airlines has flights from Boulder City, Nevada, near Las Vegas, to Tusayan's **Grand Canyon Airport** (www.grandcanyonairlines.com, $369, 9.5-hour tour by plane and bus), but there are no direct commercial flights into or out of the small airport, and there are no rental cars available.

Both Flagstaff and Williams have small airports as well, but most visitors fly into Sky Harbor in Phoenix, rent a car, and drive about 3.5 hours north to the South Rim.

Bus

Arizona Shuttles (928/226-8060, www.arizonashuttle.com) offers comfortable rides from Flagstaff to the Grand Canyon three times daily ($60 round-trip for adults, Mar. 1-Oct. 31). The company also goes between Phoenix's Sky Harbor International Airport and Flagstaff ($48 one-way) several times a day as well as from Flagstaff to Sedona, the Verde Valley, and Williams ($35-43 one-way).

Grand Canyon Railway

A fun, retro, and environmentally conscious way to reach the park, the **Grand Canyon Railway** (800/843-8724, www.thetrain.com, $65-220 round-trip pp) re-creates what it was like to visit the great gorge in the early 20th century. It takes about 2.5 hours to get to the South Rim depot from the station in Williams, where the Grand Canyon Railway Hotel and restaurant just beyond the train station makes a good base, attempting as it does to match the atmosphere of the old Santa Fe Railroad Harvey House that once stood on the same ground.

During the trip, one is always wondering when the train is going to speed up, but it never really does, rocking at about 60 mph through pine forests and across a scrubby grassland shared by cattle, elk, pronghorn, coyotes, and red-tailed hawks, all of which can be viewed from a comfortable seat in one of the old refurbished cars. Along the way, there are ruins of the great railroad days, including

ancient telegraph posts still lined up along the tracks.

A trip to and from the Grand Canyon on the old train is recommended for anyone who is interested in the heyday of train travel, the Old West, or the golden age of Southwestern tourism—or for anyone desiring a slower-paced journey across the northland. Besides, the fewer visitors who drive their vehicles to the rim, the better. Kids seem to especially enjoy the train trip, as comedian-fiddlers often stroll through the cars, and on some trips there's even a mock train robbery complete with bandits on horseback with blazing six-shooters.

GETTING AROUND
Shuttle

The park operates excellent free shuttle services with comfortable buses fueled by compressed natural gas. It's strongly encouraged you park your car for the duration of your visit and use the shuttle. It's nearly impossible to find parking at the various sights, and traffic through the park is not always easy to navigate—there are a lot of one-way routes and oblivious pedestrians that can lead to needless frustration. Make sure you pick up a copy of the free park newspaper, *The Pocket Map*, which has a map of the various shuttle routes and stops.

March 1-September 30 a route operates from the National Geographic IMAX theater into the park, all day every day. You have to purchase your entrance ticket at the IMAX before getting on the shuttle. Just leave your car in the parking lot in Tusayan and take the free shuttles everywhere you want to go inside the park. Shuttles from the theater begin at 8am daily, and the last trip is at 9:45pm. The Tusayan shuttle drops you off at the Grand Canyon Visitors Center; the last shuttle out of the park leaves at 9:30pm.

Pretty much anywhere you want to go in the park a shuttle will get you there, and you rarely have to wait more than 10 minutes at any stop. That being said, there is no shuttle that goes all the way to the Tusayan Museum and Ruin or the Watchtower near the East Entrance. Shuttle drivers are a good source of information about the park. They are generally very friendly and knowledgeable, and a few of them are genuinely entertaining. The shuttle conveniently runs from around sunup until about 9pm, and drivers always know the expected sunrise and sundown times and seem to be intent on getting people to the best overlooks to view these two popular daily park events.

Bike

Whether you're staying in the park or just visiting for the day, consider bringing your bike along. You can park at the **South Rim Backcountry Information** **Center parking lot** and ride your bike all around the park from there using the paved **Tuyasan Greenway Trail.** Every hotel, restaurant, store and sight has a bike rack; don't forget your bike lock. If you get tired, park shuttles have racks that fit 2-3 bikes. Remember, though, that the shuttles take a lot longer because they make many stops. There's a good map of all the in-park bike routes in the free *Pocket Map* guide, and the staff at **Bright Angel Bicycles and Café** (928/814-8704, www.bikegrandcanyon. com, 6am-8pm daily Apr.-Nov., 7am-7pm daily Dec.-Mar.), right next to the **Grand Canyon Visitors Center** near the South Entrance and Mather Point, can answer your questions.

The North Rim

TOP EXPERIENCE

Standing at Bright Angel Point on the Grand Canyon's North Rim, crowded together with several other gazers as if stranded on a jetty over a wide, hazy sea, blurred evergreens growing atop great jagged rock spines banded with white and red, someone whispers, "It looks pretty much the same as the other rim."

It's not true—far from it—but the comment brings up the main point about the North Rim: Should you go? Only about 10 percent of canyon visitors make the trip to the North Rim, which is significantly less developed than the South; there aren't many activities other than gazing, unless you are a hiker and a backcountry wilderness lover. The coniferous mountain forests of the Kaibab Plateau are themselves worth the trip—broken by grassy meadows and painted with summer wildflowers, populated by often-seen elk and mule deer, and dappled with aspens that turn yellow and red in the fall and burst out of the otherwise uniform dark green like solitary flames. But it is a long trip, and you need to be prepared for a land of scant services—in return you'll find the simple, contemplative pleasures of nature in the raw.

EXPLORING THE NORTH RIM

It's all about the scenery here at 8,000 feet and above. The often-misty canyon, and the thick, old-growth forest along its rim, command all of your attention. Some of the people you'll meet here are a bit different from the South Rim visitors, a good portion being hard-core hikers and backpackers waiting for early morning to hit the North Kaibab Trail for a rim-to-rim trek.

That's not to say that there's nothing to do on the North Rim. Spend some time on the lodge's back porch, have an overpriced beer at the cantina, and hike through the highland forest on easy trails to reach uncrowded viewpoints. There are similarly lonely lookouts (at least compared to the often elbow-to-elbow scene at some the South Rim's spots) at the end of a couple of scenic drives. Only a rare few see the North Rim covered in snow, as it often is past November. The park here closes in mid-October and doesn't open again until mid-May.

Visitors Centers

The **North Rim Visitor Center and Bookstore** (8am-6pm daily May-Oct.), near the Grand Canyon Lodge, has information, maps, and exhibits on North Rim science and history. The nonprofit Grand Canyon Association operates the well-stocked bookstore. Rangers offer a full program of talks and guided hikes throughout the day and night programs around the campfire. The North Rim edition of *The Pocket Map* has an up-to-date list of topics, times, and meeting places. Try to attend at least one or two—they are typically interesting and entertaining for both kids and adults, and it tends to deepen your connection with this st oried place when you learn about its natural and human history from those who know it best. For the kids, the visitors center has the usual super-fun and educational Junior Rangers program.

Driving Tours

CAPE ROYAL SCENIC DRIVE

You can reach Point Imperial and several other lookout spots on the Cape Royal Scenic Drive, one of the most scenic, dramatic roads in the state. From the lodge to Cape Royal it's about 30 miles round-trip on a paved road that wends through the mixed conifer and aspen forests of the **Walhalla Plateau.** There are plenty of chances for wildlife-spotting, plus short trails to viewpoints offering breathtaking views of the canyon off to the east and even as far as Navajoland. Plan to spend at least half a day, and take food and water. Go to **Point Imperial** first, reached by a three-mile side road at the beginning of the Cape Royal Road. The best way to do it would be to leave the lodge just before sunrise, watch the show from Point Imperial, and then hit the scenic drive for the rest of the day, stopping often. Along the way, **Vista Encantadora** (Charming View) provides just that, rising above Nanokoweap Creek. Just beyond that is **Roosevelt Point,** where

you can hike the easy 0.2-mile loop trail to a view worthy of the man who saved the Grand Canyon. When you finally reach the point of the drive, **Cape Royal** at 7,865 feet, you'll walk out on a 0.6-mile round-trip paved trail for an expansive and unbounded view of the canyon—one of the very best, from which, on a clear day, you can spot the South Rim's Desert View Watchtower way across the gorge, and the river far below. Along the short trail you'll pass the rock arch called **Angel's Window.**

SIGHTS
★ Grand Canyon Lodge

Even if you aren't staying at the **Grand Canyon Lodge** (www.grandcanyonlodgenorth.com), a rustic log-and-stone structure built in 1927-1928 and perched on the edge of the rim at the end of the highway, don't make the trip to the North Rim without going into its warm Sun Room to view the canyon through the huge picture windows. You may want to sink into one of the comfortable couches and stare for hours. At sunset, head out to the Adirondack chairs on the lodge's back patio and watch the sun sink over the canyon; everybody's quiet, hushed in reverence, bundled up in jackets and sweaters. Right near the door leading out to the patio, check out sculptor Peter Jepson's charming life-size bronze of **Brighty,** a famous canyon burro and star of the 1953 children's book *Brighty of the Grand Canyon* by Marguerite Henry. A display nearby tells Brighty's story, and they say if you rub his bronze nose you'll have good luck. The book, along with a movie based on the story, is available at gift shops and bookstores on both the North and South Rims.

Viewpoints

There are three developed viewpoints at the North Rim, each of them offering a slightly different look at the canyon. **Bright Angel Point,** about a half-mile round-trip walk

---

1: Grand Canyon Lodge **2:** Transept Trail

outside the lodge's back door, looks over Bright Angel Canyon with a view of Roaring Springs, the source of Bright Angel Creek and fresh water for the North Rim and inner canyon; **Point Imperial**, at 8,803 feet the highest point on the North Rim, probably has the best all-around view of the canyon; and **Cape Royal**, a 23-mile one-way drive across the Walhalla Plateau, looks toward the South Rim.

RECREATION
Hiking

It's significantly cooler on the high, forested North Rim than it is on the South, making hiking, especially summer hiking below the rim, much less of a chore. There are a few easy rim trails to choose from and several tough but unforgettable day hikes into the canyon along the North Kaibab Trail.

Easy trails lead to and from all the developed scenic overlooks on the rim, their trailheads accessible and well marked. *The Pocket Map* has a comprehensive listing of the area's trails and where to pick them up. The four-mile round-trip **Transept Trail** is an easy hike through the forest from the Grand Canyon Lodge to the campground. It has a few nice views and is a good introduction to the North Rim.

UNCLE JIM TRAIL

Distance: 5 miles round-trip
Duration: 3 hours
Elevation gain: about 200 feet
Effort: easy
Trailhead: North Kaibab Trail parking lot, 3 miles north of Grand Canyon Lodge on the main park entrance road

Take this easy, flat trail through the forest to watch backpackers winding their way down the North Kaibab Trail's twisting switchbacks and maybe see a mule train or two along the way. The **Uncle Jim Trail** winds through old stands of spruce and fir, sprinkled with quaking aspen, to Uncle Jim Point, where you can let out your best roar into the tributary known as Roaring Springs Canyon.

WIDFORSS TRAIL

Distance: 10 miles round-trip
Duration: 5-6 hours
Elevation gain: negligible
Effort: easy
Trailhead: 4 miles north of the lodge; look for the sign

Named for the 1930s canyon painter Gunnar Widforss, the mostly flat and easy **Widforss Trail** leads along the rim of the side canyon called Transept Canyon and through ponderosa pine, fir, and spruce forest, with a few stands of aspen mixed in, for five miles to Widforss Point, where you can stare across the great chasm and rest before heading back.

For a shorter hike, pick up the free guide to the Widforss Trail at the trailhead or the visitors center. It proposes a five-mile round-trip hike on the first half of the trail, and includes a map and information on the natural and human history of the North Rim.

NORTH KAIBAB TRAIL

Distance: varies; 9.4 miles to Roaring Springs
Duration: a few hours to overnight
Elevation gain: 5,961 feet from Phantom Ranch
Effort: moderate to difficult
Trailhead: North Kaibab Trail parking area

The **North Kaibab Trail** starts out among the coniferous heights of the North Rim. The forest surrounding the trail soon dries out and becomes a red-rock desert, the trail cut into the rock face of the cliffs and twisting down improbable routes hard against the cliffs, with nothing but your sanity keeping you away from the gorge. This is the only North Rim route down into the Inner Canyon and to the Colorado River. Sooner than you realize, the walls close in, and you are deep in the canyon, the trees on the rim just green blurs now. A good introduction to this corridor trail and ancient native route is the short, 1.5-mile round-trip jog down to the **Coconino Overlook**, from which, on a clear day, you can see the San Francisco Peaks and the South Rim. A four-mile round-trip hike down will get you to **Supai Tunnel**, blasted out of the red rock in the 1930s by the Civilian

Conservation Corps. A little more than a mile onward you'll reach **The Bridge in the Redwall** (5.5 miles round-trip), built in 1966 after a flood ruined this portion of the trail. For a tough, all-day hike that will likely have you sore but smiling the next morning, take the North Kaibab roughly five miles down to **Roaring Springs,** the source of life-giving Bright Angel Creek. The springs fall headlong out of the cliffside and spray mist and rainbows into the hot air. Just remember, you also have to go five miles back up. Start hiking early, and take plenty of water.

The North Kaibab Trailhead is a few miles north of the Grand Canyon Lodge, the park's only accommodations on the North Rim. To get from the lodge to the trailhead, take the **hiker's shuttle** (first person $7, each additional person $4), which leaves every morning from the lodge at 5:30am and 6am. Tickets must be purchased 24 hours before at the lodge.

North Rim Mule Rides

The mules at the North Rim all work for **Canyon Trail Rides** (435/679-8665, www.canyonrides.com, May 15-Oct. 15), the park's northside trail-riding concessionaire. Guides will take you and your friendly mule on a one-hour rimside ride ($45) or a three-hour ride to Uncle Jim's Point ($90). You can also take a mule down into the canyon along the North Kaibab Trail to the Supai Tunnel (3 hours, $90). Kids have to be at least seven years old for the one-hour ride, and at least 10 for the three-hour rides. There's a 220-pound weight limit. Call ahead for a reservation if this is something you're set on doing. You might be able to hop on last-minute, though probably not in June, which is the busiest time at the North Rim.

FOOD

The **Grand Canyon Lodge Dining Room** (928/638-2611, www.grandcanyonlodgenorth.com, 6:30am-10am, 11:30am-2:30pm, and 4:30pm-9:30pm daily mid-May-mid-Oct., reservations required for dinner, $10-30) serves breakfast, lunch, dinner and a buffet every day during the too-brief North Rim season. The lodge's historic dining room is a great place to be, with its high log-mansion ceilings, exposed pinewood vigas, local-stone walls and floor-to-ceiling windows framing the canyon, and the food is pretty good too. For breakfast they have excellent omelets and breakfast burritos, along with hiker-friendly options like oatmeal and granola. Lunch and dinner feature regionally sourced and inspired creations such as elk chili, Lee's Ferry trout, and venison meat loaf. There are quite a few vegetarian options here as well. Every night in season the lodge also offers a buffet in the main auditorium.

If you're just looking for a quick bite or something simple to take back to the cabin, head over to the **Deli in the Pines** (10:30am-9pm daily, $5-15), just a few steps from the lodge. The deli has decent sandwiches and pizza in a casual, counter-service setting, and the friendly staff members from all over the world are happy to pack your meal to go. Try **The Coffee Shop and Rough Rider Saloon** (5:30am-10:30am and 11:30am-10:30pm daily, $5-15) right across from the deli for a quick and delicious breakfast burrito and a latte, and then head back to the same place in the evening for a cold beer and snacks.

The only other option within 50 miles of the park is the **Kaibab Lodge Restaurant** (928/638-2389, www.kaibablodge.com, breakfast, lunch, and dinner daily mid-May-early Nov., $10-15), about 18 miles north of the Grand Canyon Lodge. Here they serve hearty comfort fare perfect for the high, cool country. The knotty-pine dining room feels like a throwback to the days of summer camps and family lodges, and the food is homemade and flavorful: burgers, ribs, steaks, hot and cold sandwiches, big breakfasts, beer, and wine. Vegetarian options are limited to a few pasta dishes and a garden burger.

ACCOMMODATIONS

Built in the late 1930s after the original lodge burned down, the ★ **Grand Canyon**

Lodge (928/638-2611 or 888/297-2757, www.grandcanyonlodgenorth.com, mid-May-mid-Oct., $132 rooms, $146-268 cabins) is the only hotel on the North Rim. The rustic but very comfortable log-and-stone lodge has a large central lobby, high-ceilinged dining room, deli, saloon, gift shop, general store, and gas station. There are several small, comfortable lodge rooms and dozens of cabins scattered around the property, each with a bathroom and most with a gas-powered fireplace that makes things very cozy on a cold night. The lodge is open from mid-May-mid-October. You must book far in advance (at least six months), though there are sometimes cancellations allowing for a last-minute booking.

The **Kaibab Lodge** (928/638-2389, www.kaibablodge.com, mid-May-early Nov., $95-185) is a small gathering of rustic, cozy cabins (some more rustic than others) on the edge of a meadow, tucked behind the tree line along Route 67, about five miles north of the park. You can rent cabins of varying sizes and enjoy the lounge, gift shop, and warm fireplace in the lobby. The lodge closes in early November. Book very early (3-6 months in advance) if you want to stay here in summer. A small room with a bed and bathroom is included in the $95 "hiker's special" here, which is a great option if you can nab a reservation. There are no TVs and no cell service.

There is also a comfortable lodge at Jacob Lake, the **Jacob Lake Inn** (junction of U.S. 89A and Rte. 67, 928/643-7232, www.jacoblake.com, $126-144 rooms, $94-144 cabins), on the Kaibab Plateau about 42 miles from the park entrance.

Camping

The in-park **North Rim Campground** (877/444-6777, www.recreation.gov, $18-25, reservation only) has basic camping spots near the rim, with showers and a coin-operated laundry. About 25 miles south of Jacob Lake and about 7 miles north of the park entrance on Highway 67 is the **DeMotte Campground** (May-Oct., $18), operated by the U.S. Forest Service. It has 38 sites with tables and cooking grills, toilets, and drinking water. Tents, trailers, and motor homes are allowed, but there are no utility hookups or dump stations available. Reservations must be made three days ahead between September 7 and March 21.

Kaibab Camper Village (AZ 67, just south of Jacob Lake, 928/643-7804 or 800/525-0924, www.kaibabcampervillage.com, May 14-Oct. 15) has full-hookup sites ($37)

cabins at the Grand Canyon Lodge

and basic tent sites ($18). The village also has cabins ($85) and offers fire pits, tables, bathrooms, and coin-operated showers.

TRANSPORTATION

Although it's only an average of about 10 miles across the canyon from the South to North Rims for a hawk, raven, or condor, it's a 215-mile, five-hour drive for those of us who are primarily earthbound. The long route north is something to behold, moving through a corner of Navajoland, past the towering Vermilion Cliffs, and deep into the high forests of the Kaibab Plateau. Route 67 from Jacob Lake to the North Rim typically closes to vehicles by late November until May. In the winter, it's not uncommon for cross-country skiers and snowshoe hikers to take to the closed and snow-covered highway, heading with their own power toward the canyon and the North Kaibab Trail.

Between the hotel, restaurant, and gas station at Jacob Lake on the Kaibab Plateau and the entrance to Grand Canyon National Park on the North Rim, there's not much more than high-mountain scenery. But in case you forget anything before venturing into this relative wilderness, you can always stop at the well-stocked **North Rim Country Store** (Hwy. 67, milepost 605, 928/638-2383, www.northrimcountrystore.com, 7:30am-7pm

daily mid-May-early Nov.), about 43 miles along Highway 67 from Jacob Lake. The store has just about anything you'll need, from snacks to gas to camping supplies. There's also a small auto shop here in case you're having car troubles or catch a flat that you can't fix yourself. The store closes for winter, as does the whole region, around the beginning of November.

The **Trans Canyon Shuttle** (928/638-2820, www.trans-canyonshuttle.com, $90 one-way, reservations required) makes a daily round-trip excursion between the North and South Rims, departing the North Rim at 7am and arriving at the South Rim at 11:30am. The shuttle then leaves the South Rim at 1:30pm and arrives back at the North Rim at 6:30pm.

To get from the Grand Canyon Lodge—the park's only accommodations on the North Rim—to the North Kaibab Trailhead, take the **Hikers Shuttle** ($7 for first person, $4 for each additional person), which leaves the lodge twice daily first thing in the morning. Tickets must be purchased the day before at the lodge.

If you paid your park entrance fee at the South Rim, this will be honored at the North as long as you go within seven days. If not, you'll have to pay again. A North Rim edition of the park's helpful newspaper *The Pocket Map* is passed out at the North Rim entrance.

The Inner Canyon

Inside the canyon is a strange desert, red and green, pink and rocky. It's those sheer rock walls, tight and claustrophobic in the interior's narrowest slots, that make this place a different world altogether. A large part of a canyon-crossing hike takes place in Bright Angel Canyon along Bright Angel Creek. As you hike along the trail beside the creek, greenery and the cool rushing water clash with the silent heat washing off the cliffs on your other side.

On any given night there are only a few hundred visitors sleeping below the rim—at either Phantom Ranch, a Mary Colter-designed lodge near the mouth of Bright Angel Canyon, or at three campgrounds along the corridor trails. Until a few decades ago visiting the inner canyon was something of a free-for-all, but these days access to the interior is strictly controlled; you have to purchase a permit ($10, plus $8 pp per night), and they're not always easy to get—each year the park receives 30,000 requests for backcountry permits and issues only 13,000.

No matter which trail you use, there's no avoiding an arduous, leg- and spirit-punishing hike there and back if you really want to see the inner canyon. It's not easy, no matter who you are, but it is worth it; it's a true accomplishment, a hard walk you'll never forget.

EXPLORING THE INNER CANYON

If you want to be one of the small minority of canyon visitors to spend some quality time below the rim, stay at least one full day and night in the inner canyon. Even hikers in excellent shape find that they are sore after trekking down to the river, Phantom Ranch, and beyond. A rim-to-rim hike, either from the south or from the north, pretty much requires at least a day of rest below the rim. The ideal inner canyon trip lasts three days and two nights: one day hiking in, one day of rest, and one day to hike out.

River trips range from three days up to three weeks and often include a hike down one of the corridor trails to the river. Depending on how long you want to spend on the river, plan far, far in advance, and consider making the river trip your only major activity on that particular canyon visit. Combining too much strenuous, mind-blowing, and life-changing activity into one trip tends to water down the entire experience.

Permits and Reservations

The earlier you apply for a permit, the better, but you can't apply for one prior to the first of the month four months before your proposed trip date. The easiest way to get a permit is to go to the **park's website** (www.nps.gov/grca), print out a backcountry permit request form, fill it out, and then fax it first thing in the morning on the date in question—for example, if you want to hike in October, you would **fax** (928/638-2125) your request May 20-June 1. Have patience; on the first day of the month the fax number is usually busy throughout the day—keep

trying. On the permit request form you'll indicate where you plan to stay. If you are camping, the permit is your reservation, but if you want to stay at Phantom Ranch, you must get separate reservations, and that is often a close-to-impossible task. For more information on obtaining a backcountry permit, call the **South Rim Backcountry Information Center** (928/638-7875, 8am-5pm daily).

HIKING
Into the Inner Canyon

Although there are lesser-known routes into and through the canyon, most hikers stick to the **corridor trails—Bright Angel, South Kaibab,** and **North Kaibab.** A classic Grand Canyon backpacking journey begins at either the Bright Angel Trailhead or the South Kaibab Trailhead on the South Rim. Consider going up the one you don't use going down, mostly for variety's sake. Via the Bright Angel Trail, it's a 9.5-mile hike to the Bright Angel Campground, which is just a short walk from the Colorado River and also from Phantom Ranch. Ideally, spend at least two days—the hike-in day and one full day after that—and two nights in the Phantom Ranch area, hiking up the North Kaibab a short way to see the narrow and close walls, talking to the rangers, sitting on the beach watching the river-trippers float by, and losing yourself to the calm, quiet soul of the wilderness.

When it's time to leave the oasis that is Bright Angel Campground and Phantom Ranch, a question arises: Should you rise headlong to the rim (7 miles up on the South Kaibab or 9.5 miles up on the Bright Angel) or move on leisurely to the next oasis? Those inclined to choose the latter should stay an extra night below the rim at the campground at Indian Garden, a green and lush spot 4.7 miles up the Bright Angel Trail from the Bright Angel Campground. The small

---

1: the inner canyon **2:** mule rides from the bottom of the Grand Canyon

campground is primitive but charming, and the area around it is populated by deer and other creatures. After setting up camp and resting a bit, head out on the flat, three-mile round-trip hike to Plateau Point and a spectacular view of the canyon and river, especially at sunset. When you wake up beneath the shady trees at Indian Garden, you face a mere 4.9-mile hike to the rim.

From the **North Rim**, the **North Kaibab** is the only trail to the river and Phantom Ranch.

Rim to Rim

For an epic, **23.9-mile** rim-to-rim rim hike, you can choose, as long as the season permits, to start either on the north or south. Starting from the South Rim, you may want to go down the **Bright Angel** to see beautiful Indian Garden; then again, the **South Kaibab** provides a faster, more direct route to the river. If you start from the north, you may want to come out of the canyon via the South Kaibab; it is shorter and faster, and at that point you are probably going to want to take the path of least resistance. Remember though, while it's shorter, the South Kaibab is a good deal steeper than the Bright Angel, and there is no water available.

No matter who you are or what trail you prefer, the hike out of the Grand Canyon is, at several points, a brutal trudge. It's even worse with 30-40 pounds of stuff you don't really need on your back. Try to take only the essentials to keep your pack weight down. The best rim-to-rim hikes include at least one full day at Phantom Ranch or the Bright Angel Campground. You could do the hike without a permit with a bit of preplanning: Reserve a room on the North Rim and hike there from the South Rim in one day. Then after a day of rest and another night, hike back to the South Rim in one day.

No matter how you do it, when you finally gain the final rim after a cross-canyon hike, a profound sense of accomplishment washes away at least half of the fatigue. The other half typically hangs around for a week or so.

Day Hikes Around Phantom Ranch

Some people prefer to spend their time in the canyon recovering from the hard walk or mule ride that brought them here, and a day spent cooling your feet in Bright Angel Creek or drinking beer in the cantina is not a day wasted. However, if you want to do some exploring around Phantom Ranch, there are a few popular day hikes from which to choose. When you arrive, the friendly rangers will usually tell you, unsolicited, all about these hikes and provide detailed directions. If you want to get deeper out in the bush and far from the other hikers, ask one of the rangers to recommend a lesser-known route.

RIVER TRAIL

Distance: 1.5 miles round-trip
Duration: 1-2 hours
Elevation gain: negligible
Effort: easy

This rather short hike is along the precipitous **River Trail**, high above the Colorado just south of Phantom Ranch. The Civilian Conservation Corps (CCC) blasted this skinny cliffside trail out of the rock walls in the 1930s to provide a link between the Bright Angel and the South Kaibab Trails. Heading out from Phantom, it's about a 1.5-mile loop that takes you across both suspension bridges and high above the river. It's an easy walk with fantastic views and a good way to get your sore legs stretched and moving again. And you are likely to see a bighorn sheep's cute little face poking out from the rocks and shadows on the steep cliffs.

CLEAR CREEK TO PHANTOM OVERLOOK

Distance: about 1.5 miles
Duration: 1-2 hours
Elevation gain: 826 feet
Effort: easy to moderate
Trailhead: about 0.25 mile north of Phantom Ranch on the North Kaibab Trail

Another popular CCC-built trail near Phantom, the 1.5-mile **Clear Creek Loop,** takes you high above the river to Phantom Overlook, where there's an old stone bench and excellent views of the canyon and Phantom Ranch below. The rangers seem to recommend this hike the most, but, while it's not tough, it can be a little steep and rugged, especially if you're exhausted and sore. The views are, ultimately, well worth the pain.

RIBBON FALLS

Distance: 11 miles round-trip
Duration: 5-6 hours to all day
Elevation gain: 1,174 feet
Effort: easy to moderate
Trailhead: look for the sign 5.5 miles north of Phantom Ranch on the North Kaibab Trail

If you hiked in from the South Rim and you have a long, approximately 11-mile round-trip day hike in you, head north on the North Kaibab from Phantom Ranch to beautiful **Ribbon Falls,** a mossy, cool-water oasis just off the hot, dusty trail. The falls are indeed a ribbon of cold water falling hard off the rock cliffs, and you can scramble up the slickrock and through the green creekside jungle and stand beneath the shower. This hike will also give you a chance to see the eerie, claustrophobic "Box," one of the strangest and most exhilarating stretches of the North Kaibab.

Guides

You certainly don't need a guide to take a classic backpacking trip into the Grand Canyon along one of the corridor trails. The National Park Service makes it a relatively simple process to plan and complete such a memorable expedition, and, while hikers die below the rim pretty much every year, the more popular regions of the inner canyon are as safe as can be expected in a vast wilderness. Then again, having some friendly, knowledgeable, and undoubtedly badass canyonlander plan and implement every detail of your trip sure couldn't hurt. Indeed, it would probably make the whole expedition infinitely more enjoyable. As long as you're willing to pay for it—and it is never cheap—hiring a guide is an especially good idea if you want to go places where few tourists and casual hikers dwell.

There are more than 20 companies authorized, through a guide permit issued by the National Park Service, to take trips below the rim. If your guide does not have such a permit, do not follow him or her into the Grand Canyon. For an up-to-date list, go to www. nps.gov/grca.

The **Grand Canyon Field Institute** (928/638-2481, www.grandcanyon.org, $690-815), which is operated by the nonprofit Grand Canyon Association, offers several three- to five-day guided backpacking trips to various points inside the canyon, including trips designed specifically for women, for beginners, and for those interested in the canyon's natural history. Operating out of Flagstaff, **Four Season Guides** (1051 S. Milton Rd., 928/779-6224, www.fsguides.com, $799-1,450) offers more than a dozen different backpacking trips below the rim, from a three-day frolic to Indian Garden to a nearly weeklong, 36-mile expedition on some of the canyon's lesser-known trails. The experienced and friendly guides tend to inspire a level of strength and ambition that you might not reach otherwise. These are the guys to call if you want to experience the lonely, out-of-the-way depths of the canyon but don't want to needlessly risk your life doing it alone.

MULE RIDES

For generations the famous Grand Canyon mules have been dexterously picking along the skinny trails, loaded with packs and people. Even the Brady Bunch rode them, so they come highly recommended. A descent into the canyon on the back of a friendly mule—with an often-taciturn cowboy-type leading the train—can be an unforgettable experience, but don't assume because you're riding and not walking that you won't be sore in the morning. You can hire a mule for one night at Phantom Ranch, meals included, and a ride down costs $588 per person or $1,378 for two. Two nights at Phantom, meals, and a mule ride costs $838 per person or $1,229 for two. For reservations call 888/297-2757 or visit www.grandcanyonlodges.com. You can make a reservation up to 13 months in advance, and you really should do it as soon as you know your plans. There's a 225-pound weight restriction.

RIVER TRIPS

People who have been inside the Grand Canyon often have one of two reactions—either they can't wait to return, or they swear never to return. This is doubly true of those intrepid souls who ride the great river, braving white-water roller coasters while looking forward to a star-filled evening—dry, and full of gourmet camp food—camping on a white beach deep in the gorge. To boat the Colorado, one of the last explored regions of North America, is one of the most exciting and potentially life-changing trips the West has to offer.

Because of this well-known truth, trips are neither cheap nor easy to book. Rafting season in the canyon runs April-October, and there are myriad trips to choose from—from a 3-day long-weekend ride to a 21-day full-canyon epic. An Upper Canyon trip will take you from River Mile 0 at Lee's Ferry through the canyon to Phantom Ranch, while a Lower Canyon trip begins at Phantom, requiring a hike down the Bright Angel with your gear on your back. Furthermore, you can choose between a motorized pontoon boat, as some three-quarters of rafters do, a paddleboat, a kayak, or some other combination. It all depends on what you want and what you can afford.

If you are considering taking a river trip, the best place to start is the website of the **Grand Canyon River Outfitters Association** (www.gcroa.org), a nonprofit group of about 16 licensed river outfitters, all of them monitored and approved by the National Park Service, each with a good safety record and relatively similar rates. Expect to pay about $1,400 per person for a three-day motor trip, $2,600 per person for a six-day motor trip, $2,000 per person for a six-day oar

trip, and up to $4,000 per person for a 13-day oar trip. Your guide takes care of all the permits you need to spend nights below the rim. After you decide what kind of trip you want, the website links to the individual outfitters for booking. Most of the companies offer trips lasting 3-18 days and have a variety of boat styles. It's a good idea to choose two or three companies, call them up, and talk to someone live. You'll be putting your life in their hands, so you want to make sure that you like the spirit of the company. Also consider the size of the group. These river trips are very social; you'll be spending a lot of time with your fellow boaters. Talk to a company representative about previous trips so you can get a gauge of what kind of people, and how many, you'll be floating with.

If you are one of the majority of river explorers who can't wait to get back on the water once you've landed at the final port, remember that the National Park Service enforces a strict limit of one trip per year, per person.

FOOD AND ACCOMMODATIONS

Designed by Mary Colter for the Fred Harvey Company in 1922, ★ **Phantom Ranch** (888/297-2757, www.grandcanyonlodges.com, dormitory $51 pp, 2-person cabin $149, $13 each additional person), the only noncamping accommodations inside the canyon, is a shady, peaceful place that you're likely to miss and yearn for once you've visited and left it behind. Perhaps Phantom's strong draw is less about its intrinsic pleasures and more about it being the only sign of civilization in a deep wilderness that can feel like the end of the world, especially after a 17-mile hike in from the North Rim. It would probably be an inviting place even if you could get there without hiking into the canyon, and it's all the better because it's not.

Phantom has several rustic, air-conditioned cabins and dormitories, one for men and one for women, both offering restrooms with showers. The lodge's center point is the **Phantom Ranch Canteen,** a welcoming, air-conditioned, beer- and lemonade-selling sight for anyone who has just descended one of the trails. The Canteen offers two meals per day—breakfast, made up of eggs, pancakes, and thick slices of bacon ($23.65), and dinner, with a choice of steak ($47.91), stew ($29.43), or vegetarian ($29.43). The cantina also offers a box lunch ($20.85) with a bagel, fruit, and salty snacks. Reservations for meals are also difficult to come by.

Most nights and afternoons, a ranger based at Phantom Ranch will give a talk on some aspect of canyon lore, history, or science. These events are always interesting and well attended, even in the 110°F heat of summer.

Phantom is located near the mouth of Bright Angel Canyon, within a few yards of clear, babbling Bright Angel Creek, and shaded by large cottonwoods planted in the 1930s by the Civilian Conservation Corps. There are several day hikes within easy reach, and the Colorado River and the two awesome suspension bridges that link one bank to the other are only about 0.25 mile from the lodge.

A **lottery system** governs Phantom Ranch **reservations.** You have to enter the lottery between the 1st and 25th of the month 15 months prior to your proposed trip. You'll be notified at least 14 months before your trip if you won a stay. Go to www.grandcanyonlodges.com/lodging/phantom-ranch/lottery for more details.

Camping

There are three developed campgrounds in the inner canyon: **Cottonwood Campground,** about seven miles from the North Rim along the North Kaibab Trail; **Bright Angel Campground,** along the creek of the same name near Phantom Ranch; and **Indian Garden,** about 4.5 miles from the South Rim along the Bright Angel Trail. To stay overnight at any of these campgrounds you must obtain a permit from the **South Rim Backcountry Information Center** (928/638-7875, $10 plus $8 pp per night). All three campgrounds offer restrooms, a freshwater spigot, picnic tables, and food storage bins to keep the critters out. There are no showers or other amenities.

The best campground in the inner canyon is Bright Angel, a shady, cottonwood-lined setting along cool Bright Angel Creek. Because of its easy proximity to Phantom Ranch, campers can make use of the Phantom Ranch Canteen, even eating meals there if they can get a reservation, and can attend the ranger talks offered at the lodge. There's nothing quite like sitting on the grassy banks beside your campsite and cooling your worn feet in the creek.

Grand Canyon West

Since the Hualapai Tribe's Skywalk opened in 2007, the remote Grand Canyon West has become a busy tourist attraction. The Skywalk is about two hours of dirt-road driving from the Hualapai Reservation's capital, Peach Springs, located along Route 66 east of Kingman. If you want to experience Grand Canyon West during your trip to the Grand Canyon National Park, remember that it is about 250 miles from the South Rim and will take at least an extra two days. Along the way, you can drive on the longest remaining portion of Route 66 and, if you have a few days on top of that, hike down into Havasupai Canyon and see its famous, fantastical waterfalls.

HAVASUPAI INDIAN RESERVATION

Havasu Creek is heavy with lime, which turns the water an almost tropical blue-green. It passes below the weathered red walls of the western Grand Canyon, home these many centuries to the Havasupai (Havasu 'Baaja), the "people of the blue-green water."

The creek falls through the canyon on its way to join the Colorado River, passing briefly by the ramshackle, inner-canyon village of **Supai,** where it is not unusual to see horses running free in the dusty streets, where reggae plays all day through some community speaker, and where the supply helicopter alights and then hops out again every 10 minutes or so in a field across from the post office. Then, about two miles on from the village, the creek plunges 120 feet into a misty turquoise pool. It does it again after another mile, but not before passing peacefully through a cottonwood-shaded campground.

Thousands of people from all over the world visit **Havasupai** (928/448-2121, http:// theofficialhavasupaitribe.com, entry fee $50 plus $10 environmental fee) every year just to see these blue-green waterfalls, to swim in their pools, and to see one of the remotest hometowns in America. The trip is all the more enticing and memorable because it's rather an expedition, or near to it. Still, there are those who return year after year, as if going home.

Reservations

The tribe requires that you **stay overnight** and have a **reservation** to visit Supai and the falls; no day trips are allowed. To make a reservation to camp in Havasupai Canyon, you have to reserve a space online at www. havasupaireservations.com beginning at 8am on February 1 of the year you want to go. Camping permits sell out fast! To make reservations at the Havasupai Lodge, call 928/448-2111.

Planning Tips

A visit to Havasupai takes some planning. It's unbearably hot in the deep summer, when you can't hike except in the very early morning; the **best months** to visit are **September-October** and **April-June.** If you aren't into **backpacking,** you can hire a **pack horse** ($242 round-trip) or take the **helicopter** ($85 one-way). A popular way to visit is to hike in and take the helicopter out. It's a five-minute thrill ride through the canyon to the rim, and the helipad is only about 50 yards from the trailhead parking lot.

Most visitors stay the night at one of the motels along Historic Route 66 before hiking in. Get an early start, especially during the summer. It's a **60-mile drive** to the trailhead at Hualapai Hill from Route 66. The closest hotel is the **Hualapai Lodge** (900 Route 66, 928/769-2230 or 928/769-2636, www. grandcanyonwest.com, $150-170) in Peach Springs, about seven miles west of Highway

Havasu Falls

18, which leads to the trailhead. You'll find cheaper accommodations in **Seligman**, about 30 miles east.

Hiking to Supai

The **eight-mile one-way hike** to the village of Supai from Hualapai Hilltop is one of the easier treks into the Grand Canyon. A few miles of switchbacks lead to a sandy bottomland, where you're surrounded by eroded humps of seemingly melted, pockmarked sandstone. This is not Grand Canyon National Park: You'll know that for sure when you see the trash along the trail. It doesn't ruin the hike, but it nearly breaks the spell. When you reach the village, you'll see the twin rock spires, called Wii'Gliva, that tower over the little farms and homes of Supai.

The Waterfalls

What used to be Navajo Falls, just down the trail from the village, was destroyed in a 2008 flash flood. Now there's a wider set of falls and a big pool that sits below a flood-eroded hill. Perhaps the most famous of the canyon's falls, **Havasu Falls** comes on you all of a sudden as you get closer to the campground. Few hikers refuse to toss their packs aside and strip to their swimming suits when they see Havasu Falls for the first time. The other major waterfall, **Mooney Falls,** is another mile down the trail, through the campground. It's not easy to reach the pool below; it requires a careful walk down a narrow rock-hewn trail with chain handles, but most reasonably dexterous people can handle it. **Beaver Falls,** somewhat underwhelming by comparison, is another two miles toward the river, which is seven miles from the campground.

Food and Accommodations

The **Havasupai Lodge** (928/448-2111, up to 4 people $145) has air-conditioning and private baths. The village also has a small **café** that serves decent breakfast, lunch, and dinner, and a **general store.** Most visitors pack in and stay at the primitive **campground** (first-come, first-served, $25) not far from the main waterfall, which is another 1.5 miles from the village.

HUALAPAI INDIAN RESERVATION

Although Peach Springs is the capital of the Hualapai (WALL-uh-pie) Reservation, there's not much there but a lodge and a few scattered houses. The real attractions are up on the West Rim about 50 miles and two hours away. Peach Springs makes an obvious base for a visit to the West Rim, which has several lookout points, the famous Skywalk, and a kitschy Old West-style tourist attraction called Hualapai Ranch. The tribe's **Hualapai River Runners** (928/769-2219) will take you on a day trip on the river, and there are several all-inclusive package tours to choose from. Check out the **tribe's website** (www. grandcanyonwest.com) for more information.

Tour Packages

To visit Grand Canyon West, the Hualapai require you to purchase one of the rather overpriced **Legacy Packages** ($50-83 pp), and only the more expensive Gold and VIP packages include the Skywalk. The lesser packages allow you to ride a shuttle from **Eagle Point,** where the Skywalk juts out, to **Guano Point,** a nice view of the western canyon, and **Hualapai Ranch,** where fake cowboys will entertain you with Old West clichés, take you on a ride in a wagon, or lead a horseback ride in a corral or to the canyon rim ($10-75). You can stay the night in one of the ranch's rustic cabins ($100). A couple of the packages include a meal, or you can add one for $15 per person. You can also add the Skywalk to your package for $22 if you get up there and decide you really have to try it. Frankly, the packages that don't include the Skywalk are definitely not worth the price or the drive. The views from the South and North Rims are much more dramatic and memorable, and cost only $30.

The Skywalk

The Skywalk (928/769-2636, www.

The Hualapai Nation

Before the 1850s, northwestern Arizona's small Hualapai Nation didn't really exist. It was the federal government's idea to group together 13 autonomous bands of Yuman-speaking Pai Indians, who had lived on the high dry plains near Grand Canyon's western reaches for eons, as the "People of the Tall Pines."

Before the colonial clampdown and the Hualapai Wars of the 1860s, the Pai bands were independent, though they "followed common rules for marriage and land use, spoke variations of one language, and shared social structures, kin networks, cultural practices, environmental niches, and so on," according to Jeffrey Shepherd's *We Are an Indian Nation: A History of the Hualapai People*, which the scholar spent 10 years researching and writing.

The U.S. Army nearly wiped out the bands during the land wars of the 1860s, and the internment of the survivors almost finished the job. But the bands persisted, and in 1883 the government established the million-acre Hualapai Reservation, with its capital at Peach Springs. Then it spent the next 100 years or so trying to take it away from them for the benefit of Anglo ranchers, the railroad, and the National Park Service.

These days the Hualapai Nation, though still impoverished, is a worldwide brand—Grand Canyon West. How did this happen?

The small, isolated tribe has always been willing to take economic risks, one of the many ways, as Shepherd argues, that the Hualapai have twisted colonial objectives for their own survival. A few years ago they partnered with Las Vegas entrepreneur David Jin and built the Hualapai Skywalk, a 70-foot-long glass walkway hanging from the Grand Canyon's western rim. Now you can't walk two steps along the Vegas strip without a tour guide offering to drive you to one of the most isolated sections of Arizona.

Throughout their relatively short history as a nation, the Hualapai have consistently tried to make their windy and dry reservation economically viable, sometimes with the assistance of the government but often in direct contradiction to its goals. For generations they were cattle ranchers, but they could never get enough water to make it pay. They successfully sued the Santa Fe Railroad over an important reservation spring in a landmark case for indigenous rights. For a time in the 1980s they even hesitantly explored allowing uranium mining on their reservation. Now, they have bet their future on tourism.

grandcanyonwest.com, $75) is as much an art installation as it is a tourist attraction. A horseshoe-shaped glass and steel platform jutting out 70 feet from the canyon rim, it appears futuristic surrounded by the rugged, remote western canyon. It's something to see for sure, but is it worth the long drive and the high price tag? Not really. If you have time for an off-the-beaten-path portion of your canyon trip, it's better to go to the North Rim and stand out on Bright Angel Point— you'll get a somewhat similar impression, and it's cheaper. There is something of the thrill ride to the Skywalk, however. Some people can't handle it: They walk out a few steps, look down through the glass at the canyon 4,000 feet below, and head for (seemingly) more solid ground. It's all perfectly safe, but

it doesn't feel that way if you are subject to vertigo. Another drawback of this site is that they won't let you take your camera out on the Skywalk. If you want a record of this adventure, you have to buy a "professional" photo taken by somebody else. You have to store all of your possessions, including your camera, in a locker before stepping out on the glass, with covers on your shoes.

Recreation

Though the Skywalk may not be worth the high price of admission and the long drive to reach it, the Hualapai offer one adventure that is worth the steep price tag: the canyon's only **one-day river rafting experience** (928/769-2636, www.grandcanyonwest.com, May-Oct., $450 pp). It generally takes up to a year of planning and several days of roughing it to ride the river and the rapids through the inner gorge, making a Colorado River adventure something that the average tourist isn't likely to try. Not so in Grand Canyon West. For about $450 per person, Hualapai river guides will pick you up in a van early in the morning at the Hualapai Lodge in Peach Springs and drive you to the Colorado via the rough Diamond Creek Road, where you'll float downstream in a motorboat over roiling white-water rapids and smooth and tranquil stretches. You'll stop for lunch on a beach and take a short hike through a watery side canyon to beautiful Travertine Falls. At the end of the trip, a helicopter picks you out of the canyon and drops you on the rim near the Skywalk. It's expensive, yes, but if you want to ride the river without a lot of preplanning and camping, this is the way to do it. Along the way the Hualapai guides tell stories about this end of the Grand Canyon, sprinkled with tribal history and lore.

You can drive to the river's edge yourself along the 19-mile **Diamond Creek Road** through a dry, scrubby landscape scattered with cacti. The road provides the only easy access to the river's edge between Lee's Ferry, not far from the North Rim, and Pearce Ferry, near Lake Mead. The route is best negotiated in a high-clearance SUV; they say you can do it in a regular sedan, but you have to cross Diamond Creek six times as the dirt road winds down through Peach Springs Canyon, dropping some 3,400 feet from its beginning at Peach Springs on Route 66. The creek is susceptible to flash floods during the summer and winter rainy seasons, so call ahead to check **road conditions** (928/769-2230). At the end of the road, where Diamond Creek marries the Colorado, there's a sandy beach by an enchanting, lush oasis, and, of course, there's that big river rolling by.

Food and Accommodations

The **Hualapai Lodge** (900 Route 66, 928/769-2230 or 928/769-2636, www. grandcanyonwest.com, $150-170) in Peach Springs has a small heated saltwater pool, an exercise room, gift shop, 57 comfortable, newish rooms with soft beds, cable, free wireless Internet access, and train tracks right out the back door. The lodge is a good place to stay the night before hiking into Havasupai, as it's only about seven miles west of the turnoff to Hualapai Hill and the trailhead.

The lodge's restaurant, **Diamond Creek** (6am-9pm daily, $10-15), serves American and Native American dishes. They offer a heaping plate of delicious spaghetti if you're carbo-loading for a big hike to Havasupai; the Hualapai taco (similar to the Navajo taco, with beans and meat piled high on a fluffy slab of fry bread) and the Hualapai stew (with luscious sirloin tips and vegetables swimming in a delicious, hearty broth) are both recommended. They also have a few vegetarian choices, good chili, and pizza.

More food and lodging options are available in **Kingman** and **Seligman** along Old Route 66.

TRANSPORTATION

The best way to get to **Grand Canyon West** from the South Rim is to take I-40 to the Ash Fork exit and then drive west on Route 66. Starting at Ash Fork and heading west to Peach Springs, the longest remaining portion of Route 66 moves through **Seligman,** a small roadside town that's caught in the heyday of the Mother Road. The route through Seligman, which stands up to a stop and a walk around if you have the time, is popular with nostalgic motorcyclists, and there are a few eateries and tourist-style stores in town. Once you reach Peach Springs, take Antares Road 25 miles, head right on Pearce Ferry Road for 3 miles, and then turn east onto Diamond Bar Road for 21 miles, 14 of it on dirt. Diamond Bar Road ends at the only entrance to Grand Canyon West. The 49-mile trip takes about two hours. For park-and-ride reservations, call 702/260-6506.

To reach **Havasupai Canyon,** turn north on Highway 18 just before Peach Springs and drive 60 miles north to a parking area at

Hualapai Hilltop. From there it's an eight-mile hike in to Supai Village and the lodge, and another two miles to the campground. The trail is moderate and leads through a sandy wash with overhanging canyon walls. For the first two miles or so, rocky, moderately technical switchbacks lead to the canyon floor. Then it's easy and beautiful the rest of the way. If you don't want to hike in, you can arrange to **rent a horse** (928/448-2121, 928/448-2174, or 928/448-2180, www.havasupaitribe.com, $120 round-trip to lodge, $150 round-trip to campground), or even hire a **helicopter** (623/516-2790, $85 pp one-way).

Hualapai Reservation's Skywalk is only 125 miles from Las Vegas (about a 2.5-hour drive), so it makes sense to include this remote side trip if you're headed to the South Rim from Vegas anyway. To reach Grand Canyon West from Las Vegas, take U.S. 93 out of the city, heading south for about 65 miles to mile marker 42, where you'll see the Dolan Springs/Meadview City/Pearce Ferry exit. Turn north onto Pearce Ferry Road. About 30 miles in, turn east on Diamond Bar Road. Then it's about 20 miles, 7 or so miles of it unpaved, to Grand Canyon West.

The Arizona Strip

If there is any wild loneliness left in the United States, it is holed up on the Arizona Strip. This five-million-acre wilderness of crumbling red-rock walls, fallen boulders, and long sagebrush sweeps, humpbacked by the evergreen Kaibab Plateau, has only been accessible by highway from within Arizona since 1929 and the opening of the old Navajo Bridge across the Colorado River. Before that, only Latter-day Saints and Paiutes made a go of it here on any serious scale. The region is still inhabited primarily by ranchers, polygamists, hermits, river guides, and residents of the Kaibab Paiute Indian Reservation.

Think of the "strip" as exactly that: a narrow band of Arizona territory hemmed on the north by Utah's southern border, the south by the Grand Canyon, the east by the Colorado River, and the west by Nevada's eastern border. Within that band are several semidesert grassland valleys; the long red-rock southern escarpment of the Paria Plateau, a vast tableland protected as the Vermilion Cliffs National Monument; a green and meadowy forest, smothered by deep snow in winter; and a historic human crossing point where the Paria River washes into the Colorado, the only rest in the great river's canyon-cutting ways for hundreds of miles.

The first Europeans to enter the strip were the path-finding priests of the Dominguez-Escalante expedition in 1776, looking for a northern route from New Mexico to California. In the later 1800s Mormon pioneers from Utah were encouraged by their church leaders to settle in the region. Some found the isolation of the strip to their advantage after the official LDS church outlawed polygamy in the 1890s; others raised cattle, cut wood, and fought with the Navajo and Paiute over the land's scant resources. When construction on a Mormon temple began in St. George, Utah, to the west, the fruits of the Mormon ranch at Pipe Spring, now a national monument, were used to feed the workers, and the trees on Mount Trumbull provided the lumber. In the years before the railroad, the red-dust wagon road across this territory was known as the "Honeymoon Trail," as it was beaten and smoothed by a stream of LDS couples making the long journey from settlements along the Little Colorado River to St. George, where their unions would be officially sealed in the temple.

These days the strip isn't that different from the way it was before the bridge put

1: the Skywalk 2: the Vermilion Cliffs Highway

Lee's Ferry out of business and any Arizonan with a sedan and a canteen could explore it. It remains lonely, isolated, and unpaved, for the most part. There are a few exceptions, of course; about 15 miles upstream from the Lee's Ferry crossing, Glen Canyon Dam has stopped the old warm and muddy Colorado and impounded its water in a 186-mile, canyon-flooding reservoir, where millions of boaters, anglers, and water lovers play year-round. The river that trickles out the other side of the dam is far from what it was in the old days, now running mostly clear, cold, and predictable through its great, sculpted canyons.

A place of outlander history, desolate beauty, and long, quiet spaces, the Arizona Strip isn't for everyone. But for those who take the time and effort to explore it, it can become a haunting landscape, magnetic and well remembered in both dream and waking life.

PLANNING TIPS

This is classic road-trip territory, and if you're already in state with a rental car or your own vehicle, consider taking time to at least drive the **Vermilion Cliffs Highway,** a paved two-lane route that runs, more or less, from St. George, Utah, to Lee's Ferry and Marble Canyon, using Route 59 in Utah, AZ 389, and U.S. 89A. Along the way you'll pass through the entire strip, ascending and coming back down the Kaibab Plateau and crossing the Colorado River. This can be done in one long day from either the west or the east, but if you want to stop and really see the landscape, take at least two days. If you're heading west to east, you might want to stay the night in Fredonia or in Kanab, Utah; St. George, Utah; or even Mesquite, Nevada, near the Virgin River Gorge. If you're heading east to west, the Cameron Trading Post and hotel on U.S. 89, near the Little Colorado River and the Eastern Entrance to Grand Canyon National Park's South Rim, makes a good stopping destination. The most logical way to see the strip is to fold it into an excursion from the South Rim to the North Rim. Leave the South Rim early

in the morning, cross the eastern strip, spend the night and the next day at the North Rim, and then keep heading west down the Kaibab Plateau to Pipe Spring National Monument and on to St. George. From there it's easy to go on and explore western Arizona and the lower Colorado.

If you plan on doing more than road-tripping, such as hiking the empty spaces of the Vermilion Cliffs or standing on the unfenced edge of the Grand Canyon at Toroweap, it's best to plan ahead and to have at least a high and tough SUV, if not a four-wheel-drive vehicle.

THE VERMILION CLIFFS HIGHWAY

Don't think of this scenic journey in terms of political boundaries, for it clips two other states. Rather, it is a journey over a landscape, through a region with a history that cannot be understood without seeing the formidable barriers thrown up by nature. If you begin your drive of the highway from the west, the best place to start is Mesquite, Nevada, along I-15. (From the east start at Cameron.) Mesquite is a small but accommodations-packed town full of gambling senior citizens and cheap but nice casino-hotels on the order of Laughlin. It's common to find a comfortable room in the **Virgin River Casino** (100 Pioneer Blvd., Mesquite, Nevada, 877/438-2929, www.virginriver.com) for $27-60, especially on a weekday, and there is a buffet, pool, and theater, as well as dog-friendly rooms. From Mesquite, head north on I-15 toward St. George, Utah. Just outside of town, you'll enter a corner of Arizona through which the Virgin River flows, cutting through the rocks to create the spectacular Virgin River Gorge.

Virgin River Gorge

On its way to Lake Mead and the lower Colorado, the Virgin River, the strip's only perennial stream other than the Colorado River, cuts a dramatic rock maze through the Virgin and Beaver Dam Mountains in the far northwest corner of Arizona. For several miles along I-15 between Mesquite and St. George, the views are towering and car crash-inducing: high and dry rock mountains, rough and jagged and molded haphazardly by the river, covered with holdout Mojave Desert vegetation, tripped over by desert big-horn sheep and mountain lions. Few sections of the speedy interstate move through such precipitous, wild scenery, and it's best to stop and look around at one of the several pullouts rather than craning your neck while trying to keep your eyes on the road. A good place to stop is Exit 18 (the Cedar Pocket Interchange) at the **Virgin River Canyon Recreation Area** (435/688-3200, www.blm.gov), about 20 miles south of St. George and halfway through the gorge. This Mojave Desert riverside preserve has a few easy and sandy trails leading down to the river—its flow varies by season—and great views of the cliffs and mountains. It is snugged in between two of the wildest wildernesses anywhere—the 19,600-acre **Beaver Dam Wilderness Area** and the 84,700-acre **Paiute Wilderness Area**—and has about 75 campsites for $8 per night.

St. George to Pipe Spring

Interstate travel ends at St. George, the capital of Mormon expansion into southern Utah and Northern Arizona. Here you can visit the beautiful white **LDS temple** (250 E. 400 S., 435/673-5181, 9am-9pm daily, free), dedicated in 1877 and built using supplies and wood gathered on the strip. Continuing east out of St. George, you can either take the northeast route along Route 9 to swing by the otherworldly **Zion National Park** (435/772-3256, www.nps.gov/zion, $30 per car), or head straight to the heart of the strip southeast on Route 59, past the tiny polygamist town of Colorado City-Hilldale on the Arizona-Utah border, and on to Highway 389 and **Pipe Spring National Monument.**

★ Pipe Spring National Monument

A shady, watered spot on an otherwise dry and windy bunchgrass plain, **Pipe Spring**

National Monument (928/643-7105, www.nps.gov/pisp, 8am-5pm daily June-Aug., 8:30am-4:30pm daily Sept.-May, $7) is the strip's best historic site. A museum and visitors center fronts a well preserved fortified ranch house and a few historic outbuildings, a compound built in the 1860s and 1870s by Mormon pioneers who raised cattle for meat and cheese here, much of it taken west weekly to feed workers building a temple in St. George.

An excellent museum inside the visitors center has several displays telling the history of both Native American and Mormon settlement on the strip, with artifacts of both cultures. For an in-depth introduction to the history and politics of the strip, this museum can't be beat. After looking over the displays, bookstore, and gift shop, you can head out to the fort for a personal tour by a volunteer (about every half hour in the busy season). The guide takes you through each room in the fortified home, called **Windsor Castle,** furnished with period furniture and still displaying rifle notches in the walls. The tour also takes you into the factorylike rooms where cheese and other provisions were made and stored, recalling the hardscrabble life on the 19th-century strip. The fort had the first telegraph in Arizona, part of which is still here. There is also a trail that goes about half a mile up a rise behind the fort, where there's an expansive view of the vast plain stretching out toward lonely Mount Trumbull to the south. It is a beautiful, isolating view, quiet except for the wind and the crunch of your feet on the rocky red ground. The rangers at Pipe Spring are also excellent sources for tips on touring the strip.

Grand Canyon-Parashant National Monument and Toroweap

Way off to the south and west of Pipe Spring rises the Shivwits Plateau and the vast **Grand Canyon-Parashant National Monument** (BLM Arizona Strip District, 345 E. Riverside Dr., St. George, Utah, 435/688-3200, www.

The Mystery of Everett Ruess

Everett Ruess (pronounced Roos) disappeared in 1934 into the canyonland wilderness around Escalante, Utah. He was 20 years old and a seasoned desert rat. Friends, strangers, and newspaper reporters searched long hours and many miles looking for the talkative, eccentric young artist. But nobody ever saw him again.

At the astonishing age of 16, Ruess embarked on a series of epic solo journeys across the Colorado Plateau. He employed companionable mules to carry his camping gear and ventured into the uninhabited sandstone wilds for weeks at a time, searching for beauty and Puebloan ruins to inspire his watercolors, linocuts, sketches, photographs, and poetry.

Reuss came to the great Southwest during the worst days of the Great Depression. He never had much money and was often destitute, doing odd jobs and befriending tourists for his meals. He received a steady stream of books and art supplies from his parents back home in Hollywood, packages that he regularly picked up at some of America's most isolated outposts of proto-civilization. Obsessed with art and literature, he read Thomas Mann's *Magic Mountain* while working as a cowboy on Arizona's Mogollon Rim, and recited T.S. Eliot's "The Love Song of J. Alfred Prufrock" to the stones and stars in Canyon de Chelly.

Ruess was talkative and easy company, and he managed to know several of the era's great artists, including the painter Maynard Dixon and photographers Dorothea Lang, Ansel Adams, and Edward Weston. He briefly lived in San Francisco and tried to make it as an artist, but the canyons kept calling his name.

We know about Ruess and his romantic travels because he wrote eloquent letters to family and friends and kept a detailed and compelling diary. *Desert Magazine* published a few of his letters in 1939, about five years after he disappeared. Hundreds of readers called for more, so the next year the magazine published a book-length collection: *On Desert Trails with Everett Ruess*, edited by Hugh Lacy. When R. L. Rusho's edition of the letters, *A Vagabond for Beauty*, appeared in 1983, and later the *Wilderness Journals of Everett Ruess*, the artist's cult grew mightily, and his story became a favorite mystery and legend of the canyonlands.

The early search parties found his two burros grazing in an isolated canyon, but his gear and body have never been recovered. Strangely, he carved the word NEMO in at least two places, in a cave and near a ruin around the area where he was last seen. His father later wrote that Ruess was probably referring to Captain Nemo from *20,000 Leagues Under the Sea*, by Jules Verne. While most experts believe he died as a result of an accident or foul play and that his body sank forever beneath the roiling waters of the Colorado River, the carvings and Reuss's own words have fueled speculation over the years that he disappeared by choice. If he had planned to run away and live out his life as a desert hermit, this magical canyon country would have been the ideal setting for such a spiritual quest.

Just before he walked off into desert and the unknown, Ruess wrote what would be his last letter to his brother Waldo.

"As to when I shall revisit civilization, it will not be soon, I think," he wrote. "I have not tired of the wilderness; rather I enjoy its beauty and the vagrant life I lead more keenly all the time. I prefer the saddle to the streetcar, and the star-sprinkled sky to the roof."

nps.gov/para, 7:45am-5pm Mon.-Fri., 10am-3pm Sat.). There are no paved roads within this million-acre wilderness, no visitors centers, no well-stocked campgrounds, and no concessionaires—truthfully, no services of any kind. There are, however, opportunities for the intrepid and well-prepared visitor to see nature in the raw.

The plateau, rising to heights between 6,000 and 7,000 feet and covered by semidesert sweeps, short piñon forests, and stands of ponderosa pine on its mountains, marks the transition from the Mojave Desert basin and range province to the Colorado Plateau and is home to one of the loneliest and most inspiring Grand Canyon views anyone with a tough vehicle and several hours of hard travel in them can see. In the monument's western reaches, southwest of Pipe Spring, the Toroweap Valley stretches out toward the rim and **Toroweap Point** (sometimes both are called Tuweap, after an abandoned town nearby), a hard-won but amazing viewpoint, without fence or crowd, from which to see the canyon and the Colorado rushing by about 3,000 feet below. There are a few campsites right on the unhemmed rim and more at a nearby **campground** (www.nps.gov/grca, backcountry permit required), which are free but have no water or much of anything else. The mighty Lava Flow Rapids stir up the river just below the point, and nearby Vulcan's Throne, a volcanic remnant, rises 50 feet or more from the plain. There is a ranger station near the viewpoint, and a few short trails run along the rim. While this is a truly wondrous place to visit, it's not easy getting here.

There are a few different ways to get to Toroweap Point (which is technically within Grand Canyon National Park), all of them rough, washboarded, and possibly impassable during bad weather. Make sure you take supplies, tools, and a map. The most popular route to the viewpoint is nine miles west of Fredonia off Highway 389, Road 109. It's about 60 miles of rough, slow travel from there, following the signs. This is an all-day, if not multiday, trip that should not be taken lightly or on a whim.

Also within the monument, mountains Trumbull and Logan both reach around 8,000 feet and in the old days were the only source of lumber on the strip. Both rise within federal Wilderness Areas in the scrub south of Pipe Spring; you'll pass by them on the way to Toroweap, and you can take a side trip to hike the short trails to both mountaintops or to walk to the half-mile trail to **Nampaweap,** a petroglyph site. For practical, local advice on visiting these areas, talk to a ranger at the **North Kaibab Ranger District** (430 S. Main St., Fredonia, 928/643-7395), one of the rangers at Pipe Spring National Monument, or the folks at the BLM office in St. George.

KANAB, UTAH

About seven miles north of the Arizona border along 89A in Utah, Kanab is the pleasant, relatively bustling capital of the Arizona Strip. Here you'll find varied accommodations, including several chain hotels and restaurants. It's a tiny, rural burg, far from the real world. Isolated out here on the western end of the Colorado Plateau, Kanab is home to only about 4,000 year-round residents. It is nonetheless well set up for travelers and tourists. Kanab makes an ideal base for visiting Grand Canyon National Park's North Rim, just 80 miles or about two hours away; Zion National Park, just 40 miles to the northwest; Bryce Canyon National Park, 77 miles to the northeast; and Lake Powell, which is 70 miles off to the east.

Food and Accommodations

The **Rocking V Café** (97 W. Center St., 435/644-8001, www.rockingvcafe.com, 11:30am-10pm daily, $15-48) serves fresh and delicious food, and there's an interesting art gallery upstairs. They make a good burger, including a Boca burger, as well as tasty chicken and pasta dishes, veggie enchiladas, creamy mac-and-cheese, and more. They also have a decent selection of beer and wine, including microbrews.

The **Quail Park Lodge** (125 N. 300 W., 435/215-1447, www.quailparklodge.com, $109-129), along Highway 89 as it rolls through Kanab, is clean, affordable, and has a freshly painted, retro motor lodge look to it that draws in the fan of American road culture and popular architecture. A small pool, tasteful motel-style rooms with TVs and free Wi-Fi and a location that can't be beat make this one of the best places to stay on the Arizona Strip. Right next door and owned by the same folks, the **Canyons Lodge** (236 N. 300 W., 435/644-3069, www.canyonslodge.com, $89-179) is less nostalgic than its sister, choosing instead a nattier, posh-wilderness look that is warm and stylish. There's also a small pool, and the comfortable rooms offer flat-screens, free Wi-Fi, and crisp, relaxing beds for the end of a hard day of outdoor play. Free breakfast comes with every room.

FREDONIA

Fredonia is a small settlement of about 1,000 residents at the junction of State Highway 389 and U.S. 89A, about seven miles south of Kanab. It's a former polygamist holdout, these days a mostly tumbledown, friendly village offering brief respite and gear storage for river guides and canyonland explorers. The name means "free woman" in Spanish. It is Arizona's northernmost town, just four miles south of the border with Utah. It was originally settled by residents of Kanab. Though it has fewer services than Kanab, it is a fine place to base your visit to the Arizona Strip, southern Utah, and the Grand Canyon's North Rim.

Food

The **Cowboy Butte Grill & Steakhouse** (165 N. Main St., 928/643-6848, hours vary, $13-30) serves good burgers and sandwiches, chicken-fried steak smothered in rich gravy, excellent french fries and fried chicken, pork ribs, steaks, and more—superior, home-style comfort food to fill you up and warm your soul after exploring the landscape. If you are planning on staying the night in this region, head back to Kanab.

THE KAIBAB PLATEAU

After Fredonia, U.S. 89A begins to rise into a piñon-juniper woodland that quickly becomes a ponderosa pine forest as the highway climbs the massive upsweep in the land known as the Kaibab Plateau. This island-like highland, surrounded by arid valleys and giving way on its southern edge to the Grand Canyon, measures about 60 miles from north to south and roughly 45 miles east to west, ranging in height, and so climate and flora, from 3,000 to 9,200 feet. In the plateau's highest ranges along Route 67 from Jacob Lake to the North Rim, dark evergreen forests, mixed with white and yellow aspens, hedge the wide

green meadows. One of the state's best forest landscapes, the Kaibab has long been logged and hunted; there are old logging and Jeep trails crisscrossing the tableland, which make backcountry exploring relatively easy, though only with four-wheel drive and not in the winter. After November you'll find Route 67 to the North Rim closed, but U.S. 89A usually stays open year-round, even when the plateau is covered in a thick blanket of snow.

While negotiating the steep and twisty highway on the west side of the plateau—or descending it, if you're coming from the east—look for the sign for the **Le Fevre Overlook** and stop at the pullout for a great view.

Food and Accommodations

The main oasis on the Kaibab Plateau is the **Jacob Lake Inn** (junction of U.S. 89A and Rte. 67, 928/643-7232, www.jacoblake.com, $128-165 rooms, $96-144 cabins), about 42 miles from the North Rim. It features rustic cabins as well as motel-style rooms with outside entrances easily accessible from the parking lot. There are no televisions, phones, or Internet access in these accommodations. However, the Jacob Lake Inn also has a hotel-style building which does offer these amenities. Also here are a bakery, gift shop, small general store, and gas station, as well as a **restaurant** (6:30am-9pm daily) with excellent homemade bread and soups and hearty, delicious scratch creations for breakfast, lunch, and dinner ($8-15), with a few vegetarian options, including a delicious garden burger.

Information

Next to the Jacob Lake Inn, the rangers at the **Kaibab Plateau Visitors Center** (Rte. 67 and U.S. 89A, Jacob Lake, 928/643-7298, 8am-5pm daily May-Sept., 8am-1pm Sat.-Sun. Oct.-Dec.) can give you advice on hiking and exploring the plateau, and there's a good selection of books for sale and a few displays on the area's flora and fauna.

VERMILION CLIFFS NATIONAL MONUMENT

Most Arizona Strip visitors see only the southern escarpment of the Paria Plateau as they cut through the valley along U.S. 89A. That edge's high, crumbling sandstone cliffs give this national monument of swirling slickrock and narrow, high-walled river canyons its name. The cliffs are best viewed from an established viewpoint about 10 miles east of Jacob Lake, as the highway begins to descend to the House Rock Valley.

The Paria River cuts through the northeast portion of the 294,000-acre monument, creating Paria Canyon, one of the most popular canyonland backpacking trips (38 miles, about five days, reserved $5 permit required)—red and purple and black sandstone cliffs rising high above narrow slots of sand and water. There are no services or visitors centers on this remote monument, and much of it is within the **Paria Canyon-Vermilion Cliffs Wilderness Area** and so can't be accessed by car. The area is best explored from the north, along U.S. 89 in Utah between Kanab, Utah, and Page, Arizona. From Page, head west on U.S. 89 for about 30 miles to reach the BLM's **Paria Canyon-Vermilion Cliffs Wilderness Ranger Station,** where you can get advice on visiting the area; it serves as a kind of visitors center and crossroads for backpackers and day hikers. This is really the kind of place you have to plan ahead for; most of the best areas require a permit, and those are given out on a lottery system for some of the most popular attractions. You can also access the monument from the west on the compacted-dirt House Rock/Coyote Valley Road (BLM Road 1065), off the south side of U.S. 89A at House Rock, which leads to the **Coyote Buttes Permit Area.** Coyote Buttes has a north and south section—the north is best gained via U.S. 89 in Utah. This is a world-famous trekking area where there are several trails that lead through a strange rock world of twisted, undulating, multicolored sandstone formations, often appearing as if rough red, yellow, and pink water has been

held up and petrified. Along these trails you'll see all the sandstone arches, alcoves, spires, domes, amphitheaters, and buttes that make the canyonlands so exotic and enticing. A limited number of people are allowed in each day, even for day hiking, so make sure to get a permit (www.blm.gov, $5) before traveling. For more information on the monument, talk to the folks at the BLM's **Arizona Strip Field Office** (345 E. Riverside Dr., St. George, UT, 435/688-3200) or the **Kanab Field Office** (435/644-4600).

★ CLIFF DWELLERS AND HOUSE ROCK VALLEY

U.S. 89A continues on through the red-dirt and sagebrush **House Rock Valley** at the base of the Kaibab Plateau, overlooked by the Vermilion Cliffs. Just after passing the lodge in the tiny settlement of **Cliff Dwellers,** you'll see a little sandstone-brick structure tucked beneath a fallen boulder. Like some kind of canyon-country Hobbit house, the red-rock slabs and sculpted boulder blend with the cliffs and the chipped light-blue trim paint matches the empty sky. This little rock house, nearly melding into the vermilion scenery, is one of the most enchanting structures in all of Arizona. There's usually a Navajo or two selling jewelry here, and you can walk around and duck in and out of the strange rock hovels, as long as you remember this is private property. The house and other little shelters were built by Blanche and Bill Russell, the area's original homesteaders. Operating a trading post out of the little rock house, the Russells also catered to Mormon travelers moving through the valley on their way to the St. George temple.

★ LEE'S FERRY

Reached via paved road past high red buttes just east of Cliff Dwellers—look for the sign— **Lee's Ferry** (www.nps.gov/glca) is the only spot in hundreds of miles of canyonland where you can drive down to the Colorado River. It's named for a man who occupied the area briefly in the early 1870s, Mormon outlaw

John D. Lee, one of the leaders of the infamous Mountain Meadows Massacre in Utah. Lee was exiled to this lonely spot after he and others attacked and murdered more than 100 westbound Arkansas emigrants moving through Utah Territory during a period when relations between the Utah Mormons and the U.S. government were strained, to say the least. One of Lee's wives, Emma Lee, ended up running the ferry more than Lee ever did; he soon lit out and lived as a kind of fugitive until he was finally, in 1877, recalled home and sentenced to death. The proclamation was carried out by firing squad on the same ground as the massacre. To the end and in a published memoir, Lee insisted that he was a scapegoat, and many believe Brigham Young ordered the massacre.

The Lee family operated a small ranch and orchard near the crossing, the remnants of which can still be seen on a self-guided tour of the **Lonely Dell Ranch Historic Site,** which includes the rusting remains of a mining operation, several old boat ruins, and a graveyard. There are a few rocky hiking trails around the area, but one of the best things to do here is to simply sit on a soggy beach and watch the river flow by the sun-spattered cliffs. There's a nice campground ($16, no hookups, no reservations) if you feel like staying, and a ranger station and launch ramp as well.

For long before and after Lee lent his name to the crossing, this two-mile stretch near the mouth of the Paria River was one of the few places to cross the river in southern Utah and Northern Arizona, and it remained so until the bridging of the Colorado at Marble Canyon in 1929. Today the area is the starting block for thousands of brave river-trippers who venture into the Grand Canyon on the Colorado River every year. It's also a popular fishing spot, though the trout here have been introduced and were not native to the warm, muddy flow before the dam at Glen Canyon changed the Colorado's character. For guides, gear, and any other information about the area, try **Lee's Ferry Anglers** (928/355-2261 or 800/962-9755, www.leesferry.com,

6am-9pm daily), located at the Cliff Dwellers Lodge.

Lee's Ferry marks the divide between the upper and lower states of the Colorado River's watershed, inasmuch as they were divided by the compact that divvied up the river's water for human use. This has made Lee's Ferry "River Mile 0," the gateway and crossroads to both the upper and lower Colorado and the place where its annual flows are measured and recorded.

Food and Accommodations

The small **Cliff Dwellers Lodge** (928/355-2261 or 800/962-9755, https://leesferry.com, $90) is nearly drowned by the scenery around it, tucked beneath the base of the red cliffs. This lodge offers charming, rustic-but-comfortable rooms with satellite television, and the restaurant serves good breakfasts, lunches, and dinners ($10-30), with everything from fajitas and ribs to falafel and halibut. They also serve liquor, beer, and wine, which you can sip on the little patio here at what seems like the very end of the world.

The **Lee's Ferry Lodge at Vermilion Cliffs** (U.S. 89A near Marble Canyon, 928/355-2231 or 800/451-2231, www.vermilioncliffs.com, $65) has romantic little rooms in a retro-West little rock-built structure that blends into the tremendous background wonderfully. This is a fine place to stay but consider that it has been undergoing extensive remodeling under new management since the summer of 2019.

The trading post first established by Lorenzo Hubbell at **Marble Canyon Lodge** (U.S. 89A near Marble Canyon, 800/726-1789, www.marblecanyoncompany.com, $82-185) has been open for business since 1920—nearly 100 years of serving wanderers under the ever-blue sky, which is the only thing bigger out here than the wide-open landscape. This is a friendly and comfortable place to stop. They offer rooms with kitchenettes and have an

---

1: Cliff Dwellers **2:** Lee's Ferry Lodge at Vermilion Cliffs **3:** Marble Canyon **4:** Horseshoe Bend

excellent restaurant serving tasty fry bread and other Southwestern staples ($10-20). The trading post here has a superior selection of books about the region. The lodge also operates a gas station and convenience store just up the road.

NAVAJO BRIDGE AND MARBLE CANYON

A few miles before U.S. 89A runs into U.S. 89 south toward Navajoland and the Grand Canyon, two bridges span Marble Canyon, where the Colorado River digs deep again after its surfacing at Lee's Ferry. This is the exit from or the entrance to the heart of the strip, depending on which way you're headed. The original Navajo Bridge was opened in 1929, the first bridge to cross this part of the Colorado, putting Lee's Ferry out of business for good. By 1995, a new bridge had opened, as the original was not up to the increased traffic along Highway 89A. The original bridge is now kept open for sightseers, and you can walk over it and look down at the river flowing through magnificent Marble Canyon, here at the very start of the Grand Canyon. The **Navajo Bridge Interpretive Center** (928/355-2319, www.nps.gov/glca, 9am-5pm daily Apr.-Oct.) has a book shop and displays about the bridge, and there are usually several booths selling Native American arts and crafts.

PAGE AND LAKE POWELL

The town would not exist without the lake, and the lake would not exist without the dam: Such is the symbiotic chain of existence here in the slickrock lands around sunken Glen Canyon, where water lovers come to play among the red and pink sandstone labyrinths.

Page is a small, tidy town with a higher-than-normal number of churches for its size; they are all lined up along one long block at the beginning of this resort burg's main drag. The population here was once composed primarily of dam builders and their families, for the town was founded in 1957 as a government-run camp for Glen Canyon Dam workers, built on land formerly owned by the Navajo but traded for a slice of property in Utah. These days Page has sizable Latter-day Saint and Navajo communities, and the population swells with boaters, water skiers, swimmers, and houseboat loungers in the spring and summer. The business life of Page is now dedicated to that influx, so there are plenty of chain hotels and restaurants here if you don't want to stay and eat at Wahweap Marina, the lake's largest marina and the center of most Arizona visits to the lake, most of which is in Utah.

Sights
JOHN WESLEY POWELL MUSEUM
Just off Page's main drag is the **John Wesley Powell Museum** (6 N. Lake Powell Blvd., 928/645-9496 or 888/597-6873, www.powellmuseum.org, 9am-5pm daily, free, donation welcomed), named, as is the nearby reservoir, for the one-armed Civil War veteran, scientist, writer, and explorer who led the first two river expeditions through the Grand Canyon. The center has an excellent bookstore, and the friendly staff can help you book boat and air tours, but the museum itself takes a little more effort to enjoy. There is a lot of fascinating information on Powell and the river runners who followed in his path, but most of the displays are made up of long articles that you have to stand there and read. Children will likely be impatient, though there's a small interactive display on the natural science of the area. Inside the museum is Page's **Visitor Information Center** (www.visitpagelakepowell.com).

HORSESHOE BEND
As you drive into Page from the south along U.S. 89, look for milepost 545 (about four miles south of town), where you can walk 0.75 mile one-way to a viewpoint above the famous, much-photographed **Horseshoe Bend,** where the Colorado River curves like a horseshoe around a lonely pink butte far below. You'll likely know you're there by the

crowds. In recent years this barrier-free road-side lookout has become very popular. It's of course incredibly beautiful—the green river meanders in a tight curve around red rock—but it's also thrilling because there's nothing between you and the river far, far below. If you're hoping to get a good photograph here, make sure to bring a wide-angle lens. Take water, a hat, and sunscreen with you; though short, the hike moves over sand and up and down a few inclines.

ANTELOPE CANYON NAVAJO TRIBAL PARK

A color-swirled, water-worn slot in a mesa on Navajoland, **Antelope Canyon Navajo Tribal Park** (928/698-2808, 8am-5pm daily Apr.-Oct., $8 admission, required guided tours extra) is a few miles south of Page on Highway 98. This popular crevice of twisting and twirling slickrock requires a Navajo guide, but it's easy to find one. You pile into a big four-wheel drive with your guide and others and ride several bumpy miles down a sandy wash to the slit in the rocks rising up out of the ground—the entrance to a wonderland. The guide then takes you through the short slot canyon, out the other side, and then back again. It's an easy walk along a sandy bottomland, with the canyon walls rising 130 feet and impossibly narrow in some stretches. It's a strange, fantastic, and very memorable stroll, and one that is highly recommended despite the relatively high cost of a tour. The tours are staggered, so you are never crammed in there with too many other people. The earlier you go the better; the light and the colors are said to be at their best between 10am and noon, but it's really only important for serious photographers to go at these ideal times of the day.

The slot canyon's unique undulations and warm reds and pinks, especially in the summer with the sun high in the sky and shining in laser-like shafts through small gashes high above, make it one of the most photographed in the canyonlands, if not the world. It is a very popular attraction, and you'll find no

shortage of guides in Page. Still, it's a good idea to make a reservation. Park admission is generally wrapped into what you pay the guide. You can also go to the park yourself and hire a guide there.

Antelope Canyon Navajo Tours (928/698-3384, http://navajotours.com, tours 8:45am-4pm daily, $60, $30 children) start about three miles east of Page off Highway 89 at Antelope Canyon Navajo Tribal Park. Knowledgeable Navajo guides drive you through the desert landscape in a big four-wheeler for a 1.5-hour general tour.

Antelope Canyon Tours (22 S. Lake Powell Blvd., 928/645-9102, www.antelopecanyon.com, $60, $50 ages 8-22, $42 under age 8) offers two different tours every day, year-round, departing from Page. The 1.5-hour general tour leaves at 7am, 8am, 9:30am, 11:30pm, 1:30pm, 3:30pm, and 4:30pm.

One of the better photography tours of Antelope Canyon is offered by **Adventurous Antelope Canyon Photo Tours** (Hwy. 98, milepost 302, 928/380-1874, www.navajoantelopecanyon.com, $158-297), and they will also take you out to a few other, though lesser, slot canyons that aren't as well known and heavily visited as Antelope Canyon. This company is recommended for serious amateur and professional photographers.

LOWER ANTELOPE CANYON

Across Highway 98 from the tribal park, a few tour operators offer hike-in access to Lower Antelope Canyon, a similarly beautiful and mysterious slot canyon. Tours ($40, $20 children 8-12, plus $8 Navajo permit fee) run about every 20 minutes and last 1.25 hours. The 1.1-mile round-trip hike is easy and okay for kids. **Dixie Ellis' Lower Antelope Canyon Tours** (928/640-1761, http://antelopelowercanyon.com) has tours 10am-4:10pm daily. **Ken's Tours** (928/606-2168, www.lowerantelope.com) operates in the same area and has tours 8:20am-4pm daily.

ANTELOPE POINT MARINA

The Navajo Nation's **Antelope Point** (537 Marina Pkwy., Navajo Rte. N22b, 928/645-5900, www.antelopepointlakepowell.com, $25) has a tasteful sandstone welcome center (8am-4pm daily) and offers a variety of services as well as access to Lake Powell in a starkly beautiful setting. The **Ja'di' Tooh Restaurant** (11am-8pm daily in summer, $14-28) serves decent American food (burgers, sandwiches, steaks, salads) and looks out over the stark, red land and the glowing blue lake. A hotel is planned for the future. You can rent houseboats and other watercraft or get flicked across the water at the wakeboarding park, and there are slips to park your boat and a store to purchase supplies.

The marina is about 9 miles outside Page on Navajo land. Take Route 98 east to Navajo Route 222. It's not far from Antelope Canyon Navajo Tribal Park.

★ Glen Canyon National Recreation Area

Sprawling over the Arizona-Utah border and some 1.25 million acres, **Glen Canyon National Recreation Area** (928/608-6200, www.nps.gov/glca, $30 per car for a seven-day pass, $25 motorcycles, $15 bikes) is a popular boating, fishing, and hiking area centered on **Lake Powell,** the continent's second-largest artificial lake. Created by the damming of the Colorado River and the destruction of the river-sculpted Glen Canyon, the lake is 186 miles long and has more than a thousand miles of meandering desert shoreline. Its waters run through a red-rock maze of narrow side canyons, like canals around an ornate sandstone city, now abandoned. During the spring and summer months the lake is crowded with sometimes rowdy Jet Skiers, water-skiers, and houseboat residents, but you could also visit the area and never get wet—the canyon-country scenery is enough to draw and keep even the most water-averse visitors. The whole area resembles one vast, salmon-pink sand dune frozen and petrified at once—it is a desolate, lonely place

sometimes, beautiful and sacred but also a reminder of how humans can change a seemingly unalterable landscape at their will.

Probably the most popular activity on Lake Powell is houseboating. The floating mansions chug around the buttes and spires, while their residents shoot water cannons at each other and stop at night for parties on the beaches around the lake. As it is on the nearby Navajo Reservation, some places around Lake Powell are an hour off of Arizona time during daylight saving time.

GLEN CANYON DAM

Looking out at **Glen Canyon Dam** through large picture windows in Glen Canyon's **Carl Hayden Visitor Center** (928/648-6404 or 928/608-6072, www.nps.gov/glca, 8am-5pm daily, free tours offered), it's difficult not to be impressed. The great concrete slab shimmed into the narrow Navajo-sandstone channel allows for the storage of some 27 million acre-feet of water (an acre-foot of water is roughly the amount that a family of four uses in a year); it's a brash reclamation feat if there ever was one. But it is also difficult to see Lake Powell, the reservoir and playground created by the dam, and not feel that something was lost in the flooding of once-spectacular Glen Canyon and the irrevocable alteration of the Colorado River's ecosystem.

The writer and desert-country anarchist Edward Abbey, whose famous 1975 trickster-novel *The Monkey Wrench Gang* envisions the destruction of Glen Canyon Dam by a group of ecowarriors, described the long-lost canyon, waiting silent about 300 feet below Lake Powell's glassy surface, as a "once lovely wonderland of grottoes, alcoves, Indian ruins, natural stone arches, cottonwood groves, springs and seeps and hanging gardens of ivy, columbine, and maidenhair fern—and many other rare things."

Along with sinking this natural wonderland, the dam severely altered the character of the Colorado River downstream. A sediment-laden river—a characteristic of the mighty flow that allowed it to carve those famous canyons—the Colorado River once ran warm and muddy, filled with native fish and lined by beaches, sandbars, and groves of cottonwood and willow. Now that the flow stops at the dam, the once sediment-heavy river runs cool and clear coming out of the other side, which has encouraged invasive plant and fish species to thrive to the detriment of the native flora and fauna. Beaches that are eroded don't come back so easily because of the lack of sediment in the river flow, and a controlled flow has replaced the natural flood cycle of the river, leading to the disappearance of an entire ecosystem.

Many people, including some who once supported the dam's construction, now believe that too much was lost for what was gained. The dam is surely an awesome sight, and it will either draw your admiration for the brave and tough laborers who built it from 1957 to 1964 or your disgust for the loss of a once-wild river that it changed forever. More likely, you'll feel a little bit of both, and you will agree with Abbey, who conceded that "though much has been lost, much remains."

Since the 1990s the river below the dam has been purposely flooded several times with timed releases of flows from the reservoir. An army of scientists then moves into the canyon along the river to determine the flood's effects on the ecosystem. While these experiments have been helpful, many scientists believe they happen too infrequently to make much of a difference in combating the dam's negative influence downriver.

WAHWEAP MARINA AND LAKE POWELL RESORT

The largest marina in the recreation area and the center of Arizona-side visits to Lake Powell, the **Wahweap Marina** (928/645-2433, www.lakepowell.com) offers lodging, food, boat and other watercraft rentals, camping, RV parking, tours, and shopping all within one area. Aramark is the main concessionaire at the marina, running the ★ **Lake Powell Resort and Marina** (100 Lakeshore Dr., 928/645-2433, $154-250), where you can rent the equipment to do just about anything on the lake. The hotel has two heated pools, a sauna, a hot tub, and a workout room. The marina's **Rainbow Room** (100 Lakeshore Dr., 928/645-2433, 6am-2pm and 5pm-10pm daily in season, 7am-1:30pm and 5pm-9pm daily winter, $10-32) at the Lake Powell Resort has lakeview tables and serves delicious fish, steak, pork chops, and pasta for dinner and a buffet at lunch. The hotel also has a stylish,

Glen Canyon Dam

relaxing bar, the **Driftwood Lounge,** inside with good drinks and tasty tapas. The marina has a sandy beach with chairs and cabanas, and it offers guided fishing tours and waterskiing instruction, among myriad other activities.

BOATING ON LAKE POWELL

If you make the drive to these remote corners of the Colorado Plateau, crossing Indian lands and canyonlands just to see the drowned landscape, and fail to get out on the water, you are indeed missing something.

Many otherwise landbound folks who visit Lake Powell have their own boats, including a large contingent of locals and near-locals from the surrounding region. Others become lake-top locals for a week every year, conspiring with friends to lounge in luxury under the relentless sun, blushed in a more or less permanent buzz. Most of the houseboats available for rent here sleep up to 12 people and have all the comforts of home. On average, expect to pay about $150-200 per person per day for a houseboat, which you can rent from three days up to seven days. The least expensive are about $1,800-2,500 for three days, while the luxury models are about $10,000 for five days. You can rent a boat at **Wahweap Marina** (www.lakepowell.com/houseboats), and it's essential to plan far ahead (about six months in advance) and make a reservation (888/896-3829).

The **boat rental facility** (8am-6pm daily Arizona time) at Wahweap, which is just a short drive from the resort along Lake Shore Drive, also rents **Jet Skis** ($180 for two hours, $375 all day, plus $500 deposit) and **powerboats** $600 all day, plus $500 deposit). While these vehicles are pricey and a bit obnoxious, exploring the canyons and alcoves of Lake Powell on a speedy boat or Jet Ski seems otherwise ideal. There's no easier, or faster, way to see the whole lake and to explore its mysterious corners and beaches.

A more peaceful and contemplative activity, which also has the virtue of being great exercise, is **kayaking** on Lake Powell. It's

even better with a loved one; the double sit-upon kayak here is perfect for couples, especially if one of the pair is not inclined to do much paddling ($60 all day, plus $100 deposit). Make sure to take some water and food along with you. You can buy groceries in Page, and they sell a small selection of snacks and drinks at a store near the rental office, which also has bathrooms. Two or three hours is more than enough time to paddle across the lake to one of the white beaches spreading out from sheer white rock faces nearby, have a picnic, climb into the shallow caves in the rock face, and paddle back again. Don't forget the sunscreen.

Between April and October, the marina offers several boat tours of the lake, including dinner and breakfast cruises and day trips to Rainbow Bridge and elsewhere. The red rocks grow warm and flash their deep hidden colors during sunrise and sunset, and a boat tour is a great way to experience this. There are nighttime tours of the lake for a view of the city of stars that emerges from the huge, clear sky. Depending on their length and destination, boat tours from Wahweap run $41-125. There's a booking desk inside the Lake Powell Resort at Wahweap Marina.

RAINBOW BRIDGE NATIONAL MONUMENT

Rainbow Bridge, the world's largest arched-rock span and one of the true wonders of the natural world, is a sacred site to the Navajo, who call it *Nonnezoshi* (rainbow turned to stone). An improbable arch of reddish-orange sandstone 290 feet high, the "bridge" is one of the most popular sites within the recreation area, even with the difficulty in getting there and the admonitions against walking under it in deference to Navajo beliefs. While you can gear up for a multiday backpack trip across the hot, rugged land to reach the wonder on foot, most visitors take a 50-mile, all-day boat tour from Wahweap Marina or take their own boat to the well-signed port of call. **Aramark** (800/528-6154, www.lakepowell.com, $122) is in charge of tours. The trip includes an easy two-mile round-trip hike from the dock to the arch.

DAM OVERLOOK

An easy but mildly strenuous walk to the Dam Overlook is worth the effort to see the front of the massive dam and the Colorado River going its merry way beyond it. Catch the trailhead off Highway 89, about 1.5 miles south of the Carl Hayden Visitor Center on Scenic View Road. It's a 940-foot walk, one-way, down some relatively steep steps.

HANGING GARDEN

Hanging Garden is an unlikely oasis out on the hard land where greenery hangs from the seeping rocks, providing a cool place to kick back and study the landscape. It's an easy walk, a one-mile, one-way trek on a slickrock trail that's okay for kids. The trailhead is 0.5 mile from Glen Canyon Bridge on Highway 89. Just look for the sign.

Events

Every year on the first weekend in November, about 50 hot-air balloonists bring their colorful crafts to Page for the **Page Balloon Regatta** (928/645-2741, www.pagechamber. com, early Nov.). The highlight of the event is the Balloon Glow, when the balloonists light up their balloons on the ground, creating dozens of glowing orbs. There's also a street festival and other events that attend this busy weekend near Lake Powell.

Food

Millions of tourists drive through Page every season to see Lake Powell and the canyonlands, and as a result the area has all the usual chain hotels and several chain restaurants—more than is usual for a small town in the middle of nowhere. You'll find most of Page's services along Lake Powell Boulevard, the main drag through town.

The **Dam Bar & Grille** (644 N. Navajo, 928/645-2161, www.damplaza.com, 11am-11pm daily, $13-34) is the small resort town's entertainment complex, featuring a surf-and-turf restaurant (with well-made baby back ribs, steaks, prime rib, sandwiches, and salads).

For dinner or lunch try ★ **Strombolli's Italian Restaurant & Pizzeria** (711 N. Navajo Dr., 928/645-2605, https:// strombollisrestaurant.com, 11am-10pm daily, $10-20) for toothsome Italian entrées like baked ravioli with meat sauce, calzones, New York-style pizza, chicken parmigiana, stuffed eggplant parmigiana, burgers, steaks, salads, and a decent wine list.

Accommodations

Most of the many chain accommodations outside the marina are midrange, but expect prices higher than other locations.

Canyon Colors B&B (225 S. Navajo Dr., 928/645-5979, www.canyoncolorsbandb. com, $99-159, two-night minimum) rents two bright and homey rooms in Page and has an outdoor barbecue area and a pool, friendly hosts, and big, delectable breakfasts. The **Dreamkatcher Lake Powell Bed & Breakfast** (66 S. American Way, Big Water, Utah, 435/675-5828, www. dreamkatcherslakepowell.com, $99-215) is about 20 minutes from Page on the Utah side of the recreation area. There are three pleasant rooms with private baths, a library with views of Lake Powell, and a hot tub with a spectacular view of the canyonlands.

Information and Services

The **Page Lake Powell Tourism Bureau** (647-A Elm St., 928/660-3405, www. visitpagelakepowell.com) has all kinds of information on Page, Glen Canyon, and the rest of the region, and the staff there can help you book tours. The bureau runs the **Visitor Information Center** (10am-4pm Mon.-Fri., 10am-2pm Sat.), located inside the Powell Museum (6 N. Lake Powell Blvd.).

Transportation

The best and really the only practical, freewheeling way to travel to and explore the Lake Powell region is by car. If you're flying into

Phoenix, it's a long, lonely five-hour drive from the teeming metropolis northward to poor, drowned Glen Canyon, now called Lake Powell. Take I-17 out of the valley to Flagstaff, about a two-hour drive from the desert to the forest; then take Highway 89A from Flagstaff north across the western edge of the Navajo Reservation to Page, a total of 327 miles that passes through Arizona's three great landscapes—the Sonoran Desert, the pine forest, and the Colorado Plateau.

A trip north to Lake Powell can easily be folded into a visit to the Grand Canyon's South Rim, but it's a bit closer to the North Rim, which is just as spectacular in its way but without the crowds. Lake Powell is 187 miles from the South Rim. Take Highway 64 east through the Desert View gate to Cameron, about 60 miles, then head north on Highway 89 for 45 miles to Page. The total distance is 136 miles and will take about three hours. The North Rim is 154 miles from Lake Powell along Highway 89A. It will likely take you just as long as the drive from the South Rim; figure on three hours without stops.

If you're visiting the North Rim along with Zion National Park and Bryce Canyon National Park, consider a side trip to Lake Powell, especially if you're staying in Kanab, Utah, a central base camp for visiting all of the Arizona Strip and southern Utah. Kanab is 74 miles from Lake Powell along Highway 89, just to the north of the Arizona border. The drive across the vast sagebrush plain takes about 1.5 hours. From Kayenta and Monument Valley on the Navajo Reservation, east of Lake Powell, take U.S. 160 west to Highway 98 for about 100 miles, a two-hour drive. You'll reach the region right near Antelope Canyon, one of its top sights.

Navajo and Hopi Country

Here is the Arizona you often see on vintage
travel posters and in old Westerns: Monument Valley, the Painted
Desert, the railroad tracks, and Route 66. This is also the Arizona you
won't see unless you make a concerted effort to do so.

From the vast, arid grasslands of the high desert to the pink and red
sandstone guardians of Indian Country, the scenery here gets top bill-
ing, but there are also comforts to be had in this region that was once an
exotic, longed-for destination for generations of Americans and still is a
major draw for those looking for something just a bit off the beaten path.

Here you can gaze at weather-formed canyons with rock features that
seem deliberately molded according to a strange, thrilling aesthetic;
hike into Canyon de Chelly (pronounced "de Shay"), a sacred place

Navajo and Hopi Country

Highlights

Look for ★ to find recommended sights, activities, dining, and lodging.

★ **Navajo National Monument:** Stand on the edge of sacred Tsegi Canyon and gaze at an ancient city rising out of the rock, hidden and forgotten (page 327).

★ **Monument Valley Navajo Tribal Park:** Drive the red-dirt loop around a barren valley populated by crumbling stone giants, a landscape rooted deeply in the American imagination (page 330).

★ **Canyon de Chelly National Monument:** Hike to the White House Ruin along a precipitous rock trail hewn out of the cliffside, circled endlessly by ravens and silence (page 336).

★ **Second Mesa:** Walk through the oldest continually inhabited village on the continent, where thousand-year-old traditions are a part of everyday life (page 342).

★ **Petrified Forest National Park:** The slickrock remains of a swampy forest are now a parched land strewn with reminders of the earth's unfathomable age (page 344).

© MOON.COM

where pueblo ruins sit below sheer, multicolored walls; or visit the Hopi in their remote mesa-top villages, living in some ways just as their ancestors did a thousand years ago. This place is not for the lazy, easy-come traveler but rather those looking for something different. The region's challenges, and its sometimes foreign feel, only make a trip out here all the more memorable and meaningful.

PLANNING YOUR TIME

You could easily spend five days to a week in this region, hiking the canyons and exploring the ruins, following native guides to out-of-the-way sights, searching for handmade treasures, and touring all the parks and monuments; however, a long weekend would suffice to hit all of the essentials and to gain an unforgettable impression of Indian Country.

One of the most important things to remember while traveling in Indian Country is that the Navajo Nation recognizes **daylight saving time**, unlike the rest of Arizona. That means that March-November, the reservation observes Mountain Daylight Saving Time, while the rest of Arizona observes Mountain Standard Time (MST) all year.

TRANSPORTATION

It's relatively easy to navigate Indian Country, as long as you have a steady vehicle and a good map. Remember that the distances between stations, much as it was in the old days of the territory, are generally long, so take advantage of off-road respite when it presents itself.

To reach the high-desert railroad towns and the sights nearby, stick to I-40, which is well signed for tourist sights. To reach the Navajo and Hopi Reservations from the west, take U.S. 89 north from I-40 at Flagstaff to Cameron, at the entrance to the Navajo Nation. Past Cameron, turn east on U.S. 160, which will take you through Tuba City and Kayenta, past the Navajo National Monument and Monument Valley Navajo Tribal Park. Take U.S. 191 south from Highway 160 east of Kayenta to reach Chinle and Canyon de Chelly National Monument. From there take Highway 191 farther south to Ganado and the Hubbell Trading Post, and then head east on State Highway 264 to Window Rock, the Nation's capital.

If you're entering the Nation from the east, take Indian Route 12 north to Window Rock from I-40 and then go north and west to hit the sights.

Hopi land can be reached from the west by way of State Highway 264 from Highway 160 at Tuba City and Moenkopi; from the east, pick up State Highway 264 at Window Rock.

The best map of this area is the American Automobile Association's (AAA) Indian Country Guide Map.

The Navajo Nation

Though it has been visited by tourists regularly for more than a century, the 27,000-square-mile Navajo Nation still feels like the American outback. This is one of the most isolated, undeveloped regions in the country, a land of red-dirt roads, scrubby gray-green sweeps of arid plain, and pink-rock spires reaching for the persistent, glaring blue-white sky. To visit "Indian Country" one must enter without expectations, remaining open and ready for sudden bolts of strange beauty and spiritual recognition.

The appeal of the sprawling Nation is primarily scenic. Understanding this, the Navajo, or Diné, have not overly exploited

Previous: Monument Valley; Navajo National Monument; Petrified Forest National Park.

The Diné

The Diné (the name the Navajo give to themselves, meaning "The People") are the largest and most populous Native American nation. They migrated down from Canada to the Colorado Plateau about a century before the Spanish arrived from the south, and lived a seminomadic life of hunting, gathering, and raiding that sometimes had them at odds with their neighbors, who were sedentary, pueblo-dwelling farmers.

After contact with the Spanish and the Pueblos, the Diné also became pastoralists and farmers, one of many occasions when these resilient people borrowed from another culture to expand their own. As the anthropologist Edward T. Hall explains: "In their natural state all people are highly adaptable, but the Navajos seem to be the most adaptable people on earth—not simply in adapting to new technologies . . . but in their ability to live with, even absorb into their society, people who are different."

The Nation's modern story is largely one of survival in the face of government antagonism and neglect. In 1863, Col. Kit Carson was sent in to exert government control over the Navajo, loosing a brutal campaign to round up what remained of the tribe and forcibly march them some 300 miles toward isolation and death at Fort Sumner, New Mexico Territory. This event, called the "Long Walk" in Navajo lore, remains an indelible scar on the collective heart of the Diné, a before-and-after dividing line in the Nation's modern history. About 8,000 Navajo were interned at Fort Sumner. Four years later, when the tribe returned to Navajoland, some 5,000 remained.

After years of extreme privation, they eventually returned to their adapting ways, becoming very successful pastoralists, weavers, and artists. They were encouraged and helped by the Anglo traders who found worldwide markets for high-quality Navajo crafts and brought modern goods to the remote reservation. The Diné have thrived and grown, and now, less than 150 years after the Long Walk, they number 298,000 (about 180,000 of whom live on the reservation).

Still, despite the large mineral and energy mining operations on their lands, nearly half of all Diné families live below the federal poverty line, and many still live without modern conveniences most of us take for granted. For some this is because they choose a traditional Navajo existence; for others it is more about the lack of jobs and opportunity on the reservation, whose economy is often compared to that of a developing nation. Those who leave the reservation often do so to attend college in Flagstaff, Tempe, Tucson, and Albuquerque. Education remains one of the best future hopes for the Nation and a source of pride and advocacy for Navajo leaders.

their homeland for the sake of more dollars and euros. The comforts are few and far between, and the landscape is all the better for it. Moreover, the land here is sacred in a very real sense to the Diné. This is where they live; it is not a tourist attraction but a homeland, a birthright, and a cathedral. Respectful visitors will find this seemingly empty land to be full of wonder.

But then again, the Nation isn't as remote as it seems. Just as it was before paved highways traversed the land, a trip to the reservation today is a journey between springs. The few population centers have all grown up naturally where stores of cool water flow beneath the otherwise parched high desert—semigreen places like Tuba City, Kayenta, Chinle,

and Window Rock, the Nation's capital on the eastern border. These towns, while not much to look at—dusty accumulations of houses and businesses along the highway, dwarfed in this land of great rock giants—offer the usual chain hotels (though nearly all rooms are on the expensive side) and some homegrown restaurants serving foods unique to the region.

There are rare opportunities here to go beyond—beyond time when you contemplate the abandoned cities hanging from the cliffs of Navajo National Monument and Canyon de Chelly, and beyond reality as you watch the sun set at Monument Valley, surrounded by an alien beauty.

For shoppers, collectors, and treasure hunters, the Nation probably has the most working artists this side of Santa Fe. The best and most memorable items—famous Navajo rugs and overlay jewelry, Hopi baskets and pottery—can be found at trading posts, co-op stores, and sometimes even on the artist's doorstep—but you have to keep your eyes open for homemade signs out in all that vastness.

As guests of the Diné, tourists are expected to be respectful and follow a few simple but nonnegotiable rules of the reservation. One should not, however, overreact to these rules in a way that keeps you from interacting with the Navajo people. If you simply remember that you are not in a living diorama—that these are real people with real lives to live—then you should be fine. Think about how you'd feel if strangers showed up and started photographing your house. It is never appropriate to photograph Diné individuals or their property without first obtaining permission. The federal parks and monuments are an exception, though there are farms in Canyon de Chelly that you can't photograph. This is a hard-and-fast rule, so if you break it, expect to have your camera gear confiscated. Also, even though the reservation may seem wild and open at times, it's not appropriate to drive off-road or across the land. The land here provides many a Diné family's livelihood, and it should not be disturbed by visitors. If you are invited to witness a religious ceremony of some kind, all due respect is expected—take off your hat and watch silently, as you would at a Catholic mass. Drugs and alcohol are not allowed anywhere on the reservation.

CAMERON

If you're heading north on U.S. 89 from Flagstaff to the Nation, the **Cameron Trading Post** (466 U.S. 89, 877/221-0690), while usually crowded with folks on their way to the Grand Canyon, makes for a handy first stop for gas and snacks and a look at the beautiful old bridge that crosses Little Colorado Gorge. There's also a restaurant, a hotel, shops, and a gallery to browse.

TUBA CITY AND VICINITY

The Navajo call Tuba City *Tonaneesdizi* (Weaving Water or Water Scattered), due to its many life-giving underground natural springs that coax greenery out of the rocky ground and make this small town a kind of dusty oasis. For centuries an agricultural center for the Hopi (who would run from the mesas to nearby Moenkopi to tend their corn), in the late 1800s the area was settled by Mormons. They named their town after a Hopi leader called Tuuvi, who had become a Latter-day Saint and invited others to settle here. In 1903 the federal government sent off the settlers because the town was located on part of the expanded Navajo Reservation. Today Tuba City, with a population of about 9,000 residents, serves as the administrative and cultural center of the western portion of the reservation. Its location at the junction of Highway 264 and U.S. 160 and proximity to the essential Navajo National Monument (about 65 miles to the northeast) makes it a natural stop for travelers. Nearby you can witness the marks ancient beasts have left on the landscape. Tuba City may not look like much—it isn't, really—but there are a few places to eat and stay, and trading posts to browse.

Sights

Approaching Tuba City from the west (from U.S. 89 North from Flagstaff to U.S. 160 East), you'll drive through a wondrous stretch of **Painted Desert,** red, dusty-orange, and gray mounds rising above the ruins of washes, like the humped, craggy backs of buried dinosaurs, with not a shrub in sight. There are several natural turnoffs along the road to take pictures of this strange landscape. In downtown Tuba City, you'll find the **Explore Navajo Interactive Museum** (Main St. and Moenave Rd., 928/640-0684, www.explorenavajo.com, 9am-5pm Mon.-Fri. Mar.-May and Sept.-Nov., 8am-7pm Mon.-Fri., 8am-5pm Sat. June-Aug., by appt. Mon.-Fri. Dec.-Feb., $4.50 adults, $3 children 7-12). The museum offers interesting displays on Navajo history and culture, created with the assistance of Navajo scholars and artists, which explain the various stages of a traditional Navajo life. It's worth it if you have a particular interest in the tribe's traditions. The museum is next to the Quality Inn and the Tuba City Trading Post.

About five miles west of Tuba City on U.S. 160, look for a sign that says **Dinosaur Tracks.** Turn north onto the dirt road and expect to be greeted by one of several Navajo guides who hang around the area, especially during the busy summer season. You can follow one of the friendly guides onto a great red sandstone slab, where eons ago raptor dinosaurs and other ancient monsters populated this land, back when it was swampy and fertile. Their birdlike tracks were sealed forever in the stone, and the guides, many of whom learned details about the tracks from Northern Arizona University archaeologists working in the area, will spray water on the dozens of claw prints to bring them out of the red rock while explaining exactly what you're seeing. Expect to tip $10-20 for the tour (it seems a bit excessive, but think about sitting out on that hot high desert all day). Off to the northeast look for the lush green hillsides of **Moenave,** where several Navajo families live off the natural springs for which this area is known. This is also where Mormon farmers settled in the 1870s, and it was for generations prior to that a Hopi farming area.

Events

The **To'Nanees'Dizi Diné Fair** (aka the Western Navajo Fair, 928/283-3305, http://westernnavajonationfair.net), held once a year in mid-October, is the social event of the season in this corner of the reservation. It's not easy to secure reservations over the three-day fair, which brings hundreds of Navajo families to Tuba City from around the reservation for a rodeo, parade, traditional food and ceremonies, live bands, cutest baby and Miss Western Navajo pageants, and sporting events. It's a fun and illuminating time to be in Tuba City.

Shopping

The **Historic Tuba City Trading Post** (10 N. Main St. and Moenave Rd., 928/283-5441, 8am-5pm daily) in downtown Tuba City has been selling native crafts and a vast array of staples since the 1870s. It's still open, and though it has changed a lot these last 140 years, it offers a great assortment of handmade jewelry, rugs, and other popular Indian Country souvenirs and collectibles. **Van's Trading Post** (928/283-5343, 8am-8pm daily) along Highway 160 is like a lesser Walmart, half grocery store and half other merchandise like clothing and furniture. There's a coin laundry next door, and a pawn shop is also operated on-site.

Food and Accommodations

The nicest hotel in Tuba City is the **Quality Inn Navajo Nation** (10 N. Main St. and Moenave Rd., 928/283-5260, www.choicehotels.com, $130-150), right next to the Historic Tuba City Trading Post. The two-story hotel has clean rooms decorated in a soft Southwestern style, free Wi-Fi and free continental breakfast. On the same property is the **Hogan Restaurant** (928/283-5260, 6am-10pm daily, $10-20), a diner-style place that serves decent food for breakfast, lunch, and dinner daily, including everything from burgers and fries to Navajo tacos and mutton stew as well as a few Mexican favorites. Next door you can get a cappuccino or a latte at **Hogan Espresso** (10 N. Main St., 928/283-4545, 7am-7pm Mon.-Fri., 9am-7pm Sat., 9am-4pm Sun., $5-10). The inn, restaurant, and on-site museum are all operated by the Navajo Nation Tribal Council's **Navajo Nation Hospitality Enterprise,** so while they seem like chains, the money you spend generally stays on the reservation.

A note about reserving a room: Every room in town is booked weeks before the Western Navajo Fair, and expect to pay extra if you manage to find one for yourself.

Elephant Feet

On the north side of Highway 160 at mile

marker 345, about 24 miles east of Tuba City near Tonalea, you'll see the two sandstone spires called **Elephant Feet,** side by side and similarly eroded with wide, red-banded bases tapering up to slender, flat peaks. They really do look like elephant feet, as if they were the last remains of some great mammoth turned to stone. They are improbable landmarks, yes, but they are merely two of the hundreds of rock formations you will soon see that will have you wondering at the seemingly random, though nonetheless artistic, forces of erosion that formed this strange, thrilling land.

★ NAVAJO NATIONAL MONUMENT

Though it's within the Navajo Reservation, beautiful **Tsegi Canyon,** an eroded pink-rock landscape carpeted with gray-green piñon pine and juniper forests, was once home to the Hisatsinom, ancestors of the Hopi. These Ancestral Puebloans (sometimes referred to by the Navajo name Anasazi) are credited with building the three cliffside villages in the canyon—some of the best-preserved and most awe-inspiring ruins in the Southwest. The Hopi, Navajo, Zuni, and Paiute cultures still consider this a sacred place, so only a few short hikes to promontories above the canyon are open to the general public. If you want to explore the area more deeply, you can sign up to take guided hikes to two of the ruins with a park ranger.

Only the ruins of the village called **Betatakin** by the Navajo and Talastima by the Hopi are visible from the canyon rim, tucked in a south-facing natural rock alcove that kept the village cool in the summer and warm in the winter; just below the village is a white-and-green aspen forest. Deeper in is Keet Seel, an older and larger village than Betatakin and one of the largest cliff dwellings in the Southwest. It's called Kawestima by the Hopi. **Inscription House,** or Tsu'ovi, is also perched in the canyon, but it has been closed to the public since the late 1960s.

Archaeologists believe that the Kayenta culture (one of three Ancestral Puebloan subgroups, along with Chaco and Mesa Verde) lived in the canyon as early as AD 950, with major building projects getting under way around AD 1250. But by AD 1300, for reasons only guessed at, all of the villages had been abandoned.

Visiting the Monument

The park is about 50 miles northeast of Tuba City and 30 miles southwest of Kayenta. Approaching from either way on U.S. 160, take Route 564 nine miles to the park entrance. Unlike most parks and monuments off the reservation, admission here is free. The **visitors center** (928/672-2700, www. nps.gov/nava, 9am-5pm daily, free) has a gift shop that sells books, T-shirts, hats, and small water bottles, as well as an interesting museum featuring items used in everyday life by the Puebloans and found in their left-behind villages.

Just outside the visitors center there are three short hiking trails that allow for optimum viewing of the canyon. The one-mile round-trip **Sandal Trail** is paved and leads to an overlook perfect for viewing the village of Betatakin/Talastima sleeping in its alcove. It's steep going back up, and the hike should not be treated lightly just because it's short. Take water, especially in the summer. The 0.8-mile round-trip **Aspen Forest Overlook** descends about 300 feet to provide a good look at the forest below the village, but you can't see the ruins; the **Canyon View Trail** leads 0.6 mile round-trip to a nice view of the ruins near the **Canyon View Campground.**

Hiking

If viewing Betatakin from the ridge top isn't enough for you, you can sign up to take one of two hikes into the canyon to explore the ruins up close. The hike to Betatakin is five miles round-trip and takes three to five hours to complete. A ranger guides you 700 feet down into the canyon and then on to the ruins. It is a mildly strenuous hike, but the outing is memorable for its scenery, not its difficulty. Two hikes are available daily in the summer

May-September, leaving from the visitors center at 8:15am and 10am. During the rest of the year one hike leaves from the center daily at 10am. It's required that you sign up beforehand with the rangers at the visitors center if you want to take the hike.

The trek to **Keet Seel** (which roughly translates to "shattered house") is a bit more involved. One of the best-preserved ruins in the Southwest, Keet Seel was "discovered," for the Anglo world anyway, by the famous Southwestern ruin-hunter Richard Wetherill while he was chasing a runaway burro.

Reaching the ruin involves a 17-mile round-trip hike through the canyon bottomlands along a meandering stream—with several small waterfalls—that you have to cross dozens of times. You will get your feet wet early and often on this hike; there's no way to avoid it. Many hikers take along a sturdy pair of hiking sandals and change into them after descending 1,000 feet into the canyon along a rock-hewn trail. When you arrive at the primitive campground within sight of the ruin, a volunteer ranger who lives in a hogan-shaped log cabin nearby will take you on an hour-long tour of the ruin, which you reach by climbing a steep ladder into a cliffside rock alcove. He explains all about the people who once lived in this hidden canyon and usually shows off a few astounding items found at the site from the everyday lives of the stone village's builders and residents. This is as close as you're likely to get to the ancients.

If you are some kind of world-champion hiker, you could go in and out in the same day, but a stay overnight at the campground, with the ruins dark and mute just across the wash, is a memorable experience. (There is no water available at the campground, nor are fires allowed, but there is a compost toilet.) You have to attend a short orientation meeting either the morning of your hike at 8am or the afternoon prior at 4pm. It's best to arrive the day before so you can get an early start. The best place to stay is at one of the chains in Kayenta, about a half-hour drive from the monument.

It's a good idea to purchase and pack all your backpacking supplies before arriving on the reservation, as there aren't any good places to do so nearby.

Reservations and a backcountry permit are required for Keet Seel and are limited to 20 people per day. Call ahead for best results (928/672-2700). The hike is offered daily in the summer, May-September, but after September 15 it's offered every second weekend of the month only.

Accommodations

The monument has two small campgrounds, free and open year-round, with spaces available first come, first served. Spaces have charcoal grills, but open campfires aren't allowed. It's a good idea to get supplies in either Tuba City or Kayenta before traveling to the monument for an overnight visit. The best hotel options are in Kayenta, about 30 miles from the entrance to the monument.

KAYENTA AND VICINITY

Called *Tohdineeshzhee* (Water Going in Different Directions) by the Diné, Kayenta is the reservation town nearest to Monument Valley and is a good base for a visit to the northern reservation. John Wetherill, who with his brother Richard was one of the first Anglos to explore (and exploit) the Ancestral Puebloan ruins of Mesa Verde and Chaco Canyon, opened a trading post here in 1910. Today it's the only town on the reservation with a U.S.-style township government, home to about 5,000 people.

Shopping

The Navajo Arts and Crafts Enterprise has a retail store at Kayenta (928/697-8611, www.gonavajo.com, 9am-7pm Mon.-Sat., noon-6pm Sun.) at the junction of Highways 160 and 163. Operated by Navajos, the company sells all kinds of local handmade arts

---

1: Elephant Feet **2:** Navajo National Monument **3:** Blue Coffee Pot Restaurant in Kayenta **4:** The Three Sisters in Monument Valley Navajo Tribal Park

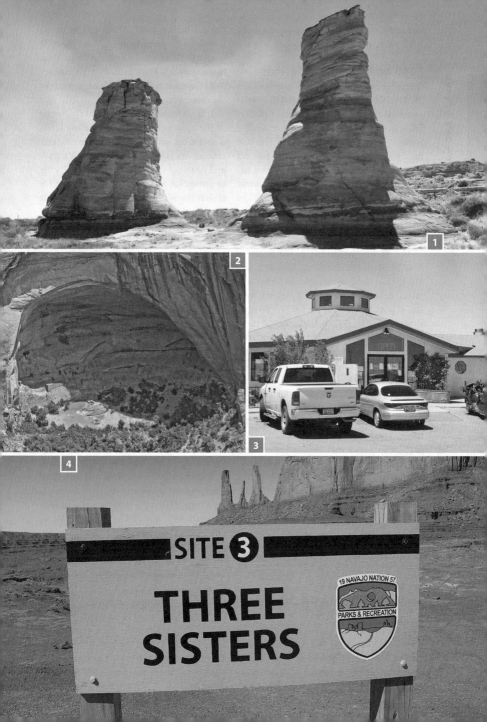

and crafts, curios, rugs, silver jewelry, concha belts, bolo ties, pottery, and more.

Food and Accommodations

One of the best restaurants on Navajoland, the ★ **Blue Coffee Pot Restaurant** (0.25 mile east of U.S. 160 and 163 junction, 928/697-3396, $4-12) in Kayenta serves outstanding home-style Navajo, American, and Mexican food in a hogan-shaped building just off Highway 160. You might find yourself sitting at a table next to a 90-something Navajo woman dressed like it's the 19th century. The Navajo taco here is simply terrific, as are the beef ribs. The staff is friendly, if a bit harried in this busy place.

The ★ **Amigo Café** (U.S. 163, 928/697-8448, 10:30am-9pm Mon.-Fri., 8am-9pm Sat., $10-15) just north of the junction serves fantastic Mexican, Navajo, and American food and is popular with the locals. The **Burger King** (928/697-3534) on Highway 160 (near the Hampton Inn) has the usual, with the added feature of a **Navajo Code Talkers** exhibit, which you can view as you chow down on your french fries.

Because it is so close to Monument Valley, there are several nice chain hotels in Kayenta, most of them along Highway 160 as you enter town. The **Hampton Inn** (928/697-3170, $215-220) is very comfortable and offers wireless Internet, a pool, a gift shop, a restaurant, and free continental breakfast. The **Wetherill Inn** (U.S. 163, 1000 Main St., 928/697-3231, www.wetherill-inn.com, $149) has comfortable rooms, an indoor pool, wireless Internet, a gift shop, and free breakfast.

TOP EXPERIENCE

★ MONUMENT VALLEY NAVAJO TRIBAL PARK

The **scenic drive** north 22 miles from **Kayenta** along **U.S. 163** to **Monument Valley Navajo Tribal Park** ($20 per car with four people) is almost as dramatic as the destination itself. About a third of the way along the paved route you'll see the aptly named **Owl Rock** to the west and the hulking, jagged **Agathla Peak** to the east (also known as El Capitan), which tribal lore says marks the center of the world.

If there were any question that this is one of the most celebrated and enticing landscapes in the world, listen to the conversations around you as you visit Monument Valley—and you must visit Monument Valley, if only to prove that all the images you've seen are real. It sounds like "It's a Small World" out on this arid, dusty valley. Japanese, Chinese, Italian, German, British, and various Eastern European visitors gather at every lookout, looking for something distinctly Western, or American, in the iconic jutting red rocks.

It was the director John Ford who brought this strange, remote place to the world and made it a stand-in for the West's dueling freedom and danger, most memorably in *The Searchers*. Now, to drive around the park is to enter a thousand car commercials, magazine layouts, road films, and Westerns, a landscape that's comfortably, beautifully familiar even if you're seeing it for the first time.

The Navajo have thankfully not overdeveloped this sacred place—some would argue it's underdeveloped for its potential—so the only way to see the park without a Navajo guide is to drive the 17-mile unpaved **loop road** with pullouts for scenic views of the rock spires and lonely buttes. Upon entering the park you'll get a map of the drive with the name of each "Monument"—names like Wetherill Mesa, John Ford's Point, and The Thumb. If you can, it's worth arriving about an hour or so before sundown to see sunset over the valley—you'll wonder how you got here, and you'll stay until the lights go out. Be warned, though, that with the constant stream of cars driving the dry, dirt road, the air tends to get dusty.

You're allowed to take photographs here, but only of the natural wonders. Remember to ask permission before taking pictures of any Navajos or their private property.

Visitors Center

The park's **visitors center** (435/727-5874 or 435/727-5870, 6am-8pm daily Apr.-Sept., 8am-5pm daily Oct.-Mar.), perched on a promontory overlooking the valley and the dirt road that snakes through it and around the eroded-sandstone sculptures, is an obvious place to start your visit. There's a small museum with displays on Navajo culture and history, as well as the history of Hollywood's use of this iconic landscape, and a wall or two showing contemporary Navajo art. Staff here can set you up with a guide if you want to go deeper into the valley and learn about the tribe's religious, cultural, and economic ties to it. There's a small patio outside the visitors center, which is right next to The View Hotel, restaurant, and trading post/gift shop, where you can sit and contemplate the natural art before you.

The Valley Drive

The best way to see the valley and its monuments up close and on your own time is to head out into the hazy red lands via the 17-mile, self-guided **Valley Drive** (6am-8pm daily Apr.-Sept., 8am-5pm daily Oct.-Apr., $20 per car with up to four people). The route, which is all dirt and a bit rough in some spots, has 11 pullouts for longer views of some of the more famous mesas, buttes, and spires. At many of these numbered stops, which otherwise have no services, you'll find Navajo families selling jewelry and souvenirs. Plan to spend at least two hours exploring the valley. If dust bothers you, so too will the Valley Drive, but try not to let that stop you: This is one of the most scenic, inspirational, and absolutely essential drives in the Southwest. Take water and food along, and check your tires before you head out. The roughest part of the drive is at the start, going down a steep hill into the valley, but the rest is easy and flat. Don't follow too close behind other cars; you'll be buried in red dust if you do. The tribe does not allow motorcycles or RVs on the Valley Drive.

The road into the valley starts just past the visitors center parking lot and has two lanes until Camel Butte, where it becomes a one-way loop around **Rain God Mesa.** The first stop, just as you enter the valley, provides a classic, much-photographed view of the "mittens," **West Mitten Butte** and **East Mitten Butte,** named because of the spires that rise from the side of each butte to form what looks like a hand in a mitten. Just a short scoot up the road is **Merrick Butte,** named, according to Richard Klinck in his classic history of the valley, *Land of Room Enough and Time Enough,* for James Merrick, a soldier turned prospector who was killed near the butte for trespassing on a Navajo silver mine. The huge mesa opposite Merrick Butte is called **Mitchell Mesa,** for it is said that at its base died Ernest Mitchell, Merrick's partner in trespass and violent death.

The second stop on the drive, **Elephant Butte,** is supposed to look like the titular pachyderm. The third and fourth numbered stops, **The Three Sisters** and **John Ford's Point,** are two of the best. The sisters are side-by-side spires on the edge of Mitchell Mesa, and the point is named for the famous director who revealed this valley to the world through his Westerns. The fifth stop is **Camel Butte,** named for the stone-frozen ungulate that to many it resembles. Just a bit up the road from the fifth stop, a ramshackle hut and corral provides **horseback tours of the backcountry** (30-minute to 6-hour tours, $45-165, credit cards accepted). You can also stop here and take pictures of the horses, but make sure to ask first, and be prepared to pay $5.

The sixth numbered stop on the drive provides a view of the formation called **The Hub,** which looks somewhat like the center of a wagon wheel, and of huge **Rain God Mesa,** marking the center of the valley. Here the road turns to loop around Rain God Mesa, with pull-offs at **Thunderbird Mesa** and the edge of **Spearhead Mesa.** Here you'll see red sand dunes and, far off in the valley beyond the road, the impossibly delicate spire called the **Totem Pole,** which rises next to a gathering of thicker spires the Navajo call **Yei Bi Chei** ("dancers emerging from a hogan"). The ninth stop is at the far tip of Spearhead Mesa, where there's a short, easy trail out to **Artist Point Overlook.** The view here is spectacular, and it's easy to see how the promontory got its name. Continuing on around the other side of Rain God Mesa, you'll see **Cly Butte,** at the base of which is buried "Old Cly," a beloved Navajo medicine man who died in 1934. Cly Butte is the last numbered stop, seen from a short side road up to the penultimate stop, the **North Window Overlook,** which provides a breathtaking view of the valley's northern section. The loop ends at Camel Butte, behind which rises a spire called **The Thumb.** Then it's back to the visitors center along the two-lane route from Camel Butte. You'll pass the same monuments on the way back, obviously, and feel free to stop at them again.

Wildcat Trail

The only hiking you can do in the absence of a hired Navajo guide is along this 3.2-mile loop trail around **West Mitten Butte.** It's an easy, quiet walk along a red-dirt path among gray-green scrub and sagebrush, with the spires and buttes looming close and lizards whipping over red rocks. The trail starts 0.4 mile north of the visitors center. It's easy enough for kids, but there's no shade, and it can get windy out there. Take water with you, and plan on being out for two hours or more.

Tours

As impressive as the buttes and jutting rock castles along the main road around the valley are, they are but a small sampling; many more hulking, crumbling buttes, as well as wondrous arches, delicate spires, petroglyphs, and traditional Navajo homesteads, are scattered throughout this vast, remote land, accessible only with a Navajo guide at your side. Be sure to make reservations at least a week in advance.

There is no shortage of Navajo guides, and you can easily hire one inside the park at the visitors center. Also, the **Navajo Parks and Recreation Department** has a list of reputable, Navajo-owned guide companies on its website (www.navajonationparks.org). Prices vary slightly between the different companies, but you can generally expect to pay about $50 for a 1.5-hour ride in an open Jeep around the main road, to about $115-165 for an all-day backcountry immersion tour. You have to book a 2.5-hour tour or longer (generally around $75 pp) to go anywhere you can't go on your own. The **View Hotel in Monument Valley** also has a list of reputable guides on its website (http://monumentvalleyview.com/navajo-guided-tours).

Serious photographers should consider booking a guide, lest they return home with images not considerably different from those snapped by a tourist with a cell phone. Guide Tom J. Phillips of **Keya-Hozhoni Tours** (928/429-0665, 928/429-0040, or 928/429-0042, www.monumentvalley.com, $125, 3.5 hours), which also offers regular Jeep and horseback tours, charges about $30 an hour to show photographers the best shots outside the mainstream.

Food and Accommodations

For all its fame, Monument Valley is still a considerably remote place, and there aren't a lot of services out here. Don't come hungry; eat in Kayenta before you head out, or bring your own food with you. That's not to say that there's nothing to eat at all. The **View Restaurant** (435/727-3468, www.monumentvalleyview.com, 7am-2pm and 5pm-8pm daily, $10-25) inside the park has decent Navajo, Mexican, and American food for breakfast, lunch, and dinner. In between meals there are only packaged sandwiches, fruit, and snacks available. At the junction of Highway 163 and the park entrance road, there's a small shopping center where you can get snacks and fry bread, and there are a few gift shops selling local crafts and curios.

When the tribe developed **The View Hotel** (435/727-5555, www.monumentvalleyview.com, $249 and up), the only in-park, non-camping accommodations available at

Monument Valley, they probably could have thrown up a few trailers and a kiddy pool and charged $100 per night. The location alone is the attraction; everything else just gets in the way. But they didn't do that, thankfully. The View is instead a complement to the landscape, a low and tucked-away line of rooms near the Mitten Buttes, with patios facing east over the valley where the sun comes alive in the morning. The color of the hotel fairly merges with that of the buttes, monuments, and vast red dunes, making it appear inevitable. The rooms are comfortable and decorated in a generic Southwestern style. It's the view that you're paying for, obviously, and you will pay a lot, if you can get a reservation. There are no cheap rooms, especially during the spring and summer high season. The hotel also rents out cabins with their own amazing views near the Wildcat Trail. These are a good option for families and groups ($199 for a cabin that sleeps four).

CAMPING

Campsites are available at the **Mitten View Campground** (435/727-5802, www.monumentvalleyview.com, $20 tent sites, $40 RV sites) year-round, first come, first served. Each site has a table, grill, ramada, and trash can, and there are restrooms and coin-operated showers. No hookups are available, but a dump station is open during the summer. Check in at the visitors center to get a campsite.

GOULDING'S LODGE

This compound just outside the park features a hotel with luxury amenities, a campground, a museum, and a trading post selling Navajo crafts. It keeps the name of the first trader to settle in the valley, Harry Goulding, who opened a trading post here in 1928, exchanging staples for Navajo jewelry and rugs. The story goes that in the late 1930s Goulding himself went to Hollywood to convince Ford to come to Monument Valley to film *Stagecoach*.

Goulding's Lodge (435/727-3231, www.gouldings.com, $175-250) has 62 rooms and eight family-friendly, multiroom suites with kitchenettes. There's an indoor heated swimming pool and exercise room, wireless Internet, and satellite TV. The **Stagecoach Dining Room** serves American and Navajo food (such as lamb stew, Navajo tacos, and fry bread) for breakfast, lunch, and dinner. The well-equipped **Goulding's Campground** offers tent sites for $19 per night and full hookup sites for $48 per night. There's also a convenience store, a gas station, a coin laundry, a car wash, and an indoor pool at the campground.

Goulding's offers various tours of the monument with Navajo guides for about $70 per person for 2.5-hour tours.

MEXICAN HAT, UTAH

This very small town on the San Juan River is just 27 miles north of Monument Valley along Highway 163, about 40 minutes from the tribal park. As such, Mexican Hat, named for a precariously balanced rock near town that looks like a sombrero, is an excellent place to base your visit, especially if you are approaching from the north or the east rather than from Phoenix. Another virtue of Mexican Hat is that it lacks the Navajo Reservation's prohibition on alcohol. The tiny conglomerate of buildings stretches out along Highway 163 near the San Juan for a mile or so, and there really isn't much to it. There are, however, a few places to stay and eat and a few scenic sites to whet your appetite for a tour of those red sandstone monuments just to the south.

The vista at **Goosenecks State Park,** about eight miles or 15 minutes north of Mexican Hat, provides a jaw-dropping, head-scratching look at the San Juan River wrapping around large buttes from 1,000 feet above. The park is nothing more than the vista and has no services save for bathrooms. Take Highway 163 east out of town, turn left on UT 261 and then left on State Highway 316, following the signs. Along the way look for the eponymous rock wearing a sombrero off to the east along Highway 163.

Another place near Mexican Hat worth a visit is the remote **Valley of the Gods,** a kind of lesser Monument Valley. You can drive through the valley and view its buttes and mesas along a 17-mile dirt road, which is a bit rough but safe for most passenger cars. There are no services out here, so bring your own water and food, and make sure you have enough gas. There is a gas station in Mexican Hat along Highway 163. From Mexican Hat take Highway 163 east of town eight miles to Valley of the Gods Road and turn left; it's another five miles from there.

Food and Accommodations

The few accommodations in Mexican Hat are generally less expensive than the chain hotels in Kayenta and are much less expensive than The View Hotel in Monument Valley. Moreover, a few restaurants here serve alcohol, which is prohibited on the reservation.

The ★ **San Juan Inn and Trading Post** (Hwy. 163 and the San Juan River, 800/447-2022, www.sanjuaninn.net, $130-145) is right on the banks of the beautiful San Juan River and next to a picturesque bridge. Offering basic rooms with air-conditioning, TV, and free but spotty Wi-Fi, the San Juan Inn is the best place to stay near Monument Valley for the money. It's in a quiet and relaxing setting, with red cliffs hovering above the bushy green riverbank and the river rolling by—plus there are always a few other explorers around here to talk to. The inn also rents well-appointed yurts, which are located on a different property nearby ($110). A couple steps from the inn, The **Old Bridge Bar & Grill** (7am-9pm daily, $5-20), serves a big, filling breakfast, tasty Mexican food, Navajo tacos, burgers, and all the other grill-style mainstays, plus a few vegetarian options. It also has a full bar and pool.

The **Mexican Hat Lodge** (Hwy. 163 across from the Shell gas station, 435/683-2222, www.mexicanhatlodge.com, $98-134) has comfortable and clean rooms with TVs and minifridges in most rooms. It offers a fun, laid-back, and friendly vibe more akin to a bed-and-breakfast than a regular motel. They offer free Wi-Fi, an indoor pool, and a hot tub outside. The restaurant here is called **The Swinging Steak** (5pm-9pm daily Apr.-Sept., $13-40), and it has a pleasant patio where you can watch your steak being cooked over a swinging grill. It serves wine and beer, but it's of the low-alcohol Utah variety.

Four Corners Monument

About 70 miles east on Highway 160 from Kayenta is the **Four Corners Monument** (928/871-6647, 8am-5pm daily Sept.-May, 7am-8pm daily June-Aug., $5), the only place in the United States where, if you do a little bit of Twister-style contorting, you can exist briefly in four states at once—Arizona, Colorado, New Mexico, and Utah. You're not likely to stay long after you take the obligatory picture. In the summer months there are usually Navajo artisans and others selling crafts.

CHINLE AND VICINITY

Like most town names on the arid Navajo Reservation, Ch'inlih refers to moisture, in this case "Water Flowing." There isn't much here for the tourist save a few chain hotels and the gateway to Canyon de Chelly. Chinle has been a center for canyon visitors since the early 20th century, when the famous trader Lorenzo Hubbell operated a stagecoach from the train stop at Gallup to bring tourists to see the ancient cliff dwellings and the other wonders of the canyon.

Food and Accommodations

Chinle is the best place to base a multiday visit to Canyon de Chelly National Monument. The town's not much to look at, but it does have two comfortable, long-established chain hotels, both with good restaurants: **Best Western Canyon de Chelly** (100 Mina St., 928/674-5875, www.canyondechelly.com, $66-109) and **Holiday Inn Canyon de Chelly**

1: horses for Monument Valley backcountry tours 2: the rock that gave Mexican Hat its name 3: view from Spider Rock Overlook at Canyon de Chelly 4: Canyon de Chelly National Monument

(Rte. 7, 928/674-5000, www.holiday-inn.com, $100-150).

Near the visitors center on Canyon de Chelly National Monument, ★ **Thunderbird Lodge** (3.5 miles east of U.S. 191 on Indian Rte. 7, 928/671-5841, http://thunderbirdlodge.com, $90-120) is the only hotel within the monument and feels faraway and rural with its grassy and shady grounds. The basic rooms come with free Wi-Fi, refrigerators, and TVs, and they are clean and comfortable. There's a decent cafeteria-style restaurant here, and a trading post-gift shop where you can book tours of the canyon.

Also on the monument is the **Cottonwood Campground,** a free, first-come, first-served campground with running water and flush toilets in the summer only.

★ CANYON DE CHELLY NATIONAL MONUMENT

The most visually impressive wind- and water-worn canyon in Arizona save for the one they call Grand, Canyon de Chelly (pronounced "de Shay"; the name is a Spanish approximation of the Navajo word for canyon, *tsegi*), is a labyrinth of eroded sandstone mesas, buttes, and spires, washed in pink and red and varnished with black and purple. The canyon's fertile bottomlands and safe, hidden alcoves, seemingly designed beforehand to host stone cliff dwellings, have drawn people here for some 4,000 years. The greatest among the Southwest's ancients, the Ancestral Puebloans, built several hanging villages against the red-rock cliffs, the remains of which are still slowly crumbling in their shady alcoves.

About 40 Navajo families call the canyon and its rimlands home. You'll pass some of their homesites and hogans as you drive the two scenic roads along the rim. Free-roaming horses like to munch on the grasses and weeds that grow along the side of the road; they will generally ignore you until you get out of your car for a photo, when they will promptly turn and trot away. The federal monument comprises about 84,000 acres of the canyon; however, as with the other federal parks on the reservation, the Navajos' interests trump all others here. Nearly all of the canyon is off-limits without a hired Navajo guide.

Visitors Center

The **visitors center** (928/674-5500, www.nps.gov/cach, 8am-5pm daily, free) is a good place to start your visit. Here you can find out about guided tours (a ranger will give you a long list if you ask), learn about the history and science of the canyon, and browse a small bookstore stocked well with volumes on the Southwest and the Colorado Plateau. A map of the park's scenic drives is available here for free.

White House Ruin Trail

The short but steep **White House Ruin Trail** (2.5 miles round-trip) down a skinny trail hewn out of petrified pink sand dunes, to the **White House Ruin,** is the only route to the sandy, shady canyon bottomlands that you can take without a guide, and it is one of the highlights of a visit to Indian Country. The trail offers a rare chance to see Ancestral Puebloan ruins up close and on your own. Once on the canyon bottom, you pass a traditional Navajo hogan and farm, and the canyon walls, streaked with purple, black, and orange, rise hundreds of feet above you. Hawks and ravens circle overhead as black and brown dots high in the bright blue sky. Cave-like hideouts built by natural forces in sandstone alcoves call for you to rest and sit back in their cool shade. Cottonwoods, willows, and peach trees grow in the bottomlands, while piñon pine, juniper, scrub oak, cholla, and prickly pear cling to the sides of the precipitous trail, a dusty green set against the reddish-pink of the de Chelly sandstone. Although you can also take two scenic drives to see all the canyon's wonders, there is no substitute for hiking in. Pick up the trailhead at the **White House Overlook,** the fourth signed stop along the South Rim Drive, about six miles from the visitors center. If you're on the hunt for Navajo arts, take some cash with you on the hike; there are often artists sitting beneath the shady trees near the White House Ruin, offering their creations for sale.

Scenic Drives

Two paved scenic rimside drives offer the most comprehensive look at Canyon de Chelly without hiring a guide. The visitors center has a free map of the easy drives, and both can be done in a regular car. The 37-mile round-trip **South Rim Drive** will take you to the **Spider Rock Overlook,** where you can see the eponymous 800-foot red-rock spire, a must-see of any visit to the canyon. The south drive has seven overlooks, while the 34-mile round-trip **North Rim Drive** has three: **Antelope House Ruin, Mummy Cave Overlook,** and **Massacre Cave Overlook,** each with a view of ruins. Many of the lookouts are at the end of a short but relatively strenuous hike, and most have no barriers whatsoever between you and the edge.

Tours

You need a Navajo guide with you to travel deep into the canyon, and there are many available for hire throughout the year. Expect to pay about $50-60 per hour for 1-3 people for a private Jeep tour along the canyon bottom to some of the out-of-the-way ruins, caves, and rock-art sites. **Canyon de Chelly (Unimoq) Tours** (Chinle, 928/349-1391 or 928/349-1600, http://canyondechellytours.com, $75 pp) offers a three-hour group tour in a big four-by-four (you ride with about 10 other passengers in the open bed). They'll take you from Antelope Ruin to White House Ruin.

Antelope House Tours (Chinle, 928/674-5231, www.canyondechelly.net, $157 for three people) offers three-hour Jeep tours of all the ruins and three-hour hiking tours ($99 for three people) with guides versed in the lore and culture of the Navajo and the other peoples that lived in this spectacular place before them. It's a good idea to call ahead for reservations.

Tsalie and Diné College

At the end of the scenic drive along the Canyon de Chelly's north rim (Indian Rte. 64), past the last established lookout, you'll come to **Diné College,** a Navajo-run junior college that has been educating tribal members and preserving tribal traditions since 1968. The circular, hogan-shaped campus is designed to reflect traditional Navajo philosophy, which the **Ned Hatathli Museum and Gallery** (Diné College Tsalie campus, 1 Circle Dr., Indian Rte. 12, 928/724-6600, 8am-5pm Mon.-Fri., closed for the lunch hour, free)—itself housed in a six-story glass hogan—interprets, as well as showing off historic tribal artifacts and contemporary Navajo arts and crafts.

HUBBELL TRADING POST NATIONAL HISTORIC SITE

When you walk into the rustic building in Ganado that has housed the **Hubbell Trading Post** (928/755-3475, www.nps.gov/hutr, 8am-6pm summer, 8am-5pm winter, free entry, $2 adults over 16 for Hubbell Home Tour) since 1876, you expect to enter a museum or a typical visitors center. Instead, you enter the "bull pen," a working trading post that looks much like it did 100 years ago, still selling jewelry, rugs, and staples and still an important commercial spot to the Diné. The area has a fascinating history, and this is the best place to learn about the impact Anglo traders—J. L. Hubbell and his family the most famous and beloved among them—had on Navajo lifeways and the reservation economy. You can tour the homestead with a ranger or with a self-guided tour book and peek into the Hubbell Home, laden with Navajo rugs, old books, and original paintings by the famous artist E. A. Burbank. There's also a small museum and bookstore operated by the National Park Service.

WINDOW ROCK

Window Rock, the capital of the Navajo Nation, is a lot like the other population centers on the Navajo Reservation: small, utilitarian, and surrounded by scenery that dwarfs the buildings. The town of about 4,000 persons is right on the Arizona-New Mexico border and just 27 miles northwest of Gallup, New Mexico, a fairly large city (with about 25,000 persons) by the standards of this remote, rural corner of the world. At nearly 8,000 feet, Window Rock has a cooler climate than the lower western reservation, and in winter the ponderosa pine and piñon-juniper forests that decorate the artfully eroded sandstone buttes and spires around the town are often dusted with a thin layer of snow.

Sure, it's a long drive to get here from Phoenix (300 miles), Tucson (355 miles), or the Grand Canyon (234 miles). But it is a scenic drive, and one that must be undertaken by anyone truly interested in what the Navajo Nation is all about. It has the best museum on the reservation in the Navajo Nation Museum and is a fun stop for families with small kids for its free zoo featuring the reservation's most famous and prevalent creatures.

Sights

The famous **Window Rock** that gives the town its name—a 200-foot-high red sandstone monument with an unlikely 47-foot-diameter wind- and water-chipped hole in it (called *Tseghahodzani* by the Navajo, roughly translating to "the rock with the hole in it")—is at the **Window Rock Navajo Tribal Park,** just a short drive north on Indian Route 12 from its intersection with State Highway 264. It stares down like an oracle. You can't climb it or anything, but it is a ready-made photograph: pink-red and towering against the usually bright blue sky, with gnarled, deep-green junipers and piñons and little yellow wildflowers stretched out in front of it. There's also an evocative statue here of a Navajo soldier kneeling with a radio to his ear and a look of serious intensity on his face. It is the centerpiece of a **memorial to the Navajo Code Talkers** of World War II and is instantly recognizable as a depiction of those celebrated men.

Window Rock has been the center of the Navajo Nation government since the 1930s, when the Civilian Conservation Corps built the rough-hewn but stylish native-stone and pinewood **Navajo Nation Council Chambers** and its surrounding buildings, which sit in the shadow of the one-eyed red rock and are used intermittently when the council is in session.

About three miles west of Window Rock in St. Michaels (a small town along Hwy. 264), you'll see the **St. Michael's Mission,** a Franciscan mission established in 1896 by St. Katharine Drexel. The **St. Michael's Historical Museum** (3 mi. west of Window Rock on Hwy. 264, 928/871-4171, 9am-5pm Mon.-Fri. Memorial Day-Labor Day) on the mission grounds has a small, interesting museum about Navajo and Catholic interactions and the history of the mission.

NAVAJO NATION MUSEUM

The tribal members could charge $10 per person or more for a look around the sleek and informative **Navajo Nation Museum** (Hwy. 264 and Loop Rd., 928/871-7941, http://navajopeople.org, 10am-5pm Mon.-Sat., free), but instead they let everybody in for free. That's just the first of many surprises here. Another is that there is plenty of space dedicated to contemporary reservation life—a subject that many tourists tend to overlook in favor of the romantic, story-filled past. The museum's art gallery hosts revolving shows featuring Navajo artists and photographers, and throughout the museum there are examples of silverwork and weaving by many living artists. The museum reaches into the past to tell the story of the harrowing Long Walk and the tribe's near fatal exile at Fort Sumner in the 1860s, showing actual artifacts and ephemera related to the events that help make the traumas suffered seem recent, as they still are from the Navajo perspective. There is also a fascinating display that explains the traditional Navajo way of life. This is simply the best museum on the reservation, and it should be visited by anyone with an interest in the Navajo Nation. Even if you have no interest before entering, it's likely that you will upon exiting. Just outside the museum's front entrance, there's a traditional hogan that you are allowed to enter and examine up close; it's surprising how cool it is inside, even at the height of summer.

NAVAJO NATION ZOOLOGICAL AND BOTANICAL PARK

Tall, fat cylinders of beige-colored sandstone stand just to the north of the museum. They are called, for reasons that will be obvious to anyone who sees them, **The Haystacks.** These photo-worthy monoliths watch over a tiny zoo run by the tribe. The **Navajo Nation Zoological and Botanical Park** (Hwy. 264 and Loop Rd., 928/871-6574, www.navajozoo. org, 10am-4:30pm Mon.-Sat., free) houses examples of many of the animals that share these wild, open lands with the Navajos, most of which occupy a sacred place in the traditional Navajo belief system. A short, easy trail leads around a small open area overlooked by the Haystacks, past fenced-in habitats with raccoons, bobcats, a cougar, a black bear, prairie dogs, and other common Colorado Plateau wildlife. Along the trail there are interpretive signs naming the animals and various native plants and explaining their presence and use in traditional Navajo life. You really get up close to the often playful animals, and the kids will love it here. The zoo is just a short walk across from the entrance to the museum.

Events

The population of Window Rock swells every year in early September as the **Navajo Nation Fair** (http://navajopeople.org, general admission $5-12) brings Navajos and others to one of the largest Native American cultural fairs anywhere. The weeklong event features a rodeo, horticulture contests, pageants for babies, teens, and Miss Navajo, a parade, a midway and carnival, native foods, arts and crafts, drumming, dancing, and myriad other events. Don't count on getting a hotel room in town, or even in nearby Gallup, New Mexico, unless you book far ahead of the fair.

Shopping

The headquarters of the **Navajo Arts and Crafts Enterprises** (928/871-4090, 9am-5pm Mon.-Fri.) and a well-stocked outlet are located east of the junction of Highway 264 and Indian Route 12, just across from the Quality Inn, as is the **Chi Hoo Tso Indian Market** (928/871-5443, hours vary by vendor), where there's a flea market on the weekends.

Food and Accommodations

The **Quality Inn Navajo Nation Capital** (48 W. Hwy. 264, 928/871-4108, $83-111) offers wireless Internet and a full breakfast. It has comfortable, clean rooms decorated in a generic Southwestern style, and the staff is very friendly and helpful. This is definitely the best place to stay in town. The **Diné Restaurant** (928/871-4108, $10-14) inside the Quality Inn serves American and Navajo food for breakfast, lunch, and dinner and is a popular spot with the locals. Guests of the inn may partake in the restaurant's breakfast buffet at no additional cost, but the price is its most attractive feature.

Some visitors choose to stay in nearby Gallup, New Mexico, about 27 miles to the southeast, which, as an I-40 stop, has loads of hotels and restaurants.

INFORMATION AND SERVICES

Contact the **Navajo Tourism Department** (P.O. Box 663, Window Rock, AZ 86515, 928/810-8501, www.discovernavajo.com) for advice and information about traveling in this region.

The **Navajo Area Indian Health Service** (Hwy. 264 & St. Michael Rd., St. Michael, 928/871-4811, www.ihs.gov) operates six hospitals on the vast Navajo Reservation. In Arizona, the **Fort Defiance Indian Hospital** (928/729-8000), eight miles north of Window Rock on the eastern reservation, has a Level 2, 24-hour emergency room; on the western reservation, the **Kayenta Health Center** (928/697-4000), in Kayenta, has the same.

Hopi Villages

When you visit Hopi, you step out of normal time into a kind of sacred time in which the Hisatsinom still speak to their modern-day descendants, the "People of Peace," and the lessons and stories of the ancients still guide and rule life in the 21st century, the dawning of which has mostly been ignored around Hopi.

The Hopi are a very religious, conservative people on the whole, and what many of them want, it seems, is to be left alone to mark their sacred time and grow their small plots of corn in their washes and valleys—which is a Hopi religious rite in itself. Signs are everywhere of Hopi pleading with visitors to show respect for the present in this land that seems so rooted in the past. Go to Hopi if you want to have a quiet, spiritual experience touring crumbling villages occupied for centuries, interacting with the friendly and creative people whose direct and well-remembered ancestors built and lived in most of the spectacular Pueblo ruins around Indian Country, and searching for artistic treasures built on patterns and narratives laid down before time began.

The Hopi do not allow any photography, sketching, or recording in the villages, and they don't like it when you enter their villages without first asking a village leader or at least someone at a crafts store or gallery. Talk to the folks at the **Hopi Cultural Center** on Second Mesa or the **Moenkopi Legacy Inn & Suites** in Moenkopi if you have any questions about the rules. Be respectful, and remember, as it is with the Navajos, the Hopi people are living their lives, not participating in an anthropological experiment. Don't bring any drugs or alcohol onto the reservation, and don't take any pottery shards off of it.

MOENKOPI

The **Moenkopi Legacy Inn & Suites** (junction of Hwy. 160 and Hwy. 264, Tuba City, 928/283-4500, www.experiencehopi.com,

$152) in the Upper Village of Moenkopi, at the junction of Highway 160 and Highway 264 near Tuba City, has become the gateway to visiting Hopi. The all-Hopi staff at this gorgeous hotel and visitors center can help you book a guide to take you on an unforgettable tour of the Hopi mesas. It makes sense, now that the Moenkopi Legacy Inn is open, to start any tour of Hopi from the west and head east along Highway 264, which will take you to each of the mesas.

HOPI MESAS

Many Hopi live on three remote mesas on the southern tip of **Black Mesa,** a separate reservation carved out of the southwest portion of the Navajo Nation. There are 10 villages on the mesas, which are numbered east to west.

You can drive yourself up and over the mesas, and enter many of the villages, but this is not an ideal, or even a very interesting way to visit Hopi. Without a bit of historical and cultural context, many of the mesa villages simply look like rundown rural outposts. But with a **guide,** a whole ancient, hidden world that exists beneath the rather hardscrabble surface opens up, and the mesas become sacred, mysterious ground.

About 15 miles from Moenkopi along Highway 264, look for milepost 336 and a dirt road that leads to **Coal Mine Canyon,** a spectacular gorge with magnificently eroded, multicolored hoodoos that's worth a few hundred snapshots from a sitting area near the rim.

Tours

It's essential to call ahead to book a tour. The Hopi religious calendar is rather full, and often one village or another will close to outsiders for days at a time. Weather on the remote mesas can also cancel tours. The best

1: Coal Mine Canyon 2: Moenkopi Legacy Inn & Suites

place to book a tour is through the **Moenkopi Legacy Inn & Suites** (junction of Hwy. 160 and Hwy. 264, Tuba City, 928/283-4500, www.experiencehopi.com) or the **Hopi Cultural Center** (928/734-2401, www. hopiculturalcenter.com, 8am-5pm daily) on Second Mesa. The Moenkopi Legacy Inn's website has a comprehensive list of approved guides and their prices.

Left-Handed Hunter Tour Company (Second Mesa, 928/734-2567, $120-195 pp for 4-8 hours) offers exceedingly informative and memorable tours of the Taawaki Petroglyph Site, Moenkopi, Old Oraibi, Hotevilla, Bacavi, Kykotsmovi, Sipaulovi, and Musangnuvi, as well as visits with local artists. The Moenkopi Hotel offers a highlight-filled **Experience Hopi Tour** ($145 pp, www.experiencehopi. com/tours), which includes a comprehensive exploration of the land, people, history and art of the Hopi, plus lunch at the Hopi Cultural Center. A guide picks you up at the hotel in the morning and brings you back in the late afternoon.

Third Mesa

The first of the mesa villages along Highway 264, and the first you reach on the road from Moenkopi, are **Hotevilla, Bacavi,** and **Kykotsmovi.** All are a mix of mostly ramshackle homes next to ancient, stacked-rock half-ruins hundreds of years old. The best place to stop on Third Mesa is **Oraibi,** also called Old Oraibi. Twenty-four families still live in the village, which sits at the edge of the mesa and looks out over the hazy flatland sea below. There's no electricity and no running water. "Our elders want no webbing above us and nothing buried in the ground," a Hopi woman who had been born and raised in the village explained. Some villagers have installed solar panels on the roofs of their small homes—each one built next to or on top of the ruin of an older one—to bring a little modern comfort. There are several kivas in the village that look exactly like those seen in the Hisatsinom ruins, with their rough ladders sticking out of their trapdoor entrances,

except these are still in use. A walk around this village, in which people have made lives since at least AD 1100, is a strangely humbling experience. You may come away from it wondering why most of us think we need so much stuff to live that elusive good life.

★ Second Mesa

The **Hopi Cultural Center** (928/734-2401, www.hopiculturalcenter.com, 8am-5pm daily) on Second Mesa has a small museum ($3) featuring blown-up photographs of Hopi taken in the 19th and early 20th centuries and displays on Hopi culture as well as many artifacts from around the mesas. It provides one of the few stops along the road through Hopi that can be enjoyed without a guide. The museum is an essential stop for anyone interested in Hopi culture. The center also has a restaurant serving traditional Hopi dishes and other food, and a small hotel. There are several interesting shops in the cultural center complex, including an excellent silversmith. The village of **Shongopavi** on Second Mesa is believed to have been the first Hopi village, and the village of **Sipaulovi** on Second Mesa offers walking tours and other information about visiting Hopi.

First Mesa

Polacca, just below First Mesa, is one of the younger villages on Hopi, founded in 1890. There are many Hopi and Tewa potters living in Polacca. If you're interested in buying direct from the artists, keep a lookout for handmade signs outside of homes. Next you'll come to **Hano,** founded in 1680 after the Pueblo Revolt by Tewas from New Mexico. The Hopi said the fleeing Tewas could stay in exchange for their vigilance in keeping enemies and attackers off the mesa trails. Hano is the home of the famous Tewa potter **Nampeyo;** in the early 1900s, Fred Harvey convinced Nampeyo to move to the Grand Canyon to demonstrate pottery making for tourists, creating a kind of living diorama at the famous Mary Colter-designed "Hopi House." The area is still a center of pottery making, and artists directly related to Nampeyo—who is credited, even as a Tewa, with beginning a renaissance in Hopi pottery and thus creating a major modern art form and economy—still reside and work here, selling pottery out of their homes.

Just above Hano is **Sichomovi,** founded in 1750 by citizens of **Walpi.** This village has running water and electricity, unlike Walpi, a traditional village at the very edge of the mesa founded in the 1600s when villagers moved up the mesa from their village below to escape the predations of their neighbors.

Walpi Guided Walking Tour

If you have time for just one tour, make it of Walpi, a traditional Hopi village where the old ways live on. You will also meet several Hopi artists on the tour of Walpi, sitting on the steps in front of their rock-carved homes, carving kachina dolls from cottonwood root. The people here are remarkably friendly—everybody says hello and smiles, welcoming visitors and inviting you into their homes to show you their art. If you are at all interested in Hopi art, this is the place to buy it. Not only will the price be significantly less than at a museum store or trading post, but you'll also get to meet the artist—and maybe even watch the final stages of creation. Take cash with you. Your Hopi tour guide will take you on a slow walk around the clifftop village, a time warp on the edge of the world. You'll learn all about the traditions and history, both temporal and spiritual, of this ancient place. It's a fascinating and memorable experience.

You should book a tour a day in advance if you can, and don't be surprised if the village is closed due to weather or for religious reasons. Tours run through **First Mesa Consolidated Village Office** (928/737-2670, 9am-3pm daily, last tour at 2pm daily winter, 8am-4:30pm daily summer, $20 adults, $10 children under 18), about 71 miles from Moenkopi in Polacca at the base of First Mesa, where you must stop and check in before heading up to Walpi. Take Highway 264 west to mile marker 390.8, turn north at the

stop sign, and go a quarter of a mile to the office, which is next to the post office.

Shopping

The Hopi are world renowned for their pottery, baskets, overlay jewelry, and kachina dolls. There are dozens of artists on the Hopi Reservation making and selling collectible, museum-quality crafts for much, much less than you are likely to pay in a museum store or trading post. Look for homemade signs advertising crafts for sale at homes in most villages, and take lots of cash with you.

In recent years many Hopi artists have banded together to form the **Hopi Arts Trail,** a marketing campaign that has made it easier than ever to meet and buy art from Hopi artists living on and below the mesas. A free pamphlet guide to the trail is available online at www.hopiartstrail.com or at the Moenkopi Inn. The guide features eight galleries spread out around Hopi in 12 villages along Highway 264 and lists the name, phone number, and specialty of 18 different Hopi artists. An artist will typically invite you into his or her home, where you can view the work and learn about the process.

Another great way to meet artists on Hopi is by taking the **Walpi Guided Walking Tour** on First Mesa.

PRACTICALITIES

There are few services on Hopi, but it isn't far from any of the Navajo towns, and it's close to the high-desert towns as well.

The **Moenkopi Legacy Inn & Suites** (junction of Hwy. 160 and Hwy. 264, Tuba City, 928/283-4500, www.experiencehopi.com, $152) set a new standard for accommodations on Hopi when it opened a few years ago. It has luxury rooms with big, comfortable beds, tastefully decorated with photographs of Hopi and featuring a patio door that opens to a heated, saltwater pool and spa. There is a small eating area where a continental breakfast is served in the morning, or there's a café at the gas station across the street (also operated by the Hopi) that serves diner-style fare and some Hopi dishes. Each room has free wireless and a flat-screen TV, and there are some excellent examples of Hopi arts throughout the beautiful lobby. This is the best hotel in Indian Country for the price.

The **Hopi Cultural Center on Second Mesa** is a hotel ($115-120 Mar.-Oct.) and restaurant (6am-9pm daily summer, 7am-8pm winter) that serves American and Hopi food for breakfast, lunch, and dinner. The **Hotevilla Village Co-Op Store** (928/734-2350) on Third Mesa has a convenience store with a gas station, and **The Kykotsmovi Village Store** (928/734-2456) on Third Mesa has a deli and a gas station.

The High Desert

HOLBROOK AND VICINITY

Long ago, by most accounts, Holbrook was a rough and violent cowboy town; then it profited, like everything else in this region, from the railroad and Route 66, back when tourists would necessarily stay a while. These days it's not much more than a convenient gateway and stopover for those visiting the nearby Petrified Forest National Park and Indian Country, offering several chain hotels and mostly fast food. For those interested in the history of both the old and the modern West, a trip to the **Navajo County Historical Society's Museum** (100 E. Arizona St., 928/524-6558 or 800/524-2459, 8am-4pm daily, free) in the 1880s Navajo County Court House is a must. Donations are encouraged and rewarded with free chips of petrified wood. It's a strange, crowded place without a lot of context—you feel like you're wandering around an abandoned government building after the population has died out. Sitting in the old jail, used until the 1970s and still decorated with the graffiti and sketches of its former inmates, is an eerie, thrilling experience.

Food and Accommodations

American popular architecture like that employed at the **Wigwam Motel** (811 W. Hopi Dr., Holbrook, 928/524-3048, www.galerie-kokopelli.com/wigwam, $69-76) had its postwar heyday along Route 66, and, like the route itself, it is mostly gone from the landscape these days in favor of cookie-cutter chains. But the kitschy tradition still has a hold on these dry high-desert plains at the Wigwam Motel in Holbrook, one of the last of many similarly designed motor courts that once lined the Mother Road. It's clean and comfortable, with all the updated amenities, but a stay here is mostly about its retro appeal. It should not be missed by Route 66 enthusiasts, road-trip scholars, chroniclers of fading Americana, and the like.

There are a number of chain hotels off I-40 in and around Holbrook, most of them located on Navajo Boulevard, the town's main drag.

★ PETRIFIED FOREST NATIONAL PARK

What once was a swampy forest frequented by ancient oversize reptiles is now **Petrified Forest National Park,** a blasted scrubland strewn with multicolored, quartz-wrapped logs some 225 million years old, each one possessing a smooth, multicolored splotch or swirl seemingly unique from the rest. You can walk among the logs on several easy, paved trails and view a small ruin and petroglyph-covered rocks (best with binoculars, but there are viewing scopes provided). Then, while driving through the pastel-hued badlands of the **Painted Desert,** which, seen from a promontory along the park's 28-mile scenic drive, will take your breath away, stop at the **Painted Desert Inn Museum.** The historical interest in this Pueblo Revival-style structure is more modern than primordial. Redesigned by Mary Colter, the great genius of

Southwestern style and elegance, the inn was a restaurant and store operated by the Fred Harvey Company just after World War II, and before that it was a rustic, out-of-the-way hotel and taproom built from petrified wood. There's a gift shop and bookstore at the inn now, and you can walk through it and gaze at the evocative, mysterious murals, full of Hopi mythology and symbolism, painted by Fred Kabotie, the great Hopi artist whom Colter commissioned to decorate the inn's walls. The park's proximity both to a major railroad stop at Winslow and to Route 66 have made it a popular Southwestern tourist attraction since the late 19th century, and the lore and style of that golden age of tourism pervades the park with a pleasant nostalgia, adding an extra, unexpected dimension to the overwhelming age all around you.

Visiting the Park

Approaching **Petrified Forest National Park** (928/524-6228, www.nps.gov/pefo, daily year-round, $20 per vehicle for 7 days) from the west, take I-40 to U.S. 180 from Holbrook to the south entrance, past numerous shops featuring all things petrified. A paved road leads 28 miles north through the park, past several points of interest, back to I-40. From the east take I-40 Exit 311 to the north entrance and then head south through the park. There are two **visitors centers,** one at the south entrance and one at the north, both showing a short movie about the park and passing out free maps of all the stops.

PARK ROAD DRIVING TOUR

It doesn't really matter which direction you enter the park from. To really see this understated masterpiece of a national park, you should drive the entire 28-mile route, stopping at the pullouts along the way, with time out for short hikes into the colorful badlands. Consider starting your tour at the south entrance and the **Rainbow Forest Museum,** which has some amazing fossils and displays about the dinosaurs that once ruled this land.

Take a stroll on the **Giant Logs Trail,** an easy, half-mile loop trail just outside the visitors center that features a few of the largest stone trees in the park. Also near the south visitors center, the **Long Logs Trail** is an easy, aptly named 1.6-mile loop. Up the road a bit is **Crystal Forest,** which has a paved, 0.75-mile loop trail among the petrified logs.

Strange, multicolored cliffs, worn and sculpted into fantastic shapes, are the main attraction of **Blue Mesa.** See it via a one-mile, fairly steep loop trail or a 3.5-mile loop road off the main road through the park. Farther south, the **Agate Bridge** pullout features a 110-foot-long bridge made of petrified logs. The **Newspaper Rock** petroglyphs and **Puerco Pueblo ruin** preserve the cultural leftovers of the people that once lived and thrived on this high-desert plain.

Cross over the usually dry Puerco River and the Santa Fe Railroad tracks, and watch out for the rusted husk of a **1932 Studebaker** sitting alone off the side of the road. This artifact marks the line that old Route 66 once took through the park, roughly visible now in the alignment of the power lines stretching west behind the car. Now you've entered the **Painted Desert** section of the park. The views are long, subtle, colorful, and barren. It is a wondrous, exotic landscape. Make sure to stop at the **Painted Desert Inn Museum,** where you'll see one of the most dramatic petroglyphs in the state—a large, stylized mountain lion etched into a slab of rock. There is free Wi-Fi available here and at the Painted Desert Visitor Center.

PRACTICALITIES

Both visitors centers have excellent gift shops, and rangers are always on hand to answer your questions. The only place to get a meal in the park is the south entrance's **Fred Harvey Company** restaurant, ★ **Painted Desert Diner** (928/524-3756, 8am-4pm daily, $5-10), which serves delicious fried chicken, Navajo tacos, burgers, and other road-food favorites in a cool Route 66 retro dining room. The south entrance visitors center has snacks for sale, but consider bringing your own food and

especially water, as the park is spread out and it is a 28-mile drive between visitors centers.

WINSLOW AND VICINITY

Stop at this small, ex-Route 66, ex-railroad town if you happen to be in the area. Much of its historic downtown remains intact, if not too busy, and there are a few off-track treasures to be found if you have time to walk around. The town seems committed to celebrating the fact that its name appeared in the song "Take It Easy," an Eagles hit co-penned by Jackson Browne. There are reminders in nearly every business, and there's even **Standin' on the Corner Park** along the town's main street, featuring a statue of a man doing just that. The primary reason to stop in Winslow is to see **La Posada**, Southwestern architect Mary Colter's masterpiece and a place where Fred Harvey-style outback elegance is kept alive.

Sights

The **Old Trails Museum** (212 Kinsley Ave., 928/289 5861, www.oldtrailsmuseum.org, 10am-4pm Tues.-Sat., free) in downtown Winslow is a treasure trove of strange and thrilling artifacts, photographs, and stories about life in the high desert, with a special emphasis on the region's Route 66 past and its connection with the stylish railroad era of the Fred Harvey Company. The museum also has a fine collection of Navajo arts and crafts, and all kinds of weird and forgotten items that take on new historical meaning and emotional color simply by virtue of being old and saved. It's a small museum but definitely worth a stop for anyone interested in Route 66, the railroad, and Fred Harvey, and a visit here should be paired with a look around the restored Harvey House, **La Posada.**

Food

The independently operated ★ **Turquoise**

1: Painted Desert in the Petrified Forest National Park 2: a 1932 Studebaker along old Route 66 in the Petrified Forest National Park

Room (303 E. 2nd St., 928/289-2888, www.theturquoiseroom.net, 7am-9pm daily, $21-34 for dinner, $8-18 breakfast), just off La Posada's main lobby, serves Southwestern- and Native American-inspired twists on prime rib, lamb, steak, pasta and fish dishes in an elegant space that riffs on the great Fred Harvey days. Chef John Sharpe does his best to find his largely organic ingredients semi-locally from central Arizona, the Valley of the Sun, and nearby New Mexico. In a nod to the Hopi people who live on the mesas just north of Winslow, Sharpe serves piki bread, a traditional Hopi staple, made by a Hopi baker from Second Mesa, along with a hummus prepared with tepary beans grown on the Hopi Reservation. This is the best restaurant in the region and one of the best in the state. Reservations are required for dinner.

Slowly but surely over the long years since the La Posada Hotel put this small town back on the map, Winslow's downtown has been crawling toward becoming a tourist draw, and it has made some mighty progress lately. These days there's even the obligatory brewpub just across the street from Standin' on the Corner Park. **RelicRoad Brewing Company** (107 W. 2nd Street, 928/224-0045, 11am-10:30pm daily, $8-15) brews terrific beers and serves mouthwatering burgers, salads, tacos, and other delicious brewpub staples. **Las Marias Mexican Food** (122 E. 2nd Street, 928/289-6496, $6-15) serves fantastic and authentic Mexican food in a casual downtown setting filled with locals.

Accommodations

There are several chain hotels and fast-food places off the interstate at Winslow for those in a hurry.

People travel to this lonely, ramshackle high-desert town just to stay at ★ **La Posada** (303 E. 2nd St., Winslow, 928/289-4366, www.laposada.org, $137-177) and eat at the **Turquoise Room,** so it's essential to call ahead for a reservation. Built in 1929 and obsessively restored by its current owners, the hacienda-style hotel is truly an Arizona

The Last of the Fred Harvey Railroad Hotels

Now owned by Allen Affeldt and his wife, the brilliant painter Tina Mion (whose paintings fill the arched hallways of the hotel), La Posada (303 E. 2nd St., Winslow, 928/289-4366, www.laposada.org, $129-169) has been beautifully restored and is a reminder of the days when Indian Country was a chic travel destination for the rich and famous.

La Posada

This was largely the result of the genius of Fred Harvey. He and his "Harvey Girls"—well-trained professional young women imported to the West to serve train passengers at Harvey's restaurants along the Santa Fe Railroad's right-of-way—made a trip to this barren, underdeveloped high desert an experience quite beyond merely comfortable. The Harvey Company lunch counters and hotel restaurants offered fine dining and fresh, gourmet food prepared by European chefs, along with the unmatched service of the Harvey Girls, many of whom ended up marrying their customers. Using the talents of Mary Colter, the Southwest's greatest designer and architect, Harvey built fine hotels in decidedly out-of-the-way places, allowing passengers on the Santa Fe's popular Los Angeles-to-Chicago line to live well even when stopping in Needles, California, and Winslow, Arizona.

Harvey also hired attractive, educated young women who knew their history, anthropology, ethnology, and art as tour guides. Intrepid tourists who could pay, in 1936, about $45 per person were packed into tough but comfortable limousines, along with gourmet box lunches, and driven in style deep into Indian Country. These trips were famously called "Indian Detours"—three days of adventure and exoticism billed, according to surviving marketing pamphlets, as "the most distinctive motor cruise service in the world . . . off the beaten path in the Great Southwest."

The crowning achievement of the Harvey-Colter partnership came just before the stock market crash with the construction of La Posada (The Resting Place) at Winslow, the headquarters of the Santa Fe Railroad and the gateway to Arizona's Indian Country. Howard Hughes, Frank Sinatra, Albert Einstein, Bob Hope, and the crown prince of Japan all stayed in Colter's masterpiece, along with many other luminaries of American and world culture. They'd hop off the train right outside the hotel, tour the Hopi Mesas and Navajoland, and then return to the Spanish hacienda-inspired hotel and enjoy supreme comfort in a land that knew little of that luxury.

Eventually train travel fell off, and Route 66 gave way to the interstate. Not long after that everything was the same, and the interstate became the province of chain hotels and those restroom machines that blow hot air on your hands. La Posada closed in the 1950s and sat disused until 1997, when Affeldt and Mion saved it. Now the old hotel has been restored beyond even its original glory, and it's booked up often with guests from all over the world. The hotel is especially popular these days with Europeans, many of whom rent motorcycles and ride the remainders of Route 66, searching for some lost version of the "America Road." Affeldt said recently that the irony of this phenomenon was not lost on a modern-day celebrity visitor to La Posada: the "Easy Rider" himself, Peter Fonda.

treasure. The rooms all have that rare touch of retro style, and each is named for some famous person who visited the hotel back in the golden age of train travel. But they also have up-to-date amenities, including deep tubs and heavenly beds. Never mind that there's still not much to see in Winslow; you could spend two full days exploring this hotel—walking its tiled and arched corridors; looking at co-owner and artist Tina Mion's gallery of strange and thrilling paintings; eating locally sourced, Fred Harvey-inspired meals at the Turquoise Room; sitting outside on the back platform watching the trains go by; or taking a long and peaceful stroll through the hotel's large and surprisingly lush grounds. Over the years the owners of La Posada have attempted not only to restore the gardens and grounds but to expand them based on original architect Mary Colter's vision of a desert-adapted oasis. The native dryland plant communities throughout the beautiful grounds create a sustainable explosion of green on this otherwise high and dry desert. Just one of the many reasons why it's hard to leave this special place.

Information and Services
The Winslow Visitor Center & Hubbell Trading Post (523 W. 2nd St., 928/289-2434, https://winslowarizona.org, 9am-5pm daily) has much useful information about traveling these high desert plains and driving the remains of the Mother Road. The visitor center is housed in a historic building that was once a Hubble Trading Post and the center of the world for the pioneers of these lonely grasslands.

METEOR CRATER
Meteor Crater (I-40 and Meteor Crater Rd., 928/289-4002, www.meteorcrater.com, 7am-7pm in summer, 8am-5pm the rest of the year, $18 adults, $16 seniors, $9 children 6-17), though impressive, is perhaps best viewed prior to a visit to, say, Canyon de Chelly or the Grand Canyon. Compared to those nearby attractions, built over eons by wind and water, this pockmark has trouble looking like more than the hole in the ground it is, isolated on the plain off I-40.

But the crater is an interesting hole nonetheless, being born from the collision of an asteroid with the high-desert grasslands about 50,000 years ago. A small museum examines this and other meteor sites and explores the role the crater and its owner played in the study of meteors and in the U.S. space program. There's a 10-minute film about the crater, and rangers offer short interpretive hikes but insist that you have closed-toe shoes to tag along. A Subway on-site sells sandwiches and drinks. Unlike most of the outdoor sights in Arizona, Meteor Crater is run by a private corporation. The $15 adult entrance price is, truthfully, a bit steep for what you get.

HOMOLOVI RUINS STATE PARK
Here in the grasslands south of the Hopi mesas, along the banks of the Little Colorado River, the ancient Hisatsinom settled for a time in the 1200s and 1300s before moving on northward to Black Mesa. A few crumbling rock aggregations and beds of shattered pottery, what remains of decades of looting, sit on dry promontories. It's a beautiful place, windy and desolate, but the ruins aren't as impressive as others nearby. This is a good place to start a trip to Indian Country and its ancient structures; afterward, it pales in comparison to what you've already seen. The **visitors center** (I-40 to U.S. 87 North at Winslow, 928/289-4106, http://azstateparks.com, 8am-5pm daily, $7 per car) has one of the best selections of books on Southwestern archaeology in the region and offers a chance to converse with Hopi artists. There are picnic tables and trails on the park, plus a 53-site campground ($25) with hookups and showers.

The White Mountains and the Gila Valley

The high pine forests of eastern Arizona's White Mountains have for generations been a cool summer getaway for the state's lowlanders and city dwellers.

It was in these still largely unbroken stands of evergreens, high on the Colorado Plateau, that the idea of wilderness for its own sake began in the United States with the great conservationist and writer Aldo Leopold. He arrived in Springerville in 1909, a young man just starting out in the newly created U.S. Forest Service. Still moved years later by these mountains, forests, and meadows, he would write of them in his 1949 classic *A Sand County Almanac*, one of the prime movers of a then-nascent campaign to preserve the West's wild places. Leopold predicted the fate of Arizona as a state and its slow, ongoing

Highlights

Look for ★ to find recommended sights, activities, dining, and lodging.

★ **White Mountain Trail System:** Hike, bike, or ride a horse through thick, cool green forests on this renowned series of trails (page 356).

★ **Apache Cultural Center and Museum:** Learn about the lifeways and history of the Western Apache (page 359).

★ **Sunrise Park Resort:** In the winter, slide down dozens of ski runs on three high, forested peaks. In the summer, do the same on a mountain bike (page 361).

★ **Casa Malpais Indian Ruins and Archaeological Park:** Explore a basalt-rock village built by the ancestors of the Hopi and the Zuni tribes (page 365).

★ **The Coronado Trail:** Drive 120 miles of twisting, two-lane switchbacks from the desert to the high pine forests (page 368).

★ **Gila Box Riparian National Conservation Area:** Hike beside the slow, lazy flow of the Gila River, watching wildlife hiding out in the cool shade (page 376).

departure from a mining, ranching, and logging economy when he wrote of the predator control agent who killed the last known grizzly bear in the state, around 1910: "He did not foresee that within two decades the cow country would become tourist country, and as such would have greater need of bears than of beefsteaks."

Now, just over a century since Leopold rode these forests on horseback, his observations still ring true. For the White Mountains are known today as a wilderness playground, a place where the real Old West—the Old West not of gunfights and cardsharps but of wilderness, solitude, and natural beauty—lives on. The region still lacks grizzlies, but the wolf has returned. On a dark, quiet night in these ancient forests, all snuggled up and safe in your rented-cabin bed, you might happen to hear a long-forgotten howl at the moon from deep in the rural darkness. Then you'll know why you came here, and you will never forget again.

PLANNING YOUR TIME

Unless you're a snow lover, the best time to visit the White Mountains is during the summer months, when the cool, green highlands offer respite from the desert heat. May-September you'll find gorgeous, temperate days and nippy nights in the high country, and you won't be alone. The campgrounds, cabins, and lakesides of the region are a big draw for campers, hikers, hunters, and anglers, so it's best to plan ahead. The snow starts falling (ideally) around December and can last until March or thereabouts. During these months skiers and snowboarders crowd the region, mostly on the weekends.

If you're coming from Phoenix or Tucson, a weekend is enough to see the glorious mountains and forests of the region. This is the perfect destination for a road trip—cruising slowly along twisty mountain roads, taking in the scenery, and keeping a sharp eye for wildlife.

The Gila Valley's charms are less obvious. It's hot in this desert river valley in the summer but cool and temperate in the fall and winter. The best way to see the Gila Valley is to drive through it on your way to the mountains along the Coronado Trail. It's a slow, winding route but one that won't be forgotten soon.

If you have more time—say, five days to a week—consider renting a cabin beside one of the high-country lakes or setting up a camp deep in the forest and sampling the White Mountains' many trails for hikers and mountain bikers. Or grab your kayak or canoe and float down the remaining wild sections of the Gila River. If you're interested in seeing the huge telescopes that scan the heavens from the heights of the Gila River Valley's Mount Graham, make sure you reserve a spot far in advance and plan to be in the region for at least one full day and night.

TRANSPORTATION

You really must have your own car to visit this out-of-the-way mountainous playground. Pinetop-Lakeside, the capital village of the White Mountains region, sits about 200 miles northeast of Phoenix, the capital city of Arizona, but it is a scenic 200 miles that stretches from the desert to the cool mountain pines. Plan on the drive taking at least 3.5 hours, longer on the weekends. Take U.S. 60 east to Mesa, pick up State Highway 87 north to the Mogollon Rim, and then head east on State Highway 260 to Show Low, which is right near Pinetop-Lakeside.

Previous: hiking in the White Mountains; Sunrise Park Resort; the Gila River.

The White Mountains and the Gila Valley

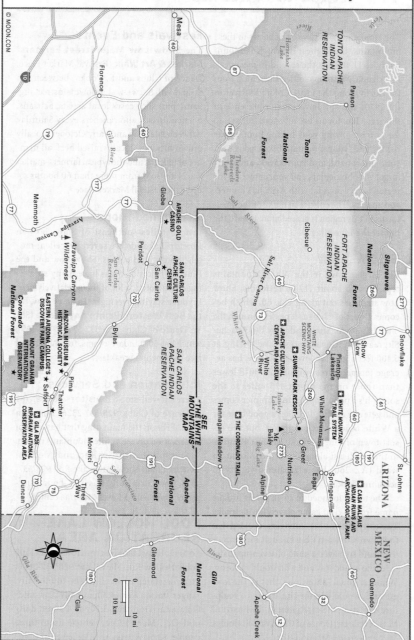

© MOON.COM

The White Mountains

The Hopi and Zuni have ancient ties to these mountains, the highest of which is Mount Baldy, at 11,409 feet the second-highest peak in Arizona. Mormons settled the region from the north along the Little Colorado River in the 1870s and still have a major presence in the area. The towns are all small but set up for tourists. Bring your hiking boots, your fishing rod, your mountain bikes, your skis, your snowboard, and your kayak, and don't forget your binoculars and your camera. This region is very popular with Arizona's hunters and anglers. The culture in many of the small towns in this region is geared more toward the hunter than the hiker.

SHOW LOW

The largest town in the White Mountains region, with about 11,000 residents, Show Low stretches out along U.S. 60, which becomes Deuce of Clubs as it passes through the one-strip town. Surrounded by the Apache-Sitgreaves National Forests and sitting at 6,400 feet above sea level, Show Low has average temperatures running 25-30°F lower than those on the desert 175 miles to the south. It's a popular place for summer homes and getaway cabins. It makes a good base for a White Mountains excursion, but the resort town of Pinetop-Lakeside just 10 miles to the southeast along the White Mountain Road (AZ 260) has a greater diversity of accommodations.

The town, founded in 1870, got its unique name from a card game played for its spoils. Two early settlers, the story goes, decided that the town site wasn't big enough for both of them and so played a hand of seven-up to decide who would stay and who would move on. Whoever could "show low," that is, the lowest card, would win the site. There's a sculpture depicting the card game at the Festival Marketplace (Deuce of Clubs and E. Cooley St., between 9th St. and 11th St.).

Festivals and Events

The **Show Low Main Street Farmers' Market & Art Walk** (Festival Market Place, Deuce of Clubs and E. Cooley, between 9th St. and 11th St., www.showlowmainstreet.org, 9am-1pm) showcases local artists, artisans, horticulturists, and ranchers every Saturday between late May and early October. Locally grown produce, locally raised beef, all manner of folk art, and the typical farmers-market wares are sold from more than 60 booths set up at the Festival Market Place.

Accommodations

Just 10 miles southeast of Show Low in Pinetop-Lakeside are several excellent motels, hotels, and cabins. Show Low and the Pinetop-Lakeside areas have many sprawling chain hotels, a lot of them relatively new. If you're staying overnight. In Show Low, try the **Best Western Paint Pony Lodge** (581 W. Deuce of Clubs, 928/537-5773, $116-129), which has 50 standard rooms, free Wi-Fi, and free continental breakfast.

Information and Services

There's a well-stocked **visitors center** (81 E. Deuce of Clubs, 928/537-2326, 9am-5pm Mon.-Fri.) on the main drag that has a lot of information on the White Mountains region.

Summit Healthcare Regional Medical Center (2200 Show Low Lake Rd., 928/537-4375, www.nrmc.org) has a 24-hour emergency room with a Level 4 trauma center.

FOOL HOLLOW LAKE RECREATION AREA

Fool Hollow Lake Recreation Area (1500 Fools Hollow Rd., Show Low, 928/537-3680, http://azstateparks.com, 5am-10pm daily, ranger station 8am-4:30pm daily Apr.-mid-Oct., 8am-11am and 3:30pm-4:30pm daily mid-Oct.-Mar., $7 per vehicle up to three people, $3 bicyclists), with its jewel-like blue

The White Mountains

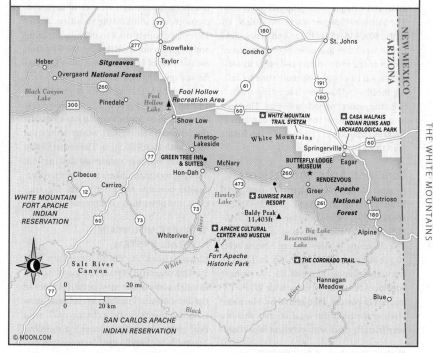

© MOON.COM

highland lake surrounded by tall pines, offers fishing, camping, picnicking, swimming, and hiking. A dam at the meeting of Show Low Creek and Fool Hollow Wash (named so because people said the original settlers were fools to attempt to farm here) created the 150-acre lake in 1957, and it has since become a popular spot for outdoor types, especially in the summer months. There's a 1.5-mile trail along the south and west sides of the lake that's worth a stroll. This is a family-oriented place with a playground and interpretive programs on natural history and wildlife. There always seem to be a lot of parents and kids fishing together for rainbow trout, large- and smallmouth bass, sunfish, catfish, and other species. Only nonmotorized boats are allowed. Canoe and kayak rentals are available at the **East Dock** (928/892-9170, 9am-5pm Mon.-Thurs.,

8am-6pm Fri.-Sat., 8am-4pm Sun., $20-25 per hour).

Camping

Fool Hollow is an ideal spot for **car camping** ($33-35, electricity available), as it's just a few miles from Show Low and only 15 miles from Pinetop-Lakeside and the area's best trails and restaurants. There are 31 tent sites tucked among the evergreens, with fire rings and picnic tables, and 92 RV spots for rigs up to 40 feet long. All the sites have water and are just a short walk from relatively clean restrooms and showers.

SNOWFLAKE

Founded in 1878 by Mormon pioneers sent south from Utah by Brigham Young to establish colonies throughout the arid west, this small roadside village 18 miles north of

Show Low on State Highway 77 is home to the Latter-day Saints' 108th temple (there are 133 total) and Arizona's only pulp and paper mill. The **Stinson Pioneer Museum** (102 N. 1st St. E., 928/536-4881, 10am-4pm Tues.-Sat., free) offers a free tour of some of the restored homes of the early settlers and other historic sites—you can book a specific time by calling ahead—and has some interesting artifacts from the pioneer period on display. The town is in the foothills of the White Mountains at 5,600 feet and enjoys a more moderate climate than those higher up.

Food and Accommodations

A stay at the **Heritage Inn Bed and Breakfast** (161 N. Main St., 928/536-3322 or 866/486-5947, www.heritage-inn.net, $110-140) is reason enough to stop in Snowflake. The charming pioneer-Victorian home rents 10 rooms, each decorated with antiques in frontier elegance. Three of the rooms have whirlpool tubs, and all come with Wi-Fi, TV, and DVD players. Frequented by Mormons visiting the beautiful local temple, this is a very friendly place with excellent breakfasts.

PINETOP-LAKESIDE

This small resort village marks the beginning of the **White Mountain Scenic Road,** otherwise known as State Highway 260. Pinetop-Lakeside, one incorporated community, stretches out along the highway at more than 7,000 feet, a high-forest getaway with just 4,000 year-round residents. When the snow melts, however, more than 35,000 call this place home, mostly on summer weekends. This is the White Mountain region's tourism capital, and there are quite a few distinctive shops and restaurants here. This burgeoning mountain village offers forest-and-meadow trails beside glimmering lakes, country comfort food, and adorable little antiques shops run by friendly senior citizens and big-city runaways.

Recreation

Surrounded by the Apache-Sitgreaves National Forests, Pinetop-Lakeside offers a pine needle-paved antidote to hikers and mountain bikers who are sick of saguaros, creosote, and unrelenting sunshine. About 180 miles of single-track trails and old mining and logging roads wind through the wrinkled, rocky forest of tall ponderosa pine, Douglas fir, and quaking aspen.

From the highland town's strip of hotels and resorts it's a scenic 30-mile drive east along Highway 260 to **Sunrise Park Resort,** the center of the region's winter recreation scene with its 65 ski runs. The resort is also a popular summer recreation destination, drawing mountain bikers to its steep, roller-coaster descents and offering fishing, trail rides, and other high-country pursuits.

★ WHITE MOUNTAIN TRAIL SYSTEM

Closer to town, the **White Mountain Trail System** organizes 19 trails into loops that run through some of the most beautiful areas of the forest around Pinetop-Lakeside and Show Low, and there's always a chance you'll see a deer or two bounding through a meadow. The trails are heavily used by mountain bikers, horseback riders, and hikers, especially in the summer. They can get muddy during the late-summer rainy season, turning a ride into a chore. The trails run from 1.5 miles to 14 miles, and several of them wind along babbling brooks with spongy green banks and up highland ridgeways overlooking the pine tops.

TRACKS (www.tracks-pinetop-lakeside. org), the heroic local group that organized the trail system in response to encroaching development on the forest, keeps a guide to the trails on their website. The **Lakeside Ranger District** (W. White Mountain Blvd., 928/368-5111, www.fs.usda.gov/asnf) sells a paperback guide to the trail system ($2) that has detailed directions on how to get to the trailheads, and the rangers are usually easy with the advice. **Cycle Mania** (100 N. White Mountain Rd., Show Low, 928/537-8812, http://cyclemaniaaz. com, 10am-6pm Tues.-Fri., 11am-3pm Sat.) has bike equipment, repairs, and rentals.

The small **Woodland Lake Park** (Pinetop-Lakeside Parks and Recreation, 928/368-6700, sunrise-10pm Apr.-Oct., sunrise-sunset Nov.-Mar., free) offers the best of the White Mountains in miniature, and it's an ideal place to hike around and get a deep impression of the forest if you don't have the time or inclination to mount a major expedition. The little reservoir attracts wildlife and anglers, and the trails are easy—especially the 1.25-mile **Lake Loop Trail**, a paved route around the lake that's perfect for families with young children. Hiking the two-mile **Hitching Post Loop Trail** is an excellent way to introduce yourself to the forest, and there's a side trail off the loop that leads to the marshy meadow of the **Big Springs Environmental Study Area.** The park has bathrooms, picnic tables, and charcoal grills. To get there, take Highway 260 south to Woodland Lake Road.

Festivals and Events

Over July 4-7 every year, artists and artisans congregate in Pinetop and sell their creations at the **4th of July Arts and Crafts Festival** (480/816-4165, www.highcountryartgallery. com). The long-running juried festival features more than 75 booths with unique arts and crafts, live music, and food from Charlie Clark's, a legendary local bar and grill. The artisans set up in The Orchard, a cool, grassy area behind the restaurant and saloon to which those who are averse to craft fairs can retire for a cool one.

In fall the quaking aspens turn red and yellow, flashing like flames from their evergreen surroundings. This inspiring time of year brings the **Pinetop-Lakeside Fall Artisans Festival** (Orchard at Charlie Clarks, 1701 E. White Mountain Blvd., 928/367-4290, www. pinetoplakesidechamber.com, late Sept.) to the Mountain Meadow Recreation Complex, with more than 150 artists and artisans selling their unique wares. The festival includes the **Run to the Pines Car Show** and antiques and quilt shows—all around a great weekend to be in Pinetop.

Shopping

There are a number of antiques stores, boutiques, gift shops, and galleries scattered along Highway 260 through Pinetop-Lakeside, one of the sure signs that you're in a resort community. As such, the scene here tends to be seasonal; if you're planning a visit in the dead of winter, you could find some places closed. Many stores are open only from April until October.

Stop at the **High Country Art Gallery and Gift Shop** (592 W. White Mountain Blvd., 928/367-3916, www. highcountryartgallery.com, 10am-5pm Tues.-Sun.) to check out paintings, jewelry, clothing, pottery, and other arts and crafts for sale by local artists. At **Harvest Moon Antiques** (392 W. White Mountain Blvd., 928/367-6973, 10am-5pm Tues.-Sat.), you'll find some of the best Native American and historic Old West pieces in the region.

The **Red Door Consignment Shops** (2701 N. Porter Mountain Rd., 928/368-2477, 10am-5pm Tues.-Sat.) has 6,000 square feet of resale furniture, antiques, clothes, jewelry, and all manner of treasures waiting to be found. There's also a coffee bar and hot dog stand inside.

The **Orchard Antiques** (1664 White Mountain Blvd., 928/368-6563, 10am-5pm Tues.-Sat.) is one of the oldest and best of the area's many antiques stores and has a fairly representative sampling of what you'll find in most of the area's shops: high-quality furniture, glass, knickknacks, art, and other staples, many with a Western influence.

If you're up for something truly unique, have the "master chainsaw artist" at **The Burly Bear** (1545 S. Adair, at White Mountain Blvd., 928/367-2327, www.theburlybear.com, Mon.-Sat., 10am-5pm) carve you a 15-foot-tall cuddly faced wooden bear or some one-of-a-kind furniture.

Food

More and more varied restaurants are opening in Pinetop-Lakeside all the time, it seems, and the area certainly has more food choices than any other White Mountains community. You'll find Italian food and pizza, Thai food, seafood, fast food, and just about any other style (within reason) that you're in the mood for as you drive slowly through the one-strip town spread out along Highway 260. The places listed below are the leading lights of this moderately bustling food scene—local favorites, many of which have been serving the townies and tourists alike for generations.

The oldest continually operating restaurant in the White Mountains, **Charlie Clark's Steakhouse** (Hwy. 260, 928/367-4900, www.charlieclarks.com, 11am-3pm and 5pm-10pm daily, $11-32) serves up some of the best steaks, barbecue beef, and prime rib in the area on a site that disguised a distillery during Prohibition. A casual Western-style place that's popular with tourists and locals alike, Charlie's has been open in one form or another since the late 1930s. Lunch is served daily in the saloon and enclosed log cabin patio, and there's a garden-style bar out back called **The Orchard.** For lunch they serve a full menu of sandwiches and salads, plus some really excellent fish tacos and other specials. Sitting in the saloon, you'll hear regulars and cowboys joshing each other; make sure to check out all the cartoon caricatures that line the walls depicting favored customers throughout the years.

Darbi's Café (235 E. White Mountain Blvd., 928/367-6556, http://darbiscafe.com, 6am-2pm Sun.-Tues., 6am-8pm Wed.-Sat., $7-16) is a favorite among locals for big American-style breakfasts and burgers, sandwiches, soups, and salads for lunch, all at a fair price. There's often a wait for breakfast, especially on the weekends.

El Rancho Restaurant (1523 E. White Mountain Blvd., 928/367-4557, www.elranchorestaurantpinetop.com, 11am-8:30pm Mon.-Sat., noon-8pm Sun., $8-20) serves reliably tasty and filling Mexican favorites like enchiladas, burritos, and fajitas, and has a fairly extensive selection of tequila and brain-freezing margaritas. This has been a favorite spot for locals since the early 1960s.

Accommodations

There are more than 40 hotels, motels, and country-cabin resorts in this tiny sylvan burg—so many that it seems like the whole town is for rent by the night. Rates fluctuate somewhat according to season, with the prices highest during summer months (roughly mid-May-Sept.) and the ski season (late Dec.-Mar.). It's a good idea to make reservations long in advance, especially for cabin rentals.

★ **GreenTree Inn & Suites** (431 E. White Mountain Blvd., 928/367-6077, www.greentreeinn.com, $113-135) is part of a small Southwestern chain of boutique hotels with a fairly extensive sustainability mission. The Pinetop property is sleek, fresh, and comfortable, with an indoor pool and hot tub, free Wi-Fi, and immaculate rooms with refrigerators and microwaves. You'll eat your free hot breakfast with compostable plates, cups, cutlery, and napkins, and the hotel's tailor-made recycling program goes through a local waste management company. Tasteful LED lighting illuminates the rooms and corridors, and you'll find only waste-reducing pump dispensers in the shower and at the sink.

The **Antlers Inn** (1023 E. White Mountain Blvd., 928/367-4146, www.antlersinnpinetop.com, $89-104) is a basic motor lodge-style hotel with affordable, clean, and comfortable rooms, offering free Wi-Fi, a fridge, TV, and microwave, and free breakfast. The little courtyard has minigolf and barbecue grills. This is a great place to base your hiking- or mountain-biking weekend.

At the **Moonridge Lodge** (596 W. White Mountain Blvd., 928/367-1906, www.moonridgelodge.com, $129-199) you can rent your own one-, two-, or three-bedroom cabin, a few of which also have lofts. The three-bedroom can hold groups or families of up to 12 people. The cabins have pinewood interiors, comfy old chairs and couches, and TVs; many have covered porches and picnic tables, and all are surrounded by the whispering forest and close to restaurants, shopping, and trailheads. This place is very pet-friendly, allowing dogs for no extra charge.

The Hidden Rest Resort (3448 White Mountain Blvd., 928/368-6336, www.hiddenrest.com, $89-129) rents 11 country-quaint and comfortable knotty-pine-paneled cabins on a forested property along Highway 260. Four of the cabins have in-room whirlpool tubs, and most will sleep up to four people. All the cabins have private bathrooms, a gas or a wood fireplace, and a stocked kitchen. Pets are allowed for a fee.

Information and Services

The **Pinetop-Lakeside Chamber of Commerce Visitor Center** (102-C W. White Mountain Blvd., 800/573-4031, www.pinetoplakesidechamber.com, 8:30am-4:30pm Mon.-Fri., 8:30am-2:30pm Sat.-Sun.) has all the information you will need on visiting this area.

WHITE MOUNTAIN APACHE INDIAN RESERVATION

The homeland of the White Mountain bands of the Western Apache, who call themselves the Ndee (the People), comprises some 2,600 square miles of tall pines and lush, green, flower-strewn meadows in and below the White Mountains. Established in the 1880s, the reservation is home to about 12,000 of the tribe's more than 15,000 members. There's not much to see save for beautiful high-elevation forests and a few scattered, often dilapidated homes and trailers, most of them with a corral and several perfectly posed horses peeking through the screen of pine trees along the highway. The tribe operates two of the region's top stops—**Hon-Dah Resort and Casino** and **Sunrise Park Resort**. The reservation is also home to **Salt River Canyon**, a 2,600-foot-deep wild mountain gorge, and the sacred 11,409-foot-high Mount Baldy, the second-highest mountain in Arizona. The reservation begins just south of Pinetop along Highway 260, and its capital is the tiny roadside village of **Whiteriver**, along State Highway 73 about 30 miles south of Pinetop.

★ Apache Cultural Center and Museum

The Western Apache preserve and interpret their history at the **Apache Cultural Center and Museum** (Indian Rte. 46, about five miles south of Whiteriver, 928/338-4625, www.fortapachearizona.org, 8am-5pm Mon.-Fri., 11am-3pm Sat. summer, 8am-5pm Mon.-Fri. winter, $5 adults, $3 children) in Whiteriver, part of **Fort Apache Historical Park** (7am-sunset daily).

Called **Nohwike' Bágowa** (the House of Our Footprints), the cultural center and museum has a fascinating collection of Apache artifacts and historic photographs and features revolving exhibits on Apache history and culture. Apache artists-in-residence show their work here, and a gift shop sells locally made baskets, beadwork, Crown Dancer figures, and books about the tribe. You'll come away from this small but well-managed museum with an introductory understanding of the tribe's hard-fought and often tragic history, especially if you spend some time perusing the exhibit "Ndee Bike'/Footprints of the Apache," which traces the tribe's epic journey from creation to the present day.

The surrounding 288-acre historical park is a National Register Historic District; a self-guided tour reveals something of what it was like to be a soldier at this far-flung mountain outpost of the Apache wars of the 1870s. The oldest building here is the 1871 log cabin called "General Crook's Cabin," where the exhibit **The Fort Apache Legacy** explains the history of the fort. There's even an old cemetery here, and a 1.4-mile loop trail through a small canyon that goes past an old scout camp. About four miles west of the park, the **Kinishba Ruins National Historic Landmark** preserves a small Pueblo ruin occupied until about 1400. Admission to the historic park includes the ruin. Apache tour guides are sometimes available to take you around if you call in advance.

Scenic Drive

Highway 73 through the reservation's

western section becomes the **Whiteriver Scenic Road** as it winds through the lumpy green landscape and hooks up with U.S. 60/ State Highway 77 South through **Salt River Canyon** toward Globe and the desert. This is the most scenic route out of the region, and a stop at the pullout about an hour south of Whiteriver provides a breathtaking view of Salt River Canyon. Make sure to gas up and fill up first, though. There are no gas stations until Globe after Whiteriver (almost 100 miles), where gas is expensive, and there's nothing much to eat past the casino. One of the more impressive roadside natural wonders in a state chock-full of them, the canyon was once used as a hideout by the Apache during the Indian wars. The 2,600-foot-deep jagged desert gorge is where the Salt River runs free and wild. There's a parking area before the bridge where you can learn about the canyon and take pictures, and easy paved trails lead down to the flowing river. If you've got four-wheel drive, you can head off on a riverside Jeep trail and explore the canyon in more depth. The traffic along Highway 77 near the canyon bridge can get heavy and frustrating, especially on the weekends. The canyon is about 40 miles north of Globe and about 60 miles from Whiteriver.

Events

Thousands head to the tiny town of Whiteriver in late August and early September for the **White Mountain Apache Fair and Rodeo** (S. Chief Ave. and Mint Rd., 928/338-4346, early Sept., $3-5) at the White Mountain Apache Rodeo Grounds, which started in 1925. Apaches of all ages compete in and watch bull riding, roping, barrel racing, and other rodeo events, and there's a fry bread-making competition, traditional dancing, food, and handmade local arts and crafts.

Recreation

Elk, deer, black bears, bobcats, wild turkeys, and a host of other beasts share these coniferous mountains with the Apaches, and hunters from all over the Southwest fill the region's campgrounds in all seasons. The same goes for anglers, for the reservation has 12 stocked lakes and some 800 miles of cold-water trout streams renowned for giving up various river monsters, including the Apache trout, Arizona's official state fish.

The tribe operates the Southwest's largest ski resort at Sunrise Park, where the temperate summer months find mountain bikers whipping down the runs and hikers and horseback riders taking a slower tack through the highland forests and meadows. The still and the patient have a reasonable chance of seeing a group of deer, heads lowered to graze in some flowery meadow, and maybe, if you're really lucky, a chubby black bear waddling toward the tree line. If you do see a bear, take your obvious good luck and your hard-earned money straight to the tribe's Hon-Dah Resort and Casino and see how the one-armed bandits and the blackjack tables react.

PERMITS

You must purchase a recreation permit (fishing $9 per day; camping $8 per day; boating $5; hiking, mountain biking, and sightseeing $15 per day; rafting $20 per day) from the tribe to do just about anything within the boundaries of the reservation. **White Mountain Apache Wildlife & Outdoor Recreation** (100 West Fatco Rd., 928/338-4385, www.wmatoutdoors.org) in Whiteriver controls outdoor recreation on the reservation and issues the permits; state fishing and hunting licenses hold no authority here. You can secure a permit online (www.wmatoutdoors.org) or at **Hon-Dah Ski and Outdoor Sport** (787 Hwy. 260, 928/369-7669, www.hon-dah.com, 7am-5pm daily), where you can also rent and buy equipment and get some local advice. The shop also organizes rafting and canyoneering trips deep into Salt River Canyon and other remote corners of the reservation. Hunters should contact the tribe's recreation department or check the website for detailed information on elk, deer, small game, and predator hunt permits. The tribe offers guided hunts, but you can also go out on your own.

Permits are available throughout the region, including at **Pinetop Sporting Goods** (747 E. White Mountain Blvd., 928/367-5050, 8am-5pm Tues.-Fri., 8am-noon Sat.) and **Sportsman's Warehouse** (4421 S. White Mountain, Show Low, 928/537-0800, 9am-8pm Mon.-Thurs., 9am-9pm Fri.-Sat., 10am-6pm Sun.).

★ Sunrise Park Resort

Like drunken migratory birds, skiers and snowboarders from the desert flock north to the White Mountains every winter to slide down the 65 high-mountain (10,700-11,100 ft.) ski runs scratched into Sunrise, Cyclone, and Apache Peaks. **Sunrise Park Resort** (Hwy. 273, four miles south of Hwy. 260, 30 miles east of Pinetop, 928/735-7669, http://sunriseskiparkaz.com), which is usually at least ankle deep in snow by January, has a separate **Terrain Park** for snowboarding, with a half-pipe, wood and metal rails, and jumps. The trails, the longest of which is the 1.2-mile "Sidewinder" from 10,700-foot Sunrise Peak, are somewhat diverse, with about 20 percent strictly for the expert skier. There are a fair number of runs for beginners and a few just for kids, and there are cross-country trails through the high pine forests for those strange folks who prefer a cardio workout to a whooshing rush. The park has 10 ski lifts running up the peaks (tickets $23-49). If you are willing to throw yourself down a mountain but lack the necessary equipment, there are rentals available at the Sunrise Park Lodge, or you can go to the folks at **Hon-Dah Ski and Outdoor Sport** (787 Hwy. 260, 928/369-7669, www.hon-dah.com/sos.html) at the casino for your gear.

The lifts creak to life Thursday-Monday Memorial Day-Labor Day. A slow, cool-breeze ride up one of the three peaks, high above the green-carpeted land on a summer's day, is a romantic and relaxing way to spend an hour or so (10am-4pm Sat.-Sun., $19). Also on summer weekends, the park welcomes **mountain bikers** for about the most fun you can have on two wheels. Sunrise is one of the few places in Arizona where the obvious benefits of going down can be had without a lot of heart-pounding ground work: Bikers can attach their rides to the **lift chairs** (10am-4pm Sat.-Sun., $36.50 for an all-day pass) for an easy ride up the peaks and a high-speed roller-coaster ride down.

Summer also finds anglers vying for a spot along the shore of **Sunrise Lake,** the state's largest cold-water lake, stocked with big fat trout and other species and the only lake on the reservation that allows gas-powered motorboats (10 hp or less). The park's **Snowy Mountain Stables** (928/205-760, $22-180, half hour-all day) offer horseback rides through the cool forests and meadows during the summer months.

Hon-Dah Resort and Casino

On a rainy day in the White Mountains **Hon-Dah Resort and Casino** (junction of Hwy. 260 and Hwy. 73, 928/369-0299, www.hon-dah.com) can seem a bit dour, with dead-eyed RV gypsies and chain-smoking octogenarians watching emotionless as a bleeping and blinking machine takes their retirement money. At other times it seems a bit brighter, but it rains quite a bit here. Hon-Dah, which means "welcome" in the Apache language, has a good restaurant (with a casino-style buffet Thurs.-Sun.), a store and gas station, an RV park, and a lodge with clean, basic rooms, but in truth it offers little for those not drawn to games of chance. It's relatively clean and features the usual slot machines, poker, and blackjack. Middling Las Vegas-style music acts, many of them with a country-western bent, play to the dance floor at the **Timbers Lounge and Showroom** Tuesday-Saturday.

Food and Accommodations

Hunters and anglers, the reservation's primary block of annual visitors, prefer to rough it in fishing cabins, tent camps, and RVs. For a comprehensive list of the reservation's **camping** options, reach out to the tribe's

recreation department (928/338-4385, www.wmatoutdoors.org). Camping permits cost $8 per day, and most sites on the reservation are first come, first served. Ice fishing is somewhat popular on reservation lakes in the winter, but not all the campgrounds are open and accessible during the snowy months.

The **Hawley Lake Recreation Area** (928/369-1753) rents out rustic but reasonably comfortable cabins along the shores of the reservation's highest lake. At 8,200 feet the 300-acre mountain lake is stocked with trout and a popular spot for serious solitary anglers and families alike. The tribe rents 20 cabins that sleep from 2 to 14 people ($125-300) as well as a few two-person motel rooms ($65). There's also a large campground around the lake and an RV park. There are no phones, TVs, or microwaves in the cabins, but they are fully furnished with dishes, pans, utensils, coffeemakers, and toasters. There's a small store and gas station on-site, but it's best to come prepared with food and drinks just in case. To reach Hawley Lake from Pinetop-Lakeside, take Highway 260 through McNary to State Highway 473, then turn right on State Highway 473/Hawley Lake Road. From there it's about nine miles to the lake.

Hon-Dah Resort and Casino (junction of Hwy. 73 and Hwy. 260, www.hon-dah.com, $109-199) offers standard, clean, and comfortable rooms with free wireless Internet, room service, and a swimming pool. Check the website for special ski and fishing packages. The rooms, though nothing special, are a half-notch above the region's decidedly midrange knotty-pine rental cabins, and the **Indian Pine Restaurant** (928/369-0299, 6am-10pm daily, $7-20) puts out a decent weekday Vegas-style buffet ($7-14 Sun.-Thurs.), as well as has crab legs, shrimp, and other fruits of the far-off sea on Fridays; succulent prime rib on Saturdays; and champagne brunch on Sundays. The Indian Pine serves a fair plate of

eggs, potatoes, and bacon for breakfast, as well as omelets and other staples, and sandwiches, pizzas, calzones, salads, and, of course, Indian fry bread for lunch. At dinner, the menu features tasty pizzas and calzones, prime rib, burgers, and ribs.

The tribe's **Sunrise Park Lodge** (928/735-7669 or 800/772-7669, www.sunriseskipark.com, $89-250 Mon.-Fri. winter, $124-295 Sat.-Sun. winter) at the base of the three-peaked skiscape has basic, clean rooms. Some of the more pricey rooms have whirlpool tubs. Though the accommodations are underwhelming and in need of a remodel, the mountains, forests, and ski runs at Sunrise Park are not, so you're probably not going to spend too much time in your room. There's nothing like rolling out of bed onto the slopes. Otherwise you waste precious downhill time driving 30 icy-road miles from Pinetop. The lodge has two decent restaurants.

GREER

Turn south off Highway 260 onto Highway 273 to reach the little village of **Greer** (www.greerarizona.com), a log-cabin hamlet nestled in the forest and green meadows around 7,000-9,000 feet, below the peaks of the White Mountains, through which flows the Little Colorado River. The area is outlandishly beautiful and picturesque. It could just as well be snuggled in the Alps, and the babbling forks of the river support a lush riparian belt with overgrowing greenery and flat, narrow trails along the moss-covered waterway. In spring and summer, Greer is perfect for hiking, horseback riding, and lying around in highland meadows, surrounded by colorful wildflowers. In winter the snow comes, and Greer makes a good base for trips to the ski hills and for cross-country expeditions into the forest.

Sights

While the forests and meadows tend to push everything else of interest off the radar, the strange and quaint **Butterfly Lodge Museum** (Hwy. 373 and County Rd. 1126, 928/735-7514, http://butterflylodgemuseum.

1: Whiteriver Scenic Road through Salt River Canyon **2:** the White Mountains near Greer **3:** Rendezvous in Greer org, 10am-5pm Thurs.-Sun. Memorial Day weekend-Labor Day weekend, $2 adults, $1 youth 12-17, children under 12 free) is worth a look if you're in Greer during the summer. The little log house was once the hunting lodge of James Willard Schultz, an early-20th-century writer of adventure stories about the West for magazines, known primarily for his 1907 book *My Life as an Indian*. The home was later used as a studio by Schultz's equally interesting son, Hart Merriam Schultz, or Lone Wolf, a famous Indian painter and artist. The home is set up with all kinds of artifacts and everyday items that show what life was like in this remote green mountain valley years ago. There are several of Lone Wolf's paintings on display, and a gift shop selling the elder Schultz's nostalgic writings.

On a guided tour of the **Little House Museum** (928/333-2286, www.xdiamondranch.com, $15) and the **Little Bear Archaeological Site**, you'll get an entertaining course on the whole long history of human habitation in the White Mountains region, from the proto-Pueblo inhabitants to the tough pioneers, ranchers, and cattle rustlers. The museum, a cluster of restored pioneer-style buildings filled with all kinds of strange and wonderful Old West and pioneer-era furniture, household items, and collectibles, is on the grounds of the **X Diamond Ranch** and is only accessible with a reservation. The museum tour includes a jaunt out to the Little Bear site, where the rubble of several dwellings dates back to AD 500. A tour of the museum is $8 without the ruins.

Recreation

The best hiking in Greer is along the forks of the Little Colorado River. Pick up several trailheads where Main Street enters the National Forest on the south end of Greer. Head south until the end of the main road and follow the well-worn footpaths along the river. In some places the ground is so spongy and overgrown with greenery that it seems like you're in a rainforest. But walking is so lowland. Here,

not 20 miles from where John Wayne himself raised prize Hereford cattle on the 26 Bar Ranch, consider letting a mountain-bred horse take you deep into the pines.

The **X Diamond Ranch** (928/333-2286, www.xdiamondranch.com, $30-155) offers guided rides ranging from one hour to all day, and they'll on occasion let a greenhorn do some ranch work à la *City Slickers*. The historic ranch, started by White Mountain pioneers John and Molly Butler in the early 1900s, also operates a catch-and-release fly fishery on the Little Colorado ($40 pp half day, $50 full day).

Food and Accommodations

There are several lodges in Greer and a host of cabins for rent, whether for the night or the season. For a complete list check out the official town website (www.greerarizona.com).

The historic **Molly Butler Restaurant and Bar** (109 Main St., 928/735-7226 or 866/288-3167, www.mollybutlerlodge.com) is a fantastic, beloved restaurant that's been serving hearty mountain food since 1910. It's open for dinner nightly (5pm-9pm daily, $13-30), serving excellent fish, steaks, chili, prime rib, and more. The restaurant is also open for lunch 11am-2:30pm Monday-Saturday and brunch 10am-2pm on Sundays. Reservations are a good idea.

Also make reservations for a memorable lunch at ★ **Rendezvous** (117 Main St., 928/735-7483, 8am-3pm Wed.-Mon., $9-15), which is often crowded, especially on summer weekends—you'll know you've arrived when you see all the cars parked along the street. This small restaurant serves some of the best food in the White Mountains, offering a creative array of sandwiches, burgers, and salads, as well as a popular Friday fish fry and famous green bean "fries." Sit on the cool and shady patio or inside the small, historic home with its quirky country style.

The **X Diamond Ranch** (928/333-2286, www.xdiamondranch.com, $125-175 Apr.-Oct., $110-160 Nov.-Mar.), where Molly Butler once lived and raised cattle in the early

1900s, rents out seven comfortable and scenically placed cabins along the Little Colorado River. Each cabin is a unique structure surrounded by the outlandish grandeur of the area. All sleep up to four people and can accommodate eight, and they all have kitchens and fireplaces.

SPRINGERVILLE-EAGAR

The Round Valley opens up at the base of the mountains near the junction of U.S. 191 and 60; nestled there at about 7,000 feet are the sister villages of Springerville and Eagar. The ancestors of the nearby Zuni and Hopi found this Little Colorado River valley to their liking in the 1250s, and Basque settlers arrived in 1870 and gave the area its moniker, *Valle Redondo*. By 1879 ranchers and farmers from New Mexico and Utah had trickled in to homestead and raise cattle and crops to supply nearby Fort Apache. A dramatic reminder of the frontier beginnings of these rural Arizona towns is the **Madonna of the Trails** statue, dedicated in 1928 and located on Main Street in Springerville across the street from the post office. John Wayne was famously a partial owner of the 26 Bar Ranch in Eagar, where the Duke and his partners raised high-quality Herefords in the 1960s and 1970s. The Hopi purchased the ranch in the late 1990s in a campaign to reclaim their ancestral lands in the Little Colorado River region.

A short drive north of Springerville on Highway 191/180 leads to the vast and lonely **Springerville Volcanic Field.** Covering some 1,200 square miles of basaltic badlands, the field, whose activity dates from more than 3 million to just about 13,000 years ago, has 405 vents, some of which look like giant anthills rising out of the sweeping plains strewn with black rocks. A pamphlet-guide for a driving tour of the volcanic field, the third largest in North America, is available at the **Springerville-Eagar Regional Chamber of Commerce** (7 W. Main St., 928/333-2123, www.springerville-eagarchamber.com, 9am-5pm daily).

★ **Casa Malpais Indian Ruins and Archaeological Park**

The volcanic badlands around Springerville and Eagar were once home to several stone-built villages occupied by the ancestors of New Mexico's Zuni and Arizona's Hopi people. The upper Little Colorado River region was occupied on and off from at least AD 900 until about 1400, with the largest villages constructed from about 1275 to 1400. The remains of one of these basalt outposts overlooking the river are preserved by the city of Springerville at **Casa Malpais Indian Ruins and Archaeological Park** (418 E. Main St., 928/333-5375, www.casamalpais.org, tours 9am and 1pm Tues.-Sat. Mar.-Nov. weather permitting, $10, advance reservations required). The "house of badlands" had about 50 rooms, a square kiva (a structure used for rituals), and an accurate solar calendar. It was constructed in the late 1270s and early 1280s and occupied for about 50 years. Archaeologists believe that most of its residents had left the area by about 1400 and settled at Zuni, about 140 miles to the northeast, while some moved to the Hopi villages, about 180 miles to the northwest. When Coronado came through the area in 1540 searching for the Seven Cities of Cibola, he found no permanent residents in the valley. Today both the Zuni and the Hopi consider the Little Colorado River region to be an integral part of their historic homelands. The tour is a fascinating and memorable way to learn more about the early settlers of this beautiful, harsh land, and the museum preserves some of the artifacts that they left behind. The tour lasts about two hours and requires walking up a steep and rocky trail.

Recreation

A popular site for fishing, boating, and camping, the **Big Lake Recreation Area** is open May-November and has several campgrounds around the 400-acre **Big Lake** and nearby **Crescent Lake,** about 19 miles southwest of Eagar off Highway 261. At 9,000 feet, the highlands here can get cold, even in the

The Wolves of the White Mountains

"We reached the old wolf in time to watch the fierce green fire dying in her eyes," wrote renowned conservationist and author Aldo Leopold in his classic *A Sand County Almanac*. Leopold, a founding hero of the wilderness movement in America, did his first tour of duty as a U.S. Forest Ranger in the White Mountains in 1909, back when the only good wolf in Arizona was a dead wolf.

"I was young then, and full of trigger itch," Leopold continued. "I thought that because fewer wolves mean more deer, that no wolves would mean hunters' paradise. But after seeing that green fire die, I sensed that neither the wolf nor the mountain agreed with such a view."

Though ahead of his time in the early 20th century, Leopold's hard-learned lesson—that a healthy ecosystem needs predators as well as prey to remain so—is today an accepted scientific fact (though there are still a few rural ranchers who would disagree). And the wolves, gone from these mountains and forests since the 1970s, have returned.

In 1998, several Mexican gray wolves were reintroduced into the White Mountains region in the Blue Range Wolf Recovery Area, near Hannagan Meadow along the Coronado Trail, and in a nearby New Mexico wilderness. According to the U.S. Fish and Wildlife Service, as of the end of 2007, there were 12 known wolf packs in the reintroduction area, 6 in Arizona and 6 in New Mexico—about 32 total wolves—plus 4 known single wolves in New Mexico. And the most exciting news is that "approximately 75 percent of the radio-collared individuals and 90 percent of all documented wolves (in the recovery area) were born in the wild."

summer. Still, it's one of the most popular fishing and camping areas in the region and is often crowded with families during the summer months. **Big Lake Tackle and Supply** (at the junction of U.S. 191 and 180, Alpine, 928/339-4338, www.biglakeaz.com) has all the bait, tackle, and other supplies you'll need for a day fishing on Big Lake. They also rent four- and five-person rowboats, motorboats, and kayaks ($16-43 per hour).

Serious hikers should not miss a trek up Arizona's second-highest mountain, 11,409-foot **Mount Baldy.** The high peak is sacred to the Apaches, and the actual tip-top of Mount Baldy is closed to the public. You can, however, make it to within a quarter mile or so of the peak, which most agree is good enough once they see the sweeping views from the near-top. There are a couple of routes up the mountain, but the most scenic is the 13.5-mile round-trip **West Fork Trail,** which follows the Little Colorado River for several miles through thick old-growth forests and high green meadows. The grade is mostly moderate, though you climb more 2,000 feet from the bottom to the top, which is above the tree line and rocky and

cold, with short and gnarled subalpine trees and a blasting wind. To reach the trailhead, drive 3.1 miles west on Highway 260 from Eagar, then south on Highway 261 for 18.2 miles to Highway 273. Then head 7.2 miles northwest on Highway 273, cross the river, and drive 1 mile to Mount Baldy Wilderness Trailhead. From Pinetop-Lakeside, take Highway 260 26 miles east to Highway 273 (toward Sunrise Ski Resort), turn right on Highway 273, and head south for about 11 miles.

Shopping

At the retro-rural **Western Drug & General Store** (106 E. Main St., 928/333-4321, www. westerndrugstore.com, 9am-7pm Mon.-Fri., 9am-6pm Sat., 9am-5pm Sun.) on Springerville's main drag you can buy a deer rifle, pick up a bag of chips and a soda, and fill a prescription. Even if you need none of these things, this 1934 precursor to Walmart is worth a stop, if only to wonder at the bagged-and-stuffed menagerie featuring a mountain lion, an elk, a bighorn sheep, and other Arizona wildlife frozen in midgrandeur by some loving taxidermist.

Food and Accommodations

Booga Red's Restaurant and Cantina (521 E. Main St., 6am-9pm daily, cantina 10am-11pm daily, $6-11) has been family owned since the 1970s and serves delicious, familiar Mexican and American fare from passed-down recipes. This place is a favorite with locals.

Goob's Pizza (211 S. Mountain Ave., 928/333-1502, www.goobspizzas.com, 11am-8pm Tues.-Wed., 11am-9pm Thurs.-Sat., $13-28) serves top-notch pizza, wings, and breadsticks, and has a salad bar. It's located in the Safeway Shopping Plaza in Springville and is a great place to fill up after a day of hiking or playing in the snow. Along with mouthwatering specialty pizzas and create-your-own options, Goob's offers a small pizza with gluten-free dough.

There are a few small motels along the main route through Springerville and Eagar. You could do worse for a base, as the Round Valley is just 23 miles east of Sunrise Park, 17 miles from Greer, and is situated at the junction of U.S. 60 and 191. **Reed's Lodge** (514 E. Main St., 928/333-4323, www.k5reeds.com, $50-120) has been welcoming travelers since 1949, and, reportedly, the Duke played cards here on occasion back when he owned the nearby 26 Bar Ranch. You probably won't see any celebrities these days, but there's a gallery featuring work by local artists and lots of Old West memorabilia, collectibles, and books. There's a big fireplace in the lobby, the rooms have free wireless, microwaves, and refrigerators, and outside there's a hot tub in which to soak your road-weary bones.

CAMPING

There are five campgrounds in the **Big Lake Recreation Area** (www.fs.usda.gov/asnf), which offer hundreds of sites for everything from monster RVs to pup tents and can be reserved at www.recreation.gov. **Apache Trout Campground** ($26 per vehicle per night, $42 with hookup) has full hookups and can handle big RVs, while **Rainbow Campground** ($20-22 per vehicle per night) and **Grayling Campground** ($20 per vehicle per night) can hold small RVs and cars but don't have hookups. The campgrounds offer bathrooms and showers a short walk from your site, and there's a store nearby in case you forgot some supplies. **Brookchar Campground** ($16 per vehicle per night), with 12 sites right on the water, is for tent camping only, as is **Cutthroat Campground** ($16 per vehicle per night).

At most of the campgrounds on Big Lake you can rent an old-school white canvas tent cabin, just like the ones homesteaders in the area used while they built their cabins, complete with cots, lanterns, and a stove, all for $55 per night (Springerville Ranger Station, 928/333-6200, www.fs.usda.gov).

Services

The **White Mountain Regional Medical Center** (118 S. Mountain Ave., 928/333-4368, www.wmrmc.com) in Springerville has a 24-hour emergency room.

LYMAN LAKE STATE PARK

North of Springerville-Eagar along U.S. 191/180, the landscape flattens out and opens wide as the crumpled mountains begin to give way to high desert. About 11 miles south of the small town of St. Johns, 1,500-acre **Lyman Lake,** a reservoir formed by the damming of the Little Colorado River, is stocked with bass and catfish and is one of the only lakes in the region with no boat restrictions. The lake is the centerpiece of the large **Lyman Lake State Park** (928/337-4441, http://azstateparks.com, $7 per vehicle) where you can camp lakeside in a small log cabin ($55 per night) with electricity and air-conditioning. There are also regular campsites and RV spots available ($28-33, electric, water, and sewer hookups available).

At a mere 6,000 feet above sea level, Lyman Lake State Park has a more temperate climate than the mountain towns, and it gets relatively hot here in the summer. The **visitors center** (8am-5pm daily May-Sept., 9am-4pm daily

Oct.-Apr.) has lots of information and a few displays about the prehistory of the area and its natural history. A small store in the park sells ice, snacks, and fuel, but you should bring all your food with you.

There are also a number of ancient, mysterious petroglyphs etched into boulders throughout the park, some of which can be seen on the quarter-mile self-guided **Peninsula Petroglyph Trail** near the campground. You'll need a boat to reach the spectacular **Ultimate Petroglyph Trail,** a half-mile trail on the lake's eastern shore, but it's worth the trip over to see the rocks covered with those cryptic figures.

Apache County Historical Museum

Woolly mammoth tusks, frontier fashions, pioneer-era farming equipment and household items, rock slabs covered in petroglyphs, refurbished historic log cabins, and all manner of other artifacts and ephemera from prehistory to the near present are preserved at the **Apache County Historical Museum** (180 W. Cleveland St., St. Johns, 928/337-4737, 8am-4pm Mon.-Fri., free). It's worth a stop to learn about the people's history of northeastern Arizona—from proto-Pueblos to Mormon homesteaders and beyond. St. Johns has just 3,000 residents, but it has an outsize historical presence in the state because it's the hometown of the Arizona Udall clan, Mormon Democrats who produced two national politicians: congressman (1961-1991) and presidential candidate (1976) Mo Udall and secretary of the interior (1961-1969) Stewart Udall.

★ THE CORONADO TRAIL

When Francisco Vazquez de Coronado spurred his prancing mount north from Compostela, Mexico, in 1540, he had reason to believe that the vast unknown northern lands into which he would lead his crowded retinue held riches and glory quite beyond those even of Mexico itself. A few years later he returned, after having traversed what is now the great American Southwest, with nothing but saddle sores and a secure place in the history of North American exploration and conquest.

Nobody knows for sure the exact route that the Coronado expedition took on its way north in search of the sadly nonexistent Seven Cities of Cibola, but scholars believe that he passed through, or at least nearby, the White Mountains, perhaps following the San Francisco River drainage along what is now the border between Arizona and New Mexico. And they aren't just guessing: Ranching families, homesteaders, and other longtime residents of the region have been digging up and tripping over left-behind and discarded items from the Spanish colonial era for generations.

So it is not wholly unreasonable, as you slowly negotiate the switchbacks and hairpins along the twisty two-lane U.S. 191 from the desert grasslands to the high pinelands, to feel a certain connection to the hard-bitten Spanish explorer. And the 120-mile route from the copper mines of Clifton to the U.S. 60 junction near Springerville, which takes 3-5 hours to complete, is often as deserted as it must have been when there was no road at all, the haunt of more wildflowers than vehicles.

Along the way you'll pass the tiny settlements of **Alpine, Nutrioso,** and **Hannagan Meadow,** and to the east, between Clifton and Hannagan Meadow, is the vast **Blue Range Primitive Area,** a coniferous wildland cut through by the Blue River. The scenery is really the attraction here; it's best to take it slow, stopping often at the lookouts and pullouts set up along the route, marveling at the deep green meadows splashed with yellow, red, and purple in the spring and summer. With so much beauty it's hard to keep your eyes on the road, so be careful, and look out for motorcycles; the route is understandably quite popular with that growing tribe.

Don't take this route if you're in a hurry to hit the lakes or the slopes (indeed, don't take it

1: Big Lake in the White Mountains 2: Blue Range Primitive Area along the Coronado Trail

in winter at all), if you are an impatient driver, or if you're susceptible to car sickness.

Recreation

Most of the Coronado Trail is surrounded by the **Apache-Sitgreaves National Forests.** As you drive along Highway 191 you'll see a number of trailhead signs on both sides of the road. The helpful folks at the **Alpine Ranger Station** (42634 Hwy. 191, Alpine, 928/339-5000, www.fs.usda.gov/asnf) give away a handy 66-page guide to the hiking, mountain biking, and equestrian trails along the Coronado Trail and environs that has detailed descriptions of nearly 20 different trails and information on the area's many lakes.

The best hike in this section of the White Mountains, and one that serious hikers should not miss, is the **Escudilla National Recreation Trail** to the top of **Escudilla Mountain,** a storied regional landmark and the state's third-highest peak. The six-mile round-trip hike takes you through aspen groves and deep stands of fir and spruce, through wide green mountain meadows, and into the Escudilla Wilderness Area (no bikes allowed here). The hike is relatively easy, especially compared to the monumental trek up Mount Baldy, Escudilla's big-sister peak to the west. When you reach the top, at about 10,900 feet above sea level, you'll see the **Escudilla Lookout,** a fire lookout that offers an even higher view of the green land spreading out below. To reach the trailhead, take Highway 191 north from Alpine for 5.5 miles to Forest Road 8056, then turn right and drive 3.6 miles to Terry Flat. Take the left fork past Toolbox Draw about a half mile to the trailhead.

Just three miles east of Alpine on Highway 180, the 154-acre **Luna Lake** is stocked with trout and a popular camping, fishing, hiking, and biking spot. A few loop trails around the lake, which attracts bald eagles and other exotic wildlife to its shores, offer easy hiking and biking for families with children.

If you're dead set on seeing some of the region's abundant but typically shy wildlife, the best place to do so is at the **Sipe White Mountain Wildlife Area** (928/367-4281, www.azgfd.com, visitors center 8am-5pm daily mid-May-mid-Oct.). Two miles south of Eagar off the Coronado Trail, this 1,362-acre former Hereford ranch has been converted by the Arizona Game and Fish Department into a prime wildlife-viewing area with several easy trails and developed lookouts. Bring your binoculars to spot elk, deer, bald eagles, hawks, wild turkeys, and other wildlife. This is another ideal place to bring the kids, as the trails are relatively flat, easy, and short, and everybody knows that kids love animals. The visitors center, which is open only in the summer months, has displays about the area's natural history. It's all free, and you can bring your horse or your bike along if you want, but the best way to see wildlife is to sit still and quiet, waiting.

Food and Accommodations

Most of the services along the Coronado Trail are in the tiny mountain village of **Alpine,** about 94 miles north of the scenic byway's beginnings in Clifton. If you're headed up the trail from the desert, there isn't much in the way of food or even gas between Clifton and Alpine, a drive that could conceivably take three hours. But once you reach the tiny highland settlement, at 8,050 feet and near the headwaters of the San Francisco River, there are several excellent restaurants to choose from for a leisurely lunch or dinner after a long day of driving and forest play. Alpine, which is just six miles or so west of the New Mexico border, has a few rustic rural hideaways, and there are dozens of cabins for rent throughout the area. Some of the restaurant owners in Alpine also rent cabins, and the **Alpine Area Chamber of Commerce** (928/339-4330, www.alpinearizona.com) has information about rentals on its website. Many of the businesses in Alpine have seasonal hours and are often closed in the deep winter.

About four miles north of Alpine off Highway 191, the **Tal-Wi-Wi Lodge & Saloon** (40 County Rd. 2220, just off Hwy.

191, 928/339-4319, www.talwiwilodge.com, $80) has nice rooms with blond knotty-pine interiors and some with whirlpool tubs next to the bed. There's free Wi-Fi in all the rooms. Tal-Wi-Wi is popular with car and motorcycle clubs traveling the trail. The staff is friendly and helpful, and the convivial **Tal-Wi-Wi Restaurant and Saloon** (11am-8pm Tues.-Wed., 11am-9pm Thurs., 11am-10pm Fri., 7am-10pm Sat., 7am-8pm Sun., $10-23) is a good spot for a rib-sticking meal and a few drinks.

Foxfire at Alpine (42661 Hwy. 180, 928/339-4344, http://foxfireatalpineaz.com, 4pm-8pm Mon.-Thurs., 11am-8pm Fri.-Sun., $9-15) serves delicious burgers, sandwiches, salads, soups, pasta, and pizza, all with a homemade touch and care for details. It's a pleasant and cozy little place close to the junction of Highway 180 and the Coronado Trail

at Alpine. They offer vegetarian, vegan, and gluten-free dishes.

Hannagan Meadow Lodge (Hwy. 191 near mile marker 232, 22 miles south of Alpine, 928/339-4370, www.hannaganmeadow.com, $85-130) is a historic, cozy forest getaway with a backcountry atmosphere and antique country-style decor. It's been open since 1926 and sits right off the trail about 22 miles south of Alpine, lost to the mad world down below. The rates change according to the season by about $5-10 per night, lowest in winter (early Nov.-Apr.) and fall (mid-Aug.-early Nov.), slightly higher in spring (May-early June), and highest in summer (early June-mid-Aug.). The lodge rents seven suites named for figures from Arizona history, and there are cabins named for luminaries of local history. The lodge's country-comfort dining room is open 8am-8pm daily.

The Gila Valley

There are only about 40,000 people living in the Gila Valley (pronounced "Hee-la"), a meeting ground of the Sonoran and Chihuahuan Deserts near Arizona's border with New Mexico. Tiny towns, many of them moribund long ago, stand dusty and forgotten along the Old West Highway (Hwy. 70). Former Supreme Court justice Sandra Day O'Connor grew up near Duncan, the last station before New Mexico, on the Lazy B Ranch. The whole lonely region is watched over by the largest of Southern Arizona's sky islands, Mount Graham, where telescopes scour the heavens for signs and wonders. Hot springs bubble up from beneath the hot sand, and the Gila River, a once mighty Southwestern river now dammed to oblivion and sucked mostly dry, still runs year-round here in a few lush, riparian oases.

SAFFORD AND VICINITY
Safford, a rural town with about 8,000 inhabitants near the Gila River, has been a farming,

mining, and ranching area since the 1870s. Cotton is still grown in this hot desert valley, and a mighty chunk of the nation's copper is ripped from the ground just to the northeast. While Safford still has a quaint downtown strip, an old courthouse building, and some residential neighborhoods with historic bungalows, most of the town is a jumble of chain stores, restaurants, hotels, and strip malls strung out along U.S. 70 between the New Mexico border (about 45 miles east) and the San Carlos Apache Reservation (about 60 miles west). Safford is the bright light of the upper Gila Valley, to which all the outliers, holding tight to something in the nearly empty old communities of Pima and Thatcher to the west and Solomon, Duncan, and Clifton-Morenci to the east, look toward for company and supplies. As such, it makes a good base for your Gila Valley adventures.

Sights
Not even the dust kicked up by all that

uninterrupted open-pit mining less than 50 miles to the northeast can spoil the clear and dark rural skies here, and the 10,720-foot sky island peak that hems the valley to the southwest, Mount Graham, holds a few of the world's most powerful telescopes. **Eastern Arizona College's Discovery Park Campus** (1651 W. Discovery Park Blvd., Safford, 928/428-6260, www.eac.edu/discoverypark, 8am-5pm Mon.-Fri., 4pm-9:30pm Sat., free) celebrates and explains the area's astronomical benefits, the science of astronomy, the beginnings of life, and the mysteries of the universe at its **Gov Aker Observatory.** It costs nothing to take a look at the sun through a telescope equipped with eye-saving filters, or to listen to the eerie sounds of space. The highlight of a visit is a ride on the **Space Shuttle Polaris** simulator, in which you tour the solar system after buzzing Mount Graham. This is a great place to take kids. The grounds have several trails along which the public can stroll at will during business hours; the campus shows off the desert at its best, with a restored riparian area alive with birds and, if you are patient, maybe a few other animals. You can also book an all-day tour of the Mount Graham International Observatory here.

For a more down-to-earth, human-centric view of the valley, visit the **Eastern Arizona Museum and Historical Society** (2 N. Main St., Pima, 928/485-9400, www.easternarizonamuseum.com, 10am-3pm Thurs.-Sat.), which preserves relics and stories from the valley's long history of habitation, from hunter-gatherer tribes to the Apaches, Mormon pioneers to cotton farmers and cattle ranchers.

An even deeper look at the valley's history is offered on the **Graham County Historic Walking and Driving Tour,** a self-guided tour of Highway 70 through Solomon, Safford, Thatcher, and Pima. Along the way you'll see just about every old building of note in the tiny old towns as well as Safford's 1916 neocolonial courthouse and several historic homes. The **Graham County Chamber of Commerce**

(1111 Thatcher Blvd., Safford, 928/428-2511 or 888/837-1841, www.visitgrahamcounty.com, 9am-5pm Mon.-Fri.) has a free 11-page booklet describing the tour, along with a plethora of other information about the area.

Festivals and Events

The whole valley celebrates its Mexican restaurants and heritage with **SalsaFest** (www.salsatrail.com) in late September, during which local chefs compete in salsa-making competitions, eaters try to outdo one another in a jalapeño-eating contest, children bounce around in castles, and bands play to crowds stuffed with food and fun.

Food

The Gila Valley has some of the finest Mexican food restaurants in Arizona, most of them small, casual family-owned spots along Highway 70 and frequented by locals. Some valley restaurants have grouped together to form **The Salsa Trail,** a marketing campaign to draw visitors and diners to this lonely region. One can hardly imagine a more worthy public service. Uniformly first-rate, the Trail's member eateries serve up fresh and familiar Mexican fare with local and familial twists, and many of them offer American dishes as well. There is really no reason to eat anywhere else, and that's a good thing because the non-Mexican choices in Safford are for the most part chains and fast food. A brochure and map of the Salsa Trail are available at the **Graham County Chamber of Commerce** (1111 Thatcher Blvd., Safford, 928/428-2511 or 888/837-1841, www.visitgrahamcounty.com, 5am-9pm Mon.-Fri.) or at any of the eateries listed below.

In Safford's retro and quiet old downtown, **El Coronado** (409 W. Main St., Safford, 928/428-7755, 7am-8pm Mon. and Wed.-Fri., 7am-5pm Sat.-Sun., $7-15) has superlative breakfasts: big fat burritos stuffed with egg, potato, cheese, and peppers, legendary

1: downtown Safford **2:** the Old Safford Bridge in Gila Box Riparian National Conservation Area

huevos rancheros, or a simple plate of eggs and bacon if you're not into early morning spice. The Mexican dishes here are delicious and, of course, filling.

For tortillas that might convince you to buy a trailer in Safford, just to be nearby, visit the famed **Mi Casa Tortilla Factory** (621 S. 7th Ave., Safford, 928/428-7915, www. micasatortilla.com, 8am-5:30pm Mon.-Fri., $5-10). Fresh and hot, simple and handmade, the tortillas you get here are known far and wide. Buy a few dozen to chomp on in the car as you head out to the river or up to Mount Graham.

Valley locals love **El Charro** (601 W. Main St., Safford, 928/428-4134, www.elcharrogrill. com, 11am-8:30pm Mon.-Thurs., 11am-9:30pm Fri.-Sat., $7-15) in downtown Safford because they've been open, and serving pretty much the same food, since 1955. It's the oldest restaurant in the region. Their enchiladas, red- and green-chili burritos, and other standard dishes are tasty and fresh, and their special chalaca, a fried masa bowl stuffed with beans and chili meat, is worth a try if you're in the mood for something slightly different.

To the east along Highway 70 a few miles, the family-owned and operated **La Paloma** (5185 Clifton St., Solomon, 928/428-2094, 10:30am-8pm Mon.-Thurs., 10:30am-9pm Fri.-Sat., $7-16) has superior Mexican food, cold and delicious margaritas, and friendly service in a laid-back atmosphere.

Accommodations

The **Cottage Bed & Breakfast** (1104 S. Central Ave., Safford, 928/428-5118 or 800/814-5118, www.cottagebedandbreakfast. com, $90) in Safford has the most distinctive and drive-worthy accommodations in town. This very small bed-and-breakfast, in a red-brick Western Colonial Revival home on the National Register of Historic Places, has a pleasant kind of Old West ambience. A wonderful bakery on-site serves homemade bread and pastries, espresso, and tea.

But nothing beats Duncan's **Simpson Hotel** (116 Main St., Duncan, 928/359-3590, www.simpsonhotel.com, $75-105), about 40 miles east of Safford on Highway 70, for that rural-West atmosphere. The owner has beautifully restored an old hotel first opened in 1915 and decorated its small, cozy rooms (including one named for writer Cormac McCarthy) with a tasteful country simplicity. Plus, the breakfasts are worth waking up for, made as they are with all-natural and often local ingredients.

The **Essence of Tranquility Natural Hot Spring** (6047 S. Lebanon Loop, Safford, 928/428-9312, www.azhotmineralspring. com), in the shadow of 10,720-foot-high Mount Graham, offers private, clothing-optional hot spring baths in which you can soak away all your stress and troubles. The baths are charmingly decorated and private; a bigger communal bath requires clothing. Though a bit on the rustic side, Essence of Tranquility is a wonderful place to visit if you love hot springs and want to meet like-minded soakers. If you want to stay the night or longer at the baths, you can camp for $15 per night, which includes use of a communal kitchen and barbecue area and unlimited use of the tubs. Rustic but comfortable casitas are also available for $50-70 per night. You can make a reservation for ear coning (an alternative-medicine method of cleaning and detoxifying the ears), shiatsu, and Swedish massage, or a detoxifying sweat wrap. If you're just going for the day, expect to pay $8-10 per person for use of the baths. While most of the baths are clothing optional, the owners don't allow any "open nudity." They also discourage bringing children along.

Services

The **Mount Graham Regional Medical Center** (1600 S. 20th Ave., Safford, 928/348-4000, www.mtgraham.org) in Safford has a full-service, 24-hour emergency room with 17 treatment bays.

ROPER LAKE STATE PARK

Desert-valley **Roper Lake State Park** (101 E. Roper Lake Rd., Safford, 928/428-6760, http://azstateparks.com, $10 per car) has decent fishing in a 30-acre reservoir and rents small but comfortable (more so than a tent, anyway) log cabins that sleep up to six people ($65-70, reservations required). The lake is stocked with trout and bass, and there are clean shower facilities and both electric ($30) and nonelectric ($20) campsites.

But Roper Lake is also a fun spot to stop for a day of swimming from its sandy swimming beach and soaking in its stone-lined hot tub filled by underground hot springs. There are about five miles of mostly flat, easy desert trails around the park, including a nearly two-mile loop trail at nearby **Dankworth Pond** (a unit of the park three miles south on Hwy. 191) that winds around a re-created village from the Paleo-Indian and Mogollon periods.

HOT WELL DUNES RECREATION AREA

Another developed hot spring bubbles up deep in the desert about 35 miles southeast of Safford in the middle of 2,000 acres of shifting sand dunes at **Hot Well Dunes Recreation Area.** This is a stark and hot landscape popular with off-road vehicle enthusiasts, who crowd the dunes in fall, winter, and spring to tear around on their sandrails and ATVs. The recreation area is often quite busy for being so remote, and if you're just looking to soak in the three developed, fenced-in tubs fed by a warm artesian well, it's not a good idea to go out on the weekends during the beautiful months. During summer it's blistering hot out here and not too welcoming. There's no electricity, drinking water, food, gas, or phones, so bring all your own supplies. There are several developed camping spots with fire rings and picnic tables, or you can camp in undeveloped spots. There are toilets on-site. If you're planning to rip around the dunes, you need an OHV decal ($25); regardless, a recreation use fee of $3 per day is required. From Safford,

head seven miles east on Highway 70, then turn south on Haekel Road, from which it's 25 miles to the recreation area.

Despite the distance to and isolation of the dunes, if you're a natural hot spring enthusiast, you should make the effort. The artesian well, discovered in 1928 by workers drilling for oil (you can still see the ancient drilling equipment nearby), spews out more than 250 gallons of 106-degree water every minute. It fills two developed tubs and overflows into a pond to make a cooler third pool.

For more information contact the **Safford BLM office** (711 14th Ave., 928/348-4400, www.blm.gov/az). You can purchase an OHV decal at www.servicearizona.com.

PINALENO MOUNTAINS AND MOUNT GRAHAM

The largest of Southern Arizona's sky islands, the Pinaleno range guards the upper Gila Valley from the west, an often-snowcapped Olympus for the lowlanders in the desert scrub below to ponder and worship. The range has seven peaks, all of them over 7,000 feet but none as high as 10,720-foot Mount Graham, which residents here often use to refer to the entire range, its influence over the valley below being that strong.

Mount Graham, atop which astronomers scan the universe with some of the most powerful telescopes in the world, can be reached by just about any vehicle via the Civilian Conservation Corps-constructed **Swift Trail Parkway.** The steep, twisting two-lane road rises from the scrubby desert floor at just under 3,000 feet, to more than 9,000 feet near the top of Mount Graham, and along the way it passes through most of the state's major ecosystems, finally reaching the high evergreen forest, where the air is cool and thin. The road (State Hwy. 366, off Hwy. 191 about 8 miles south of Safford) is 35 miles one-way, a trip that typically takes about two hours. You'll twist past old summer cabins, trailheads, campgrounds, lookouts, and picnic tables, and it's essential to stop along the way and take your time, noticing as the scrub gives way to oak woodlands, which give way to tall and thin pines, which pass on to majestic stands of fir and spruce. Snow usually closes the Swift Trail by November 14; it opens for the driving season on April 15. Most passenger cars can make it; 21.85 miles of the route are paved, and 13.35 miles are graded dirt. At the end of the trail you'll see **Riggs Lake**, a small highland fishing hole stocked with trout. The **Safford Ranger Station** (711 14th Ave., Ste. D, Safford, 928/428-4150, 8am-4pm Mon.-Fri.) has a lot of information on traveling, hiking, and camping in the mountains, including a booklet on driving the Swift Trail. The folks at the **Columbine Visitor Information Station,** about three-quarters of the way toward the end of the road, are also helpful.

Operated by the University of Arizona in Tucson, the **Mount Graham International Observatory** sits near the top of Mount Graham, its powerful telescopes pointed at the heavens. Indeed, the **Vatican Advanced Technology Telescope** may be literally aimed heavenward. Also scanning the galaxy and beyond are the **Heinrich Hert Submillimeter Radio Telescope** and the **Large Binocular Telescope,** humankind's strongest eye on the great unknown. **Eastern Arizona College's Discovery Park Campus** (1651 W. Discovery Park Blvd., Safford, 928/428-6260, https://mgio. arizona.edu/visiting-public) organizes infrequent tours of the observatory complex on Fridays and Saturdays, May-October, when the mountain weather cooperates. The tour, in groups of six or more, lasts all day (9am-4:30pm, $40 pp, no children under 8) and includes a sack lunch and a fair bit of the natural and human history of the area as well as an in-depth look at the observatory. You ride in a van along the Swift Trail to the top, and the guide points out all the interesting sights along the way. The tour begins in Safford at Discovery Park. It's a good idea to call far ahead to make a reservation.

★ GILA BOX RIPARIAN NATIONAL CONSERVATION AREA

You can't visit the Gila Valley without at least a glimpse at the sad river that drew, in turn, Apaches, trappers, and Mormon farmers to this area long ago. The Gila was once a mighty desertland river, but Phoenix's thirst, along with the irrigation needs of the valley's farmers, has dammed and sucked the Gila to death. In a few places it still runs wild and free through wilderness that isn't too different from that seen by the natives and pioneers. One of those places is the BLM-monitored **Gila Box Riparian National Conservation Area** (BLM Safford Field Office, 711 14th Ave., 928/348-4400, www.blm.gov/az), a 23,000-acre nature preserve off U.S. 70 just 20 miles northeast of Safford.

A popular spot for kayakers and other river runners, the Gila Box offers streamside hiking, cool riparian coves, and a chance to see a few bighorn sheep clinging to rocky cliffs. Cottonwood stands, mesquite bosks, and sandbars line the mud-brown flow, hemmed by high, beige cliffs. The best way to see the river and possibly some wildlife is to take Sanchez Road off Highway 70, about five miles east of Safford (you'll see signs) to the **Spring Canyon Picnic Area** (it's about nine miles from the turnoff; along the way you'll pass an entrance kiosk). From there you can walk along the river on the two-mile-loop **Cottonwood Trail** through the **Riverview Campground** and past the **Kearny Monument,** a tribute to General Stephen Watts Kearny, who led 300 soldiers along the Gila, camping nearby at Bonita Creek, to California during the Mexican-American War. Then it's on to the **Bonita Creek Watchable Wildlife Area,** which has interpretive signs about the area's animals. You can also drive all through the area on dirt roads, and there are two developed campgrounds ($5 per day). If you're a floater, make sure to check

1: Pinaleno Mountains **2:** a mining tractor at Morenci Mine

out the website for more information. There's a $3 per day recreation fee.

A rugged and scenic alternative route to the river is the **Black Hills Back Country Byway,** a 21-mile bumpy dirt road that passes over the river at the **Old Safford Bridge,** a historic concrete bridge built in 1918. You don't reach the river until 17 miles in, but along the way the dry scrublands provide some sweeping, lonely views, including of the postapocalyptic Morenci Mine. There's a picnic area and campground with a bathroom below the bridge, and this is also a popular place for boaters to put in. The byway ends just outside of Morenci on Highway 191 and makes a good scenic detour.

CLIFTON AND MORENCI

These two small towns along U.S. 191, bisected by the lazy San Francisco River and marking the start of the Coronado Trail into the White Mountains, were founded in the late 1800s as a copper mining complex, and they remain so today: Freeport-McMoran's Morenci Mine is the nation's largest, producing around 800 million pounds of the useful metal every year. There's a turnout about five miles north of town from which to view the monumental hole in the ground that is the result.

Clifton, with only about 2,000 residents, is full of boarded-up old buildings from the late 19th and early 20th centuries. Drive around slowly and wonder at the fix-up potential of these grand old structures. There's a small local-history museum and some really cool old buildings in the old downtown and several across the bridge on the east side of the river. The town's old jail, chunked out of the cliffside, is still visible along the highway, and on the east side of the bridge there's a huge old digger that helped open up the pit. Up the hill a few miles in **Morenci,** the modern mineworks moan all day and night; about two-thirds of the approximately 4,500 residents of the two towns work for the mine. Driving up or down the twisting road through Morenci at night, while the

lit-up mine works on, is an unsettling—and thrilling—experience.

Sights

You can see for yourself the toll paid for cell phones and computers, both of which use a lot of copper, on a tour of the huge **Morenci Mine** (4521 U.S. Hwy. 191, Morenci). During the tour (call 877/646-8687), which lasts about 2.5 hours, you'll ride around the dusty mine site in a bus as a tour guide explains the mining process and peppers you with staggering statistics. Reservations are required, and the tours are only offered Friday-Saturday at 9am and 1pm.

SAN CARLOS APACHE RESERVATION

Before 1871, the Western Apache bands that call this 1.8-million-acre reservation along the Gila River northwest of Safford home used to live and migrate across the valley's desert grasslands, creeksides, and oak woodlands, hunting game and gathering the land's many edibles. These days the San Carlos Apache Tribe welcomes visitors to recreate on their sparsely populated lands, and they operate a casino-resort complex with a golf course. To hike, fish, swim, and drive the backcountry here you need to purchase a permit from **San Carlos Apache Tribe Recreation & Wildlife Department** (Hwy. 70 and Geronimo Rd., San Carlos, 928/475-2343 or 888/475-2344, www.scatrecreation.org, $10 per day). Permits are also sold at the Apache Gold Casino's convenience store and at the Express Stop in Globe.

The **San Carlos Apache Culture Center** (Hwy. 70, milepost 272, 928/475-2894, www.sancarlosapache.com, 9am-5pm Mon.-Fri.) has interesting displays about the tribe's history and culture. Here you can also see and purchase examples of the locally made peridot jewelry. The world's largest deposit of the August birthstone is located near the reservation capital of **San Carlos,** and there are a few places in the small town that sell jewelry, Apache burden baskets, cradle

The Western Apache and the Settlers

All over Southern and Central Arizona, where the Western Apache once wandered unchallenged according to a seasonal schedule held deep in their cultural memories, there is food: acorns, agave, wild spinach, wild onions, mesquite beans, cactus fruit, and more—all integral to the once-diverse Apache larder.

Once settlers—Spanish then Mexican then American—began claiming this land as their own, the Western Apache found it increasingly difficult to gain unfettered access to their traditional gathering grounds, and they drew the unending ire of the new arrivals when they stole livestock, which many Apache saw as little different from hunting any other ungulate grazing in the desert.

Really, the Western Apache never had much of a chance. Their lifeways were about thin-line subsistence, living lightly so as to conserve the relative abundance of the desert for future generations. The capitalist settlers couldn't have been more different; they wanted wealth, surplus, and the power that comes with it. Furthermore, settlers never really got the fact that not all Apaches were the same. The Western Apache, one of the few agricultural-minded bands in Apacheria, were often blamed for the depredations of the less sedentary Chiricahua Apache, who claimed Geronimo as one of their leaders.

Thus we have the general circumstances, building over generations, that led to the Camp Grant Massacre in 1871, an infamous slaughter of more than a hundred Western Apache, mostly women and children, who were peacefully camped close to a U.S. Army fort near Aravaipa Canyon (south of San Carlos Lake on the San Carlos Apache Reservation).

The outrage was planned and perpetrated by the leading lights of Tucson's business community and justified by the half-mad screeds of *Tucson Citizen* editor John Wasson. In the aftermath of the largely unprovoked massacre, Tucson's murderous elite didn't even bother to attempt to name the victims for the laughable trial that saw all the perpetrators acquitted; instead, they listed them as John Doe Apache or Mary Doe Apache—names that reveal just how unknown the Western Apache were to their new neighbors.

boards, and other local arts and crafts. The culture center has a good gift shop selling all of these items and more, as does the Apache Gold Casino.

Apache Gold Casino

Apache Gold (5 miles east of Globe on Hwy. 70, 800/272-2438, www.apache-gold-casino.com) is the center of activity on the reservation, offering the usual Indian casino-style slots, blackjack, poker, bingo, and live entertainment. The **Apache Stronghold Golf Course** is lovely and affordable, and the resort's rooms ($109-179) and restaurants offer the best accommodations and meals on the reservation. The resort has a gift shop that sells local Apache crafts, and **Wickiup Buffet** ($6-18) lays out prime rib on Saturdays, seafood on Fridays, and brunch on Sunday. The always-open **Apache Grill** serves native and Southwestern dishes along with standard American fare.

San Carlos Lake

Formed by the damming of the Gila, **San Carlos Lake** is a large reservoir, with 158 miles of desert shoreline and surrounded by the jagged Gila, Mescal, and Santa Teresa Mountains. It has good fishing, and there's a tackle shop with snacks and other supplies on site. The nearby **Coolidge Dam**, dedicated by its namesake commander-in-chief in 1930, is a feat of engineering that's worth seeing. Follow the signed road south off of Highway 70 at Peridot to the **San Carlos Reservoir Recreation Area**, where you can boat and swim, water-ski, fish, camp, and walk around the rocky scrublands.

The Lower Colorado River

The great river is the chief draw of this region,

with much to see and do in the small resort communities along its banks—especially if you like getting wet.

Here you can marvel at the engineering audacity of Hoover Dam, which sought to tame the Colorado and bring hydroelectricity, irrigation, and predictable flows to the desert. Spend hot, lazy days by the water at Lake Havasu City, and stroll across London Bridge, rebuilt here in the desert in the 1970s. Discover the Old West in Yuma and the history of American road culture in Kingman, Seligman, and along the lonely remains of old Route 66.

Hikers, bikers, desert rats, and winter bird-watchers can explore several vast desert wildlife refuges as well as nine wilderness areas

Highlights

Look for ★ to find recommended sights, activities, dining, and lodging.

★ **Hoover Dam:** One of the largest concrete dams in the world holds back the Colorado River in a barren desert canyon (page 385).

★ **Driving Historic Route 66:** On the longest remaining stretch of the old Mother Road, nostalgia rules (page 392).

★ **Seligman:** This small town is a throwback to the Route 66 era—and one of the models for the town of Radiator Springs in the hit Disney-Pixar film *Cars* (page 398).

★ **London Bridge:** The picturesque bridge that once spanned the Thames now reaches across the Lake Havasu channel (page 406).

★ **Yuma Territorial Prison State Historic Park:** Witness how the rapscallions and outlaws of Arizona's wild territorial days lived in this legendary Old West prison (page 410).

The Lower Colorado River

© MOON.COM

M E X I C O

C A L I F O R N I A

To San Diego

To Los Angeles

To Los Angeles

0
0   20 km

20 mi

8

10

78

ALGODONES
SAND DUNES

S34

FORT YUMA INDIAN RES.

IMPERIAL DAM
Recreation Area

LAGUNA DAM

95

Algodones

San Luis

Somerton

Yuma

YUMA TERRITORIAL PRISON
STATE HISTORIC PARK

Imperial Dam
Recreation Area

Imperial National
Wildlife Refuge

Martinez Lake

Martinez
Lake

Yuma Quartermaster
Depot State
Historic Park

Colorado River

Cibola National
Wildlife Refuge

Cibola

Blythe

Ehrenberg

78

95

COLORADO RIVER INDIAN
TRIBES MUSEUM AND LIBRARY

COLORADO
RIVER INDIAN
RESERVATION

Poston

95

95

62

Parker Strip
Recreation Area

Havasu
Landing

Lake Havasu

Lake Havasu

Lake Havasu City

Cattail Cove SP

Lake Havasu SP

95

Topock

LONDON BRIDGE

Havasu National Wildlife Refuge

PARKER DAM

Parker

95

Parker

Bill Williams
River National
Wildlife Refuge

Bill Williams River

Alamo
Lake

ALAMO CROSSING RD

ALAMO RD

SIGNAL RD

Santa Maria River

93

JOSHUA TREE
FOREST PARKWA

Quartzsite

Kofa National
Wildlife Refuge

Castle Dome Peak
3,788ft

72

Bouse

Salome

Wenden

SALOME RD

EAGLE EYE RD

ALAMO RD

60

Wickenburg

60

National

Prescott

Forest

Gila

River

Dateland

8

GILA BEND
RESERVATION

10

Gila Bend

GILA INDIAN
RESERVATION

TOHONO O'ODHAM
INDIAN RESERVATION

To Tucson

PHOENIX

GILA RIVER
INDIAN
RESERVATION

17

10

THE LOWER COLORADO RIVER

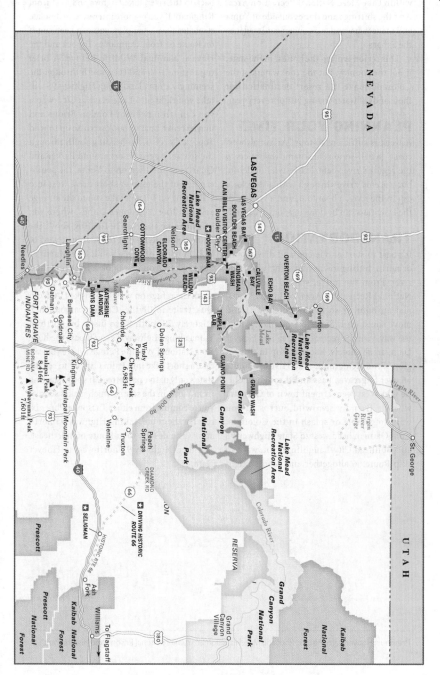

within Lake Mead National Recreation Area. And the shifting sand dunes outside of Yuma will make you wonder if you've wandered into the Sahara.

This region is often the hottest in the state, if not the country, but the cool waters of the Colorado make it a resort destination for thousands of water-loving visitors every year.

PLANNING YOUR TIME

A week is sufficient to tour "Arizona's west coast" (a half-serious nickname that refers to the region's river-centric lifestyle) in depth, but a scenic drive-through with a stop for a dip in the river, a boat tour, and a visit to all the essentials can be done in a long weekend.

TRANSPORTATION

It's best to start at one end and drive south or north, hitting towns and sights along the river. From the north, start at Lake Mead National Recreation Area (or in Las Vegas, just an hour or so to the northwest) and move south on U.S. 93 to Kingman. Along the way, visit the recreation area and Hoover Dam, an absolutely essential stop in this region. From Kingman, take Historic Route 66 over Sitgreaves Pass and through the little Old West reenactment town of Oatman, with its friendly semiwild burros. If you want to gamble or splash in the Colorado, from Oatman head west to State Highway 95 and Bullhead City-Laughlin; if you want to skip Route 66 altogether and head straight

back to the river, take Highway 68 west from Kingman. If you're more interested in desolate stretches than river play, you can keep south on Route 66 from Oatman to Topock and the Havasu National Wildlife Refuge. A brief tug east on I-40 and then south through the seemingly empty land along Highway 95 will take you right into Lake Havasu City, where you can stroll beneath London Bridge and maybe rent a boat or book a cruise up to wild Topock Gorge. Keep heading south through the sparse, jagged desert around Parker and Quartzsite and then on to Yuma, the southern end of the tour. A short drive west into California on I-8 will take you to the strange and thrilling Algodones Dunes, where you can imagine that you're floating above the Dune Sea in *Return of the Jedi*. Just west of U.S. 95 north of Yuma you'll find Martinez Lake, where you can book a boat tour into the Imperial National Wildlife Refuge. To reach the refuge on your own, take I-10 from Quartzsite to Blythe, California, and then Highway 78 south. Also just a bit north of Yuma along Highway 95 you'll pass the huge Kofa National Wildlife Refuge, where you can take a short hike into Palm Canyon to see the state's only native palm trees. If you're starting from Yuma in the south, which makes sense if you're coming from either Tucson or Phoenix, reverse the route, taking Highway 95 north across the desert, then Route 66 northeast, and then Highway 93 northwest to Hoover Dam.

Lake Mead National Recreation Area

Water spreads like exploring fingers over the dry, scrubby land, molding a wet playground out of the necessities of industry and progress. It wasn't enough for those reclaimers of the 1930s to stop the Colorado River dead in its tracks and impound all the water the imagined Southwestern empire would need. Why not create a boating and fishing empire while we're at it? And so we have this 290-square-mile, 2.5-million-acre national recreation area, the nation's first.

There are two desert lakes here: Mead, at 112 miles long the continent's largest artificial body of water, and the smaller Mohave (pronounced "Mo-hah-vee"), 67 miles downriver. Two dams hold the waters back: Hoover, some 70 stories high, keeps Lake Mead in check, while the smaller Davis Dam has its back to Mohave. The placid waters lap at more than 700 miles of Mojave Desert shoreline in two states and stretch north toward a third. The Mojave Desert is named after the desert tribe that lived along the Colorado River—the word means something like "alongside the water." The folks that established Mohave County in 1864 used a variant spelling of the word. Throughout this region you'll see the word spelled both ways.

Millions of waterborne and sun-stained revelers find this place every year, flocking from nearby Las Vegas and the Arizona cities. There is excellent fishing here no matter the season, plus boating, swimming, scuba diving, sunbathing, and houseboat touring. If you're not a water type, a tour of Hoover Dam or a slow drive along Lake Mead's scenic Northshore Road—the sun igniting the red-rock cliffs of the Bowl of Fire, bighorn sheep picking along the rough rock spines along the road—are enough to justify a visit.

Due to prolonged drought in the Southwest, the recreation area has been plagued in recent years by low water levels—in some places it is 60 feet below normal levels—causing the closure of a few areas. It's a good idea to call the **Lake Mead National Recreation Area headquarters** (601 Nevada Way, Boulder City, NV, 702/293-8907, www.nps.gov/lame, $25 per vehicle for 7 days) or check the website before making your travel plans.

★ HOOVER DAM

Once the largest dam of its kind just about anywhere, **Hoover Dam** is still one of the nation's greatest engineering and construction feats and stands today as a testament to the brawn and ambition of a people set on taming a wild river. The Southwest as we know it simply would not exist without this dam. During its construction, an epic human story played out, with thousands of workers climbing the sheer rock walls of an overheated canyon in the middle of nowhere, holding back a river with concrete and will. Some say more than 700 workers died during the dam's construction (a number higher than the official estimates), which took five years and about 3.2 million cubic yards of concrete to complete.

Not only is Hoover Dam an engineering audacity of the highest order, it's a rather stylish one at that. Heading northwest out of Kingman along U.S. 93, suddenly the walls of Black Canyon close in, and the huge concrete slab of the dam comes into view. You must drive over the dam to reach Nevada and the **parking garage** (8am-5:15pm daily, $10 cash only), passing along the way sculptor Oskar J. W. Hansen's soaring work *Winged Figures of the Republic*. The two 30-foot-high bronze angels, with the strained muscles of dam builders and upstretched wings, are meant to symbolize, according to the artist, "the enormous power of trained physical strength, equally enthroned in placid triumph of scientific accomplishment."

The **Hoover Dam Visitor Center** (702/494-2517 or 866/730-90979, www.usbr. gov, 9am-5pm daily, $10 without tour) has numerous exhibits on the building of the dam and the scientific and social justifications behind the enormous undertaking. There's a short movie and an elevator to the roof and the best overview of the dam complex and the river flowing beyond it on down to Lake Mohave. If you're there already, it's worth it to take one of two tours offered. The **Powerplant Tour** ($15 adults, $12 children 4-16) lasts about 30 minutes and gives a comprehensive view of the dam and an explanation of how it works. The **Hoover Dam Tour** ($30, no children under 8 allowed) lasts about one hour and goes deep into the dam, revealing the inner workings of the huge complex. This tour is highly recommended and worth the extra money; it includes a booklet about the dam for each participant. You get to walk the rounded and brightly lit low-ceilinged corridors inside the damworks and view the lazy band of river from high up in the dam. This tour also provides a chance to see all the beautiful art deco touches folded into the design of the dam complex in the 1930s, an arguably more stylish era than our own. The entire inner complex is floored with a gray Italian marble flecked with reds and yellows, and there are stylized Native American-inspired designs etched into the floor in even the most out-of-the-way corners. In summer, the first tour begins at 9am, and the last tour begins at 5:15pm. In winter, the last tour begins at 4:15pm. The last tickets are sold an hour before the last tour. There's a standard gift shop near the parking garage and a little café that serves good but expensive hamburgers, sandwiches, hot dogs, and other tasty eats.

Hoover Dam Bypass/ Colorado River Bridge

The Colorado River Bridge spans Black Canyon about 900 feet above the Colorado River just south of Hoover Dam. Officially named the **Mike O'Callaghan-Pat Tillman Memorial Bridge** (after Nevada governor Mike O'Callaghan and Pat Tillman, a former Arizona Cardinals player and Army Ranger killed by friendly fire in Afghanistan), it is one of the longest and highest arch bridges in the Western Hemisphere. On the Nevada side there's a path and viewing area where you can stop and look at the dam and the river rushing by far below.

LAKE MEAD

The larger of the two lakes in the recreation area is **Lake Mead.** When full (which it hasn't been since the early 1980s because of

Hoover Dam

drought), the lake is 112 miles long and some 500 feet deep, with 247 square miles of surface area. It is very hot here in the summer, despite all the splashing and frolicking going on in the water. There is little shade in the Mojave, and the sun is incessant and unforgiving. The vegetation is sparse—nothing but rocks, scrub, and barren red, pink, and blue hills, sharp and jagged. The native terrain seems out of touch with the artificial oases around the lake, with their imported palm trees and other assorted lush touches, creating a contradictory atmosphere that is strange and thrilling. Throngs flood the lake country, with speedboats, sailboats, and fishing boats in tow, on any given spring or summer weekend. From April through October the high temperatures are generally in the 80s, then the 90s, then up to the triple digits in deep summer, then back down to the 90s and then 80s. By November and through March the weather is cooler, though certainly not cold during the day. Water temperatures range from 45°F in winter to 85°F in the summer. One of the least crowded times of year to visit is January and February, though you might not want to get in the water during this time. The best place to start is the **Alan Bible Visitor Center** (U.S. 93 and Lakeshore Scenic Dr., four miles southeast of Boulder City, NV, 702/293-8990, www.nps.gov/lame, 8:30am-4:30pm daily, $25 per vehicle, good for 7 days, boats and other vessels $16) just west of Hoover Dam along U.S. 93. Here you'll find helpful rangers and volunteers with all the information and maps you'll need for your visit.

NORTHSHORE ROAD

If you're only going to be in the area for a day or so, or if you're not the water sports type, the best way to see the recreation area's natural wonders is to take a slow, scenic drive along Lake Mead's **Northshore Road.** From the entrance station near the Alan Bible Visitor Center, head north on Lakeshore Scenic Drive, which turns into Northshore Road. You'll pass all the major west- and north-end bays and beaches, and you can turn off at any

point and stop. The road extends more than 50 miles along the shore and eventually becomes Route 169 near Overton, Nevada. Try to make it as far as the spectacular **Bowl of Fire** at the base of the Muddy Mountains, about 25 miles from the entrance. The Bowl of Fire is so named for the deep red rocks jutting up off the desert, which light up as if ablaze, especially as the sun is dropping in the west. Climb up about half a mile to the overlook on the **Northshore Summit Trail** (it's well signed at the trailhead) for one of the best views in the region. Keep your eyes open along the rocky spines of the mountains on both sides of the road, for you're likely to see a few bighorn sheep negotiating the rugged terrain.

RECREATION
Hiking and Biking

One of the longer hikes in the recreation area will take you to natural hot springs in a slot canyon below Hoover Dam. The hike to **Arizona Hot Springs,** in White Rock Canyon, is a six-mile round-trip, moderately rough trek to the Colorado River and into a side canyon with nearly vertical walls and the spare and rocky landscape typical of this inhospitable but strangely beautiful land. This isn't for the weak, though—you have to climb down a 20-foot ladder stuck in the rocks to reach the best pools, and the walk back to the car can be a tough trudge even for well-worn hikers. To reach the trailhead go east from the visitors center about eight miles, four miles past Hoover Dam on U.S. 93, to a dirt parking lot, which is at the head of White Rock Canyon (the trailhead is on the map you'll get when entering the recreation area). The trail is closed during the high heat of summer. Just outside the visitors center is the trailhead for the **Railroad Tunnel Trail,** which leads along the disused right-of-way built during the construction of Hoover Dam, and through five spooky old train tunnels. From the visitors center to the entrance of the fifth tunnel is just over two miles one-way. A hike from the visitors center through all five tunnels to the dam is just over three miles one-way. The recreation area's newspaper, *Desert Views,* has a comprehensive listing of the trails around Lake Mead, most of which are quite short and lead to some overlook or scenic feature. Be careful hiking here, especially in the summer, when you probably won't want to do much walking, let alone long hard desert trekking.

There are more than 800 miles of backcountry dirt roads through the Mojave Desert in the recreation area, perfect for touring on a mountain bike. Ask at the visitors center for a map of the backcountry roads. Also try the Railroad Tunnel Trail for biking.

Boating

You can rent boats for fishing, exploring, waterskiing, and living the easy lake-top life at **Callville Bay** (702/565-8958, www.callvillebay.com)—everything from 16-foot fishing crafts to big patio cruisers and 18-foot speedsters. Prices range $25-95 per hour for wakeboard boats, pontoon boats, Jet Skis and kayaks.

A leisurely sightseeing cruise around Lake Mead on the *Desert Princess,* a replica of an old Mississippi paddleboat, is a popular way to take in the stark scenery. **Lake Mead Cruises** (866/292-9191, www.lakemeadcruises.com, $28-65) offers several different options, including brunch and dinner cruises.

You can rent a **houseboat** for three days or up to a week ($750-4,000); most sleep between 6 and 14 people and come with all kinds of extras, depending on how much you want to spend. Contact **Forever Houseboats** (800/255-5561, www.foreverhouseboats.com).

If you're more into a guided tour or skimming across the water by your own power, look into **Black Canyon/Willow Beach River Adventures** (Hacienda Hotel, Hwy. 93, 702/494-2204, 10:30am-5pm Mon.-Fri., or call 702/293-8204, www.blackcanyonadventures.com). They rent kayaks and canoes at the **Willow Beach Marina** (928/767-4747, www.willowbeachharbor.com, $25-35 for 2 hours,

minimum 2 hours, plus deposit). They also offer group raft trips on the Colorado River, along the starkly beautiful **Black Canyon National Water Trail,** which stretches from Hoover Dam to Willow Beach, with several stops at beaches for swimming and frolicking and a waterside box lunch ($69 pp for a 1.5-hour trip, $114 pp for a 3-hour tour with lunch).

Those with their own paddle craft need to get a **permit** ($12, plus $10 entrance fee) to launch at Black Canyon; you can get one through Black Canyon/Willow Beach River Adventures in its office at the Hacienda Hotel just west of Hoover Dam.

Swimming and Scuba Diving

The best place to swim and scuba dive is around **Boulder Beach,** not far from the visitors center, which has a cordoned swimming area that's popular with families. The area has been lately adversely affected by low water levels, but swimming there remains viable. There's a **Dive Park** at North Boulder Beach that's a great place for beginners and experts alike, and a few watercraft have been deliberately submerged here for exploring and pretending. **Boulder Islands,** large concrete tanks that were used to store water during the construction of the dam, are also a popular area for scuba enthusiasts. More experienced and adventuresome scuba divers have many options around the two lakes. Check out **Lake Mead's website** (www.nps.gov/lame) for more scuba information.

Fishing

Sport anglers launch on Lake Mead in search of striped and largemouth bass, rainbow trout, channel catfish, and other fish. The biggest striped bass in Lake Mead have been known to weigh up to 50 pounds. Each of the marinas has fishing gear for sale and rent, boats for rent, fishing guides, and information. **Lake Mead's website** (www.nps.gov/lame) has an up-to-date fishing report.

FOOD AND ACCOMMODATIONS

The food options are rather scarce around Lake Mead National Recreation Area, and it's a good idea to bring your own victuals with you. There are restaurants, snack bars, bars, and small stores at the marinas on Lake Mead and Lake Mohave, but they are far apart and should not be relied on for all of your sustenance while visiting the park. Remember that restaurants at the marinas have seasonal hours, being open daily roughly from Memorial Day to Labor Day, and then truncated hours after that.

On the Arizona side of the lake, **Temple Bar Marina Restaurant** (31409 N. Temple Bar Rd., 928/767-3211, 7am-8pm daily Mar.-Sept., 8am-5pm Fri.-Sun Oct., 8am-3pm Fri-Sat. Nov., $9-18) is a typical and decent bar-and-grill-style place serving burgers, sandwiches, pizzas, and the like. **Harbor House Café** (490 Horsepower Cove, Boulder City, 7am-8pm Mon.-Thurs. and Sun., 7am-10pm Fri.-Sat., $8-15), located at Las Vegas Boat Harbor on the Nevada side of the lake, is another decent restaurant also serving bar-and-grill-style food and offering a nice lakeside view for breakfast, lunch, or dinner. Back in Arizona at the Lake Mohave marina at Katherine Landing, the **Tail O' the Whale** (8am-5pm Mon.-Thurs., 8am-9pm Fri.-Sat., and 8am-8pm Sun. Memorial Day-Labor Day, $8-20) has pretty good food and offers a full bar with views of the lake while you eat.

There's just one lakeside lodge left within the Lake Mead portion of the recreation area. The **Temple Bar Resort and Marina** (928/767-3211, www.templebarlakemead.com, $65-150 during high season) near the eastern part of the lake, offers standard rooms, fishing cabins, and suites with kitchens, some with lake views and some with desert views.

There are hundreds of **camping** spots around Lake Mead ($20-45). The campgrounds—with showers, tables, grills, and all the other amenities a camper needs—are at **Boulder Beach** (154 sites), **Callville Bay** (80 sites), **Temple Bar** (153 sites), and **Las Vegas Bay** (89 sites). Visitors with RVs will find sites with full hookups at **Callville Bay Resort** (702/565-8958, www.callvillebay.com).

LAKE MOHAVE

This lake doesn't really seem like a lake at all but more like the river it's filled with. Mohave is thin and runs long through Black Canyon as if it were the untamed Colorado, widening at Arizona Basin and Cottonwood Basin to seem more lakelike. The scenery around Mohave is similar to that around Mead: spare and rocky, ruled by creosote and other scrub, with sandy beaches and hidden coves. The recreation opportunities are similar as well—fishing and waterskiing, houseboating and floating in the calm, warm water.

A boat launch and placid waters ringed by ragged rock cliffs make **Willow Beach** a fine place for an easy day on the water with your canoe, fishing near a fish hatchery, or just lounging and picnicking on the hot desert beach. Waterfowl and other birds abound. Take U.S. 93 west toward Hoover Dam and turn at the sign for Willow Beach.

Food and Accommodations

Lake Mohave has two major marinas, both with small hotels with basic and clean lakeside rooms, stores, restaurants, bars, and boat and watercraft rentals (including houseboats)—everything you'll need for a perfect time on the water.

Cottonwood Cove Resort & Marina (702/297-1464, www.cottonwoodcoveresort. com, $89 in winter, $150 in summer) is on the Nevada side and has a nice little lodge and campground, plus a great swimming beach popular with kids. On the Arizona side just outside of Bullhead City is **Lake Mohave Resort at Katherine Landing** (2690 E. Katherine Spur Rd., Bullhead City, 928/754-3245, www.katherinelanding.com, $115 in winter, $145 in summer), a modest waterside stop with plenty of boat rentals and water activities. This is a popular place for families with kids. Make sure to ask for one of the remodeled rooms, as the older ones reek of stale smoke.

Kingman and Vicinity

Spread across a dry desert basin below pine-topped mountains and cut through by I-40, Kingman and its environs have long been a stopover for those traveling the two famous American trails along the 35th Parallel: the Santa Fe Railroad and Route 66. Indeed, the town, mostly a transportation hub and county government center these days, has secured its place in Americana, along with a few other Arizona towns, by appearing in the song "Route 66," certainly one of the most frequently covered tunes of all time, written in 1946 by Bobby Troup and first recorded by the great Nat King Cole.

Kingman's identity, at least for the sake of tourism, is all wrapped up in being the "Heart of Route 66," and there are a few nostalgic sights here harking back to a time when cross-country travel was slower and, in a sense, more meaningful than it is today. The town, which isn't much to look at, sits near the junction of two scenic drives that will show you an unvarnished Arizona, rolling through large swaths of left-alone desert and old mining ghost towns taken over by artisans and actors, up over mountain passes held together by strange cacti, across bridges swaying high above dry arroyos, and past abandoned outposts and tourists traps, the rusted shells of long-dead vehicles, and all those tiny white roadside crosses remembering road-weary tragedies.

SIGHTS

Peruse museums and stores featuring the artifacts and stories of the heyday of Route 66 travel, then hop in your car and drive the rough and lonely remains of the Mother Road, through squat-cactus forests and old lost towns still pining for the region's long-gone gold- and silver-mining days. Paying $4 for one museum gets you into all three local museums.

Historic Route 66 Museum

The serious-faced manikins that populate the life-sized dioramas at the small **Historic Route 66 Museum** (Powerhouse Visitors Center, 120 W. Andy Devine Ave., 928/753-9889, www.route66museum.net, 9am-5pm daily, $4 adults, children under 13 free) are a bit unsettling, but they create an evocative picture of how Arizona was influenced, and to a major degree populated, by one long strip of road. Plastic pioneers, decked out in authentic frontier-era outfits, walk beside real wagons, while sad dust-bowl migrants gather their possessions and their children into a rickety truck and look plaintively toward a new life in the gardens of California. The curators here have stuffed a lot of history, and a good deal of local artifacts and ephemera, into a relatively small space, using detailed scenes to depict the historic movement of people and culture along the 35th Parallel—from the Native Americans to Lt. Edward Beale's 1857 trek across what was then a wagon road, at the helm of a company of 25 camels, to the well-remembered golden age of postwar car culture. One of the museum's best scenes recreates the style and design of 1950s Route 66, the heyday of the cross-country family road trip that brought so many easterners to the still-wild West to see the Grand Canyon and the Petrified Forest. Though much of the road romance found in those eras is dead and gone now, thanks to this excellent little museum we can relive it all just a bit.

Those interested in American car culture and road culture should not miss this sight.

Mohave Museum of History and Arts

A diverse local history museum, the **Mohave Museum of History and Arts** (400 W. Beale St., 928/753-3195, www.mohavemuseum.org, 9am-4:30pm Mon.-Fri., 1pm-5pm Sat., $4

Kingman

© MOON.com

To Lake
Havasu City and
Needles, CA

To Bullhead City,
Hoover Dam,
and Las Vegas

To I-40 Exit 44
and Oatman

EXIT 48

EXIT 51

EXIT 53

93

40

66

66

66

SILVER ST
GOLD ST
SPRING ST
LEAD ST

GRANDVIEW AVE

PARK ST
N 5TH ST
N 7TH ST

SEE DETAIL

ANDY DEVINE AVE
BEALE ST

RAMBLIN ROSE
MOTEL

HILL TOP MOTEL

HUALAPAI MOUNTAIN RD

POST
OFFICE

DAMBAR &
STEAKHOUSE

To Hualapai
Mountain Park

WESTERN AVE

GOLF DR

COUNTRY
CLUB DR

GREENWAY DR

ARIZONA ST
GATES AVE
CLUB AVE
MOTOR AVE
DETROIT AVE
STOCKTON HILL RD

FAIRGROUNDS BLVD

HARRISON ST

AIRFIELD AVE

ANDY DEVINE AVE

TOWNSEND ST

KINGMAN REGIONAL
MEDICAL CENTER

MOHAVE COUNTY
DISTRICT LIBRARY

Centennial
Park

BLM KINGMAN
RESOURCE
AREA OFFICE

BUS
STATION

AIRWAY

BURBANK ST

RUTHERFORD ST

BEVERLY AVE

ROOSEVELT ST

AVE

To Northern Ave

To Airport and
Peach Springs

To Seligman
and Flagstaff

0   0.5 km
0   0.5 mi

Metcalfe
City Park

THE CELLAR DOOR
WINE BAR

MOHAVE MUSEUM OF
HISTORY AND ARTS

POWERHOUSE
VISITOR CENTER &
ROUTE 66 MUSEUM

LOCOMOTIVE
PARK

MR. D'Z
ROUTE 66
DINER

MATTINA'S
RISTORANTE ITALIANO

REDNECK'S
SOUTHERN
BARBECUE

POST
OFFICE

COURTHOUSE

66

ANDY DEVINE AVE
BEALE ST
OAK ST

N 1ST ST
SPRING ST

N 2ND ST

3RD ST

4TH ST

5TH ST

adults, children under 12 free) has a lot to look at, including a detailed display on the life and career of Kingman's favorite son, actor Andy Devine (there are even original telegrams sent by the famous screen cowboy on display here).

About a block away from the Powerhouse Visitors Center, the museum has several rooms crowded with the history of northwestern Arizona as well as a gallery of portraits depicting each U.S. president and first lady and some stuffed examples of the region's wildlife. Other displays explain the history of mining and ranching in the area, and there are some first-rate examples of Hualapai basketry and locally mined turquoise. You could spend a few hours lost among the eclectic collections if you're not careful. Southwestern artist Roy Purcell, a former director of the museum, painted the museum's wonderful murals showing life as it used to be here in this forgotten frontier, and a gallery features the work of a rotating group of local artists.

Bonelli House

A pioneer Mormon family that settled in Kingman in the 1890s, the Bonellis built this territorial-era home after their first home burned down in 1915. They rebuilt better and stronger, using tufa stone from the rocky hills nearby to create an interior that was cool in the summer and warm in the winter. Local history buffs have restored the **Bonelli House** (430 E. Spring St., 928/753-1413, 11am-3pm Mon.-Fri., included in price of admission to Mohave Museum) with exacting detail, giving visitors an authentic look at what middle-class family and home life was like on the high-desert frontier.

TOP EXPERIENCE

★ Driving Historic Route 66

The longest remaining stretch of Route 66 runs through the dry grasslands, cholla forests, and barren rocky mountains of northwestern Arizona, about 165 miles between Ash Fork on the east and Topock on the Colorado River to the west.

Ash Fork sits just off I-40, 94 miles east of Kingman. From there head west to the Colorado River, following the Route 66 signs. Or, you can start from Topock, near the Havasu National Wildlife Refuge, and drive east, ending at Ash Fork. Either way, you'll pass through sleepy Peach Springs, capital of the Hualapai Indian Reservation, and the nearly abandoned Truxton and Valentine, a few buildings dating from the 1930s to the 1950s moldering along the road. You'll pass Hackberry, with its famous and much-photographed Hackberry General Store, and climb up a scrubby, rocky mountain, where the road is like a washboard and steep and curvy beyond reason, passing old ghost homes, mine shafts, and a few sprawling junkyard compounds. Then climb up over Sitgreaves Pass and down the other side of the mountain to Oatman, home of the wild burros of Route 66, each descended from the beasts of burden that helped prospectors fight these desert hills more than a century ago.

HACKBERRY GENERAL STORE

Try *not* to stop at this picture-ready old store and junkyard museum. It can't be done. Maybe it's the cherry-red, 1957 Corvette parked conspicuously out front. Maybe it's because it's the only sign of life for miles in either direction along this forgotten stretch of the old Mother Road. Maybe it's the root beer.

Cluttered with Route 66 and American road culture memorabilia, including several rusting old cars that once made their way along the Route, the **Hackberry General Store** (11255 E. Hwy. 66, Hackberry, 928/769-2605, www.hackberrygeneralstore.com, 9am-6pm daily) looks like it belongs to another era. Inside you'll find cold sodas, snacks, souvenirs, and a lot to look at, including some really cool road-map murals on the walls by artist Bob Waldmire. The owners, who bought the place on a whim years ago while driving Route 66, encourage visitors to walk around the property, examine the memorabilia, and take pictures. The store is 28 miles east of Kingman and 60 miles west of Seligman.

Driving Historic Route 66

© MOON.COM

COOL SPRINGS STATION

Twenty miles west of Kingman and 16 miles east of Oatman, on the way up over the Black Mountains, **Cool Springs Station** (8275 W. Oatman Hwy., 928/768-8366, 10am-5pm Tues.-Sun., free) is a photogenic replica of a gas station that served this stretch of Route 66 in the 1920s. The station eventually fell to ruin and later played a fiery role in the 1990s film *Universal Soldier*. New owners built a detailed replica of the old station in 2004, and now it's a small museum and gift shop worthy of a brief stop.

OATMAN

Between 1904 and 1931 about $36 million in ore, mostly gold and silver, came out of these dry rocky hills. At its peak, the town of Oatman had some 10,000 residents. It went ghostly for a while after the mines shut down, but, as it was with so many mining towns in the Southwest, Oatman was rediscovered in the 1960s and 1970s as a tourist stop along one of the roughest stretches of Historic Route 66. There are a few resale shops and gift boutiques here, a restaurant or two, and a saloon. Some latter-day gunfighters will stage duels in the

street on most days, and you can check out the old **Oatman Hotel,** where Clark Gable and Carole Lombard spent their honeymoon. But the real fun in Oatman—which is a touch kitschy and has few genuinely authentic buildings left anymore—is to feed and commune with wild **burros.** They're not really "wild" anymore—they'll walk right up and say hello, letting you pet their heads and feed them snacks sold by various vendors in town. There are usually a few baby burros milling around too.

Leaving Oatman and descending along Route 66 to the desert floor just east of the river, the foothills are covered with cholla, which blooms, along with a few dormant wildflowers, in the spring and adds a bit of bright, shocking color to the landscape, making those warm and clear months the perfect time for a visit.

Keepers of the Wild Nature Park

Though tawny cougars are known to occasionally haunt these windy high-desert plains and some stretches of Historic Route 66 could perhaps stand in for a sweeping African savanna, one doesn't expect to encounter a shaggy-maned lion here, or for that matter a flitting lemur or a thoughtful baboon—except perhaps at this hospital, retirement home, and haven for abused, neglected, and abandoned exotic animals. **Keepers of the Wild Nature Park** (13441 E. Route 66, milepost 87, www.keepersofthewild.org, 9am-5pm Wed.-Mon., $20 all-day pass, $12 children over 12) has tigers, a bear, a wolf, a whole village full of squealing, playful monkeys, and much more. The animals live in large, fenced-in habitats, with big boulders and pools and mostly native trees and shrubs. The paths are easy, but there isn't a lot of shade, so bring a hat. The whole park is wheelchair accessible, and there's a gift shop with snacks and drinks. They encourage picnicking, so feel free to bring a basket. The

1: Historic Route 66 2: semi-wild burro in Oatman 3: Oatman, originally a mining camp 4: Cool Springs Station

last tickets are sold at 4pm. For $10 more per person, a guide will take you on a driven "safari" tour of the park that lasts about an hour and a half (10am, 1pm, and 3:30pm). This is an ideal stop for families with kids. Most of the animals here have cute names and sad life stories, so you run the risk of falling in love.

RECREATION
Hiking and Camping

If you missed North-Central Arizona's pinelands, head to northwest Arizona's answer at **Hualapai Mountain Park** (6250 Hualapai Mountain Park, 928/681-5700, www.mcparks.com), about 12 miles from Kingman. This sap-and-campfire-scented 2,300-acre mountain park is high in the pines overlooking the scrub valley. The titular mountain range rises from the plain southeast of town to heights between 5,000 and nearly 8,500 feet, cloaked in the conifers typical of such elevations in Arizona. There are 19 cabins for rent through the **Mohave County Parks Division** (877/757-0915, www.mcparks.com, $85-115), built of stacked stone and wood by the Civilian Conservation Corps in the 1930s and sleeping 2-12 people, most with rustic old fireplaces—but also with kitchens and electricity. You can camp here, too, or park your RV among the pines ($20-35); most of the camping spots don't have water and are obtained on a first-come, first-served basis.

The park's trail system leads high into the mountains for some inspiring views. The trails are well worn and forested, with huge slabs and half-buried outcroppings of granite dropped in everywhere as if there was a rock fight among giants here long ago. The 8,417-foot **Hualapai Peak** is the highest point in the park and in the region. The 4.3-mile round-trip **Potato Patch Loop Trail** is a moderate and representative hike, running through ponderosa pines, aspens, and high stands of spruce and fir, strewn with needles and cones and watched over by boulders covered in dry lichen. Start out on the switchbacks of the **Aspen Springs Trail** and then meet up with the loop at the

Who Is Andy Devine?

Kingman's favorite son was one of those great American character actors that most of us recognize but often can't name. His strained, gravelly but high voice, the result of a childhood accident that permanently damaged his vocal cords, and his size—a former football star, he was corpulent his entire adult life—make Andy Devine (1905-1977) stand out more than most.

While film buffs will remember Devine as the driver in John Ford's 1939 Western classic *Stagecoach,* John Wayne's breakout film made partly in Monument Valley, or as one of the soldiers in John Huston's *The Red Badge of Courage* in 1951, his career was long and diverse, encompassing radio, both B- and A-grade movies, and television. He started out as a bit player in silent films during the 1920s and went on to entertain several generations.

Those of us who grew up in the 1970s and 1980s will likely remember Devine by his voice alone, which became that of the gentle and funny Friar Tuck in Disney's animated *Robin Hood* in 1973. Those who grew up in the 1950s and 1960s, on the other hand, remember Devine as "Jingle Jones" from the Western television series *Wild Bill Hickok* or as the host of the Saturday morning show *Andy's Gang.* If you remember the 1930s and 1940s, you'll recognize that voice again as a regular on the Jack Benny radio show, where his greeting "Hiya, Buck!" made him famous, and of course you'll know Devine as the funny sidekick in many Roy Rogers Westerns.

Though Devine was born in Flagstaff a couple hours northeast of Kingman, where his father worked for the railroad, he moved to Kingman when he was just one year old. An on-the-job accident had taken the elder Devine's leg, and a settlement with the railroad helped the family buy the Beale Hotel in Kingman, where Devine grew up and is celebrated in the local museum and during an annual festival and parade.

Aspen Springs-Potato Patch Junction after about a mile. You go up about 800 feet in the first mile and half, but it levels out on the loop. A map of the entire system, which has about 16 miles of developed and undeveloped trails, is available at the park office. There's really no time of year to stay away from this pleasant, heavily used mountain park (there will be ATV riders here, so be forewarned). It's hot in the summer, but with the breezy moderation that its elevation allows; it's cold and sometimes snowy in the winter, but not to any uncomfortable degree.

ENTERTAINMENT AND EVENTS

A focal point of Kingman's downtown, **Diana's Cellar Door Wine Bar** (414 E. Beale St., 928/753-3885, www.dianascellardoor.com, 4pm-10pm Mon.-Wed., 11am-10pm Thurs., 11am-midnight Fri.-Sat.) adds a bit of urban class to this rural region. It offers wine, beer and cocktails, and live music (Tues.-Sat. 7pm). You can sit at the tasteful bar and listen to a laid-back local musician, or take your bottle with you.

The month of May brings thousands of Route 66 nostalgics and classic-car lovers to the old stretch of the Mother Road from Seligman to Topock for the **Historic Route 66 Fun Run** (928/753-5001, www.azrt66. com, May). Far-flung drivers in a riot of old and new vehicles—many of them gorgeous and classic, and many of their owners in some kind of recycled 1950s wear—gather in Seligman for the kickoff of this popular regional event. After eating and dancing to the live bands, a host of roaring two- and four-wheelers makes its slow way along Historic Route 66 west to Kingman, where they park en masse for show-and-tell in the parking lot of the Powerhouse Visitors Center. In downtown Kingman there's more eating, bands and other entertainment, and vendors. Come Sunday morning, hangover or not, everybody gets up, climbs back behind the wheel, and heads east to Topock and the end of the road, stopping of course to give some love to the burros in Oatman.

In late September Kingman celebrates itself and its favorite son during **Andy Devine Days Parade & Community Fair** (928/757-7919, late Sept.), which features food vendors, arts and crafts, and entertainment in the town's historic, if usually a bit desolate, downtown.

SHOPPING

There are two shops in the **Powerhouse Visitors Center** (120 W. Andy Devine Ave., 928/753-6106, 9am-5pm daily) where you'll find items you might not be able to get too many other places. For Route 66 and American road-culture gifts and souvenirs check out the **Historic Route 66 Association of Arizona Gift Shop** inside the Powerhouse.

If you're into finding the treasures that other people have given up, there are a few antiques and resale shops along East Beale Street in the historic old town area that are definitely worth wandering through.

FOOD

The **Dambar & Steakhouse** (1960 E. Andy Devine Ave., 928/753-3523, www.dambarsteakhouse.com, 11am-10pm daily, $15-33) is local favorite that serves great steaks, prime rib, lobster, cowboy beans, and burgers. The bar has excellent regionally brewed beers, and the sawdust on the floor, cowboy kitsch, and Route 66 memorabilia add a bit of character to this popular place. They offer patio seating in the summer and live country music on the weekends.

Mattina's Ristorante Italiano (318 E. Oak St., 928/753-7504, www.mattinasristorante.com, 5pm-9pm Tues.-Sat., $14-38) serves expertly prepared Italian food, including outstanding beef medallions and rack of lamb. It's difficult to choose among the diverse and outlandishly appetizing selection of pasta dishes, but it's equally difficult to pass up the lobster ravioli or the thick, creamy fettuccini alfredo. Don't leave without trying the tiramisu or key lime pie, and consider sampling liberally from the well-stocked wine cellar.

Floyd & Co. (420 E. Beale St., 928/757-8227, 11am-8pm Tues.-Sat., www.floydandcompany.com, $7-25) in Kingman's small downtown serves excellent wood-fired pizza and tasty barbecue plates and sandwiches, as well as fantastic sweet potato fries, corn nuggets, and other scrumptious sides. It also has six taps with Arizona-made beer.

It is widely known throughout this flat and windy region that the retro Route 66 drive-in ★ **Mr. D'z Route 66 Diner** (105 E. Andy Devine, 928/718-0066, 7am-9pm daily, $9-18) serves the best burger in town, but they also have a large menu with all manner of delectable diner and road food, like chili dogs, pizza, hot sandwiches, baby back ribs, chicken-fried steak, and a big plate of spaghetti. Plus, breakfast is served all day. The portions are big, but save room for a thick shake or a root-beer float. Don't leave your camera in the car; the turquoise-and-pink interior and the cool old jukebox here are snapshot-ready.

Beale Street Brews Coffee Shop (510 E. Beale St., 928/753-1404, http://bealestreetbrews.net, 6am-6pm Sun.-Sat.) has fair-trade coffee, pastries, free Wi-Fi, poetry readings, local art on the walls, local music in the air, and a cool old art deco building—perfect for relaxing the day away.

ACCOMMODATIONS

There are several very affordable, basic hotels located on Andy Devine Avenue, Route 66, in Kingman's downtown area, some of them with retro road-trip neon signs and Route 66 themes. There are a good many chain hotels in town as well.

The **Ramblin' Rose Motel** (1001 E. Andy Devine Ave., 928/753-4747, www.ramblinrosemotel.com, $42-48) doesn't look like much, just another roadside place to park and snooze. It's inexpensive and clean, with big, comfy beds, refrigerators, and free Wi-Fi.

The ★ **Hill Top Motel** (1901 E. Andy Devine Ave., 928/753-2198, $52-68) has a bit of character. Its 1950s-era neon sign calls out to all Route 66 road-trippers, clicking something far back in the American memory, convincing them to stop and stay. This small, affordable motel, near the top of a hill looking out on the Hualapai Mountains, has a connection to the dark side of American culture as well: Oklahoma City bomber Timothy McVeigh stayed here for a few nights in 1995 while planning his attack on the Alfred P. Murrah Building for April of that same year. The bombing killed 168 people. Built in the 1950s but refurbished since then, the Hill Top has standard, comfortable rooms with refrigerators, microwaves, free Wi-Fi, and a pool.

Along Hualapai Mountain Road on the way up to the piney mountains, the **Hualapai Mountain Resort** (4525 Hualapai Mountain Rd., 928/757-3545, www.hmresort.net, $79-159) rents eight rustic but comfortable and clean rooms in a quiet, secluded setting. They have an on-site **restaurant** (11am-8pm Wed.-Thurs., 11am-10pm Fri., 8am-10pm Sat., 8am-8pm Sun., $6-22) serving steaks and burgers, salads, sandwiches, and other standard American fare.

INFORMATION AND SERVICES

Built in 1907 to supply power to the region's mines, the **Powerhouse Visitors Center** (120 W. Andy Devine Ave., 928/753-6106, 9am-5pm daily) has information on all the sights, accommodations, and attractions in Kingman and environs, plus a model train circling the inside perimeter.

Kingman Regional Medical Center (3269 Stockton Hill Rd., 928/757-2101, www.azkrmc.com) has a full-service emergency room.

★ SELIGMAN

This tiny roadside settlement 87 miles east of Kingman holds on tight to its Route 66 heritage. Fewer than 500 full-time residents live in this old ranching hub, railroad center, and Route 66 stop, but there is often, especially on summer weekends, twice that number in tourists driving through and stopping for a

bite to eat and a look around the gift shops. Tour buses and large gangs of motorcycling Europeans even stop here and crowd up the one-strip town on occasion, as Seligman has become in recent years one of the top stops for a burgeoning subculture of classic car nuts, fortysomething *Easy Rider* role players, and lovers of mid-20th-century commercial architecture and road culture, all of whom prefer to eschew the interstate and take to the back roads.

John Lasseter, codirector of the 2006 Disney-Pixar film *Cars,* has said that he based the movie's fictional town of **Radiator Springs** partly on Seligman, which, like Radiator Springs, nearly died out when it was bypassed by I-40 in the late 1970s.

Sights

Stop in at the **Route 66 Gift Shop & Visitor's Center** (217 E. Route 66, 928/422-3352, www.route66giftshop.com, 8am-6pm daily) to buy a Route 66 souvenir and learn about the history of the area from Angel and Vilma Delgadillo, longtime residents who are largely responsible for keeping Seligman on the map.

In 2005 Seligman's commercial center, a three-block area off of Chino Street (Historic Route 66) that's hemmed by First Street on the west, Lamport Street on the east, Picacho Street on the north, and Railroad Avenue on the south, made the National Register of Historic Places as "an important reminder of how transportation systems influenced the development of communities in the American West." Pick up a pamphlet for the self-guided tour of the **Seligman Historic District** (www.seligmanazhistoricdistrict.com) at the **Historic Seligman Sundries** and other places in town, and walk the district with your camera, snapping shots of all the retro signs and buildings from the pre-interstate era.

About 22 miles west of Seligman along Historic Route 66, **Grand Canyon Caverns**

1: Hill Top Motel in Kingman 2: Grand Canyon Caverns, west of Seligman

(Route 66, mile marker 115, 928/422-3223, www.gccaverns.com, 8am-6pm daily summer, 10am-4pm daily winter, $16-21) offers guided underground tours of North America's largest dry cave, where crystals and other strange rock formations hide in the darkness. The main tour lasts about 45 minutes and takes you about three-quarters of a mile through the limestone cavern, but not before you descend 21 stories (210 feet) beneath the earth in an elevator. There's a lot of history here, too: During the Cold War the cavern served as a bomb-shelter-in-waiting, packed with enough food and water to sustain hundreds of blast-weary survivors if the unthinkable occurred. The friendly folks here at this old-school Route 66 tourist trap (in the best sense of the phrase) also offer an off-trail tour ($99) that goes much deeper into the caverns. And they'll be happy to take you out into the nearby ranchlands on horseback or in a Jeep.

Shopping

Inside the turquoise-and-pink 100-year-old **Historic Seligman Sundries** (22495 Historic Route 66, 928/853-0051, www.seligmansundries.com, 8am-7pm daily Apr.-Oct.), you'll find a plethora of Route 66 memorabilia as well as motorcycle- and car-culture items, Native American jewelry, cowboy kitsch, and really good coffee and malts. There's a small museum, and the walls are covered with old advertisements and other reminders of the mid-20th-century heyday of American popular culture.

That sprawling building with all the dressed-up manikins standing around on the roof, and Elvis kicking back on the bumper of a classic pink roadster, is **The Rusty Bolt** (115 E. Route 66, 928/422-0106, www.rustybolt66.com, 8am-4pm daily), where they sell the usual local Route 66 memorabilia and a large selection of items for motorcyclists.

Food

A majority of the Route 66 argonauts who slide through Seligman stop at ★ **Delgadillo's**

Snow Cap Drive-In (301 E. Chino Ave., 928/422-3291, 10am-6pm daily, $5-10), a famous food shack whose family of owners have been dedicated to feeding, entertaining, and teasing Route 66 travelers for generations. They serve a mean chili burger, a famous "cheeseburger with cheese," hot dogs, malts, soft ice cream, and much more, but the food's not really the point. Originally built in 1953 out of found lumber, the Snow Cap has become one of the stars of the back-to-Route-66 movement. There's a lot to look at outside: a 1936 Chevy and other old cars (all of them with big eyes on their windshields, à la Disney-Pixar's 2006 homage to Route 66, *Cars*), railroad junk, and several very silly signs; and inside, the close walls are covered with the business cards of customers from all over the world. Don't go here if you're grumpy: There will likely be a stand-up wait, especially on summer weekends, and you *will* be teased, especially if you have a question that requires a serious answer.

The **Roadkill Café** (502 W. Route 66, 928/422-3554, 7am-9pm daily, $8-24) is more than just a funny name; it's a popular place for buffalo burgers, steaks, sandwiches, and other typical Old West-themed bar-and-grill eats. Have a few drinks in the **OK Saloon** and a look around at the cluttered interior.

The majestic, if stuffed, mountain lion that watches over diners at **Westside Lilo's Café** (415 W. Chino Ave., 928/422-5456, www.westsidelilos.com, 6am-9pm daily, $8-23), a popular diner-style eatery (complete with counter service), was shot not far from the restaurant by a member of the owners' family. It's just one of the backcountry touches that add to the ambience here, where they serve good burgers, excellent homemade potato salad, and other standard American fare. They are famous for their carrot cake, which is moist and flavorful.

Accommodations

There are several small, locally owned motels in Seligman, many of them with historic, retro signs and, of course, a Route 66 theme. The accommodations here are nothing special, though they are typically quite affordable.

The **Supai Motel** (134 W. Chino St., 928/422-4153, www.supaimotelseligman.com, $69-82), named for the nearby Grand Canyon-bottom village inhabited by the Havasupai tribe, has clean and comfortable rooms at a fair price.

The **Historic Route 66 Motel** (22750 W. Route 66, 928/422-3204, www.route66seligmanarizona.com, $69-82) offers free wireless Internet and refrigerators in clean, comfortable rooms.

The **Canyon Lodge** (114 E. Chino St., 928/422-3255, www.route66canyonlodge.com, $70-100) has free wireless Internet in its themed rooms (which means posters on the walls of James Dean, Marilyn Monroe, John Wayne, and other pop-culture icons), along with refrigerators and microwaves. They also serve a free continental breakfast.

U.S. HIGHWAY 93

Though not as popular as Route 66, U.S. 93 between Wickenburg, an hour north of Phoenix, and Hoover Dam, about an hour northwest of Kingman, has 200 miles of spectacular desert scenery. Just north of Route 71 before the town of Wikieup, U.S. 93 becomes the **Joshua Tree Forest Parkway.** Look out your window and you'll see why. A few miles north of Kingman, Mohave County Road 125 leads to **Chloride** (four miles east from U.S. 93), an old mining town turned tourist trap in the foothills of the Cerebat Mountains. Here you can browse through some shops and galleries; explore the ruins of mine shafts and a brothel; watch gunfights (high noon the first and third Sat. July-Aug., and every Sat. Sept.-June); and look at all the artwork and found-art in town, including famous rock-face murals by renowned Southwestern artist Roy Purcell.

Food

As you pass through the wide spot in the road known as Wikieup, stop at **Luchia's** (15797 S. Hwy. 93, Wikieup, 928/765-2229, 9am-5pm Sun.-Fri., $5-20), where tasty American and Mexican dishes are served on a lush and shady outdoor patio. It's known for homemade pies (when in doubt, get the apple) and also sells Indian jewelry, rugs, pottery, kachinas, and baskets.

Bullhead City and Laughlin

You pretty much have to be interested in either river games or games of chance to get anything out of a visit to Laughlin or Bullhead City, often two of the hottest spots in the nation during the summer months. On August 11, 1983, at 2:21pm, the shade temperature in Bullhead City reached 132°F—the hottest on record. However, if you'd like nothing more than to skim and spray around the river on a Jet Ski during the day and play poker and slots when the unforgiving sun finally dips away, then you'll want to follow the many Arizona families from Phoenix and elsewhere who head for this desert playground several times a year, with their kids, speedboats, and Jet Skis in tow. Bullhead City, which has little

to offer otherwise, is also a good choice for river rats, though without the gambling and Vegas aesthetic. (It has more of a strip-mall aesthetic, unfortunately.) It borders the Lake Mead National Recreation Area and is right near Lake Mohave, with its marinas and boat rental shops, and has one of the best river parks in the region at Davis Camp.

CASINOS

There are nine resorts and 13 casinos in Laughlin, most of them relatively affordable. The best of the bunch stretch out along the river's west bank, and there's a riverside walkway between them with streetlights, public art, and boat docks. Room prices vary,

402

THE LOWER COLORADO RIVER
BULLHEAD CITY AND LAUGHLIN

but you can often find a relatively nice bed on the river for under $50. Prices generally go up on holidays. Most of the resorts offer a variety of packages that include meals and river cruises. These aren't the Indian casinos that you've seen in Arizona; Laughlin's gambling halls are pure Vegas clones. What with the heat and the desert and all, it's possible to forget you're not in Sin City, especially if you've been head-down at the blackjack table for two days straight. But then you look out the window and see that blue river, and you know exactly where you are.

The **Pioneer Hotel and Gambling Hall** (2200 S. Casino Dr., 800/634-3469, www.pioneerlaughlin.com) is a step or two down from the likes of the Aquarius and the other newer luxury places in town but has the usual slots, poker, blackjack, roulette, and more. This is a good overnight choice for folks with boats and other watercraft because you can park close to your room.

The **Riverside Resort Hotel and Casino** (1650 S. Casino Dr., 800/227-3849, www.riversideresort.com) was the first casino built in Laughlin, way back in 1966. Of course, it's been built up mightily since then. It has a movie theater, a classic car collection, a bowling alley and game room, and two swimming pools. The 80,000-square-foot casino has slots, blackjack, table games, and more, and a concert venue hosts music, comedy, and burlesque shows.

The **Colorado Belle Hotel and Casino** (2100 S. Casino Dr., 877/460-0777, www.coloradobelle.com), a nonfloating replica of a 19th-century Mississippi paddlewheel, is a wonder of popular architecture. It has a swimming pool and spa and a huge casino with the usual games. It's right on the riverwalk.

The **Aquarius Casino Resort** (1900 S. Casino Dr., 800/662-5825, www.aquariuscasinoresort.com) has slots, blackjack, poker, keno, and a variety of table games and offers frequent concerts in its pavilion (Foreigner, ZZ Top, Carrie Underwood, Rascal Flatts). There's a big pool on the roof with cabanas and some amazing views of the stark desert cut through by that shining band of blue river.

RECREATION

People come here for the river: to float on it, speed over it, and swim in it. Every other truck barreling down the melting blacktops around here tows a speedboat, and the kids walk around in their life vests because they are rarely out of the water long enough to bother removing them.

Davis Camp

If you're not staying in one of the casino resorts, the best place to spend a day playing in the river and seeing if your boat still floats is **Davis Camp** (2251 Hwy. 68, Bullhead City, 928/754-7250, www.mcparks.com, dawn-dusk, $10 per car) in Bullhead City, which was built in the 1940s to house workers building nearby Davis Dam. You can fish here, ride your Jet Ski (or rent one), and swim and lounge in the sun on the park's sandy beaches, which all have charcoal grills and picnic tables. There's a mile and half of shoreline here, and it's the easiest and most convivial way to get a taste, though hopefully not a mouthful, of the Colorado. Just east of the park's boat dock **BestJetz** (702/208-0333, www.bestjetz.com, 8am-11pm daily, $69 per hour, $189 per day, reservations suggested) rents Jet Skis and kayaks.

Boat Tours

Along the riverwalk in Laughlin and in many of the casino resorts, you can book speedboat tours of the river. One of the best is **London Bridge Jet Boat Tours** (888/505-3545, http://laughlinboattours.com, 9:30am to 4:30 pm, $75 adults, $55 children 12 and under). The fully enclosed boats run 58 miles downriver to London Bridge in Lake Havasu City, passing through spectacular **Topock Gorge,** with its bighorn sheep dancing on the cliffs above, along the way. The trip takes all day—two hours each way and a two-hour layover at the bridge for lunch and sightseeing—but is worth the time away from the casino for all the beautiful scenery.

EVENTS

In late April thousands of Harley-Davidson enthusiasts gather in the desert along the river for the **Laughlin River Run** (714/694-2800 or 800/357-8223, http://laughlinriverrun.com, late Apr.), which includes concerts, festivals, and all sorts of general revelry.

In early August, just as the hot dog days take hold, thousands of revelers gather from both sides of the river for the **River Regatta Roundup** (855/924-6882, www.bullheadregatta.com, early Aug.), a floating party of tubers and boaters and various other floaters, all drifting together along the Colorado River in one big traffic jam.

SHOPPING

Nearly all of the casino resorts in Laughlin have several different retail shops and gift shops selling local souvenirs and T-shirts with silly slogans, cowboy gear, and the necessities of river play.

If you're more inclined to drop your money at the shoe store than in a slot machine, check out the **Laughlin Outlet Center** (1955 S. Casino Dr., 702/298-3650, www.laughlinoutletcenter.com, 9am-8pm Mon.-Sat., 10am-7pm Sun.). The 68 outlet stores in this air-conditioned mall across the street from the Aquarius will keep bargain hunters busy and out of the heat and sun.

FOOD
Laughlin

Most of the casinos have chain restaurants, but the Vegas-style buffets are really where it's at. Typically one night of the weekend is prime rib night and one night offers seafood, and your dinner usually comes with a free drink or two. Three of the best in town are the **Windows on the River Buffet** (1900 S. Casino Dr., 800/662-5825, www.aquariuscasinoresort.com, $14-20) at the Aquarius or the **Riverside Buffet**

(1650 S. Casino Dr., 800/227-3849, www.riversideresort.com, $9-20) or **Gourmet Room** at the Riverside ($25-30).

For nonbuffet eating, try the **Pints Brewery and Sports Bar** (2100 S. Casino Dr., 877/460-0777, www.coloradobelle.com, 11am-11pm daily, late night service 3am-11am daily, $9-30) at the Colorado Belle, which has well-crafted beers and serves appetizing and tasteful pub eats, including pizza, buckets of deep-fried shrimp, and amazing onion rings. Their motto: "Vegetarian: an old Indian word for bad hunter."

Bullhead City
The **Black Bear Diner** (1751 W. Hwy. 95, 928/763-2477, www.blackbeardiner.com, 6am-10pm Sun.-Thurs., 6am-11pm Fri.-Sat., $8-16) serves a fantastic breakfast.

ACCOMMODATIONS
Laughlin

In Laughlin, your best bet for accommodations is the casinos.

The **Pioneer Hotel and Gambling Hall** (2200 S. Casino Dr., 800/634-3469, www.pioneerlaughlin.com, $80-132) has some of the most affordable rooms in Laughlin, many of them looking out over the riverwalk and the river with the hotel's landmark "River Rick" sign looking down from high above. This is a good choice for visitors with boats and other watercraft because you can park close to your room.

The rooms at the **Riverside Resort Hotel and Casino** (1650 S. Casino Dr., 800/227-3849, www.riversideresort.com, $50-119), many of them high in the sky and overlooking the dry land and the river, are standard, clean, and comfortable. The 80,000-square-foot casino has slots, blackjack, table games, and more.

The **Colorado Belle Hotel and Casino** (2100 S. Casino Dr., 877/460-0777, www.coloradobelle.com, $30-130) has nice rooms that overlook the river along with a swimming pool and spa. It's right on the riverwalk, so you can look down from your room and watch the crowds go by and the water-skiers go down.

The **Aquarius Casino Resort** (1900 S. Casino Dr., 800/662-5825, www.aquariuscasinoresort.com, $50-170) has elegant rooms with river views and an adults-only tower. There's a large pool on the roof with cabanas and amazing views of the desert.

Bullhead City

There are several chain hotels in town, but you can probably find a better deal and a nicer, more entertaining place to stay just across the river in Laughlin. **Davis Camp** (2251 Hwy. 68, Bullhead City, 928/754-7250, www.mcparks.com), which is right on the river, rents rustic 1940s-era two- and three-bedroom bungalows ($100-215) that are perfect for a weekend family getaway. There are also rustic but air-conditioned "bunkhouses" for rent ($50 pp), plus dry camp spots ($17) and an RV park ($25-30). Reservations for a bungalow are recommended far in advance.

INFORMATION AND SERVICES

Stop in at the **Laughlin Visitor Information Center** (1555 Casino Dr., 702/298-3321, www.visitlaughlin.com, 8am-4:30pm Mon.-Fri.) for information on Laughlin and the surrounding area.

Lake Havasu City and Vicinity

This riverside haven for snowbird retirees and boat-cruising vacationers sprang up from the hot and sandy desert in 1963. A few years later, Havasu's developer, Robert McCulloch Sr., secured the master-planned community's place in history by bringing a bit of history to its brand-new shores. He purchased the London Bridge and shipped it to Arizona, where he installed it brick by brick across the channel at Pittsburgh Point, a peninsula now referred to locally as "the island." McCulloch also hired a former Disneyland designer to help create an "English Village" in the bridge's shadow, and the whole package has been a popular tourist draw ever since. These days, the state parks and walkways and beaches along the reservoir are crowded most weekends in spring and even in summer—when the triple digits rule for three months or more—with boaters, anglers, and Jet Ski enthusiasts. During the college universe's annual spring break bacchanalia, hordes of bikini- and board short-clad students descend on the town, while at other times it seems as though everyone is over 60.

Lake Havasu City, like many other once-sleepy communities along the state's west coast, has grown immensely over the last decade or so, and there are more and more working families living here now, and so more chain stores and restaurants. For the visitor, however, it is still Lake Havasu—born from the building of Parker Dam and holding water that travels across the desert in canals to Phoenix and Tucson—that is the main draw. If you're not into water sports and if you wilt easily in the sun, consider spending no more than an afternoon here, strolling over and beneath the bridge and along the walkway next to the channel, watching the ducks dip and bob. If you want to get to know the reservoir, though, there are all manner of wet and cool things to do here.

SIGHTS AND RECREATION

If you're not boating, fishing, swimming, or generally worshipping the sun here, you may find things a bit dull. The water is the place to be, but you can easily get on it without getting wet. All along the main walkway under the bridge you'll find boat rentals, fishing guides,

1: Laughlin, a mini-Vegas on the Colorado River
2: London Bridge

excursion cruises, and even a singing gondola ride. There are also unique shopping opportunities near the lake, and a few great places to eat. This is where you'll want to head first—just follow the signs to London Bridge, where the parking is generally free.

★ London Bridge

London Bridge (McCulloch Blvd., 928/453-8883, free) began its long life in 1831, spanning the Thames River in London. First, horses pulled carriages across it, then the first cars chugged its length, and then, inevitably, the modern world caught up with it. By the early 1960s the old bridge no longer had what it takes to serve such a busy crossing, so the city of London sold it to Robert McCulloch, a chainsaw manufacturer just then entering the lucrative trade of master-planned retirement and resort communities. Now it spans an artificial channel of the Colorado River, walked and driven over by millions of sun-baked tourists every year. It's a strange sight, the old-world urban structure stuck out here in the middle of the desert. The best views are from below, where the scene has a bit of a picturesque old London look to it—but not quite. The bridge's seeming incongruity isn't as strange as it appears, however. In the 19th century, the lower Colorado and the Arizona Strip, not too far north of this region, were settled by Mormon pioneers from Salt Lake City, many of whom were English. That has little to do with the bridge's travels, though. Take a half hour or so to walk across and under it, and read the plaques placed at either end that explain how these bricks from the North Atlantic wound up stacked here in the desert.

Lake Havasu State Park

Popular **Lake Havasu State Park** (99 London Bridge Rd., 928/855-2784, http://azstateparks.com, sunrise-10pm daily, $15 per car Mon.-Fri., $20 Sat.-Sun. and holidays, camping $30-35) stretches along the river north and south of the bridge and includes **Windsor Beach,** an excellent riverside campground and sunning and swimming spot. If you're looking to laze around on the beach for a while and watch the people and the waterfowl, Windsor Beach is the place to do it.

Jet Ski rentals are available at the park through **Windsor Beach Rentals** (928/453-5558, www.windsorbeachrentals.com). Call for daily rates, as they offer a lot of specials.

Cattail Cove State Park

About 15 miles south of the bridge along Route 95 the telltale cattails that give **Cattail Cove State Park** (Rte. 95, 928/855-1223, http://azstateparks.com, sunrise-10pm daily, $10 per car Mon.-Fri., $15 Sat.-Sun. and holidays, camping $30-35) its name rise up out of the water. Here you'll find camping, boating, and fishing opportunities just a bit outside the main town area, including several primitive campsites along the shores accessible only by boat. There's a nice beach and good swimming here—a perfect place for a laid-back day or overnight riverine outing with the family.

Havasu National Wildlife Refuge

Havasu National Wildlife Refuge (317 Mesquite Ave., Needles, California, 760/326-3853, www.fws.gov) protects 30 river miles of Colorado River habitat from Needles, California, to Lake Havasu City, Arizona, where one of the last remaining natural sections of the lower Colorado River flows through the 20-mile-long spectacle that is **Topock Gorge,** where you might see bighorn sheep and other native animals.

Watercraft Rentals

One of the better outfitters is **London Bridge Watercraft Tours and Rentals** (928/453-8883, http://londonbridgewatercraft.com), which operates out of **Crazyhorse Campgrounds** (1534 Beachcomber Blvd., 928/855-4033, www.crazyhorsecampgrounds.com, $15 day use) on "the island" on the west side of the bridge. There are a number of other rental places along the walkway beneath the bridge offering all-day and dining excursions, fishing trips, expeditions into the Lake Havasu Wildlife Refuge upriver, and paddleboats and canoes for sticking closer to the shore. The rental prices may change according to the season, with spring break and other crowded times ushering in higher fees. All of the rental places are going to require some kind of deposit, typically taken care of by handing over your credit card number.

There are several concessionaires beneath the bridge in Lake Havasu City that offer **guided tours** of **Topock Gorge,** a gorgeous river canyon with towering walls and dramatic formations.

It's essential to prebook a tour at least a day ahead and plan to be gone for several hours. The **Bluewater Jet Boat Tours** (926/855-7171, www.coloradoriverjettours. com, Oct.-May, 10:30am and 1:30pm, $45 pp, $25 children 6-12) offers a 2.5-hour air-conditioned excursion into the gorge in a 49-passenger speedboat, while **Rubba Duck Safari** (928/208-0293, 9am-5pm year-round, $69 pp double, $119 single) lets you pilot your own inflatable speedboat as you follow a guide. The latter is definitely not recommended in summer.

EVENTS

Not surprisingly, most of Lake Havasu's annual events have something to do with the water. The biggest event of the year is probably spring break, which happens throughout March and April. The population skews young during this time of year, and if you're not looking for a party and crowds, you might want to stay away. In late February the **Mark Hahn Memorial Havasu 300 APBA National Team Endurance Race** (www.pwcoffshore.com, late Feb.) brings together the nation's best Jet Ski pilots for a big race. April brings the **Lake Havasu Marine Associations Annual Boat Show** (928/453-8833, Apr.), a three-day event featuring the best in watercraft, food, concerts, and all sorts of other fun.

SHOPPING

Stick around the water to find distinctive gifts and souvenirs at the **English Village Shoppes** (1477 Queens Bay, 928/855-0888). Under the bridge and across the channel you'll find the **Island Mall & Brewery** (1425 McCulloch Blvd., 928/855-6274), a two-story enclosed mall.

Away from the bridge and water area, the **Main Street in the Uptown District** (upper McCulloch Blvd., one mile east of London Bridge) has more than 200 shops, including Shambles Village, which has all kinds of antiques galleries.

FOOD

★ **Ójala** (2144 N. McCulloch Blvd., 928/846-3916, www.ojala108.com, 11am-2pm Mon.-Fri., $8-15) is a plant-based all-vegan restaurant with a small lunch menu featuring largely organic, sustainable, and local ingredients. Head 1.6 miles inland from London Bridge along North McCulloch to sample chef Karla Pada's creative and healthy appetizers, salads, sandwiches, and other plant-based delights—with dishes like cauliflower ceviche, Greek salad with garbanzo beans and lime dressing, and a chipotle hummus burger.

Juicy's River Café (42 Smoketree Ave. S., 928/855-8429, www.juicysgreatfood.com, 7am-9pm Mon.-Sat., 7am-7pm Sun., $12-40) serves delectable breakfasts, sandwiches, and homemade comfort fare such as ribs and fish-and-chips, for those who've worn themselves hungry playing on the river.

Shugrue's (1425 McCulloch Blvd., 928/453-1400, 11am-close daily, $12-40) has great views of the water and bridge, delicious seafood, burgers, and other American fare, plus homemade pastries and bread.

ACCOMMODATIONS

Though you could definitely do it, it is not necessary to spend a lot of money to find a nice place to stay on the lake.

The **Island Inn Hotel** (1300 McCulloch Blvd., 928/680-0606 or 800/243-9955, www. islandinnhotelaz.com, $89-109) has basic, affordable rooms available near the water and right in the middle of all the fun.

The nicest and most popular place to stay in town is the **London Bridge Resort** (Rte. 95, 928/855-0888, www.londonbridgeresort. com, $139-239 plus $30 per night resort fee), right near the bridge and overlooking the lake. It has a beautiful lobby with a replica of the "queen's carriage," comfortable suite-style rooms with bridge and channel views, a good restaurant, and a lot of extras, like a waterslide for the kids.

The **Heat Hotel** (1420 McCulloch Blvd., 928/854-2833, www.heathotel.com, $179-250 plus $15 per night resort fee) is a boutique hotel that's bringing a bit of badly needed style to this desert waystation. Many of the bright rooms have wonderful views of the water and feature natural light and sleek modern furnishings. The outdoor but covered **Heat Bar** off the lobby is a great place to drink and watch the boats go by, and if you brought your own boat the hotel has its own docks.

INFORMATION AND SERVICES

The **Lake Havasu City Convention and Visitors Bureau** (314 London Bridge Rd., 928/453-3444 or 800/242-8278, www. golakehavasu.com, 8am-5pm Mon.-Fri.) can help you with all your questions and provide plenty of literature on sights and events in Lake Havasu. There's also a **Visitor Information Center** (422 English Village, 9am-5pm daily).

PARKER AND THE PARKER STRIP

The small resort town of Parker looks out on about 16 miles of swift-flowing Colorado River called the Parker Strip, where retirement and vacation homes line the banks between the town and Parker Dam to the north. Most of the land below and around Parker comprises the **Colorado River Indian Reservation**, 270,000 acres that include the beautiful 16,400-acre **Swansea Wilderness Area**, about 25 miles northeast of town.

This is one of the best stretches of the lower Colorado, and it's packed with boaters and other river lovers most weekends in season. Again, though, if you're not a river rat or trying to be one, there's not much of an incentive to stop.

Sights and Recreation

The small **Colorado River Indian Tribes Museum and Library** (1007 Arizona Ave., Parker, 928/669-8770, www.crit-nsn.gov, 8am-5pm Mon.-Fri., 10am-3pm Sat., free) has some interesting exhibits and artifacts of these often-overlooked tribes.

Buckskin Mountain State Park (5476 Hwy. 95, 928/667-3231, http://azstateparks. com, $10 per car) and its **River Island Unit** (5200 Hwy. 95, 928/667-3386), about 12 miles north of Parker, have excellent camping, fishing, and boating opportunities.

You can also drive over **Parker Dam** (Hwy. 95, 760/663-3712) just north of the town; it's open to passenger vehicles only 5am-11pm. On the California side of the dam, there's a rough but scenic drive that will take you along the river and past a few historic sites and shoreline oases.

Just north of Parker, the Bill Williams River flows from the east into the Colorado River. A beautiful thin ribbon of water moving through a marshy forest of cattails announces the **Bill Williams River National Wildlife Refuge** (60911 Hwy. 95, Parker, 928/667-4144, www.fws.gov), which protects a thick cottonwood-willow forest and has excellent bird-watching and kayaking opportunities. The refuge is located between mileposts 160 and 162 on State Highway 95, about 17 miles south of Lake Havasu City.

Food and Accommodations

The place to be in the Parker area is the Colorado Indian Tribe's **BlueWater Resort & Casino** (Hwy. 95, 928/669-7000, www. bluewaterfun.com, $140), which has affordable and clean, but chilly, rooms that look out over the river and the marina, where you can rent boats and Jet Skis and park your own

The Naked Bookseller of Quartzsite

Paul Winer, the nearly nude proprietor of the **Reader's Oasis** (690 E. Main St., 928/927-6551) in Quartzsite, has been selling books along the tiny desert town's main drag since the 1990s.

"I used to wear very brief shorts," he said. "I didn't drop them and feel free to be who I am until I had 180,000 books; then I thought I could do it."

Winer spent 25 years back East playing boogie-woogie piano, nude, under the name "Sweet Pie." He fought a protracted public indecency battle and eventually prevailed, he said. In lieu of recompense he chose to settle a rather large IRS bill free and clear; then he headed out to Arizona to see his parents. He started selling his mom's paperbacks at the big swap-meet gem shows that give Quartzsite one of the largest populations in Arizona for a few weeks every winter, when the desert becomes a tent city and there are all manner of strange and interesting itinerant merchants around. Paul is here to stay, however; he's open year-round, he said, even when the heat reaches 120°F, which it is wont to do here in the summer. Arizona, he said, "is one of the few states that would tolerate someone like me on the main street of a town. It has a history of having the most obstinate, stubborn, off-the-wall people. There is still quite a tolerance for outsiders."

He has a lot of good books for sale, including an excellent selection of used books about the Southwest and children's books. Book lovers who might otherwise be put off by Winer's lack of clothing—he usually wears a small thong-style loincloth and not much else on his thin and tanned frame—will want to think twice about missing this unique store. Winer is a smart, friendly fellow, and he won't hesitate to tell you his crazy story and recommend a book.

craft if you have one. Inside the hotel there's a buffet; slots, blackjack, and poker, along with a multitiered pool and waterslide that the kids won't want to leave behind. There's also a movie theater and a sports bar.

QUARTZSITE

This quiet desert spot on Highway 95 between Parker and Yuma, right off I-10, is nearly deserted in the summer, when temperatures can and do reach 120°F fairly regularly. When the mercury dips, however, this wide spot in the road becomes crowded with itinerant retirees, roaming bands of gem and mineral dealers, and other assorted swap-meet entrepreneurs.

Throughout January and February, the streets in town are lined with booths and tables selling all manner of gems and jewelry and just about anything else you can think of, and on through the winter the RV tribe of retirees makes Quartzsite a temporary boomtown.

Even if it's summer and 110°F in the shade, if you happen to be passing through this settlement around lunch or dinnertime, make sure to stop at the ★ **Grubstake Social Club** (725 N. Central, Hwy. 95, 928/927-4485, www.grubstakeaz.com, 11am-close daily, $10-30), which serves delicious bar-and-grill-style food and has karaoke, pool tables, live bands, and a fun local vibe.

Yuma and Vicinity

Yuma has long been an important place. For centuries the area where the once wild Colorado and Gila Rivers found each other and merged was a natural crossing point for Native Americans, and during the great gold rush of 1849 the riverside desert became a crucial crossing and lifeline for all those prospectors and adventurers going to California. For a time steamboats chugged up and down the Colorado, docking at Yuma to load and unload supplies important to the settling of the Southwest. Some of the Wild West's most despicable characters found themselves sweltering in the hell of the Yuma Territorial Prison. In the era of reclamation Yuma became an important agricultural center, and it still is, producing winter lettuce and other crops. In 1915 Yuma became an important link in the nation's commercial scene with the opening of the famous Ocean-to-Ocean Highway Bridge over the Colorado. To most Arizonans who don't live near the state's western border, Yuma is known mostly as a place to stop and get gas on the way to the cool ocean breezes of San Diego.

Today Yuma is a growing city of about 105,000 people with an economy based largely on agriculture and the service industry. From about November through March the city's population swells by some 90,000 people, many of them retirees and snowbirds seeking the easy life in one of Yuma's more than 80 RV and mobile home parks. While the town boasts sunny skies 95 percent of the year, and winter temperatures are often in the 70s and even the 80s, it is not a place that you want to visit during the height of summer. You'll find the temperature hovering many days around 110°F, cooling off very little at night. Consequently, some businesses and attractions truncate their hours or shut down altogether when the heat reigns.

SIGHTS
★ Yuma Territorial Prison State Historic Park

They say Yuma Prison wasn't as bad as its reputation suggests, that the more than 3,000 outlaws, polygamists, gunfighters, robbers, and murderers housed here between 1876 and 1909 were afforded three squares a day, health care, and education, conveniences many of their pioneer counterparts on the outside sorely lacked. But spend a little time exploring popular **Yuma Territorial Prison State Historic Park** (100 Prison Hill Rd., 928/783-4771, http://azstateparks.com, 9am-5pm daily, $6 adults, $3 children 7-13) and you'll likely come to a different conclusion: This wasn't a place where you'd want to spend any time, especially in an era long before air-conditioning. If you think it's hot in Yuma today, just imagine being confined to a dark, airless cell, the heat as incessant as the din from the cell block, full of half-mad prisoners and constant tubercular coughing.

There's not a lot left of the original buildings; Yuma citizens used the old prison as a kind of free lumberyard for years before it was made into a state park. During the Depression the cells served as temporary homes for hobos and destitute families. But the real interest here is the lore of the lawless territorial days, and there is much of it in the museum, where you'll learn all about the various characters who once called the dark cells home as well as the colorful doctors and prison administrators who managed the place. You can climb up to the large guard tower, look over the slowly meandering Colorado as it snakes through wetlands below, and feel what it was like (sort of, anyway) to be confined to a prison cell way out here in the middle of the desert, far from home and grace. Plan on spending at least an hour or two here, as there is much to discover in the stories and artifacts of crime and punishment on the Southwestern frontier.

Yuma

To Algodones
Sand Dunes
and San Diego

ARAZ RD

Winterhaven

WINTERHAVEN DR

Colorado River

CALIFORNIA

ARIZONA

Yuma Quartermaster
State Historic Park

YUMA LANDING
RESTAURANT

BEST WESTERN
CORONADO
MOTOR HOTEL

RIVER CITY
GRILL

1ST ST

3RD ST

SEE DETAIL

YUMA TERRITORIAL
PRISON STATE
HISTORIC PARK

EXIT 1

S MAIN ST

S GILA ST

QUECHAN DR

1ST AVE

BUS.
8

8TH ST

YUMA CABANA
MOTEL

10TH ST

12TH ST

SHILO INN
HOTEL

EXIT 2

0   0.5 mi

0   0.5 km

To Quartzsite →

AVENUE C

AVENUE B

AVENUE A

E 1ST ST

W 2ND ST

S MAIN ST

LUTE'S
CASINO

SANGUINETTI
HOUSE MUSEUM

S MAIDEN LN

S GILA ST

I-8

16TH ST

4TH AVE

ARIZONA AVE

95

To Phoenix →

EXIT 3

280

S 1ST AVE

W 3RD ST

S MADISON AVE

YUMA CONVENTION
AND VISITORS
BUREAU

HOTEL LEE

HAROLD C GISS PKWY

24TH ST

THE PRESS
CAFE & BISTRO

PACIFIC AVE

AVENUE 3 E

BUS.
8

95

COUNTY 11TH ST

32ND ST

© MOON.COM

YUMA INT'L AIRPORT ✈

Yuma Quartermaster Depot State Historic Park

A small historic park on Yuma's main drag, **Yuma Quartermaster Depot State Historic Park** (201 N. 4th Ave., 928/329-0471, http://azstateparks.com, 9am-5pm daily, $4 adults, $2 children 7-13) preserves the history of the U.S. Army's presence in Yuma from 1864 to 1883, when riverboat steamers brought supplies up from the mouth of the Colorado to serve army outposts throughout the region. Before the railroad entered the

Southwest, a six-month supply of food, clothing, ammunition, and other staples was quartered here for distribution to forts in Arizona, Utah, Nevada, and New Mexico. At the park you can see the old commanding officer's quarters and a few other historic buildings and artifacts related to the army's long occupation of the wild open West.

The most interesting story told at the park, which until the summer of 2007 was called Yuma Crossing Historic Park, is about the construction of the audacious Yuma Siphon, an engineering project that would sound ambitious even today. Using old Captain Nemo-style diving gear, workers built a concrete tunnel underneath the Colorado River in order to divert the river for use in agriculture, changing the fate of Yuma forever and securing the town's survival beyond being a way station for goods and people headed to California. At the park there are some excellent displays on the project, and a few of the old diving suits and other artifacts of this incredible reclamation feat.

Sanguinetti House Museum

The history of Yuma is on display at the **Sanguinetti House Museum** (240 S. Madison Ave., 928/782-1841, www. arizonahistoricalsociety.org, 10am-4pm Tues.-Sat., $6 adults, children 12 and under free) in the city's quiet historic downtown. Named after the home's former owner, pioneer merchant E. F. Sanguinetti, the little adobe house has informative displays on the history of the lower Colorado region from prehistory through modern times, with period rooms and a shady garden patio and aviary with talking birds in cages. If you're really interested in the history of the region, make sure to converse with one of the volunteer docents who staff the main desk; they are usually longtime residents or natives of the area and can provide personal context to the historical displays. A separate adobe next door, formerly the residence of a riverboat captain, houses an excellent local- and regional-history bookshop.

Historic Downtown

Yuma's downtown has been going through a planned rebirth for a few decades now, and there are some cool old buildings from various eras still standing, including the art deco **Yuma Theatre** built in 1936. It has been restored and now shows movies, and nearby, the **Yuma Downtown Art Center** has four galleries showing the work of local and regional artists. Other buildings show the influence of Spanish Colonial Revival style, and there are

even a few old adobes still standing from the territorial days. It's easy to walk around the downtown. Start at **Main Street Plaza** and just explore—there are a few shops, antiques stores, galleries, and boutiques along the narrow streets, and on the edges of the downtown you'll see a few old historic homes. That being said, on most days the downtown is a bit quiet and deserted, especially in the summer. Still, it's a good place to get a feel for what Yuma used to be.

Algodones Dunes

Desert country neophytes might be a little disappointed with the relative lushness of the typical Arizona desert landscape, which defies with its diversity the daydream of Saharaesque dunes with nothing but white sand for miles and miles. If you were hoping for a "real desert," something on the order of Luke Skywalker's home planet of Tatooine, head across the bridge into California for a look at the southeastern end of the great, shifting stretch of sand known as the Algodones Dunes, also called the Imperial Dunes. About 17 miles west on I-8 outside of Yuma take the Gray's Well exit to a parking lot on the edge of the dunes near the Midway campground, part of the **Imperial Dunes Recreation Area.** Here you can park your car and witness the 45-mile by 6-mile dunes—but don't go far. There is literally nothing out here but sand and then more sand. If you think it looks like Tatooine, that's because it is: George Lucas filmed portions of *Return of the Jedi* near here in the 1980s. These days the dunes are popular with motorcycle and ATV enthusiasts, who tear around nearby Glamis on holiday weekends in a great rumbling and rolling party. A few miles west on the frontage road from Gray's Well (follow the signs) you can see what remains of the old **Plank Road,** a movable highway of wooden planks once placed on top of the dunes so early car travelers could pass without sinking into the sand, this before highway technology advanced enough to build the interstate that now bisects the area. It's not recommended that you go here in the summer, nor should you take off across the dunes on foot. Just look, or maybe scamper up a tall dune near the parking lot and see what an expanse of nothing looks like—it's preternaturally beautiful, and a good place for meditating on, well . . . nothingness.

RECREATION

The **riverfront trail** follows the Colorado River past wetlands and historic sites, parks, and Yuma's downtown—a lighted, paved path for biking and walking in perfect winter weather. There are several interesting stops along the way, including a wetlands park, a small plaza marking the spot where in 1877 the first railroad car passed into Arizona, and Gateway Park, a riverside greenspace with great views of the Ocean-to-Ocean Highway Bridge. A walk or ride here is a perfect way to get a sense of what the river is like and how important it has been to the history of the Yuma. You can rent bikes along the trail at the **Quartermaster Depot State Historic Park** (201 N. 4th Ave., www.mrbsbicycles.com, 9am-5pm daily except Mon. June-Sept., $10 per hour, $25 for 24 hours). The trail begins at Joe Henry Memorial Park at 23rd Avenue and First Street and goes to Pacific Avenue/ Avenue 2E.

A popular and fun way to see the river and the refuge is to take a boat tour with **Yuma River Tours** (1920 Arizona Ave., 928/783-4400, www.yumarivertours.com, $38-89). Make sure to call ahead in summer, as they have limited hours during the hot months. The best tour is the 4- to 5-hour, 32-mile boat trip to **Norton's Landing** ($75 pp, includes lunch), an old steamboat port and mining ghost town. The tour takes you deep into the refuge, and the guides are expert at spotting and pointing out birds and mammals along the way. Reservations are required. Yuma River Tours also offers day and dining cruises on an old stern-wheeler ($48-63 pp) and overnight guided kayak and canoe trips.

About 35 miles north of Yuma on U.S. 95 is **Martinez Lake**, where you can fish, boat, and view wildlife, among other activities.

The Imperial National Wildlife Refuge is just north of the lake and extends for 30 miles upriver, teeming with water-loving birds and other wildlife. At **Fisher's Landing** (928/782-7049, www.fisherslandingresort.com) on Martinez Lake you can rent a boat for the day ($50). You can also rent or buy fishing gear and book a guide to show you the best hideouts of bass, crappie, bluegill, stripers, and flathead catfish. There's a restaurant serving burgers, sandwiches, fish, and steaks ($5-18) and a general store. The boat shop and a gas dock are open daily 8am-4pm. Other facilities at Fisher's Landing are open daily but hours vary seasonally, so it's best to call ahead.

Wildlife Refuges

While the many dams built along the Colorado River during the era of reclamation in the 1930s and 1940s made it possible for the Southwest to grow and thrive as a habitat for humans, the loss of the river's natural and wild flow ruined much of the essential riparian habitat downstream. In an effort to restore what was lost and hold on to what remains, the U.S. Fish and Wildlife Service has established a number of wildlife refuges in western Arizona. These are wild and rugged places, not for the unprepared or the uninitiated. But for those looking for something far off the track, these protected lands provide some of the best bird-watching, wildlife-viewing, and nature communing—especially of the desert and riverine kind—in the entire state.

Two of the refuges—Imperial and Havasu—feature well-established tour companies that will take you along the river and point out all there is to see.

Just north of Yuma along U.S. 95, the ruggedly beautiful **Kofa National Wildlife Refuge** (356 W. 1st St., Yuma, 928/783-7861, www.fws.gov) includes 665,400 acres of rough desert landscape, home to the dexterous bighorn and legions of reptiles who couldn't live anywhere else but this dry and sharp-rock land. Within the refuge is **Palm Canyon,** in the west end of the Kofa Mountains, where grow the only native palm trees in Arizona—a

state that probably has more than its fair share of palms imported to its city streets. The half-mile hike into Palm Canyon to see the trees is one of the region's best. Along U.S. 95 north of Yuma, watch for the Palm Canyon sign, then follow the dirt road east for nine miles toward the mountains and the trailhead.

Heading west to the river, you will find the 25,768-acre Imperial National Wildlife Refuge (Martinez Lake, 928/783-3317, www.fws.gov), a 30-mile desert-meets-wetland landscape that is renowned as a stop for various migratory bird species and full of desert mammals like bighorn sheep, mountain lions, bobcats, deer, wild horses, and burros. There's a visitors center here, a rough-and-tumble scenic drive that takes you through an unvarnished Sonoran Desert stretch, and a few awesome lookouts with views of the river valley. The 1.3-mile Painted Desert Trail leads to a grand view as well. Yuma River Tours (1920 Arizona Ave., 928/783-4400, www.yumarivertours.com) offers boat tours into the refuge.

Farther upriver is the Cibola National Wildlife Refuge (66600 Cibola Lake Rd., Cibola, 928/857-3253, www.fws.gov), where you'll find some of the best birding in the region. Just outside the visitors center there's a short, scenic drive (called Canada Goose Drive), along which you can stop and hike the one-mile loop nature trail, moving through a beautiful riparian habitat of cottonwood, willow, and mesquite forests. In winter, thousands of Canada geese, snow geese, ducks, and sandhill cranes are usually visible from an observation deck here.

The Cabeza Prieta National Wildlife Refuge (1611 N. 2nd St., Ajo, 520/387-6483, www.fws.gov), about 90 miles east of Yuma, is a forbidding landscape hugging the U.S.-Mexico border. If you're looking for the Sonoran Desert in the raw, you'll find it here. The Cabeza Prieta (meaning "dark head" in Spanish, for the area's volcanic coloring) is

a hot and sparse land, covered in cacti and creosote (and wildflowers and other blooming desert show-offs in the spring). The refuge provides 860,010 acres of habitat for desert creatures to roam, including bighorn sheep and the cactus-pollinating lesser long-nosed bats. There's a small visitors center and short interpretive trail at the refuge office, where you have to stop first to pick up a permit to explore the refuge. Most of the refuge is within the airspace of the Barry M. Goldwater Air Force Range, so there are often low-flying aircraft in the area, crossing the refuge on their way to the bombing ranges to the north. Somewhere out in that sublimely wild swath of Sonoran Desert, that great advocate of wild desert, the author Edward Abbey, is said to be buried in an unmarked grave.

ENTERTAINMENT AND EVENTS

For Vegas-style entertainment and games of chance, head over to Quechan Paradise Casino (450 Quechan Dr., 888/777-4946, www.paradise-casinos.com), where popular bands of yesteryear play often, and there are slots, blackjack, poker, and lots of food and drinks. To get there, take I-8 to the 4th Avenue exit, then go north on Imperial County Route S-24.

In early January Yuma's historic downtown hosts the Old Town Jubilee, with artisans, entertainment, and activities for the whole family. If you're in town in mid-February, when the weather in Yuma is perfect, don't miss Yuma River Daze and the Yuma Crossing Days Festival, three days celebrating local history and culture that includes river races, swimming, and a block party downtown.

FOOD

The must-visit restaurant in downtown Yuma is ★ Lute's Casino (221 S. Main St., 928/782-2192, www.lutescasino.com, 9am-8pm Mon.-Thurs., 9am-9pm Fri.-Sat., 10am-6pm Sun., $5-15), a place popular with locals and visitors alike. Even if you aren't hungry,

1: Algodones Dunes 2: Kofa National Wildlife Refuge

you'll enjoy sitting at one of the tall tables and drinking a brew, your neck craning to look at all the strange and hilarious—and even a bit bawdy—pictures covering the walls. The menu offers everything from burgers and hot dogs to burritos and tacos, all served up in huge portions. If you like hot dogs, don't miss Bob's Polish Kraut Dog—it's awesome. Lute's is also a good place to enjoy some nightlife with the locals.

The ★ **Yuma Landing Restaurant** (195 S. 4th Ave., 928/782-7427, www.yumalanding. com, 6am-9pm Sun.-Thurs., 6am-midnight Fri.-Sat., $10-14) is on the site where the first airplane landed in Yuma, and it has all sorts of memorabilia about that and other town history on the walls. It serves an eclectic mix of salads, sandwiches, steaks, prime rib, and Mexican dishes and has a bar with a good happy hour.

The **River City Grill** (600 W. 3rd St., 928/782-7988, www.rivercitygrillyuma.com, 11am-2pm and 5pm-10pm Mon.-Fri., 5pm-10pm Sat.-Sun., $18-30) serves top-notch seafood, sushi, lamb, beef, chicken, and vegetarian dishes in a cool contemporary setting, with a great patio for dining in the warmth of winter. It also has a fairly large selection of vegetarian and vegan options.

The Press Café & Bistro (121 E. 24th St., 928/726-2960, www.thepressyuma.com, 7am-4pm daily, $5-10) is a great place for breakfast, lunch, and a relaxing coffee or tea. They serve an assortment of pressed sandwiches—including the Yuman with avocado dressing, romaine lettuce, and pepper jack—as well as creative and filling salads for lunch, and breakfast burritos and homemade biscuits for breakfast. The Press uses all-recyclable, compostable, or biodegradable paper products.

ACCOMMODATIONS

Yuma has all the chain hotels and motels a town its size would ever want, and many of them are located just off I-8 or along 4th Avenue, the town's main commercial thoroughfare.

The best independent hotel in town is the historic **Coronado Motor Hotel** (233 4th Ave., 928/783-4453, www. coronadomotorhotel.com, $89-200). Built in 1938, this retro road-culture gem has comfortable rooms with free Wi-Fi and refrigerators. The staff is very friendly and helpful, and it's within minutes of the Yuma's historic downtown and the river. Breakfast at Yuma Landing comes with the room.

INFORMATION AND SERVICES

The **Visitor Information Center at Yuma Quartermaster Depot State Historic Park** (201 N. 4th Ave., 928/783-0071 or 800/293-0071, www.visityuma.com, 9am-5pm Tues.-Sun. June-Sept., 9am-5pm daily Oct.-May) downtown has all kinds of pamphlets and advice for enjoying Yuma and the lower Colorado River region.

TRANSPORTATION

Yuma International Airport (YUM, 2191 E. 32nd St., 928/726-5882, www.yumaairport. com) offers a few flights each day to Phoenix, but you really need a car to explore this region and to get around Yuma. The main line in and out of the city is I-8, and if you're going north along the river, use U.S. 95.

Background

The Landscape

The Arizona landscape is more varied than most, changing, with rises in elevation, from hot, cactus-choked **deserts** to scrubby bushlands to open **ponderosa pine forests** to coniferous, snowy highlands. Dry **grasslands** and long stretches of sagebrush plains spread across the higher deserts.

While it snows and rains much more in the high country than it does in the desert belt, the entire state is subject to what Lawrence Clark Powell called a "wrinkled dryness." Aridity is a constant no matter where you go. Spread thinly across the land, a few life-giving river

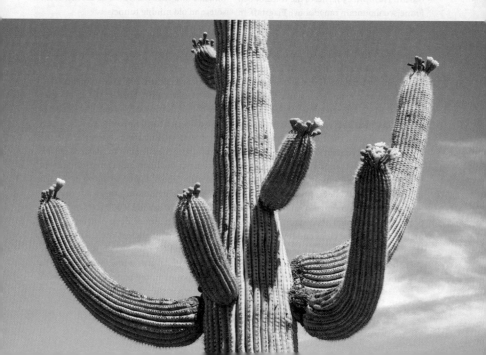

ways and **riparian areas** are treasured as oases and predictably exploited.

Arizona has 114,000 square miles, making it sixth in size among the states. Large tracts of wild, open land remain and likely always will.

GEOGRAPHY AND GEOLOGY

When dinosaurs roamed the earth, this desert was a swampy and wet place. Over the eons different portions of Arizona were covered by shallow seas that flowed in, flourished, and then dried up and retreated. Eventually the Arizona you see took shape—mountains rose, volcanoes burst and created new land, and plates slid apart and crashed into each other, creating upland plateaus and digging deep canyons with the erosional help of rivers, wind, and aridity.

Mountains

Few places have such extremes in elevation: You could travel from sea level along the lower Colorado to the 12,600-foot peak of **Mount Humphreys,** part of the volcanic San Francisco mountain range above Flagstaff, in a matter of a day or so. The White Mountains in the central-eastern part of the state tower higher than 10,000 feet and are often snow-capped. The Santa Catalinas, north of Tucson, rise to similar heights and feature the nation's southernmost ski run. A bit south of Tucson toward the U.S.-Mexico border, the Santa Rita Mountains tower above the Santa Cruz Valley, and just to the east the Huachuca Mountains do the same over the San Pedro Valley. Farther east the Pinaleno range rises above 10,000 feet, with towering Mount Graham watching over the Gila Valley. Many of these high Southern Arizona mountain ranges have important international observatories on their high reaches, so the cities and towns around them, Tucson included, are encouraged to keep their street lights and other "light noise" to a minimum so as to keep the sky dark and

clear. These southern ranges are often referred to as sky islands because they are exactly that: islands of biological diversity surrounded, and isolated, by vast seas of harsh, hot desert. In these sky islands can be found flora and fauna that exist in few other places in North America. Subtropical birds and other animals use these mountains as the northern reaches of their ranges, so it's not uncommon to find quetzal-like birds and even jungle-loving jaguars flitting and stalking around the misty creeksides of these forested ranges.

The central and north-central region of Arizona is also very mountainous, though the ranges here are somewhat smaller and older than those in the south. Around Prescott the Bradshaws and the Sierra Prieta reach to about 9,000 feet and are covered in pine. They were once, and perhaps still are, strewn with the precious minerals that became the impetus for one of the state's first mining booms. Throughout the state there are several other ranges and many detached, lonely peaks, many of them high and timbered and others midsize and rocky, covered in cactus, creosote, and old mining tunnels.

The Colorado Plateau

The plateau country dominates the northern portion of the state, covering about two-fifths of its area; its nearly 200-mile southern edge, the **Mogollon Rim,** borders the scrub-and-pine belt of the transition zone. Below that is the **basin and range province** of the desert country, stretching from the western to the eastern border and south to Mexico. The elevations in the basin and range swing from sea level to about 4,000 feet above it, though several large mountain ranges dot the lowlands and rise beyond 9,000 feet. In the uplands of the plateaus, deep canyons plunge into the layers of ancient rock. The bottom of the Grand Canyon, which is cut into the Colorado Plateau, is a low, hot desert. The highest points in the plateau country reach above 12,000 feet and are dominated by tundra and bare, cold boulders.

It is the contrast between the plateau and the basin and range provinces that makes Arizona such a rare landscape. Both have their origins deep in geologic time. The plateau country began to form in its current shape around 600 million years ago, when the continent was relatively flat and layer after layer of limestone, sandstone, siltstone, and shale were deposited by tropical seas moving in and then receding, leaving behind dunes and stream deposits and eroding the older layers for some 300 million years. Then the dune deposits started to harden and petrify, creating the strange, swirling rock-dune sandstone one sees all over the plateau region. Volcanic eruptions around the plateau added to the great piling of sediment while rivers and lakes and inland seas flushed in and then dried up or receded. But the plateau itself, while it was eroded and cut and sculpted and formed, remained relatively stable in contrast to the other lands around it, which changed mightily. About 70 million years ago the land all around the Southwest began to rise, pushing the plateau from about sea level to more than 10,000 feet above it. Great mountains were thrust up out of the ground all around the region, and the earth stretched with underground tension to create the basin and range province to the west and south of the plateau. According to the U.S. Geological Survey, about 20 million years ago a "great tension developed in the [earth's] crust . . . and the basin and range province broke into a multitude of down-dropped valleys and elongated mountains" similar to what we see today in Arizona's desertlands. But the Colorado Plateau remained stable and eventually rose nearly a mile higher than the basin and range. The Colorado River fell through the plateau and cut deep into the rock, carving the Grand Canyon—a process that started less than six million years ago.

The Grand Canyon

A visit to the Grand Canyon reveals much of the story of the continent's geologic formation. The top layers of rock, through which the Colorado first cut, called the Kaibab Formation, are around 270 million years old, while the gneiss and schist of the inner canyon are about 1.8 billion years old. Many geologists believe that the lower 2,000 feet or so of the canyon was cut and eroded just in the last 750,000 years—the blink of a geologist's eye. The canyon was formed by the great cosmic need of all water to return to the sea from whence it came. Water falls—that's its sole mission in life—and huge torrents of water carrying loads of dry, rocky sediment fall hard and fast, cutting deep into the rocks of an uplifted plateau. As the cuts get deeper, the land around it gives way and falls apart, thus creating the deep, wide, and wonderful hole in the plateau that has made Arizona famous.

Deserts

Arizona is the only state where three major deserts converge: The **Sonoran Desert** stretches across the southern portion of the state and includes the Phoenix and Tucson areas, while the **Mojave Desert** dominates on the western reaches. The **Chihuahuan Desert** of Mexico stretches north into southeastern Arizona.

The Sonoran Desert comprises about 120,000 square miles across the southwestern and south-central parts of Arizona. It is a woody desert, full of mesquite and paloverde trees, creosote, and, of course, the famous saguaro cactus. A small portion of the Mojave Desert dominates northwestern Arizona and is marked by creosote and other small bushes, cholla, and Joshua trees. The Chihuahuan Desert spreads out through southeastern Arizona and into Mexico, dominated by arid grasslands.

Rivers

The state's rivers, though many of them are dry for much of the year these days, have made human culture possible in Arizona. The **Gila River,** nearly dead today, was the main east-west waterway, stretching from the mountains of New Mexico all the way to the lower Colorado, which forms the western border. The banks of the Gila's tributaries, the Verde, the San Pedro, the Salt, and the Santa Cruz, saw the rise of several complex and creative cultures over the centuries, including the Hohokam, the Salado, the Sinagua, and the Mogollon. The state's main river, the **Colorado River,** drains the vast Colorado Plateau and stretches from Wyoming all the way to Mexico. Much of the river through Arizona, about half of its total length, has historically been difficult to access because it flows deep within intricately carved canyons. Tributaries of the Colorado, like the Little Colorado in the northeastern portion of the state and the Bill Williams River in the central-west portion, have also been important to human settlement in Arizona. The Little Colorado provided a reasonable water supply for the early Puebloan cultures that settled on the high plains and, much later, was the source of life for Mormon pioneers in the 19th century.

Most of the state's rivers are no longer wild, having been dammed and controlled, a process that started, on a major scale, in the late 19th and early 20th centuries with the era of reclamation. Because wild desert rivers like the Gila, Salt, and Colorado were subject to intense flooding and severe drought, it was difficult for European settlers to rely on their quirky flows for agriculture. The federal government was also eager to harness the rivers' power to create hydroelectricity and to build vast reservoirs of water that could be sent to the growing agricultural and urban areas of Arizona, California, and elsewhere. Beginning at the turn of the 20th century with the building of Roosevelt Dam on the Salt, which helped make Phoenix and the Valley of the Sun first an agricultural boomtown and then an urban megalopolis, the era of reclamation saw most of the state's rivers dammed, ending with the damming of the Colorado River at Glen Canyon in the mid-20th century. Earlier, the biggest dam of them all, Hoover, was constructed in Black Canyon on the

Colorado at the Arizona-Nevada border, creating the world's largest artificial lake, **Lake Mead,** and making the agricultural blunder called the Imperial Valley, in California, possible. The damming of any river changes that river irrevocably; the damming of the Colorado at Glen Canyon altered the stretch of the West's greatest river that created the Grand Canyon so much that it is unrecognizable from its previous form. Even the color of the river is different. The red Colorado River used to flow muddy and warm through the canyon, hence its name of "Colored River," because it was full of the sediment that helped cut the great gorge. Since the dam was built, most of that sediment has been deposited behind the dam in the reservoir known as **Lake Powell,** and the river flows cool and green through the inner gorge. This has led to a complete change in the river's downstream ecosystem, as the ancient cycles of flood and drought have changed to a predictable, constant flow, thus altering the very character of the river and making it difficult for native species to survive.

CLIMATE

Contrary to popular belief, many regions of Arizona experience four seasons. Even on the desert, while summers are long and hot below 5,000 feet or so, the sky island mountain ranges experience little pockets of seasonally based weather.

Spring is the best time to be on Arizona's lowland deserts. From late February until May temperatures typically hang around the high 70s and 80s from the lower Colorado River region across the desert belt to the New Mexico border.

The highland summer is warm—even hot—during the day and cool at night, ranging from the mid to high 80s to the low 60s at night. In late summer the smell of wet pine needles precedes each late-afternoon "monsoon" rainstorm, and a mist rises when the cold raindrops hit the warm rocks.

While it also rains during the late summer on the deserts, during the beloved

The Desert at Risk

Many scientists in the Southwest these days are busy researching how climate change and prolonged drought will affect the region's arid life zones over the long term. One of these scientists is Travis Huxman, director of the University of California, Irvine's Huxman Lab, which studies ecology and evolution of plant functional traits.

For many years Huxman has been interested in how plants translate climate into ecosystem behavior—how plants respond to temperature fluctuation, carbon dioxide concentration, animals, and microbes, and how a plant's interaction with all these elements affects how an ecosystem processes water, which is probably the single most important question here in the arid, thirsty Southwest.

"Plants can tell us a lot about ourselves, especially in the desert," Huxman says. "Deserts are very sensitive to change; you see big impacts in deserts before you might see them somewhere else."

Huxman and others argue that, because of climate change, big, representative species of the Sonoran Desert, most notably the mighty saguaro, are living under a very real threat.

We could lose the saguaro and other celebrities of the desert because of fires sparked by invasive grasses, the spread of which is a direct impact of global climate change. It's happening in North America's other deserts as well. In the Mojave Desert to the west, the great Joshua tree is similarly threatened, according to Huxman.

"I don't have a projection for how long it would take, but you can hardly drive a freeway through the North American deserts and not see this change and the impact of fire on these landscapes," Huxman says. "It's fairly obvious."

So far in Arizona, such changes are most evident in the high deserts of the state's north-central pine belt. There, the largest ponderosa pine forest in North America is on the verge of total collapse. The conifers are stressed due to drought, and that stress allows bark beetles and other killers to dig in, which in turn leaves this typically fire-resistant species ready to burn. And once they're gone, will they grow back, or has the ecosystem changed irrevocably?

But that's not even the biggest problem, Huxman says. What we don't know yet is how the water cycle will react if a single dominant species like the ponderosa pine is no longer part of the ecosystem. "That's the big research question," he says. "How will all this affect water?"

And that, according to Huxman, points to the most important fact we can learn from plants: what he calls the water-energy problem.

"Plants take up carbon dioxide in order to grow, but to do so they have to lose water to the atmosphere," he explains. "That's our problem on many different scales: How water and energy are related; so the most important thing we can do now is to remember that when we are thinking about energy efficiency, we are also thinking about water efficiency at the same time."

"monsoon" season, the storms only serve to make an already unbearable heat humid as well. Summers in the desert are intensely hot and listless. The daytime highs range from the high 90s to 110°F or even 120°F at their worst, while at night the lows rarely fall below the 80s. In Tucson and Phoenix it is not uncommon to experience several months straight of 100°F or higher temperatures with little or no rainfall.

The monsoon season, which, to be strictly correct, should be called simply the summer rainy season, occurs when shifting winds from the south encourage late-afternoon downpours, often attended by thunder and lightning, nearly every day from July into September. During this time of year the dry washes and riverbeds throughout the state are subject to flash flooding as torrents of rain flow through the channels from the uplands to the desert. Never stop or park in a dry wash during this time of year—it could become a raging river rather quickly, even if the sun is shining overhead. Monsoon storms are highly localized—so much so that it is sometimes raining in the backyard and not in the front yard. Hiking up a canyon during this time of year can also be dangerous and sometimes deadly; you never know if it's raining in the mountains above you, and that water could show up anytime, falling off the mountain and rushing through the canyon, taking hikers with it. Washes fill up quickly during the rainy season, and trapped drivers necessitate rescues that are expensive and dangerous for first responders. Never venture into a flooded wash, no matter how shallow it appears. However, unless you visit Arizona during the two months or so of the summer rainy season, or during the couple months in winter when it may be snowing in the highlands and raining intermittently on the deserts, you're not likely to experience anything but sunshine.

In the highlands during spring you'll encounter cool days and cold nights, and it has even been known to snow across the pine belt in April or later. Depending on the length and strength of the winter, there will typically be snow in the north-central high country in February and even into March.

Fall (Oct.-Dec. or Jan.) comes on cold and barren in the highlands, and the ground crunches with fallen leaves. The "second spring" begins on the desert. The weather gets perfect again, from the high 60s to the 80s, with cool, light-jacket nights. This is the time of year when the snowbirds arrive from the Midwest to set up camp until it starts to get hot. After December, the winter rains come to the desert, and it starts to snow in the high country. For a very brief couple of weeks, everybody in the state is cold and housebound.

Winter temperatures can fall below freezing in the highlands and regularly reach lows of 20°F or below and highs in the 40s and 50s. On the deserts during this time, highs fall to the low 60s and even into the 50s, and lows regularly fall below 30°F. Only a few places in the state receive significant snowfall—Flagstaff, the Kaibab Plateau, and the White Mountains. In these places the snow can be deep enough to close roads and halt normal life.

ENVIRONMENTAL ISSUES

With its delicate and finely balanced biomes and some of the most dramatic and exotic scenery on earth, Arizona has over the generations been a haven, a laboratory, and a rallying point for environmentalists and ecologists. One of the biggest threats to the state's extremely varied ecosystems is simple growth; much of the desert has been paved over and crowded with homes, while the upland forests host droves of overbuilt homes just waiting for a wildfire to burn them to their foundations. It may seem strange that a land so naturally inhospitable to human occupation is, year after year, listed as one of the top two or three fastest-growing states in the nation. There are no signs that this trend is going to let up anytime soon. The constant influx of people has led over the years to environmental problems far beyond the mere pavement of desert and clearing of forests. Growth and the state's founding impetus to glean profit from the land have led to the overpumping of groundwater and the damming and taming of most of the state's rivers. This has altered the green riverways so completely that many species of native fish are now as good as gone, and nonnative plants line the mostly dry riverbeds, crowding out native riverine flora like cottonwoods and willows.

Climate change, scientists say, is likely to increase the state's environmental woes and, coupled with an ongoing drought that has been eating away at the state for more than a decade, may lead to shortages on the Colorado River, water from which the vast majority of urban Arizonans depend. Some scientists have recently predicted that Lake Mead may dry up by 2025, while others believe the current human culture in Arizona may, one day in the future, suffer the same collapse as did the Ancestral Puebloans, the Hohokam, and other complex societies who have tried to make a go of it here, leaving behind the ambitious ruins of their rise and fall but not much else.

There are numerous organizations fighting to save Arizona and its rare natural beauty from destruction and overuse, and over the last few decades the state, many local governments, and especially the diverse citizenry have taken a more proactive approach to conservation. Visiting neighborhoods in Tucson, Phoenix, and elsewhere in the desert gives the best evidence of this, where one can see a slowly increasing number of homes with solar panels on their roofs and rainwater tanks rising from behind their fences. The federal government, which controls many of the state's most famous environmental treasures, has over the last several years set aside more and more of the remaining open and wild lands as wilderness areas and national monuments. However, as ever the fluctuating price of copper and energy lead to periodic renewed explorations and plans to dig strip mines on public lands. These familiar debates over resource conservation have been raging for decades. Groups like the Nature Conservancy and the Tucson-based Sky Island Alliance and Center for Biological Diversity are using a variety of methods, including simple capitalism, science-based advocacy, and the federal courts, to make sure that large swaths of Arizona remain open and wild.

Visitors to Arizona can help keep the state beautiful and clean by adhering to a few simple, commonsense rules. First of all, as always, pack out what you pack in. Always stay on the trails, don't feed wild animals, and never, ever take any vehicle off the road or the trail, including a bike. If you're an off-highway vehicle (OHV) enthusiast, stick to the set-aside off-road areas in the national forests (which can be identified through the U.S. Forest Service's Arizona websites or at the local offices). Also, if you're visiting any of the state's many national forests during the summer, there are likely to be campfire and smoking restrictions enforced throughout the state due to high temperatures and ongoing drought. Make sure that you are familiar with these restrictions and that you follow them to the letter. Nearly all of the state's huge, catastrophic wildfires in recent years have been caused by humans.

Plants and Animals

PLANTS

The state's flora is, like the land itself, extremely diverse, ranging from weird desert rarities to tall, thick evergreens.

If you pay attention to your elevation—and the "wrinkled" nature of the state assures that you are changing elevation all the time—you can generally predict what the weather will be like and which plants you are likely to see; of course, it's not all strictly delineated, and the various life zones often bleed into one another. Between 4,500 and about 7,000 feet you're in the **Upper Sonoran zone,** characterized by scrub oak, piñon pine, juniper, manzanita, and sagebrush grasslands; this zone is often called the chaparral. The midlands of the state, at around 6,000 feet and higher, are marked by the **transition zone,** a scrubby land of short dry bushes stretching into the ponderosa pines. Above 8,500 feet or so, thick stands of evergreen conifers and white aspen are common. Above 9,500 feet or so, a height reached in Arizona primarily by climbing up towering mountains, the **subalpine zone** has tough Engelmann spruce and bristlecone pine, and above that it's all barren rocks and tundra.

Trees and Bushes

The official Arizona state tree is the paloverde, a green-skinned desert dweller that can grow up to 25 feet high. The tree proliferates throughout the Lower Sonoran zone and is often a close neighbor to the saguaro, the baby buds of which use the paloverde's cover to hide and grow. Other common desert trees are the ubiquitous mesquite, which has often been used for firewood and building and whose beans have nourished people and animals alike. Both the mesquite and the paloverde bloom yellow in the spring.

Ironwood trees, drought-resistant evergreens, grow along slopes and washes in the desert. Bushy plants crowd the desert as well: Creosote is everywhere, as are stickery, **catclaw,** and **rabbitbrush,** all of which bloom yellow. Adding a little red to the bloom time is the **ocotillo,** which is everywhere in the desert and resembles a sprouting group of pipe cleaners. Throughout the desert and into the chaparral of the transition zones you'll see several sword-cluster species of **agave,** an important plant to the human population in that it can be turned into mescal and tequila. The *Agave parryi,* or **century plant,** blooms only once with a tall stalk of yellow flowers.

In the scrublands and chaparral and higher you'll see scrub oak, piñon pine, juniper, manzanita, and other brushy trees. In the high country, above 6,000 feet or so, you'll see ponderosa pine mainly. Higher still, in the mountain forests near the North Rim of the Grand Canyon, in the White Mountains and elsewhere, fir, spruce, and aspen forests dominate. Along many waterways you'll see big cottonwoods and willows and sycamores.

Cacti

The most famous of Arizona's cacti, the **saguaro,** looks like it does because it is perfect: Every form has a function. Its green skin allows for photosynthesis, normally the job of leaves on less individualistic plants. Its spongy flesh and ribbed contours encourage water storage; the saguaro can collect and store up to 200 gallons of water from a single rainfall, which can maintain it throughout the year. Its telltale needles protect it from the incessant gnawing of hungry desert creatures. Its splashy white blossoms (seen in April, May, and June—the blossoms are Arizona's official state flower) and its juicy red fruits (eaten for eons by the desert's native inhabitants) assure the rising of another generation. The

best place to commune with these perfectly adapted desert plants is Saguaro National Park near Tucson.

You'll see various species of cactus throughout the Lower and into the Upper Sonoran zones. Most cacti are easily recognizable if you know their names: **organpipe, barrel, beavertail, claret cup,** and **hedgehog** cacti generally look like their sobriquets suggest, albeit spiky and standoffish versions. The famous **prickly pear** cactus can be identified by its red fruit-blooms, which are turned into jellies and even margarita mix.

Wildflowers

In the early spring, especially after a rainy winter, the desert *bajadas,* the sloping flatland that stretches out from the desert mountain ranges, and valleys bloom with color as dormant wildflowers burst back to life. Various shades of photogenic whites, yellows, blues, reds, and purples contrast with the uniform rich green of the well-watered springtime desert to create a truly beautiful but ephemeral scenery. Some of the most common bloomers are the light-purple **Arizona lupine,** the deep yellow **Mexican gold poppy,** the dark pink **Parry's penstemon (or Parry's beardtongue),** and the virginal white **desert lily.** In summer the northland meadows and grasslands bloom with wild color as well. The best, most accessible places to see wildflowers in the spring are Picacho Peak State Park between Phoenix and Tucson and the Superstition Mountains east of Phoenix. You'll also see the desert in bloom in places like Saguaro National Park near Tucson and throughout the Santa Cruz Valley south of Tucson.

ANIMALS
Mammals

Arizona's official state mammal is the **ringtail,** a relative of the raccoon often called a ringtailed cat or a miner's cat because of its rodent-eating proclivities. Its huge, bushy, white-and-black-ringed tail is its identifying feature, but it's not likely you'll see one unless you're nocturnal. The **mountain lion,** or cougar, is found, and hunted, throughout Arizona; smaller **bobcats** are often seen lounging near water features in Sonoran Desert backyards, and scrawny **coyotes** can be spotted quickly crossing highways throughout the state. In the western deserts a few **bighorn sheep** still cling to the dry rocky cliffs.

A few different species of **jackrabbit** can be found all over, and **white-tailed deer** and **mule deer** live from the bottom of the Grand Canyon to the mountain heights and most places in between. **Pronghorn** live on the high grasslands in herds. The **collared peccary,** or **javelina** (which resembles a wild pig), is everywhere in the desert and the transition zone, so much so that they are generally considered pests. The **black bear** lives in the mountains throughout the state, and various species of **bats** come out in the Arizona night, responsible for pollinating and continuing the state's signature cactus forests.

Birds

The small, flitting **cactus wren,** which lives among the spiky plants, is the Arizona state bird, while the tall **roadrunner** may be its most recognizable. The **red-tailed hawk** proliferates in the desert sky, hunting rodents. The **California condor** has been reintroduced into the wild around Grand Canyon country. Though the condor is not a native to the state, the jagged canyon country was deemed a perfect place to acclimate the threatened, prehistoric-looking bird into the wild.

Waterbirds, including the elegant **great blue heron,** hang around the state's riparian areas, and **wild turkeys** are somewhat common in oak and pine woodlands. One of the most common birds in the desert is the **Gambel's quail,** which can often be seen crossing streets followed by a ragged line of tiny offspring. The **turkey vulture** is constantly soaring slowly in the ever-blue dryland sky. Various owl species are common in the woodlands and the deserts, and the **gila** and the **acorn woodpecker** are always tapping away at some tree or woodland home.

Southern Arizona is a mecca for bird enthusiasts, who stalk the region's sky island mountain ranges looking for rare subtropical birds like the **elegant trogon,** a green, red, white, and black bird related to the jungle-loving quetzal.

Fish

The **apache trout,** a gold-and-black native Arizona species, is the official state fish. Because of changes to the ecosystem and other factors, 28 of the state's 31 native fish are threatened, endangered, or as good as extinct. Still, in the mountain streams and lakes popular with anglers, you'll find rainbow and brown trout, bass, and others. In the lowland lakes there's bass, crappie, sunfish, catfish, and trout.

Reptiles

The desert is known as the home of the rattlesnake, seen more and more these days as the suburban attack on the desert continues. A few species of rattlesnake are found in Arizona. The **western diamondback,** which has lent its name to the state's world-champion professional baseball team, lives in the desert and the mountains and has deadly venom. Its skin is gray with brown diamond-shaped splotches along the back and a series of black-and-white bands just above its rattle. As with nearly all animals, the diamondback will leave you alone if you afford it the same courtesy. The light-brown **western rattlesnake** lives throughout the state, and the **Arizona ridge-nosed rattlesnake** lives in the woodlands of southeastern Arizona, a reddish-brown or gray hunter of rodents and lizards.

Several different species of **lizard** can be seen all over the lowlands, doing push-ups on hot rocks. The desert's most recognizable residents, these tiny leftover dinosaurs come in many shapes and sizes. One of the biggest is the fat and venomous **Gila monster,** with its beady skin and languid looks. The monster can be seen sunning itself sometimes in and around Tucson. The only venomous lizard in the United States should be given a wide berth if encountered.

The slow and wise **desert tortoise** hides out from the desert sun in its burrow, and if it makes it past its soft-shell youth—when it's a favorite of predatory birds—it can live up to a hundred years or more. Frogs and toads in Arizona include the **Arizona tree frog,** a lime-green forest resident, and the **western spadefoot toad,** which lives in the desert in a burrow, a blotchy greenish-brown with gray tints.

Insects and Arachnids

The **bark scorpion** is the crabby, pinching demon of the desert underworld; its venom is dangerous if it finds its way to the blood. The **grand western cicada** makes a racket in the woodlands on summer evenings. The hirsute **desert tarantula** looks much meaner than it is, cruising about in the early morning and early evening. You're bound to encounter gnats, mosquitoes, and other tiny pests in desert riparian areas and around upland lakes.

History

PREHISTORIC CULTURES

Small bands of ice-age migrants were probably moving through North America as many as 20,000 years ago, but the pioneer Southwesterners are still widely considered to be the **Clovis** people (named for their spear points, first found in Clovis, New Mexico), who hunted big game in what is now Arizona about 10,000 to 16,000 years ago. Climate change and the overexploitation of the mammoths and great ground sloths of the Pleistocene ended this epoch by about 8,000 BC. From then until pottery-making cultures began to rise around the time of Jesus, the Archaic-era hunter-gatherers made a long, successful go of it here, moving between the forested highlands and the deserts seasonally to hunt and gather wild foods. By the late Archaic period these bands were living in semipermanent camps in pit houses and were growing corn likely introduced by migrants from Mesoamerica.

The first millennium AD saw the rise of several sophisticated and mostly sedentary cultures in Arizona, the most successful of which were the **Ancestral Puebloans** on the Colorado Plateau, the **Sinagua** in the Verde Valley and volcanolands around Flagstaff, the **Mogollon** in eastern Arizona and New Mexico, the **Salado** in the region around the Little Colorado River, and the **Hohokam** in the river valleys of the Sonoran Desert. These cultures would rise and fall in stages, with rises generally coinciding with wet times and falls subsequent to droughts.

By AD 700 or so the Ancestral Puebloans were building above-ground, rock-and-mud urban-like villages that would become known as pueblos, from the Spanish for town or city. The Ancestral Puebloan culture would briefly rise to become something of an empire in the plateau country, with New Mexico's Chaco Canyon as its ruling capital.

A separate culture, but one related in many ways to the Ancestral Puebloans, flourished in the Flagstaff and Verde Valley regions from around AD 500 to 1425. Called the Sinagua, which means "without water" in Spanish, the group mostly lived around Sunset Crater near Flagstaff until AD 700, when several bands migrated below the Mogollon Rim to live along the Verde River and among the red rocks of Sedona. The Sinagua built impressive cliff dwellings and huge sandstone apartment-style pueblos that can still be seen and visited today. The Sinagua culture survived the eruption of Sunset Crater in 1064 and thrived as part of an important regional trade route for centuries.

Known for their elegant black-and-white Mimbres pottery, the Mogollon people lived in scattered villages in the pine forests of

West-Central New Mexico and East-Central Arizona from around AD 150 to about 1400, when they are thought to have been absorbed into the Ancestral Puebloan regime. The Salado people lived in the Tonto Basin northeast of Phoenix from about AD 1150 to the 1400s. One of their cliff dwellings above the Salt River can still be seen today at Tonto National Monument. On the low deserts, the Hohokam constructed a network of irrigation canals in the river valleys around what are now Phoenix and Tucson and lived in complex, hierarchical agricultural societies that built adobe great houses and ceremonial ball courts.

Around AD 1150 many of the dramatic cliff dwellings, built by various cultures and scattered from the desert to the pines to the rocky lands of the Colorado Plateau, began to appear throughout the Southwest. These cultures had mostly run their course by AD 1450 due to a variety of factors—ecological, climatic, and social. For generations the monuments and ruins they left behind have fascinated scientists and tourists alike.

Sometime in the 1400s or before, the Athapaskan culture migrated south to the area from the far north in Canada; these tribes would later become those known as the **Apache** and the **Navajo.** These tribes were not related to any of the cultures living in the region at the time they arrived. The Apache eventually moved to southeastern Arizona, where they would have an epochal battle for supremacy with the U.S. Army in the late 19th century, while the Navajo stayed in the Colorado Plateau area and learned about dryland farming from their Puebloan neighbors while also spending a good amount of time raiding those same neighbors. They would eventually be nearly killed off by the U.S. Army under the direction of Kit Carson. After a long and brutal internment outside of their harsh but beloved Four Corners lands, the Navajo signed a treaty with the United States in 1868 that allowed them to return to the plateau country, where they remain today and have grown to become North America's largest tribe. The **Hopi,** who live on a small reservation on three mesas in the middle of the Navajo Nation, are the descendants of the Ancestral Puebloans who lived in the region's dramatic cliff dwellings and pueblos. They were never forced off the land that they consider to be their homeland—the same harsh and seemingly inhospitable mesas they still live on today—but they were subject, as were the Navajo and Apache, to periodic attempts by the federal government to "Americanize" them by sending their children to government-run schools off the reservation, forcing them into a cash and labor economy very different from their subsistence lifestyle and converting them to Christianity. A large number of Navajo today are Christians, and there are churches throughout the reservation. Many Hopi have held on to their native religious beliefs and seem to live in a separate, more ancient time.

EUROPEANS ARRIVE

The impenetrable northern reaches of the Spanish Empire in Mexico were essentially unexplored by Europeans when **Alvar Nuñez Cabeza de Vaca** found himself shipwrecked and lost in the grasslands and deserts of what is now the southwestern United States and northern Mexico in the 1520s. And though he and his companions—one of them, Estevan, was a Moorish slave or indentured servant—probably never made it to Arizona proper, the tales they told of their adventures when they finally returned to Mexico City inspired subsequent explorations in the great north. In 1539 Fray Marcos de Niza and Estevan trekked north to discover the Seven Cities of Cibola, rumors of which Estevan and Cabeza de Vaca had heard during their ordeal. Estevan scouted ahead and was killed by the Zuni, who lived not in golden cities but in regular old mesa-top pueblos not too different from those that still exist on the Hopi reservation in Arizona and in the Rio Grande Valley of New Mexico. Nevertheless, de Niza's report suggested that the golden cities might indeed be a reality, and that was enough to inspire an ambitious expedition in 1540 led by **Francisco Vasquez de Coronado** in search of the reported riches. Coronado found none, but his expedition moved through what is now eastern Arizona. In the 1690s **Father Eusebio Francisco Kino** began his journeys into Southern Arizona and Sonora, bringing cattle to the region for the first time and establishing several long-lasting missions, including San Xavier del Bac near Tucson, to this day still celebrating mass in its dark, cool interior. By the 1750s the Spanish crown had established a presidio or fort at Tubac, which was moved to the Santa Cruz Valley near Tucson in 1775. Southern Arizona comprised the northern reaches of the Spanish New-World empire, though it was sparsely populated and was a violent, dangerous place to live. Spanish cattle ranchers and other hardy settlers fought Apaches and others for the right to live in the region, but for decades the north would remain too isolated and too dangerous to grow much. The Mexicans won their independence from Spain in 1821 and so took over administration of the vast northlands. The wilderness was exploited somewhat for its resources, used for cattle ranching and placer mining by tough Mexican explorers, but mostly it was too far from the center of power and too dangerous to be of much worth to the new nation.

In the later 1820s trappers, hunters, and mountain men like James Ohio Pattie, Antoine Leroux, and Pauline Weaver became some of the first Anglo Americans to venture through Arizona, in search of beaver pelts. Such men would in turn guide the **Army of the West** and the Mormon Battalion through the state in 1846 and 1847 during the Mexican-American War, which was fought primarily in Mexico. After the war ended in 1848, much of what is now the Southwest became U.S. property, and in 1850 a huge area that included Arizona and New Mexico became the New Mexico Territory. In 1854 the land between the Gila River and the Mexican border—Southern Arizona, basically—was added to the territory through the **Gadsden Purchase.**

In 1849 and for several years afterward, thousands of Americans passed through Arizona headed for gold and glory in California. Those hard-rock, hard-luck miners would return east to the state a few years later in search of the gold and silver most of them had failed to find on the coast. Several boundary, land, railroad, and scientific surveys of Arizona and the West during the 1850s brought this far corner of the continent greater attention and interest from the East.

TERRITORIAL YEARS

It was the increasing mining activity in the state that, among other factors, led President Lincoln to establish the Arizona Territory in 1863, disconnecting it from the huge conglomerate of land called New Mexico. The capital was established at Prescott, in the state's mineral-laden midlands, and the East's economic exploitation of the land, albeit on a much smaller scale than it would become, commenced. During the Civil War, Tucson was a Confederate hotbed for a time before being occupied by the U.S. Army. After the Civil War ended, immigration and exploration of the Southwest picked up considerably. Still, when **John Wesley Powell** completed the first river run through the Grand Canyon in 1869, the population of the territory was fewer than 10,000 persons.

Settlers trickled in over the coming years, spurred here to find treasure, to cure their tuberculosis, and for adventure, science, and cheap land made available by the federal Homestead and Desert Land Acts. Despite this, the territory remained a wild and dangerous place for most. The Apache, Navajo, and other tribes didn't feel they should have to give up the land they had conquered to settlers, many of whom were looking to get rich quick by exploiting the land and then leave. From 1871 until **Geronimo**'s final surrender in 1886, the U.S. Army fought a brutal war with the Apache and other tribes. The Apache were eventually defeated at a high cost to both parties, and some bands were sent to Oklahoma, where they became prisoners of war for many years. They struggled to hold to their traditional ways and remain a strong culture, but privation and the machinations of a government that did not understand them took their toll. Eventually the Apache were allowed to return to Arizona to reservations that include parts of their traditional homelands, and today they operate successful casinos and resorts.

With the end of the Apache wars the territory moved one step closer to large-scale settlement and development. In the 1880s the railroad arrived and transformed the region, bringing in more people and materials than ever before. By 1889 the Phoenix area had already begun to dominate the territory, and with the construction of Roosevelt Dam on the Salt River in 1911, the valley's agricultural boom was just on the horizon. In 1912, Arizona entered the union as the 48th state.

STATEHOOD AND BEYOND

The first half of the 20th century in Arizona was dominated by the era of reclamation. The federal government used taxpayer money to develop the state's water resources, damming rivers for irrigation, water storage, and hydroelectric power, creating a huge agricultural industry in the process. Phelps Dodge and other mining giants ripped huge holes in the land to extract low-grade copper, while Anglo owners and managers on the whole treated the Mexican and Native American miners and those who worked in the agricultural industry as seasonal laborers—without whom Arizona agriculture would not have been possible—poorly, even criminally on many occasions.

At the same time, more residents and visitors began to realize that there was more to the fantastic Arizona landscape than profit and loss, and this era saw the rise of national parks and monuments, national forests, and state-level protection of important lands. Beginning around the 1920s, boosters in Phoenix, Tucson, and elsewhere began to see the economic benefits of attracting tourists to the sunny state, and by 1950 or so tourism had replaced the extractive industries in importance. During the two world wars the federal government set up training bases and military installations in the state that led to a growth spurt, and the advent of swamp coolers and air conditioners stimulated a population boom in Arizona that has yet to really let up.

Government and Economy

GOVERNMENT

Arizona's government has had a contrary relationship with the federal establishment since before statehood. The state's entrance into the union was delayed for some time because the legislature, backed by a majority of the public, refused to give up a section of its constitution that allowed for the popular recall of judges. Today the bickering between the two continues over public land issues and border control. The truth is that the federal government made Arizona, and it still controls a good portion of the land in the state. With history as an example, it's easy to see that had the federal government not protected huge portions of the state as national forests, monuments, parks, and wilderness areas, outside (mostly eastern) economic interests would have used that land for their own profit, as they have the majority of Arizona's natural resources since long before statehood.

The state's government for most of its history has been interested, like nearly everybody else, in developing and taking from the land, and the various land-hungry interests who at one time or another were in favor—be they mining, agricultural, ranching, or military—have dictated policy. This is not as true today as it has been in the past, however.

While Arizona is known today as a

staunchly "red" state, that has not always been the case and it likely won't be for much longer. Progressive Democrats ruled the state for a few generations until **Barry Goldwater** and the conservative revolution found success here and on the national stage in the 1960s. Since then the state has been a Republican stronghold and a conservative one at that. There are a few "blue" enclaves, notably Tucson and the Navajo Nation. However, the state's demographics are changing, and the voter rolls are swelling not with Republicans and Democrats, but with Independents. Evidence of this slow purpling of Arizona came in 2018 when Arizona elected Kyrsten Sinema to the U.S. Senate, the first Democrat since 1995 to hold the seat.

ECONOMY

Arizona's economy for much of the past was ruled by the boom-and-bust realities of the extractive and agricultural industries. Worldwide prices, the fickleness of the market, and the constant threat of a destructive act of nature made economic life here before World War II a wild ride. Booms in the cattle industry in the 1890s and cotton before and during World War I created large industries in the state virtually overnight. The overgrazing of an arid open range and monocultural agriculture took their individual tolls, and both of these members of the state's well-known "Five C" economy (the Five Cs being cotton, cattle, copper, citrus, and climate) actually influenced life here on a major scale for a relatively short time. The other members of the Five Cs have fared better than cotton and cattle, both of which are now very minor elements of the state's economy. Copper mining, the state's claim to fame in economic circles for several generations, faces an ever-precarious future. The extractive and agricultural industries are no longer the primary economic engines of Arizona and the western states and haven't been for some time. According to a report by the Tucson-based Sonoran Institute, fewer than 5 percent of the West's counties have more than 20 percent of employment in traditional extractive industries.

A boom in single-family housing and urban and suburban development has enraptured the state for several decades, but the deep truth of the Arizona economy, and one that holds for the entire West, is that the service industry (much of it tourism related), with its low wages and transient workers, is the hottest-running economic engine here and has been for many years. All over the West, nonlabor income like investments, disability, and retirement payments come in a close second to the service industry as a top economic driver.

The median household income in Arizona is about $56,000, with 2.6 people per household. Some 15 percent of Arizonans live below the poverty line.

Local Culture

Most Arizona residents are immigrants to the state, and most have lived here a relatively short time. The majority of the state's 6.7 million residents live in Pima and Maricopa Counties, in and around the two large urban areas of Tucson and Phoenix. About a million people live in Pima County, and some four million live in Maricopa. About 16 percent of Arizonans are 65 and over, but 24 percent are under 18. The former statistic is expected to rise significantly as more and more baby boomers retire and move to the sunbelt, just as their parents did in the 1960s and 1970s. About 86 percent of Arizonans are high school graduates, and 27 percent have at least a bachelor's degree. A full 64 percent of Arizonans own their homes.

While the majority of Arizonans are still in most corners of the West referred to as Anglos, and the state was largely founded and developed by Anglos—much more so than was its neighbor New Mexico—people of Latino origin have a significant influence on the economy and culture here, especially in Southern Arizona and in both large urban areas. According to the U.S. Census Bureau, 30 percent of Arizonans are of Hispanic or Latino origin, compared to 15 percent nationwide. The influence of Latino culture, especially that of Mexico, can be seen throughout the state. Much of the finest art, music, and food to be found in Arizona has its origins in Mexico, to which the entire land area of the state used to belong, not too long ago.

Native Americans make up about 5 percent of the population; the largest tribe, the Navajo Nation, has some 350,000 members. Other tribes include the O'odham people, formerly called the Papago and Pima. The **Tohono O'odham** (the Desert People) live on a large reservation southwest of Tucson and operate casinos near the city. In the Phoenix area, the **Akimel O'odham** (the River People), or the Gila River Indian Community, live on a reservation and operate casinos as well. Other tribes in the state include the Hopi, the Yavapai near Prescott, the Western Apache bands, and the Colorado River tribes of western Arizona.

Unlike many of the other Native American nations on the continent, Arizona's tribes are still living today on what they consider their ancestral homelands, albeit smaller portions of that homeland set aside by the federal government under the reservation system. And while poverty is generally the rule on these reservations, Arizona's Native Americans have made important contributions to the artistic, cultural, political, and economic life of the state. The finest artists to come out of Arizona are Native American, and many are known the world over for their arts and crafts based on traditional designs and patterns but adapted and evolved to speak to a contemporary world.

Most of the state's Native American tribes have compacts allowing them to operate casinos, and those casinos are popular and profitable; still, many Arizona Native Americans live below the poverty line, even though access to education, health care, and jobs has increased somewhat over the years.

RELIGION

Religious life in Arizona is diverse and complex. **Catholicism** is popular among Latino residents and with many Anglos as well, while the **Church of Jesus Christ of Latter-day Saints,** or the Mormons, has been established in some rural areas of the state since the 19th century.

A Pew Forum survey in 2014 found that 20 percent of Arizonans identified as Catholics, and 25 percent identified as Evangelical Protestants. Mainline Protestants make up about 15 percent of the religious population,

Native American Arts and Crafts

There are hundreds of Native American artists living in Arizona. The majority are Hopi and Navajo, and they live on reservations in the far northeastern corner of the state. Many Indian artists sell their work at markets and fairs held throughout the year in Phoenix, Tucson, Flagstaff, and elsewhere. Silverwork, carvings, pottery, rugs, and paintings of the Hopi, Navajo, and others have been highly desired since territorial days.

Because it's made by Native Americans, many people approach this art with a lot of preconceived notions; especially prevalent are notions about authenticity and tradition. Some people expect every Indian artist and artisan to be adhering to some ancient set of guidelines set down before real time began, a method that washes each squash-blossom necklace and kachina doll carving with some undeniable spiritual patina. As with most artistic movements, however, the provenance of the Southwestern Indian Arts and Crafts tradition is far more complex.

Think of these artists as working within similar confines as did painters and sculptors of the Western European tradition before and during the Renaissance. Such artists were bound more often than not to paint and sculpt imagery from the Bible or Greek and Roman mythology, and they could count on their public immediately recognizing the scenes and characters they depicted. However, within this rather narrow tradition, there existed astonishing variety.

Consider, as an example, the story of how silverwork was introduced to the Navajo. In the 1850s, Navajo ironworker Atsidi Sani (Old Smith) added silver to the old Navajo tradition of making jewelry out of shell and stone. The Hopi and Zuni later learned from the Navajo. The oral tradition says the Southwest's Indians were taught metalwork in general by the Europeans; Atsidi Sani is said to have learned silversmithing from a smith called Nakai Tsosi or "Thin Mexican." More and more Navajo learned the art during the tribe's tragic imprisonment at Fort Sumner at Bosque Redondo, and the Navajo are said to have taught their Pueblo neighbors, mostly the Hopi and the Zuni, to work silver.

The silver in the early days and for a long time after mostly came from Mexican and U.S. coins. Reservation traders like John Lorenzo Hubbell, at Ganado, paid the Navajo to teach it to each other, then sold the products to tourists. Some of the best silversmiths gave up raising livestock and farming and were able to become full-time artisans, a pattern that still plays out today.

It was during the golden age of Southwestern tourism that the authenticity of Indian jewelry became an issue. The artists were, of course, encouraged to create work specifically for tourists, who flocked to the reservations and pueblos on the Fred Harvey Indian Detours. Writer and trader Mark Bahti writes that these pieces were often lightweight, with "horses, tipis, arrows, thunderbirds . . . designed to fit the tourist notion of what Indian jewelry was *supposed* to look like." But, as Bahti points out, what was Indian jewelry actually "supposed" to look like? Nobody could really say, and they still can't. By the 1920s, manufactured copies were being made outside the Southwest and then shipped in to be sold as authentic, spurring the artists to join together in co-ops and guilds, many of which are still in operation and are still training new artists.

The 1970s brought about a boom in the market for Pueblo and Navajo jewelry, and today there is a really diffuse sense of what is traditional and what is innovative. Innovation—the artist responding not only to tradition but to the world around him or her—can be seen everywhere at Indian markets throughout Arizona.

and LDS adherents constitute about 4 percent. A surprising 22 percent see themselves as "unaffiliated." Members of historically Black Protestant churches make up 2 percent of the population, 2 percent are Jewish, and 1 percent is Buddhist. Jehovah's Witnesses also make up 1 percent of the population.

LANGUAGE

The majority of Arizonans speak English, though some 27 percent of residents speak a language other than English at home (likely Spanish), according to the U.S. Census Bureau. From time to time over the years there have been calls for and votes on making

English the official language of the state, usually attending some new round of anger and fear over illegal immigration, which, owing more than anything else to Arizona's proximity to Mexico, is an ever-present political issue. The reality is that Spanish is used throughout the state and especially in the urban areas. You'll see and hear it everywhere. You may also hear several Native American languages as you travel around the state, including the intricate Hopi language and the Navajo tongue, which was used by the famous code talkers of World War II—one of the only "codes" never to be broken.

THE ARTS

Most of the prominent non-Native American artists and writers associated with Arizona were émigrés. **Edward Abbey,** author of the *Monkey Wrench Gang* and many other books, continues, nearly two decades after his death, to influence writing and environmental politics in the state. A friend of Abbey's, Doug Peacock (Hayduke from Abbey's novel) has written an excellent war memoir, *Walking It Off,* and several books about grizzly bears. Another Abbey friend, Tucsonan **Charles Bowden,** has a national reputation as a nonfiction writer and has produced some of the best books ever about the disaffection and dark ironies of sunbelt culture. Tucson resident **Leslie Marmon Silko** wrote the closest thing we yet have to an Arizona epic: her *Almanac of the Dead* examines the ancient and contemporary Southwest and the confluence of the two. The prolific **Zane Grey,** one of the progenitors of the Western genre, spent a lot of time in Arizona's Rim Country and based many of his books in the state.

The German painter **Max Ernst** came to Arizona in 1946, settling in Sedona and painting the state's surrealistic landscapes in the manner they deserved. His work is on display at the **Phoenix Art Museum.** There are hundreds of painters and sculptors living and working in Arizona today. Many of them congregate in Sedona, Tucson, Tubac, Bisbee, and Jerome. Each of these towns and cities has many galleries dedicated to individual artists, styles, and groups. The famed **Cowboy Artists of America** group was founded in Sedona in 1965, and the aesthetic traditions of the group are still highly visible in the state's galleries and museums.

Arizona has produced a few pop stars, most notably **Linda Ronstadt,** whose family has deep roots in Tucson. **Alice Cooper** grew up in the Valley of the Sun and still resides there, operating a popular downtown rock-and-jock-themed restaurant and bar. The Tempe music scene had a minor worldwide reputation in the 1990s thanks to bands like the **Gin Blossoms** and the **Refreshments.** Singer **Stevie Nicks** is from the Phoenix area, as is **Wayne Newton.**

Thanks to its desert scenery and always-clear skies, Arizona has had a vibrant movie-making scene on and off since the silent era. Classic films like *Arizona, Stagecoach,* and *Oklahoma* were filmed in the state, along with *The Planet of the Apes, The Three Amigos,* and hundreds of others. The fortunes of Arizona's film industry tend to rise and fall with the popularity of the Western.

Essentials

Transportation

AIR

If you're flying into Arizona, you'll likely find yourself at **Phoenix Sky Harbor International Airport** (PHX, 3400 E. Sky Harbor Blvd., 602/273-3300, www.skyharbor.com). One of the Southwest's largest airports, Sky Harbor has three terminals served by many domestic and international airlines. The airport is just three miles east of downtown Phoenix and easy to find. There's a free shuttle system that will take you between terminals.

The only other serious choice is **Tucson International Airport**

(TUS, 7250 S. Tucson Blvd., 520/573-8100, www.flytucson.com), which hosts a few airlines and offers daily flights to both coasts and other destinations. If you book a flight to Tucson, it may be slightly more expensive than flying into Sky Harbor in Phoenix, and you probably won't get a direct flight; in many cases, you'll have to fly into Sky Harbor, switch planes, and then fly south to Tucson—just a 1.5-hour drive on I-10. If you're renting a car anyway, it's probably a better idea to fly into Phoenix and then drive from there, unless you are just going to Tucson and Southern Arizona; then a direct flight into Tucson makes more sense.

Flagstaff, Prescott, Tusayan near the Grand Canyon, Yuma, and other towns have airports, though they are small and offer mostly regional routes. There are also several smaller regional airports around the Valley of the Sun, offering regional flights to Southwestern and West Coast ports. If you're coming from the West Coast or some other Southwestern city, you might look into regional flights to your Arizona destination; otherwise, Sky Harbor and then a rental car will be your best bet no matter where you're headed in Arizona.

TRAIN

The *Southwest Chief* route of **Amtrak,** which mirrors the old Santa Fe Railway's *Super Chief* route of the grand Fred Harvey days, stops twice daily (one eastbound, one westbound) at Flagstaff's classic **downtown depot** (1 E. Route 66, 800/872-7245, www.amtrak.com), the former Santa Fe headquarters and also the town's visitors center (800/842-7293). The route crosses the country from Chicago to L.A., dipping into the Southwest through northern New Mexico and Northern Arizona. There are long-term plans for a high-speed railway between Phoenix and Tucson, and possibly to other parts of the state, though likely such a useful project is a generation or more away from being realized. The

Southwest, while built and populated largely by the railroads, continues to hold strong to the car culture, and that isn't going to change anytime soon.

CAR

You need a personal vehicle to get around in Arizona. A significant part of the fun of a visit to the great Southwest is the road trip, and there's just too much scenery and too many spur-of-the-moment stops to go any other way. It's a good idea to reserve a rental car before you travel. But don't rent it at the Phoenix Sky Harbor International Airport; the airport charges exorbitant taxes and fees that make a short taxi ride to an off-airport rental place well worth it.

If you'd like to carry your home along with you on the Arizona road, or if you desire to relive a favorite sitcom moment or two, look into renting an RV. All over the state these days you'll see rented RVs touring the monuments and landscapes of the West, packed with families and groups of friends. In Phoenix, check out **RV Rental Outlet** (2126 W. Main St., Mesa, 480/461-0023, 480/461-0025, or 888/461-0023, www.rvrentaloutlet.com).

From Los Angeles: The major road routes into and through the state are I-10, I-40, and I-8. I-10 is the best and really the only practical way to get from Los Angeles to Phoenix and Tucson, a distance of 373 miles (five hours) and 488 miles (seven hours), respectively. To reach Flagstaff and the Grand Canyon from Los Angeles, take I-40, a distance of 486 miles (seven hours) to Flagstaff, with another 78 miles (1.5 hours) to the Grand Canyon. I-40 also passes by Williams, another gateway to the Grand Canyon. L.A. is 431 miles (six hours) from Williams, all of it along the interstate, and it's another 60 miles (one hour) to the South Rim from there.

From Las Vegas: The main route from Las Vegas to Flagstaff, Williams, and the Grand Canyon runs along Highway 93 to

I-40. The popular South Rim section of Grand Canyon National Park is 277 miles from Las Vegas (4 hours from Las Vegas to Flagstaff, then 1.5 hours to the Grand Canyon).

The drive across the rocky, jagged desert from Las Vegas to Phoenix is 300 miles (about five hours). Most of the drive, save for a short jog on I-40 near Kingman, is on U.S. 93, a scenic desert highway that moves through some of the most ruggedly beautiful outbacks in the Southwest and crosses the Colorado River near Hoover Dam.

From Phoenix: To reach Arizona's northland (which includes Flagstaff, the Grand Canyon, Prescott, the Mogollon Rim, and Sedona) from Phoenix, take I-17 out of the valley. I-17 goes all the way to Flagstaff, where it hooks into I-40, a distance of about 150 miles (two hours).

BUS

Greyhound (www.greyhound.com) provides bus service between major towns, mostly along the interstate routes. This isn't a very efficient way to travel around Arizona, but you could do it. Check out the website for schedules and station locations.

BIKE

The most bike-friendly towns in Arizona are Tucson and Tempe, in the southern, desert portion of the state, and Flagstaff, in the cool, mountainous pine forest. They have large and active biking communities that consistently push for more trails and lanes. And each has hundreds of miles of bike paths and bike lanes, making it possible to live in these cities with just a bike for transportation. However, for about three months out of the year it is either too hot in Tucson and Tempe or too cold in Flagstaff to ride much.

Grand Canyon National Park's South Rim has become increasingly bike friendly in recent years. You can take your own bike or rent one inside the park. Biking is actually an ideal way to see the park—much better than driving to each of the lookouts and having to park and get out of the car, and it's faster than walking. It's mostly a summertime activity, however, considering the park's relatively high elevation; come early November, you'll likely find it too cold to enjoy the ride.

TOURS

If you're looking for the knowledgeable assistance of an expert, you can hire **Open Road Tours** (602/997-6474, http://openroadtoursusa.com) to guide and shuttle you in comfort all over the state. Such tours are only recommended for those who enjoy groups. Arizona's tourist track is well established and easy to negotiate, and a tour guide is not necessary. Most of the best sights are controlled by the federal government, specifically the National Park Service, and rangers are always on hand to answer questions and give free, informative tours.

Food and Accommodations

FOOD

Mexican food reigns supreme in Southern Arizona. But the local-food revolution has not missed Arizona either; throughout the state you'll find numerous restaurants dedicated to using local and all-natural ingredients, harking back to a simpler time when we knew a bit more about our food. In the old mining towns of Bisbee in Southern Arizona and Jerome in Northern Arizona, you'll find a few high-style restaurants serving an eclectic blend of Southwestern and haute cuisine. In Scottsdale, Phoenix, and throughout the Valley of the Sun, your head will spin from all the options, most of them highly creative and dedicated to a fusion of the native and the new. Head to either the Navajo or Hopi Reservation, and you can sample the native cuisine, centered

Clothing-Optional Accommodations

There's something about the powerful Arizona sun, especially when it shines hard on the desert country, that makes one want to wear as little clothing as possible. While this usually isn't recommended, what with society's conventions and the danger of overexposure to the dastardly rays, those who enjoy the popular world of "naturism" will want to check out the clothing-optional resort in the desert just north of Phoenix. **Shangri La Ranch** (44444 N. Shangri La Rd., New River, 623/465-5959, www.shangrilaranch.com, office hours 9am-5pm daily, $32 per couple daily fee, $70-105 for a room, $10 per night camping, $15 RV hookup) is a family-oriented nudist resort with rooms, camping, and an RV park. It offers numerous activities, a huge swimming pool, and a friendly staff. Although no bathing suits are allowed in the pool, the philosophy of Shangri La seems to be live and let live, so you can "ease into" the nudist lifestyle if you're not already a committed naturist. The setting is gorgeous, way out in the scrubby desert about 45 minutes north of Sky Harbor International Airport off I-17 near New River. This is most definitely a family place, so they expect you to be respectful and adhere to the rules of conduct.

mainly around mutton and corn and a kind of Mexican-Native American amalgam called the Navajo (or Hopi) taco—a delicious hunk of fry bread piled high with meat and beans. If you're looking for gluten-free options, you'll find that many of the best restaurants in Phoenix and Tucson offer choices or will make a gluten-free version for you. As you move into the outback, which is most of Arizona, the choices dwindle, but it never hurts to ask. Some venues in Arizona's small towns offer gluten-free dishes, and their numbers appear to be growing.

ACCOMMODATIONS

Arizona is famous for its luxury resorts. The best of these all-inclusive, posh spa-resorts in Phoenix, Scottsdale, Tucson, and Sedona are listed in the chapters for those cities.

The state is also fortunate to have a number of historic hotels still in operation, though updated and remodeled, and there are many boutique hotels and bed-and-breakfasts operating out of historic buildings that used to serve some important territorial function.

Bed-and-breakfast inns proliferate throughout Arizona, and nearly every region has several. Many of the best B&Bs can be contacted through the **Arizona Association of Bed and Breakfast Inns** (www.arizona-bed-breakfast.com).

If you're just looking for a place to flop between adventures, there is an abundance of chain hotels in every major city and town, and in small towns near national parks and monuments and off the interstates.

Travel Tips

In many ways Arizona was saved by tourists. If travelers didn't love the state's scenery and history so much, the Grand Canyon may have long ago been strip-mined and the last of the desert paved over. Instead, the natural wonders have been to a large degree preserved forever, and a vibrant and busy tourism industry has grown up here. Because of this, it's easy to be a tourist in Arizona. Here you'll find a few tips to make it even easier.

TIME ZONES

Arizona is in the Mountain Time Zone (MST) and is one of the few places in the country that does not switch over to daylight saving time from the second Sunday in March to the first Sunday in November. The Navajo Nation in northeastern Arizona, because it spreads across three states, does switch to daylight saving time, adding even a time change to complete the foreign-country feel of that region.

INTERNATIONAL TRAVELERS

The many national parks and monuments in Arizona are well equipped for international tourists. They all offer guides and other literature in a variety of major languages and are used to working with international travelers. Arizona and the Southwest in general are very popular destinations for European, Japanese, and Chinese travelers especially, and in the summer, no matter where you're from, you could very well meet one of your compatriots on the South Rim or at Monument Valley.

The U.S. government's **Visa Waiver Program** allows tourists from 37 countries to visit without a visa for up to 90 days. To check if your country is on the list go to http://travel.state.gov. Even with a waiver, you still need to bring your passport and present it at the port of entry.

ACCESS FOR TRAVELERS WITH DISABILITIES

Many of the best sights in Arizona are accessible to disabled travelers in one way or another. The Grand Canyon and most of the other major federal parks have accessible trails and viewpoints. For advice and links to other helpful Internet resources, go to www.disabledtravelers.com, which is based in Arizona and is full of accessible travel information, though it's not specific to the state. The **National Accessible Travelers Database** may also be helpful. For questions specific to Arizona, you may want to contact the state Department of Administration's **Office for Americans with Disabilities** (100 N. 15th Ave., Ste. 361, Phoenix, 602/542-6276 or 800/358-3617, TTY 602/542-6686).

TRAVELING WITH CHILDREN

A family trip around Arizona is necessarily a road trip. Is there such a thing as an entirely kid-friendly road trip? At any rate, Arizona is an ideal place for an active, outdoor vacation involving the whole family. Most of the major sights, especially the national parks and monuments, cater to families and offer a host of fun and educational programs for kids. Phoenix and Tucson both have excellent zoos, both of them kidcentric. Rangers at all the parks and monuments are usually eager to explain and illuminate the sights for kids, and the **Junior Rangers** program, offered at most of the parks, is a fun and educational way to get your kids engaged with nature—it even includes a photo-ready swearing-in ceremony. Children under 16 are admitted free to federal parks, monuments, and recreation areas.

SENIOR TRAVELERS

The best thing those 62 years old or older can do before visiting Arizona is to purchase

Arizona's sights, restaurants, and accommodations offer the traveler plenty of opportunities to consider the state's fragile, arid environment. The challenges inherent in keeping that environment healthy amid the frenzy of consumerism and growth are in your face and hard to miss: The rivers are dry; the city is hotter than it used to be; the freeways are choked with cars carrying a single passenger. But don't get discouraged or overwhelmed. There are ways to leave fewer footprints in this desert country.

Your green-travel strategy begins with **planning** and **packing.** Look for **hotels** that list their **sustainable practices** on their website or in their literature. Businesses that are serious about the environment want you to know about it. Consider staying in an **independent, locally owned hotel or motel** that has made **new use of an old space** rather than wasting nonrenewable resources to build yet another shining tower. You will find several such quirky and enchanting accommodations in Tucson, Phoenix, Jerome, Prescott, and Flagstaff. There are also about 20 hotels, many of them high-end resorts in Tucson, Phoenix, and Scottsdale, that have been **Certified Green** under the Arizona Hotel & Lodging Association's fairly new Green Lodging Program. To earn the certification hotels and motels work through a long list of criteria that include stepping up recycling and energy and water saving and generally reducing their impact on the state's environment. You will find many of these Certified Green in this guidebook.

Once you've chosen your ecofriendly hotel, the first item you should pack is a **reusable water bottle**—and then you should use it all the time. All of Arizona's national parks and monuments have water stations for refills.

One of the most meaningful, and difficult, green choices you can make while traveling in Arizona is to **drive less.** It's actually possible these days in Phoenix and Tucson to use **public transportation** most of the time, as long you confine yourself to just a few areas. In Tucson, if you stay in a hotel downtown and seek to go no farther afield than the University of Arizona campus, you could ride the SunLink Modern Streetcar all around the city's historic core. In the Valley of the Sun, you could explore the essential parts of central Phoenix, Tempe around the University, downtown Mesa, and downtown Scottsdale via the Valley Metro light rail system.

Tucson, Flagstaff, Prescott, and other Arizona towns make it easy to get around on a **bike,** as does Tempe and a few parts of Phoenix. If you're visiting Arizona's national parks, consider taking a bike along and parking your car. This is especially easy to do in Grand Canyon National Park, whose South Rim section has excellent paved trails leading into and out of the park. If you don't have your bike with you, there's a place to rent one in the park.

When it's time for breakfast, lunch, and dinner, consider a **locally owned eatery** that uses **locally sourced ingredients** and humane practices. Or skip the meat and eat at **plant-based restaurants,** of which there are several in Arizona. Back at the hotel, ask housekeeping not to wash your bedding for the duration of your stay, within reason of course.

Finally, when you are out in the deserts, pine forests, and red rocks, **pack out what you pack in, stay on the trail,** and **leave wild animals alone.**

an **America the Beautiful—National Parks and Federal Recreational Lands Senior Pass.** This golden ticket will get you and up to three adults into every national park and monument for the rest of your life (non-seniors can buy an America the Beautiful Pass as well, but that version is only valid for one year). It costs $80,

paid once in person at any federal park. In Arizona, where most of the best attractions and sights are under federal control, this adds up to big savings.

Road Scholar (800/454-5768, www.roadscholar.org) offers guided trips to Grand Canyon, Sedona, the Navajo Reservation, and elsewhere in Arizona.

GAY AND LESBIAN TRAVELERS

The gay community is strong and diverse in both Phoenix and Tucson, the state's two major cities. There aren't really LGBT districts, as such, though in Phoenix the **Melrose District,** on 7th Avenue between Camelback and Indian School Roads, is sometimes considered one.

The **Greater Phoenix Gay & Lesbian Chamber of Commerce** (P.O. Box 2097, Phoenix, AZ 85001, 602/266-5055, www.gpglcc.org) has lists of the state's LGBT and LGBT-friendly accommodations. The Valley of the Sun's *Echo Magazine* (602/266-0550, www.echomag.com) is an excellent source of news and culture for the community.

In Tucson, www.tucsongaynews.com and www.gaytucson.com have news and information about the local offerings.

CONDUCT AND CUSTOMS

Be polite and friendly and you'll get along in Arizona just fine; it may not look like other places, but Arizona is very much a typical U.S. state. Most of the rural areas are ruled by conservative values and politics, though a strong and vocal minority of more liberal wilderness lovers and runaway hippies exists in nearly every forest and desert town of any size. The college towns—Tucson, Flagstaff, and Tempe—tend to be more liberal than the rest of the state.

On the Navajo, Hopi, Western Apache, and other Native American reservations throughout the state, don't take pictures without asking first, and don't drive off road for any reason—that's somebody's land and livelihood. On the Hopi Reservation, don't enter a village without first stopping at a store or a village office to ask permission. It's a good idea to hire a guide to take you around, as there are many places that are off limits without one.

Health and Safety

THE ARIZONA SUN

Whether you're hiking deep into Grand Canyon, walking sun-splattered paths through a saguaro forest, or simply strolling through the Phoenix Zoo, you must be aware that the incessant sun, the driving reason for most visits to Arizona, can quickly become a dangerous threat to your health. To eliminate this threat, thus allowing you to bask only in the sun's friendly attributes, practice moderation and prevention. Rather than worship, the sun requires timidity: Stay in the shadows, covered from head to toe. If you're not willing to do this, as most aren't, then at least wear a hat with a wide brim, use high-SPF sunscreen, cover your neck, and, preferably, wear long sleeves. This applies not only to backcountry desert adventurers and hikers; mere sightseers, especially those with fresh-faced children in tow, are just as susceptible to sun- and heat-related health issues—more

so, in fact: The less fit you are, the higher the danger.

The least of what the sun can do to you is not to be taken lightly. A **sunburn,** which comes on quicker than you'd think, can lead to skin cancer, and that can lead to death. If you get a sunburn, there's little you can do save try to make yourself more comfortable. Stay out of the sun, of course, and try to keep cool and hydrated. There are dozens of over-the-counter balms available, but simple aloe works as well as anything. A popular home remedy is to gently dab the burned areas with vinegar. If the burn starts to blister, reaching the dreaded third-degree stage, skin cancer becomes a very real threat. Again, the best way to avoid sunburn is to stay out of the sun; barring that, cover up and follow common sense. Those with fair skin and children should be even more cautious.

Hikers, shoppers, sightseers, golfers, and

anybody else exerting themselves under high-heat conditions should watch out for **dehydration.** When your body becomes dangerously depleted of fluids, you'll notice first that you are not urinating regularly and your saliva has dried up. You may become irritable and confused; your skin may turn gray, and your pulse may race. Children especially can become dehydrated quickly. The best way to avoid dehydration is to limit your exertion during the hottest part of the day and to drink a lot of water. If you feel the symptoms of dehydration coming on, get to a cool, comfortable place, take in fluids, and rest.

Hikers should take along a few packets of electrolyte powder, similar to Gatorade and the like, and a separate water bottle to mix it in—these can be lifesavers. If you exert yourself in the heat and sun and fail to replace the fluids flowing out, your body can become depleted of electrolytes and fluids. Such is the path to **heat exhaustion,** a dangerous condition that can turn fatal if not treated. You begin to feel nauseated, dizzy, and weak, and your muscles cramp. Again, if you experience any of these symptoms, get to a cool, comfortable place quickly and drink water and something with sodium and potassium in it, like an electrolyte drink.

Dehydration and heat exhaustion, while dangerous and unpleasant, pale when compared to **heatstroke,** sometimes called sunstroke or heat hyperpyrexia, a severe, dangerous health threat that is frequently fatal or, if not fatal, often changes a victim's future health significantly and irrevocably. Heatstroke occurs when the body's temperature-regulating capacity fails; this can be caused by either relatively short exposure to extremely high heat—like, say, a short, strenuous run on a 120°F July afternoon in Yuma—or prolonged exposure to relatively high temperatures, as in a 15-mile hike in 90°F heat. And that's only if you're in good shape. It would take far less to cause heatstroke in most of us. The first and most important sign of heatstroke is a lack of sweating. If you stop sweating in a situation

where you *should* be sweating, take notice. Sweating is your body's way of regulating its temperature, so it stands to reason that if you stop sweating, there may be something wrong with your body. Your heart rate will speed up noticeably, and your skin will become dry; you'll get a headache and become confused. At its worst, heatstroke leads to unconsciousness, convulsions, and death. Once you notice you're not sweating, you must get help immediately: Get to an emergency room as soon as possible.

ALTITUDE SICKNESS

The mountains in Arizona reach up to 12,000 feet rarely, and more frequently up to 10,000 feet. Though most visitors won't be going that high, you should be aware that a few of the state's mountain towns sit between 5,000 and 8,000 feet above sea level. Lowlanders in relatively good shape may get headaches, a little dizziness, and shortness of breath while walking around Flagstaff or other of the state's mountain towns, but very few will experience serious altitude sickness—the result of not getting enough oxygen, and therefore not enough blood flow to the brain. Still, take it easy in the higher elevations if you begin to feel tired and out of breath, dizzy, or euphoric. If you have heart or lung problems, you need to be more aware in the higher elevations; the best thing to do is to get a prescription for oxygen from your doctor and carry it with you if you plan on spending a lot of time in the mountains.

HIKING SAFETY

Most hiking safety is based on common sense: Take enough water, wear a hat and good shoes, take along something to eat, don't go alone, and make sure somebody knows where you're going and when you're planning on being back. In the desert, such common sense takes on added meaning. It's best to avoid taking long, strenuous hikes in the desert between May and September. Unless you're a masochist or a tough guy or girl without mercy, you probably won't enjoy it, and it can get very dangerous very fast. If you do go out in the summer, however, don't go out during the hottest part of the day—stick to early morning or evening, though even at these times the heat can be brutal.

Besides the usual hiking gear that every hiker should have—water, food, a hat, shoes, and so forth—Arizona hikers should carry a **tourniquet** with them; if you happen to get bitten by a rattlesnake or a scorpion—not a very likely occurrence at all—you'll want to tie the tourniquet around the area to slow the blood flow, and the venom, until you can get to a hospital and the antivenin. The best way to avoid a snakebite is to avoid snakes. They are not going to bother you unless you bother them or surprise them. Keep an eye on the ground while you're hiking; if a snake, rattler or otherwise, is in your general vicinity, leave the area. Cover your ankles, keep your hands and feet out of dark holes, and don't put your hands on a rock without looking at it first.

OTHER CONCERNS

West Nile virus and the **hantavirus** are the long-shot threats to your health in Arizona, and both can be avoided by taking precautions. Use insect repellent to ward off the former, and simply stay away from rodents to avoid the latter.

Threats from humans come in all the usual forms. Lock your vehicle wherever you go, even in the remotest locations. Don't pick up hitchhikers, anywhere.

Information and Services

MAPS AND TOURIST INFORMATION

The **Arizona Office of Tourism** (1110 W. Washington St., Ste. 155, Phoenix, 866/275-5816, www.visitarizona.com) will send you a free print or electronic version of the official state guide, and its website is full of information and lists of accommodations, events, and restaurants throughout the state.

If you're planning to spend a lot of time in the state's national forests, you can get maps and information beforehand from the **National Forest Service, Southwestern Region** (333 Broadway SE, Albuquerque, New Mexico, 505/842-3292, www.fs.usda.gov/r3), or from the websites for the individual forests, listed in the chapters in which they appear.

The **Arizona BLM State Office** (1 N. Central Ave., Ste. 800, Phoenix, 602/417-9200, www.blm.gov) also has a lot of information on the state's wildlands, and the **Arizona State Parks Department** (1300 W. Washington St., Phoenix, 602/542-4174, http://azstateparks.com) has information on all the parks managed by the state. Passes and reservations for state and federal parks can be obtained and made online or at the parks themselves.

COMMUNICATIONS

Arizona has five **area codes.** For eastern Maricopa County, including Tempe, Mesa, and most of Scottsdale, dial 480; for Phoenix proper, dial 602; for western Maricopa County, dial 623; for all of Southern Arizona, including Tucson, dial 520; and for all of Northern Arizona, including Prescott, Flagstaff, Jerome, the Grand Canyon, and western Arizona (including Yuma and Lake Havasu City), dial 928.

Your **cell phone** will work in most parts of Arizona, though there are large swaths of the Navajo and Hopi Reservations where cell service is spotty at best and mostly nonexistent. Cell phones don't usually work in the backcountry, but it's worth taking them along just in case.

You'll find high-speed wireless **Internet** service throughout the state at the majority of hotels and motels and in cafés and libraries everywhere. Even the remote reservation lands are wired in.

MEDIA

Arizona has just two major daily newspapers, the *Arizona Republic* in Phoenix and the *Arizona Daily Star* in Tucson. The *Republic* is more of a statewide newspaper, while the *Star* focuses on Southern Arizona. You'll find the *Republic* at newsstands and newspaper vending machines throughout the state, while the *Star* is typically available only in Southern Arizona. In North-Central Arizona, the daily *Prescott Courier* and the *Daily Sun* in Flagstaff cover the northland well, including all the happenings at the Grand Canyon and the Navajo Nation. In western Arizona, the *Yuma Sun* is the only daily newspaper.

For alternative news, commentary, and arts and entertainment coverage, check out the free weekly *Phoenix New Times,* covering the Valley of the Sun. In Tucson, the free *Tucson Weekly* offers in-depth coverage of the news and art and entertainment scene in Southern Arizona. Both weeklies publish annual "best of" issues, which list readers' picks of the best restaurants, bars, shops, and attractions in the state's two major urban areas.

Tucson and Phoenix both have network television affiliates, as does Flagstaff. Outside of Southern Arizona, which looks toward Tucson for all its television news, you'll mostly see the local news out of Phoenix.

All three of the state's universities operate National Public Radio stations (Phoenix: KJZZ FM 91.5; Tucson: KUAZ FM 89.1; Flagstaff: KNAU FM 88.7), which offer public radio news programs throughout the day.

MONEY

Despite its largely rural character, Arizona is set firmly in the 21st century. Even in the most out-of-the-way areas, you'll be able to use your credit or debit card with impunity. However, it's always a good idea to carry some cash, especially if you're headed to the Navajo and Hopi Reservations, where it is not uncommon for phone lines, and therefore credit card machines, to go down, and you may find yourself in need of gas but with no way to pay for it.

Foreign travelers can exchange their money at banks throughout the state; check the website www.xe.com for up-to-date exchange rates.

If you cross the border into Mexico and remain in the tourist and shopping areas, you don't need to exchange your money. Shops and restaurants in Nogales and other border towns are happy to take your dollars.

BUSINESS HOURS

While the majority of businesses in Arizona keep regular hours, in many areas the business hours change with the season. In Tucson, Phoenix, Yuma, and all the other desert cities and towns, you may find some places closed during the hottest months of the summer (July and August). Call ahead, and don't take anything for granted if you're planning a trip to the desert during those infernal months. In winter, some of the small towns of the White Mountains go into hibernation, and many businesses close for weeks or months at a time. Again, it's best to call ahead.

Resources

Suggested Reading

HISTORY

Armstrong, William Patrick. *Fred Harvey: Creator of Western Hospitality.* Bellmont, AZ: Canyonlands Publications, 2000. A slim introduction to Harvey and his accomplishments. Available at many Grand Canyon bookstores, it puts a positive spin on the "Civilizer of the West" and the marketing of the Southwestern style.

Bandelier, Fanny, trans. *The Journey of Alvar Nuñez Cabeza de Vaca.* Chicago: Rio Grande Press, 1964. This strange first-person account marks the true beginnings of American literature. The conquistador spent years of privation with various northern Mexico Indian tribes after being shipwrecked near Florida in the late 1520s. He became a slave, a shaman, and a trader before finally finding his way back to Mexico and inspiring the later explorations of the Southwest by the Spanish.

Corel, Edwin. *The Gila: River of the Southwest.* New York: Holt, Rinehart and Winston, 1951. Using Arizona's once-mighty east-west riverway as his hub, Corel jumps off in many directions, exploring human history and culture under the influence of the Gila, which, along with its major tributaries—the Salt, the Santa Cruz, the San Pedro, and the Verde—has been the main pumping artery of Arizona civilization for centuries.

Hall, Sharlot M. (Crampton, C. Gregory, ed.). *Sharlot Hall on the Arizona Strip: A Diary of a Journey Through Northern Arizona in 1911.* Flagstaff: Northland Press, 1975. Hall, a semifamous regional writer of the frontier and early statehood, took an arduous trip to the isolated Arizona Strip and lived to write about it. The editor's notes provide a short but thorough introduction to the human history of the region.

Jones, Billy M. *Health-Seekers in the Southwest 1817-1900.* Norman: University of Oklahoma Press, 1967. A scholarly but readable study of health migration in the 19th century. It turns out, according to Jones, that the Wild West was really a "health frontier" full of reluctant settlers who ventured west to cure TB and other ailments.

Limerick, Patricia Nelson. *The Legacy of Conquest: The Unbroken Past of the American West.* New York: Norton, 1987. An unromantic reconsideration of the history of the Western frontier. Limerick finds that it was a distinctly American hunger for resources, profit, and real estate that built and ruled the West, not the six-gun and its stoic, free-shooting hero.

Luckingham, Bradford. *The Urban Southwest.* El Paso: Texas Western Press, 1982. A study of the rise of four major Southwestern cities, including Phoenix and Tucson.

Martin, Douglas D. *An Arizona Chronology: The Territorial Years, 1846-1912.* Tucson: University of Arizona Press, 1962.

Martin, Douglas D. (Patricia, Paylore, ed.). *An Arizona Chronology: Statehood 1913-1936.* Tucson: University of Arizona Press, 1966. A retired journalist, Douglas spent years searching through old Arizona newspapers, gathering the major headlines from 1846 to 1936. The series provides a general and surprisingly entertaining understanding of the march of Arizona history.

Powell, Lawrence Clark. *Arizona: A History.* Albuquerque: University of New Mexico Press, 1990. A more recent edition of the book first published in 1976, Powell's history is not a definitive blow-by-blow but rather a series of essays on various chapters in Arizona's history and culture. A much-admired Southwestern writer, librarian, and scholar, Powell lived in Tucson for many years. His *Southwest: Three Definitions* (Benson, AZ: Singing Winds Bookshop, 1990) is an excellent trilogy of essays on the landscape and culture of the Southwest.

Sheridan, Thomas. *Arizona: A History.* Tucson: University of Arizona Press, 1995. A very well-written and informative general history.

Smith, Dean. *The Great Arizona Almanac: Facts About Arizona.* Portland, OR: West-Winds Press, 2000. Former journalist Smith compiled this almanac, with entries on Arizona history, travel, current events, famous residents, mileage charts, zip codes, and area codes. It's in dire need of a new edition but is still very useful and interesting.

Sonnichsen, C. L. *Tucson: The Life and Times of an American City.* Norman: University of Oklahoma Press, 1982. A thorough telling of the Old Pueblo's long history from its founding in 1776 as a presidio up to the early 1980s.

Waters, Frank. *The Colorado.* New York: Holt, Rinehart and Winston, 1951. The great Western writer known for his novel *The Man Who Killed the Deer,* Waters was also a master of nonfiction. Though he penned this book about the Colorado River and all that it influences in the 1940s, in a Southwest unrecognizable from what it is today, the greater part of his story still seems true—a classic of that "sense of place" all writers seek.

NATIVE AMERICANS, ANTHROPOLOGY, AND ARCHAEOLOGY

Dentdale, Jennifer Nez. *Reclaiming Diné History: The Legacies of Navajo Chief Manuelito and Juanita.* Tucson: University of Arizona Press, 2007. A compelling account of the Navajo Nation written by the first Navajo woman to earn a PhD in history. Dentdale gives the oral history of her people just as much, if not more, credence than she does the mostly Anglo-written accounts that claim to be official and complete. This method reveals, among other things, that women played a much larger role in traditional Navajo society than "colonial" records credit.

Hall, Edward T. *West of the Thirties: Discoveries Among the Navajo and Hopi.* New York: Doubleday, 1994. The great anthropologist tells stories about his work with the Navajo and Hopi during the Great Depression, evoking a time when the remote Indian Country was practically inaccessible.

Houk, Rose. *Sinagua.* Tucson: Western National Parks Association, 1992. Pick up this short volume at any of the national parks or monuments you're sure to visit in Arizona; it's a concise introduction to the Sinagua and their land, part of a series sold throughout the state.

Kosik, Fran. *Native Roads: The Complete Motoring Guide to the Navajo and Hopi Nations.* Tucson: Rio Nuevo, 2005. Kosik knows the reservation lands well and includes a lot of fascinating historical tidbits;

recommended to anyone wishing to go deeper than most into Indian Country.

Lamb, Susan. *A Guide to Navajo Rugs.* Tucson: Western National Parks Association, 1992.

Lamb, Susan. *A Guide to Pueblo Pottery.* Tucson: Southwest Parks and Monuments Association, 1996. These handy guides, available at park and monument bookshops and most of the gift shops and tourist attractions in Indian Country, explain the basics of rug and pottery identification—just enough to hook you in and whet your appetite for collecting the arts and crafts of the Navajos and Pueblos.

Waters, Frank. *Book of the Hopi.* New York: Penguin, 1963. Though this history of the Hopi and retelling of their myths and legends sometimes gets a cold shoulder from scholars, Waters's book has a narrative thrust that makes the Hopi story seem immediate and meaningful not just to the Hopi and a few anthropologists but to all of us.

Wright, Barton. *The Complete Guide to Collecting Kachina Dolls.* Flagstaff: Northland Press, 1977. A classic guide to the kachina spirits and what they mean.

GRAND CANYON

Ghiglieri, Michael P., and Thomas M. Myers. *Over the Edge: Death in Grand Canyon.* Flagstaff: Puma Press, 2001. A popular collection of macabre stories about tumblers, jumpers, drowners, and killers in the Grand Canyon. One of the few books of its kind that is updated quite regularly.

Grattan, Virginia L. *Mary Colter: Builder upon Red Earth.* Grand Canyon: The Grand Canyon Association, 1992. A very readable account of architect Mary Colter's life and career. Colter seems to be little known outside the Southwest, though she deserves a wider reputation for her fanciful Grand

Canyon creations and the rustic Arts and Crafts elegance of her Harvey Houses.

Hughes, Donald. *In the House of Stone and Light.* Grand Canyon Natural History Association, 1978. A relatively short, well-written account of the human history of the Grand Canyon, concentrating mainly on the Anglo development of the South Rim and the evolution of Grand Canyon National Park.

Powell, John Wesley. *The Exploration of the Colorado River and Its Canyons.* New York: Dover, 1961. A reprint of Powell's 1895 classic *Canyons of the Colorado,* this firsthand account of two journeys through the canyon on the Colorado River is essential reading (and it is surprisingly readable) for anyone interested in the continuing story of the confluence of humans and Grand Canyon.

Schullery, Paul. *The Grand Canyon: Early Impressions.* Boulder: Colorado Associated University Press, 1981. Includes essays by John Muir and others, showing that writers and other visitors have struggled mightily to describe and comprehend the canyon since people have been visiting it.

THE ENVIRONMENT AND NATURAL HISTORY

Carter, Jack L., et al. *Common Southwestern Native Plants: An Identification Guide.* Silver City, NM: Mimbres Press, 2003. A thorough but easy-to-use guide to plants you're likely to see in Arizona; includes common species of the deserts, the forested mountains, and the plateau country.

Grubbs, Bruce. *Desert Sense: Camping, Hiking & Biking in Hot, Dry Climates.* Seattle: The Mountaineers Books, 2004. If you're going to be hiking or riding a bike in the desert, especially if you're doing it in the summer, consider picking up this or a similar book to familiarize yourself with desert survival beyond the basics of bringing water and wearing a hat.

Kavanagh, James, ed. *The Nature of Arizona.* Blaine, WA: Waterford Press, 1996. A useful all-in-one guide specific to the state; most guides attempt to lump everything together under "Southwest." Lists and provides illustrations of the state's flora and fauna, including mammals, snakes, fish, birds, and spiders.

Logan, Michael F. *The Lessening Stream: An Environmental History of the Santa Cruz River.* Tucson: University of Arizona Press, 2002. A professor paints an attractive and elegiac portrait of what the river used to be like and explains why it isn't like that anymore.

Olin, George. *50 Common Mammals of the Southwest.* Tucson: Western National Parks Association, 2000. An introduction to Arizona's mammals; slim with attractive illustrations, part of a series available throughout the state.

Quinn, Meg. *Wildflowers of the Southwest.* Tucson: Rio Nuevo, 2000. If you're going to be hiking in the desert in spring, pick up this guide to the many wildflowers that bloom throughout the state.

HIKING

Berkowitz, Alan. *Grand Canyon North Kaibab Trail Guide.* Grand Canyon Association, 2005.

Menconi, Lilia. *Moon Take a Hike Phoenix: Hikes within Two Hours of the City.* Berkeley, CA: Avalon Travel, 2013.

Thybony, Scott. *Grand Canyon Bright Angel Trail Guide.* Grand Canyon Association, 2004.

Thybony, Scott. *Grand Canyon Hermit Trail Guide.* Grand Canyon Association, 2005.

Thybony, Scott. *Grand Canyon South Kaibab Trail Guide.* Grand Canyon Association, 2006. Pick up these small, inexpensive guides to the major Grand Canyon trails at most canyon-area bookstores. They contain a lot of information for being so small, and several color photos show you what's ahead. Each guide also includes an interesting history of the trail.

Tessmer, Martin. *50 Hikes in Arizona.* Woodstock, VT: The Countryman Press, 2004. An excellent guide to the best hiking trails in the state, with detailed descriptions of each trail and precise directions to the trailheads. Includes all regions of the state.

Warren, Scott, S. *100 Classic Hikes in Arizona.* Seattle, WA: The Mountaineers Press, 2000. Has 50 more hikes than *50 Hikes in Arizona.* For those looking not only for the best, most popular hikes but also the less known and little used.

LITERATURE

Abbey, Edward. *The Monkey Wrench Gang.* New York: Harper Collins, 2000. Abbey's best-known novel, first published in 1975, is a crazy comic Western with radical environmentalists as its heroic gang of outlaws.

Abbey, Edward. *One Life at a Time, Please.* New York: Henry Holt and Company, 1987. Abbey was the Southwest's resident poet-provocateur, a major influence on a few generations of Western writers and environmentalists. It has yet to be decided if he was writing literature disguised as polemics or the other way around, but he is an essential voice in the long project to justify the ways of the West to the rest of the country. This volume of essays from the late 1970s and the 1980s includes his thoughts on Lake Powell.

Bowden, Charles. *Blue Desert.* Tucson: University of Arizona Press, 1986.

Bowden, Charles. *Frog Mountain Blues.* Tucson: University of Arizona, 1987. Bowden's voice is overwhelming once you get into it. His essays, reportage, and nature writing chronicle the darker side of the sunbelt.

Internet Resources

TOURISM SITES

Arizona Office of Tourism
www.visitarizona.com
The official site for the state's Office of Tourism has basic information on the state's regions and lists various possible itineraries.

Discover Navajo
www.discovernavajo.com
The official site of the Navajo Nation's tourism group has basic information about visiting the nation—where to stay, what to do, and what not to do. It has a large number of links to tour companies.

Flagstaff Convention
and Visitors Bureau
www.flagstaffarizona.org
This site has general information on visiting Flagstaff, the northland, and the Grand Canyon along with helpful listings.

Grand Canyon National Park
www.nps.gov/grca
The Grand Canyon's official website has basic information on the park; go here for information about backcountry permits. For reservations and information on the park's accommodations, go to the Xanterra South Rim site at www.grandcanyonlodges.com.

Greater Phoenix Convention
& Visitors Bureau
www.visitphoenix.com
The official site for Phoenix and the Valley of the Sun has a pretty comprehensive list of restaurants and hotels in the valley.

Metropolitan Tucson Convention
and Visitors Bureau
www.visittucson.org
This is Tucson and Southern Arizona's official tourism site.

Sedona Chamber of Commerce
www.visitsedona.com
The official site for Sedona tourism has general information on Sedona, Oak Creek Canyon, Red Rock Country, and the Verde Valley.

Yuma Visitors Bureau
www.visityuma.com
The official site for Yuma and the lower Colorado River region.

NEWS AND CULTURE

Arizona Daily Star
www.azstarnet.com
Tucson's morning daily is free on this site, with news and information on all of Southern Arizona.

Arizona Republic
www.azcentral.com
The state's largest newspaper is free online every day, and the site has a robust Arizona travel guide and a useful dining and entertainment section.

Phoenix New Times
www.phoenixnewtimes.com
This site is the best place to go for entertainment and cultural listings and alternative news and commentary about life in the Valley of the Sun.

Tucson Weekly
www.tucsonweekly.com
Southern Arizona's best source of alternative news, political blogs, and cultural and entertainment news and listings.

Index

List of Maps

Photo Credits

Acknowledgments

This edition is dedicated, with love and thanks, to my wife, Katie Sanderson. Thanks also to all the folks at Avalon for their help, confidence, and patience. And thanks as always to Ryan Lord for the road trips.

Get inspired for your next adventure

Follow **@moonguides** on Instagram or subscribe to our newsletter at **moon.com**

ROAD TRIPS AND DRIVE & HIKE GUIDES

MOON

Drive & Hike
APPALACHIAN TRAIL

THE BEST TRAIL TOWNS, DAY HIKES,
AND ROAD TRIPS IN BETWEEN

TIMOTHY MALCOLM

MOON

BLUE RIDGE PARKWAY
Road Trip

INCLUDING SHENANDOAH & GREAT SMOKY
MOUNTAINS NATIONAL PARKS

JASON FRYE

MOON

CALIFORNIA
Road Trip

SAN FRANCISCO, YOSEMITE, LAS VEGAS,
GRAND CANYON, LOS ANGELES,
& THE PACIFIC COAST HIGHWAY

STUART THORNTON

MOON

NASHVILLE TO NEW ORLEANS
Road Trip

NATCHEZ TRACE PARKWAY • MEMPHIS •
TUPELO • MISSISSIPPI BLUES TRAIL

MARGARET LITTMAN

MOON

NEW ENGLAND
Road Trip

BOSTON, ACADIA NATIONAL PARK, WHITE
MOUNTAINS, BERKSHIRES, NEWPORT, AND CAPE COD

JEN ROSE SMITH

MOON

NORTHERN CALIFORNIA
Road Trip

SAN FRANCISCO, WINE COUNTRY, SONOMA, REDWOODS,
LAKE TAHOE, SHASTA, LASSEN, YOSEMITE, BIG SUR

STUART THORNTON & KAYLA ANDERSON

MOON

PACIFIC COAST HIGHWAY

CALIFORNIA,
OREGON & WASHINGTON

IAN ANDERSON

MOON

Drive & Hike
PACIFIC CREST TRAIL

THE BEST TRAIL TOWNS, DAY HIKES,
AND ROAD TRIPS IN BETWEEN

CAROLINE HINCHLIFF

MOON

PACIFIC NORTHWEST
Road Trip

SEATTLE, VANCOUVER, VICTORIA,
THE OLYMPIC PENINSULA, PORTLAND,
THE OREGON COAST & MOUNT RAINIER

ALLISON WILLIAMS

MOON.COM | ROADTRIPUSA.COM

ROUTE 66
Road Trip

JESSICA DUNHAM

SOUTH FLORIDA & THE KEYS
Road Trip

WITH MIAMI, WALT DISNEY WORLD, TAMPA & THE EVERGLADES

JASON FERGUSON

SOUTHERN CALIFORNIA
Road Trips

DRIVES ALONG THE BEACHES, MOUNTAINS, AND DESERTS WITH THE BEST STOPS ALONG THE WAY

IAN ANDERSON

SOUTHWEST
Road Trip

LAS VEGAS, ZION & BRYCE, MONUMENT VALLEY, SANTA FE & TAOS, AND THE GRAND CANYON

TIM HULL

VANCOUVER & CANADIAN ROCKIES
Road Trip

VICTORIA, BANFF, JASPER, CALGARY, THE OKANAGAN, WHISTLER & THE SEA-TO-SKY HIGHWAY

CAROLYN B. HELLER

YELLOWSTONE TO GLACIER NATIONAL PARK
Road Trip

JACKSON HOLE, CODY, THE GRAND TETONS & THE ROCKY MOUNTAIN FRONT

CARTER G. WALKER

Road Trip USA

Covering more than 35,000 miles of blacktop stretching from east to west and north to south, *Road Trip USA* takes you deep into the heart of America.

This colorful guide covers the top road trips including historic Route 66 and is packed with maps, photos, illustrations, mile-by-mile highlights, and more!

Road Trip USA

CROSS-COUNTRY ADVENTURES ON AMERICA'S TWO-LANE HIGHWAYS

Jamie Jensen

Trips to Remember

BALI & LOMBOK
CHANTAE REDEN

ECUADOR
& THE GALÁPAGOS ISLANDS
BETHANY PITTS

ICELAND
JENNA GOTTLIEB

TRIP OF A LIFETIME
MACHU PICCHU
ISA DORE

MOROCCO

NEW ZEALAND
JAMIE CHRISTIAN DESPLACES

NORWAY
DAVID NIKEL

TRIP OF A LIFETIME
PATAGONIA
Including the Falkland Islands
WAYNE BERNHARDSON

PRAGUE, VIENNA & BUDAPEST
JENNIFER D. WALKER & AUBURN SCALLON

ROME, FLORENCE & VENICE
ALEXEI J. COHEN

ZION & BRYCE
Including Arches, Canyonlands, Capitol Reef, Grand Staircase-Escalante & More
W. C. MCRAE & JUDY JEWELL

Epic Adventure

CAMINO DE SANTIAGO
SACRED SITES, HISTORIC VILLAGES, LOCAL FOOD & WINE
BEEBE BAHRAMI

ROUTE 66
Road Trip
JESSICA DUNHAM

YELLOWSTONE TO GLACIER NATIONAL PARK
Road Trip
JACKSON HOLE, CODY, THE GRAND TETONS & THE ROCKY MOUNTAIN FRONT
CARTER G. WALKER

AMALFI COAST
With Capri, Naples & Pompeii
LAURA THAYER

ARUBA

BAHAMAS
MARIAH LAINE MOYLE

BAJA
Tijuana to Los Cabos
JENNIFER KRAMER

BELIZE
LEBAWIT LILY GIRMA

BERMUDA
ROSEMARY JONES

COSTA RICA

DOMINICAN REPUBLIC
LEBAWIT LILY GIRMA

FIJI

FLORIDA KEYS
With Miami & the Everglades
JOSHUA LAWRENCE KINSER

FRENCH RIVIERA: NICE, CANNES, MONACO & ST-TROPEZ
JON BRYANT

JAMAICA

MAUI
With Moloka'i & Lāna'i
GREG ARCHER

PUERTO VALLARTA
With Sayulita, Riviera Nayarit & Costalegre
MADELINE MILNE

YUCATÁN PENINSULA

Travel with Moon in the Rockies, the Southwest, and Texas

Or go big and go abroad

#TravelWithMoon